For selected older vintages, refer to the …

ITALY	13	12								
Barolo, Barbaresco	8	7								
Chianti Classico Ris.	7	7								
Brunello	7	8								
Amarone	5	8	7	8	6	8	6	8	5	9
SPAIN										
Ribera del Duero	6	8	7	8	9	7	6	6	9	8
Rioja (red)	6	7	7	9	8	7	6	6	9	9
PORTUGAL										
South	8	8	8	6	7	8	8	7	8	8
North	7	8	9	7	8	9	8	5	8	8
Port	6	7	9	7	8	8	10	7	7	8
USA										
California Cabernet	9	10	7	8	9	8	9	9	8	8
California Chardonnay	10	10	9	9	9	8	9	9	7	8
Oregon Pinot Noir	7	9	7	6	8	8	6	8	7	8
Wash. State Cabernet	8	9	7	8	8	8	8	8	8	7
AUSTRALIA										
Coonawarra Cabernet	8	9	6	9	9	9	6	8	9	10
Hunter Semillon	9	6	9	9	9	7	8	8	9	8
Barossa Shiraz	8	9	6	9	8	9	6	8	10	8
Marg. River Cabernet	9	9	10	10	9	9	9	6	10	9
NEW ZEALAND										
M'lborough Sauvignon	9	9	8	10	8	5	9	9	7	8
H'kes Bay Cab/Merlot	10	4	5	8	9	8	9	8	7	8
SOUTH AFRICA										
Stellenbosch Cabernet	8	9	8	9	10	7	9	8	7	8
S'bosch Chardonnay	9	9	8	9	10	8	9	8	8	9

Numerals (1–10) represent an overall rating for each year.
◐ Not ready ◕ Just ready ● At peak ◑ Past best ○ Not generally declared

HOW TO USE THIS BOOK

The **World of Wine** section, starting on page 22, gives an overview of all the world's significant wine-producing countries. The most important countries are followed by a full list of the relevant entries in the A–Z section. Remember that regional A–Z entries guide you to further recommended producers in each region or appellation.

The A–Z section starts on page 61 and includes over 1600 entries on wines, producers, grapes and wine regions from all over the world. It is followed on page 328 by a **Glossary** of winemaking terms.

Detailed **Vintage Charts**, with information on which of the world's top wines are ready for drinking in 2015, can be found on the inside front and back covers; the front chart features vintages back to 2004; the back chart highlights some of the best older vintages for premium wines.

Glass Symbols   These indicate the wines produced.

🍷 Red wine   🍷 Rosé wine   🍷 White wine

The order of the glasses reflects the importance of the wines in terms of volume produced. For example:

🍷🍷   White followed by rosé wine

🍷🍷🍷   Red followed by rosé, then white wine

Grape Symbols   These identify entries on grape varieties.

⣿ Red grape   ⣿ White grape

Star Symbols   These indicate wines and producers that are highly rated by the author.
- ★   A particularly good wine or producer in its category
- ★★   An excellent wine or producer in its category – one especially worth seeking out
- ★★★   An exceptional, world-class wine or producer

Best years   Recommended vintages are listed for many producer and appellation entries. Those listed in bold, e.g. **2013, 05**, indicate wines that are ready for drinking now, although they may not necessarily be at their best; those appearing in brackets, e.g. (2013), (09), are preliminary assessments of wines that are not released at the time of going to press.

Cross References   Wine names, producers and regions that have their own entries elsewhere in the A–Z are indicated by SMALL CAPITALS. **Grape varieties** are not cross-referred in this way, but more than 70 varieties, from Aglianico to Zinfandel, are included.

Special Features   The A–Z section includes special 2-page features on the world's most important wine styles, regions and grape varieties. These features include recommended vintages and producers, as well as lists of related entries elsewhere in the A–Z.

Index   The Index contains over 4500 recommended producers. Some of the world's most famous brand names are also included.

CONTENTS

INTRODUCTION

I have just seen the future. It is the smiling face of a vineyard owner proudly strolling among his vines. In Fife. In Scotland. Where last July the local weather station recorded highs of 21.4°C – ideal conditions for gently coaxing your vines to ripeness. You think I jest? Why? Southern Sweden already has a healthy network of small vineyards. I've tasted the wines, some are rather good – so why not Scotland? Canada's supposedly icy Nova Scotia – New Scotland, geddit? – has 16 thriving wineries.

And I've seen another future. On 15 January 2014, Adelaide in South Australia was officially the hottest city in the world, sweltering in the mid 40°Cs as all around her South Australia's most famous vineyard regions struggled to stop their crops expiring on the vine. Bush fires raged. Wineries could see the flames and smell the smoke in the Barossa and Eden Valleys. Over in Victoria the fires stayed further from the vines, but cool-climate areas like Mornington Peninsula had unprecedented runs of days as hot as 41°C. Usually anything over 30°C is regarded as on the warm side, and the fragrant delicacy of their Pinot Noirs and Chardonnays is built on typical summer days in the 20°Cs. What on earth is going on?

These are obviously two extremes. We could dismiss them as isolated freak events. But they're not. Drought stalks California. 2013 was its driest year for one and a half centuries. Typhoons hammered Bordeaux in 2013. Hail ravaged Burgundy. Frost destroyed at least 20% of Chile's crop in 2014 and vicious weather may have destroyed a considerable chunk of New York State's actual vines. Hang on: I thought we were talking about global warming. No, we're not. I haven't mentioned global warming. Now, climate change – that's a very different matter. And that's what I'm talking about. It's getting hotter, it's getting colder, it's getting wetter, it's getting drier, it's getting windier – and often all in the same place, one year to the next. For climate change, read climate chaos.

And is this good or bad for wine? Well, typically, it's both. In the short term. But in the long term it's very worrying indeed. In the short term, the warming section of the change means vineyards are becoming viable closer to both poles. The Canadians and the Scots are delighted. The Germans record one fine ripe vintage after another. Polish and Scandinavian winemaking prospers, and vineyards sprout further and further south in Chile and Argentina. Bordeaux's wines get riper and riper. Burgundy's growing seasons are up to 1.4°C warmer than in the 1970s.

So Bordeaux and Burgundy are doing OK, then? Well, no. It's no good if all Bordeaux's heat comes at the wrong time – as in 2011 – or if the heat only arrives after a winter that never ends, as in 2013, so that the vines can never catch up their ripening before the autumn storms put an end to it and you just have to harvest, whether the grapes are ripe or not. Burgundy's warming pattern is no good if a mixture of hails, frosts and rains at the wrong time mean you can't pick more than half a normal crop in 2010, 11, 12 and 13. Rain events in Europe are becoming more and more violent, often accompanied by destructive wind. The frequency of hailstorms hasn't changed much in 20 years but their intensity has increased by 70%.

So what's the wine world supposed to do? Firstly we need to admit that change is occurring. You don't have to accept that the world is inexorably warming – but change is all around us, and much of it seems to concern warming patterns, however erratic they may be. Some scientists put the period 1982–2012 as our warmest 30-year stretch for 1400 years. Other scientists suggest that by 2050 up to 73% of today's vineyards will either have to dramatically change their vineyard practices and the varieties they grow, or they will simply no longer be fit for purpose. This so-called 'loss of suitability' would, by 2050, affect most of central and eastern Spain, most of south-western and southern France, most of Italy, and also great swathes of Eastern Europe, as their continental climates simply become too extreme.

So is this a death knell? It doesn't have to be. It is entirely possible that considerable swathes of land that are already semi-desert and prone to drought and which rely crucially on irrigation in an ever-drying environment may have to give up growing vines. Australia's Murray-Darling river basin, California's Central Valley and much of central Spain are three

> 'In the future, dirt-cheap wine may simply be a luxury we can't afford.'

areas at risk. Not coincidentally, they are each primarily involved with producing high volumes of forgettable wine at low cost. In the future, dirt-cheap wine may simply be a luxury we can't afford.

But even they might survive if the weather patterns which today are starving them of water, change. The Sierra Nevada mountains that feed California's Central Valley with snow meltwater had snowfalls only 20% of average in the winter of 2013–14, but there were still some big, unexpected, late falls. With climate chaos, things might reverse next year.

But all these examples of extreme weather conditions show one thing. How difficult it is going to be to plan for the future. In which case the wine world must become more flexible. And we, the wine drinkers, must help. Territorial appellations, particularly those in countries such as France, Spain and Italy, must become more flexible about what grape varieties can be planted in them, because all grape varieties need differing amounts of nourishment and heat to ripen well. If we are looking at a warming world, then regions that have planted the same grape varieties for centuries may have

Bien Nacido vineyard in Santa Maria Valley, California, is famous for Pinot Noir and Chardonnay.

to become more open-minded, and at least consider allowing varieties that can flourish in greater heat into their vineyards. People talk of Burgundy eventually having to open its doors to Syrah or to Viognier and Roussanne. Syrah and Tempranillo might be needed in Bordeaux. But don't stop there. If we're talking of vines that are well adapted from ancient times to heat and water stress, then countries like Italy, Portugal and Greece have a treasure trove that future generations may need to call upon, not only in France but also in California, Australia, South Africa, Chile and Argentina.

These countries lead the New World, and all of them rely far too heavily on a few French classic grapes from the temperate French regions of Bordeaux, Burgundy and the northern Rhône Valley – Cabernet, Merlot, Pinot Noir, Syrah, Malbec, Chardonnay, Viognier, Sauvignon Blanc. Why? Because that's what we, the consumers, demand. Cabernet Sauvignon is now the most widely planted variety in the world, followed by Merlot. Nearly 40% of the global vineyard is made up of French varieties, and the top 35 varieties occupy two thirds of the global area. Because that's what we'll drink. Experiments with wonderful heat- and drought-tolerant varieties such as the Portuguese Touriga Nacional, the Spanish Bobal, Monastrell and Garnacha,

Cabernet Sauvignon is now the most planted grape variety in the world.

the Italian Nero d'Avola, Sangiovese, Fiano and Falanghina, the Greek Assyrtiko and Agioritiko are being carried out by enthusiastic and concerned wine producers all round the world. But we, the consumers, will have to put aside our obsession with the safe varieties of Cabernet, Chardonnay and their ilk and take the plunge and embrace these unfamiliar beauties.

If we are prepared to become flexible drinkers, the producers of the world who look with increasing concern on what is happening around them will have the courage to open their vineyards to different varieties, maybe grown in different ways, as the dangers of wind, rain and hail also challenge the status quo. And the flavours we enjoy will be different. Initially in countries such as Australia, South Africa, Chile, but eventually – not soon, but eventually – in such bastions of tradition as the great wine areas of France. If the whole wine world decides to approach climate change as one of the great challenges of our age, there is no reason to doubt that the greatest vintages and the greatest wines of all time can yet be in the future.

And while I wait for these to arrive, I'll try to enjoy what cool-vintage wines that I can. Bordeaux's dry whites and the basic reds of both 2010 and 2012 are frequently delicious, Burgundy's 2010s and 12s are similarly good, even at less exalted levels, and Beaujolais 2013 is a juice bomb. Add to that some fantastic fresh Languedoc 2013s.

Spain's Rioja is motoring at the moment, in warm vintages and cool, and there's still lots of beautiful 2010 to be had, along with good fresh Albariño, and the trickle of great sherry is becoming faster and fuller. Portugal's Douro reds – 2010 and also 2011 – are tip top.

Italy's white wine revolution gathers pace, and I'll drink as much as I can before hopping to Greece for increasingly arresting reds and whites, then taking an increasingly lucky dip with unexpected delights from Croatia, Slovenia, Serbia and Macedonia.

California made positively restrained 2011s and more extravagant 2012s. Oregon and Washington had their coolest vintage ever in 2010 – until 2011, which was even cooler. I'll enjoy their taut, precise flavours before wallowing a bit in the 2012s. On the East Coast I'll be snaffling Viognier, Cabernet Franc, Petit Verdot and Nebbiolo from Virginia and zesty, fragrant Rieslings from New York's Finger Lakes.

In Argentina it's the high-altitude 2013 reds and whites I'm after; in Chile the 2013's crisp coastal freshness will get my mouth watering.

In South Africa I'll stick to the cool coastal areas for snappy whites and crunchy reds, but I'll also pack in a few old-vine beauties from Swartland.

In Western Australia, cool 2013 whites and lush 2012 reds will do me. There's a new bunch of young guns in Barossa and McLaren Vale who'll wrestle with whatever nature throws at them. My kind of guys. I'll drink their wine. And it's the same in Victoria. Welcome to a new breed of Aussie. As for New Zealand, cool 2012 and sunny but not hot 2013 will have me supping both red and white.

And then I'm back to England and its ever-increasing array of truly original sparklers. Oh; I forgot Scotland. Well, if that guy sends me a bottle, I'll sure as hell try it.

SOME OF MY FAVOURITES

The following are some of the wines I've enjoyed most this year. They're not definitive lists of 'best wines', but all the wines, regions and producers mentioned here are on an exciting roll in terms of quality. Some are easy to find; others are very rare or expensive – but if you get the chance to try them, grab it! You can find out more about them in the A–Z on pages 62 to 327: the cross-references in SMALL CAPITALS will guide you to the relevant entries.

WORLD-CLASS WINES THAT DON'T COST THE EARTH
- Quinta do CRASTO Reserva Old Vines, Portugal
- CVNE Rioja Imperial Reserva, Spain
- Hatzidakis Vinsanto, Santorini, Greece
- Dom. de Marcoux CHÂTEAUNEUF-DU-PAPE, France
- Moreau-Naudet CHABLIS, France
- MUGA Rioja Reserva, Spain
- Ossian RUEDA, Spain
- Giovanni ROSSO, Barolo Serralunga, Italy
- Eben SADIE single-vineyard releases, South Africa
- Le Soula, CÔTES CATALANES, France
- Te Whare Ra Gewurztraminer MARLBOROUGH, New Zealand
- Dom. Tempier BANDOL, France
- TORRES Priorat Salmos, Spain
- Viñalba Gran Reservado/Bodegas FABRE, Argentina

OZ'S ODDBALLS
- Ch. Burgozone Viognier, Bulgaria
- Camin Larredya, Jurançon Sec, South-West France
- Cayetano del Pino Palo Cortado, JEREZ, Spain
- COOPERS CREEK Albariño 'Bell Ringer', New Zealand

- Daniel Dugois, ARBOIS Vin Jaune Jura, France
- Vignerons d'Estézargues, CÔTES DU RHÔNE Blanc 'Plein Sud', France
- Filliatreau SAUMUR-CHAMPIGNY, Loire, France
- Fox Gordon, Fiano 'Princess', ADELAIDE HILLS, Australia
- Francuska Vinarija, Obecanje, Serbia
- GEMTREE Savagnin 'Moonstone', McLaren Vale, Australia
- Leventhorpe Madeleine Angevine, Yorkshire, England
- Dom. de Montbourgeau, l'ETOILE Savagnin, Jura, France
- NIEPOORT Vinho Verde Dócil, Portugal
- Puklavec & Friends, Sauvignon Blanc-Furmint, Slovenia
- RIDGEVIEW Pimlico Sparkling Red, England
- Telmo RODRÍGUEZ Al-muvedre, Alicante, Valencia, Spain
- SCHOFFIT Chasselas, Alsace, France
- Suertes del Marqués, La Solana, Tenerife, CANARY ISLANDS
- Tbilvino, Qvevris, Georgia
- Tsantali Cabernet Sauvignon (organic), Halkidiki, Greece
- Ch. Viranel, Arômes Sauvages Alicante Bouschet, Languedoc, France

High in the Uco Valley in the Andes foothills, Tupungato is one of Mendoza's regions to watch.

BEST LOOKALIKES TO THE CLASSICS

Bordeaux-style red wines
- CATENA Alta Cabernet Sauvignon, Argentina
- Le Riche Cabernet Sauvignon, STELLENBOSCH, South Africa
- OPUS ONE, California

Burgundy-style white wines
- CULLEN, Kevin John, Australia
- HAMILTON RUSSELL, South Africa
- LEEUWIN ESTATE Art Series, Australia
- Littorai, Charles Heintz Vineyard, SONOMA COAST, California
- TE MATA Elston, New Zealand

Champagne-style wines
- Jansz (Vintage), YALUMBA, Australia
- NYETIMBER Classic Cuvée, England
- ROEDERER ESTATE L'Ermitage, California

TOP-VALUE WINES
- ALENTEJO and VINHO VERDE, Portugal
- CAMPANIA And SICILY whites, Italy
- CORBIÈRES, France
- CÔTES DE GASCOGNE whites, France
- ENTRE-DEUX-MERS and GRAVES whites, France
- Old-vines Garnacha reds, CALATAYUD and CAMPO DE BORJA, Spain
- Hungarian whites
- Leyda whites and reds, SAN ANTONIO, Chile
- White RIOJA, Spain
- SICILY reds, Italy

REGIONS TO WATCH
- ACONCAGUA Costa, Chile
- Brazil, for sparkling wine
- DOURO, Portugal
- Hampshire, Kent, Sussex, England
- LANGUEDOC-ROUSSILLON, for whites such as PICPOUL DE PINET, France
- LODI, California, USA
- MAULE, Chile
- Ribeiro and Valdeorras, GALICIA, Spain
- SWARTLAND, South Africa
- TASMANIA, Australia
- Tupungato and Gualtallary, UCO VALLEY, Argentina
- VIRGINIA, USA

PRODUCERS TO WATCH
- Alheit, WALKER BAY, South Africa
- Anduluna, MENDOZA, Argentina
- ASTROLABE, New Zealand
- BENEGAS, Argentina
- Bressia, MENDOZA, Argentina
- CHAMONIX, South Africa
- Collector, CANBERRA, Australia
- DE MARTINO, Chile
- Elephant Hill, HAWKES BAY, New Zealand
- FURLEIGH ESTATE, England
- K Vintners/Charles SMITH, USA
- LOMA LARGA, Chile
- Maycas del LIMARÍ, Chile
- MONTES (Outer Limits), Chile
- Quinta da Pellada, DÃO, Portugal

AUSTRALIA
- BROKENWOOD Semillon and Graveyard Vineyard Shiraz
- HENSCHKE Hill of Grace Shiraz and Louis Semillon
- McLean's Farmgate barr-Eden red, EDEN VALLEY
- MCWILLIAM's Mount Pleasant Lovedale Semillon
- Charles MELTON Nine Popes
- S C PANNELL Nebbiolo
- PRIMO ESTATE Moda Cabernet-Merlot
- ROCKFORD Basket Press Shiraz
- ROSEMOUNT Graciano-Mataro-Grenache, McLaren Vale
- TYRRELL's Vat 1 Semillon
- YABBY LAKE Chardonnay and Pinot Noir
- YALUMBA Bush Vine Grenache

RED BORDEAUX
- Ch. ANGÉLUS
- Ch. AUSONE
- Ch. CANON-LA-GAFFELIÈRE
- Ch. GRAND-PUY-LACOSTE
- Ch. Feytit-Clinet, POMEROL
- Ch. FIGEAC
- Les Forts de LATOUR
- Ch. LÉOVILLE-BARTON
- Ch. LÉOVILLE-POYFERRÉ
- Ch. LYNCH-BAGES
- Ch. la MISSION-HAUT-BRION
- Ch. MONTROSE
- Ch. PICHON-LONGUEVILLE
- TERTRE-RÔTEBOEUF

BURGUNDY
- Blain-Gagnard, PULIGNY-MONTRACHET (white)
- Jean-Claude BOISSET, Clos de la Roche (red)
- Confuron-Cotetidot, Charmes-CHAMBERTIN (red)
- B Dugat-Py, Charmes-CHAMBERTIN (red)
- Comte LIGER-BELAIR, Échezeaux (red)
- MÉO-CAMUZET, Clos de Vougeot (red)

- de MONTILLE, Beaune Les Grèves (red)
- de MONTILLE, Puligny-Montrachet Le Cailleret (white)
- J-F MUGNIER, Nuits-St-Georges Clos de la Maréchale (red)
- Pernot-Belicard, MEURSAULT Les Perrières (white)
- Chantal Remy, CLOS DE LA ROCHE (red)
- de Villaine, La Digoine BOURGOGNE-CÔTE CHALONNAISE (red)
- de VOGÜÉ, Bonnes-Mares (red)

CALIFORNIA
- Cline, Bridgehead ZINFANDEL, Contra Costa County
- CORISON Kronos Vineyard Cabernet Sauvignon
- Donelan Syrah, Obsidian and Richards Family Vineyard, SONOMA COUNTY
- Littorai, SONOMA COAST
- Rubissow, MOUNT VEEDER
- Rudd, Samantha's Cabernet Sauvignon, NAPA VALLEY
- SHAFER Hillside Select Cabernet Sauvignon
- SPOTTSWOODE
- TABLAS CREEK, Esprit
- Sean Thackrey, SONOMA COAST
- VIADER
- WIND GAP

ITALIAN REDS
- ALLEGRINI Amarone and La Poja
- Benanti, Rovittello ETNA, Sicily
- Fenocchio BAROLO
- GIACOSA Falletto Barolo
- Illuminati, Zanna, MONTEPULCIANO d'Abruzzo
- ISOLE E OLENA Cepparello
- ORNELLAIA Masseto
- Quintodecimo, CAMPANIA
- Francesco Rinaldi BAROLO
- Terre Nere, ETNA, Sicily
- Vajra BAROLO
- Viviani AMARONE DELLA VALPOLICELLA

RHÔNE VALLEY
- CLAPE Cornas
- Clos du Caillou CHÂTEAUNEUF-DU-PAPE
- Dom. du Colombier CROZES-HERMITAGE and HERMITAGE (red and white)
- CUILLERON Condrieu and St-Joseph
- JAMET Côte-Rôtie
- Dom. de la Mordorée CHÂTEAUNEUF-DU-PAPE
- Dom. du Mortier ST-JOSEPH Soulane
- Niéro CONDRIEU
- PERRET Condrieu and St-Joseph
- Raspail-Ay GIGONDAS
- Marc Sorrel HERMITAGE (red and white)

CABERNET SAUVIGNON
- BALNAVES, Australia
- CATENA Alta, Argentina
- Col Solare/CHATEAU STE MICHELLE, Washington State
- DIAMOND CREEK, California
- GROSSET Gaia, Australia
- HEDGES FAMILY ESTATE Red Mountain, Washington State
- RIDGE Monte Bello, California
- SANTA RITA Casa Real, Chile
- STAG'S LEAP WINE CELLARS Fay, California
- VASSE FELIX, Australia
- VERGELEGEN, South Africa

CHARDONNAY
- BERGSTRÖM, Oregon
- Dog Point, MARLBOROUGH, New Zealand
- FELTON ROAD, New Zealand
- FLOWERS Camp Meeting Ridge, California
- Norman Hardie, PRINCE EDWARD COUNTY, Canada
- HdV, California
- MARIMAR ESTATE, California
- NEUDORF, New Zealand
- Ocean Eight, MORNINGTON PENINSULA, Australia
- Payten & Jones Paul's Range, YARRA VALLEY, Australia
- PIERRO, Australia
- RAMEY Hyde Vineyard, California
- Rijckaert Vignes des Voises, CÔTES DU JURA, France
- YABBY LAKE, Australia

MERLOT
- Buccella, NAPA VALLEY, California
- CONO SUR 20 Barrels, Chile
- CRAGGY RANGE Sophia, New Zealand
- Fermoy Estate, MARGARET RIVER, Australia
- LEONETTI CELLAR, Pedestal, Washington State
- Le MACCHIOLE Messorio, Italy
- Sacred Hill Brokenstone, HAWKES BAY, New Zealand
- TAPANAPPA Whalebone Vineyard, Australia
- WOODWARD CANYON, Washington State

PINOT NOIR

- ATA RANGI, New Zealand
- Bethel Heights, WILLAMETTE VALLEY, Oregon
- Burn Cottage, CENTRAL OTAGO, New Zealand
- Crystallum Bona Fide, WALKER BAY, South Africa
- FELTON ROAD, New Zealand
- FLOWERS Camp Meeting Ridge, California
- Moorooduc, MORNINGTON PENINSULA, Australia
- Rippon Tinker's Field, CENTRAL OTAGO, New Zealand
- TEN MINUTES BY TRACTOR, Australia
- Valli, WAITAKI, New Zealand
- WILLIAMS SELYEM Westside Road Neighbors, California

RIESLING

- Tim ADAMS, Australia
- Ch. Belá/Egon Müller, Slovakia
- BRÜNDLMAYER Zöbinger Heiligenstein, Austria
- Larry CHERUBINO, Australia
- DÖNNHOFF Oberhäuser Brücke, Germany
- Fielding Estate, NIAGARA PENINSULA, Canada
- GROSSET, Australia
- JACOB'S CREEK Steingarten, Australia
- Toni JOST Bacharacher Hahn, Germany
- LEITZ Rudesheimer Rosengarten , Germany
- WEINBACH Schlossberg Cuvée Ste Catherine, France

SAUVIGNON BLANC

- Alpha Estate, Greece
- ASTROLABE Kekerengu Coast, New Zealand
- BRANCOTT Late Harvest, New Zealand
- CASA MARÍN Cipreses, Chile
- Cedarberg David Nieuwoudt Ghost Corner, ELIM, South Africa
- Gladstone Vineyard Sophie's Choice, MARTINBOROUGH/WAIRARAPA, New Zealand
- Greywacke, MARLBOROUGH, New Zealand
- Ch. MALARTIC-LAGRAVIÈRE, France
- MONTES Outer Limits, Chile
- Ch. SMITH-HAUT-LAFITTE, France
- TE MATA Cape Crest, New Zealand
- TerraVin, MARLBOROUGH, New Zealand

SYRAH/SHIRAZ

- Bilancia La Collina, HAWKES BAY, New Zealand
- CLONAKILLA, Australia
- FROMM, New Zealand
- JAMSHEED Garden Gully, Silvan and Warner, Australia
- KONGSGAARD, California
- Viña LEYDA Reserva, Chile
- MAN O'WAR Dreadnought, New Zealand
- MATETIC EQ, Chile
- Moon Curser, OKANAGAN VALLEY, Canada
- MULLINEUX Schist and Granite, South Africa
- Porseleinberg, SWARTLAND, South Africa
- TRINITY HILL Homage, New Zealand

FORTIFIED WINE

- Alvear Pedro Ximénez 1927 MONTILLA
- Argüeso MANZANILLA Las Medallas
- CHAMBERS Rutherglen Muscat
- Cossart Gordon Vintage Bual, MADEIRA WINE COMPANY
- Fernando de Castilla Antique sherries
- GONZÁLEZ BYASS Noé Pedro Ximénez
- GRAHAM'S 20-year-old Tawny
- HENRIQUES & HENRIQUES 15-year-old Madeira
- MAURY, Pla del Fount
- PENFOLDS Grandfather Rare Tawny

SPARKLING WINE

- ARGYLE Blanc de Blancs, Oregon
- Baud, CRÉMANT DU JURA, France
- Benjamin Bridge Brut Reserve, Nova Scotia, Canada
- CA'DEL BOSCO, Franciacorta Cuvée Annamaria Clementi, Italy
- Deviation Road, ADELAIDE HILLS, Australia
- Geisse Brut Rosé, Brazil
- GUSBOURNE, England
- Charles HEIDSIECK Champagne, France
- Lilbert CHAMPAGNE, France
- Meonhill Chardonnay, England
- POL ROGER Champagne, France
- QUARTZ REEF Vintage, New Zealand
- SCHRAMSBERG Blanc de Blancs, California
- SYNCLINE Scintillation, Washington State

11

TODAY'S WINE STYLES

Not so long ago, if I were to have outlined the basic wine styles, the list would have been strongly biased towards the classics – Bordeaux, Burgundy, Sancerre, Mosel Riesling, Champagne. But the classics have, over time, become expensive and unreliable – giving other regions the chance to offer us wines that may or may not owe anything to the originals. *These* are the flavours to which ambitious winemakers the world over now aspire.

WHITE WINES

Ripe, up-front, spicy Chardonnay is the main grape and fruit is the key: apricot, peach, melon, pineapple and tropical fruits, spiced up with the vanilla and butterscotch richness of some new oak to make a delicious, approachable, fruit cocktail of taste. Australia, South Africa and Chile are best at this style, but all, Australia in particular, have begun to tone down the richness. Oak-aged Chenin from South Africa, Semillon from Australia and Semillon-Sauvignon from South-West France can have similar characteristics.

Green and tangy New Zealand Sauvignon was the originator of this style – zingy lime zest, nettles and asparagus and passionfruit – and coastal South Africa and Chile's coastal valleys and Casablanca regions now have their own tangy, super-fresh examples. Good, less expensive versions from southern France and Hungary. Bordeaux and the Loire are the original sources of dry Sauvignon wines, and an expanding band of modern producers are matching clean fruit with zippy green tang. Spain's Rueda is zesty. Riesling in Australia is usually lean and limy; in New Zealand, Chile and Austria it's a little more scented and full.

Bone-dry, neutral Chablis is the most famous, and most appetizing. Unoaked Chardonnay in cool parts of Australia, New Zealand and the USA does a good, but fruitier, impression. Many Italian and Greek whites from indigenous varieties fit this bill in a minerally way. Southern French wines are often like this, as are basic wines from Bordeaux, South-West France, Muscadet and Anjou. Modern young Spanish whites and dry Portuguese Vinho Verdes are good examples. Cheap South African and California whites can be 'superneutral'. More interesting are Verdelhos and Chenins from Australia.

White Burgundy By this I mean the nutty, oatmealy-ripe but dry, subtly oaked styles of villages like Meursault at their best. Few people do it well, even in Burgundy itself, and it's a difficult style to emulate. California makes the most effort. Washington, Oregon, New York State and British Columbia each have occasional successes, but the best New World producers are in Australia and New Zealand, followed by South Africa.

Perfumy, dry or off-dry Gewürztraminer, Muscat and Pinot Gris from Alsace or Gewürztraminer, Scheurebe, Grauburgunder (Pinot Gris) and occasionally Riesling in southern Germany will give you this style. In New Zealand look for Riesling, Pinot Gris and Gewürztraminer. Irsai Olivér from Hungary and Torrontés from Argentina are both heady and perfumed. Albariño in Spain is leaner but heady with citrus scent. Viognier is apricotty and scented in southern Europe, Australia, Chile and California. Croatian Malvasia and Greek Malagousia are bright and subtly scented.

Mouthfuls of luscious gold Good sweet wines are difficult to make. Sauternes is the most famous, but Monbazillac, the Loire, and sometimes Alsace, can also come up with rich, intensely sweet wines that can live for decades. Top sweeties from Germany and Austria are stunning. Hungarian Tokaji has a wonderful sweet-sour smoky flavour. Australia, California and New Zealand produce some exciting examples and South Africa, the USA and Croatia have a few excellent sweeties. Canadian Icewines are impressive.

RED WINES

Juicy, fruity Beaujolais – and other wines from the Gamay grape – can be the perfect example, but leafy, raspberryish Loire reds, and simple Grenache and Syrah are also good. Modern Spanish reds from Valdepeñas, Bierzo and La Mancha, and old-vine Garnachas from Campo de Borja and Calatayud, do the trick, as do unoaked Douros from Portugal and young Valpolicella and Teroldego in Italy. Young Chilean Merlots are juicy, and Argentina has some good examples from Bonarda, Tempranillo, Sangiovese and Barbera.

Soft, strawberryish charmers Good Burgundy tops this group. Pinot Noir in California, Oregon, Chile and New Zealand is frequently delicious, and South Africa and Australia increasingly get it right. German Spätburgunder (Pinot Noir) can thrill. Rioja, Navarra and Valdepeñas in Spain sometimes get there. In Bordeaux, St-Émilion, Pomerol and Blaye can do the business.

Spicy, warm-hearted Australia's Shiraz reds are ripe, almost sweet, sinfully easy to enjoy, though they're becoming lighter and more scented. France's southern Rhône Valley and the traditional appellations in the far south of France are looking good. In Italy, Piedmont produces rich, beefy Barbera, Puglia has chocolaty Negroamaro and Sicily has Nero d'Avola. Portugal's Tejo and Alentejo also deliver the goods, as does Malbec in Argentina. California Zinfandel made in its most powerful style is spicy and rich; Lebanese reds have the succulent scent of the kasbah.

Deep and blackcurrant Chile has climbed back to the top of the Cabernet tree, though good producers in cooler parts of Australia and South Africa produce Cabernets of thrilling blackcurranty intensity. New Zealand Merlot and Cabernet Franc are dense and rich yet dry. California and Argentina too frequently overripen their Cabernet and Merlot, though restrained examples can be terrific, as can the best from Washington and Virginia. Top Bordeaux is on a rich blackcurranty roll since 2000: it's expensive but exciting – as is top Tuscan Cabernet.

Tough, tannic long-haul boys Bordeaux leads this field, and the best wines are really good after 10 years or so – but minor properties rarely age in the same way. Top wines in Tuscany and Piedmont age well – especially Brunello di Montalcino, Vino Nobile di Montepulciano, some IGT and Chianti Classico, Barolo and Barbaresco. Portugal has some increasingly good Dão and Douro reds, and Spain's Toro and Ribera del Duero reds need aging. Top Cabernet- and Malbec-based blends from Chile and Argentina are burly and dark and may age well.

Rosé There's been a surge in rosé's popularity, probably led by California's blush Zinfandel and Grenache. But far better, drier rosés are also becoming popular, with Spain, Italy and France leading the way for drier styles and Chile and New Zealand the best for fuller pinks.

SPARKLING AND FORTIFIED WINES

Fizz White, pink or red, dry or sweet; I sometimes think it doesn't matter what it tastes like as long as it's cold enough and plentiful. Champagne can be best, but frequently isn't – and there are lots of new-wave winemakers making good-value lookalikes. California, Tasmania, England and New Zealand all produce top-quality fizz. Spain can also excel. Prosecco is a lively party fizz. New kid on the block is Brazil.

Fortified wines Spain is unassailable as the master of dry fortifieds with its fino sherries. Ports are the most intense and satisfying rich red wines – but Australia, California and South Africa have their own versions of both these styles. Madeira's fortifieds have rich, brown smoky flavours, and luscious Muscats are made all round the Mediterranean and in Rutherglen, Australia.

13

GOOD MATCHES: FOOD AND WINE

Give me a rule, I'll break it – well, bend it anyway. So when I see the proliferation of publications laying down rules as to what wine to drink with what food, I get very uneasy and have to quell a burning desire to slosh back a Grand Cru Burgundy with my chilli con carne.

The pleasures of eating and drinking operate on so many levels that hard and fast rules make no sense. What about mood? If I'm in the mood for Champagne, Champagne it shall be, whatever I'm eating. What about company? An old friend, a lover, a bank manager – each of these companions would probably be best served by quite different wines. What about place? If I'm sitting gazing out across the shimmering Mediterranean, hand me anything, just as long as it's local – it'll be perfect.

Even so, there are some things that simply don't go well with wine: artichokes, asparagus, spinach, kippers and mackerel, chilli, salsas and vinegars, salted peanuts, chocolate, all flatten the flavours of wines. The general rule here is avoid tannic red wines and go for juicy young reds, or whites with plenty of fruit and fresh acidity. And for chocolate, liqueur Muscats, raisiny Banyuls or Italy's grapy, frothy Asti all work, but some people like Argentine Malbec or powerful Italian reds such as Barolo or Amarone. Don't be afraid to experiment. Who would guess that salty Roquefort cheese is perfect with rich, sweet Sauternes? So, with these factors in mind, the following pairings are not rules – just my recommendations.

FISH

Grilled or baked white fish White Burgundy or other fine Chardonnay, white Bordeaux, Viognier, Australian and New Zealand Riesling and Sauvignon, South African Chenin.

Grilled or baked oily or 'meaty' fish (e.g. salmon, tuna, swordfish) Alsace or Austrian Riesling, Grüner Veltliner, fruity New World Chardonnay or Semillon; reds such as Chinon or Bourgueil, Grenache/Garnacha, or New World Pinot Noir or Cabernet Franc.

Fried/battered fish Simple, fresh whites, e.g. Soave, Mâcon-Villages, Verdelho, Vinho Verde, Pinot Gris, white Bordeaux, or a Riesling Spätlese from the Pfalz.

Shellfish Chablis or unoaked Chardonnay, Sauvignon Blanc, Pinot Blanc; *clams and oysters* Albariño, Aligoté, Vinho Verde, Seyval Blanc; *crab* Riesling, Viognier; *lobster, scallops* fine Chardonnay, Champagne, Viognier; *mussels* Muscadet, Pinot Grigio.

Smoked fish Ice-cold basic fizz, manzanilla or fino sherry, Riesling, Sauvignon Blanc, Alsace Gewurztraminer or Pinot Gris.

MEAT

Beef and lamb are perfect with just about any red wine.

Beef/steak *Plain roasted or grilled* tannic reds, Bordeaux, New World Cabernet Sauvignon, Shiraz, Ribera del Duero, Chianti Classico.

Lamb *Plain roasted or grilled* red Burgundy, red Bordeaux, especially Pauillac or St-Julien, Rioja Reserva, New World Pinot Noir, Merlot or Malbec.

Pork *Plain roasted or grilled* full, spicy dry whites, e.g. Alsace Pinot Gris, lightly oaked Chardonnay; smooth reds, e.g. Rioja, Alentejo, Sicily; *ham, bacon, sausages, salami* young, fruity reds, e.g. Beaujolais, Lambrusco, Teroldego, unoaked Tempranillo or Garnacha, New World Malbec, Merlot, Zinfandel/Primitivo.

Veal *Plain roasted or grilled* full-bodied whites, e.g. Pinot Gris, Grüner Veltliner, white Rioja; soft reds, e.g. mature Rioja or Pinot Noir; *with cream-based sauce* full, ripe whites, e.g. Alsace or New Zealand Pinot Gris, Vouvray, oaked New World Chardonnay; *with rich red-wine sauce* (e.g. *osso buco*) young Italian reds, Zinfandel.

Venison *Plain roasted or grilled*
Barolo, St-Estèphe, Pomerol,
Côte de Nuits, Hermitage, big
Zinfandel, Alsace or German
Pinot Gris; *with red-wine sauce*
Piedmont and Portuguese reds,
Pomerol, St-Émilion, Priorat, New
World Syrah/Shiraz or Pinotage.
Chicken and turkey Most red
and white wines go with these
meats – much depends on the
sauce or accompaniments. Try
red or white Burgundy, red
Rioja Reserva, New World Pinot
Noir or Chardonnay.
Duck Pomerol, St-Émilion, Côte
de Nuits or Rhône reds, New World
Syrah/Shiraz (including sparkling)
or Merlot; also full, soft whites from
Austria and southern Germany.
Game birds *Plain roasted or grilled*
top reds from Burgundy, Rhône,
Tuscany, Piedmont, Ribera del
Duero, New World Cabernet or
Merlot; also full whites such as
oaked New World Semillon.
Casseroles and stews Generally
uncomplicated, full-flavoured
reds. The thicker the sauce, the
fuller the wine. If wine is used in
the preparation, match the colour.
For strong tomato flavours
see Pasta.

HIGHLY SPICED FOOD

Chinese Riesling, Sauvignon,
Pinot Gris, Gewürztraminer,
unoaked New World Chardonnay
or Semillon; fruity rosé; light Pinot
Noir.
Indian Aromatic whites,
e.g. Riesling, Sauvignon Blanc,
Gewürztraminer, Viognier;
non-tannic reds, e.g. Valpolicella,
Rioja, Grenache.
Mexican Fruity reds, e.g. Merlot,
Cabernet Franc, Grenache,
Syrah/Shiraz, Zinfandel.
Thai/South-East Asian Spicy
or tangy whites, e.g. Riesling,
Gewürztraminer, New World
Sauvignon Blanc, dry Alsace
Muscat. Coconut is tricky: New
World Chardonnay may work.

EGG DISHES

Champagne and traditional-method
fizz; light, fresh reds such as
Beaujolais or Chinon; full, dry
unoaked whites; New World rosé.

PASTA, PIZZA

With tomato sauce Barbera,
Valpolicella, Soave, Verdicchio,
New World Sauvignon Blanc; *with
meat-based sauce* north or central
Italian reds, French or New World
Syrah/Shiraz, Zinfandel; *with cream-
or cheese-based sauce* gently oaked
Chardonnay, Soave, Verdicchio,
Campania whites, Valpolicella or
Merlot; *with seafood/fish* dry, tangy
whites, e.g. Verdicchio, Vermentino,
Grüner Veltliner, Istrian Malvasia
from Croatia; *with pesto* New World
Sauvignon Blanc, Campania whites;
Dolcetto, Languedoc reds.
*Basic pizza, with tomato, mozzarella
and oregano* juicy young reds, e.g.
Grenache/Garnacha, Valpolicella,
Austrian reds, Languedoc reds.

SALADS

Sharp-edged whites, e.g. New
World Sauvignon Blanc, Chenin
Blanc, dry Riesling, Vinho Verde.

CHEESES

Hard Full reds from Italy, France
or Spain, New World Merlot or
Zinfandel, dry oloroso sherry,
tawny port.
Soft LBV port, Zinfandel, Alsace
Pinot Gris, Gewürztraminer.
Blue Botrytized sweet whites such
as Sauternes, vintage port, old
oloroso sherry, Malmsey Madeira.
Goats' Sancerre, Pouilly-Fumé,
New World Sauvignon Blanc,
Chinon, Saumur-Champigny.

DESSERTS

Chocolate Asti, Australian Liqueur
Muscat, Banyuls, Cabernet Franc
Icewine, Malbec, Barolo.
Fruit-based Sauternes, Eiswein,
fortified European Muscats.
Christmas pudding Asti,
Australian Liqueur Muscat.

MATCHING WINE AND FOOD

With very special bottles, when you have found an irresistible bargain or when you are casting around for culinary inspiration, it can be a good idea to let the wine dictate the choice of food.

Although I said earlier that rules in this area are made to be bent, if not broken, there are certain points to remember when matching wine and food. Before you make specific choices, think about some basic characteristics and see how thinking in terms of grape varieties and wine styles can point you in the right direction.

In many cases, the local food and wine combinations that have evolved over the years simply cannot be bettered (think of ripe Burgundy with *coq au vin* or *boeuf bourguignon*; Chianti Riserva with *bistecca alla Fiorentina*; Muscadet with Breton oysters). Yet the world of food and wine is moving so fast that it would be madness to be restricted by the old tenets. Californian cuisine, fusion food, and the infiltration of innumerable ethnic influences coupled with the re-invigoration of traditional wines, continuous experiment with new methods and blends and the opening up of completely new wine areas mean that the search for perfect food and wine partners is, and will remain, very much an on-going process.

Here are some of the characteristics you need to consider, plus a summary of the main grape varieties and their best food matches.

Body/weight As well as considering the taste of the wine you need to match the body or weight of the wine to the intensity of the food's flavour. A heavy alcoholic wine will not suit a delicate dish, and vice versa.

Acidity The acidity of a dish should balance the acidity of a wine. High-acid flavours, such as tomato, lemon or vinegar, should need matching acidity in their accompanying wines, but, almost by mistake, I've tried a few reds with salad dressing and the wine's fruit was enhanced, not wrecked. Was I lucky? More research needed, I think. Use acidity in wine to cut through the richness of a dish – but for this to work, make sure the wine is full in flavour.

Sweetness Sweet food makes dry wine taste unpleasantly lean and acidic. With desserts and puddings, find a wine that is at least as sweet as the food (sweeter than the food is better). However, many savoury foods, such as carrots, onions and parsnips, taste slightly sweet and dishes in which they feature prominently will go best with ripe, fruity wines that have a touch of sweetness.

Salt Salty foods, such as blue cheese, and sweet wines match. Salty foods and tannic reds are definitely best avoided.

Age/maturity The bouquet of a wine is only acquired over time and should be savoured and appreciated: with age, many red wines acquire complex flavours and perfumes and simple food flavours are the best accompaniment.

Tannin Red meat, when cooked rare, can have the effect of softening tannic wine. Mature hard cheeses can make rough wine seem gentle. Avoid eggs and fish with tannic wines.

Oak Oak flavours in wine vary from the satisfyingly subtle to positively strident. This latter end of the scale can conflict with food, although it may be suitable for smoked fish (white wines only) or full-flavoured meat or game.

Wine in the food If you want to use wine in cooking it is best to use the same style of wine as the one you are going to drink with the meal (it can be an inferior version though).

RED GRAPES

Barbera Wines made to be drunk young have high acidity that can hold their own with sausages, salami, ham, and tomato sauces. Complex, older or oak-aged wines from the top growers need to be matched with rich food such as beef casseroles and game dishes.

Cabernet Franc Best drunk with plain rather than sauced meat dishes, or, slightly chilled, with grilled or baked salmon or trout.

Cabernet Sauvignon All over the world the Cabernet Sauvignon makes full-flavoured reliable red wine: the ideal food wine. Cabernet Sauvignon seems to have a particular affinity with lamb, but it partners all plain roast or grilled meats and game well and would be an excellent choice for many sauced meat dishes such as beef casserole, steak and kidney pie or rabbit stew and substantial dishes made with mushrooms.

Dolcetto Dolcetto produces fruity purple wines that go beautifully with hearty meat dishes such as calves' liver and onions or casseroled pork, beef or game.

Gamay The grape of red Beaujolais, Gamay makes wine you can drink whenever, wherever, however and with whatever you want – although it's particularly good lightly chilled on hot summer days. It goes well with pâtés, bacon and sausages because its acidity provides a satisfying foil to their richness. It would be a good choice for many vegetarian dishes.

Grenache/Garnacha Frequently blended with other grapes, Grenache nonetheless dominates, with its high alcoholic strength and rich, spicy flavours. These are wines readily matched with food: barbecues and casseroles for heavier wines; almost anything for lighter reds and rosés – vegetarian dishes, charcuterie, picnics, grills, and even meaty fish such as tuna and salmon.

Merlot Merlot makes soft, rounded, fruity wines that are some of the easiest red wines to enjoy without food, yet are also a good choice with many kinds of food. Spicier game dishes, herby terrines and pâtés, pheasant, pigeon, duck or goose all team well with Merlot; substantial casseroles made with wine are excellent with Pomerols and St-Émilions; and the soft fruitiness of the wines is perfect for pork, liver, turkey, and savoury foods with a hint of sweetness such as Iberico, Parma or honey-roast ham.

Nebbiolo Lean but fragrant, early-drinking styles of Nebbiolo wine are best with Italian salami, pâtés, *bresaola* and lighter meat dishes. Top Barolos and Barbarescos need substantial food: *bollito misto*, rich hare or beef casseroles and *brasato al Barolo* (a large piece of beef marinated then braised slowly in Barolo) are just the job in Piedmont, or anywhere else for that matter.

Pinot Noir The great grape of Burgundy has taken its food-friendly complexity all over the wine world. However, nothing can beat the marriage of great wine with sublime local food that is Burgundy's heritage, and it is Burgundian dishes that spring to mind as perfect partners for Pinot Noir: *coq au vin*, *boeuf bourguignon*, rabbit with mustard, braised ham, chicken with tarragon, *entrecôtes* from prized Charolais cattle with a rich red-wine sauce … the list is endless.

Pinot Noir's subtle flavours make it a natural choice for complex meat dishes, but it is excellent with plain grills and roasts. New World Pinots are often richer and fruitier – good with grills and roasts and a match for salmon or tuna.

17

In spite of the prevalence of superb cheese in Burgundy, the best Pinot Noir red wines are wasted on cheese.

Sangiovese Only in Tuscany does Sangiovese claim to be one of the world's great grapes, though Australia and Argentina are starting to succeed. Sangiovese definitely 'needs' food and Chianti, Rosso di Montalcino, Vino Nobile di Montepulciano and the biggest of them all, Brunello, positively demand to be drunk with food. Drink them with grilled steak, roast meats and game, calves' liver, casseroles, hearty pasta sauces, *porcini* mushrooms and Pecorino cheese.

Syrah/Shiraz Modern Syrah/Shiraz can be rich and exotic or scented and savoury, but it always offers loads of flavour and is superb with full-flavoured food. France and Australia lead the pack, followed by South America, South Africa, California and Washington, and even New Zealand. The classic barbecue wine, also brilliant with roasts, game, hearty casseroles and charcuterie. It can be good with tangy cheeses such as Manchego or Cheshire.

Tempranillo Spain's best native red grape makes juicy wines for drinking young, and matures well in a rich (usually) oaky style. Good with game, cured hams and sausages, casseroles and meat grilled with herbs, particularly roast lamb. It can partner some Indian and Mexican dishes.

Zinfandel California's much-planted, most versatile grape is used for a bewildering variety of wine styles from bland, sweetish pinks to rich, succulent, fruity reds. And the good red Zinfandels themselves may vary greatly in style, from relatively soft and light to big and beefy, but they're always ripe and ready for spicy, smoky, unsubtle food: barbecued meat, haunches of lamb, venison or beef, game casseroles, sausages, Tex-Mex, the Beach Boys, The Eagles – anything rowdy – Zin copes with them all.

WHITE GRAPES

Albariño Light, crisp, aromatic in a grapefruity way, this goes well with crab and prawn dishes as well as Chinese-style chicken dishes.

Aligoté This Burgundian grape can, at its best, make very versatile food wine. It goes well with many fish and seafood dishes, smoked fish, salads and snails in garlic and butter.

Chardonnay More than almost any other grape, Chardonnay responds to different climatic conditions and to the winemaker's art. This, plus the relative ease with which it can be grown, accounts for the marked gradation of flavours and styles: from steely, cool-climate austerity to almost tropical lusciousness. The relatively sharp end of the spectrum is one of the best choices for simple fish dishes; most Chardonnays are superb with roast chicken or other white meat; the really full, rich, New World-style blockbusters need rich fish and seafood dishes. Oaky Chardonnays are, surprisingly, a good choice for smoked fish.

Chenin Blanc One of the most versatile of grapes, Chenin Blanc makes wines ranging from averagely quaffable dry whites to the great sweet whites of the Loire. The lighter wines can be good as aperitifs or with light fish dishes or salads while the medium-sweet versions usually retain enough of their acidity to counteract the richness of creamy chicken and meat dishes. The sweet wines are superb with foie gras or blue cheese, and with fruit puddings – especially those made with slightly tart fruit.

Gewürztraminer Spicy and perfumed, Gewürztraminer has the weight and flavour to go with such hard-to-match dishes as *choucroute* and smoked fish. It is also a good choice for Chinese or any lightly spiced Oriental food, with its use of lemongrass, coriander and ginger, and pungent soft cheeses, such as Munster from Alsace.

Grüner Veltliner In its lightest form, this makes a peppery, refreshing aperitif. Riper, more structured versions keep the pepper but add peach and apple fruit, and are particularly good with grilled or baked fish.

Marsanne These rich, fat wines are a bit short of acidity, so match them with simply prepared chicken, pork, fish or vegetables.

Muscadet The dry, light Muscadet grape (best wines are *sur lie*) is perfect with seafood.

Muscat Fragrant, grapy wines in a multitude of styles, from delicate to downright syrupy. The drier ones are more difficult to pair with food, but can be delightful with Oriental cuisines; the sweeties really come into their own with most desserts. Sweet Moscato d'Asti, delicious by itself, goes well with rich Christmas pudding or mince pies.

Pinot Blanc Clean, bright and appley, Pinot Blanc is very food-friendly. Classic fish and chicken dishes, modern vegetarian food, pasta and pizza all match up well.

Pinot Gris In Alsace, this makes rich, fat wines that need rich, fat food: *choucroute*, *confit de canard*, rich pork and fish dishes. Italian Pinot Grigio wines are light quaffers. New World Pinot Gris is often delightfully fragrant and ideal with grilled fish.

Riesling Good dry Rieslings are excellent with spicy cuisine. Sweet Rieslings are best enjoyed for their own lusciousness but are suitable partners to fruit-based desserts. In between, those with a fresh acid bite and some residual sweetness can counteract the richness of, say, goose or duck, and the fuller examples can be good with Oriental food and otherwise hard-to-match salads.

Sauvignon Blanc Tangy green flavours and high acidity are the hallmarks of this grape. Led by New Zealand, New World Sauvignons are some of the snappiest, tastiest whites around and make good, thirst-quenching aperitifs. Brilliant with seafood and Oriental cuisine, they also go well with tomato dishes, salads and goats' cheese.

Sémillon Dry Bordeaux Blancs are excellent with fish and shellfish; fuller, riper New World Semillons are equal to spicy food and rich sauces, often going even better with meat than with fish; sweet Sémillons can partner many puddings, especially rich, creamy ones. Sémillon also goes well with many cheeses, and Sauternes with Roquefort is a classic combination.

Viognier Fresh, young Viognier is at its best drunk as an aperitif. It can also go well with mildly spiced Indian dishes or chicken in a creamy sauce. The apricot aroma that typifies even inexpensive Viognier suggests another good pairing – pork or chicken dishes with apricot stuffing.

MAKING THE MOST OF WINE

Most wine is pretty hardy stuff and can put up with a fair amount of rough handling. Young red wines can knock about in the back of a car for a day or two and be lugged from garage to kitchen to dinner table without coming to too much harm. Serving young white wines when well chilled can cover up all kinds of ill-treatment – a couple of hours in the fridge should do the trick. Even so, there are some conditions that are better than others for storing your wines, especially if they are on the mature side. And there are certain ways of serving wines that will emphasize any flavours or perfumes they have.

STORING

Most wines are sold ready for drinking, and it will be hard to ruin them if you store them for a few months before you pull the cork. Don't stand them next to the central heating or the cooker, though, nor on a sunny windowsill, as too much warmth will flatten the flavour and give a 'baked' taste.

Light and extremes of temperature are also the things to worry about if you are storing wine long-term. Some wines, Chardonnay for instance, are particularly sensitive to exposure to light over several months, and the damage will be worse if the bottle is made of pale-coloured glass. The warmer the wine, the quicker it will age, and really high temperatures can spoil wine quite quickly. Beware in the winter of garages and outhouses, too: a very cold snap – say –4°C (25°F) or below – will freeze your wine, push out the corks and crack the bottles. An underground cellar is ideal, with a fairly constant temperature of 10°–15°C (50°–59°F). And bottles really do need to lie on their sides, so that the cork stays damp and swollen, and keeps out the air. You can store screwcaps upright if you want.

TEMPERATURE

The person who thought up the rule that red wine should be served at room temperature certainly didn't live in a modern, centrally heated flat. It's no great sin to serve a big, beefy red at the temperature of your central heating, but I prefer most reds just a touch cooler. Over-heated wine tastes flabby, and will lose some of its more volatile aromas. In general, the lighter the red, the cooler it can be. Really light, refreshing reds, such as Beaujolais, are nice lightly chilled. Ideally, I'd serve Burgundy and other Pinot Noir wines at larder temperature (about 15°C/59°F), Bordeaux and Rioja a bit warmer (17°C/62°F), Rhône wines and New World Cabernet at a comfortable room temperature, but never more than 20°C (68°F).

Chilling white wines makes them taste fresher, emphasizing their acidity. White wines with low acidity especially benefit from chilling, and it's vital for sparkling wines if you want to avoid exploding corks and a tableful of froth. Drastic chilling also subdues flavours, however – a useful ruse if you're serving basic wine, but a shame if the wine is very good. A good guide for whites is to give the cheapest and lightest a spell in the fridge, but serve bigger and better wines – Australian Chardonnays or top white Burgundies – perhaps halfway between fridge and central-heating temperature. If you're undecided, err on the cooler side, for whites or reds. To chill wine quickly, and to keep it cool, an ice bucket is much more efficient if filled with a mixture of ice and water, rather than ice alone.

OPENING THE BOTTLE

There's no corkscrew to beat the Screwpull, and the Spinhandle Screwpull is especially easy to use. Don't worry if bits of cork crumble into the wine – just fish them out of your glass. Tight corks that refuse to budge might be loosened if you run hot water over the bottle neck to expand the glass. If the cork is loose and falls in, push it right in and don't worry about it.

Opening sparkling wines is a serious business – point the cork away from people! Once you've started, never take your hand off the cork until it's safely out. Remove the foil, loosen the wire, hold the wire and cork firmly and twist the bottle. If the wine froths, hold the bottle at an angle of 45 degrees, and have a glass at hand.

AIRING AND DECANTING

Contact with air *does* change wine. Opening a bottle and pouring out half a glass will help mix oxygen with the wine and improve the flavour. Screw-capped wines are greatly improved by exposure to oxygen – the screw cap is such an efficient closure that the wine won't have experienced air before it's opened and typically its flavours will blossom after 5 or 10 minutes – i.e. by the second glass.

Decanting is good fun – and makes the wine look lovely. Some older wines with sediment need decanting to separate the liquid from the deposit: mature Bordeaux, Rhône, Burgundy and Vintage Port usually benefit. Ideally, if you are able to plan that far in advance, you need to stand the bottle upright for a day or two to let the sediment settle in the bottom. Draw the cork extremely gently. As you tip the bottle, shine a bright light through from underneath as you pour in a single steady movement. Stop pouring when you see the sediment approaching the bottle neck. Contrary to many wine buffs' practice, I would decant a mature wine only just before serving; elderly wines often fade rapidly once they meet with air, and an hour in the decanter could kill off what little fruit they had left.

A good-quality young white wine can benefit from decanting, and mature white Burgundy looks fabulous – all glistening gold – in a decanter.

GLASSES

If you want to taste wine at its best, to enjoy all its flavours and aromas, to admire its colours and texture, choose glasses designed for the purpose and show the wine a bit of respect. The ideal wine glass is a fairly large tulip shape, narrower at the top, to concentrate aromas, and is made of fine, clear glass, with a slender stem. When you pour the wine, fill the glass no more than halfway to allow space for aromas. For sparkling wines choose a tall, slender flute glass, as it helps the bubbles to last longer.

KEEPING LEFTOVERS

Leftover white wine keeps better than red, since the tannin and colouring matter in red wine is easily attacked by the air. Any wine, red or white, keeps better in the fridge than in a warm kitchen. And most wines, if well made in the first place, will be perfectly acceptable, if not pristine, after 2 or 3 days re-corked in the fridge. Young, screw-capped wines, especially whites, might even improve and can easily last a week and still be good to drink.

A variety of gadgets are sold for the purpose of keeping wine fresh. The ones that work by blanketing the wine with heavier-than-air inert gas are much better than those that create a vacuum in the air space in the bottle.

FRANCE

I've visited most of the wine-producing countries of the world, but the one I come back to again and again, with my enthusiasm undimmed by time, is France. The sheer range of its wine flavours, the number of wine styles produced, and indeed the quality differences, from very best to very nearly worst, continue to enthral me, and as each year's vintage nears, I find myself itching to leap into the car and head for the vineyards of Champagne, of Burgundy, of Bordeaux and the Loire. France is currently going through a difficult period – aware that the New World is making tremendous strides and is the master of innovation and technology, yet unwilling to admit to the quality and character of this new breed of wines. But the best French producers learn from the newcomers while proudly defining their Frenchness.

CLIMATE AND SOIL

France lies between the 40th and 50th parallels north, and the climate runs from the distinctly chilly and almost too cool to ripen grapes in the far north near the English Channel, right through to the swelteringly hot and almost too torrid to avoid grapes overripening in the far south on the Mediterranean shores. In the north, the most refined and delicate sparkling wine is made in Champagne. In the south, rich, luscious dessert Muscats and fortified wines dominate. In between is just about every sort of wine you could wish for.

The factors that influence a wine's flavour are the grape variety, the soil and climate, and the winemaker's techniques. Most of the great wine grapes, like the red Cabernet Sauvignon, Merlot, Pinot Noir and Syrah, and the white Chardonnay, Sauvignon Blanc, Sémillon and Viognier, find conditions in France where they can ripen slowly but reliably – and slow, even ripening always gives the best flavours to a wine. Since grapes have been grown for over 2000 years in France, the most suitable varieties for the different soils and mesoclimates have naturally evolved. And since winemaking was brought to France by the Romans, generation upon generation of winemakers have refined their techniques to produce the best possible results from their different grape types. The great wines of areas like Bordeaux and Burgundy are the results of centuries of experience and of trial and error, which winemakers from other countries of the world now use as role models in their attempts to create good wine.

WINE REGIONS

White grapes generally ripen more easily than red grapes and they dominate the northern regions. Even so, the chilly Champagne region barely manages to ripen its red or white grapes on its chalky soil. But the resultant acid wine is the ideal base for sparkling wine: with good winemaking and a few years' maturing, the young still wine can transform into a golden, honeyed sparkling wine of incomparable finesse.

Alsace, on the German border, is warmer and drier than its northerly location might suggest (the vineyards sit in the Vosges mountains' rain shadow). It produces mainly dry – and some sweet – whites, from grapes such as Riesling, Pinot Gris and Gewurztraminer that are seldom encountered elsewhere in France, plus a little Pinot Noir red. With its clear blue skies, Alsace can provide ripeness, and therefore the higher alcoholic strength of the warm south, but also the perfume and fragrance of the cool north.

South-east of Paris, heading into limestone country, Chablis marks the northernmost tip of the Burgundy region, and the Chardonnay grape here produces very dry wines, usually with a streak of green acidity and minerality, but nowadays with a fuller, softer texture to subdue any harshness.

It's a good 2 hours' drive further south to the heart of Burgundy – the Côte d'Or, which runs between Dijon and Chagny. World-famous villages such as Gevrey-Chambertin and Vosne-Romanée (where the red Pinot Noir dominates) and Meursault and Puligny-Montrachet (where Chardonnay reigns) produce the great Burgundies that have given the region renown over the centuries. Lesser Burgundies – but they're still good – are produced further south in the Côte Chalonnaise, while between Mâcon and Lyon are the Mâconnais white wine villages (Pouilly-Fuissé and St-Véran are particularly tasty) and the villages of Beaujolais, famous for bright, easy-going red wine from the Gamay grape, and less well known for their whites. The 10 Beaujolais Crus or 'growths' produce wine with more character and structure.

East of Burgundy, Jura makes unusual whites, good sparkling and light reds; further south, Savoie and Bugey make crisp whites and light, spicy reds.

South of Lyon, in the Rhône Valley, red wines take over. The Syrah grape makes great wine at Côte-Rôtie, Hermitage and Cornas in the north, while in the much warmer south the Grenache and a host of supporting grapes (most southern Rhône reds add at least Syrah, Mourvèdre or Cinsaut to their blends) make profound, densely flavoured reds, of which Châteauneuf-du-Pape is the richest, most famous and most expensive. Viognier makes scented whites at Condrieu and Château-Grillet in the north, where Marsanne is the foundation for the long-lived white wines of Hermitage.

The whole of the south of France has undergone considerable change over the last 25 years. New ownership and a new generation are producing exciting wines from previously unpromising lands. The traditional Provence,

23

Languedoc and Roussillon vineyards make increasingly impressive reds from Grenache, Syrah, Mourvèdre and Carignan, as well as some surprisingly fragrant whites from varieties such as Rolle, Marsanne, Roussanne, Grenache Blanc and Gris and even Carignan Blanc. Rosés, previously overproduced and underflavoured, are now some of France's most elegant. And with the new Languedoc appellation (covering the whole of Languedoc and Roussillon), the freedom to improve by blending will be extended. Many tasty and affordable vins de pays/IGP wines come either from international grapes such as Cabernet and Chardonnay or traditional southern varieties; Viognier is increasingly finding its way into Provençal white wines. Roussillon also makes fine sweet Muscats and Grenache-based fortifieds.

The South-West is finally taking its rightful place as a producer of some of France's most original and unusual wines, from as many as 50 different grape varieties. Dry whites from Gascony, Bergerac and Gaillac are crisp and fresh, while Monbazillac, Saussignac and Jurançon make fine sweet wines. Madiran, Cahors, Fronton, Gaillac and Bergerac produce top-quality reds.

But Bordeaux is the king here. Cabernet Sauvignon and Merlot are the chief grapes, the Cabernet dominating the production of deep reds from the Médoc peninsula and its famous villages of Margaux, St-Julien, Pauillac and St-Estèphe on the left bank of the Gironde river. Round the city of Bordeaux are Pessac-Léognan and Graves, where Cabernet and Merlot blend to produce fragrant refined reds. On the right bank of the Gironde estuary, the Merlot is most important in the plump rich reds of St-Émilion and Pomerol. Sweet whites from Sémillon and Sauvignon Blanc are made in Sauternes, with increasingly good dry whites produced in the Entre-Deux-Mers, and especially in Graves and Pessac-Léognan.

The Loire Valley is France's northernmost Atlantic wine region but, since the river rises in the heart of France not far from the Rhône and extends over 1000km (600 miles), styles from its 77 appellations vary widely. Sancerre and Pouilly in the east produce tangy, *terroir*-influenced Sauvignon whites and some surprisingly good Pinot Noir reds and rosés. The river Cher, which joins the Loire at Tours, grows Sauvignon and Romorantin for whites, Gamay and Côt/Malbec for reds. In central Touraine, Saumur and Anjou the focus is on Chenin Blanc in styles which range from bone dry to lusciously sweet, even sparkling, and for reds (and rosés), Cabernet Franc with a little Cabernet Sauvignon. Down at the mouth of the river, as it slips past Nantes into the Atlantic swell, the vineyards of Muscadet produce dry whites that take on the salty notes of the sea. At the vanguard of the natural wine movement – some 2415 hectares (6000 acres) are cultivated organically – the Loire Valley is teeming with producers working as naturally as possible both in the vineyard and winery; look out for ambitious, characterful vins de France.

CLASSIFICATIONS

Not for the first time, France is making an attempt to simplify its wine classification system, this time in partnership with general changes in the EU wine industry. The basic category is **Vin de France** and this can now show both grape variety and vintage on the label, covering both everyday wines and exciting non-mainstream innovations (see page 162). The middle-ranking **Vin de Pays** category has been morphed into a pretty similar **IGP** (Indication Géographique Protégée) category. For instance, Vin de Pays d'Oc may now appear with Pays d'Oc IGP on the label. It'll taste exactly the same, but there'll be another gaggle of contented bureaucrats somewhere in Europe. The top classification is Appellation d'Origine Protégée, or **AOP**, which will gradually replace **AC** (Appellation d'Origine Contrôlée).

2013 VINTAGE REPORT

2013 was the most onerous vintage the Bordelais have experienced in the last 20 years. Nothing seemed to go right from start to finish. Flowering was blighted by rain and unseasonably cold weather, which continued until the end of June. This meant poor fruit set and pressure from mildew. Warmer weather in July and August brought a moment of optimism but the delay in the ripening cycle was never fully recouped. A hailstorm in early August caused a huge amount of damage in the Entre-Deux-Mers and Castillon. Then semi-tropical conditions in September encouraged grey rot, inciting growers to harvest before the grapes were fully ripe. The consequences were a tiny crop (25% less than 2012) and a small amount of satisfactory red wine at the highest level, where draconian selection could be applied. Otherwise, finding a positive note is difficult. There's some decent fruity rosé, and dry whites are fresh and aromatic. Sauternes also returned with a respectable year. Most of the reds, though, need to be looked at with a wary eye.

In South-West France a long, cool but mostly dry winter gave way to a cold, dry spring, which retarded the budding of the grapes. There was little warmth until July. The harvest was punctuated with rain. Frost and hail devastated the crop in many areas, particularly Bergerac and Cahors. Much-reduced volume, but the quality is expected to be fair. A difficult year.

Poor old Burgundy. We start to wonder whether the vignerons will ever produce a full crop again. This time the problems were poor, damp flowering conditions, which restricted the potential size of the crop, and then a catastrophic hailstorm across Volnay, Pommard, Beaune, Savigny and into the Corton and Corton-Charlemagne vineyards. It is going to be hit and miss everywhere else, though once again the Côte de Nuits seems to have had the best of conditions. Whites in the Côte de Beaune may prove interesting; Chablis was difficult as rot started to set in.

After a couple of trying vintages, Beaujolais is back on form in 2013. Things weren't looking that promising early in the year, with an extremely cold spring delaying growth. However, a hot and sunny summer resulted in very healthy grapes. Growers were grateful for rainy spells during the relatively cool September: these helped bring the crop to full maturity in time for a later-than-usual harvest. The only catch is that yields are modest, so the best wines will be in short supply.

The northern Rhône reds have good colour, agreeable depth and last pretty well on the palate. It is a cool style of vintage. The southern Rhône reds are lighter than usual; the right bank around Lirac fared OK; elsewhere the signature is loose-knit fruit, a juicy style. 2012 is superior to both 2013 and 2011. The 2013 whites are fresh, clear, aromatic.

In Provence, a slow, wet start to the year meant that flowering, fruit set and ripening were all delayed, resulting in a harvest 2 weeks later than usual. Regional storms in June caused some damage, but less than in 2012. The wet spring meant the vines were not water-stressed, while moderate temperatures allowed for slow and consistent ripening. Rain in September gave a final boost to the development of the fruit, although in some regions, such as Bellet, the heavy rain caused harvest delays. Balanced, fresh, fruity and aromatic wines epitomize the 2013 vintage.

The Languedoc fared significantly better than the rest of France. One of the wettest springs for 30 years avoided any problems of water stress during the summer. However, the summer was late to arrive, so the flowering was late and uneven, making for smaller yields, especially from Grenache. Limoux had hail. A fine September brought on a very late but very good harvest, with many fresh, fragrant wines.

In the Loire, a cold spring and late frosts delayed budbreak and flowering by up to 4 weeks, and led to some uneven ripening. Vouvray suffered a devastating hailstorm in mid-June, resulting in a loss of some 70% of the crop. A hot, dry summer came to the rescue, and growers across the region saw their grapes ripen steadily, though lack of rainfall threatened to block full maturity, so when the rains began to fall in late September they were welcomed in many quarters, despite the threat of rot. Overall, yields are fairly low, and alcohol levels are a little lower than usual, while acidity is on the high side, especially in Muscadet and the Sauvignon Blancs. Reds had to be picked earlier than usual to avoid the risk of rot, but are balanced. Dry Chenin Blanc is, arguably, the star style of the vintage, but this is not a great year for sweet wines.

In Alsace a poor flowering and hailstorms produced a reduced crop of fairly high-acid wines. Attempts to leave the grapes to ripen in an Indian summer were threatened by early October rains. Few sweet wines, high acids all round.

In Champagne a cold wet spring led to a late harvest, with picking continuing until mid-October. Yields in the Chardonnay-dominated Côte des Blancs were hit by poor weather during flowering, and hail, but while quality is uneven there is some excellent Chardonnay and Pinot Noir with good ripeness and acidity levels in the best sites. Aube Pinot Noir was hit by September rain.

French entries in the A–Z section (pages 62–327), by region.

ALSACE	PRODUCERS	Mann, Albert	Trimbach
ACs	Deiss, Marcel	Muré, René	Turckheim, Cave de
Alsace	Hugel	Ostertag, Dom.	Weinbach
Crémant d'Alsace	Josmeyer	Schoffit, Dom.	Zind-Humbrecht

BORDEAUX	Médoc	Batailley	Falfas
ACs	Montagne-St-	Beau-Séjour Bécot	de Fargues
Barsac	Émilion	Belair-Monange	Ferrière
Blaye-Côtes de	Moulis	Beychevelle	de Fieuzal
Bordeaux	Pauillac	le Bon Pasteur	Figeac
Bordeaux	Pessac-Léognan	Bonnet	La Fleur de Boüard
Bordeaux Supérieur	Pomerol	Branaire-Ducru	la Fleur-Pétrus
Cadillac	Premières Côtes de	Brane-Cantenac	Gazin
Cadillac-Côtes de	Bordeaux	Calon-Ségur	Gilette
Bordeaux	Puisseguin-St-	Canon	Gloria
Canon-Fronsac	Émilion	Canon-la-Gaffelière	Grand-Puy-Ducasse
Castillon-Côtes de	St-Émilion	Cantemerle	Grand-Puy-Lacoste
Bordeaux	St-Émilion Grand	Chasse-Spleen	Gruaud-Larose
Cérons	Cru	Cheval Blanc	Guiraud
Côtes de Bourg	St-Estèphe	Dom. de Chevalier	Haut-Bages-Libéral
Entre-Deux-Mers	St-Georges-St-	Clarke	Haut-Bailly
Francs-Côtes de	Émilion	Climens	Haut-Batailley
Bordeaux	St-Julien	La Conseillante	Haut-Brion
Fronsac	Ste-Croix-du-Mont	Cos d'Estournel	Haut-Marbuzet
Graves	Sauternes	Coutet	d'Issan
Haut-Médoc		Doisy-Daëne	Kirwan
Lalande-de-Pomerol	CHATEAUX	Doisy-Védrines	Lafaurie-Peyraguey
Listrac-Médoc	Angélus	Ducru-Beaucaillou	Lafite-Rothschild
Loupiac	d'Angludet	Duhart-Milon	Lafleur
Lussac-St-Émilion	l'Arrosée	l'Église-Clinet	Lafon-Rochet
Margaux	Ausone	l'Évangile	Lagrange

la Lagune
Langoa-Barton
Lascombes
Latour
Latour-Martillac
Latour-à-Pomerol
Laville-Haut-Brion
Léoville-Barton
Léoville-Las-Cases
Léoville-Poyferré
la Louvière
Lynch-Bages
Magdelaine
Malartic-Lagravière
Malescot St-Exupéry
Margaux
Maucaillou

Meyney
la Mission-Haut-
  Brion
Monbousquet
Montrose
Moueix, J P
Mouton-Cadet
Mouton-Rothschild
Nairac
Palmer
Pape-Clément
Pavie
Pavie-Macquin
Petit-Village
Pétrus
de Pez
Pichon-Longueville

Pichon-Longueville-
  Lalande
le Pin
Pontet-Canet
Potensac
Poujeaux
Prieuré-Lichine
Rauzan-Ségla
Reynon
Rieussec
Roc de Cambes
St-Pierre
Siran
Smith-Haut-Lafitte
Sociando-Mallet
Suduiraut
Talbot

Tertre-Rôteboeuf
la Tour Blanche
Troplong-Mondot
Trotanoy
Valandraud
Vieux-Château-
  Certan
d'Yquem

SEE ALSO
Bordeaux Red
  Wines
Bordeaux White
  Wines
St-Émilion Premier
  Grand Cru Classé

**BURGUNDY AND
BEAUJOLAIS**
ACs
Aloxe-Corton
Auxey-Duresses
Bâtard-Montrachet
Beaujolais
Beaujolais-Villages
Beaune
Blagny
Bonnes-Mares
Bourgogne
Bourgogne-Côte
  Chalonnaise
Bourgogne-Côte
  d'Or
Bourgogne-Hautes-
  Côtes de Beaune
Bourgogne-Hautes-
  Côtes de Nuits
Brouilly
Chablis
Chablis Grand Cru
Chambertin
Chambolle-Musigny
Chassagne-
  Montrachet
Chénas
Chiroubles
Chorey-lès-Beaune
Clos des Lambrays
Clos de la Roche
Clos St-Denis
Clos de Tart
Clos de Vougeot
Corton
Corton-Charlemagne
Côte de Beaune
Côte de Beaune-
  Villages
Côte de Brouilly

Côte de Nuits-
  Villages
Coteaux
  Bourguignons
Coteaux du
  Lyonnais
Crémant de
  Bourgogne
Échézeaux
Fixin
Fleurie
Gevrey-Chambertin
Givry
Irancy
Juliénas
Ladoix
Mâcon
Mâcon-Villages
Maranges
Marsannay
Mercurey
Meursault
Montagny
Monthelie
Montrachet
Morey-St-Denis
Morgon
Moulin-à-Vent
Musigny
Nuits-St-Georges
Pernand-Vergelesses
Pommard
Pouilly-Fuissé
Pouilly-Vinzelles
Puligny-Montrachet
Régnié
Richebourg
la Romanée
la Romanée-Conti
Romanée-St-Vivant
Rully

St-Amour
St-Aubin
St-Bris
St-Romain
St-Véran
Santenay
Savigny-lès-Beaune
la Tâche
Viré-Clessé
Volnay
Vosne-Romanée
Vougeot

PRODUCERS
d'Angerville,
  Marquis
Bachelet
Bellene
Boisset
Bouchard Père & Fils
Brocard, Jean-Marc
Buxy, Vignerons de
Carillon
Cathiard, Sylvain
Chablisienne, La
Chandon de Briailles
Clair, Bruno
Coche-Dury, J-F
Colin
Dauvissat, Vincent
Drouhin, Joseph
Duboeuf, Georges
Dujac
Faiveley, Joseph
Gagnard, Jean-Noël
Girardin, Vincent
Grivot, Jean
Gros
Hospices de Beaune
Jadot, Louis
Lafarge, Michel

Lafon
Laroche, Dom.
Latour, Louis
Leflaive, Dom.
Leflaive, Olivier
Leroy, Dom.
Liger-Belair
Méo-Camuzet
Montille, Dom. de
Morey
Mortet, Denis
Mugneret
Mugnier, J-F
Noëllat
Ramonet
Raveneau, Dom.
Rion
Romanée-Conti,
  Dom. de la
Roulot, Dom.
Roumier, Georges
Rousseau, Armand
Sauzet
Tollot-Beaut
Vogüé, Comte
  Georges de
Vougeraie, Dom. de
  la

SEE ALSO
Aligoté
Beaujolais Nouveau
Burgundy Red
  Wines
Burgundy White
  Wines
Côte de Beaune
Côte de Nuits
Côte d'Or
Gamay

CHAMPAGNE
Champagne AC
Champagne Rosé
Coteaux
  Champenois AC
Rosé des Riceys AC

PRODUCERS
Billecart-Salmon
Bollinger
Deutz
Duval-Leroy
Gratien, Alfred
Gosset
Heidsieck, Charles
Henriot
Jacquesson
Krug
Lanson
Laurent-Perrier
Moët & Chandon
Mumm, G H
Paillard, Bruno
Perrier, Joseph
Perrier-Jouët
Philipponnat
Piper-Heidsieck
Pol Roger
Pommery
Roederer, Louis
Ruinart
Taittinger
Veuve Clicquot

JURA AND SAVOIE
Arbois AC
Bugey AC
Château-Chalon
  AC
Côtes du Jura AC
Crémant du Jura AC
l'Étoile AC
Roussette de Savoie
  AC
Savoie

LOIRE VALLEY
ACs
Anjou Blanc
Anjou Rouge
Anjou-Villages
Bonnezeaux
Bourgueil
Cabernet d'Anjou
Cheverny
Chinon
Côte Roannaise
Coteaux de
  l'Aubance
Coteaux du
  Giennois
Coteaux du Layon
Crémant de Loire
Jasnières
Menetou-Salon
Montlouis-sur-Loire
Muscadet
Pouilly-Fumé
Pouilly-sur-Loire
Quarts de Chaume
Quincy
Reuilly
Rosé de Loire
St-Nicolas-de-
  Bourgueil
Sancerre
Saumur
Saumur-Champigny
Saumur Mousseux
Savennières
Touraine
Val de Loire, IGP
Vouvray

PRODUCERS
Baudry, Bernard
Blot, Jacky
Bourgeois, Dom.
  Henri
Chidaine, François
Clos Naudin, Dom.
  du
Coulée de Serrant,
  Vignobles de la
Dagueneau, Didier
Druet, Pierre-
  Jacques
Huet
Hureau, Ch. du
Luneau-Papin, Dom.
Mabileau, Frédéric
Mellot, Alphonse
Ogereau, Dom.
Pierre-Bise, Ch.
Ragotière, Ch. de la
Roches Neuves,
  Dom. des
Vacheron, Dom.
Villeneuve, Ch. de

RHÔNE VALLEY
ACs
Beaumes-de-Venise
Château-Grillet
Châteauneuf-du-
  Pape
Clairette de Die
Collines
  Rhodaniennes,
  IGP des
Condrieu
Cornas
Costières de Nîmes
Côte-Rôtie
Coteaux de
  l'Ardèche, Vin de
  Pays des
Côtes du Rhône
Côtes du Rhône-
  Villages
Côtes du Vivarais
Crémant de Die
Crozes-Hermitage
Gigondas
Grignan-les-
  Adhémar
Hermitage
Lirac
Lubéron
Muscat de
  Beaumes-de-
  Venise
Rasteau
St-Joseph
St-Péray
Tavel
Vacqueyras
Ventoux
Vinsobres

PRODUCERS
Allemand, Thiérry
Beaucastel, Ch. de
Chapoutier, M
Chave, Jean-Louis
Clape, A
Clos des Papes
Colombo, Jean-Luc
Coursodon, Pierre
Cuilleron, Yves
Delas Frères
Font de Michelle,
  Dom.
Graillot, Alain
Guigal
Jaboulet Aîné,
  Paul
Jamet
Oratoire St-Martin,
  Dom.
Perret, André
Rayas, Ch.
Réméjeanne,
  Dom. la
Rostaing, Réné
Saint Gayan, Dom.
Sang des Cailloux,
  Dom. le
Tain, Cave de
Vidal-Fleury
Vieux Télégraphe,
  Dom. du

SEE ALSO
Cairanne

SOUTHERN FRANCE

SOUTH-WEST
AOPs
Béarn
Bergerac
Buzet
Cahors
Coteaux du Quercy
Côtes du Brulhois
Côtes de Duras
Côtes de Gascogne
Côtes du
  Marmandais
Entraygues-et-du-
  Fel, Estaing
Fronton
Gaillac
Irouléguy
Jurançon
Madiran
Marcillac
Monbazillac
Montravel
Pacherenc du Vic-
  Bilh
Pécharmant
Rosette
Saussignac
St-Mont
Tursan

PRODUCERS
l'Ancienne Cure,
  Dom. de
Arretxea, Dom.
Aydie, Ch. d'
Berthoumieu, Dom.
Cauhapé, Dom.
Causse Marines,
  Dom. de
Cèdre, Ch. du
Clos de Gamot
Clos d'un Jour
Clos Triguedina
Cosse-Maisonneuve,
  Dom.
Elian da Ros, Dom.
Jardins de Babylone
Labranche-Laffont,
  Dom.
Lapeyre
Montus, Ch.
Peyres Roses, Dom.
Plageoles, Dom.
Plaimont,
  Producteurs
Plaisance, Ch.
Ramaye, Dom. de la
Souch, Dom. de
Tariquet
Tirecul la Gravière,
  Ch.
Tour des Gendres,
  Ch.
Verdots, Vignoble
  des

LANGUEDOC-
  ROUSSILLON
ACs and IGPs
Banyuls
Blanquette de
  Limoux
Cabardès
Clape, La
Collioure
Corbières
Coteaux du
  Languedoc
Côtes Catalanes,
  IGP des
Côtes du Roussillon
Côtes du
  Roussillon-Villages
Côtes de Thongue,
  IGP des
Crémant de
  Limoux
Faugères
Fitou
Gard, IGP du
Grès de Montpellier
Hérault, IGP de l'
Languedoc
Limoux
Maury
Minervois
Muscat de
  Frontignan
Muscat de
  Rivesaltes
Muscat de St-Jean-
  de-Minervois
Oc, IGP d'
Pézenas
Pic St-Loup
Picpoul de Pinet
Rivesaltes
St-Chinian
Terrasses du Larzac

PRODUCERS
Alquier, Dom. Jean-
  Michel
Antugnac, Dom. d'
Bertrand, Gérard
Borie la Vitarèle
Casenove, Dom. la
Cazes, Dom.
Clos de l'Anhel
Clos Centeilles
Clos Marie
Clot de l'Oum
Denois, J-L
Estanilles, Ch. des
Gauby, Dom.
Grange des Pères,
  Dom. de la
l'Hortus, Dom. de
Mas, Dom. Paul
Mas Blanc,
  Dom. du
Mas Bruguière
Mas la Chevalière
Mas de Daumas
  Gassac
Nizas, Dom. de
Prieuré de St-Jean
  de Bébian
Sieur d'Arques, les
  Vignerons du
Tour Boisée, Ch.

SEE ALSO
Roussillon

PROVENCE
ACs
Bandol
les Baux-de-
  Provence
Bellet
Bouches-du-Rhône,
  IGP
Cassis
Coteaux d'Aix-en-
  Provence
Coteaux Varois-en-
  Provence
Côtes de Provence
Palette
PRODUCERS
d'Eole, Dom.
Esclans, Ch. d'
Pibarnon, Ch. de
Richeaume,
  Dom.
Romanin, Ch.
Sorin, Dom.
Trévallon, Dom.
  de
Vannières, Ch.

CORSICA
Corse AC, Vin de
PRODUCERS
Arena, Dom.
  Antoine
Clos Canarelli

ITALY

What a great moment to re-appraise, explore and enjoy Italy's classic wines. An over-reliance upon international grapes and technology to make an ocean of faceless 'global' wines (coinciding with 30 years of unprecedented affluence) seems to be behind Italy, along with the bursting of the economic bubble. Now we're celebrating the return of authentic, traditional Italian wines: wines that speak of a unique and ancient (viti)culture, born of noble indigenous varieties, reflecting their fine *terroir* and rich patrimony.

Aided by the internet, climate change and a shift in the domestic market away from bulk quantity towards bottle quality, today even the smallest artisan producers (of which Italy has many) are able to communicate their philosophy and reach their ideal customers. They appear less impressed by the trappings of fame and fortune sought by the previous generation, finding a renewed sense of belief in what's right under their feet, recalling what their grandfathers told them, and motivated by making wines that are a pleasure to drink, not just to admire.

GRAPE VARIETIES AND WINE REGIONS

Best think of Italy not in terms of 20 political regions but of the 'North', 'Centre' and 'South'. The North leads with the black Nebbiolo (Barbaresco and Barolo) and frothy white Moscato grapes of Piedmont, ubiquitous Barbera, Veneto's Corvina (Valpolicella) and bubbly Glera (Prosecco), while Friuli breeds the workhorse Pinot Grigio. In the Centre, Tuscany's most

famous wines, such as Chianti, are based on Sangiovese, while trendy Cabernets proliferate on the coast; the Marche is a sea of Verdicchio; in Abruzzo white Trebbiano and black Montepulciano are now turning heads; and Umbria is home to swarthy Sagrantino. The South, still a Euro bulk supplier, is raising its game thanks to emerging estate-bottled Greco, Fianco and Falanghina (in Campania), Aglianico (in Campania and Basilicata), Puglian Primitivo and Negroamaro, Calabrian Gaglioppo (Cirò), Sicilian Nero d'Avola and Nerello Mascalese.

CLASSIFICATIONS

Introduced in 1963, updated in 1992, the Italian classification system was overhauled in 2010, leading to four levels:

Vino (generic wine) is at the bottom of the pyramid: it may be produced anywhere in the EU, and must not show indication of origin, nor vintage, nor the grapes used, but only the colour of the wine.

Varietali (varietal wines) are made from at least 85% of one authorized international grape (Cabernet, Chardonnay, Merlot, Sauvignon Blanc, Syrah), or a blend of two or more of them; grape(s) and vintage may be shown on the label.

IGP (Indicazione Geografica Protetta/Protected Geographical Indication), replacing IGT, refers to the production of wine from a specific territory (of which there are 118), and following regulations on viticultural and vinification practices.

DOP (Denominazione di Origine Protetta/Protected Designation of Origin) comprises two quality subcategories – **DOC** and **DOCG** – from smaller zones (within an IGP area) with notable climatic and geological characteristics and a tradition of quality winemaking. At the time of writing there are 330 DOCs (Denominazione di Origine Controllata/Controlled Designation of Origin). The top quality level is DOCG (Denominazione di Origine Controllata e Garantita/Controlled and Guaranteed Designation of Origin), which must be assessed by a panel of tasters to guarantee its authenticity and quality. There are currently 73 DOCGs. The term '**Classico**' is applied to wines from an historic area; '**Superiore**' wines have 0.5% more alcohol than the regular DOP wine due to lower yields; '**Riserva**' wines have extended aging. No hierarchical classification yet exists in Italy but from Barbaresco vintage 2006 and Barolo vintage 2010, the *'menzioni geografiche aggiuntive'*, or subzone delimitation of vineyards, was officially introduced in the Langhe: mention of a single vineyard/subzone on a Barbaresco or Barolo guarantees that at least 85% of the fruit comes from that vineyard.

2013 VINTAGE REPORT

North (Piedmont, Valle d'Aosta, Lombardy, Trentino-Alto Adige, Veneto, Friuli-Venezia Giulia): a late harvest, recalling the years before global warming. Cold and wet spring weather brought downy mildew and lower yields; a burst of summer heat was followed by a mild August; more rain in September and October spoilt most of the crop, and even the late-ripening Nebbiolo had to be picked before the berries burst. Reds needed good sites; whites are light and perfumed.

Centre (Tuscany, Emilia-Romagna, Marche, Umbria, Lazio, Abruzzo, Molise): a similar story in Italy's *pancia* ('belly'), where successive rain showers made disease control near-impossible, necessitating strict selection and reducing yields. Conditions seemed more favourable for reds in southern Tuscany and Abruzzo, and in Umbria whites fared best.

South (Campania, Puglia, Basilicata, Calabria, Sicily): seems to have enjoyed the best of the weather in 2013. It started slowly, despite the preceding mild winter, before hotting up over summer, relieved by regular showers during August and September. A hot October wrapped up the vintage, with Aglianico harvested in late October/early November.

Italian entries in the A–Z section (pages 62–327).

GERMANY

The dull semi-sweet wines with names like Liebfraumilch and Niersteiner Gutes Domtal that used to dominate the export market are rapidly vanishing off all but the most basic radar screens. Instead, we are seeing an expanding range of single-estate wines of fine quality, although the choice, except at specialist wine merchants, remains limited. Throughout Germany, both red and white wines are year by year, region by region, grower by grower, becoming fuller, better balanced and drier.

GRAPE VARIETIES

Riesling makes the best wines, at least in northerly regions such as the Mosel and Rheingau, in styles ranging from dry to intensely sweet. Other white wines come from Grauburgunder/Ruländer (Pinot Gris), Weissburgunder (Pinot Blanc), Gewürztraminer, Silvaner, Scheurebe and Rieslaner, although Müller-Thurgau produces much of the simpler wine. Plantings of red grape varieties now account for over 35% of the nation's vineyards. Good reds are being made throughout the wine regions, mostly from Spätburgunder (Pinot Noir) and Dornfelder.

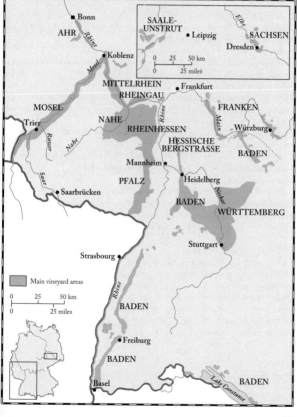

WINE REGIONS

Many of the most delectable Rieslings come from villages such as Bernkastel, Brauneberg, Ürzig and Wehlen on the Mosel, and Kiedrich, Johannisberg and Rüdesheim in the Rheingau. Characterful dry Mosel Rieslings, once the speciality of villages such as Winningen near Koblenz, are increasingly common throughout the region. The Nahe makes superb Rieslings in Schlossböckelheim and Traisen, and Niederhausen has the region's best vineyards. Rheinhessen's most celebrated wines are the excellent racy Rieslings produced on riverside slopes in Nackenheim and Nierstein, but growers such as Keller and Wittmann have shown the remarkable potential of some inland sites. Franken is the one place the Silvaner grape excels, often made in a powerful, dry, earthy style. The Pfalz is climatically similar to Alsace and has a similar potential for well-rounded, dry whites, plus rapidly improving reds. Baden also produces fully ripe but dry wine styles, which, were they better marketed, should enjoy wider international success. In Württemberg many red wines are thin and dull, but a few producers understand the need for weight and flavour. The other smaller wine regions make little wine and little is exported, although the Ahr has a well-deserved reputation for Pinot Noir.

CLASSIFICATIONS

Germany's classification system is based on the ripeness of the grapes and therefore their potential alcohol level.

Deutscher Wein (German wine) is the most basic term.

Landwein (country wine) is a slightly more upmarket version, linked to 19 regional areas (only Franken being excluded). These must be Trocken (dry) or Halbtrocken (medium-dry).

QbA (Qualitätswein bestimmter Anbaugebiete) is 'quality' wine from one of 13 designated regions, but the grapes don't have to be very ripe, and sugar can be added to the juice to increase alcoholic content.

QmP (Qualitätswein mit Prädikat) or 'quality wine with distinction' is the top level; in 2007 the term was replaced by 'Prädikatswein'. There are 6 levels of QmP (in ascending order of ripeness): **Kabinett**, **Spätlese**, **Auslese**, **Beerenauslese**, **Eiswein**, **Trockenbeerenauslese** (**TBA**). The addition of sugar is forbidden.

The Rheingau introduced an official classification – Erstes Gewächs (First Growth) – for its best sites, but this is now being absorbed into the more widely adopted classification called Grosses Gewächs (GG), restricted – except in the Mosel – to dry and nobly sweet wines of the highest quality.

2013 VINTAGE REPORT

A cold spring caused late and somewhat uneven flowering, but was followed by a hot, dry summer. Cool wet weather returned in mid-September, provoking rot or dilution, which persuaded some growers to harvest in haste. Quality was satisfactory overall, but the crop was reduced, severely in some cases. Expect lighter, fruity wines rather than wines of power and structure. Acidity levels are quite high, but alcoholic degrees in warmer southern Germany were moderate.

German entries in the A–Z section (pages 62–327).

AUSTRIA

I can't think of a European nation where the wine culture has changed so dramatically in recent times as it has in Austria. Austria still makes great sweet wines, but a new order based on world-class medium- and full-bodied dry whites and increasingly fine reds has emerged.

WINE REGIONS AND GRAPE VARIETIES

The Danube runs through Niederösterreich. Here the Wachau produces great Riesling and excellent pepper-dry Grüner Veltliner. The Riesling is powerful and ripe, closer in style to Alsace than Germany. Next up the Danube are Kremstal and Kamptal, both increasingly reliable sources of lush dry whites plus a few good reds. The Weinviertel, in the north-east, produces large quantities of Grüner Veltliner whites. South of Vienna, the Thermenregion, known for exotic whites from Zierfandler and Rotgipfler, has a growing reputation for reds. Burgenland, south-east of Vienna, produces the best reds, mostly from local varieties Zweigelt, Blaufränkisch and St-Laurent. Also, around the shores of the Neusiedler See, Burgenland produces some superb dessert wines. Further south, in Steiermark (Styria), Chardonnay and Sauvignon are increasingly oak-aged, though many drinkers still prefer the racy unoaked 'classic' wines from these varieties.

CLASSIFICATIONS

Wine categories are similar to those in Germany, but in practice the only ones frequently encountered are those defining the sweeter styles: **Auslese**, **Beerenauslese**, **Ausbruch** (a style only found around Rust in the Burgenland), **Trockenbeerenauslese (TBA)**, **Eiswein** and **Strohwein**. The Wachau has its own ripeness scale for dry whites: Steinfeder wines are made for early drinking, Federspiel wines can last three years or so, and the most powerful wines are known as Smaragd. Over recent years Austria has developed a geographical appellation system with stylistic constraints, called DAC. As each DAC has different rules and restrictions – for example, there are 3 different Blaufränkisch DACs in the Mittelburgenland alone – the system, which includes a strictly defined Reserve category, is hard to understand and often ignored even by producers.

2013 VINTAGE REPORT

An exceedingly hot, dry July was fortunately followed by a cooler August, which revived the grapes, as did some rain in September. In some regions the rain caused berries to split, so growers rushed to pick. But most reds were picked in early October in better conditions. Lower Austria and Styria produced fruity wines with fine aromas and moderate alcohols. Reds are good but sometimes lack flesh. In most regions grape selection was essential to produce high-quality wines. Excellent sweet wines in the Burgenland.

Austrian entries in the A–Z section (pages 62–327).

SPAIN

The early 21st century was marked by the technical makeover of Spain's long-dormant wine scene. Since then, there has been a progressive refinement of the wines, as more producers eschewed the over-oaked and ultra-powerful style that had been a hallmark of Spain's wine revolution. Not coincidentally, forgotten regions and native grape varieties have now come to the fore.

WINE REGIONS

Galicia in the green, hilly north-west grows Spain's most aromatic whites. The heartland of the great Spanish reds – Rioja, Navarra and Ribera del Duero – is situated between the central plateau and the northern coast. Further west along the Duero, Rueda produces fresh whites and Toro has good, sometimes chunky but often surprisingly refined reds. Cataluña is principally white wine country (much of it sparkling Cava), though there are some great reds in Priorat and increasingly in Terra Alta, Empordà-Costa Brava, Costers del Segre and Montsant. Aragón's reds are looking good too, with an impressive relaunch of Aragón's great (but long-neglected) native grape Garnacha. In the Madrid region, the sleepy Vinos de Madrid DO has sprung to life, with some remarkable reds from Garnacha and whites from Albillo. The central plateau of La Mancha makes mainly cheap reds and whites, though smaller private estates are improving spectacularly and neighbouring Manchuela is on the march with beefy reds. Valencia and Murcia, known for simple, inexpensive wines, are now producing increasingly ambitious and rich reds, for example from Utiel-Requena and Jumilla. Andalucía's specialities are fortified wines – sherry, Montilla and Málaga. There has been a notable rebirth of viticulture and winemaking in both the Balearics and the Canary Islands.

CLASSIFICATIONS

New European Union rules about wine classification are causing havoc as former appellations have been allowed to continue or adopt the new name, as they wish. So you may find a confusing array of names:

Basic, generic wine, formerly known as **Vino de Mesa** (table wine) may now be called simply **Vino** (wine) and may include grape varieties and vintage on the label. Most producers have switched.

Vino de la Tierra or **VT** (country wine) with a geographical designation may now appear as **Indicación Geográfica Protegida** (IGP) or **Vino de Calidad**. **Denominación de Origen** (DO), the main classification for wines from demarcated regions, can now be called **Denominación de Origen Protegida** (DOP), but only recently created appellations are using this: the older ones, for now, are not.

Denominación de Origen Calificada (DOCa) is a super-category. Only two regions (Rioja and Priorat) have been promoted.

2013 VINTAGE REPORT

As the Spanish saying goes, 'it never rains to everyone's liking', and after two drought-stricken years, the spring of 2013 was exceptionally wet and favoured a very abundant crop. After a reasonably dry and not overly hot summer, large-scale rainfall before harvest produced much mildew and grey rot, particularly in the normally arid south. Rioja had its wettest, latest vintage for 100 years. So quality was very uneven – rotten luck in the year where for the first time in history Spain surpassed Italy and France as the world's largest producer.

Spanish entries in the A–Z section (pages 62–327).

REGIONS			
Andalucía	Montilla-Moriles	Contino	Raïmat
Aragón	Navarra	CVNE	Remelluri
Balearic Islands	Penedès	Faustino	Rioja Alta, La
Canary Islands	Priorat	Fournier, O	Riojanas, Bodegas
Castilla-La Mancha	Rías Baixas	Freixenet	Rodríguez, Telmo
Castilla y León	Ribera del Duero	González Byass	Sandeman
Cataluña	Rioja	Hidalgo	Terroir al Límit
Galicia	Rueda	López de Heredia	Torres
Valencia	Somontano	Lustau	Valdespino
	Toro	Marqués de	Vall Llach
DO/DOCa	Utiel-Requena	Cáceres	Vega Sicilia
Bierzo	Valdepeñas	Marqués de Griñón	
Calatayud		Marqués de	**SEE ALSO**
Campo de Borja	**PRODUCERS**	Murrieta	Airén
Cariñena	Aalto	Marqués de Riscal	Albariño
Cava	Allende	Martínez Bujanda	Bobal
Costers del Segre	Artadi	Mas Doix	Graciano
Jerez y Manzanilla	Barbadillo	Mauro	Grenache Noir
Jumilla	Campo Viejo	Muga	Mencía
Madrid, Vinos de	Chivite	Osborne	Mourvèdre
Málaga	Clos Erasmus	Palacios, Alvaro	Tempranillo
Mancha, La	Clos Mogador	Pérez, Raúl	Verdejo
Manchuela	Codorníu	Pesquera	Xarel-lo
	Contador	Pingus, Dominio de	

PORTUGAL ▬▬▬▬▬

Investment and imagination have paid off in this attractive country, with climates that vary from the mild, damp Minho region in the north-west to the subtropical island of Madeira. Use of native grapes, occasionally blended with international varieties, means that Portugal is now a rich source of characterful wines of ever-increasing quality.

WINE REGIONS

The lush Vinho Verde country in the north-west gives very different wine from the winding valleys of the neighbouring Douro, with its drier, more continental climate. The Douro, home of port, is also the source of some of Portugal's best unfortified red and white wines. In Bairrada, Dão and Beira Interior, soil types are crucial in determining the character of the wines. Lisboa and Tejo (formerly known as Estremadura and Ribatejo), influenced either by the maritime climate or by the river Tagus, use native and international varieties. South of Lisbon, the Península de Setúbal and Alentejo produce some exciting table wines – and the Algarve is waking up. Madeira is unique: a volcanic island 850km (530 miles) out in the Atlantic Ocean.

CLASSIFICATIONS

Vinho is the lowest level, but commercially important as so much off-dry to medium-dry rosé is exported in this category.

Vinho Regional, or **Indicação Geográfica Protegida** (IGP), is the next level, with laws and permitted varieties much freer than for DOC/DOP. There are currently 14 IGPs.

Denominação de Origem Controlada/Protegida (DOC/DOP) is the most strictly regulated; there are now 30 DOC/DOPs.

2013 VINTAGE REPORT

Portugal had a wet, cold winter and early spring, with flowering delayed, and yields lowered as a result. Summer was cool until August, then hot until significant rain fell at the end of September and in the first weeks of October. Most whites were picked before the rain, and are attractive. Some late-ripening grapes (Touriga Franca in the western Douro, Antão Vaz and Alicante Bouschet in the Alentejo) were caught by the rains and suffered dilution and rot problems. Vinho Verde made tasty whites before the rain, as did Lisboa and the Tejo. Reds, too, were reasonably successful here. Bairrada whites were successful, with some top, early-picked reds. Dão whites are serious, and most reds good but lightened by rain. In the Douro, whites are excellent, and some reds classy, but it's not a year for vintage port. The Alentejo made attractive whites and juicy, early-drinking reds.

Portuguese entries in the A–Z section (pages 62–327).

USA

The United States has more varied growing conditions for grapes than any other country in the world, which isn't so surprising when you consider that the 50 states of the Union cover an area that is larger than Western Europe; and although Alaska doesn't grow grapes in the icy far north, Washington State does in the north-west, as do Texas in the south and New York State in the north-east; even Hawaii, way out in the Pacific Ocean, manages to grow grapes and make wine. Every state, including Alaska (thanks to salmonberry and fireweed), now produces wine of some sort or another; it ranges from some pretty dire offerings, which would have been far better distilled into brandy, to some of the greatest and most original wines in the world today.

GRAPE VARIETIES AND WINE REGIONS

California is far and away the most important state for wine production. California winemakers have proved they can match the best that the Old World has to offer, giving the classic European grape varieties a distinctive California accent. While covering the top-end wines, California has not neglected the everyday wines. The interior Central Valley, a vast winegrowing region between the coastal mountain ranges and the Sierra Nevada, produces the majority of the simple but gulpable wines that still dominate the American market, but the northern end around Lodi and Clarksburg is proving that real quality is possible here. Napa and Sonoma Counties, north of San Francisco

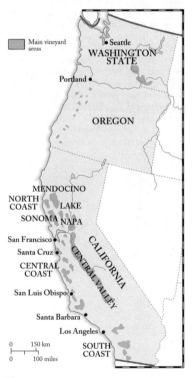

Bay, produce great Cabernet Sauvignon and Chardonnay, but grapes like Zinfandel and Merlot also make their mark; the Carneros, Russian River Valley and Sonoma Coast areas are highly successful for Pinot Noir, Chardonnay and sparkling wines. In the north, Mendocino and Lake Counties produce good grapes and Anderson Valley is superb for fizz and Pinot Noir. South of San Francisco, in the cool, foggy valleys between Santa Cruz and Santa Barbara, and in the Santa Lucia Highlands in Monterey County, Chardonnay, Pinot Noir and Syrah are producing exciting cool-climate but ripe-flavoured wines.

Oregon, with a cooler and more capricious climate than most of California, perseveres with Pinot

Noir, Chardonnay, Pinot Gris, Pinot Blanc and Riesling, with increasing success. Washington State, so chilly and misty on the coast, becomes virtual desert east of the Cascade Mountains and it is here, in irrigated vineyards, that superb Cabernet Sauvignon, Merlot and Syrah can be made, with thrillingly focused fruit.

In New York State, winemakers in the Finger Lakes continue to develop a regional style and national reputation for dry Riesling, and they're working on reds – I've even tried a Finger Lakes Syrah. Long Island impresses with classically styled Merlot, Cabernet Sauvignon and Cabernet Franc, as well as Chardonnay to pair with the local lobster. Improved vineyard practices have enabled growers to cope with the vagaries of the region's inconsistent weather, resulting in an overall increase in quality from year to year.

A growing consumer appreciation of wines from 'The Other 47' states (not California, Oregon or Washington) has helped fuel a 'locapour' movement. Virginia's wine industry nearly doubled in size over the last 5 years, and Maryland, Texas, Colorado, Arizona, Missouri and Michigan grew dramatically. Nearly anywhere you go in the USA today, 'local' wine is worth trying. I'm not saying it will always be quite what you're used to, but hey, where's your spirit of adventure?

CLASSIFICATIONS

The AVA (American Viticultural Area) system does not guarantee a quality standard, but merely requires that at least 85% of grapes in a wine come from the specified AVA. New AVAs are added every year. Currently there are well over 200 AVAs nationwide and more than 120 in California. AVAs come in all shapes and sizes, varying from the largest, Upper Mississippi Valley, which spans an area of 77,477 sq km (29,914 sq miles) to the smallest, Cole Ranch in California, which covers a little less than a quarter of a square mile.

2013 VINTAGE REPORT

Winemakers from all parts of California report an outstanding vintage. Harvest was early, following a warm, dry spring and ideal growing conditions during the summer. The yield was one of the largest ever, with the young wines showing great balance and acidity. The glowing reports of the 2013 harvest follow on the heels of similar reports to the 2012 harvest, meaning that California should have outstanding wine at all levels – and plenty of it.

In Oregon, spring was warm and sunny and vine growth was vigorous, but a cool spell in June extended the flowering period. The summer season was one of the driest on record and many grapes for white and sparkling wines were harvested before 22 September, when a series of storms pummelled the region and monsoon-like conditions dropped record rainfall. It dried out again after 2 October, and those who were prepared were able to collect clean fruit. White wines will have vibrant acidity and lots of stone fruit flavour. The red wines are surprisingly dark in colour, taste fresh and clean, and have zesty acidity.

In Washington, early budbreak was followed by a dry, warm spring and summer, with some record high temperatures. Many white varieties were harvested in the first week of September. A cold front moved in on 15 September and this slowed the pace of ripening. The resulting wines have lower alcohol levels than 2012, but snappy acidity.

The Eastern US experienced a depressingly rainy and cool spring, with frost damage and extreme disease pressure. Amazingly, the skies parted and the sun emerged in early July, and the rest of the season was about as ideal as possible. So vintners who kept a close eye on their vines emerged with low yields but good quality.

41

USA entries in the A–Z section (pages 62–327) by state.

AUSTRALIA

Australia finds itself at a bit of a crossroads nowadays. Its reputation, which soared sky-high on a relatively small volume of wine produced, began to teeter as volumes mushroomed. Its ability to overdeliver quality at a fair price, which fuelled the New World wine revolution, was undermined by the need to soak up excess production from poorly thought-out expansion of vineyards. And despite the fact that its winemakers, especially those of independent companies and estates, are creating some of Australia's best-ever wine, the country has increasingly been saddled with the downmarket reputation of 'critter' brands, based on whatever marsupial had not yet featured on a label, and deep-discounted junk. But a significant amount of vines have been pulled out in the last few years, yields are down and attitudes are changing. Consequently, Australia is moving from a position of oversupply to one where demand can't quite be met. Now is the time to rediscover Australia's genius, sometimes rough and ready, but frequently finely balanced and sublime, and unlike the wines of any other country in the world.

GRAPE VARIETIES

Varietal wines remain more prized than blends. Shiraz has long been a key varietal and is more fashionable than Cabernet Sauvignon, especially in its ever-increasing cool-climate manifestations. Renewed respect for old-vine Grenache and Mourvèdre has seen these former workhorse varieties transformed into sought-after stars. Cool-climate Pinot Noir leads the pack of alternative red varieties, along with prospective show-stealers in Petit Verdot, Tempranillo, Nebbiolo and Sangiovese. Among white grapes, the position of Chardonnay has been challenged by the upstart Sauvignon Blanc, despite the fact that modern Australian Chardonnay is some of the best in the

world and modern Australian Sauvignon isn't. However, one in four of the whites Australians drink is Chardonnay, and at the top end of the market, tauter, finer, ultra-cool Chardonnay is fighting back with world-class wines. The number of Pinot Grigios is increasing at an amazing rate as an alternative to cheaper Chardonnay. Semillon and Riesling remain popular, with the Italians Fiano and Vermentino and Rhône varieties Marsanne and Viognier (now fashionably included in blends with Shiraz) both impressing. Sweet whites are produced from Semillon, Riesling and Muscat – both the top-class Brown Muscat (a sub-variety of Muscat Blanc à Petits Grains) and the more workaday Muscat Gordo Blanco. Fizzy moscatos are the big mover here.

WINE REGIONS

South Australia dominates the wine scene – it grows the most grapes, makes the most wine and is home to most of the nation's biggest wine companies. There is more to it, however, than attractive, undemanding, gluggable wine. Clare Valley produces outstanding cool-climate Riesling, as well as excellent Shiraz and Cabernet. The Barossa has some of the planet's oldest vines, particularly Shiraz and Grenache. Eden Valley is great for Riesling, Coonawarra for Cabernet, Adelaide Hills for Chardonnay and Pinot Noir.

Victoria was Australia's major producer for most of the 19th century until her vineyards were devastated by phylloxera. Victoria has now regained her position as provider of some of the country's most startling wine styles: stunning liqueur Muscats; thrilling dark reds from Central Victoria; impressive Chardonnays and Pinots from Yarra Valley, Mornington Peninsula, trendy Beechworth and up-and-coming Geelong.

New South Wales (specifically the Hunter Valley) was home to the revolution that propelled Australia to the front of the world wine stage; a clutch of new regions in the Central Ranges are now grabbing headlines. The state is also a major bulk producer in Riverina.

Western Australia's viticultural heartland, Margaret River and the Great Southern, has a short history, stretching back little more than 40 years, but produces some of the country's finest wines. Margaret River has a thriving wine tourism industry thanks largely to the quality of its Chardonnay and Cabernet Sauvignon; the Great Southern excels with increasingly impressive Shiraz and Riesling; both regions make outstanding Semillon-Sauvignon Blanc blends. Pemberton is gaining a reputation for its whites and its Pinots.

Tasmania, with its cooler climate, is benefiting from more mature vines and better viticultural expertise, and attracting attention for top-quality Pinot Noirs and Champagne-method sparkling wines – and there is excellent potential for Riesling, Pinot Gris and Gewürztraminer.

CLASSIFICATIONS

The Label Integrity Program (LIP) guarantees all claims made on labels and the Geographical Indications (GI) committee is busy clarifying zones, regions and sub-regions – albeit with plenty of lively, at times acrimonious, debate about where some regional borders should go. But inter-regional blending for commercial brands is still the order of the day.

2014 VINTAGE REPORT

As always, it's hard to generalize about the 2014 vintage in Australia because conditions vary so much from region to region. However, it's fair to say that quality should be good to very good in spite of the challenges that nature threw at growers, while yields will generally be below average. In South Australia, for example, the Barossa and Clare Valleys experienced two heatwaves and a few days of heavy rainfall in the lead-up to harvest but the warm days and cool nights that followed are likely to have delivered a fine vintage. Cool conditions during flowering in the Adelaide Hills kept yields substantially lower than usual, but a slow, dry ripening season meant quality was excellent. Just to the south, the warmth of Langhorne Creek was moderated by the impact of a replenished Lake Alexandrina, full after 10 years of drought, and the region is expecting big things, especially of its Cabernet Sauvignon. Spring rains set up Coonawarra to withstand the heat of January and expectations there are also high.

In Victoria, the Yarra Valley, Mornington Peninsula and Gippsland – as well as Tasmania – suffered from rain during flowering, so yields are down, but ideal conditions followed and this suggests fine, elegant whites and attractive, plush reds. A spell of extreme heat may have damaged Beechworth, but growers are optimistic.

In New South Wales, Orange was hit by October frosts and a small January earthquake, before a warm, dry growing season was finished off with refreshing rain. After grumbling loudly early on, Brokenwood's Iain Riggs has declared 2014 an 11 out of 10 vintage for the Hunter Valley.

Western Australia continues its run of excellent vintages, with adequate spring rainfall, cool dry summer ripening conditions and consistently cool nights in regions as diverse as Margaret River and the Great Southern.

Australian entries in the A–Z section (pages 62–327).

NEW ZEALAND

New Zealand's wines, though diverse in style, are characterized by intense fruit flavours, zesty acidity and pungent aromas – the product of cool growing conditions and high-tech winemaking.

GRAPE VARIETIES

New Zealand is a small, cool-climate wine-producing country which has done a brilliant job of selling itself on rarity, exclusivity, high quality and high price. Its fame was based firmly on Sauvignon Blanc – deservedly so, because Sauvignon's explosion onto the world's consciousness during the 1980s and 1990s changed forever our views of how tangy and refreshing a white wine could be. Sauvignon Blanc is still the Kiwi flag-waver and dominates the country's main wine region, Marlborough. Despite a quality blip in 2008, serious Sauvignon producers are making their best ever wines, but there remains a danger of too much cheap, mediocre wine reaching the market. Sauvignon Blanc's dominance can mask the fact that the country also produces superb, full-bodied, oatmealy Chardonnay, succulent Pinot Gris, fragrant Riesling and Gewürztraminer, and excellent fizz.

For a long time thought of as too cool for high-quality reds, New Zealand is now creating sensational, scented Pinot Noir, dark, serious Bordeaux-style blends usually based on Merlot and Cabernet Sauvignon, and a small amount of exquisite Syrah. Wines of such quality are rare and should be high-priced.

WINE REGIONS

Nearly 1600km (1000 miles) separate New Zealand's northernmost wine region from the country's (and the world's) most southerly wine region, Central Otago. In terms of wine styles it is useful to divide the country into two parts. The warmer climate of Hawkes Bay and one or two pockets around Auckland produce the best Cabernet Sauvignon, Merlot and Cabernet Franc, as well as increasingly good Syrah. Waiheke Island and Hawkes Bay's Gimblett Gravels have some of the most exciting red wine vineyards. Martinborough and Wairarapa are noted for Pinot Noir. In the South Island, Nelson is good for Pinot Noir and aromatic whites, while Marlborough is the hub of the industry, famous for Sauvignon Blanc, but also excellent for fizz, Chardonnay, Riesling and Pinot Noir. Waipara is small but produces very characterful reds and whites, while Central Otago produces fabulous Pinot Noir, vibrant Riesling and an increasing amount of flavoursome Pinot Gris.

CLASSIFICATIONS

Labels guarantee geographic origin. The broadest designation is New Zealand, followed by North or South Island. Next come the 10 or so regions. Labels may also name specific localities and individual vineyards.

2014 VINTAGE REPORT

Heavy rain struck parts of the country in mid-April after an extended spell of near-perfect ripening conditions. Many winemakers who harvested before the rain describe it as a 'truly great vintage'. Those who harvested after the rainfall, which in some regions, particularly Marlborough, exceeded 130mm/5 inches in just 11 days, are less enthusiastic.

The North Island generally enjoyed plenty of sun and not too much rain. Late varieties such as Cabernet Sauvignon appear to have survived fairly well, even if they were caught in the downpour. An outbreak of powdery mildew on Waiheke Island marred an otherwise perfect vintage. Marlborough set a large crop, although the more quality-conscious producers fruit-thinned to reduce quantity and increase quality. That strategy paid off: lighter crops of Sauvignon Blanc were harvested before the rain. Expect excellent wine, particularly at the upper end of the price range. At lower prices, high volumes may mean over-cropped, rain-affected wines not delivering acceptable quality. Central Otago was unaffected by rain and enjoyed a very good vintage that some claim will produce wines similar to those from the excellent 2012.

New Zealand entries in the A–Z section (pages 62–327).

REGIONS	PRODUCERS		
Auckland	Astrolabe	Jackson Estate	Saint Clair
Awatere Valley	Ata Rangi	Kumeu River	Seresin
Canterbury/	Babich	Man O'War	Stonyridge
Waipara	Brancott Estate	Martinborough	Te Mata
Central Otago	Church Road	Vineyard	Trinity Hill
Gisborne	Cloudy Bay	Matua Valley	Vavasour
Hawkes Bay	Coopers Creek	Millton	Villa Maria
Kumeu/Huapai	Craggy Range	Morton Estate	Wither Hills
Marlborough	Delegat	Neudorf	Yealands
Martinborough/	Dry River	Ngatarawa	
Wairarapa	Felton Road	Nobilo	
Nelson	Framingham	Palliser Estate	
Waiheke Island	Fromm	Pask, C J	
Waitaki	Hunter's	Pegasus Bay	
		Quartz Reef	

SOUTH AFRICA

The good news for the South African wine industry in 2013 was a record harvest of good quality. It was also a year of record-breaking exports – a 26% increase on 2012 (a record year in itself) – in part thanks to demand from some European countries, which had suffered serious shortfalls in their 2012 harvest. Despite the word about South Africa's much-improved quality and increasingly distinctive wines being spread by the large number of visiting international journalists, there is a feeling among some that the country's top wines are underrated and undervalued. However, the number of fired-up, enthusiastic youngsters joining the winemaker ranks continues to increase, their wines being in high demand.

GRAPE VARIETIES AND WINE REGIONS

The Cape's winelands run roughly 400km (250 miles) north and east of Cape Town, although small pockets of new vineyards are taking the winelands way outside their traditional territory. Wine, albeit in tiny quantities, is now being produced from grapes grown in the mountains above the Eastern Cape town of Plettenberg Bay – better known for its beaches and holidaymakers than its vines – from vineyards in the Drakensberg region of KwaZulu-Natal, and most recently near the northern Cape town of Sutherland, home also to the South African Astronomical Observatory, where the vineyards, 1500m (5000ft) above sea level, are covered in snow in winter.

Plantings overall continue to decrease. The ratio of white to red is now 55:45. Major white varieties are Chenin Blanc (paradoxically still the most planted and uprooted of all varieties), Sauvignon Blanc, Colombard and Chardonnay, with Cabernet Sauvignon and Shiraz way ahead of the red pack, though the recent increase in Pinotage plantings continues. Rhône varieties still generate the most excitement: as well as Shiraz/Syrah, there's Grenache,

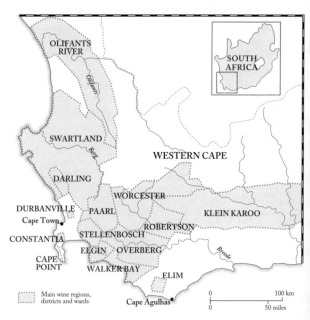

Cinsaut and Mourvèdre for reds, and Viognier, Grenache Blanc and Roussanne for whites, with Marsanne making a welcome appearance in vineyards. Mindful of climate change, varieties suited to warmer climates are being trialled: small quantities of the Greek varieties Assyrtiko, Xinomavro and Agiorgitiko have been planted, as has the Spanish Mencía grape. Another Spanish variety, Albariño, is already bearing fruit but not yet available in the market. Much interest is being shown in old vines, which include rare varieties such as red Semillon. There are approximately 3550ha (8770 acres) of vines 35 years or older, the oldest dating back to 1900.

Some areas are historically associated with specific varieties or styles. Stellenbosch lays claim to some of the best red wines; maritime-influenced Constantia, Cape Point, Elim and Darling produce exhilarating Sauvignon Blanc, as do other coastal areas, from Upper Langkloof in the Klein Karoo, right round to Bamboes Bay near the mouth of the Olifants River. Many of these areas are also producing distinctive blends of Semillon and Sauvignon Blanc. In cool Walker Bay, the focus is on Chardonnay and Pinot Noir. Chardonnay is also important in Robertson and Elgin, and for Cap Classique sparkling wines. Warmer areas such as Worcester are recognized for fortifieds, mainly Muscadel (Muscat). Calitzdorp in the Klein Karoo makes highly regarded port styles. Inland areas such as Swartland along the west coast have considerable plantings of old bush vine reds and whites, and exhibit real affinity for Rhône varieties such as Syrah.

CLASSIFICATIONS

The Wine of Origin (WO) system divides wine-producing areas into regions, districts, wards and single vineyards. Varietal, vintaged wines must be made from at least 85% of the named grape and vintage.

2014 VINTAGE REPORT

A milder than usual January saw harvest start around 10 to 14 days late. The pace of ripening was hastened by the second of two short February heatwaves, when many varieties ripened together, putting pressure on cellars already struggling with space, although the overall crop size was slightly down on 2013. Those who picked before the heavy, wintry March rainfall are delighted with quality in both whites and reds, which show bright aromatics, good flavour, freshness and excellent balance, with lower-than-usual alcohols. The late spring and March rainfalls did cause some fungus and rot, leaving timing as 2014's biggest challenge.

SOUTH AMERICA

ARGENTINA

Argentina has been a major wine producer since the 19th century, but its current success is very much a 21st-century phenomenon, with Malbec its cheerleader. Basic Malbec is attractive, juicy and damsony; at its best it is thrilling, perfumed, complex and long lived. The best hail from Mendoza, in particular the Upper Mendoza River region and the Uco Valley in the shadows of the Andes mountains. The cooler regions of Neuquén and Río Negro in Patagonia are noted for minerally, deep Malbecs, while the extreme altitude vineyards of Salta in the north produce the most dense yet scented expressions. Argentina has other treasures: Bonarda with its sweet-sour juicy fruit, and aromatic, perfumed white Torrontés. Add those to Cabernet Sauvignon, Tempranillo, Shiraz, Cabernet Franc, Tannat and over 100 other grape varieties and the possibilities are endless. Foreign investment and personnel made this possible, but now many of the most thrilling wines, those with the purest expressions of *terroir*, are coming from a new generation of hugely talented Argentine winemakers and viticulturalists, enthusiastically exploiting the wealth of different soils and local climates recent research has revealed, not least in the form of single-vineyard wines.

CHILE

In a remarkably short space of time, Chile has taken on the leadership of South America's wine community, in terms of the personality of its different wine types, innovation in its winemaking and in establishing new vineyard areas, and in the influence its wines are having on wine lovers' drinking habits worldwide. Looking at Chile, that long, thin pencil of a nation tacked on to the Pacific edge of South America, with most of its landmass seeming to comprise mighty mountain ranges, led by the majestic Andes, you might wonder where exactly there was room for any expansion

50

of vineyards. But from the Andes great rivers flow to the sea, and with every mountain range they cut through, they create valleys, broad or narrow, ripe for planting vines, from Copiapó, 665km (413 miles) north of the capital Santiago, way down to the Osorno Valley 820km (510 miles) to the south. It is in these numerous valleys, the sunshine tempered by the cold Pacific winds, that many of Chile's most exciting wines are being made, often from vineyards so young the vines have scarcely taken root. However, there is a traditional wine scene too, based south of Santiago in Maipo and spreading down the Central Valley through Rapel, Curicó and Maule, hemmed in by the Andes and the Coastal Ranges, that is also shaking off its cobwebby past and beginning to contribute numerous challenging, thought-provoking wines to Chile's heady mix.

Carmenère, with its dark, rich, savoury flavours, is called Chile's flagship grape variety, but Merlot and Cabernet Sauvignon from Maipo, Syrah from Elqui, Limarí, Leyda and Colchagua, Carignan from Maule, and Pinot Noir from Leyda and Casablanca all offer superbly individual flavours. Chile's Chardonnay, especially from Limarí, Leyda and the south, is world class. Sauvignon Blanc from the coastal valleys such as San Antonio, Casablanca and Aconcagua can be stunning, and Riesling and Gewürztraminer from the south are delicate and delightful. There are other grape varieties, too, which will increasingly make their mark, particularly with the revival of old bush vines in the south.

2014 VINTAGE REPORT

Yields in Argentina were significantly lower than in 2013. It was in general a challenging harvest, with late frosts and an unusually high amount of rain in Mendoza in February. However, later-budding varieties such as Malbec and Cabernet Sauvignon were not affected. Slow maturity of the Bordeaux varietals meant a late harvest in some regions, resulting in intense, medium-bodied wines that will mature very well. The sparkling wines that were made before the rains are excellent and fresh.

In Chile, horrific frosts in mid-September may have caused crop loss of between 40 and 50%, with Chardonnay, Sauvignon Blanc, Pinot Noir and Merlot worst affected. But a warm and dry growing season helped the buds that survived to produce a small crop of good, healthy grapes. The Central Valley's harvest was 10 days earlier than normal. Northern regions like Elqui were the least hit by frosts. We can expect intense, concentrated and highly aromatic wines at the premium end, while lower-priced white wines will be the first to suffer, as the supply and demand effect will drive prices up.

BRAZIL
Brazil dominates the map of South America, and you'd have thought there'd be loads of places ideal for growing grapes. But the country largely straddles the Equator and the Tropic of Capricorn, and is tropical, subtropical or desert. Add in the world's largest tracts of rainforest, and you'd expect it to be pretty humid – most of it is. Remarkably, there is a fascinating subtropical operation at Vale do São Francisco, only 9° south, which in blistering conditions produces two crops a year of pretty tasty wine – the Moscato is particularly juicy. Otherwise you have to head way south to find decent stuff. The traditional area – the Rio Grande do Sul, centred on the mountain city of Bento Gonçalves – was settled by Italians in the 1840s. It's still pretty humid, but good wines are increasingly possible, and the need to pick early in wet conditions means that lowish-alcohol reds from grapes like Merlot, Cabernet Franc and Teroldego can be delightful, as can the Moscatos. Sparkling wine, dry or sweet, from Pinot Noir and Chardonnay, or Moscato, is always good, and sometimes outstanding. The most promising areas for dry reds and whites are the high Planalto Catarinense vineyards north of Bento Gonçalves and the dry and temperate vineyards of the Serra do Sudeste down near the Uruguayan border. Further inland along the border is the Campanha region: also promising, but less temperate, drier and hotter, giving ripeness but less perfume and character than the grapes of the Sudeste.

URUGUAY
Most of the vines are on very fertile clay soils in the rainy, coolish Canelones region around Montevideo. Those soils plus that climate is not a great recipe for ripening most grape varieties before they rot on the vine, which is why the thick-skinned, rot-resistant black Tannat grape is the leading variety. Modern wineries have managed to soften the tannic Tannat; they are also producing snappy Sauvignon Blanc and fresh Cabernet Franc and Merlot. Efforts to find more suitable vineyard areas initially focused on inland sites, especially in the Cerro Chapeu region right on the Brazilian border. However, the most exciting new plantings are on the Atlantic seaboard around Maldonado in the south-east. The area is barely developed and thinly populated, but could end up as Uruguay's finest wine region. Best producers: Bouza, Carrau, Castillo Viejo, Filgueira, Juanicó, Pisano, Stagnari, Toscanini, Viñedo de los Vientos.

OTHER COUNTRIES
Peru has seemingly good vineyard sites in the Ica Valley south of Lima. I first tasted wines from the Tacama vineyards donkey's years ago; they're a lot better now. Colombia makes a bit of wine. Bolivia has few vineyards, but they're incredibly high. Venezuela's chief claim to fame is that some of her subtropical vines give three crops a year – which makes a vintage chart rather complicated!

OTHER WINE COUNTRIES

ALGERIA With many vines over 40 years old, there should be great potential here, but political uncertainty hinders progress. The western coastal province of Oran produces three-quarters of Algeria's wine, including the soft but muscular Coteaux de Tlemcen wines and dark, beefy reds of the Coteaux de Mascara.

BELGIUM Belgium's vineyards were established by the Romans, but it is only within the past 20 years that climate change has once again allowed vines to thrive, and the country now has a budding wine industry, admittedly on a very small scale. Pinot Noir and Chardonnay are grown for sparkling and still wines, most notably some Chablis-like Chardonnay.

BULGARIA After success in the 1980s and disarray in the 90s, some progress followed the introduction of new wine legislation in 2001, and investment in new vineyards is beginning to gather pace. New World influences are having some effect, although few wines shine. Cabernet Sauvignon and Merlot dominate, but local grapes – plummy Mavrud, meaty Gamza, deep Melnik, fruity white Dimiat and Misket – can be good. Established wineries such as Domaine Boyar, Khan Krum and Lovico Suhindol are being joined by new operations, some financed locally, others, like the promising Edoardo Miroglio, with international backing. Stork Nest and Bessa Valley are two of the largest, and anyone doubting Bulgaria's potential should taste the excellent Enira wines from Bessa Valley (owned by Stephan von Neipperg of Ch. CANON-LA-GAFFELIÈRE in St-Émilion in France).

CANADA The strict VQA (Vintners Quality Alliance) maintains high standards in British Columbia and Ontario, and there is continuing progress in the two most important regions – OKANAGAN VALLEY in British Columbia and the NIAGARA PENINSULA in Ontario. Also jutting into Lake Ontario is the up-and-coming PRINCE EDWARD COUNTY. Sweet Icewine, made primarily from Vidal and Riesling, but increasingly from Cabernet Franc and other varieties, is still Canada's trump card. But producers have realized they also make high-quality Chardonnay and have begun to market Canadian Chardonnay more aggressively. Next up should be Riesling, Pinot Gris, Sauvignon Blanc and Gewurztraminer; Merlot, Cabernet Franc, Cabernet Sauvignon, even Syrah in British Columbia and Pinot Noir in Ontario, are producing tasty red wines. As a cold country, Canada should be a nirvana for sparkling wine. Now, led by the East Coast – and not just Ontario, but seriously east: Nova Scotia – it's starting to happen. England may have a rival in the cool-climate fizz stakes.

CHINA With its massive population, burgeoning middle class and taste for luxury, China is unquestionably an appealing prospective market for wine producers throughout the world. In 2005 China's tariffs on imported wines were reduced from 64% to 14%, widening the door for imported wines. Currently wine from grapes only accounts for about 1.5% of alcohol consumed in China and consumption is 0.69 litres per person each year – but it is growing at an exciting rate, despite a blip in 2013. Interest remains overwhelmingly for red wine, encouraged by the commonly used translation of wine as 'red alcohol', with Bordeaux reds still perceived as 'the best'. However, tastes are now maturing beyond the Classed Growths of the MÉDOC, with notable interest in wines from POMEROL, ST-ÉMILION and even the great estates of BURGUNDY. An increase in whites is also being seen, especially in the economically developed areas of the South East.

Production of wine in China has been stepped up to meet the increase in demand. Around 80–85% of wine consumed in the country is produced domestically from locally grown grapes that are often blended with a large proportion of cheap bulk wine imports and sold as 'Chinese wine'. There is, however, a growing number of wineries that are seeking to make genuine China-reared wines. Cabernet Sauvignon is the emphasis, with plantings rocketing – regardless of suitability of vineyards and climates. The best results of recent vintages range from drinkable wines that are recognizably Cabernet to some very good efforts indeed, but even the finest are nothing to strike fear in the hearts of Bordeaux First Growths just yet. That said, in 2009 Domaines Barons de Rothschild (DBR) Lafite famously partnered with CITIC, China's biggest state-owned investment company, to establish vineyards in China with the aim of producing 'Chinese Grand Cru' for domestic consumption.

China currently has more than 500 wineries. Vineyards are mainly located in Ningxia, Hebei, Shanxi and Shandong provinces, south-west and south-east of Beijing. Many larger operations, international companies and joint ventures, including DBR Lafite, have based themselves around the city of Penglai in the coastal province of Shandong. This area has a relatively mild climate compared to the frigid winters in regions further north, which avoids

the need to bury the vines in winter, but summer rains and ensuing rot frequently prove troublesome. Moving inland, drier, temperate-to-warm continental parts of China, such as parts of Hebei and Shanxi provinces as well as the Mount Helan region in Ningxia province, seem climatically compatible with the production of quality red wine grapes. Slightly cooler than Bordeaux, Ningxia has had impressive results, such as Silver Heights' The Summit and Helan Qingxue's Jia Bei Lan. Also promising is the Xinjiang area, which is considerably further inland, to the extreme west of China. This is warmer and even drier, receiving just 150mm (6 inches) of rain annually, with a particularly dry late summer/autumn spell during the critical ripening period. It also has significant diurnal swings in temperature, with hot summer days and very cool nights, which could slow the ripening process and extend hang-time but hampers attempts to grow late-ripening varieties such as Cabernet Sauvignon and Carmenère, which are still not especially well suited even to this pretty favourable climate.

Dynasty, Changyu and Great Wall are the major producers in China in terms of volume, controlling around half of grape wine production. Top boutique wineries that are making real quality inroads include Grace Vineyards in Shanxi province and Silver Heights, Helan Qingxue, Chateau Zhihui Yuanshi and Helan Mountain in Ningxia province. China's first major sparkling wine joint venture has been set up in Ningxia with LVMH, with its first Chardonnay-Pinot Noir based wine to be released in 2014.

CROATIA Croatia has a strong viticultural heritage and an undercurrent of rising potential; bulk whites dominate, but small private producers are emerging and big companies are improving as investment brings better technology and more winemakers gain experience of other parts of the wine world and develop their own visions of flavour. Buoyant tourism is helping, though labels in Serbo-Croat are not exactly easy to understand.

The most established red vineyards are on the Dalmatian coast, where international varieties are being planted alongside gutsy indigenous grapes: deep, tannic Plavac Mali – related to Zinfandel – has long produced the best-known red wines, but there are numerous other indigenous varieties; further north, Istrian Merlot is surprisingly good. The most popular white grapes are Malvazija (Malvasia) from Istria up toward the Italian border – ideally zippy and fresh or glowing amber and challenging – and the fleshier Graševina (Welschriesling) in the centre of the country. On the Serbian border at Fruska Gora there is good Traminac (Traminer). Frano Miloš on the Pelješac peninsula, Zlatan Otok on Hvar island, Krauthaker in Kutjevo, and Coronica, Kozlovic, Vina Laguna, Pilato and Matoševic in Istria are names to look for.

CYPRUS The larger wineries have reduced production and moved their winemaking to the hills, but to no great effect. It is enterprising small wineries like Hadjiantonas, Kyperounda, Tsiakkas, Vlassides and Zambartas, that are succeeding in taking Cyprus forward, by investing in vineyards and with hands-on winemaking. Local red grape Maratheftiko has more potential than the mass-planted Mavro, while Shiraz is the best of the international varieties.

CZECH REPUBLIC The vineyards of Bohemia in the north-west and Moravia in the south-east are mainly planted with white varieties – Grüner Veltliner, Müller-Thurgau, Riesling, Pinot Blanc, Pinot Gris – with pockets of red such as St-Laurent and Lemberger (Blaufränkisch).

DENMARK Grapes shouldn't grow this far north. But as global warming pushes the threshold for viticulture ever northward and new grape varieties are developed to thrive here, the EU permitted commercial wine production in 2000. The industry is still tiny, with about 50 growers taking advantage of the long hours of sunshine to ripen their grapes. Southern Sweden, with very similar conditions, is also getting in on the act, with both white and red wines.

ENGLAND The first UK vineyard of the modern era was planted in 1952 and since then the tiny industry has come a long way. Today, the UK has around 1,650 ha (4,075 acres) of vines with over 500 vineyards (many very small), 125 wineries and an average annual output of around 2.5 million bottles – and rising – 2013 produced nearly 4.5 million bottles. Gone are most of the old German crosses and hybrids, with the majority of new plantings being the three Champagne varieties, Chardonnay, Pinot Noir and Pinot Meunier, for excellent quality sparklers. The best varieties for still whites are Bacchus, Reichensteiner, Schönburger and Seyval Blanc; for still reds and rosés, Rondo, Regent, Dornfelder and Pinot Noir. English (and a few Welsh) sparkling wines have shown they can equal Champagne in quality and the area planted to the classic Champagne varieties is now approaching 60% of the UK total. Although growers from Champagne have been taking notice, only one French producer so far has planted (at Meonhill in Hampshire, now owned by Hambledon Vineyard), but you hear a lot more French accents in the wineries now than a few years ago.

The most popular winemaking counties are: East Sussex (Bluebell Estates, BREAKY BOTTOM, Davenport, HENNERS, PLUMPTON COLLEGE), West Sussex (Bolney, Nutbourne, NYETIMBER, RIDGEVIEW, WISTON), Kent (BALFOUR, BIDDENDEN, CHAPEL DOWN, GUSBOURNE, Meopham Valley, Sandhurst), Surrey (DENBIES), Hampshire (COATES & SEELY, Hambledon, Hattingley Valley, Jenkyn Place, Meonhill), Dorset (FURLEIGH ESTATE, Kenton), Devon (SHARPHAM), Cornwall (CAMEL VALLEY), Berkshire (Stanlake Park), Gloucestershire (THREE CHOIRS),

Worcestershire (Astley), Essex (NEW HALL) and Suffolk (Lavenham Brook). The investment potential is shown by Rathfinny Estate developing 160ha (395 acres) in East Sussex and building a £5.5m winery.

2009 was an amazing year (the best year that UK vineyards have ever had) and the sparkling wines are generally excellent and long-lasting. 2010 had excellent early conditions, with a good flowering, and then a wet, indifferent summer leading to grapes with surprisingly high sugars, but also very high acidities. 2011 had a very warm dry spring and early summer, followed by a terrible flowering and very small crops. However, a very warm September and October saw the grapes achieve record sugar levels (but also high acids), which resulted in some good wines. 2012 was *the* year to forget for many growers; many vineyards, including the UK's largest, Nyetimber, picked nothing. However, some well-sited and managed vineyards in Kent fared reasonably well. The wines that were produced are good, with firm fruit flavours and balanced acidity. Having said that 2012 was a year to forget, 2013 also threatened to be a stinker, with a very late spring and flowering resulting in an extremely late (and wet) vintage with lower sugar levels and higher acids than anyone expected. Some growers were still picking on 19 November! However, despite these conditions, yields were good – a warm July and August helped – and most vineyards produced clean wines; sparkling base wines are looking good.

GEORGIA Georgia faces many challenges – lack of regulation, counterfeiting, and a 7-year ban (lifted in 2013) on exports to Russia, its biggest market – but its diverse climates (from subtropical to moderate continental) and soils could produce every style imaginable, and there is increasing evidence that Georgia is the cradle of winemaking. The tourist industry is helping introduce Georgian wines to a wider audience. International and indigenous varieties abound; the peppery, powerful red Saperavi could be a world-beater. Most wine is still pretty rustic, but investment is having an effect. A number of remarkable wines made in fat earthenware '*qvevri*' jars are starting to appear, giving us some idea of what ancient wine might have tasted like – and it's not for the faint-hearted.

GREECE The reputation, distribution and sales of Greek wines, both red and white, continue to improve, particularly in the US, but the Greek financial crisis has badly affected their domestic market. The new generation of winemakers and grape growers, many of them trained in France, Australia or California, have a clear vision of the flavours they want to achieve and their wines are modern but marvellously original too. Polarization between cheap bulk and expensive boutique wines continues, but large companies such as Boutari, Kourtaki and Tsantali are upping the quality stakes, and flavours improve every vintage. More vineyard and marketing work – many labels are still difficult to understand – is needed. Retsina – resinated white and rosé wine – is common throughout Greece; poor retsina is rough stuff but the best are deliciously oily and piny. There are successful blends of international and indigenous varieties, but also tremendous unblended examples of the red Agiorgitiko, Limnio and Xynomavro, and white Assyrtiko, Malagousia, Moschofilero and Roditis. Quality areas: Santorini and Macedonia for whites, Nemea and Naoussa for reds, SAMOS for sweet Muscats, Patras for dessert red Mavrodaphne. Wineries to watch include: Aidarinis, Alpha Estate, Argyros, Antonopoulos, Biblia Chora, Gaia, Gentilini, GEROVASSILIOU, Hatzidakis, Hatzimichalis, Kyr Yianni, Domaine Costa LAZARIDI, Mercouri, Papaïoannou, Strofilia and Tselepos.

HUNGARY Hungary makes remarkably good whites and reds and outstanding sweet TOKAJI wines. Stringent regulations and investment/advice from Australian and western European companies and consultants have put Hungary back on the international wine map. It has had some success with Sauvignon Blanc and Pinot Gris (also known as Szürkebarát) and there is renewed interest in native varieties such as Furmint, Hárslevelü and Irsai Olivér for whites, Kékfrankos (Blaufränkisch) and Kadarka (the traditional grape used in BIKAVÉR) for reds, and top Hungarian winemakers – Akos Kamocsay (at HILLTOP), Vilmos Thummerer, Attila Gere and others – are now a solid force. But price and reputation remain low and many vineyards are being abandoned out of desperation.

INDIA In spite of a population of about 1.3 billion people, wine consumption in India is minuscule. The urban/tourist centres of Delhi, Mumbai (Bombay), Bangalore and Goa account for about 80% of the country's wine consumption. Around 25% of wine is imported, the remainder is produced domestically. There is a long tradition of growing table grapes, but wine grape production is very recent. The major area of wine grape production is in the state of Maharashtra, focused around the town of Nashik. The vineyards are located at around 600m (2000ft) above sea level and so are relatively cool – certainly cooler than nearby Mumbai. In 2001 there were 6 wineries in India. Today there are more than 50, most of them in Maharashtra.

India is now starting to produce some consistent, decent-quality wines, thanks mainly to the groundbreaking work of major player Chateau Indage in Maharashtra and concerted efforts in recent years of two quality-focused producers, Sula Vineyards in the Nashik area and Grover Vineyards located in the Nandi Hills just outside of Bangalore in the state of Karnataka. Newcomer Fratelli at Akluj, south of Pune, is worth keeping an eye on. But there's nothing thrilling here yet.

ISRAEL Israeli wines have benefited from the country's advanced technology and agricultural skills, and from young winemakers who have studied and worked abroad. The quality wine industry is young and moving forward fast. Wineries such as Carmel, CASTEL, Clos de Gat, Flam, Margalit, Tzora, Yarden and YATIR are leading the way, while new start-ups such as Lewinsohn, Shvo and Sphera are showing promise.

Cabernet Sauvignon is still king, but Syrah/Shiraz is proving more adaptable to the climate. There is a move to blends of Mediterranean grapes, a trend fanned by Carmel, Chateau Golan, Lewinsohn, Recanati, Shvo and Vitkin. These may feature old-vine Carignan, Petite Sirah, Grenache and Mourvèdre for red wines and Viognier and Roussanne for whites. The quality regions are the higher-altitude, cooler-climate Upper Galilee, Golan Heights and Judean Hills.

The word kosher means 'pure', and kosher wines are necessary for observant Jews. These are the oldest wine laws, some of which come from the Bible. In fact, winemaking is the same for kosher or non-kosher wine, but the winery workers touching the wine have to be religious Jews and materials have to be certified as kosher. Kosher wines may be world-class; they are not necessarily sweet and sickly. Arguably the finest kosher wines are produced by CASTEL, Yarden and YATIR in Israel, Covenant and Herzog in California and Capçanes in CATALUÑA, Spain. LAURENT-PERRIER in Champagne, and Ch. PONTET-CANET and Ch. LÉOVILLE-POYFERRÉ in Bordeaux have also made kosher cuvées.

JAPAN It's not easy to grow wine grapes in Japan. The major viticulture regions, Nagano and Yamanashi, are located near the centre of the main island of Honshu, and producers face a number of climate challenges during the growing season. 90% of the grapes grown in Japan are table grapes; very few are of the European wine grape species *Vitis vinifera*. Some wineries do try to use table grapes or wine grape hybrids (which are easier to grow than *vinifera*), and wines made from Delaware, Kyoho, Ryugan and Muscat Bailey A are common, but can have that distinctive and generally unappealing 'foxy' or chemical/epoxy character that is found in species other than *vinifera*.

Some fairly interesting Japanese wine is made from Koshu, a pink-skinned, predominantly *vinifera* grape, believed to have come to Japan from Europe many centuries ago, via the Silk Road. Koshu usually produces a clean, dry, light-bodied wine with a delicate citrus character that pairs very well with sushi and sashimi. Good Koshu producers include Grace, Château Mercian, Katsunuma Winery (good sparkling Koshu), Marufuji Rubaiyat and Asagiri Wine Company. Also worth trying are red and white wines from Suntory in Yamanashi, Yamazaki Winery in Hokkaido, and some of the upper level Château Mercian wines – their Private Reserve Chardonnay is surprisingly good.

LEBANON Lebanese wine has always been centralized in the Bekaa Valley, but new vineyard areas have been planted, particularly in Batroun and Mount Lebanon in the west and Jezzine in the south. Lebanon's speciality is spicy red wine blends, but whites are improving. Chateau Musar and Kefraya's Comte de M are still the most sought-after wines, but investment is paying off in Ixsir and Château Marsyas (with the same owners as Domaine de Bargylus in Syria) and other wineries such as Massaya, Clos St. Thomas, Dom. des Tourelles and Château

Ka are also improving in quality. A number of new small wineries making characterful wines include Ch. Belle-Vue, Karam and Dom. de Baal.

LUXEMBOURG With one of the world's highest levels of wine consumption per capita, very little wine is exported. Co-operatives dominate here and quality is about what you would expect. Plantings of Elbling and Rivaner (Müller-Thurgau) are in decline, and are being replaced with quality varietals such as Riesling, Pinot Noir, Chardonnay and Gewürztraminer. *Crémant* (sparkling) wines continue to increase in quality and popularity.

MALTA The first impression of Malta is of an arid rocky island squeezed full of people and with barely enough soil to grow basic food crops. And it *never* seems to rain. Well, it does rain, and its limestone rock is able to absorb and hold a significant amount of water in reserve. Even so, water is scarce, but the vine doesn't need much – often the morning and evening dews from the sea breezes is enough to keep it going. Most wines used to be made from imported Italian grapes, and they weren't bad. But, especially on the small island of Gozo, vineyards are being developed and attractive wines are now available from 100% Maltese grapes. They're good, but you can taste the sun.

MEXICO In the far north-west of Mexico, in Baja California, some good reds are made by L A CETTO as well as by smaller companies such as Monte

Xanic and Casa de Piedra. In the rest of the country, only high-altitude areas such as the Parras Valley and Zacatecas have the potential for quality wines. Casa Madero, in the Parras Valley, has some success with Cabernet Sauvignon. Other promising grape varieties include Nebbiolo, Petite Sirah, Tempranillo, Zinfandel and Barbera, with Viognier and Chardonnay also planted.

MOLDOVA Standards of winemaking and equipment leave much to be desired, but fruit quality is good, and international players, including PENFOLDS and winemakers Jacques Lurton, Hugh Ryman and Alain Thiénot, have worked with local wineries. However, chaotic social conditions have led to many attempts being abandoned.

MONTENEGRO This red-wine-dominated part of the former Yugoslavia shows some potential in the beefy Vranac grape with its bitter cherry flavours – but the worst wines are really poor.

MOROCCO Known for big, sweet-fruited reds that once found a ready blending market in France. France is still the biggest export market, but the wines have improved dramatically since the 1990s and domestic consumption is increasing, especially among young urban professionals. Massive investment by Castel Frères kickstarted the renaissance, and quality is on the rise at Morocco's leading producer, Celliers de Meknès. Domaine el Baraka and Domaine Larroque are promising, and French producers Bernard Magrez (sometimes in harness with Gérard Depardieu) and Alain GRAILLOT (Tandem) are making some good wines here, especially from Syrah.

NETHERLANDS The vineyard area has expanded rapidly in the past decade: there are currently around 175ha (430 acres) in the hands of more than 150 commercial growers, most of whom sell all their wines locally. The best vineyards are in the southern part of the country, in the rolling hills of Limburg. Chardonnay is the most promising grape variety.

ROMANIA *Vitis vinifera* grapes such as Pinot Noir, Cabernet Sauvignon, Merlot and the native Feteasca Negra for reds, Pinot Gris, Chardonnay and the fragrant Tamaiosa Romaneasca for whites are rapidly replacing hybrid varieties. International-backed ventures such as Cramele Recas, Cramele Halewood (Prahova Valley) and Carl Reh are a sign of a mini-revolution, but challenges remain. Recent forays into the export market showed marked improvements but no really memorable flavours yet. The appellation system is of limited value, although Dealul Mare, Murfatlar and Cotnari all have ancient reputations.

SLOVAKIA The eastern part of the old Czechoslovakia, with its cool-climate vineyards, is dominated by white varieties – Pinot Blanc, Riesling, Grüner Veltliner, Irsai Olivér – with the occasional fruity Frankovka (Blaufränkisch) red. Western investment is rapidly improving the quality.

SLOVENIA Many of the old Yugoslav Federation's best vineyards are here. Potential is considerable, and some interesting wines are emerging, with whites generally better than reds. The increasing popularity of Slovenia as a holiday and second-home region should improve availability. On the Italian border, Brda and Vipava have go-ahead co-operatives, and Kraski Teran is a red wine of repute. The Movia range, from the Kristancic family, looks promising. Inland, nearer the Hungarian border, Puklavec produces tasty whites.

SWITZERLAND Fendant (Chasselas) is the main grape for spritzy but neutral whites from the VALAIS and VAUD. Like the fruity DÔLE reds, they are best drunk very young. German-speaking cantons produce whites from Müller-Thurgau (sometimes labelled Riesling-Sylvaner) and mostly light reds and rosés from Pinot Noir (Blauburgunder); an expanding group of top producers, such as Daniel GANTENBEIN, make more powerful versions. Italian-speaking TICINO concentrates on Merlots, which are increasingly impressive. Serious wines, especially in Valais, use Pinot Noir, Syrah, Chardonnay, Marsanne and traditional varieties like Amigne and Petite Arvine. Indeed, the numerous traditional varieties are undergoing a revival. See also NEUCHÂTEL.

THAILAND The very concept of growing wine grapes anywhere within Thailand's tropics calls for a suspension of disbelief, but Thailand, close to the equator, has no less than 8 major wineries, producing nearly a million bottles of wine a year. The first still wines appeared in 1995 from Chateau de Loei in north-eastern Thailand, using Chenin Blanc and Syrah. Siam Winery, which had begun producing wine coolers in 1986, launched its Monsoon Valley label in 2003; the wines are now exported to more than 15 countries. Entry-level red and white blends are made mainly from hybrid grapes, but premium range wines made from grapes such as Colombard and Shiraz grown in the Hua Hin Hills vineyard show potential.

TUNISIA Ancient wine traditions have had an injection of new life from international investment. Tourism soaks up most of the production. It remains to be seen what effect recent political upheaval has had.

TURKEY Turkey is a blessing for anyone tired of the globalization and sameness of the wine world. It is a country with an enormous range of *terroirs*, from Thrace in the west to tribal lands in the east. There are some fascinating indigenous grape varieties: the muscular yet scented Bogazkere, softer, plummy Öküzgözü, and juicy, fruity Kalecik Karasi. The best whites are the aromatic Emir and the fatter Narince. There is certainly a new desire for improvement. The three largest wineries – Kavaklidere, Kayra and Doluca – are leading the quality drive. Other wineries that are part of the new wave include Baküs Butik, Büyülübag, Corvus, LA (formerly Idol), Likya, Pamukkale, Prodom, Sevilen, Umurbey, Urla and Vinkara.

UKRAINE Political events have disrupted Ukraine's wines, since Crimea's vineyards are the most important, producing hearty reds, sparkling reds and whites, and tremendous sweet stickies from Muscatel and other varieties, especially under the Massandra label. Good sparkling wines include Inkerman, Novyi Svet and Zolotaya Balka. The Odessa region also has vineyards. Kolonist has raised the stakes for high-quality reds on the Moldovan border, and Trubetskoy is waking things up on the Dnieper.

A–Z

OF WINES, PRODUCERS, GRAPES & WINE REGIONS

In the following pages there are over
1600 entries covering the world's top wines, as well as leading
producers, main wine regions and grape
varieties, followed on page 328 by a glossary of wine terms
and classifications.

*On page 2 you will find a full explanation of
how to use the A–Z.
On page 337 there is an index of all wine producers
in the book, to help you find the world's best wines.*

AALTO *Ribera del Duero DO, Castilla y León, Spain*   From the outset this winery, created in 1999, has produced dense but elegant reds, Aalto★★ and old vines cuvée Aalto PS★★. Best years: 2010 09 08 07 **06** 05 04 03 01 00 99.

ABACELA *Umpqua Valley AVA, Oregon, USA*   Earl and Hilda Jones planted the first Tempranillo vines in the Pacific Northwest, in the Umpqua Valley, southern OREGON, in 1995. Today they grow Tempranillo★ (Reserve★★), Albariño★★ (surprisingly similar to those of GALICIA), Syrah, Merlot, Dolcetto, Malbec, Grenache and Viognier. Best years: (2012) 11 10 **09** 08.

ABEJA *Walla Walla Valley AVA, Washington State, USA*   Modern winery located on a century-old farmstead in the foothills of the Blue Mountains. Winemaker John Abbott produces crisp Viognier★★ in small quantities, rich and concentrated Chardonnay★, spicy Syrah★, supple Merlot★ and fine Cabernet Sauvignon★★, plus a tiny amount of Cabernet Sauvignon Reserve★★. Best years: (Cabernet Sauvignon) (2012) 11 10 **09 08** 07.

ABRUZZO-MOLISE *Italy*   Abruzzo, with its neighbour Molise, is part maritime, part mountainous. White Trebbiano d'Abruzzo, dry with elegant hay and white currant characters, can reach great heights of quality, but is increasingly overlooked in favour of more immediately characterful and fashionable local grapes Coccociola, Passerina and Pecorino. The fruity, full-coloured Montepulciano d'Abruzzo DOC, despite high production, can be a red of real quality, as can its *rosato* partner, Cerasuolo. The creation of subzone COLLINE TERAMANE DOCG for Montepulciano d'Abruzzo from the 2003 vintage reinforces the region's potential for quality wine. Good producers include Cirelli★, Col del Mondo, Contesa★, Faraone★, Illuminati★, Marramiero★, Masciarelli★, Nicodemi, Emidio Pepe★★, Orlandi Contucci Ponno★, Tollo★, VALENTINI★★★. See also MONTEPULCIANO.

ACHAVAL FERRER *Mendoza, Argentina*   Founded in 1998, and now one of Argentina's most sought-after labels. 80-year-old vines in the La Consulta area of UCO VALLEY produce Finca Altamira★★, a dark, rich Malbec. Also very good single-vineyard Malbecs Bella Vista★★ and Mirador★★, as well as regular Malbec★★ and a more approachable red blend, Quimera★. Best years: 2011 **10 09** 08 06 05.

ACONCAGUA *Chile*   A warm region and home to some of Chile's best reds, from Cabernet Sauvignon, Syrah and Carmenère. Recent vineyard developments in the cool Aconcagua Costa region, close to the sea, are proving very exciting for Sauvignon Blanc and Syrah. Best producers: ERRÁZURIZ★★, MONTES★ (Outer Limits), VON SIEBENTHAL★.

TIM ADAMS *Clare Valley, South Australia*   Important maker of fine, traditional wine, whose need to buy in grapes has disappeared since his bargain purchase of 75ha (185 acres) of vines from Leasingham in 2009. He subsequently snapped up the Leasingham winery (closed by Constellation), which he uses for contract winemaking. Classic dry Riesling★★★, oaky Semillon★★ and rich, opulent Shiraz★★ (both often ★★★) and Cabernet-Malbec★★. Newcomers Tempranillo★★ and Pinot Gris★ are exciting. The Fergus★★ red blend is based on Grenache and Tempranillo and can be glorious, while minty, peppery Aberfeldy Shiraz★★ (can be ★★★) is a remarkable, at times unnerving, mouthful of brilliance from 100-year-old vines. The botrytis Riesling★ can be super. Protégé★ label is used for some of his newly acquired vineyards' fruit. Best years: (Aberfeldy Shiraz) (2013) 12 10 09 08 06 **05** 04 03 02 01 00 99 98 96 94.

ADELAIDE HILLS *South Australia* Small, exciting region; high altitude affords a cool, moist climate ideal for superb sparkling wine, consistently good Sauvignon Blanc and Chardonnay, promising Pinot Noir, small amounts of classy Nebbiolo, and increasingly exciting, fleshy Shiraz from warmer southern vineyards. Best producers: Ashton Hills★, Barratt, Bird in Hand★, Deviation Road★, Fox Gordon, HENSCHKE★★, The Lane★, Longview★, Nepenthe★, PETALUMA★★, SHAW & SMITH★★, Geoff Weaver★.

ADELSHEIM *Willamette Valley AVA, Oregon, USA* Over the past 3 decades, Adelsheim has established a reputation for excellent, generally unfiltered, Pinot Noir – especially cherry-scented Elizabeth's Reserve★ and Bryan Creek Vineyard★ – and for rich Chardonnay Caitlin's Reserve★★. Also a bright, minerally Pinot Gris★. Best years: (Elizabeth's Reserve) (2012) 11 10 09 08.

AGLIANICO Arguably southern Italy's noblest black grape, Aglianico makes fine, ageworthy wines, particularly from Campania's calcareous/volcanic TAURASI or on the volcanic slopes of Monte Vulture in Basilicata. Puglia's CASTEL DEL MONTE and Campania's Cilento make softer versions.

AGLIANICO DEL VULTURE DOCG *Basilicata, Italy* Wine from the Aglianico grape grown on the steep slopes of extinct volcano Mt Vulture. Despite the location, the harvest is sometimes later than in BAROLO, 750km (470 miles) to the north-west, because the Aglianico grape ripens very late at altitude. Promoted from DOC to DOCG from the 2011 vintage. The best wines are structured, complex and long-lived. Compared with the elegant TAURASI, Aglianico del Vulture is broader and generous in character. Best producers: Basilium★, Bisceglia★, D'Angelo, Donato d'Angelo★★, Carbone★, Elena Fucci★, Musto Carmelitano★, Cantine del Notaio, Le Querce★, I Talenti, Consorzio Viticoltori Associati del Vulture (Carpe Diem★). Best years: (2012) 11 08 07 06 05 04 01.

AHR *Germany* The Ahr Valley is a small, 562ha (1388-acre), mainly red wine region south of Bonn, best known for Spätburgunder (Pinot Noir). Adeneuer★, Deutzerhof★, MEYER-NÄKEL★★ and STODDEN★★ are the best of a growing band of serious producers.

AIRÉN Spain's most planted white grape, Airén is grown all over the centre and south of Spain, especially in La MANCHA, VALDEPEÑAS and ANDALUCIA (where it's called Lairén). Fresh, generally neutral wines, with some eye-opening exceptions, such as Ercavio's old-vines white from Toledo and 'natural' whites by Patio in La Mancha and Ambiz in Madrid.

ALBAN *San Luis Obispo County, California, USA* Based in the cool Arroyo Grande district of Edna Valley, John Alban is a RHÔNE specialist. He offers 2 Viogniers★★, a Roussanne★★ laden with honey notes, 3 Syrahs (Reva★★★, Lorraine★★, Seymour's Vineyard★★), intense Grenache★★ and Pandora★★, a blend of about 60% Grenache, 40% Syrah. Some of America's purest expressions of Rhône varietals, though recently a little too ripe. Best years: (Syrah) (2010) 09 08 07 06 05 04 03 02 01 00.

ALBARIÑO Possibly Spain's most characterful white grape. A speciality of RIAS BAIXAS in Galicia in Spain's rainy north-west and, as Alvarinho, in Portugal's VINHO VERDE region. Australia, New Zealand, California,

Oregon and the US Mid-Atlantic region are having a go. Recently introduced into South Africa. When well made, Albariño wines have fascinating flavours of apricot, peach and grapefruit, refreshingly high acidity and highish alcohol. The danger to quality is excessive yields.

ALENQUER DOC *Lisboa, Portugal* Maritime-influenced hills north of Lisbon, producing wines from local grape varieties such as Castelão (Periquita) and Trincadeira, and from Cabernet, Syrah and Chardonnay, often simply labelled LISBOA (formerly Estremadura). Best producers: Quinta de Chocapalha★, Quinta da Cortezia★, Quinta do Monte d'Oiro★★, Casa SANTOS LIMA★. Best years: (reds) (2012) **11 09 07 05 04 03**.

ALENTEJO *Portugal* A large chunk of southern Portugal south and east of Lisbon and, along with the DOURO, one of Portugal's fastest-improving red wine regions. Already some of Portugal's finest reds come from here. Vinho Regional wines are labelled Alentejano. Best producers: (reds) ALIANÇA (Quinta da Terrugem★★), BACALHÔA★ (Tinto da Ânfora Grande Escolha★★), Borba co-op★, Cartuxa★ (Pera-Manca★★), Quinta do Centro★ (Pedra e Alma★★), CORTES DE CIMA★, Dona Maria★, ESPORÃO★, Fita Preta★, Paulo Laureano★, MALHADINHA NOVA★★, Monte da Penha, Mouchão★★, Quinta do Mouro★, Quinta da Plansel (Plansel Selecta★), João Portugal RAMOS★, Herdade do Rocim, SOGRAPE★, José de Sousa★, Terras d'Alter★. Best years: (reds) (2012) **11 09 08 07 05 04 01**.

ALEXANDER VALLEY AVA *Sonoma County, California, USA* AVA centred on the northern Russian River, which is fairly warm, with only patchy summer fog. Delightful juicy Cabernet Sauvignon, not marred by an excess of tannin. Chardonnay may also be good when not over-cropped. Merlot and old-vine Zinfandel can be outstanding from hillside vineyards. Good Sauvignon Blanc, especially from gravelly soils near the river. Best producers: Alexander Valley Vineyards★, CLOS DU BOIS★, De Lorimier★, Geyser Peak★, Hanna★, JORDAN★★, Murphy-Goode★★, RIDGE (Geyserville★★), Sausal★, SEGHESIO★★, SILVER OAK★★, Simi★, Skipstone★, Trentadue★★. See also RUSSIAN RIVER VALLEY AVA, SONOMA COUNTY. Best years: (reds) 2012 11 10 **09 08 07 06 04 03 02 01 99 97 95**.

ALGARVE *Portugal* Holiday region with mostly red wines in 4 DOCs: Lagoa, Lagos, Portimão and Tavira. Look out for reds and rosés from Sir Cliff Richard's Vida Nova, Quinta do Barranco Longo and Morgado da Torre.

ALIANÇA *Bairrada DOC, Portugal* Crisp, fresh whites and soft, approachable red BAIRRADAS★. Also reds from the DÃO (Quinta da Garrida★), DOURO (Quinta dos Quatro Ventos★) and ALENTEJO (Quinta da Terrugem★★).

ALICANTE BOUSCHET French grape, found (illegally) in Provence and in the Languedoc. This workhorse variety was largely grubbed up 20–30 years ago as lacking finesse, but a few growers are now producing robust vins de France from old vines. In Spain it's known as Garnacha Tintorera. Portugal – and South America – make good use of its dark, brooding qualities.

ALIGOTÉ French grape, found mainly in Burgundy, whose basic characteristic is a lemony tartness. It can make extremely refreshing white wine, sometimes with a mineral, buttermilk undertone, especially from old vines, but is generally rather lean. The best comes from the village of Bouzeron in the CÔTE CHALONNAISE, where Aligoté has its own appellation. Occasionally found in Moldova and Bulgaria. Drink young. **Best producers: (Burgundy)** COCHE-DURY★, A Ente★, J-H Goisot★, Ponsot★, les Temps Perdus, TOLLOT-BEAUT, de Villaine★.

ALLEGRINI *Valpolicella DOC, Veneto, Italy* High-profile producer in VALPOLICELLA Classico, making single-vineyard IGTs La Grola★★ (Corvina with a bit of Syrah) and La Poja★★★ (100% Corvina), wines that show the great potential that exists for Veronese red as a table wine. Very good AMARONE★★ and RECIOTO Giovanni Allegrini★★. **Best years: (Amarone)** 2011 10 08 07 06 04 03 01.

THIÉRRY ALLEMAND *Cornas AC, Rhône Valley, France* Thiérry Allemand has 5ha (12 acres) of prime quality granite hillside vines. He uses little sulphur, in wines that parade clear fruit and dashing depth. He produces 2 unfiltered expressions of CORNAS at its intense and powerful best: Chaillot★★ has racy, dark berry fruit and crisp, lively tannins; complex, sustained, long-lived Reynard★★★ is from very old Syrah. **Best years: (Reynard)** 2013 12 11 10 09 08 07 06 05 04 03 01 00 99 98 96 95 94 91 90.

ALLENDE *Rioja DOCa, Rioja, Spain* One of the most admired new names in RIOJA, making a mix of single-vineyard (*pago*) and high-quality blends. Scented, uncompromisingly concentrated reds include Aurus★★, Calvario★★ and fresh, vibrant Allende★★. Also a marvellous, scented white★★. **Best years: (reds)** (2011) 11 09 08 07 06 05 04 03 02 01 00 99.

ALMAVIVA★★★ *Maipo, Chile* State-of-the-art joint venture between CONCHA Y TORO and the Baron Philippe de Rothschild company (see MOUTON-ROTHSCHILD), located in MAIPO Valley's Tocornal vineyard. A memorably powerful red blend, predominantly from old Cabernet Sauvignon vines planted in alluvial, stony soils; it can be drunk at 5 years but should age for 10. **Best years:** 2011 10 09 07 06 05 03 01.

ALOXE-CORTON AC *Côte de Beaune, Burgundy, France* Important village at the northern end of the CÔTE DE BEAUNE producing mostly red wines. Its reputation is based on the 2 Grands Crus, CORTON (mainly red) and CORTON-CHARLEMAGNE (white only). There's an argument raging that some of the Grand Cru red vineyards should be 1er Cru, and some 1er Crus downgraded to village level. That's harsh, and some village wines from Boutières and Valozières are worth a second look. Almost all the white wine is classified as Grand Cru. **Best producers: (reds)** d'Ardhuy★, CHANDON DE BRIAILLES★, M Chapuis★, Marius Delarche★, Dubreuil-Fontaine★, Follin-Arbelet★, Camille Giroud★, Antonin Guyon★, JADOT★, Mallard, Rapet★, Senard★, TOLLOT-BEAUT★. **Best years: (reds)** 12 11 10 09 08 07 06 05 03 02 99.

DOM. JEAN-MICHEL ALQUIER *Faugères AC, Languedoc, France* This estate shows how good FAUGÈRES can be, with barrel aging, and low yields for the special cuvées, Les Bastides★★ and La Maison Jaune★. Whites include Grand Blanc (Marsanne-Grenache Blanc) and Pierres Blanches★ (Sauvignon Blanc). **Best years: (Bastides)** (2013) 12 11 10 09 08 07 06 05.

ALSACE AC *Alsace, France* Tucked away on France's border with Germany, Alsace produces some of the most individual white wines of all, rich in aroma and full of ripe, distinctive flavours. Alsace is almost as far north as CHAMPAGNE, but its climate is considerably warmer and drier. Wines from the 51 best vineyard sites can call themselves Alsace Grand Cru AC and account for 4% of production; quality regulations are more stringent and many individual crus have further tightened the rules. Riesling, Muscat, Gewurztraminer and Pinot Gris are generally considered the finest varieties. Pinot Blanc can produce good wines too – although confusingly, Pinot Blanc can legally be made from 100% Auxerrois. Reds from Pinot Noir are improving fitfully. Alsace labels its wines by grape variety and, apart from the Edelzwicker blends and CRÉMANT D'ALSACE fizz, most Alsace wines are made from a single variety, although blends from certain Grand Cru sites, such as Altenberg de Bergheim and Kaefferkopf, are now recognized. Vendange Tardive means 'late-harvest': the grapes (Riesling, Muscat, Pinot Gris or Gewurztraminer) are picked almost overripe, with higher sugar levels. The resulting wines are usually rich and mouthfilling and often need 5 years or more to reach their full potential. Sélection de Grains Nobles (made from botrytized grapes of the same varieties) are among Alsace's finest, but are very expensive to produce (and to buy). Best producers: Barmès-Buecher, J Becker, Léon Beyer★, A & C Binner, P Blanck★, Bott-Geyl★★, A Boxler★, DEISS★★, Dirler-Cadé★★, A Dussourt★, Pierre Frick★, Rémy Gresser★, HUGEL★, Hunawihr co-op, JOSMEYER★★, Kientzler★, Kreydenweiss★★, Kuentz-Bas★, A MANN★★, Mittnacht Frères, MURÉ★★, OSTERTAG★★, Pfaffenheim co-op, Ribeauvillé co-op, L Rieffel, Rieflé★, Rolly Gassmann★, Charles Schléret, Schlumberger★, Schoenheitz, SCHOFFIT★★, Bruno Sorg★, TRIMBACH★★, TURCKHEIM co-op★, WEINBACH★★, Zinck★, ZIND-HUMBRECHT★★★. Best years: (2013) 12 **11 10 09 08 07 05 04**.

ALTA VISTA *Mendoza, Argentina* Founded in 1998, French-owned, specializing in old-vine Malbec, with vineyards in Las Compuertas, Alto Agrelo and El Cepillo: single-vineyard Alizarine★★, Serenade★★ and Temis★ and Terroir Selection★ Malbecs are thrilling interpretations. Premium Torrontés★ from Cafayate is one of Argentina's best examples.

ALTARE *Barolo DOCG, Piedmont, Italy* Elio Altare led the winemaking revolution in traditionalist Alba, drastically shortening maceration times for Nebbiolo and other grapes. A professed modernist, Elio's wines are rich and oaky, the accent on extracted fruit rather than on *terroir*. Very good BAROLO Arborina★★ and Brunate★★ from La Morra and recently added Cerretta★ from Serralunga. Also 3 barrique-aged wines under the LANGHE DOC: Arborina★★ (Nebbiolo), Larigi★★ (Barbera) and La Villa★ (Nebbiolo-Barbera). Best years: (Barolo) 2011 10 **09 08 07 06 04 01 00 99**.

ALTO ADIGE *Trentino-Alto Adige, Italy* A largely German-speaking province, originally called Südtirol. The DOC covers dozens of different types of wine. Reds range from light and perfumed Schiava, to fruity and more structured Cabernet and Merlot, to dark and velvety Lagrein. Oak aging, once inclined to excess, is being handled ever better. Whites include Chardonnay, Gewürztraminer, Pinot Grigio, Riesling, Sauvignon Blanc and minerally, potentially long-lived Pinot Bianco (Weissburgunder) wines. There is also some good sparkling wine. Production is dominated by well-run co-ops, although there are excellent individual producers. Best producers (private): Abbazia di Novacella★, Casòn Hirschprunn★, Peter Dipoli★★, Franz Haas★★, Haderburg★★, Hofstätter★★, LAGEDER★★, Laimburg★, Loacker★, Muri-Gries★★, Josef Niedermayr★, Ignaz Niedriest★, Nössing★★, Plattner-Waldgries★, Peter Pliger/Kuenhof★★, Hans Rottensteiner★, Heinrich Rottensteiner★, Thurnhof★,

TIEFENBRUNNER★★, Elena Walch★; (co-ops) Caldaro★, Colterenzio★★, Girlan-Cornaiano★, Gries★★, Nals-Margreid★★, Prima & Nuova/Erste & Neue★, San Michele Appiano★★, Santa Maddalena★, Terlano★★★, Termeno★★.

ALTOS LAS HORMIGAS *Mendoza, Argentina* When visionary Tuscan winemaker Alberto Antonini fell in love with Argentina and its Malbec, Altos Las Hormigas was born. A relentless pursuit of *terroir* expression through Malbec has spanned 15 years and some 216ha (530 acres) of vineyards and it is now part owned by the famous soils specialist, Pedro Parra. The MENDOZA Classic★★ label is benchmark stuff, while the UCO VALLEY Terroir★★ selection shows lovely purity of fruit. At the top end the Vista Flores Single Vineyard Malbec★ is deeply perfumed and lush with blue fruit. Fine Bonarda under the Colonia Las Liebres★★ label.

ALVARINHO See ALBARIÑO.

ALZINGER *Unterloiben, Wachau, Austria* This estate is impeccably run by Leo senior and junior. Riesling and Grüner Veltliner are of equal quality and routinely ageworthy. Top bottlings – Rieslings from Loibenberg and Höhereck, and Veltliners from Loibenberg and Steinertal – are all effortlessly ★★. Best years: (2013) 12 11 **09 08 07**.

AMADOR FOOTHILL *Sierra Foothills AVA, California, USA* Outstanding Zinfandel★★, pleasing Sauvignon Blanc and a good RHÔNE-style red blend called Katie's Côte.

AMARONE DELLA VALPOLICELLA DOCG *Veneto, Italy* A brilliantly individual, bitter-rich style of VALPOLICELLA made from mainly Corvina and Rondinella grapes dried on mats or in lofts. The wine, which can reach 16% of alcohol and more, is fermented to near-dryness, unlike the sweet RECIOTO DELLA VALPOLICELLA. Wines from the hilly Classico zone are generally the best (exceptions from DAL FORNO, Corte Sant'Alda, Roccolo Grassi and Prà's Morandina). Now DOCG (from the 2010 vintage). Best producers: Accordini★★, ALLEGRINI★★, Bertani★★, Brigaldara★, Brunelli★, BUSSOLA★★★, Michele Castellani★★, Corte Sant'Alda★, Valentina Cubi★★, DAL FORNO★★★, Guerrieri-Rizzardi★★, Marion★★, MASI★★, Monte dei Ragni★★★, Novaia★, Prà★, QUINTARELLI★★★, Le Ragose★★, Roccolo Grassi★, Le Salette★★, Serègo Alighieri★, Speri★★, Tedeschi★★, Villa Monteleone★★, Viviani★★, Zenato★★. Best years: 2011 10 **08 06 04 03 01 00 99 98**.

ANAKENA *Cachapoal, Rapel, Chile* A modern winery producing one of Chile's best Viogniers★★, Ona Pinot Noir★ and the unusual Ona white blend of Riesling, Viognier and Chardonnay★. Some excellent single-vineyard★ releases.

DOM. DE L'ANCIENNE CURE *Bergerac AOP and Monbazillac AOP, South-West France* Christian Roche is best known for his luscious MONBAZILLACS★★, but his dry whites and his reds are no less remarkable. Top cuvées L'Abbaye★ and L'Extase★★ for all three styles. Best years: (reds and dry whites) 2012 11 **10 09**; (sweet whites) **2012 11 09 05**.

ANDALUCÍA *Spain* Fortified wines, or wines naturally so strong in alcohol that they don't need fortifying, are the speciality of this southern stretch of Spain. Apart from sherry (JEREZ Y MANZANILLA), there are the lesser, sherry-like wines of Condado de Huelva DO and MONTILLA-MORILES, and the rich, sweet wines of MÁLAGA. These regions also make some modern but bland dry whites; the best are from Condado de Huelva. Red and unfortified white wines are also appearing from Málaga, Cádiz, Seville, Granada and Almería provinces, often from very high-altitude vineyards around Sierra Nevada.

ANDERSON VALLEY AVA *California, USA* Small AVA in western MENDOCINO COUNTY, producing brilliant wines. Many vineyards are within 15 miles of the Pacific Ocean, making this potentially one of the coldest AVAs in California. Delicate Pinot Noirs and Chardonnays, and one of the few places in the state for first-rate Gewürztraminer and Riesling. Superb sparkling wines, combining acidity with cream. Best producers: Breggo★, Brutocao★, Goldeneye★, Greenwood Ridge★, HANDLEY★★, Lazy Creek★, Littorai★, NAVARRO★★, ROEDERER ESTATE★★, SCHARFFENBERGER CELLARS★★.

ANDREW WILL WINERY *Washington State, USA* Winemaker Chris Camarda makes delicious blends of BORDEAUX varietals from a range of older WASHINGTON vineyards. At the top are the complex Champoux Vineyard★★★ and the opulent Ciel du Cheval★★. Wine from the estate vineyard, Two Blondes Vineyard★, has improved as the vines have aged. Sorella★★, a blend of the best barrels each vintage, can be outstanding with age. Best years: (reds) (2012) 11 10 **09 08 07 06**.

CH. ANGÉLUS ★★★ *St-Émilion Grand Cru AC, 1er Grand Cru Classé, Bordeaux, France* Reached the pinnacle of Premier Grand Cru Classé 'A' in the 2012 ST-ÉMILION classification. New bell tower built to celebrate. Rich, dark, spicy, modern St-Émilion with lots of lovely old-vine Cabernet Franc. On flying form but watch prices. Best years: 2012 11 10 09 08 **07 06 05 04 03 02 01 00 99 98 96**.

MARQUIS D'ANGERVILLE *Volnay, Côte de Beaune, Burgundy, France* Succeeding generations of d'Angervilles have provided an exemplary range of elegant Premiers Crus from VOLNAY, the subtlest of the CÔTE DE BEAUNE's red wine appellations. Quality now superb, along with biodynamic approach. Clos des Ducs and Taillepieds are ★★★. All should be kept for at least 5 years. Now expanding into the JURA with Dom. du Pélican. Best years: (top reds) 12 11 10 09 **08 07 06 05 03 02 99 98 96 90**.

CH. D'ANGLUDET★ *Margaux AC, Haut-Médoc, Bordeaux, France* English-owned château making a gentle, charming style that is always good value – and on excellent form this century, sometimes achieving ★★. Ages well for at least 10 years. Best years: 2012 11 10 **09 08 06 05 04 02 00 98 96 95**.

ANJOU BLANC AC *Loire Valley, France* Wines range from bone dry to sweet, from excellent to dreadful; the best are dry or off-dry. Up to 20% Chardonnay or Sauvignon can be added, but many leading producers – some preferring the IGP VAL DE LOIRE or Vin de France labels – use 100% Chenin from top sites once dedicated to sweet COTEAUX DU LAYON. Best producers: M Angeli/Sansonnière★, P Baudouin, Bergerie, S Bernaudeau★, D Chaffardon, des Chesnaies, P Delesvaux★★, Fesles★, Dom. F L, Forges★, HUREAU★, de Juchepie★, Richard Leroy★★, Montgilet, Mosse★, OGEREAU★, de Passavant★, PIERRE-BISE★, Pithon-Paillé★, Richou★, Roulerie★, Soucherie★. Best years: (top wines) (2013) 12 11 10 09 08 07 06 05.

ANJOU ROUGE AC *Loire Valley, France* Anjou reds (from Cabernets Sauvignon and Franc or Pineau d'Aunis) are increasingly successful. Usually fruity, easy-drinking wine, with less tannin than ANJOU-VILLAGES. Wines made from Gamay are sold as Anjou Gamay. Best producers: Brizé★, B Courault, P Delesvaux★, du Fresne, La Grange aux Belles, OGEREAU★, PIERRE-BISE★ (Anjou Gamay), Putille, Richou★, Rochelles★, Roulerie. Best years: (top wines) (2013) 11 10 09 08 06 05.

ANJOU-VILLAGES AC *Loire Valley, France* Superior Anjou red (from Cabernet Franc and Cabernet Sauvignon) from 46 villages. Anjou-Villages Brissac's schist-dominated soils produce particularly firmly structured wines, which reward aging. Best producers: Bablut/Daviau★★,

P Baudouin, Brizé★, de Conquessac, Deux Arcs, Haute Perche, Montgilet★, de la Motte, OGEREAU★, PIERRE-BISE★★, Putille★, Richou★★, Rochelles★★, Sauveroy, la Varière★. Best years: (2013) **11 10 09 08 06 05 04**.

ANSELMI *Veneto, Italy* Roberto Anselmi was one of the first after PIEROPAN to show that SOAVE can have real personality when carefully made. Using ultra-modern methods he has honed the fruit flavours of his San Vincenzo★★ and Capitel Foscarino★★, and introduced small-

barrel-aging for single-vineyard Capitel Croce★★ and luscious, SAUTERNES-like I Capitelli★★ (sometimes ★★★), as well as the Cabernet Sauvignon Realdà. All sold under the regional IGT rather than Soave DOC. Best years: (I Capitelli) **2012 11 10 09 08 05 04 03 01 00**.

ANTHONY ROAD *Finger Lakes AVA, New York State, USA* Located on the west edge of Seneca Lake, Anthony Road specializes in dry★, semi-dry★ and sweet Rieslings, as well as an ALSACE-styled Gewurztraminer. A second label, Martini-Reinhardt, features some of the region's best Cabernet Franc. Winemaker Johannes Reinhardt also collaborates on TIERCE.

ANTINORI *Tuscany, Italy* Florentine wine merchants since 1385, Antinori, under the leadership of Piero, were at the forefront of the so-called 'wine renaissance' of the 1970s. Still a major force for modernization in Tuscany, with a national portfolio in Umbria (Castello della Sala, with white Cervaro★★), Piedmont (Prunotto), Puglia (Tormaresca) and Franciacorta (Montenisa). Best Tuscan offerings include Marchese Antinori CHIANTI CLASSICO Riserva★★, VINO NOBILE La Braccesca★★, BRUNELLO DI MONTALCINO Pian delle Vigne★★ and BOLGHERI's Guado al Tasso★★. But the wines that helped to revolutionize Tuscan – indeed Italian – wines are the 'super-Tuscans' TIGNANELLO★★ (Sangiovese-Cabernet) and SOLAIA★★ (Cabernet-Sangiovese): barrique-aged and aimed at the top echelons of the wine world. Best years: (reds) (2011) 10 09 **08 07 06 04 01 00 99**.

DOM. D'ANTUGNAC *Limoux AC, Languedoc, France* Jean-Luc Terrier and Christian Collovray, who own the MÂCON Domaine des Deux Roches, produce impressive Pinot Noir and Chardonnay in the cool LIMOUX region. Côté Pierre Lys★ (Pinot Noir) exhibits finesse and complexity. Chardonnay Las Gravas★ is barrel-fermented and aged, balancing richness with apples and creamy freshness. Aux Bons Hommes★ is a Merlot-based red Limoux.

ARAGÓN *Spain* Aragón stretches south from the Pyrenees to Spain's central plateau. Winemaking has improved markedly, first of all in the cooler, hilly, northern SOMONTANO, and now also further south in CALATAYUD, CAMPO DE BORJA and CARIÑENA; these 3 DO areas have the potential to be a major budget-price force in a world mad for beefy but juicy reds.

ARAUJO *Napa Valley AVA, California, USA* Boutique winery and owners of the superb Eisele vineyard. Araujo Cabernet Sauvignon★★★ is one of California's most sought-after reds, combining great fruit intensity with power. Impressive Syrah★★★ and attractively zesty Sauvignon Blanc★★.

ARBOIS AC *Jura, France* The largest AC in the Jura, with sub-appellation Pupillin. The region's best reds, from Trousseau and Poulsard, are made here. Dry whites, from Chardonnay and/or the local Savagnin, are varied in style: some sherry-like, the most concentrated being the sallow *vin jaune*; others fruity or more 'Burgundian' and mineral. Also rare sweet *vin de paille*. See also CRÉMANT DU JURA. Best producers: L Aviet★, la Borde, P Bornard, Cavarodes, Dugois★★, Gahier, Lornet★, l'Octavin★, Overnoy/ Houillon★, Pélican, la Pinte★, J Puffeney★★, Renardière★, Rijckaert★★, A & M Tissot★★, Tournelle★. Best years: 2012 11 10 09.

ARDÈCHE, IGP See COTEAUX D'ARDÈCHE.

DOM. ANTOINE ARENA *Patrimonio AC, Corsica, France* Family-owned bio-dynamic vineyard, which specializes in white wines based on Vermentino and Bianco Gentile (a local grape that had fallen into disuse) and exciting reds under Carco, Morta Maio, Zero (no added sulphites) and Grotte di Sole★ labels. Best years: (Grotte di Sole) (2013) 12 11 10 09 08.

ARGIOLAS *Sardinia, Italy* Sardinian star making DOC wines Cannonau (Costera★), Monica (Perdera) and Vermentino (Costamolino★) di Sardegna, as well as red and white Iselis blends. Top wines are powerful, spicy reds Turriga★★ and Korem★, and golden sweet white Angialis★★.

ARGYLE *Willamette Valley AVA, Oregon, USA* Founded in 1987 by Brian Croser and Rollin Soles. The cool WILLAMETTE VALLEY is ideal for late-ripened Pinot Noir and Chardonnay, used for Argyle sparkling wine★★. Also barrel-fermented Chardonnay★ and Pinot Noir★ (Reserve★★, Nuthouse★★, Spirithouse★★). Best years: (Pinot Noir) (2012) 11 10 09 08.

ARNEIS Italian grape grown in the ROERO hills in PIEDMONT. Roero Arneis is DOCG, producing dry white wines which, at best, have an attractive appley, herbal perfume. Can be expensive, and overly extracted, but cheaper versions rarely win. TRINITY HILL and VILLA MARIA make good ones in New Zealand and Crittenden, First Drop and Thick as Thieves in Australia. Best producers: Brovia★, Correggia★, Deltetto★, GIACOSA★, Malvirà★, Poderi Marcarini★, Angelo Negro★, Vietti★, Gianni Voerzio.

ARRAS See BAY OF FIRES.

DOM. ARRETXEA *Irouléguy AOP, South-West France* Michel and Thérèse Riouspeyrous are considered the stars of IROULÉGUY. Whites are crisp, full and dry; unusually, the minerally rosé is made from Grenache. High-quality reds★, with top cuvée Haitza★★ rather like a refined MADIRAN in style, but still gutsy and macho. Best years: 2011 10 09 07 05.

CH. L'ARROSÉE★★ *St-Émilion Grand Cru AC, Grand Cru Classé, Bordeaux, France* Small property making really exciting wine since 2002: rich, chewy and wonderfully luscious, with a comparatively high proportion (40%) of Cabernet. Now at an end, as l'Arrosée has been sold to the Dillons, owners of HAUT-BRION, to be integrated into their new estate, Ch. Quintus. 2012 was the last vintage. Drink after 5 years, but may be cellared for 10 or more. Best years: 2012 11 10 09 08 07 06 05 04 03 02 00.

ARTADI *Rioja DOCa, País Vasco, Spain* This former co-op is now producing some of RIOJA's deepest, most ambitious reds, but they in no way overshadow the excellent, scented and fairly priced Viñas de Gain★★. Viña El Pisón★★★ and three new single-vineyard wines are blockbusters. Best years: (2011) 10 09 08 07 06 05 04 03 01 00 98 96 95.

ASTI DOCG *Piedmont, Italy* The world's best-selling sweet sparkling wine, made from Moscato Bianco grapes, was long derided as light and cheap, though promotion to DOCG signalled an upturn in quality. Its light sweetness and refreshing sparkle made it ideal with fruit and a wide range of sweet dishes. Recently, competition from PROSECCO and FRANCIACORTA has caused a crisis of identity among producers, with wines becoming drier and less fruity. For the joyous explosion of sweet grapey fruit and bubbles, MOSCATO D'ASTI is now a better bet. Drink young. Best producers: Araldica, Bera★, Cascina Fonda★, Cascina Pian d'Or★, Cinzano★, Giuseppe Contratto★, Coppo★, Fontanafredda, Gancia★, Martini & Rossi★.

ASTROLABE *Marlborough, South Island, New Zealand* High-flying winery launched in 2001. The Province range includes a powerful Sauvignon Blanc★★, taut dry Riesling★ and subtly oaked Chardonnay. The Valleys range showcases MARLBOROUGH sub-regions and includes two excellent Sauvignon Blancs, from AWATERE★★ and Kekerengu Coast★★. The Vineyards range is as yet restricted to tiny parcels of experimental wines (some from the far south of Marlborough), but they show exciting individuality and potential. Also excellent Pinot Noir★★. Best years: (Sauvignon Blanc) **2013 12 11 10 09.**

ATA RANGI *Martinborough, North Island, New Zealand* Small, high-quality winery. Stylish, concentrated reds include seductively perfumed cherry/ plum Pinot Noir★★★ and an impressive Cabernet-Merlot-Syrah blend called Célèbre★★. Whites include big, rich Craighall Chardonnay★★, a more accessible Petrie★, delicately luscious Lismore Pinot Gris★★★ and a concentrated, mouthwatering Sauvignon Blanc★. A succulent Kahu Botrytis Riesling★★ is made when vintage conditions allow. Best years: (Pinot Noir) (2012) 11 10 **09 08 07 06 03 01 00.**

BODEGA ATAMISQUE *Mendoza, Argentina* One of the best of the new wineries in the UCO VALLEY. Entry-level Serbal unoaked whites and reds★ are great value and very pure; Catalpa range is more complex, especially the Chardonnay★ and Cabernet Sauvignon★; top wine Assemblage★★ is getting better with each vintage. Recent vintages of Atamisque Malbec ★★ from old vineyards in La Consulta are top class.

AU BON CLIMAT *Santa Maria Valley AVA, California, USA* Pace-setting winery in this cool region, run by Jim Clendenen. A range of lush Chardonnays★★ and intense Pinot Noirs★★ (Isabelle and Knox Alexander bottlings can be ★★★). He also makes BORDEAUX-style reds, Italian varietals (both red and white) and occasional exotic sweeties. Clendenen's wife Morgan runs Cold Heaven Cellars, specializing in cool-climate Viognier. Best years: (Pinot Noir) (2012) **10 09 08 07 06 05 04 03 02;** (Chardonnay) (2012) **11 10 09 08 07 06 05 04 03.**

AUCKLAND *North Island, New Zealand* Vineyards in this region are concentrated in the districts of Henderson, KUMEU/HUAPAI, Matakana on the mainland and high-quality red producer WAIHEKE ISLAND, out in the gulf. Clevedon, south of Auckland, shows promise. Best years: (Cabernet Sauvignon) **2013 10 09 08 07 06 05 04 02.**

CH. AUSONE★★★ *St-Émilion Grand Cru AC, 1er Grand Cru Classé, Bordeaux, France* Beautiful property on what are perhaps the best slopes in ST-ÉMILION. Owner Alain Vauthier has taken it to new heights since 1996 and the wines now display stunning texture and depth and the promise of memorable maturity. A high proportion (50%) of Cabernet Franc. Second wine Chapelle d'Ausone★★ is easily of Grand Cru Classé quality. Best years: 2012 11 10 **09 08 07 06 05 04 03 02 01 00 99 98 97 96 95 90.**

AUXEY-DURESSES AC *Côte de Beaune, Burgundy, France* A backwater village up a valley behind MEURSAULT. The reds should be light and fresh, but can lack ripeness. At its best, and at 3–5 years, the white is dry, soft, nutty and hinting at the creaminess of a good Meursault, but at much lower prices. Les Duresses is the most consistent Premier Cru. **Best producers: (reds)** Comte Armand★★, J-P Diconne★, Maison Leroy, M Prunier★, P Prunier★; **(whites)** d'Auvenay★★ (Dom. LEROY), J-P Diconne★, Gras, Olivier LEFLAIVE★, Benjamin Leroux★, Maison Leroy★, M Prunier★. **Best years: (reds)** 12 11 **10 09 08 05 03 02 99**; **(whites)** 12 **11 10 09**.

AVIGNONESI *Vino Nobile di Montepulciano DOCG,*
Tuscany, Italy Ex-proprietors the Falvo
brothers brought a revolutionary viticultural
system to Tuscany with their high-density,
bush-trained system known as *settonce*.
Ownership has changed but VINO NOBILE is
still the top wine, especially the Riserva
Grandi Annate★★. Fine Cortona DOC varietals from Chardonnay (Il Marzocco★), Merlot (Desiderio★) and Sauvignon. The most sought-after wine is Vin Santo★★★, with its partner (from Sangiovese) Occhio di Pernice★★★. **Best years: (Vino Nobile)** (2011) 10 **09 08 07 06 04 01**.

AWATERE VALLEY *Marlborough, South Island, New Zealand* MARLBOROUGH
sub-region that's cooler than the better-known Wairau Valley and has a greater vineyard area than HAWKES BAY. Awatere Sauvignon offers a concentrated Marlborough style with nettle, tomato leaf and green capsicum characters, while Chardonnay is taut and mineral. Pinot Noir can be good but may be lean. With climate change, Awatere's fresh, tangy style becomes ever more important, but its far southerly location also brings a frost risk. **Best producers:** ASTROLABE★★, Blind River★★, Clos Marguerite★, O:TU★, TerraVin★, Tohu★, VAVASOUR★★, VILLA MARIA★★, YEALANDS★. **Best years: (Sauvignon Blanc)** 2013 12 11 10 09.

CH. D'AYDIE *Madiran AOP, South-West France* The old-established Laplace family is spreading its wings. As well as a full-blown Tannat-based MADIRAN★★, named after the château, there is a softer Madiran called Odé d'Aydie★, a softer one still called Autour du Fruit and an IGP called Aramis. Maydie is the name they give to a sweet Tannat rather after the style of BANYULS. The Laplaces are also making excellent Madirans for Patrick Ducournau (Chapelle Lenclos★★ and Domaine Mouréou★). Also very fine PACHERENCS★ and a quaffable range of IGPs. **Best years: (reds)** 2011 10 **08 06 05**; **(sweet whites)** 2011 **10 07 06 05**.

BABICH *Henderson, North Island, New Zealand* Family-run winery with prime vineyard land in MARLBOROUGH and HAWKES BAY. Irongate Chardonnay★ is an intense, steely wine that needs plenty of cellaring, while full-flavoured reds under the Winemakers' Reserve label show even greater potential for development. Flagship wine The Patriarch★★ is a red BORDEAUX blend from Hawkes Bay. Marlborough whites include stylish Sauvignon Blanc★, tangy Riesling and light, fruity Pinot Gris. **Best years: (premium Hawkes Bay reds)** (2013) 10 **09 08 07 06 05 04**.

BACALHÔA VINHOS DE PORTUGAL *Península de Setúbal, Portugal*
Forward-looking operation, using Portuguese and foreign grapes with equal ease. Quinta da Bacalhôa★ is an oaky, meaty Cabernet-Merlot blend, Palácio da Bacalhôa★★ even better; Tinto da Ânfora★ a rich and figgy ALENTEJO red (Grande Escolha★★ version is powerful and cedary); and Cova da Ursa★ a toasty, rich Chardonnay. Portugal's finest sparkling wine, vintage-dated Espumante Loridos Chardonnay★, is a decent CHAMPAGNE lookalike. Só Syrah ('só' means 'only' in Portuguese) is characterful. Also excellent 20-year-old Moscatel de SETÚBAL★★.

BACHELET *Burgundy, France* A relatively common Burgundian name, though the families are often not related. Look out for Jean-Claude Bachelet in ST-AUBIN and the excellent Bachelet-Monnot in MARANGES, both fine domaines for white wines. Also superb, for reds, at the other end of the Côte, is Denis Bachelet in GEVREY-CHAMBERTIN.

BADEN *Germany* Very large, 15,900ha (39,290-acre) wine region stretching from FRANKEN to the Bodensee (Lake Constance). Its dry whites and reds show off the fuller, softer flavours Germany can produce in the warmer climate of its southerly regions. Many of the best non-Riesling German wines come from here, as well as many good barrel-fermented and barrel-aged wines. Gutedel (the local name for Chasselas) is a speciality, but the wines tend to be merely quaffable. See also KAISERSTUHL, ORTENAU.

BADIA A COLTIBUONO *Chianti Classico DOCG, Tuscany, Italy* Historic estate in Gaiole in Chianti. Current quality is high thanks to old Sangiovese clones, a new winery at Monti in Chianti and a certified organic regime since 2003. CHIANTI CLASSICO★★ and Chianti Classico Riserva★★★ are consistently very good examples of their type, with notable aging potential. Also good Chianti Classico Cultus Boni★ and 'Sangioveto' IGT★ and fine Vin Santo★ and Vin Santo Occhio di Pernice★★. Best years: (Chianti Classico Riserva) (2011) 10 09 **08 07** 06 05 04 01 99 98.

BAIRRADA DOC *Beiras, Portugal* Bairrada can be the source of many of Portugal's best red wines, brimming with intense raspberry and blackberry fruit, though austere tannins may take quite a few years to soften. Traditionally made from a minimum of 50% of the tannic Baga grape, but nowadays numerous international varieties are permitted. The whites are coming on fast with modern vinification methods. With an Atlantic climate, vintages can be very variable. Best producers: (reds) ALIANCA★, Quinta das Bágeiras★, Quinta de Baixo★, Campolargo★, Cantanhede co-op, Quinta do Encontro, Caves do Freixo, Caves Messias (Quinta do Valdoeiro Reserva★), Casa de Saima★★, Caves SÃO JOÃO★ (Quinta do Poço do Lobo★), SOGRAPE, Sidónio de Sousa★★; (whites) Caves SÃO JOÃO★★, SOGRAPE (Reserva★). Best years: (reds) (2012) **11 10** 09 08 05 04 03 01 00.

BALEARIC ISLANDS *Spain* Medium-bodied reds and soft rosés were the mainstays of Mallorca's 2 DO areas, Binissalem and Plà i Llevant, until Anima Negra began making impressive, deep reds from the native Callet grape. Best producers: 4 Kilos Vinícola★★, Anima Negra★★, Hereus de Ribas, Miquel Gelabert★, Toni Gelabert★, Macià Batle, Miquel Oliver, Son Bordils★.

BALFOUR *Kent, England* Consistent quality from this Kent vineyard, Hush Heath Estate, which covers 11.5ha (28 acres). Reserved, elegant Balfour Brut Rosé★★ and stylish Blanc de Blancs★. Good apple juice and ciders.

BALNAVES *Coonawarra, South Australia* Long-term residents of COONAWARRA, the grape-growing Balnaves family decided to become involved in making wine in the mid-1990s and are among the best producers in the region. Reserve Cabernet The Tally★★★ is complex, wonderfully structured and deeply flavoured; the regular Cabernet★★ is well priced and an excellent example of Coonawarra style.

BANDOL AC *Provence, France* A lovely fishing port with vineyards high above the Mediterranean, producing some of the best reds and rosés in Provence. The Mourvèdre grape gives Bandol its character – dense colour, warm, smoky black fruit and a herby fragrance. The reds happily age for 10 years, sometimes more, but should be very good at 3–4. The rosés, delicious and spicy but pricey, should be drunk young. A small amount of white wine, sometimes overpriced, is made with a blend of traditional varieties and freshened with Sauvignon and Ugni Blanc. **Best producers:** la Bastide Blanche★, la Bégude★, Bunan★, Frégate★, le Galantin★, J-P Gaussen★★, Gros' Noré★, l'Hermitage★, Lafran-Veyrolles★, la Laidière★, Mas Redonne★, la Noblesse★, PIBARNON★★, Pradeaux★★, Ray-Jane★, Roche Redonne★, Ste-Anne★, Salettes★, SORIN★, la Suffrène★, Tempier★, Terrebrune★, la Tour du Bon★, VANNIÈRES★★. **Best years:** (2012) 11 10 09 **08 07 06 05**.

BANFI *Brunello di Montalcino DOCG and Toscana IGT, Tuscany, Italy* American-owned huge estate in iconic Montalcino. Despite many awards and much work on Sangiovese clones, their BRUNELLOS (Poggio all'Oro★, Poggio alle Mura★) remain a bit stodgy and are exceeded, quality-wise, by 'super-Tuscans' Summus★★ and Excelsus★★. Also have cellars in PIEDMONT for GAVI and fizz. **Best years:** (top reds) (2011) 10 09 **08** 07 06 05 04.

BANNOCKBURN *Geelong, Victoria, Australia* The Hooper family has 27ha (67 acres) of mature vines, from which all the estate's wines are sourced. Michael Glover is proving to be an idiosyncratic and brilliant winemaker. Most notable are Sauvignon Blanc★★, Chardonnay★★, Pinot Noir★★ and Shiraz★, and four limited-release wines: my favourite, the complex and classy Alain GRAILLOT-influenced Range Shiraz★★; MEURSAULT-like SRH Chardonnay★★; powerful, gamy Serré Pinot Noir★★; and dense, tightly coiled yet elegant Stuart Pinot★★. **Best years:** (Shiraz) (2013) (12) (11) (10) 09 08 06 **05** 04 03 02 01 00 99 98 97 96 94 92 91.

BANYULS AC *Roussillon, France* One of the best *vins doux naturels*, made mainly from Grenache, with a strong plum and raisin flavour. *Rimage –* early bottlings of vintage wine – and *rancio* tawny styles are the best. Often served as an aperitif in France. **Best producers:** Cellier des Templiers★, CHAPOUTIER, Clos de Paulilles★, la Coume du Roy★, l'Étoile★, MAS BLANC★★, Piétri-Géraud★★, la Rectorie★, la Tour Vieille★, Vial Magnères★.

BARBADILLO *Jerez y Manzanilla DO, Andalucía, Spain* Sherry company in the coastal town of Sanlúcar de Barrameda with a wide range of good to excellent wines: salty, dry manzanilla styles (Solear★★, En Rama unfiltered★★★) and intense, nutty, dry amontillados and olorosos (Amontillado Príncipe★★, Oloroso Cuco★★). Neutral dry white Castillo de San Diego is a bestseller in Spain.

BARBARESCO DOCG *Piedmont, Italy* This prestigious red wine, grown in the LANGHE hills south-east of Turin, is often twinned with its neighbour BAROLO to demonstrate the nobility of the Nebbiolo grape. Barbaresco should be more feminine and fruitier than Barolo, with harvests coming earlier, and is not required by law to age as long (26 months, of which 9 must be in wood), but at the top level is often indistinguishable from Barolo. As in Barolo, traditionalists excel, led by Bruno GIACOSA. Even though the area is relatively compact (700ha/1730 acres), styles can differ significantly between vineyards and producers – although there's a trend away from the modern (concentrated fruit extract) back to traditional elegance. From vintage 2006 the mention of a vineyard on a Barbaresco label signifies that the fruit should come from that one site. **Best vineyards:** Asili, Basarin, Bricco di Neive, Crichet Pajè, Gallina, Marcorino, Martinenga, Messoirano, Moccagatta, Montefico, Montestefano, Ovello, Pora, Rabajà, Rio Sordo, Santo Stefano,

Serraboella, Sorì Paitin. Best producers: Produttori del BARBARESCO★★★, Cascina Luisin★★, Cascina delle Rose★, Ceretto★, Cigliuti, Stefano Farina★, Fontanabianca★, GAJA★★, GIACOSA★★★, Marchesi di Gresy★★, Lano★, Manuel Marinacci★, Fiorenzo Nada★, Castello di Neive★★, Paitin, Pelissero★, Punset★★, Rizzi★, ROAGNA★★★, Albino Rocca★★, Bruno Rocca★★, Roccalini★★, Sottimano★, La Spinetta, Castello di Verduno★★. Best years: (2011) 10 09 **08 07 06 04 01 00 99 98 97 96 95 90**.

PRODUTTORI DEL BARBARESCO *Barbaresco DOCG, Piedmont, Italy* Surely the finest-run *cantina sociale* (co-operative) in Italy, accounting for a sixth of the BARBARESCO zone (106ha/260 acres) and with 52 members. Only Nebbiolo, vinified traditionally, which produces a benchmark LANGHE Nebbiolo★★, Barbaresco★★ and 9 single-vineyard Barbarescos★★★: Asili, Moccagatta, Montefico, Montestefano, Ovello, Pajè, Pora, Rabajà, Rio Sordo. Best years: (2011) 10 09 **08 07 06 04 01 00 99 98**.

VINHOS BARBEITO *Madeira DOC, Portugal* Most modern of the MADEIRA producers, making elegant, pale-coloured Madeiras. Pioneer of single-harvest wines and single-cask bottlings. Good 10 Year Old★ range, excellent 20 Year Old★★ and Colheita Single-Cask★★ bottlings.

BARBERA A native of north-west Italy, Barbera vies with Sangiovese as the most widely planted red grape in the country. Great all-round food wine – its bright acidity cuts through anything fatty – but no real pretensions to age. Notable in PIEDMONT: when grown on the warm, sandy soils of Asti it can deliver the silkiest wines, while those of Alba, grown in the LANGHE zone, are more serious and structured, often needing French barriques to soften the flavours, especially where Nebbiolo has been added. Juicy and vibrant when blended with Bonarda in Lombardy. Significant plantings in California, Argentina and Australia.

BARBERA D'ALBA DOC *Piedmont, Italy* Barbera plays second fiddle to Nebbiolo among Alba wines, yet some of the finest examples from this appellation – in part due to the LANGHE (marne) soils, in part because producers are able to add 15% Nebbiolo and still label it as 'Barbera d'Alba'. Wines tend to develop well in bottle for up to 10 years from the harvest. Best producers: G Alessandria★★, ALTARE★, Azelia★★, Boglietti★, Brovia★, Burlotto★★, Cascina Fontana★★, Cascina Luisin★★★, Ceretto★, Cigliuti★, Clerico★, Elvio Cogno★, Aldo CONTERNO★★, Giacomo CONTERNO★★, Conterno-Fantino★, Corino★★, GIACOSA★, Elio Grasso★, Bartolo MASCARELLO★★, Giuseppe MASCARELLO★★, Mauro Molino★, Monfalletto-Cordero di Montezemolo★★, Oberto★, Parusso★, Pelissero★, F Principiano★★, Giuseppe RINALDI★★★, Albino Rocca★★, Bruno Rocca★, Giovanni ROSSO★★, Sandrone★, Vajra★★, Mauro Veglio★★, Vietti★, Gianni Voerzio★, Roberto VOERZIO★★. Best years: 2012 **11 09 08 07 06 04 03**.

BARBERA D'ASTI DOCG *Piedmont, Italy* In the province of Asti, Barbera gets the best sites and is capable of making outstandingly silky 100% Barbera wine. Those labelled Superiore can unfortunately suffer from being too alcoholic or too long in wood. Best examples from top sites can be kept for up to 10 years. Best producers: Araldica/Alasia★, La Barbatella★★, Pietro Barbero★★, Bava, Bertelli★, Braida★★, Cascina Castlèt★, Coppo★, Hastae (Quorum★), Martinetti★★, Il Mongetto★★, Perrone★★, Laiolo Reginin★★, La Spinetta★, Vietti★★, Vinchio-Vaglio Serra co-op★. Best years: (2013) **11 09 08 07 06 04 03**.

BAROSSA

South Australia

The Barossa Valley, an hour or so's drive north of Adelaide in South Australia, is the heart of the Australian wine industry and home to many of its giant producers – Jacob's Creek, Wolf Blass, Penfolds and Yalumba – alongside around 50 or so smaller wineries, producing or processing up to 60% of the nation's wine. However, this percentage is based mostly on grapes trucked in from other regions, because the Barossa's vineyards themselves grow less than 10% of Australia's grapes. Yet Barossa-grown grapes, once rejected as uneconomical for their low yields, are now increasingly prized for those same low yields.

Why? Well, it's highly likely that the world's oldest wine vines are in the Barossa. The valley was settled in the 1840s by Lutheran immigrants from Silesia, who brought with them vines from Europe: most importantly, as it turned out, cuttings of Syrah (or Shiraz) from France's Rhône Valley. And because the Barossa has never been affected by the phylloxera louse, which destroyed most of the world's vineyards in the late 19th century, today you can still see gnarled, twisted old vines sporting just a few tiny bunches of priceless fruit that were planted by refugees from Europe more than a century and a half ago, and are still tended by their descendants. A new wave of winemakers has taken up the cause of the Barossa old vines with much zeal and no small amount of national pride, and they now produce from them some of the deepest, most fascinating wines, not just in Australia, but in the world.

GRAPE VARIETIES

Shiraz is prized above all other Barossa grapes, able to conjure head-swirling, palate-dousing flavours. The Barossa Valley is the main source of Shiraz grapes for Penfolds Grange, the wine that began the revolution in Australian red wine in the 1950s. Cabernet Sauvignon can be very good in the best years and similarly potent, as are the Rhône varieties of heady Grenache and deliciously earthy Mourvèdre; some of the most exciting examples are from the original vines planted in the 19th century. All these varieties are largely grown on the hot, dry valley floor, but just to the east lie the Barossa Ranges, and in these higher, cooler vineyards, especially in those of the neighbouring Eden Valley, some of Australia's best and most fashionable Rieslings are grown, prized for their steely attack and lime fragrance. But even here you can't get away from Shiraz, and some thrilling examples come from the hills, not least Henschke's Hill of Grace and Mount Edelstone, and Torbreck's The Gask.

CLASSIFICATIONS

The Barossa was among the first zones to be ratified within the Australian system of Geographical Indications and comprises the regions of Barossa Valley and Eden Valley. The Barossa lies within South Australia's collective 'super zone' of Adelaide.

See also GRANGE, SOUTH AUSTRALIA; and individual producers.

BEST YEARS

(Barossa Valley Shiraz) (2013) 12
10 09 **08 06 05 04 03 02 01 00**
99 98 97 96 94 91 90 86;
(Eden Valley Riesling) **2013** 12 11
10 09 08 07 06 05 04 03 02 01
00 99 98 97 96 95

BEST PRODUCERS

Shiraz-based reds
Bethany, Rolf BINDER, Grant
BURGE, Burge Family, Chateau
Tanunda, Dutschke, John DUVAL,
Elderton (Command), GLAETZER,
Greenock Creek, Head,
HENSCHKE, Hentley Farm,
Heritage, HEWITSON, JACOB'S CREEK
(Centenary Hill), Jenke, Trevor
Jones, Kaesler, Kalleske,
Langmeil, Peter LEHMANN,
Maverick, Charles MELTON,
Murray Street, PENFOLDS (RWT,
GRANGE), Chris Ringland,
ROCKFORD, ST HALLETT,
SHOBBROOK, Tim Smith, SPINIFEX,
Teusner, Thorn Clarke,
TORBRECK, Torzi Matthews,
Turkey Flat, Two Hands, The
Willows, YALUMBA (Octavius).

Riesling
Bethany, Wolf BLASS (Gold Label),
Grant BURGE, Leo Buring (Leonay),
HENSCHKE, HEWITSON, JACOB'S
CREEK (Steingarten), Peter
LEHMANN, McLean's Farmgate,
Mesh, Radford, ROCKFORD, Ross
Estate, Ruggabellus, ST HALLETT,
SHOBBROOK, Thorn Clarke, Torzi
Matthews, YALUMBA (Heggies,
Pewsey Vale).

**Cabernet Sauvignon-based
reds**
Rolf BINDER, Grant BURGE,
Greenock Creek, HENSCHKE, Peter
LEHMANN, ST HALLETT, The Willows.

**Other reds (Grenache,
Mourvèdre, Shiraz, etc)**
Rolf BINDER, Grant BURGE, Burge
Family (Garnacha, Olive Hill),
Charles Cimicky, First Drop,
HENSCHKE, HEWITSON, Jenke
(Mourvèdre), Kalleske, Langmeil,
Peter LEHMANN, McLean's
Farmgate (barr-Eden), Charles
MELTON, PENFOLDS (Bin 138),
Teusner, TORBRECK, Turkey Flat,
Two Hands, YALUMBA.

Semillon
Grant BURGE, Burge Family,
HENSCHKE, Heritage, Jenke, Peter
LEHMANN, ROCKFORD, Turkey Flat,
The Willows.

Text on the bottle label:

YALUMBA
AUSTRALIA'S OLDEST FAMILY OWNED WINERY

BUSH VINE

GRENACHE

2009

BAROSSA   FINE WINE OF AUSTRALIA

B | BARBOURSVILLE VINEYARDS

BARBOURSVILLE VINEYARDS *Virginia, USA* Founded by Italy's Zonin winemaking family in 1976. Winemaker Luca Paschina produces an enticing range of French and Italian styles. Octagon★★, a BORDEAUX-style red, combines New World flair with Old World finesse. Good Cabernet Franc Reserve★ and Nebbiolo★, minerally, scented Viognier★ (sometimes ★★) and a crisp, lively, very Italian-style Vermentino.

BARDOLINO DOC *Veneto, Italy* Zone centred on Lake Garda, giving, traditionally, light, scented red and rosé (*chiaretto*) wines to be drunk young, from the same grape mix as neighbouring VALPOLICELLA – but some estates are now adding more character to their wines. Bardolino Superiore is DOCG. Best producers: ALLEGRINI★, Cavalchina★, Corte Gardoni★, Le Fraghe, Guerrieri-Rizzardi★, MASI, Le Vigne di San Pietro★, Zeni.

BAROLO DOCG *Piedmont, Italy* Arguably Italy's greatest wine, named after a village south-west of Alba, from the Nebbiolo grape grown in around 1800ha (4450 acres) of vineyards on the steep LANGHE hills, the best coming from near the top (*bricco*) of those hills. Having in the post-WWII period gone to excesses of austerity, Barolo in the 1990s almost threatened to go too far in the other direction, its subtle floral/wild fruit aromas being drowned all too often under expensive French barriques and compromised by excessive fruit concentration. Thankfully, in the 21st century, producers are finding their way back to the 'tar and roses' beauty of the grape, respecting its talent for expressing site perfectly, while balancing out the prominent tannins and acidity. The clay soils of Verduno, La Morra and Barolo villages tend to give more accessible, softer, perfumed wines, while Monforte, Castiglione Falletto and Serralunga wines have more structure, minerality and deep-seated power. From vintage 2010 (released in January 2014), the mention of a 'subzone' (vineyard) on a Barolo label signifies that 85% of the fruit should come from that one site. Minimum aging is 38 months from 1 November of the harvest year, of which 18 months must be in wood. Best vineyards: Bricco delle Viole, Brunate, Bussia Soprana, Cannubi, Cerequio, Conca dell'Annunziata, Francia, Ginestra, Monprivato, Monvigliero, Rocche dell'Annunziata, Rocche di Castiglione, Santo Stefano di Perno, La Serra, Vigna Rionda, Villero. Best producers: Fratelli Alessandria★★, G Alessandria★, ALTARE★, Azelia★★, Brezza★, Brovia★★, Burlotto★★, G Canonica★★, Cappellano★★, Cascina Fontana★★, Clerico★★, Aldo CONTERNO★, Giacomo CONTERNO★★★, Corino★, Fenocchio★★, GIACOSA★★★, Elio Grasso★★, Poderi Marcarini★★, Bartolo MASCARELLO★★★, Giuseppe MASCARELLO★★★, Massolino★, Monfalletto-Cordero di Montezemolo★★, Andrea Oberto★, Oddero★, Vigneti Luigi Oddero★★, Pio Cesare★, Pira★, E Pira di Chiara Boschis★★, F Principiano★, Revello★, Francesco Rinaldi★, Giuseppe RINALDI★★★, ROAGNA★★★, Rocche dei Manzoni★★, Giovanni ROSSO★★★, Sandrone★★, M Sebaste★, Trediberri★★, Vajra★★, Castello di Verduno★★, Vietti★, Gianni Voerzio★, Roberto VOERZIO★★★. Best years: (2013) 10 09 08 06 04 **01 00 99 98 97 96 95 93 91 90 89 88 86 85 83 82 78 76 71 69 67 64 58 55 45.**

BAROSSA VALLEY See pages 76–7.

JIM BARRY *Clare Valley, South Australia* Flagship white The Florita★ heads a quartet of classy, perfumed Rieslings (Watervale★★, Lodge Hill★★). Inexpensive Lodge Hill Shiraz★ is impressive, but the winery is best known for its rich, fruity McRae Wood Shiraz★★ and heady, palate-busting Armagh Shiraz★★. Best years: (Armagh Shiraz) (2013) (12) 09 06 05 **04 02 01 99 98 96 95 92.**

BARSAC AC *Bordeaux, France* Lying close to the river Garonne, and with the little river Ciron running along its eastern boundary, Barsac is the largest of the 5 communes in the SAUTERNES AC; it also has its own AC, which is used by most, but not all, of the top properties. Less power and more finesse than Sauternes (and better in 2012). Best producers: CLIMENS★★★, COUTET★★, DOISY-DAËNE★★, DOISY-VEDRINES★★, Myrat★, NAIRAC★★, Piada, Suau★. Best years: 2012 11 10 09 07 05 03 02 01 99 98 97 96 95 90 89 88 86 83.

BASILICATA *Italy* Southern Italian region best known for one wine, the potentially excellent, complex red called AGLIANICO DEL VULTURE.

BASSERMANN-JORDAN *Deidesheim, Pfalz, Germany* Famous 50ha (124-acre) estate, making rich yet elegant dry Rieslings★★ from Deidesheim and FORST. Best years: (2013) 12 11 10 09 08 07 06 05 04 03 02.

CH. BATAILLEY★ *Pauillac AC, 5ème Cru Classé, Haut-Médoc, Bordeaux, France* A byword for reliability and value for money among the PAUILLAC Classed Growth estates. Marked by a full, obvious blackcurrant fruit, not too much tannin and a luscious overlay of creamy vanilla. Lovely to drink at only 5 years old, the wine continues to age well for at least 15 years. Best years: 2012 11 10 09 08 06 05 04 03 02 00 98 96 95 90.

BÂTARD-MONTRACHET AC *Grand Cru, Côte de Beaune, Burgundy, France* This Grand Cru produces some of the world's greatest whites – full, rich and balanced, with a powerful mineral intensity of fruit and fresh acidity. There are 2 associated Grands Crus: Bienvenues-Bâtard-Montrachet and the minuscule Criots-Bâtard-Montrachet. Ages for a decade. Best producers: Blain-Gagnard★★, CARILLON★★★, DROUHIN★★, FAIVELEY★★, Fontaine-Gagnard★★, J-N GAGNARD★★★, JADOT★★, Louis LATOUR★★, Dom. LEFLAIVE★★★, Olivier LEFLAIVE★★, Marc MOREY★★, Pierre MOREY★★, RAMONET★★★, SAUZET★★★, VOUGERAIE★★★. Best years: (2013) 12 11 10 09 08 07 06 05 04 02.

BERNARD BAUDRY *Chinon AC, Loire Valley, France* Supple, elegant CHINON. Aspect and soil type differentiate four site-specific cuvées: Les Granges (sand/gravel) and Les Grézeaux★ (gravel/clay) are for earlier drinking, while Le Clos Guillot★★ (limestone/clay/tuffeau) and La Croix Boissée★★ (clay/limestone) reward patience. Good dry white and rosé too. Best years: (top reds) (2013) 12 11 10 09 08 06 05 04.

LES BAUX-DE-PROVENCE AC *Provence, France* This AC has proved that organic and biodynamic farming can produce spectacular results in a warm dry climate. Good fruit and intelligent winemaking produce some of the most enjoyable reds in Provence. Best producers: Hauvette★, Lauzières, Mas de la Dame★, Mas de Gourgonnier★, Mas Ste-Berthe★, ROMANIN★★, Terres Blanches★. Best years: (2013) 12 11 10 09 08 07 06 05 04.

BAY OF FIRES *Tasmania, Australia* The Tasmanian arm of the Accolade wine group. Complex, minerally Chardonnay★ and smooth, tightly structured, ageworthy Pinot Noir★★★. Also a sublime Riesling★★, impressive Pinot Gris★ and an intense, steely Sauvignon Blanc★. Brilliant fizz under House of Arras label (Brut Elite★★, Grand Vintage★★, EJ Carr Late Disgorged★★★).

BÉARN AOP *South-West France* Best known for quaffable rosés, sometimes from growers in MADIRAN and JURANÇON (where pink wines do not qualify for AOP). Whites mainly dull but some good reds and pinks from independent growers such as CAUHAPÉ, Guilhemas★, Lapeyre★, Nigri★.

CH. DE BEAUCASTEL *Châteauneuf-du-Pape AC, Rhône Valley, France* The Perrin family's red CHÂTEAUNEUF-DU-PAPE★★ is one of the richest, most profound of the AC, and becomes complex over time, at least a decade; there is an unusually high percentage of Mourvèdre (Hommage à Jacques Perrin★★★ is 60% Mourvèdre). The white Roussanne Vieilles Vignes★★★ is enticing, mysterious and long-lived. They also produce stylish red★ and white★ CÔTES DU RHÔNE Coudoulet de Beaucastel and GIGONDAS Dom. des Tourelles★★. Under the Famille Perrin label there are full, authentic southern reds, including organic Côtes du Rhône Nature★, VENTOUX La Vieille Ferme★, good-value CAIRANNE★, RASTEAU★ and VINSOBRES★, and white LUBÉRON La Vieille Ferme. Best years: (reds) (2013) 12 11 10 09 07 **06** 05 **04** 03 01 00 99 98 97 96 95 90 89 88 85; (whites) 2013 12 11 10 **09** 08 07 06 05 04 03 01 00 99 98 97 96 95 94 90 89.

BEAUJOLAIS AC *Beaujolais, Burgundy, France* Wine region in the beautiful hills that stretch down from Mâcon to Lyon, producing predominantly red wine from the Gamay grape. Beaujolais may once have been best known for BEAUJOLAIS NOUVEAU, but demand is now growing for the region's top wines. The better-quality reds, each having their own appellation, come from the north of the region and are BEAUJOLAIS-VILLAGES and the 10 single-Cru villages: from north to south these are ST-AMOUR, JULIENAS, MOULIN-À-VENT, CHÉNAS, FLEURIE, CHIROUBLES, MORGON, RÉGNIÉ, BROUILLY and CÔTE DE BROUILLY. There is a growing buzz about the area: standards have improved dramatically in recent years as a new wave of producers (a younger generation of locals, and winemakers from both Burgundy in the north and the Rhône in the south) have begun investing here. Growing consumer demand for food-friendly wines with lower alcohol levels has helped to spark renewed interest in the area. In good vintages simple Beaujolais is light, fresh, aromatic and delicious to drink, but in poorer vintages the wine can be drab and acidic. A little rosé is also made from Gamay, and a small quantity of Beaujolais Blanc is made from Chardonnay. Best producers: J-P Brun/Terres Dorées (l'Ancien★), A Chatoux★, H Fessy, J-F Garlon★, Y Métras★.

BEAUJOLAIS NOUVEAU *Beaujolais AC, Burgundy, France* Also known as Beaujolais Primeur, this is the first release of bouncy, fruity Beaujolais on the third Thursday of November after the harvest. Once a simple celebration of the new vintage, nouveau was badly over-hyped and, as a result, is nowhere near as popular as it once was. Quality is generally reasonable and the wine can be delicious until Christmas and the New Year, but thereafter is likely to throw a slight sediment and soon loses the vivacious fresh fruit that made it so appealing in its youth.

BEAUJOLAIS-VILLAGES AC *Beaujolais, Burgundy, France* Beaujolais-Villages can come from one of 38 villages in the north of the region. Top examples have more body, character and elegance than simple BEAUJOLAIS and represent all the pleasure of the Gamay grape at its best. Best villages: Lancié, Quincié and Perréon. Best producers: A Aucoeur, A Colonge, DUBOEUF, JADOT (Combe aux Jacques), J-C Lapalu, Ch. du Pavé★, Gilles Roux/de la Plaigne★.

BEAUMES-DE-VENISE AC *Rhône Valley, France* Area rightly famous for its scented, honeyed, sometimes elegant, fortified sweet wine, MUSCAT DE BEAUMES-DE-VENISE. The red wine from high vineyards can be potent, holds smoky dark fruit and crisp tannins, and can show well for 8–10 years. Best producers: (reds) Beaumalric, Bernardins, Cassan★, Fenouillet, Ferme Saint-Martin, les Goubert, Ch. Redortier★.

BEAUNE AC *Côte de Beaune, Burgundy, France* Most of the wines are red, with delicious, soft red-fruits ripeness. No Grands Crus, but some excellent Premiers Crus, especially Boucherottes, Bressandes, Clos des Mouches, Fèves, Grèves, Marconnets, Teurons, Vignes Franches. White-wine production is increasing – DROUHIN makes outstanding, creamy, nutty Clos des Mouches★★★. Other good whites from Chanson★★, LAFARGE★★ and Prieur★★. Best producers: (growers) BELLENE★, Croix★, Dufouleur, LAFARGE★★, de MONTILLE★★, Albert Morot★, J Prieur★, Rateau, TOLLOT-BEAUT★★; (merchants) BOUCHARD PÈRE ET FILS★★, Champy★★, Chanson★★, DROUHIN★★, Camille Giroud★★, JADOT★★. Best years: (reds) 12 11 10 09 **08 07 06** 05 03 02 99; (whites) 12 11 **10 09 08 07 06** 05.

CH. BEAU-SÉJOUR BÉCOT★★ *St-Émilion Grand Cru AC, 1er Grand Cru Classé, Bordeaux, France* Family-owned Premier Grand Cru Classé on the limestone plateau. On fine form since 1996. Gérard, Juliette and Dominique Bécot produce firm, ripe, richly textured wines that need at least 8–10 years to develop. Best years: 2012 11 10 09 **08 07 06** 05 04 03 02 01 00 98 96 95 90 89.

BEAUX FRÈRES *Willamette Valley AVA, Oregon, USA* The goal here is to make ripe, unfiltered Pinot Noir★★ that expresses the essence of their 10ha (24-acre) vineyard atop Ribbon Ridge in the Chehalem Valley. A parcel known as The Upper Terrace★★★ yields exceptional fruit from Dijon clones. Best years: (2012) 11 10 **09 08 07**.

GRAHAM BECK WINES *Robertson WO, South Africa* This large range is vinified at two cellars; fruit from STELLENBOSCH vineyards is vinified at Beck-owned STEENBERG. Top wines include spicy aromatic Cabernet Sauvignon-Shiraz blend Ad Honorem★, The Joshua Shiraz-Viognier★★, DURBANVILLE-sourced Pheasants' Run Sauvignon Blanc★★, and single-vineyard Coffeestone Cabernet★. The very popular sparkling range, under Pieter 'Bubbles' Ferreira's leadership, continues to be made at the ROBERTSON cellar and is headed by Chardonnay-based Cuvée Clive★★ with 5 years on the lees; there's also rich NV Brut★ and creamy, barrel-fermented and ageworthy Blanc de Blancs★. Single-vineyard The Ridge Syrah★ is the best Robertson table wine.

BECKMEN *Santa Ynez Valley AVA, California, USA* Estate-grown RHÔNE-style wines show beauty and structure at moderate alcohol levels. Grenache★ and Grenache-based Cuvée Le Bec★ are bright and juicy. The Purisma Mountain Syrahs★★ are richer in style, yet wonderfully balanced.

BEDELL CELLARS *Long Island, New York State, USA* Founder Kip Bedell helped establish LONG ISLAND's reputation with his BORDEAUX-style Merlot★ and red blends. Current winemaker Rich Olsen-Harbich has scaled back the use of oak and banned commercial yeasts, and the wines are getting better and receiving wider distribution and recognition.

BEECHWORTH *Victoria, Australia* Beechworth was best known as Ned Kelly country before Rick Kinzbrunner of GIACONDA planted these slopes of sub-Alpine north-east Victoria. Now boutique wineries produce tiny volumes of Chardonnay, Pinot Noir and Shiraz at high prices. BROKENWOOD sources fruit from the Indigo vineyard. Best producers: Amulet (Shiraz★★), BROKENWOOD, Castanga★ (Syrah★★), Cow Hill★, GIACONDA★★★, JAMSHEED★★, Savaterre (Chardonnay★★), Sorrenberg★.

BEIRAS *Portugal* This large region of Portugal includes the DOCs of BAIRRADA, DÃO, Távora-Varosa and Beira Interior. Wines from the coastal area, made from Portuguese varieties along with international grapes such as Cabernet Sauvignon and Chardonnay, may be labelled Beira Atlântico Vinho Regional. Inland, the cooler, high-altitude zone makes bright, fresh reds and whites under Beira Interior DOC or Terras da Beira Vinho Regional. Best producers: (Beira Atlântico) Quinta dos Cozinheiros, Quinta de Foz de Arouce★, Filipa Pato★, Luís PATO★★, Caves SÃO JOÃO; (Beira Interior) Quinta do Cardo★, Quinta dos Currais, Figueira de Castelo Rodrigo co-op, Quinta dos Termos.

CH. BELAIR-MONANGE★★ *St-Émilion Grand Cru AC, 1er Grand Cru Classé, Bordeaux, France* Acquired by négociant J-P MOUEIX in 2008. Ch. MAGDELAINE was integrated in 2012. The soft, supremely stylish wines are drinkable at 5–6 years, but also capable of long aging. Best years: 2012 11 10 09 **08** 06 05 04 03 02 01 00 99 98 95 90 89.

BELLAVISTA *Franciacorta DOCG, Lombardy, Italy* Specialist in FRANCIACORTA sparkling wines, with a very good Cuvée Brut★★ and 4 distinctive Gran Cuvées★★ (including an excellent rosé). Vittorio Moretti★★ is made in exceptional years. Also produces lovely still wines, including white blend Convento dell'Annunciata★★, Chardonnay Uccellanda★★ and red Casotte★ (Pinot Nero) and Solesine★ (Cabernet-Merlot).

BELLENE *Beaune, Côte de Beaune, Burgundy, France* New name for Nicolas Potel's own businesses. Domaine de Bellene has vineyards in BEAUNE★, NUITS-ST-GEORGES★, SAVIGNY, VOLNAY and VOSNE★★. Maison Roche de Bellene is the merchant label. Best years: (Domaine) 12 11 10 **09** 08.

BELLET AC *Provence, France* Tiny AC in the hills behind Nice; the wine is usually expensive, although domaines such as Toasc produce cheaper IGP wines from young vines. Folle Noire-based reds are bigger and more tannic, while those based on Braquet are more delicate and floral. Best producers: Ch. de Bellet★, Clos St Vincent★, Ch. de Crémat, St Jean, la Source, Toasc. Best years: (2013) 12 **11 10** 09.

BENDIGO *Central Victoria, Australia* Warm, dry, former gold-mining region, which is now home to about 40 small-scale, high-quality wineries. The best wines are rich, ripe, distinctively minty Shiraz and Cabernet. Best producers: Balgownie, Blackjack★, Bress, Leamon Estate, Passing Clouds, Pondalowie★, Turner's Crossing★, Water Wheel★. Best years: (Shiraz) (2013) 12 10 **08** 06 05 04 03 02 01 00 99 98 97 95 94 93 91 90.

BODEGA BENEGAS *Mendoza, Argentina* An old family winery, run almost single-handedly by the former owner of TRAPICHE, Federico Benegas. With some very old vineyards in the Luján de Cuyo and Maipú districts, they produce old-vine Cabernet Franc★★ and Malbec★★ and old-school red BORDEAUX-blend Meritage★★ under the top label, Benegas Lynch. Sangiovese★, Syrah and Malbec★★ lead the Benegas Estate range. New vineyards in Gualtallary in the UCO VALLEY show that Federico has big plans for the future. Best years: (2011) 10 **09** 06.

BERCHER *Burkheim, Baden, Germany* A top KAISERSTUHL estate. High points are the powerful oak-aged Spätburgunder★★ (Pinot Noir) reds, Grauburgunder★★ (Pinot Gris) and Weissburgunder★ dry whites, which marry richness with perfect balance, and elegant, tangy Muskateller★. Best years: (whites) (2013) 12 11 10 **09 08**; (reds) (2013) (12) 11 **10 09** 08 07.

BERGERAC AOP *South-West France* Bergerac's claret-like wines have a good, raw blackcurrant fruit and hint of earth, and the wines under the superior Côtes de Bergerac AOP, often oak-aged, can keep well. See also

PÉCHARMANT and MONTRAVEL for more ambitious reds. The fresh dry whites are for early drinking. The best sweet whites are produced under more specific appellations: MONBAZILLAC, SAUSSIGNAC, MONTRAVEL and ROSETTE. Best producers: (red and dry white) l'ANCIENNE CURE★, Bélingard★, Eyssards, Fontenelles★, la Jaubertie★, Marnières★, les Miaudoux★, Monestier-la-Tour★, TOUR DES GENDRES★★, VERDOTS★★. Best years: (reds) 2012 11 10 09 05.

BERGSTRÖM *Willamette Valley AVA, Oregon, USA* The Bergström family uses biodynamic farming to bring out the best character from the *terroir* of their estate vineyards. The focus is on Pinot Noir, with Bergström Vineyard★★, de Lancellotti Vineyard★★ and Temperance Hill★★ forming the greater part of the production. Cumberland Reserve★★★ is a multi-vineyard blend that can rival fine Burgundy. Also small amounts of Chardonnay★ (Sigrid★★). Best years: (reds) (2012) 11 10 **09 08 07**.

BERINGER *Napa Valley AVA, California, USA* Beringer, part of the Treasury group, mass-produces some fairly average varietal labels, but also offers a range of top-class Cabernet Sauvignons. Private Reserve Cabernet can be ★★★ and is one of NAPA VALLEY's most approachable; Chabot Vineyard★★ can be equally impressive. The Knight's Valley Cabernet Sauvignon★ is made in a lighter style and is good value. Alluvium red★★ and white★ (meritage wines) are also from Knight's Valley. Private Reserve Chardonnay★★ is powerful, ripe and toasty. Bancroft Ranch Merlot★★ from HOWELL MOUNTAIN is also very good. Best years: (Cabernet Sauvignon) (2012) **10 09 08 07 06 05 03 02 01 00 99 98 97 96 95 94 93**.

BERNKASTEL *Mosel, Germany* Both a historic wine town in the Middle MOSEL and a large Bereich. Top wines, however, come only from vineyard sites around the town – the most famous of these is the overpriced Doctor vineyard. Wines from the excellent, if less glamorous, Graben and Lay sites are often as good. Best producers: Kesselstatt★, Dr LOOSEN★★, MOLITOR★★, Pauly-Bergweiler, J J PRÜM★★, S A Prüm, Dr H Thanisch★, WEGELER★★. Best years: (2013) (12) 11 10 **09 08 07 06 05 04 02**.

DOM. BERTHOUMIEU *Madiran AOP, South-West France* Didier Barré throws down the gauntlet to Ch. MONTUS, with his more accessible reds, especially Charles de Batz★★ (the real name of d'Artagnan, fictionalized in *The Three Musketeers*). His PACHERENCS★★ are just as good. Best years: (reds) (2012) (11) **10 09 08 06 05**; (Pacherenc) 2012 **11 10 09 07 06 05**.

GÉRARD BERTRAND *Languedoc, France* Gérard Bertrand is a major vineyard owner, with an extensive range that explores the *terroirs* of the LANGUEDOC. The flagship estate, Ch. l'Hospitalet, produces red and white La CLAPE★. Red, rosé and white Cigalus★★ are from an estate run biodynamically. He also has vineyards in CORBIÈRES Boutenac (Villemajou), MINERVOIS La Livinière (Laville-Bertrou), LIMOUX (l'Aigle) and TERRASSES DU LARZAC (la Sauvageonne). Best years: (2013) 12 11 **10 09 08 07 06 05**.

BEST'S *Grampians, Victoria, Australia* Historic winery (vineyards date back to 1868). After 50 vintages, Viv Thomson handed over to his son Ben and winemaker Justin Purser. The premium range, Great Western, includes superb fleshy Bin No. 0 Shiraz★★★, good Cabernet★ and a fresh, citrus Riesling★. The Thomson Family Shiraz★★ is an outstanding cool-climate Shiraz. Best years: (Thomson Family Shiraz) (2013) 12 10 08 06 05 **04 01 99 98 97 95 94 93 91 90**.

BETZ *Columbia Valley AVA, Washington State, USA* Since 1997, Bob Betz MW has crafted wines of uniquely stylish character. Two BORDEAUX-style red blends: Clos de Betz★ and ageworthy, powerful Cabernet Sauvignon-based Père de Famille★★. The Syrah La Côte Rousse★, named for its

Red Mountain origin, is opulent; Syrah La Serenne★★ shows more polish and finesse. Best years: (2012) 11 10 **09 08 07**.

CH. BEYCHEVELLE★★ *St-Julien AC, 4ème Cru Classé, Haut-Médoc, Bordeaux, France* This beautiful château can make wine of Second Growth quality. It has a charming softness even when young, but takes at least a decade to mature into ST-JULIEN's famous cedarwood and blackcurrant flavour. Over the years, it's given me as much pleasure as any Bordeaux – I drank an awful lot of the 1961 at university with a monumentally indulgent tutor. Then it became inconsistent through the 1970s and 80s, but since 1996 has steadily regained its enticing, scented form. Second wine: Amiral de Beychevelle. Best years: 2012 11 10 09 **08 07 06 05 04 03 02 00 98 96 95 89**.

BEYERSKLOOF *Stellenbosch WO, South Africa* Variations on the Pinotage theme abound at Beyers Truter's property: the powerful yet refined Diesel★★ (named for a beloved dog), from gravel soils, sets the standard. Blended with Cabernet and Merlot, Faith★ is showy but elegant, with Pinotage-led Synergy more succulent. Pinotage also contributes to traditional PORT-style Lagare Cape Vintage. Striking Cabernet Sauvignon-based Field Blend★★ (previously named Beyerskloof). Best years: (Field Blend/Beyerskloof) 2009 **08 07 06 05 04 03**.

BIANCO DI CUSTOZA DOC *Veneto, Italy* Dry white wine from the shores of Lake Garda, made from a blend of grapes including SOAVE's Garganega and GAVI's Cortese. Drink young. Best producers: Cavalchina★, Gorgo★, Montresor★, Le Vigne di San Pietro★, Zeni★.

BIBBIANO *Chianti Classico DOCG, Tuscany, Italy* Historic, traditional CHIANTI CLASSICO producer. Brothers Tommaso and Federico Marrocchesi Marzi are now removing French grape varieties from the blend and returning to larger oak. Chianti Classico★★ (Montornello★★, Riserva Vigna del Capannino★★★), Vin Santo San Lorenzo★★ and Domino (Merlot) IGT Toscana. Best years: (Chianti Classico) (2011) 10 **09 08 07 06 05 04 01 00 99 98 97 96 95 90 89 88 85 83**.

BIDDENDEN *Kent, England* One of the oldest UK vineyards (established in 1969); produces good wines using little-known grapes such as Ortega★, Huxelrebe★ and red Dornfelder. Occasional delicious Gamay. Also great apple juices and ciders.

BIENVENUES-BÂTARD-MONTRACHET AC See BÂTARD-MONTRACHET.

BIERZO DO *Castilla y León, Spain* Sandwiched between the rainy mountains of GALICIA and the arid plains of CASTILLA Y LEÓN. The arrival of Alvaro PALACIOS, of PRIORAT fame, and his nephew Ricardo Pérez Palacios with their inspired Corullón★★★ red, shed an entirely new and exciting light on the potential of the Mencía grape, while native winemaker Raúl PÉREZ has made a name for himself on the national scene. Best producers: Bodega del Abad★, Casar de Burbia★, Castro Ventosa★, Estefanía★, Gancedo★, Losada, Luna Beberide★★, Paixar★★, Descendientes de J Palacios★★, Peique★, Raúl PÉREZ★★★, Pittacum★, Dominio de Tares★.

BIKAVÉR *Hungary* Formerly famous as Bull's Blood, Kékfrankos (Blaufränkisch) grapes sometimes replace robust Kadarka in the blend; some producers include Cabernet Sauvignon, Kékoporto or Merlot.

BILLECART-SALMON *Champagne AC, Champagne, France* High-quality family-controlled CHAMPAGNE house that makes extremely elegant wines which become irresistible with age. Greatly increased volumes diluted the non-vintage Brut★, but quality has now improved and non-vintage Brut Rosé★★, Blanc de Blancs★★★, vintage Cuvée Nicolas François

Billecart★★★ and Cuvée Elisabeth Salmon Rosé★★ are all excellent. Impressive bone-dry Extra Brut★★. Clos Saint-Hilaire★★★ is a single-vineyard vintage Blanc de Noirs. Best years: 2004 (02) **00 99 98 97 96 95 90 89 88 86 85 82**.

ROLF BINDER *Barossa, South Australia* Rolf and Christa Binder's family winery (known as Veritas until 2004), with top wines Hanisch Shiraz★★★ and Heysen Shiraz★★★. Shiraz-Mataro Pressings★★ (known locally as Bull's Blood) and Heinrich Shiraz-Grenache-Mataro★★ blends are lovely big reds; Cabernet-Merlot★★ also impresses, as does Riesling★. Under the Christa Rolf label, Shiraz-Grenache★ is good and spicy with attractive, forward black fruit.

BINGEN *Rheinhessen, Germany* This small town's vineyards fall in both the NAHE and RHEINHESSEN. The best is the Scharlachberg, which produces exciting wines, stinging with racy acidity and the whiff of minerals. Best producers: Kruger-Rumpf, Rheingraf. Best years: (2013) 12 11 **10 09 08 07**.

BÍO BÍO *Chile* One of Chile's most southerly vineyard regions, including the sub-region of Itata. Cool and wet, but showing promise for Pinot Noir, Riesling and Gewürztraminer. Itata is seeing an old-vine revolution, with Cinsault, País and Muscat leading the pack. Best producers: Agustinos, CONCHA Y TORO, CONO SUR, DE MARTINO, Veranda.

BIONDI-SANTI *Brunello di Montalcino DOCG, Tuscany, Italy* The late, great Franco Biondi-Santi's Greppo estate created both a legend and an international standing for BRUNELLO DI MONTALCINO. The Biondi-Santi style has remained deeply traditional, while that of other producers has moved on. The very expensive Riserva★★★, with formidable levels of tannin and acidity, deserves a minimum 10 years' further aging after release. Franco's son, Jacopo, has created his own range at Castello di Montepò, including Sassoalloro★★, a barrique-aged Sangiovese, and Sangiovese-Cabernet-Merlot blend Schidione★★. Best years: (Brunello Riserva) (2011) (10) (09) (08) 07 06 **04 01 99 97 95 90 88 85 75 64 55 45**.

BLAGNY AC *Côte de Beaune, Burgundy, France* Tiny hamlet above MEURSAULT and PULIGNY-MONTRACHET makes a somewhat austere red Burgundy, though it does well in the warmer years. Most producers have converted to Chardonnay to sell as Meursault-Blagny 1er Cru. Best producers: Martelet de Cherisey★★, Matrot★. Best years: (2013) 12 11 **10 09 07 06 05**.

BLANQUETTE DE LIMOUX AC *Languedoc, France* Refreshing fizz, mainly from the Mauzac grape, which gives it its striking 'green apple skin' flavour – the balance comes from Chardonnay and Chenin Blanc. The traditional (CHAMPAGNE) method is used. Best producers: Antech, Collin, Fourn★, Guinot, J Laurens, Martinolles★, Rives-Blanques★, SIEUR D'ARQUES. See also CRÉMANT DE LIMOUX AC and pages 292–3.

WOLF BLASS *Barossa Valley, South Australia* Wolf Blass, with its huge range, remains a cornerstone (with PENFOLDS) of Australia's largest wine company, Treasury Wine Estates. In ascending quality order, the wines are labelled red, yellow, silver, gold, white, platinum, black. Red and yellow labels are OK, silver can be good (Chardonnay★) and gold is usually serious (Riesling★, Shiraz★). White Label includes good Riesling★ and Chardonnay★. Black and Platinum Label reds are rich, dense and expensive and can be★★. The Eaglehawk range is reliable. Best years: (Black Label) (2013) 12 11 10 09 08 **06 03 02 01 99 98 97 96 95 91 90 88 86**.

BLAUBURGUNDER See PINOT NOIR.
BLAUER LEMBERGER See BLAUFRÄNKISCH.

BORDEAUX RED WINES

Bordeaux, France

 This large area of South-West France, centred on the historic city of Bordeaux, produces a larger volume of fine red wine than any other French region. Wonderful Bordeaux-style wines are produced in California, Australia, South Africa and South America, but the home team's top performers still just about keep the upstarts at bay. Around 650 million bottles of red wine a year are produced here. The best wines, known as the Classed Growths, account for a tiny percentage of this figure, but some of their lustre rubs off on the lesser names, making this one of the most popular wine styles.

GRAPE VARIETIES

Bordeaux's reds are commonly divided into 'right' and 'left' bank wines. On the left bank of the Gironde estuary, the red wines are dominated by the Cabernet Sauvignon grape, with varying proportions of Cabernet Franc, Merlot and Petit Verdot. At best they are austere but perfumed with blackcurrant and cedarwood. The most important left bank areas are the Haut-Médoc (especially Margaux, St-Julien, Pauillac and St-Estèphe) and, south of the city of Bordeaux, Pessac-Léognan and Graves. On the right bank, Merlot is the predominant grape, which generally makes the resulting wines more supple and fleshy than those of the left bank. The key areas for Merlot-based wines are St-Émilion, Pomerol, Fronsac and Castillon-Côtes de Bordeaux.

CLASSIFICATIONS

At its most basic, the wine is simply labelled Bordeaux or Bordeaux Supérieur. Above this are the more specific ACs covering sub-areas (such as the Haut-Médoc) and individual communes (such as Pomerol, St-Émilion or Margaux). Single-estate Crus Bourgeois (although, after a legal challenge, this is no longer a classification but as of 2008 a certificate awarded on a yearly basis) are the next rung up on the quality ladder, followed by the Crus Classés (Classed Growths) of the Médoc, Graves and St-Émilion. The famous classification of 1855 ranked the top red wines of the Médoc (plus one from Graves) into 5 tiers, from First to Fifth Growths (Crus); there has been only one change, in 1973, promoting Château Mouton-Rothschild to First Growth status. Since the 1950s the Graves/Pessac-Léognan region has had its own classification for red and white wines. St-Émilion's classification (for red wines only) has been revised several times, the latest modification being in 2012; the possibility of re-grading can help to maintain quality, but not if you can't also get relegated. Curiously, Pomerol, home of Château Pétrus, arguably the most famous red wine in the world, has no official pecking order. Many top châteaux make 'second wines', which are cheaper versions of their Grands Vins.

See also BLAYE-CÔTES DE BORDEAUX, BORDEAUX, BORDEAUX SUPÉRIEUR, CADILLAC-CÔTES DE BORDEAUX, CANON-FRONSAC, CASTILLON-CÔTES DE BORDEAUX, CÔTES DE BOURG, FRANCS-CÔTES DE BORDEAUX, FRONSAC, GRAVES, HAUT-MEDOC, LALANDE-DE-POMEROL, LISTRAC-MEDOC, LUSSAC-ST-EMILION, MARGAUX, MEDOC, MONTAGNE-ST-EMILION, MOULIS, PAUILLAC, PESSAC-LEOGNAN, POMEROL, PUISSEGUIN-ST-EMILION, ST-EMILION, ST-ESTÈPHE, ST-GEORGES-ST-EMILION, ST-JULIEN; and individual châteaux.

BEST YEARS

2012 11 10 09 08 06 05 04 03 01 00 98 96 95 90 89 88 86 85 83 82 70 66 61

BEST PRODUCERS

Graves, Pessac-Léognan Carbonnieux, Dom. de CHEVALIER, HAUT-BAILLY, HAUT-BRION, la LOUVIÈRE, MALARTIC-LAGRAVIÈRE, la MISSION HAUT-BRION, PAPE-CLÉMENT, SMITH-HAUT-LAFITTE.

Margaux BRANE-CANTENAC, FERRIÈRE, ISSAN, MALESCOT ST-EXUPÉRY, MARGAUX, PALMER, RAUZAN-SÉGLA, SIRAN, du Tertre.

Pauillac GRAND-PUY-LACOSTE, HAUT-BAGES-LIBÉRAL, LAFITE-ROTHSCHILD, LATOUR, LYNCH-BAGES, MOUTON-ROTHSCHILD, PICHON-LONGUEVILLE, PICHON-LONGUEVILLE-LALANDE, PONTET-CANET.

Pomerol le BON PASTEUR, Certan-de-May, Clinet, Clos l'Eglise, la CONSEILLANTE, l'ÉGLISE-CLINET, l'ÉVANGILE, la FLEUR-PÉTRUS, GAZIN, Hosanna, LAFLEUR, LATOUR-À-POMEROL, PETIT-VILLAGE, PÉTRUS, le PIN, TROTANOY, VIEUX-CHATEAU-CERTAN.

St-Émilion ANGELUS, l'ARROSÉE, AUSONE, BEAU-SÉJOUR BÉCOT, Beauséjour, BELAIR-MONANGE, CANON, CANON-LA-GAFFELIÈRE, CHEVAL BLANC, Clos de l'Oratoire, Clos Fourtet, la Dominique, FIGEAC, Larcis-Ducasse, MONBOUSQUET, La Mondotte, PAVIE, PAVIE-MACQUIN, TERTRE-RÔTEBOEUF, TROPLONG MONDOT, VALANDRAUD.

St-Estèphe CALON-SÉGUR, COS D'ESTOURNEL, HAUT-MARBUZET, LAFON-ROCHET, MONTROSE, Ormes de Pez, PEZ, Phélan Ségur, Tronquoy-Lalande.

St-Julien BEYCHEVELLE, BRANAIRE-DUCRU, DUCRU-BEAUCAILLOU, GRUAUD-LAROSE, LAGRANGE, LANGOA-BARTON, LÉOVILLE-BARTON, LÉOVILLE-LAS-CASES, LÉOVILLE-POYFERRÉ, ST-PIERRE, TALBOT.

BORDEAUX WHITE WINES

Bordeaux, France

 This is France's largest fine wine region, but, except for the sweet wines of Sauternes and Barsac, Bordeaux's international reputation is based almost entirely on its reds. From 52% of the vineyard area in 1970, white wines now represent only 12% of the present 112,600ha (278,235 acres) of vines. Given the size of the region, the diversity of Bordeaux's white wines should come as no surprise. There are dry, medium and sweet styles, ranging from dreary to some of the most sublime white wines of all. Bordeaux's temperate southern climate – moderated by the influence of the Atlantic and of two rivers, the Dordogne and the Garonne – is ideal for white wine production, particularly south of the city along the banks of the Garonne.

GRAPE VARIETIES

Sauvignon Blanc and Sémillon, the most important white grapes, are both varieties of considerable character and are usually blended together. They are backed up by smaller quantities of other grapes, the most notable of which is Muscadelle (unrelated to Muscat), which lends perfume to sweet wines and spiciness to dry.

DRY WINES

With the introduction of new technology and new ideas, many of them influenced by the New World, Bordeaux has become one of France's most exciting white wine areas. There are both oaked and unoaked styles. The unoaked are leafy, tangy and stony-dry. The barrel-fermented styles are delightfully rich yet dry, with custard-cream softness mellowing leafy acidity, and peach and nectarine fruit.

SWEET WINES

Bordeaux's most famous whites are its sweet wines made from grapes affected by noble rot, particularly those from Sauternes and Barsac. The noble rot concentrates the flavours, producing rich, honeyed wines replete with pineapple and peach flavours, and which develop a lanolin and beeswax depth and a barley sugar and honey richness with age. On the other side of the Garonne river, Cadillac, Loupiac and Ste-Croix-du-Mont also make sweet wines; these rarely attain the richness or complexity of a top Sauternes, but they are considerably less expensive.

CLASSIFICATIONS

The two largest dry white wine ACs in Bordeaux are Bordeaux Blanc and Entre-Deux-Mers. There are plenty of good dry wines in the Graves and Pessac-Léognan regions; the Pessac-Léognan AC, created in 1987, contains all the dry white Classed Growths. The great sweet wines of Sauternes and Barsac were classified as First or Second Growths in 1855.

See also BARSAC, BLAYE-CÔTES DE BORDEAUX, BORDEAUX, BORDEAUX SUPÉRIEUR, CADILLAC, CERONS, CÔTES DE BOURG, ENTRE-DEUX-MERS, FRANCS-CÔTES DE BORDEAUX, GRAVES, LOUPIAC, PESSAC-LÉOGNAN, PREMIÈRES CÔTES DE BORDEAUX, STE-CROIX-DU-MONT, SAUTERNES; and individual châteaux.

(dry) **2012 11 10 09 08 07 06 05 04**;
(sweet) 2011 **10 09 07 05 03 02 01 99 98 97 96 95 90 89 88**

BEST PRODUCERS

Dry wines

Pessac-Léognan Brown, de CHEVALIER, Couhins-Lurton, FIEUZAL, La Garde, HAUT-BRION, Larrivet-Haut-Brion, LATOUR-MARTILLAC, LAVILLE-HAUT-BRION (since 2009 la MISSION HAUT-BRION blanc), la LOUVIÈRE, MALARTIC-LAGRAVIÈRE, SMITH-HAUT-LAFITTE; *Graves* Archambeau, Brondelle, Chantegrive, Clos Floridène, Crabitey, Magneau, Rahoul, Respide, Respide-Médeville, St-Robert (Cuvée Poncet-Deville), Toumilon, Tourteau-Chollet, Vieux-Ch.-Gaubert, Villa Bel-Air.

Entre-Deux-Mers BONNET, de Fontenille, Landereau, Marjosse, Nardique-la-Gravière, Ste-Marie, Toutigeac, Turcaud.

Bordeaux AC Bauduc, DOISY-DAENE (Sec), LYNCH-BAGES, Ch. MARGAUX (Pavillon Blanc), MONBOUSQUET, REYNON, Roquefort, TALBOT, Thieuley, Tour de Mirambeau, VALANDRAUD.

Blaye-Côtes de Bordeaux Charron (Acacia), Haut-Bertinerie, Cave des Hauts de Gironde co-op (Chapelle de Tutiac), Tourtes (Prestige).

Sweet wines

Sauternes and Barsac CLIMENS, Clos Haut-Peyraguey, COUTET, DOISY-DAENE, DOISY-VEDRINES, FARGUES, GILETTE, GUIRAUD, LAFAURIE-PEYRAGUEY, NAIRAC, Raymond-Lafon, RIEUSSEC, Sigalas-Rabaud, SUDUIRAUT, la TOUR BLANCHE, YQUEM.

Cadillac Fayau, Manos, Mémoires.

Cérons Ch. de Cérons, Grand Enclos du Ch. de Cérons.

Loupiac Clos Jean, Dauphiné-Rondillon, Noble.

Ste-Croix-du-Mont Loubens, Pavillon, la Rame.

BLAUFRÄNKISCH Good Blaufränkisch, when not blasted with new oak, has a taste similar to raspberries and white pepper or even beetroot. Hungarian in origin, it does well in Austria, where it is the principal red grape of BURGENLAND. The Hungarian vineyards (where it is called Kékfrankos) are mostly just across the border on the other side of the Neusiedlersee. Called Lemberger in Germany, where almost all of it is grown in WÜRTTEMBERG. Croatia calls it Frankovka or Borgogna and makes crunchy, juicy reds. Also successful in NEW YORK STATE and (as Lemberger) in WASHINGTON STATE (getting better with global warming!).

BLAYE-CÔTES DE BORDEAUX AC *Bordeaux, France* Much improved AC on the right bank of the Gironde. Formerly Premières Côtes de Blaye; part of Côtes de Bordeaux AC from 2008. The fresh, Merlot-based reds are ready at 2–3 years but will age for more. Top red wines can be labelled under the quality-driven Blaye AC. Good modern whites. Best producers: (reds) Bel-Air la Royère★, Confiance★, Gigault (Cuvée Viva★), Haut-Bertinerie★, Haut-Colombier★, Haut-Grelot, Haut-Sociando, les Jonqueyres★, Monconseil-Gazin★, Mondésir-Gazin★, Montfollet★, Roland la Garde★, Segonzac★, Tourtes★; (whites) Charron (Acacia★), Haut-Bertinerie★, Cave des Hauts de Gironde (Chapelle de Tutiac★), Tourtes (Prestige★). Best years: 2012 10 09 08 05.

JACKY BLOT *Loire Valley, France* When he created Domaine de la Taille aux Loups in MONTLOUIS-SUR-LOIRE and VOUVRAY in 1988, Blot's use of barrel fermentation and new oak caused controversy. However, rigorous selection of pristine, ripe grapes produces sparkling, dry and sweet whites with tremendous fruit purity. Top Montlouis-sur-Loire cuvées Rémus (*sec*)★★ and Romulus (*liquoreux*)★★ are groundbreaking. He has recently acquired two vineyards in Montlouis: Clos de Mosny and Clos Michet. Fine Triple Zéro sparkling rosé (from Gamay), and a white version (from Chenin). Since 2002 Blot has made four powerful but ultra-refined reds at Domaine de la Butte★★ in BOURGUEIL AC. Best years: (whites) (sec) (2013) 12 11 10 08 07 06; (moelleux) 2011 09 05 03 02 97 96 95 90.

BOBAL Spain's second most widely grown red grape, surpassed only by Tempranillo. Once doomed to bulk wine's netherworld, some producers in MANCHUELA and UTIEL-REQUENA have rescued it and its fruity, vivacious, structured, somewhat rustic character.

BOEKENHOUTSKLOOF *Franschhoek WO, South Africa* Small winery, high in the FRANSCHHOEK mountains, named after the surrounding Cape beech trees. The flagship range includes punchy, savoury Syrah★★, deep, long-lived Cabernet Sauvignon★, sophisticated Semillon★★ partly from 100-year-old vines, sumptuous Noble Late Harvest★★ (Semillon) and burly, expressive Chocolate Block★ (Syrah-led-blend). Fruit-focused Porcupine Ridge★ and RHÔNE-style The Wolftrap white★ and red★ offer great value. Best years: (premium reds) 2011 10 09 08 07 06 05 04 03.

BOGLE *Central Valley AVA, California, USA* Top marks for palate-friendly everyday budget wines, especially old-vine Zinfandel★.

BOIREANN *Queensland, Australia* QUEENSLAND's most impressive boutique winery, with a 1.5ha (3.5-acre) vineyard planted to 10 red varieties plus Viognier for the flagship fragrant Shiraz-Viognier★★. Other stunning reds include Merlot★★, Cabernet Sauvignon★ and seductive Lurnea★ (a blend of Merlot, Cabernets Sauvignon and Franc and Petit Verdot).

BOISSET *Burgundy, France* Jean-Claude Boisset bought his first vineyards in 1964 and his extraordinarily successful *négociant* company has swallowed up many long-established names such as Jaffelin, Ropiteau and Héritier Guyot in the CÔTE D'OR, Moreau in CHABLIS, Rodet in Côte Chalonnaise, Cellier des Samsons and Mommessin in BEAUJOLAIS. Most of these companies produce commercially successful rather than fine wine, excepting Dom. de la VOUGERAIE and the Boisset label. Now owns Vincent GIRARDIN brand. Also projects in California, Canada, Chile and Uruguay.

BOLGHERI DOC *Tuscany, Italy* Zone named after an arty village on the Tuscan coast, with sub-zone of SASSICAIA. Until the 1980s simple white and rosé wines were made here – later, major reds based on Cabernet, Merlot and/or Syrah. Best producers: Argentiera, Ca' Marcanda★ (GAJA), Collemassari, Grattamacco★★, Guado al Tasso★★ (ANTINORI), Le MACCHIOLE★★, ORNELLAIA★★, Poggio al Tesoro★, Michele Satta. Best years: (reds) (2011) 10 **09** 08 07 06 05 04 01 00.

BOLLINGER *Champagne AC, Champagne, France* One of the great CHAMPAGNE houses, with good non-vintage (Special Cuvée★) and vintage wines (Grande Année★★★), made in a full, rich, rather old-fashioned style. (Bollinger is one of the few houses to ferment its base wine in barrels.) It also produces a range of rarer vintages, including Vintage RD★★★, and a Vieilles Vignes Françaises Blanc de Noirs★★ from ancient, ungrafted Pinot Noir vines. Delightfully soft, creamy non-vintage Brut Rosé. Bollinger bought Champagne Ayala, a neighbour in Aÿ, in 2005. Best years: (Grande Année) 2004 02 **00 99** 97 96 95 92 90 89 88 85 82 79.

CH. LE BON PASTEUR★★ *Pomerol AC, Bordeaux, France* Owned until 2013 by Michel Rolland, Bordeaux's most famous winemaker. Now in Chinese hands. The wines are expensive, but they are always deliciously soft and full of lush fruit. Best years: 2012 11 10 **09 08** 06 05 04 03 02 01 **00** 99 98 96 95 90.

BONNES-MARES AC *Grand Cru, Côte de Nuits, Burgundy, France* Large Grand Cru straddling the communes of CHAMBOLLE-MUSIGNY and MOREY-ST-DENIS; commendably consistent. Bonnes-Mares generally has a deep, ripe, smoky plum fruit, which starts rich and chewy and matures over 10–20 years. Best producers: Arlaud★★, d'Auvenay★★★ (Dom. LEROY), Bertheau★★, CLAIR★★, DROUHIN★★★, Drouhin-Laroze★★, DUJAC★★★, R Groffier★★★, JADOT★★★, ROUMIER★★★, de VOGÜÉ★★★, VOUGERAIE★★★. Best years: (2013) 12 11 10 09 **08** 07 06 05 **03 02 01** 99 98 96 95 93 90.

CH. BONNET *Entre-Deux-Mers AC, Bordeaux, France* Large volumes of consistently good, fruity, affordable ENTRE-DEUX-MERS★ and BORDEAUX AC rosé and red. Drink barrel-aged red Réserve★ at 3–4 years and the others young. Also a special cuvée, Divinus★. Owner André Lurton is also the proprietor of Ch. La LOUVIÈRE and other properties in PESSAC-LÉOGNAN.

BONNEZEAUX AC *Loire Valley, France* One of France's great sweet wines, Bonnezeaux is a zone within the COTEAUX DU LAYON AC. Quality is variable, but top wines are world class. It can age well in good vintages. Best producers: M Angeli/Sansonnière★★, Fesles★★, Les Grandes Vignes★, Petit Val★★, la Petite Croix★, Petits Quarts★★, Terrebrune★★, la Varière★★. Best years: (2013) 11 **10** 09 07 06 05 04 03 02 01 97 96 95 90 89.

BONNY DOON *Santa Cruz Mountains AVA, California, USA* Randall Grahm has a particular love for Rhône and Italian varietals: Le Cigare Volant★★ is a blend of Grenache and Syrah and is Grahm's homage to CHÂTEAUNEUF-DU-PAPE. Cigare Blanc★ is lush yet dry; Vin Gris de Cigare★ is outstanding. Also delightful Albariño★.

BORDEAUX AC *Bordeaux, France* One of the most important ACs in France, covering reds, rosés and the dry, medium and sweet white wines of the entire Gironde region. Most of the best wines are allowed specific district or commune ACs (such as MARGAUX or SAUTERNES), but a vast amount of Bordeaux's wine – delicious, atrocious and everything in between – is sold as Bordeaux AC. At its best, straight red Bordeaux is marked by bone-dry leafy fruit and an attractive earthy edge, and as global warming kicks in, raw, tannic examples are becoming less common. Good examples usually benefit from a year or so of aging. Bordeaux Blanc has joined the modern world with an increasing number of refreshing, pleasant wines. These may be labelled as Bordeaux Sauvignon. Drink young. Bordeaux Clairet is a pale red wine, virtually rosé but with a little more substance. **Best producers:** (reds) Beauregard-Ducourt, BONNET★, Dourthe (Numéro 1), Ducla, d:vin★, Fontenille★, Gadras, Girolate, Sirius, Thieuley★, Tour de Mirambeau; (whites), Bauduc★, DOISY-DAËNE★, Dourthe (Numéro 1★), LYNCH-BAGES★, MARGAUX (Pavillon Blanc★★), MONBOUSQUET★, REYNON★, Roquefort★, TALBOT★, Thieuley★, Tour de Mirambeau★, Vieux Ch. Lamothe, VALANDRAUD★. See also pages 86–9.

BORDEAUX SUPÉRIEUR AC *Bordeaux, France* Covers the same area as the BORDEAUX AC but the wines must have an extra 0.5% of alcohol, a lower yield and a longer period of maturation. Many of the best petits châteaux are labelled Bordeaux Supérieur. **Best producers (reds):** Barreyre★, Beaulieu Comtes de Tastes★, de Bouillerot★, de Courteillac★, La France★, Grand Village★, Parenchère★, Penin★, Pey la Tour★, Pierrail★, le Pin Beausoleil★, Reignac★, Roques Mauriac★, Thieuley (Réserve Francis Courselle★), Tire-Pé★.

BORIE LA VITARÈLE *St-Chinian, Languedoc, France* Several ST-CHINIANS, as well as vins de pays/IGPs, which express the different soils of the organic vineyard: Les Crès★ (Syrah-Mourvèdre) is spicy and warm; Les Schistes (Syrah-Grenache) is ripe and concentrated; white LANGUEDOC AC Le Grand Mayol (Clairette-Bourboulenc-Vermentino) has refreshing minerality. **Best years:** (2013) 12 **11 10 09 08 07 06 05**.

BOSCARELLI *Vino Nobile di Montepulciano DOCG, Tuscany, Italy* One of Montepulciano's best producers, crafting rich and stylish reds with guidance from star enologist Maurizio Castelli. VINO NOBILE★★, Riserva del Nocio★★ and the barrique-aged Boscarelli★★ are all finely tuned. **Best years:** (2011) 10 **09 08 07** 06 **04 01 99**.

BOUCHARD FINLAYSON *Walker Bay WO, South Africa* Pinotphile Peter Finlayson produces classy Pinot Noir (Galpin Peak★ and occasional Tête de Cuvée★★). Hannibal★★ is an unusual multi-cultural mix led by Sangiovese with Pinot Noir, Nebbiolo, Shiraz and others. Chardonnays (Kaaimansgaat/Crocodile's Lair★★, with citrusy freshness reflecting high, cool-climate vineyards, and minerally, nutty Missionvale★★) are plausibly Burgundian and age well. Sauvignon Blanc★ is tangy and fresh. **Best years:** (Pinot Noir) 2012 11 **10 09 08 07 06 05 04**.

BOUCHARD PÈRE & FILS *Beaune, Burgundy, France* Important merchant with superb holdings such as Chevalier-Montrachet★★, le MONTRACHET★★★, BEAUNE Grèves Vigne de l'Enfant Jésus★★, as well as a Premier Cru blend labelled Beaune du Château. Reds and whites equally good. **Best years:** (top reds) (2013) 12 11 10 09 **08 07** 06 05 **02 99**.

BOUCHES-DU-RHÔNE, IGP *Provence, France* Wines from 3 areas: the coast, a zone around Aix-en-Provence, and the Camargue. Mainly full-bodied, spicy reds, with estates like TREVALLON (now IGP Alpilles) breaking with local tradition and using a high percentage of Cabernet

Sauvignon. Unusual varieties include Caladoc (Grenache x Malbec) at la Michelle and Arinarnoa (Merlot x Petit Verdot) at Isle St-Pierre. Rosé can be good too. Best producers: Isle St-Pierre, Mas de Rey, la Michelle. Best years: (reds) (2013) 12 11 10 **09 08**.

DOM. HENRI BOURGEOIS *Sancerre AC, Loire Valley, France* A major presence with 67ha (166 acres) of domaine vineyards and a substantial *négociant* business extending into POUILLY-FUMÉ, MENETOU-SALON, QUINCY and COTEAUX DU GIENNOIS, plus Clos Henri label in New Zealand. Wonderfully mineral SANCERRE from the precipitously steep slopes of La Côte des Monts Damnés★, ageworthy Jadis★★ from *terre blanche* soils and d'Antan★★ from flint soils. Together with rare barrel-fermented Étienne Henri★★, they are among the finest in Sancerre. Good red Sancerre too. Best years: (top wines) 2013 **12 11** 10 09.

BOURGOGNE AC *Burgundy, France* Bourgogne is the French name anglicized as 'Burgundy'. This generic AC mops up all the Burgundian wine with no AC of its own, resulting in massive differences in style and quality. It is a pity that standards are not both higher and more consistent, but a top tip for value are wines from a single grower's vineyards just outside the main village ACs of the CÔTE D'OR; such wines may be the only way we can afford the joys of fine Burgundy. Pinot Noir is the main red grape. Gamay from a declassified BEAUJOLAIS Cru can use the title Bourgogne Gamay. Red Bourgogne is usually light, fruity in an upfront strawberry and cherry way, and should be drunk within 2–3 years. The rosé (Pinot Noir) can be pleasant, but little is produced. Bourgogne Blanc is a usually bone-dry Chardonnay wine and most should be drunk within 2 years. Bourgogne Passe-tout-Grains is made from Gamay with at least 30% of Pinot Noir, while the former oxymoron Bourgogne Grand Ordinaire (now renamed COTEAUX BOURGUIGNONS AC) is rarely more than a quaffing wine, drunk in local bars. Best producers: (reds/growers) Arnoux-Lachaux★★, G Barthod★★, S CATHIARD★, Dugat-Py★★, G Jourdan★, LAFARGE★, MEO-CAMUZET★★, Parent★, P RION★★, ROUMIER★, C Tremblay★, VOUGERAIE★; (reds/merchants) Roche de BELLENE, DROUHIN★, GIRARDIN, JADOT★, Maison Leroy★★; (reds/co-ops) BUXY★, Caves des Hautes-Côtes★; (whites/growers) Bachelet-Monnot★, M Bouzereau★, Boyer-Martenot★, J-M BROCARD★, COCHE-DURY★★, P-Y COLIN-MOREY★, J-P Fichet★, P Javillier★, A Jobard★, Matrot★, Ch. de Meursault★, Pierre MOREY★, ROULOT★; (whites/merchants) DROUHIN★, FAIVELEY★, JADOT★, Olivier LEFLAIVE, (whites/co-ops) BUXY★, Caves des Hautes-Côtes. Best years: (reds) (2013) 12 **11** 10 09 05; (whites) (2013) **12 11** 10 09. See also pages 94-7.

BOURGOGNE ALIGOTÉ AC See ALIGOTE.

BOURGOGNE-CÔTE CHALONNAISE AC *Burgundy, France* AC for vineyards west of Chalon-sur-Saône around the villages of Bouzeron, RULLY, MERCUREY, GIVRY and MONTAGNY. Best producers: BUXY★, Villaine (La Digoine★). Best years: (reds) (2013) 12 **11** 10 09; (whites) (2013) **12 11** 10 09.

BOURGOGNE-CÔTE D'OR AC *Burgundy, France* New AC for wines from CÔTE DE BEAUNE and CÔTE DE NUITS grapes. These should be superior to simple 'BOURGOGNE' but we are still waiting for the rules.

BOURGOGNE-HAUTES-CÔTES DE BEAUNE AC *Burgundy, France* The hills behind the great CÔTE DE BEAUNE are a good source of affordable Burgundy. The red wines are lean but drinkable, as is the slightly sharp Chardonnay. Best producers: Caves des Hautes-Côtes★, J-Y Devevey★, L Jacob★, J-L Joillot★, Mazilly★, Naudin-Ferrand★, C Nouveau★. Best years: (reds) (2013) 12 **11** 10 09 05; (whites) (2013) **12 11** 10 09.

BURGUNDY RED WINES

Burgundy, France

 Rich in history and gastronomic tradition, the region of Burgundy (Bourgogne in French) covers a vast tract of eastern France, running from Auxerre, south-east of Paris, down to the city of Mâcon. As with its white wines, Burgundy's red wines are extremely diverse, even though they almost all come from just one grape, Pinot Noir. That's partly the nature of the grape and partly the fragmentation of the vineyards between so many different growers and merchants.

WINE STYLES

Pinot Noir shows many different flavour profiles according to climate, soil and winemaking. The reds from around Auxerre (Épineuil, Irancy) in the north will be light, chalky and strawberry-flavoured. Also light, and somewhat rustic, are the generic Bourgognes from outlying areas such as the Couchois and Châtillonais, while the Côte Chalonnaise offers solid reds from Givry and Mercurey.

The top reds come from the Côte d'Or, the heartland of Burgundy. Flavours sweep through strawberry, raspberry, damson and cherry – in young wines – to a wild, magnificent maturity of Oriental spices, chocolate, mushrooms and truffles. The greatest of all – the world-famous Grand Cru vineyards such as Chambertin, Musigny, Richebourg and Clos de Vougeot – are in the Côte de Nuits, the northern part of the Côte d'Or from Nuits-St-Georges up toward Dijon. Other fine reds, especially Volnay, Pommard and Corton, come from the Côte de Beaune. Some villages tend toward a fine and elegant style (Chambolle-Musigny, Volnay), others toward a firmer, more tannic structure (Gevrey-Chambertin, Pommard).

The Beaujolais should really be considered as a separate region, growing Gamay on granitic soils rather than Pinot Noir on limestone, though a small amount of Gamay has also crept north to be included in the lesser wines of Burgundy as well as all red Mâcon.

CLASSIFICATIONS

Most of Burgundy has 5 increasingly specific levels of classification: regional ACs (e.g. Bourgogne), specified ACs covering groups of villages (e.g. Côte de Nuits-Villages), village wines taking the village name (Pommard, Vosne-Romanée), Premiers Crus (better vineyard sites) and Grands Crus (the best individual vineyard sites). At village level, vineyard names in small letters are called *lieux-dits*.

See also ALOXE-CORTON, AUXEY-DURESSES, BEAUJOLAIS, BEAUNE, BLAGNY, BONNES-MARES, BOURGOGNE, BOURGOGNE-CÔTE CHALONNAISE, BOURGOGNE-HAUTES-CÔTES DE BEAUNE/NUITS, CHAMBERTIN, CHAMBOLLE-MUSIGNY, CHASSAGNE-MONTRACHET, CHOREY-LÈS-BEAUNE, CLOS DE LA ROCHE, CLOS ST-DENIS, CLOS DE VOUGEOT, CORTON, CÔTE DE BEAUNE, CÔTE DE NUITS, CÔTE D'OR, COTEAUX BOURGUIGNONS, CRÉMANT DE BOURGOGNE, ÉCHÉZEAUX, FIXIN, GEVREY-CHAMBERTIN, GIVRY, IRANCY, LADOIX, MÂCON, MARANGES, MARSANNAY, MERCUREY, MONTHÉLIE, MOREY-ST-DENIS, MUSIGNY, NUITS-ST-GEORGES, PERNAND-VERGELESSES, POMMARD, RICHEBOURG, la ROMANÉE-CONTI, ROMANÉE-ST-VIVANT, RULLY, ST-AUBIN, ST-ROMAIN, SANTENAY, SAVIGNY-LÈS-BEAUNE, la TÂCHE, VOLNAY, VOSNE-ROMANÉE, VOUGEOT; and individual producers.

BEST YEARS

(2013) 12 11 10 09 **08 07 06** 05 **03 02 99 98 96 90**

BEST PRODUCERS

Côte de Nuits Arlaud, l'Arlot, Arnoux-Lachaux, D BACHELET, G Barthod, A Burguet, S CATHIARD, Charlopin, J Chauvenet, R Chevillon, Chopin-Groffier, B CLAIR, B Clavelier, CLOS DES LAMBRAYS, CLOS DE TART, J-J Confuron, P Damoy, Drouhin-Laroze, C Dugat, B Dugat-Py, DUJAC, Sylvie Esmonin, Eugénie, J-M Fourrier, Geantet-Pansiot, H Gouges, GRIVOT, Robert Groffier, GROS, Hudelot-NOËLLAT, Jayer-Gilles, F Lamarche, Lechenaut, Dom. LEROY, LIGER-BELAIR, H Lignier, MEO-CAMUZET, Denis MORTET, MUGNERET-Gibourg, J-F MUGNIER, G NOËLLAT, Pataille, Perrot-Minot, Ponsot, RION, Dom. de la ROMANÉE-CONTI, Rossignol-Trapet, Roty, E Rouget, ROUMIER, ROUSSEAU, Sérafin, Taupenot-Merme, Ch. de la Tour, J & J-L Trapet, Tremblay, de VOGÜÉ, VOUGERAIE.

Côte de Beaune d'ANGERVILLE, Comte Armand, BELLENE, Bize, H Boillot, J-M Boillot, CHANDON DE BRIAILLES, de Courcel, Hospices de Beaune, Michel LAFARGE, LAFON, de MONTILLE, Muzard, Parent, Pousse d'Or, J Prieur, N Rossignol, TOLLOT-BEAUT.

Côte Chalonnaise Clos Salomon, Dureuil-Janthial, Joblot, M Juillot, Lorenzon, F Raquillet, Thénard, Theulot-Juillot, de Villaine.

Merchants Roche de BELLENE, Bichot, BOISSET, BOUCHARD PÈRE & FILS, Champy, Chanson, DROUHIN, FAIVELEY, Alex Gambal, V GIRARDIN, Camille Giroud, JADOT, D Laurent, Lemoine, Benjamin Leroux, Maison Leroy, Remoissenet.

Co-ops Vignerons de BUXY, Caves des Hautes-Côtes.

BURGUNDY WHITE WINES

Burgundy, France

 White Burgundy has for generations been thought of as the world's leading dry white wine. The top wines have a remarkable succulent richness of honey and hazelnut, melted butter and sprinkled spice, yet are totally dry. Such wines are all from the Chardonnay grape and the finest are generally produced in the Côte de Beaune, the southern part of the Côte d'Or, on the Hill of Corton and in the communes of Meursault, Puligny-Montrachet, Chassagne-Montrachet and St-Aubin, where limestone soils and the aspect of the vineyard provide perfect conditions for the even ripening of grapes. However, Burgundy encompasses many more wine styles than this, even if no single one quite attains the peaks of quality of these prime locations on the Côte de Beaune.

WINE STYLES

Chablis in the north traditionally produces very good steely wines, aggressive and lean when young, but nutty and rounded – though still very dry – after a few years. Modern Chablis is frequently a softer, milder wine, easy to drink young, and sometimes enriched (or denatured) by aging in new oak barrels.

There is no doubt that Meursault and the other Côte de Beaune villages can produce stupendous wine, but there have been problems of late with wines oxidizing prematurely for various reasons still insufficiently understood. Consequently, white Burgundy from these famous villages must be approached with caution, although growers now believe they have dealt with the problem. Lesser-known villages such as Pernand-Vergelesses and St-Aubin often provide good white at lower prices. There can be interesting whites from some villages in the Côte de Nuits, such as Morey-St-Denis, Nuits-St-Georges and Vougeot, though amounts are tiny compared with the Côte de Beaune.

South of the Côte d'Or, the Côte Chalonnaise is becoming more interesting for quality white wine now that better equipment for temperature control is becoming more widespread and oak barrels are being used more often for aging. Rully and Montagny are the most important villages, though Givry and Mercurey can produce nice white too. The minor Aligoté grape makes some refreshing wine, especially in Bouzeron.

Further south, the Mâconnais is a large region, two-thirds planted with Chardonnay. There is some fair sparkling Crémant de Bourgogne, and some very good vineyard sites, in particular in Viré-Clessé, St-Véran and in Pouilly-Fuissé. Increasingly stunning wines can now be found, though there's still a lot of dross.

See also ALOXE-CORTON, AUXEY-DURESSES, BÂTARD-MONTRACHET, BEAUJOLAIS, BEAUNE, BOURGOGNE, BOURGOGNE-CÔTE CHALONNAISE, BOURGOGNE-HAUTES-CÔTES DE BEAUNE/NUITS, CHABLIS, CHASSAGNE-MONTRACHET, CORTON, CORTON-CHARLEMAGNE, CÔTE DE BEAUNE, CÔTE DE NUITS, CÔTE D'OR, CRÉMANT DE BOURGOGNE, FIXIN, GIVRY, LADOIX, MÂCON, MÂCON-VILLAGES, MARANGES, MARSANNAY, MERCUREY, MEURSAULT, MONTAGNY, MONTHELIE, MONTRACHET, MOREY-ST-DENIS, MUSIGNY, NUITS-ST-GEORGES, PERNAND-VERGELESSES, POUILLY-FUISSÉ, POUILLY-VINZELLES, PULIGNY-MONTRACHET, RULLY, ST-AUBIN, ST-ROMAIN, ST-VERAN, SANTENAY, SAVIGNY-LÈS-BEAUNE, VIRÉ-CLESSÉ, VOUGEOT; and individual producers.

BEST YEARS

(2013) 12 **11 10 09 08 07 06 05 04 02 00**

BEST PRODUCERS

Chablis and Auxerrois
Barat, J-C Bessin, S Billaud, Billaud-Simon, P Bouchard, A & F Boudin, J-M BROCARD, D Dampt, V DAUVISSAT, Droin, N & G Fèvre, W Fèvre, J-H Goisot, J-P Grossot, LAROCHE, Long-Depaquit, Malandes, Louis Michel, Christian Moreau, Moreau-Naudet, Picq, Pinson, P Piuze, RAVENEAU, Vocoret.

Côte d'Or (Côte de Beaune) M Ampeau, d'Auvenay (LEROY), BACHELET-Monnot, Blain-Gagnard, H Boillot, J-M Boillot, P Boisson, Bonneau du Martray, M Bouzereau, Boyer-Martenot, CARILLON, Coche-Bizouard, COCHE-DURY, Marc COLIN, P-Y COLIN-MOREY, Dancer, A Ente, J-P Fichet, Fontaine-Gagnard, J-N GAGNARD, A Gras, P Javillier, A Jobard, R Jobard, LAFON, H Lamy, Dom. LEFLAIVE, Matrot, B Moreau, MOREY, M Niellon, P Pernot, J & J-M Pillot, J Prieur, RAMONET, M Rollin, ROULOT, SAUZET, VOUGERAIE.

Côte Chalonnaise
S Aladame, Dureuil-Janthial, H & P Jacqueson, De Villaine.

Mâconnais D & M Barraud, Ch. de Beauregard, A Bonhomme, Bret Brothers, Cordier, Corsin, Deux Roches, J-A Ferret, Ch. Fuissé, Guffens-Heynen, Guillot, Guillot-Broux, LAFON, Merlin, Ch. des Rontets, J & N Saumaize, Saumaize-Michelin, la Soufrandière, J Thévenet.

Merchants BOUCHARD PÈRE & FILS, Champy, Chanson, DROUHIN, FAIVELEY, V GIRARDIN, JADOT, Louis LATOUR, Olivier LEFLAIVE, Maison Leroy, Rijckaert, Rodet, Verget.

Co-ops Vignerons de BUXY, la CHABLISIENNE, Lugny, Viré.

BOURGOGNE-HAUTES-CÔTES DE NUITS AC *Burgundy, France*
Attractive, lightweight wines from the hills behind the CÔTE DE NUITS. The reds are best, with an attractive cherry and plum flavour. The whites tend to be rather dry and flinty. Best producers: D Duband★, FAIVELEY★, A-F GROS★, M GROS★, A Guyon★, Caves des Hautes-Côtes★, Jayer-Gilles★★, T LIGER-BELAIR★, Thévenot-le-Brun★ (whites) A Verdet★. Best years: (reds) (2012) 11 **10 09 05**; (whites) (2012) 11 **10 09**.

BOURGUEIL AC *Loire Valley, France* Fine red from between Tours and Angers, made with Cabernet Franc, sometimes with a little Cabernet Sauvignon; expect spicy wines with plump raspberry and plum fruit. Best producers: Y Amirault★★, Audebert★, T Boucard★, P Breton★★, la Butte★★/BLOT, la Chevalerie★★, Clos de l'Abbaye★, L et M Cognard-Taluau, DRUET★★, S Guion★, Lamé-Delisle-Boucard★, la Lande/Delaunay★, F MABILEAU★, Nau Frères★, Ouches★, Raguenières★. Best years: 2013 11 **10 09 08 06 05**. See also ST-NICOLAS-DE-BOURGUEIL.

BRACHETTO An unusual Italian grape native to Piedmont, best known for Brachetto d'Acqui DOCG: sweet, frothy, perfumed light red wines.

CH. BRANAIRE-DUCRU★★ *St-Julien AC, 4ème Cru Classé, Haut-Médoc, Bordeaux, France* On full, soft, chocolaty form since the mid-1990s, with some added muscle in the new millennium and consistent in good years and poor. Best years: 2012 11 10 09 **08 06 05 04 03 02 01 00 98 96**.

BRANCOTT ESTATE *Auckland, Gisborne, Hawkes Bay and Marlborough, New Zealand* Owned since 2005 by Pernod Ricard, which replaced the well-known Montana brand with Brancott and shed a few brands, including the well-known sparkler, Lindauer. Estate bottlings of whites are generally good (Sauvignon Blanc★, some ★★, occasional Late Harvest★★) and they are now one of the world's biggest producers of Pinot Noir★ (tasty, not expensive). Letter Series★ of varietals (some ★★) is a step up. Stoneleigh label has Marlborough Sauvignon Blanc★★, Riesling★ and tasty Rapaura Series★. Waipara wines use the Camshorn label. Austere yet full-bodied Deutz Prestige Cuvée Brut★★, elegant Deutz Blanc de Blancs★★ and refreshing sparkling Sauvignon Blanc. See also CHURCH ROAD.

BRAND'S *Coonawarra, South Australia* Owned by MCWILLIAM'S, with 100ha (250 acres) of new vineyards as well as some ancient COONAWARRA vines planted in 1893. Ripe Laira Cabernet★ is increasingly attractive; One Seven One Cabernet Sauvignon★★ (formerly Patron's Reserve) is from Block One, planted in 1971, and remains excellent. Shiraz★ and opulent Stentiford's Reserve★★ (from 100-year-old vines) show how good Coonawarra Shiraz can be. Merlot★★ is often among Australia's better examples. Best years: (reds) (2013) 12 10 09 **08 06 05 04 03 02 01 00 99 98 97 96**.

CH. BRANE-CANTENAC★★ *Margaux AC, 2ème Cru Classé, Haut-Médoc, Bordeaux, France* After a drab period, Brane-Cantenac returned to form in the late 1990s when Henri Lurton took over the family property. He is making some delightful wines, particularly in 2000, 2005 and 2009, although don't expect flavours to be mainstream – 2002 and 03 are tasty but wild. Best years: 2012 11 10 09 **08 07 06 05 04 03 02 01 00 99 98 96**.

BRAUNEBERG *Mosel, Germany* Small village with 2 famous vineyard sites, Juffer and (especially) Juffer Sonnenuhr, whose wines have a honeyed richness and creaminess rare in the Mosel. Best producers: Bastgen, Fritz HAAG★★★, Willi Haag★, von Kesselstatt, Paulinshof★, M F RICHTER★★, SCHLOSS LIESER★★. Best years: (2013) 12 11 **10 09 07 06 05 04**.

BREAKY BOTTOM *Sussex, England* Small vineyard on the South Downs. Peter Hall is a quirky, passionate grower, making delicious sparkling wines★★ in two styles: Chardonnay-Pinot Noir-Meunier blends, and Seyval Blanc-based wines.

BREGANZE DOC *Veneto, Italy* This hilly zone, north-east of Verona, has reds from Pinot Nero, Cabernet and Merlot and whites from, among others, Pinot Grigio, but is best known for an amazing sweet wine called Torcolato, made from the native Vespaiolo. Main producers are Maculan and the Cantina Beato Bartolomeo da Breganze.

GEORG BREUER *Rüdesheim, Rheingau, Germany* Intense dry Riesling from RÜDESHEIM Berg Schlossberg★★★, Berg Rottland★ and RAUENTHAL Nonnenberg★★. Also a satisfying Sekt★. Best years: (Berg Schlossberg) (2013) (12) 11 **10 09 08 07 06 05 04 03 02.**

BRITTAN VINEYARDS *Willamette Valley AVA, Oregon, USA* After managing STAG'S LEAP winery in NAPA VALLEY for 16 years, in 2004 Robert Brittan fulfilled his dream of purchasing a vineyard in McMinnville, Oregon, to produce Pinot Noir. 'Gestalt Block'★ is a cherry-filled red with good balance and 'Basalt Block'★★ is black cherry scented. Best years: 2012 11 10 **09 08.**

JEAN-MARC BROCARD *Chablis, Burgundy, France* Jean-Marc built up this 80ha (200-acre) domaine almost from scratch. His son, Julien, has moved quality up a level and converted the vineyards to organic farming. The Premiers Crus (including Montée de Tonnerre★★, Montmains★★) and slow-evolving Grands Crus (les Clos★★★) are tremendous, as is the Chablis Vieilles Vignes★★. Also a range of BOURGOGNE Blancs★ from different soil types. Best years: (2013) 12 11 10 09.

BROKENWOOD *Hunter Valley, New South Wales, Australia* High-profile winery that celebrated its 40th anniversary in 2010. Delicious traditional unoaked HUNTER VALLEY Semillon★★★ (ILR Reserve ★★★). Very good Shiraz★★; the best red is classic Hunter Graveyard Vineyard Shiraz★★★. Cricket Pitch reds and whites are cheerful, fruity ready-drinkers. The Indigo vineyard at BEECHWORTH is making increasingly attractive Shiraz★, Chardonnay, Viognier and Pinot Noir. Also excellent Forest Edge Chardonnay★★ from ORANGE. Best years: (Graveyard Vineyard Shiraz) (2013) 12 11 09 07 **05 04 03 02 00 99 98 96 94 93 91 90 89 86.**

BRONCO WINE CO. *California, USA* Maker of the Charles Shaw wines – known as 'Two-Buck Chuck' because of their $2 price tag. There's now a $3.99 organic line called Green Fin. Makes you wonder how? The company is run by Fred Franzia, grand-nephew of the late Ernest GALLO. He is California's biggest vineyard owner with 16,000ha (40,000 acres), marketing 20 million cases of wine under more than a dozen brands.

BROUILLY AC *Beaujolais, Burgundy, France* Largest of the BEAUJOLAIS Crus; at its best, the wine is soft, fruity, rich and brightly coloured. Best producers: Collin-Bourisset (Terres Bleues), Demaine★, H Fessy, J-C Lapalu★★, A Michaud★, Ch. Thivin★. Best years: (2013) 11.

BROWN BROTHERS *North-East Victoria, Australia* Highly successful and energetic family winery, producing a huge range of varietal wines, which have improved significantly in recent years. Their sparkling wines have long been regarded as among Australia's best, and so the inspired 2010 purchase of Tasmania's sizeable Tamar Ridge winery is scarcely surprising. Top-of-the-range Patricia wines (Cabernet★★, sparkling Pinot-Chardonnay★★, Noble Riesling★★) are Brown's best yet.

BRÜNDLMAYER *Kamptal, Niederösterreich, Austria* Willi Bründlmayer makes wine in a variety of Austrian and international styles, but his dry Riesling (Alte Reben★★★, Lyra★★) from the great Zöbinger Heiligenstein vineyard and ageworthy Grüner Veltliner (Ried Lamm★★★) are superlative, marked by stunning fruit and mineral flavours. Also excellent Chardonnay★★ and good Sekt★. Best years: (Heiligenstein Riesling) (2013) 12 11 **10 09 08 07 06 05**.

BRUNELLO DI MONTALCINO DOCG *Tuscany, Italy* Iconic, full but elegant red 'created' by BIONDI-SANTI in the late 19th century. The number of producers soared in the late 20th century as the price of the wine (and land) took off, but the 'Brunellogate' scandal of the early 21st century (some big-name producers were accused of blending French grapes in with what is supposed to be a 100% Sangiovese wine) put a damper on sales, especially in the US, Brunello's main market. Released 4 years or more after vintage. Best producers: Agostina Pieri★★, Altesino★ (Montosoli★★), Argiano★, BIONDI-SANTI★★, Gianni Brunelli★★, Camigliano★★, Caparzo★ (La Casa★★), Casanova di Neri★, Casanuova delle Cerbaie★★, CASE BASSE★★★, Castelgiocondo★/FRESCOBALDI, Centolani★ (Pietranera★★), Cerbaiona★★★, Ciacci Piccolomini d'Aragona★★, Donatella Cinelli Colombini★, Col d'Orcia★★, COSTANTI★★, Fuligni★★, La Gerla★★, Greppone Mazzi★, Maurizio Lambardi★★, LISINI★★, Mastrojanni★★ (Schiena d'Asino★★★), Siro Pacenti★★, Pian delle Vigne★★/ANTINORI, Pian dell'Orino, Piancornello★★, Pieve Santa Restituta★/GAJA, La Poderina★, Poggio Antico★★, Poggio San Polo★★, Le Potazzine★★, Salvioni★★, San Giuseppe★★, Livio Sassetti/Pertimali★, Scopetone★, Sesti★★, Talenti★, Valdicava★★, Villa Le Prata★★. Best years: (2011) (10) (09) 08 **07 06 04 01 00 99 97 95 90 88 85**.

BUCELAS DOC *Lisboa, Portugal* Tiny but historic DOC for wines based on the high-acid Arinto grape. Attractive, modern examples from Quinta da Murta and Quinta da Romeira (Morgado de Santa Catherina★).

BUGEY AC *France* In the hills between the Jura and SAVOIE regions. Mainly Chardonnay and Altesse (also known as Roussette) for whites; Gamay, Mondeuse, Pinot Noir and Poulsard for rosés and light reds. A speciality is Bugey-Cerdon, a semi-sweet pink sparkling wine made from Gamay and Poulsard in the *méthode ancestrale*. Best producers: Angelot, Bartucci, Charlin, Lingot-Martin, Monin, Peillot★★, Renardat-Fâche★, Rondeau.

VON BUHL *Deidesheim, Pfalz, Germany* 62ha (153-acre) estate, now under the same ownership as BASSERMANN-JORDAN. Top Rieslings now invariably ★★. Best years: (Grosses Gewächs Rieslings) (2013) 12 11 **10 09 08 07 06 05**.

BUITENVERWACHTING *Constantia WO, South Africa* Beautiful old property; best known for penetrating, zesty Sauvignon Blanc★; Husseys Vlei Sauvignon Blanc★★ is bigger, more pungent, slower to develop. Also fruit-laden Chardonnay★ and classically styled reds, headed by Christine★★, one of the Cape's most accurate BORDEAUX lookalikes. Exciting experiments such as Maximus★ oak-aged Sauvignon with a drop of Semillon. Best years: (Christine) 2010 09 **08 07 06 05 04 04 03 02 01**.

BULL'S BLOOD See BIKAVÉR.

GRANT BURGE *Barossa Valley, South Australia* Leading BAROSSA producer with a wide range, including rich Meshach Shiraz★★★, chocolaty Filsell Shiraz★, Balthasar Shiraz★, Cameron Vale Cabernet★, Shadrach Cabernet★, RHÔNE-style Holy Trinity★ (Grenache-Shiraz-Mourvèdre) and fresh Thorn Riesling★. Excellent-value 5th Generation range and popular bubbly. Best years: (Meshach) (2013) 12 10 09 08 **06 05 04 02 99 98 96 95 94**.

BURGENLAND *Austria* 4 regions: Neusiedlersee, with red wines from the Zweigelt grape and sweet wines from the Seewinkel area; Neusiedlersee-Hügelland, famous for sweet wines, and now also big reds and fruity dry whites; Mittelburgenland and Südburgenland, for robust Blaufränkisch reds. Leithaberg is a recent DAC, producing exceptionally elegant Blaufränkisch. Best producers: Paul Achs★, FEILER-ARTINGER★★★, Gesellmann★★, Gernot Heinrich★★, J Heinrich★, Juris★, Kerschbaum★, KOLLWENTZ★★★, KRACHER★★★, KRUTZLER★★, Helmut Lang★★, Moric★, A & H Nittnaus★, Opitz★, Pöckl★★, Prieler★★, Schröck★★, TRIEBAUMER★★, Hans TSCHIDA★, UMATHUM★★, VELICH★★.

BURGUNDY See BOURGOGNE AC and pages 94–7.

BÜRKLIN-WOLF *Wachenheim, Pfalz, Germany* One of Germany's largest privately owned estates, with 85ha (210 acres) of vineyards in some exceptional sites in WACHENHEIM, FORST and Deidesheim. Biodynamic since 2005. The powerful, spicy dry Rieslings are ★★ to ★★★. Best years: (Grosses Gewächs Rieslings) (2013) 12 11 **10 09 08 07 06 05**.

BURMESTER *Port DOC, Douro, Portugal* Shipper established in 1730. Refined 10- and 20-year-old tawnies★, and outstanding old colheitas★★ that extend back over 100 years. Decent vintage and Late Bottled Vintage, and DOURO red, Casa Burmester. Gilberts is a range of ports aimed at younger drinkers. Best years: (Vintage) 2011 **07 03 00 97 95 94**.

CLEMENS BUSCH *Pünderich, Mosel, Germany* The little-known village of Pünderich is blessed with one exceptional site: Marienburg, with its steep grey slate soils. Initially known for powerful dry Rieslings★★, Busch has added exquisite nobly sweet Rieslings★★★ to the range. Biodynamic since the late 2000s. Best years: (2013) 12 11 **10 09 08 07**.

TOMMASO BUSSOLA *Valpolicella DOC and Amarone/Recioto DOCG, Veneto, Italy* Tommaso Bussola's AMARONE Vigneto Alto★★★ combines elegance with stunning power; Amarone Classico TB★★ is close behind, and even the basic Amarone★ is a challenge to the palate. The Ripasso VALPOLICELLA Classico Superiore TB★★ is one of the best of its genre, and the RECIOTO TB★★★ is excellent. Best years: (2011) (10) 09 **08 07 06 05 04 03 01 00**.

VIGNERONS DE BUXY *Côte Chalonnaise, Burgundy, France* One of Burgundy's top co-operatives. The light, oak-aged BOURGOGNE Pinot Noir★ and the red and white Clos de Chenôves★, as well as the nutty white MONTAGNY★, are all good, reasonably priced, and best with 2–3 years' age. Look out also for separate single-vineyard and single-domaine bottlings.

BUZET AOP *South-West France* Plummy – and affordable – BORDEAUX-style reds. Whites are rarely exciting and there's very little rosé. Buzet co-op is improving but remains uninspiring. Dom. du Pech★ is a quirky and biodynamic independent. Best years: (reds) 2012 11 **10 09 06 05**.

CA' DEL BOSCO *Franciacorta DOCG, Lombardy, Italy* Model estate, headed by Maurizio Zanella, making some of Italy's finest and most expensive international-style wines. Sparklers include FRANCIACORTA Brut★★, Dosage Zero★, Satèn★★ and the ever-improving Cuvée Annamaria Clementi★★★. Still wines include excellent Chardonnay★★★, Pinéro★★ (Pinot Noir) and BORDEAUX blend Maurizio Zanella★★★. Also a varietal Carmenère, Carmenero★, and occasional Merlot★.

CABARDÈS AC *Languedoc, France* Next door to MINERVOIS. Wines from Cabernet Sauvignon, Merlot, and Mediterranean varieties such as Syrah and Grenache. At best, full-bodied, chewy, rustically attractive – and attractively priced. Best producers: Cabrol★, Cazaban★, Font Juvénal, Jouclary, Pennautier★, Salitis★. Best years: (2013) 12 11 **10 09 08 07 06 05**.

CABERNET SAUVIGNON

Cabernet Sauvignon is now the world's most widely planted grape, and its wines – from Australia, California, Chile, South Africa, southern France – have become so popular that many people may not realize where it all started, and how Cabernet became the great, omnipresent red wine grape of the world.

WINE STYLES

Bordeaux Cabernet It all began in Bordeaux. With the exception of a lively bunch of Merlot-based beauties in St-Émilion and Pomerol, the greatest red Bordeaux wines are based on Cabernet Sauvignon, with varying amounts of Merlot, Cabernet Franc and possibly Petit Verdot blended in. The blending is necessary because by itself Cabernet makes such a strong, powerful, aggressive and assertive wine. Dark and tannic when young, the great Bordeaux wines need 10–20 years for the aggression to fade, the fruit becoming as sweet and perfumed as fresh blackcurrants, with a fragrance of cedarwood, of cigar boxes, mingling magically among the fruit. It is this character that has made red Bordeaux famous for at least two centuries.

Cabernet worldwide When winemakers in other parts of the world sought role models to try to improve their wines, most of them automatically thought of Bordeaux and chose Cabernet Sauvignon. It was lucky that they did, because not only is this variety easy to grow in almost all conditions – cool or warm, dry or damp – but that unstoppable personality always powers through. The cheaper wines are generally made to accentuate the blackcurrant fruit and the slightly earthy tannins. They are drinkable young, but able to age surprisingly well. The more ambitious wines are aged in oak barrels to enhance the tannin, and also to add spice and richness capable of developing over a decade or more. Sometimes the Cabernet is blended – usually with Merlot, sometimes with Cabernet Franc, and occasionally with other grapes: Shiraz in Australia, Sangiovese in Italy, Tempranillo in Spain, Carmenère in Chile.

Europe Many vineyards in southern France now make good, affordable Cabernet Sauvignon. In the Loire, Anjou's warmest sites produce well-structured examples in top years. Spain produces some good varietal Cabernets and blends, as does Portugal. Italy's red wine quality revolution was sparked off by the success of Cabernet in Tuscany, and all the leading regions now grow it – to the detriment, some say, of authenticity. Eastern Europe grows lots of Cabernet, but of widely varying quality, while the Eastern Mediterranean and North Africa are beginning to produce tasty examples.

New World There is a general move toward darker, denser, more serious Cabernets, even in countries like Chile and Australia, whose Cabernet triumphs have until now been based on gorgeous blackcurrant fruit. I hope they don't ditch too much of the fruit, but I have to say that a lot of these new contenders are excellent. Argentina is also pitching in with some powerful stuff, and South African Cabernets are showing better balance and ageworthiness. California's reputation was created by its strong, weighty Cabernets. It should be possible to exhibit power with balance, since thudding tannins, excess alcohol and low acid fruit defeat Cabernet's purpose. Some Napa producers are well aware of this and are creating marvellous wines of a gaudy, ferocious beauty, increasingly aided by judicious blending with other varieties. Other, more self-indulgent, producers need to be reminded: less is more.

diamond creek

Gravelly Meadow

Napa **2008** Valley

Cabernet Sauvignon

produced and bottled on diamond mountain by
DIAMOND CREEK VINEYARDS   CALISTOGA, CA.

ALCOHOL 14.1% BY VOLUME

BEST PRODUCERS

France

Bordeaux CALON-SÉGUR, COS D'ESTOURNEL, GRAND-PUY-LACOSTE, LAFITE-ROTHSCHILD, LATOUR, LÉOVILLE-BARTON, LÉOVILLE-LAS-CASES, LÉOVILLE-POYFERRÉ, LYNCH-BAGES, Ch. MARGAUX, MONTROSE, MOUTON-ROTHSCHILD, PICHON-LONGUEVILLE, PICHON-LONGUEVILLE-LALANDE, PONTET-CANET, RAUZAN-SEGLA; *South-West* TOUR DES GENDRES, VERDOTS; *Provence* TREVALLON.

Other European Cabernets

Italy CA' DEL BOSCO, GAJA, ISOLE E OLENA, LAGEDER, ORNELLAIA, San Leonardo, SASSICAIA, SOLAIA, TASCA D'ALMERITA, Tua Rita. *Spain* Abadía Retuerta, Blecua, Enate, Jané Ventura, MARQUES DE GRIÑON, TORRES.

New World Cabernets

Australia BALNAVES, CAPE MENTELLE, CULLEN, Forest Hill, Fraser Gallop, HARDYS (Thomas Hardy), HENSCHKE, HOUGHTON (Jack Mann, Gladstones), HOWARD PARK, Katnook, LEEUWIN, MAJELLA, MOSS WOOD, PARKER COONAWARRA ESTATE, PENFOLDS (Bin 707, Bin 169), PENLEY ESTATE, VASSE FELIX, VOYAGER, The Willows, WIRRA WIRRA, Woodlands, WYNNS, Xanadu, Zema.

New Zealand CRAGGY RANGE, Esk Valley, MAN O'WAR, STONYRIDGE, TE MATA, TRINITY HILL, Vidal, VILLA MARIA.

USA (California) ARAUJO, BERINGER, Bryant Family, CAKEBREAD, CAYMUS, CHIMNEY ROCK, CORISON, DALLA VALLE, DIAMOND CREEK, DOMINUS, DUNN, Grace Family, HARLAN, HARTWELL, Ladera, LAUREL GLEN, LONG MEADOW RANCH, Peter MICHAEL, MINER, NEWTON, Oakville Ranch, PHELPS, RIDGE, ST SUPÉRY, SCREAMING EAGLE, SHAFER, SILVER OAK, SPOTTSWOODE, STAG'S LEAP, Terra Valentine, Titus, VIADER; *(Washington)* ANDREW WILL, CADENCE, CORLISS ESTATES, DELILLE CELLARS, DUNHAM, Fidelitas, JANUIK, LEONETTI, QUILCEDA CREEK, Three Rivers, WOODWARD CANYON.

Chile ALMAVIVA, Altaïr, Aristos, CARMEN, CONCHA Y TORO, ERRÁZURIZ, HARAS DE PIRQUE, SANTA RITA, Miguel TORRES.

Argentina ATAMISQUE, CATENA ZAPATA, COBOS, KAIKEN, MENDEL, TERRAZAS DE LOS ANDES.

South Africa BEYERSKLOOF, BOEKEN-HOUTSKLOOF, BUITENVERWACHTING, De Toren, DE TRAFFORD, Neil Ellis, GRANGEHURST, KANONKOP, Le Riche, MEERLUST, RUSTENBERG, SAXENBURG, THELEMA, VERGELEGEN, Waterford.

103

CABERNET D'ANJOU AC *Loire Valley, France* Rosé made from both Cabernets: generally medium-dry or semi-sweet. Rosé d'un Jour is an alternative vin de France rosé, a riposte to commercial wines, made by several rebellious growers led by Mark Angeli; it is picked fully ripe and not chaptalized. Drink young. Best producers: M Angeli/Sansonnière, Bergerie, de Clayou, Hautes Ouches, OGEREAU, des Petites Grouas, Terrebrune.

CABERNET FRANC Cabernet Franc comes into its own in cool areas where the soil is damp and heavy. It can have a leafy freshness linked to raw but tasty blackcurrant-raspberry fruit; lighter wines drink well slightly chilled. In France it thrives in the LOIRE VALLEY, where single varietal wines are the norm. It is blended with Cabernet Sauvignon and Merlot in BORDEAUX, especially ST-ÉMILION (AUSONE, CHEVAL BLANC) and POMEROL (LAFLEUR, VIEUX-CHÂTEAU-CERTAN). Moderately successful where not overproduced in northern Italy, especially ALTO ADIGE and FRIULI – although some plantings here have turned out to be Carmenère – and increasingly preferred to Cabernet Sauvignon in Tuscany (LE MACCHIOLE's Paleo Rosso is an outstanding example). It is the red of choice for many winemakers in Canada and the eastern US, performing especially well in the FINGER LAKES, LONG ISLAND and VIRGINIA. Experiments with Cabernet Franc in WASHINGTON STATE and on CALIFORNIA's North Coast show promise, and it's at last gaining some respect in NAPA VALLEY. There are also some good South African, Argentine, Brazilian, Chilean, Australian, Spanish and Israeli examples.

CABERNET SAUVIGNON See pages 102–3.

CADENCE *Red Mountain AVA, Washington State, USA* A range of vineyard-specific reds. Tapteil Vineyard★★★, a powerful Cabernet Sauvignon-dominated blend, is the flagship; Ciel du Cheval Vineyard★★★ is more forward and juicy. Bel Canto★★, a Cabernet Franc-Merlot-dominant blend, and Camerata★★, based on Cabernet Sauvignon, are both from the estate Cara Mia Vineyard. Best years: (2012) 11 10 **09 08 07**.

CADILLAC AC *Bordeaux, France* Sweet wine from the southern half of CADILLAC-CÔTES DE BORDEAUX. Styles vary from fresh, semi-sweet to richly botrytized. The wines have greatly improved in recent years. Drink young. Best producers: Fayau (Réserve★), du Juge, Manos★, Mémoires★, REYNON★. Best years: **2011** 10 09 07 05 03 02 01.

CADILLAC-CÔTES DE BORDEAUX AC *Bordeaux, France* Formerly (pre-2008) Premières Côtes de Bordeaux. Hilly region overlooking GRAVES and SAUTERNES across the Garonne. For a long time the region was best known for its sweet wines, but the juicy reds have now forged ahead. Usually delicious at 2–3 years old, but should last for 5–6 years. Best producers: Bauduc★, Biac, Carignan★, Chelivette, Clos Chaumont, Clos Ste-Anne, Le Doyenné, Mont-Pérat★, Plaisance★, Puy-Bardens★, REYNON★, Ste-Marie (Alios★), Suau★. Best years: **2012** 10 09 08 05.

CAHORS AOP *South-West France* One of the oldest French wine regions and despite the bla-bla from South America, the virtual birthplace of the Malbec grape. All Cahors must contain at least 70% Malbec. The wines can be dark, austere but elegant, and have an unforgettable rich plum and tobacco flavour when ripe and well made. The best need aging, although many growers are now making softer wines for early drinking. Best producers: Armandière, la Caminade★, du CÈDRE★★, Clos la Coutale★, CLOS DE GAMOT★★, CLOS D'UN JOUR★, CLOS TRIGUEDINA★★, COSSE-

MAISONNEUVE★★, les Croisille★, Gaudou★, Lamartine★, Mas des Etoiles★, Mas del Périé★, du Prince, la Reyne★, les Rigalets★. Best years: (2012) (11) 10 09 **08 06 05 04 01 98.**

CAIRANNE *Rhône Valley, France* By far the best village in the CÔTES DU RHÔNE-VILLAGES appellation, home of full, lively, herb-scented reds and solid, food-friendly whites. Best producers: Alary★★, Ameillaud★, Armand, Berthet-Rayne, Brusset★, Camille Cayran, Cros de Romet, les Grands Bois, les Hautes Cances★, ORATOIRE ST-MARTIN★★, Famille Perrin★, Présidente★, Rabasse-Charavin★, M Richaud★★. Best years: (reds) **2012 11 10 09 07 06 05.**

CAKEBREAD CELLARS *Napa Valley, AVA, California, USA* Outstanding Cabernet★★ built for aging. Also a zesty Sauvignon Blanc. Best years: (reds) **2010 09 07 05 03 01.**

CALABRIA *Italy* Italy's poorest and most backward region. CIRÒ, Donnici, Savuto and Scavigna DOC reds from the native Gaglioppo grape, and whites from Greco, are much improved thanks to greater winemaking expertise. In a very restricted field the two leading producers remain Librandi – with reds Duca Sanfelice★ (Gaglioppo) and Magno Megonio★★ (Magliocco), and white Efeso★★ (Mantonico) – and Odoardi, with their very good Scavigna Vigna Garrone★. Two new names making fine artisan CIRÒ are À Vita★★ and Sergio Arcuri★.

CALABRIA FAMILY *Riverina, New South Wales, Australia* High-quality family winery. The 3 Bridges range includes a powerful yet scented Durif★ and lush, honeyed Botrytis Semillon★. There's also Calabria Bros Shiraz from a newly purchased 100-year-old BAROSSA vineyard, and an exciting range of warm-climate Italian varieties, including Nero d'Avola, Aglianico and Vermentino. Westend Cool Climate series includes Riesling from Eden Valley, Shiraz and Tempranillo from HILLTOPS and Pinot Noir from Tumbarumba. Richland is one of Australia's best budget ranges (especially Pinot Grigio and Sauvignon Blanc).

CALATAYUD DO *Aragón, Spain* Over 5000ha (12,500 acres) of old Grenache vines in the mountains between Madrid and Zaragoza: this is a recipe for vinous success that for too long went ignored as local co-ops made mostly bulk wines. Now, a number of more ambitious Spanish and foreign winemakers are making juicy, herb-scented reds which show some depth. Best producers: Albada★, Ateca★, Escocés Volante★, Bodegas y Viñedos del Jalón★, Langa, San Alejandro★, San Gregorio★.

CALERA *San Benito, California, USA* A pace-setter for California Pinot Noir with 6 estate wines: Reed★★, Selleck★★, Jensen★★, Mills★★, Ryan★ and de Villiers – complex, fascinating and capable of aging. Mt Harlan Chardonnay★ is excitingly original too. CENTRAL COAST Chardonnay★ and Pinot Noir★ are good value. Small amounts of Viognier★★ are succulent with sensuous fruit. Best years: (Pinot Noir) (2012) 11 **10 09 08 07 06 05 04 03 02 01**; (Chardonnay) (2012) **10 09 08 07 06 05 04 03 02.**

CALIFORNIA *USA* California's importance is not simply in being the fourth largest wine producer in the world (behind France, Italy and Spain). Most of the revolutions in technology and style that have transformed the expectations and achievements of winemakers in every country of the world – including France – were born in the ambitions of a band of Californian winemakers during the 1960s and 70s. They challenged the old order, with its regulated, self-serving elitism, and democratized the world of fine wine, to the benefit of every wine drinker. Other countries, notably Australia, now share the lead, and this rivalry is healthy. A few figures: there are around 216,506ha (535,000 acres) of wine grape vineyards, producing more than 20 million hectolitres (500 million gallons) of wine annually – about 90% of all wine made in the US. A large proportion (more than 75%) comes from the hot, inland CENTRAL VALLEY. See also CENTRAL COAST, MENDOCINO COUNTY, MONTEREY COUNTY, NAPA VALLEY, SAN LUIS OBISPO COUNTY, SANTA BARBARA COUNTY, SIERRA FOOTHILLS, SONOMA COUNTY.

CH. CALON-SÉGUR★★ *St-Estèphe AC, 3ème Cru Classé, Haut-Médoc, Bordeaux, France* Long considered one of ST-ESTÈPHE's leading châteaux, but in the mid-1980s the wines were not as good as they should have been. Vintages from the mid-1990s have been more impressive, with suppler, riper fruit and greater finesse since 2008. Sold in 2012, so let's hope it stays on top form. Second wine: Marquis de Calon. Best years: 2012 11 10 09 **08 07 06 05 04 03 02 01 00 98 96 95 90**.

CAMEL VALLEY *Cornwall, England* Top-quality producers of both still and sparkling wines. Best wines are Pinot-based sparklers★★: the Pinot Noir Rosé Brut★★ regularly wins top awards against international opposition. Single-vineyard Darnibole Bacchus★★ is their best still wine.

CAMPANIA *Italy* Three regions – PUGLIA, SICILY and Campania – lead the revolution in Italy's south. Campania forged ahead, above all with some excellent, characterful white varietals from Greco, Fiano, Falanghina and several other native grapes. On the red side, other producers besides the venerable MASTROBERARDINO have begun to realize the potential of Campania's soil, climate and grapes, especially with the red Aglianico when bottled as TAURASI or as Taburno DOC. DOC(G)s of note are Fiano di Avellino and Greco di Tufo for white wines, Taurasi for reds, and Falerno del Massico, Ischia and Vesuvio for whites, reds and a few rosés.

CAMPO DE BORJA DO *Aragón, Spain* Located to the south-east of RIOJA and NAVARRA, Campo de Borja boasts that its native clones of Grenache are the finest in all of Spain. Best producers: Alto Moncayo★★, Aragonesas★, Borsao★, Pagos del Moncayo.

CAMPO VIEJO *Rioja DOCa, Rioja, Spain* The largest producer of RIOJA is owned by Pernod Ricard. Tempranillo is a good modern young Rioja, packed with fresh, pastilley fruit; there's also an unoaked, 100% Viura white Rioja. Reserva and Gran Reserva★ are reliably good. The elegant Juan Alcorta Reserva (100% Tempranillo) is now made separately.

CANARY ISLANDS *Spain* The Canaries have a treasure trove of pre-phylloxera vines, reputedly Europe's highest vineyards, and a total of 9 DOs. The sweet Malvasia from Lanzarote DO and La Palma DO is worth a try, and there are a couple of remarkable fresh dry whites; otherwise stick with the juicy young reds. Best producers: El Grifo, Monje, Suertes del Marqués★★, Tacande★, Tanajara★, Teneguía★, Viñátigo★.

CANBERRA DISTRICT *New South Wales, Australia* Cool, high altitude (800m/2600ft) may sound good, but excessive cold and frost can be problematic. Even so, with global warming kicking in, the smart money is on Canberra really shining in the next decade or so. Lark Hill and Helm make exciting Riesling; Lark Hill and Brindabella Hills have some smart Cabernet blends; Mount Majura has classy Tempranillo; Collector, Nick O'Leary and Capital are making impressive Shiraz, and CLONAKILLA Shiraz is a world-beater. Best producers: Brindabella Hills★, Capital, CLONAKILLA★★★, Collector★★, Doonkuna★, Helm★, Lake George★, Lark Hill★, Madew★, Mount Majura, Nick O'Leary.

CANNONAU See GRENACHE NOIR.

CH. CANON★★ *St-Émilion Grand Cru AC, 1er Grand Cru Classé, Bordeaux, France* Canon can make some of the richest, most concentrated ST-ÉMILIONS, but was in decline before being bought in 1996 by Chanel (also owns RAUZAN-SÉGLA). Following extensive work on the vineyard and cellars it's now on succulent form. In good vintages the wine is tannic and rich at first, but is well worth aging for at least 10–15 years. Second wine: Clos Canon. Best years: 2012 11 10 09 **08 07 06 05 04 03 02 01 00 98**.

CANON-FRONSAC AC *Bordeaux, France* This AC is the heart of the FRONSAC region. The wines are quite sturdy when young but can age for 10 years or more. Best producers: Barrabaque (Prestige★), Canon-Pécresse, Cassagne Haut-Canon (La Trufière★), la Fleur Cailleau, Gaby★, Grand-Renouil★, Haut-Mazeris, Moulin Pey-Labrie★★, Pavillon, Vrai Canon Bouché★. Best years: 2012 11 **10 09 08 06 05 03 01**.

CH. CANON-LA-GAFFELIÈRE★★ *St-Émilion Grand Cru AC, 1er Grand Cru Classé, Bordeaux, France* Owner Stephan von Neipperg was finally rewarded for his efforts with promotion to Premier Grand Cru Classé in the 2012 ST-ÉMILION classification. The wines are firm, rich and concentrated. He also owns Clos de l'Oratoire★★, Ch. d'Aiguilhe★★ in CASTILLON-CÔTES DE  BORDEAUX, and the remarkable La Mondotte★★, now also a First Growth. Best years: 2012 11 10 09 **08 07 06 05 04 03 02 01 00 98**.

CH. CANTEMERLE★ *Haut-Médoc AC, 5ème Cru Classé, Bordeaux, France* With La LAGUNE, the most southerly of the Crus Classés. The wines are delicate in style and delightful (★★) in ripe vintages. Second wine: Les Allées de Cantemerle. Best years: 2012 11 10 09 **08 06 05 04 03 01 00 98 96**.

CANTERBURY/WAIPARA *South Island, New Zealand* The long, cool ripening season of the arid central coast of South Island favours white varieties, particularly Chardonnay, Pinot Gris, Sauvignon Blanc and Riesling, as well as Pinot Noir. The northerly Waipara district produces the most exciting wines, especially Riesling and Pinot Noir. Best producers: Bell Hill★★, Greystone★, Mountford★, Muddy Water★, Omihi Road, PEGASUS BAY★★, Pyramid Valley★, Waipara West★. Best years: (Pinot Noir) (2013) 12 **10 09 08 07 06**.

CAPE MENTELLE *Margaret River, Western Australia* Leading MARGARET RIVER winery, owned by LVMH, with Rob Mann providing winemaking expertise, has gone up a notch in recent times: superb cedary, gamy Cabernet★★★, impressive Shiraz★★ and Chardonnay★★, tangy Semillon-Sauvignon Blanc★★ and wonderfully chewy old-vine Zinfandel★★. Wallcliffe wines include taut Sauvignon Blanc-Semillon★★★ and concentrated Shiraz★★. Single-vineyard Wilyabrup Cabernet blend is rich and lush. All wines benefit from cellaring: whites up to 5 years, reds 8–15. Best years: (Cabernet Sauvignon) (2013) 12 11 10 09 08 07 **05 04 01**.

CAPE POINT VINEYARDS *Cape Point WO, South Africa*   Pioneering property influenced by bracing Atlantic breezes. Sauvignon Blanc (standard★, Reserve★★) is astonishing, ocean-fresh and original. Barrel-fermented Isliedh★★★ (Sauvignon Blanc-Semillon) effortlessly combines power with subtlety and good aging potential. Also elegant Chardonnay★ and rich, syrupy Late Harvest★. The Splattered Toad range offers drinkability and value. Best years: (whites) 2013 12 11 10 09 08 07 06 05.

CAPEL VALE *Geographe, Western Australia*   Winery with its own vineyards in Geographe, Mount Barker, PEMBERTON and MARGARET RIVER. Cheap and cheerful Debut range includes velvety Merlot★ and easy-drinking Pinot Noir. There's an impressive Regional Series, and three single-vineyard wines: intense yet fine Whispering Hill Riesling★★, elegant, powerful Whispering Hill Shiraz★★ and structured 'The Scholar' Cabernet Sauvignon★ from youngish vines in Margaret River. Best years: (Whispering Hill Riesling) 2013 12 11 10 09 08 07 06 04 03 02 01 00 98 97.

CARIGNAN   The dominant red grape in the south of France is responsible for much boring, cheap, harsh wine. But when made gently or by carbonic maceration, the wine can have delicious spicy fruit. Old vines are capable of dense, tarry, rich, impressive reds, and catch the attention of trend-setting drinkers around the world, with increasing successes in southern France, California, Lebanon, Israel and especially in Chile's Maule Valley, where dry-grown old-vine Carignan is making a serious comeback. In South Africa it is mainly used in Rhône-style blends. Although initially a Spanish grape (as Cariñena or Mazuelo), it is not that widespread there, but is useful for adding colour and acidity in RIOJA and CATALUÑA, and has gained unexpected respect in PRIORAT (some stunning cuvées from Saó del Coster, TORRES, Ferrer Bobet and TERROIR AL LIMIT). In south-west Sardinia it is behind some excellent wines, including Santadi's CARIGNANO DEL SULCIS.

CARIGNANO DEL SULCIS DOC *Sardinia, Italy*   Carignano is capable of producing wines of quite startling quality, as is demonstrated mainly by the excellent Santadi co-op, whose Rocca Rubia★, a barrique-aged Riserva with rich, fleshy and chocolaty fruit, is one of Italy's best-value reds. Baie Rosse★★ is a step up; even better is the more structured and concentrated Terre Brune★★. Best years: (2011) 10 09 08 07 06.

CARILLON *Puligny-Montrachet, Côte de Beaune, Burgundy, France*   Louis Carillon's excellent family-owned estate was split between sons Jacques and François from the 2010 vintage. Jacques was responsible for vinification at the family domaine; expect continuity of style under his own label, with delicious and affordable wines but rather less of them. Look out for PULIGNY-MONTRACHET Champs Canet★★ and Referts★★. Younger son François was responsible for the vineyards but clearly has great ambitions now he is on his own. Look out for Premiers Crus Combettes★★ and Perrières★★. Best years: (whites) (2013) 12 11 10 09 08 07 06 05 04 02.

CARIÑENA DO *Aragón, Spain*   The largest DO of ARAGÓN, baking under the mercilessly hot sun of inland eastern Spain, Cariñena has traditionally been a land of cheap, deep red, alcoholic wines from the Garnacha grape. (Confusingly the Carignan grape is called Cariñena in Spain, but accounts for only about 1% of the surface in the Cariñena region.) Since the late 1990s, however, temperature-controlled fermentation has been working wonders with the Garnacha, and Tempranillo and international grape varieties like Cabernet Sauvignon have been planted widely. Best producers: Añadas★, Monfil, Pablo★★, San Valero (Monte Ducay, Don Mendo), Solar de Urbezo★.

CARMEN *Maipo, Chile* Some of the best reds in MAIPO, including Gold Reserve★★, a limited release made with 58-year-old Cabernet Sauvignon vines, balanced, complex Winemaker's Reserve★★ and Reserva Merlot★★. Organic Nativa range (Cabernet Sauvignon★★) is now made separately. Best years: (reds) 2010 09 **07 05 03 01 99**.

CARMENÈRE An important but forgotten constituent of BORDEAUX blends in the 19th century, historically known as Grande Vidure. Widely planted in Chile, where it thrives on the warm climate and long growing season, it is sold under its own name or mixed with Merlot and Cabernet to greatly improve the blend. When ripe and made with care, it has rich blackberry, plum and spice flavours, with an unexpected but delicious bunch of savoury characters – grilled meat, soy sauce, celery, coffee bean – thrown in. Also found in northern Italy – where it has been confused with Cabernet Franc – Argentina, and China, where is it known as Cabernet Gernischt. Being replanted experimentally in Bordeaux.

CARMIGNANO DOCG *Tuscany, Italy* Red wine from the west of Florence, renowned since the 16th century and revived in the 1970s by Capezzana. The blend (Sangiovese, plus 10–20% Cabernet) gives one of Tuscany's more refined wines and can be quite long-lived. Although Carmignano is DOCG, DOC applies to a lighter red Barco Reale, rosé Vin Ruspo and fine VIN SANTO. Best producers: Ambra★ (Vigne Alte★★), Artimino★, Capezzana★★, Piaggia★★, Pratesi★, Villa di Trefiano★. Best years: (2011) **10 09 08 07 06 04 03 02 01**.

CARNEROS AVA *California, USA* Hugging the northern edge of San Francisco Bay, Carneros includes parts of NAPA and SONOMA Counties. Cool and windswept, with morning fog off the Bay, it is a top temperate area, suitable for Chardonnay and Pinot Noir as table wine and as a base for sparkling wine. Merlot and Syrah can also be exciting. Best producers: Ancien★, Artesa★, Buena Vista★, Carneros Creek★, DOMAINE CARNEROS★, Gloria Ferrer★, HdV★★, RAMEY★★, RASMUSSEN★★, SAINTSBURY★★, Tor (Las Madres Syrah★★), Truchard★★. Best years: (Pinot Noir) (2012) **11 10 09 08 07 06 05 04 03 02 01**.

CARNUNTUM *Niederösterreich, Austria* 910ha (2250-acre) region south of the Danube and east of Vienna, with sturdy Grüner Veltliner and a strong red wine tradition. Best producers: Artner★, Glatzer★, Grassl★, Markowitsch★, Netzl★.

CARSO DOC *Friuli-Venezia Giulia, Italy* Compelling if small strip of viticultural land producing fabulous wines, squeezed between the Adriatic sea and the Slovenian border, near Trieste. Fascinating Vitovska and Malvasia Istriana whites; the grape must is generally macerated on its skins. Also very good reds from the Terrano grape. Best producers: Edi Kante★, Skerk★, Vodopivec★, Zidarich★★. Best years: (2012) **11 10 09 08 07 06**.

CASA MARÍN *San Antonio, Chile* Impressive whites, led by single-vineyard Sauvignon Blancs: Laurel★★ is powerful, full of mineral and intense chilli and fruit flavours; Cipreses★★★ shows the influence of the Pacific Ocean in its haunting citrus and stony aromas. Casona Vineyard Gewürztraminer★, Miramar Riesling★, Late Harvest Riesling and Estero

Sauvignon Gris★★ are delightful too. Reds include juicy, cool-climate Lo Abarca Pinot Noir★★ and the outstanding Miramar Syrah★★★.

CASA SILVA *Colchagua, Chile* Well-run family dynasty heavily involved in the local *huaso* (horsemen) culture and protectors of COLCHAGUA style, especially with Carmenère. Much development in sub-regions such as Los Lingues, Lolol and Paredones, where they make the crisp, salty 'Cool Coast' Sauvignon Blanc★. Best wines include Los Lingues Gran Terroir Carmenère★, Edición Limitada Petit Verdot★ and red Quinta Generación★.

CASABLANCA *Chile* Coastal valley with a cool-climate personality. Whites dominate, with best results from Sauvignon Blanc, Chardonnay and Gewürztraminer. That said, the Pinot Noir is some of Chile's best, and some producers make top-quality cool-climate Syrah. **Best producers:** Viña CASABLANCA★, CASAS DEL BOSQUE★, CONCHA Y TORO★★, CONO SUR★★, EMILIANA★, ERRÁZURIZ★, Kingston★, LOMA LARGA★, MONTES★, Montsecano★, Quintay★, Veramonte.

VIÑA CASABLANCA *Casablanca, Chile* Cool CASABLANCA vineyards are the source of some top wines under the Nimbus label – quince-edged Chardonnay★, lychee-scented Gewürztraminer★ and tangy Sauvignon Blanc★ – as well as flagship red blend Neblus★. Inky-black Cabernet Sauvignon★ (from MAIPO) and fragrant Merlot★ (from COLCHAGUA).

CASAS DEL BOSQUE *Casablanca, Chile* This winery has a special focus on Sauvignon Blanc★ (Reserva★★) with Kiwi winemaker Grant Phelps. The reds are good too, especially the red blend Estate Selection★ and Pinot Noir★.

CASE BASSE *Brunello di Montalcino DOCG, Tuscany, Italy* Gianfranco Soldera unblushingly proclaims his BRUNELLO DI MONTALCINO★★★ (Riserva★★★) wines to be the best of their genre and, to be frank, he's pretty much right. A fanatical biodynamist, Soldera believes perfect grapes are all you need to make great wine. He ages his wines for a minimum of 5 years in large old (and hence neutral) oak barrels; the result is a wine of brilliant colour, amazing intensity and complexity of perfumes. Disaster struck in December 2012 when vandals destroyed ten large barrels containing six vintages of wine: 2007–12. Best years: 2006 **04 01 99 98 97 95 93 90 88 85**.

DOM. LA CASENOVE *Côtes Catalanes IGP, Roussillon, France* Former photojournalist Étienne Montès, with consultant enologist Jean-Luc COLOMBO, has developed an impressive range, including MUSCAT DE RIVESALTES★, RIVESALTES★ and CÔTES CATALANES whites and reds: a perfumed white Les Clares (Grenache Blanc-Roussanne), red La Garrigue★★ and Commandant François Jaubert★★ (100% Syrah). Drink the latter with at least 5 years' bottle age. Best years: (François Jaubert) **2009 08 07 06 05**.

CASSIS AC *Provence, France* A picturesque fishing port near Marseille. The white wine, based on Ugni Blanc and Clairette, is overpriced but can be good if fresh. Light red wine; the rosé can be pleasant. **Best producers:** Bagnol★, Barbanau, Clos Ste-Magdeleine★, la Ferme Blanche★, Fontblanche, Fontcreuse, Mas de Boudard.

DOM. DU CASTEL *Judean Hills, Israel* The Grand Vin★ is a complex and refined BORDEAUX blend from Jerusalem vineyards. Fruit-forward Petit Castel second label and barrel-fermented 'C' Blanc de Castel★★ (100% Chardonnay). New dry Rosé. Best years: (reds) 2011 **10 09 08 07 06**.

CASTEL DEL MONTE DOC *Puglia, Italy* An arid, hilly zone, and an ideal habitat for the Uva di Troia grape, producing long-lived red wine of occasionally astonishing character. There is also varietal Aglianico, some good rosé, and the whites produced from international varieties are improving. Best producers: Rivera★, Santa Lucía, Tormaresca★/ANTINORI, Torrevento★. Best years: (2012) 11 10 09 08 07 06 04 01.

CASTELL *Castell, Franken, Germany* Since medieval times the Castell family has owned the town of that name and its vineyards. The dry Silvaners and Rieslings are exemplary, especially from Casteller Schlossberg★★. Occasional powerful TBA★★ too. Best years: (2013) 12 11 09 08 06.

CASTILLA-LA MANCHA *Spain* The DOs of the central plateau, LA MANCHA and VALDEPEÑAS, make white wines from the Airén grape, and some good reds from the Cencibel (Tempranillo). Fast-improving reds and whites from Méntrida DO, MANCHUELA DO, Ribera del Júcar DO, Almansa DO and Uclés DO, as well as several single-estate (*pago*) appellations, plus a number of quality wines under the generic Vinos de la Tierra de Castilla appellation. The most ambitious single-estate wines made here are those from MARQUES DE GRIÑON's Dominio de Valdepusa★ estate near the Tagus river; the Dehesa del Carrizal and Pago de Vallegarcía★ estates, both in the Toledo mountains; Manuel Manzaneque's Cabernet-based reds and Chardonnay★ from Sierra de Alcaraz in Albacete province; and Uribes Madero's elegant Calzadilla reds★ in Cuenca province. Manzaneque and Calzadilla now have their own DOs, Finca Élez and Pago Calzadilla, as do the Dominio de Valdepusa and Dehesa del Carrizal. Other top wines are Ercavio★ and La Plazuela★★ from Toledo, Ampelos★ from VT Castilla, Adaras from Almansa, Arrayán, Canopy★ and Jiménez-Landi★★ from Méntrida.

CASTILLA Y LEÓN *Spain* This is Spain's harsh, high plateau, with long cold winters and hot summers (but always cool nights). A few rivers, notably the Duero, temper this climate and afford fine conditions for viticulture. After many decades of winemaking ignorance, with a few exceptions like VEGA SICILIA, the situation has changed radically for the better in all of the region's DOs. In addition to RIBERA DEL DUERO, RUEDA, BIERZO, Cigales and TORO, there is now a bevy of new appellations which were approved in 2009, in coincidence with new EU regulations, covering quality viticultural areas formerly lumped together under the vino de la tierra umbrella: Arlanza, Arribes, Tierra de León, Tierra del Vino de Zamora, Valles de Benavente and Valtiendas. Dynamic winemakers such as Telmo RODRIGUEZ and Mariano García (AALTO and MAURO) have won huge critical acclaim for the region.

CASTILLON-CÔTES DE BORDEAUX AC *Bordeaux, France* Area east of ST-ÉMILION that has surged in quality recently: part of Côtes de Bordeaux AC from 2008. The best wines are full and firm, yet have the lushness of St-Émilion without the high prices, though they are no longer cheap. Best producers: Dom. de l'A★★, Aiguilhe★★, Belcier, Cap-de-Faugères★, la Clarière Laithwaite★, Clos l'Eglise★, Clos Les Lunelles★, Clos Puy Arnaud★★, Côte-Montpezat★, Joanin Bécot★, Montlandrie★, Poupille★, Robin★, Veyry★, Vieux-Ch.-Champs-de-Mars★. Best years: 2012 10 09 08 06 05 04 03 02 01.

CATALUÑA *Spain* Standards vary among the region's DOs. PENEDÉS, between Barcelona and Tarragona, has the greatest number of technically equipped wineries in Spain, but doesn't make a commensurate number of superior wines. In the south, mountainous PRIORAT has become a new icon for its heady, raging reds, and the neighbouring DOs of Montsant and Terra Alta are following in its footsteps, albeit more affordably, with top wines from

Acústic, Joan d'Anguera★, Celler de Capçanes★, Espectacle★★, Europvin Falset★, Venus La Universal★ (Montsant), Bàrbara Forés★ and Celler Piñol★★ (Terra Alta). Inland COSTERS DEL SEGRE and Conca de Barberá, with top natural wine producer Escoda Sanahuja, make potentially excellent reds and whites. Up the coast, Alella makes attractive whites and Empordá-Costa Brava, by the French border, is improving noticeably. Cataluña also makes most of Spain's CAVA sparkling wines. The Catalunya DO allows (generally) inexpensive blends from anywhere in the region.

CATENA ZAPATA *Mendoza, Argentina* Owner Nicolás Catena and his daughter Laura keep Catena Zapata at the forefront of the Argentine wine industry. Mid-priced wines under the Alamos label are hugely successful. The winery also owns some of the best vineyards in the best *terroirs* of MENDOZA, where fruit for creamy Alta Chardonnay★★, superripe Alta Malbec★ and blackcurranty Alta Cabernet Sauvignon★★ is grown. Nicolás Catena Zapata★★ (sometimes ★★★) is a masterpiece based on Cabernet, and recent releases of Malbec Argentino★★ are thrilling. Very impressive single-vineyard Malbecs Adrianna★★ and Nicasia★★; White Bones★★ and White Stones★★ (from the Adrianna vineyard) are some of Argentina's best Chardonnays. Best years: (top reds) 2010 09 **08** 07 06.

SYLVAIN CATHIARD *Vosne-Romanée, Côte de Nuits, Burgundy, France* Sylvain Cathiard achieved international recognition in the late 1990s and has made brilliant wines, even in difficult vintages, since then. Son Sébastien took over from 2011. The stars are VOSNE-ROMANÉE Aux Malconsorts★★★ and ROMANÉE-ST-VIVANT★★★, but his village Vosne-Romanée★★ and NUITS-ST-GEORGES Aux Murgers★★ are excellent too. Best years: (2013) 12 11 10 09 **08** 07 06 05 03 02 00 99.

DOM. CAUHAPÉ *Jurançon AOP, South-West France* Henri Ramonteu is the largest as well as the best-known producer in JURANÇON, his complex dry whites equalling in quality his more traditional sweet wines. The dry Chant des Vignes★ and Geyser★ are raised in tank; Sève d'Automne★ is skilfully oaked. The top dry is La Canopée★★, the best sweets Noblesse du Temps★★ and the fabulous barrel-fermented Quintessence★★★. Best years: (sweet) (2012) 11 **10** 07 05 04 03.

DOMAINE
CAUHAPÉ
H. Ramonteu

2010
Noblesse du Temps
JURANÇON

DOM. DE CAUSSE MARINES *Gaillac AOP, South-West France* Patrice Lescarret continues to plough his eccentric GAILLAC furrows: famously his splendid but expensive sweet wines★★ using the rare Ondenc grape, a dry sparkler called Préambulles and his red Peyrouzelles from young vines. Best years: (2012) 11 10 09 07 05 03.

CAVA DO *Spain* Cava, the Catalan name for CHAMPAGNE-method fizz, is made throughout Spain, but most comes from CATALUÑA. Grapes are the local trio of Parellada, Macabeo and Xarel-lo, although some good Cavas in Cataluña as well as VALENCIA include Chardonnay and Pinot Noir in their blends. The best-value, fruitiest Cavas are generally the youngest, with no more than the minimum 9 months' aging, although top producers such as Gramona and Recaredo are developing ambitious, long-lived, Xarel-lo-based wines. The top Cavas are seldom seen abroad, since their prices are too close to those of Champagne to attract international customers. An exodus of sparkling producers to still-wine appellations such as PENEDÈS, accelerated in 2012 with the departure of Raventós i Blanc. These producers are protesting the downmarket strategy of the Cava DO. Best producers: Can Feixes, Can Ràfols dels Caus★, Castell de Vilarnau, Castellblanch, CODORNÍU★, FREIXENET, Gramona★★, Jané Ventura, Juvé y Camps, Marqués de Monistrol, Parxet★, RAÏMAT, Raventós i Blanc, Recaredo★★★, Rovellats, Signat★, Agustí Torelló★, Dominio de la Vega.

CAYMUS VINEYARDS *Napa Valley AVA, California, USA* Caymus Cabernet Sauvignon★ is ripe, intense and generally tannic; it can be outstanding as a Special Selection★★★. Conundrum★ (sometimes ★★) is an exotic, full-flavoured white blend. Also successful MONTEREY Chardonnay under the Mer Soleil★ label. Best years: (Special Selection) (2012) (11) **10 09 08 07 06 05 04 03 02 01 00 99 98 97 95 94 91**.

CAYUSE VINEYARDS *Walla Walla Valley AVA, Washington State, USA* Cult label created by French winemaker Christophe Baron. His superb Viognier★★★ is crisp, floral and spicy, yet he is best known for his Syrahs. Using French clones, he farms a vineyard reminiscent of some in CHATEAUNEUF-DU-PAPE for its large stones. Vineyard-designated Syrahs include Cailloux★★, with a distinctive mineral flavour and chocolate depth, and En Cerise★★, with more cherry and raspberry richness. The Bionic Frog★★ reminds me of a northern RHÔNE Syrah. Camaspelo★ is a fascinating Cabernet-based red. Best years: (Syrah) (2012) 11 10 **09 08**.

DOM. CAZES *Rivesaltes AC, Roussillon, France* The Cazes family produce outstanding MUSCAT DE RIVESALTES★★, RIVESALTES Tuilé★★ and superb Rivesaltes Aimé Cazes★★, and also a range of table wines. Soft red, white and rosé Le Canon du Maréchal★ are good, as are the CÔTES DU ROUSSILLON-VILLAGES Syrah-Grenache-Mourvèdre blends Ego★, Alter★ and Le Credo★★, and COLLIOURE Notre Dame des Anges★. Also intriguing white Libre Expression★ from Macabeo. One of the largest organic vineyard holdings in France; recently bought Clos de Paulilles.

CH. DU CÈDRE *Cahors AOP, South-West France* The brothers Verhaeghe lead the generation of modern CAHORS winemakers. Their wines are dark and richly textured, with a generous coating of chocolaty oak. The entry-level Ch. du Cèdre★★ is the most approachable; Le Cèdre, which is 100% Malbec, aged in new barrels for 20 months, and GC★, which is fermented in oak as well, need considerable aging. Also a tasty white IGP wine from Viognier. Best years: (2012) 11 10 **09 08 06 04 03 01**.

CENCIBEL See TEMPRANILLO.

CENTRAL COAST AVA *California, USA* Huge AVA covering virtually every vineyard between San Francisco and Los Angeles, with a number of sub-AVAs such as SANTA CRUZ MOUNTAINS, Santa Ynez Valley, SANTA MARIA VALLEY and Santa Lucia Highlands in MONTEREY COUNTY. See also SAN LUIS OBISPO COUNTY, SANTA BARBARA COUNTY.

CENTRAL OTAGO *South Island, New Zealand* The only wine region in New Zealand with a continental rather than maritime climate. Third largest region in vineyard area but fourth, after GISBORNE, in terms of production. Most of the vineyards are clustered in Gibbston Valley, or in the slightly warmer area around Lake Dunstan. Technically the ripening season is long and cool, suiting Pinot Noir, Gewürztraminer, Chardonnay and Pinot Gris, but there are usually periods of considerable heat during the summer to intensify flavour – and particularly in warm zones like Bendigo. Long autumns have produced some excellent Rieslings. There are nearly 100 wine producers and an explosion of plantings, both in good areas like Bannockburn and Lowburn, and in marginal zones. Best producers: Akarua★, Burn Cottage★★, Carrick★, Chard Farm★, Domain Road★, FELTON ROAD★★★, Gibbston Valley★, Kawarau Estate★, Mt Difficulty★★, Mount Edward★★, Mount Maude★, Mud House★★, Nevis Bluff, Peregrine★★, Pisa Range★, Prophet's Rock★, QUARTZ REEF★★, Rippon★★, Tarras★, Two Paddocks★, Wild Earth★. Best years: (Pinot Noir) (2013) 12 **10 09 08 07 06 05 03 02**.

CENTRAL VALLEY *California, USA* This vast area grows 75% of California's wine grapes, used mostly for cheap wine, brandies and grape concentrate. It is a hot area, where irrigated vineyards tend to produce excess tonnages of grapes. In fact, the climatic conditions in the northern half – especially LODI – are not unlike those in many parts of Spain and southern France and, viewed overall, quality has improved in recent years. Other sub-regions with claims to quality include the Sacramento Delta area, and especially Clarksburg. Best producers: BOGLE, Ficklin, R H Phillips, Quady.

CENTRAL VALLEY *Chile* (Bottles in Europe may have Valle Central on the label.) The heart of Chile's wine industry, and an appellation encompassing the valleys of MAIPO, RAPEL, CURICÓ and MAULE; many major producers are located here. The key factor determining mesoclimate differences is the distance relative to the Coastal Ranges and the Andes Mountains: the closer you get to the mountains, the cooler you are.

CENTRAL VICTORIA *Victoria, Australia* This zone comprises the regions of BENDIGO, HEATHCOTE, Goulburn Valley and the cooler Strathbogie Ranges and Upper Goulburn. Central Victoria, with its mostly warm conditions, produces powerful and individual wines. The few wineries on the banks of the Goulburn River feature fine Shiraz and Marsanne; reds from the high country are rich but scented and dry, with Heathcote excelling for texture and taste; whites are delicate and scented. Best producers: Fowles★, Heathcote Estate★★, Heathcote Winery★★, Jasper Hill★★★, Mitchelton★, Paul Osicka★, Pondalowie★, TAHBILK★, Wild Duck Creek★.

CÉRONS AC *Bordeaux, France* Sweet, soft, mildly honeyed wine from the GRAVES region of Bordeaux – not quite as sweet as SAUTERNES and not so well known, nor so highly priced. Most producers now make dry wine under the Graves AC. Best producers: Ch. de Cérons★, Chantegrive★, Grand Enclos du Château de Cérons★, Haura★, Seuil★. Best years: **2011 10 09 07 05 03 02 01**.

L A CETTO *Baja California, Mexico* One of Mexico's most successful wineries; it relies on mists and cooling Pacific breezes to temper the heat of the Valle de Guadalupe in the northern part of Baja California. Italian Camillo Magoni makes ripe, fleshy Petite Sirah★, oak-aged Cabernet Sauvignon, Zinfandel and Nebbiolo. Chardonnay and Chenin Blanc lead the whites. Also good fizz.

CHABLAIS *Vaud, Switzerland* A sub-region of the VAUD, south-east of Lake Geneva along the right bank of the Rhône. Most of the thirst-quenchingly dry whites are made from Chasselas. The reds are from Pinot Noir, as is a rosé speciality, Oeil de Perdrix. Best producers: Badoux, la Baudelière, Conne, Dillet, J & P Testuz★.

CHABLIS AC *Burgundy, France* Chablis, lying closer to CHAMPAGNE than to the COTE D'OR, is Burgundy's northernmost outpost. When not destroyed by frost or hail, the Chardonnay grape makes a crisp, dry white wine with a steely mineral fruit, which can be delicious. Several producers have taken to barrel-aging for their better wines, resulting in some full, toasty, positively rich dry whites. Others are intentionally producing a soft, creamy, early-drinking style, which is nice but not really typical Chablis. Outlying vineyards come under the Petit Chablis AC and these wines are becoming very good but should be drunk young. The better straight Chablis AC should be drunk at 2–4 years, while a good vintage of a leading Chablis Premier Cru may take 5 years to show its full potential. About a quarter of Chablis is designated as Premier Cru, the best vineyards on the rolling limestone slopes being Fourchaume, Mont de Milieu, Montmains, Montée de Tonnerre and Vaillons. **Best producers:** Barat★, J-C Bessin (Fourchaume★★), S Billaud★, Billaud-Simon★ (Mont de Milieu★★), P Bouchard★, A & F Boudin★★, J-M BROCARD★, la CHABLISIENNE★, Collet★, D Dampt★, V DAUVISSAT★★, Droin★, DROUHIN★, Duplessis★, Durup★, N & G Fèvre★, W Fèvre★★, J-P Grossot (Côte de Troesme★★), LAROCHE★★, Long-Depaquit, Malandes (Côte de Léchêt★★), Louis Michel★, de Moor★, Christian Moreau★★, Moreau-Naudet★★, Picq (Vaucoupin★★), Pinson★, Piuze★, RAVENEAU★★, les Temps Perdus, Vocoret★★. **Best years:** (Chablis Premier Cru) 2012 **10** 09 08 07 05 02 00.

CHABLIS GRAND CRU AC *Burgundy, France* The 7 Grands Crus (Bougros, les Preuses, Vaudésir, Grenouilles, Valmur, les Clos and les Blanchots) facing south-west across the town of Chablis are the heart of the Chablis vineyards. Oak barrel aging takes the edge off taut flavours, adding a rich warmth to these fine wines. Droin and Fèvre are the most enthusiastic users of new oak, but use it less than they used to. Never drink young: 5–10 years are needed before you can see why you spent your money. **Best producers:** J-C Bessin★★, Billaud-Simon★★, P Bouchard★, J-M BROCARD★★, la CHABLISIENNE★★, V DAUVISSAT★★★, Droin★, W Fèvre★★★, LAROCHE★★, Long-Depaquit★★, Louis Michel★★, Christian Moreau★★★, Moreau-Naudet★★, Pinson★★, RAVENEAU★★★, Servin★, Vocoret★★. **Best years:** (2013) 12 11 10 09 08 **07 06** 05 **02 00** 99 98 96 95 90.

LA CHABLISIENNE *Chablis, Burgundy, France* Substantial and reliable co-op producing nearly a third of all CHABLIS. The best are the oaky Grands Crus – especially les Preuses★★ and Grenouilles (sold as Ch. Grenouilles★★) – but the basic unoaked Chablis★, the Vieilles Vignes★★ and the numerous Premiers Crus★ are good, as is the red BOURGOGNE Épineuil. Makes a wide array of 'own-label' wines, sometimes a bit soft. **Best years:** (whites) 2012 **10** 09 08 07.

BODEGA CHACRA *Río Negro, Patagonia, Argentina* Small but beautiful biodynamic winery run by Hans Vinding-Diers, of nearby NOEMÍA. Barda★, Cincuenta y Cinco★ and Treinta y Dos★ ('55' and '32', from the dates the vines were planted) are the best examples of Pinot Noir in this once-proud old region. The Mainqué★ Merlot completes the range from these old vineyards.The wines from 2010 are outstanding.

CHADDSFORD WINERY *Pennsylvania, USA* This winery has gained a following across the US since its founding in 1982. Mainly Cabernet Sauvignon and Merlot, both as varietals and for red blend Merican. Proprietors Reserve is a juicy picnic red from Chambourcin. Chardonnays★ can be powerful and elegant.

CHAMBERS *Rutherglen, Victoria, Australia* Legendary family winery making sheer nectar in the form of Muscat and Muscadelle (Tokay). The secret of success is their ability to draw on ancient stocks put down in wood by earlier generations. The Grand★★ and Rare★★★ blends are national treasures. Cabernet and Shiraz table wines are good.

CHAMPAGNE AC

The Champagne region produces the most celebrated sparkling wines in the world. It is the most northerly AC in France – a place where (even with the advent of global warming) grapes struggle to ripen fully, but provide the perfect base wine to make fizz. Champagne is divided into 5 distinct areas – the best are the Montagne de Reims, where the Pinot Noir grape performs brilliantly, and the Chardonnay-dominated Côte des Blancs, south of Épernay. In addition to Chardonnay and Pinot Noir, the other main grape permitted for the production of Champagne is Pinot Meunier.

The wines undergo a second fermentation in the bottle, producing carbon dioxide which dissolves in the wine under pressure. Through this method Champagne acquires its crisp, long-lasting bubbles and a distinctive yeasty, toasty dimension to its flavour, becoming one of the most delightfully exhilarating wines of all.

That's the theory anyway, and for 150 years or so the Champenois have persuaded us that their product is second to none. It can be, too, except when it is released too young or sweetened to cover up a sour unripeness. Fortunately, among the more serious producers, there is a return to the practice of blending 'reserve' wines – from previous vintages, softened by age – into the cuvée, creating more balanced, and indeed drier, wines of often excellent quality. Champagne expertise now turns out excellent fizz all around the globe – especially in California, Australia, New Zealand and England.

The Champagne trade is dominated by large companies or houses, called négociants-manipulants, recognized by the letters NM on the label. The récolants-manipulants (RM) are growers who make their own wine, and they are becoming increasingly important for drinkers seeking characterful Champagne.

STYLES OF CHAMPAGNE

Non-vintage Most Champagne is a blend of 2 or more vintages. Quality varies enormously, depending on who has made the wine and how long it has been aged. Brut is a dry, but rarely bone-dry, style. More completely dry styles – called things like Brut Zéro, Brut Sauvage or Extra Brut – are appearing and tasting good, primarily because climate change is providing riper grapes that don't need sugar to hide their rawness. Strangely, Extra Dry denotes a style less dry than Brut.

Vintage Denotes Champagne made with grapes from a single harvest. As a rule, it is made only in the best years, but nowadays you'll find some vintage releases in all but the worst years.

Blanc de Blancs A lighter, and at best highly elegant, style of Champagne made solely from the Chardonnay grape.

Blanc de Noirs White Champagne, fuller in style, made entirely from black grapes, either Pinot Noir, Pinot Meunier, or a combination of the two.

Rosé Pink Champagne, made either from black grapes or (more usually) by mixing a little still red wine into white Champagne.

De luxe cuvée In theory, the finest Champagne and certainly always the most expensive, residing in the fanciest bottles.

See also CHAMPAGNE ROSÉ; and individual producers.

BEST PRODUCERS

Houses BILLECART-SALMON, BOLLINGER, Cattier, Delamotte, DEUTZ, Drappier, DUVAL-LEROY, GOSSET, Alfred GRATIEN, Charles HEIDSIECK, HENRIOT, JACQUESSON, KRUG, LANSON, LAURENT-PERRIER, Bruno PAILLARD, Joseph PERRIER, PERRIER-JOUET, PHILIPPONNAT, PIPER-HEIDSIECK, POL ROGER, POMMERY, Louis ROEDERER, RUINART, Salon, TAITTINGER, Thienot, VEUVE CLICQUOT.

Growers Agrapart, Michel Arnould, Barnaut, Françoise Bedel, Bérèche, Franck Bonville, Cédric Bouchard, Francis Boulard, Roger Brun, Claude Cazals, Chartogne-Taillet, Gaston Chiquet, Dehours, Paul Déthune, Diebolt-Vallois, Egly-Ouriet, René Geoffroy, Gimonnet, Henri Giraud, H Goutorbe, André Jacquart, Benoît Lahaye, Laherte Frères, Larmandier, Larmandier-Bernier, Jacques Lassaigne, Georges Laval, David Léclapart, R&L Legras, Lilbert, Maillart, Margaine, Marguet, Serge Mathieu, Bruno Michel, Moncuit, Franck Pascal, Pierre Péters, R Pouillon, Jérôme Prévost, Alain Robert, Jacques Selosse, Tarlant, G Tribaut, J-L Vergnon, Vilmart.

Co-ops Beaumont des Crayères, H Blin, Nicolas Feuillatte, Jacquart, Mailly, Le Mesnil, Union Champagne.

De luxe cuvées Belle Époque (PERRIER-JOUET), N-F Billecart (BILLECART-SALMON), Blanc de Millénaires (Charles HEIDSIECK), Celebris (GOSSET), Clos des Goisses (PHILIPPONNAT), Clos de Mesnil (KRUG), Comtes de Champagne (TAITTINGER), Cristal (Louis ROEDERER), Dom Pérignon (MOËT & CHANDON), Dom Ruinart (RUINART), Femme (DUVAL-LEROY), Grand Siècle (LAURENT-PERRIER), Grande Dame (VEUVE CLICQUOT), Josephine (Joseph PERRIER), Noble Cuvée (LANSON), RD (BOLLINGER), Sir Winston Churchill (POL ROGER), William Deutz (DEUTZ).

CHAMBERTIN AC *Grand Cru, Côte de Nuits, Burgundy, France* The village of GEVREY-CHAMBERTIN, the largest CÔTE DE NUITS commune, has no fewer than 9 Grands Crus (Chambertin, Chambertin-Clos-de-Bèze, Chapelle-Chambertin, Charmes-Chambertin, Griotte-Chambertin, Latricières-Chambertin, Mazis-Chambertin, Ruchottes-Chambertin and the rarely seen Mazoyères-Chambertin), which can produce some of Burgundy's greatest and most intense red wine. Its rough-hewn fruit, seeming to war with fragrant perfumes for its first few years, creates remarkable flavours as the wine ages. Chambertin and Clos-de-Bèze are neighbours on the slope above the village and the two greatest sites. Best producers: (Chambertin) LEROY★★★, MORTET★★★, J Prieur★, Rossignol-Trapet★★★, ROUSSEAU★★★, Trapet★★★; (Clos-de-Bèze) CLAIR★★★, Damoy★★★, FAIVELEY★★★, F Magnien★★, Prieuré-Roch★★, ROUSSEAU★★★; (other Grands Crus) BACHELET★★, Bernstein★★, Bize★★, Confuron-Cotetidot★★, Damoy★★, DROUHIN★★, Dugat★★, Dugat-Py★★, Duroché★★, FAIVELEY★★, J-M Fourrier★★, HOSPICES DE BEAUNE★★, LEROY★★, Maume★★, MUGNERET-GIBOURG★★, Perrot-Minot★★, Ponsot★★, Rossignol-Trapet★★, Roty★★, ROUMIER★★, ROUSSEAU★★, Trapet★★, Tremblay★★, VOUGERAIE★★. Best years: (2013) 12 11 10 09 08 **07** 06 05 **03 02** 01 99 98 96 93 90.

CHAMBOLLE-MUSIGNY AC *Côte de Nuits, Burgundy, France* Can produce the most fragrant, perfumed red Burgundy when in good hands – and, encouragingly, standards in the village are high. More young producers are now bottling their own wines. Best producers: Amiot-Servelle★★, G Barthod★★, Digioia-Royer★, DROUHIN★★, DUJAC★★, Felletig★, R Groffier★★, Hudelot-Baillet★, Hudelot-NOËLLAT★★, JADOT★★, Dom. LEROY★★, F Magnien★, J-F MUGNIER★★, RION★★, ROUMIER★★, Sigaut★, de VOGÜÉ★★. Best years: (2013) 12 11 10 09 **08 07** 05 **03 02** 00 99 98 96 95 93 90.

CHAMONIX *Franschhoek WO, South Africa* Recognized for seamlessly oaked, long-lived Chardonnays: citrus/creamy standard★★ and rich yet lean and ageworthy Reserve★★. Barrel-fermented Sauvignon Blanc Reserve★ shows both richness and cool minerals; new white Reserve★★ is a textured Sauvignon Blanc-Semillon blend. Reds are led by pure-fruited, silky Pinot Noir Reserve★★ and vibrant, berry-fruited Greywacke Pinotage★. Troika★ is a ripe yet fresh and firmly built BORDEAUX blend. Best years: (Chardonnay) 2013 12 **11 10** 09 08 07 06 05 04 03 02 01.

CHAMPAGNE See pages 116–17.

CHAMPAGNE ROSÉ *Champagne AC, France* Good pink CHAMPAGNE – usually a little weightier than white – can have a delicious fragrance of cherries and raspberries. The top wines can age well, but most rosé Champagne should be drunk on release, with youth to the fore. Best producers: (non-vintage) E Barnaut★★, BILLECART-SALMON★★, Chanoine★, Drappier★, Egly-Ouriet★★, Fleury★, Henri Giraud★, GOSSET★★, Charles HEIDSIECK★★, Jacquart★, KRUG★★, LANSON★, R&L Legras★★, MOËT & CHANDON, Philipponnat★★, RUINART★, TAITTINGER, Vilmart★; (vintage) BILLECART-SALMON★★, BOLLINGER★★, GOSSET★★, Charles HEIDSIECK★★, LAURENT-PERRIER (Alexandra★★★), MOËT & CHANDON★★ (Dom Pérignon★★★), PERRIER-JOUET (Belle Époque★), POL ROGER★★, POMMERY (Louise★★), Louis ROEDERER★★ (Cristal★★★), RUINART (Dom Ruinart★★), TAITTINGER (Comtes de Champagne★★), VEUVE CLICQUOT★★ (Grande Dame★★★). Best years: 2009 08 07 05 04 03 02 00 99 98 96 95 90 88 85 82. See also pages 116–17.

CHANDON DE BRIAILLES *Savigny-lès-Beaune, Côte de Beaune, Burgundy, France* François de Nicolay and his sister Claude produce old-fashioned, savoury reds, notably PERNAND-VERGELESSES★ (Premier Cru Île des Vergelesses★★)

and CORTON★★, and tasty whites from Pernand-Vergelesses★ and Corton★★. Best years: (reds) (2013) 12 11 **10 09 07 06 05 03 02 99**.

CHANNING DAUGHTERS *Long Island, New York State, USA* Boutique winery in LONG ISLAND's Hamptons AVA that uses small lots from mature vineyards to produce fascinating wines in the 'natural wine' style, including skin-fermented whites. These include a racy Sauvignon Blanc★, Muscat-based Sylvanus★ and a juicy Blaufränkisch★. Newer plantings include unusual reds such as Teroldego, Lagrein and Refosco, which made some interesting rosés from the rainy 2011 harvest.

CHAPEL DOWN *Kent, England* Important UK winery. Most grapes are grown under contract, although 30ha (74 acres) of Chardonnay and Pinot Noir were planted in 2008. Good to very good wines, especially non-vintage Chapel Down Brut, sparkling English Rosé★, vintage Pinot Reserve★, and Bacchus★★ and Rosé still wines.

CHAPEL HILL *McLaren Vale, South Australia* Powerful, classy reds: top reserve Shiraz The Vicar★★, Cabernet Sauvignon★★ and Shiraz★★ from mature MCLAREN VALE vines. Good Bush Vine Grenache★, Chardonnay★ and fascinating, bone-dry, honey-scented Verdelho★★, as well as bright, lively Savagnin★. The Il Vescovo range impresses, especially the Tempranillo and Sangiovese★. Best years: (Shiraz) (2013) 12 10 08 06 05 **04 02 01 98 97 96 95 94 93 91**.

CHAPELLE-CHAMBERTIN AC See CHAMBERTIN AC.

M CHAPOUTIER *Rhône Valley, France* Chapoutier is a big noise in the world of biodynamic viticulture, and produces serious, exciting wines. The red HERMITAGE la Sizeranne★ and special plot-specific Ermitages (les Greffieux★★, l'Ermite★★★, le Méal★★★, le Pavillon★★★), rich white Hermitage (de l'Orée★★, l'Ermite★★★ and Vin de Paille★★), CÔTE-RÔTIE La Mordorée★, CROZES-HERMITAGE les Varonniers★, ST-JOSEPH les Granits★★ (red and white) and CHÂTEAUNEUF-DU-PAPE Barbe Rac★ and Croix de Bois★ are all deep, rich and often complex. Good white ST-PÉRAY Les Tanneurs★ and old-vine CONDRIEU Coteau de Chery★★. Large-volume, lively Crozes-Hermitage la Petite Ruche★ and CÔTES DU RHÔNE Belleruche★ are good value. Also BANYULS, CÔTES DU ROUSSILLON-VILLAGES, ALSACE, plus Portuguese and Australian joint ventures. Best years: (la Sizeranne) (2013) 12 11 10 09 **07 06 05 04 03 01 00 99 98 95 91 90 89 88**.

CHARDONNAY See pages 120–21.

CHARMES-CHAMBERTIN AC See CHAMBERTIN AC.

CHASSAGNE-MONTRACHET AC *Côte de Beaune, Burgundy, France* Some of Burgundy's greatest white wine vineyards (part of le MONTRACHET and BÂTARD-MONTRACHET, all of Criots-Bâtard-Montrachet) are within the village boundary. The white Chassagne Premiers Crus are not as well known, but can offer nutty, toasty wines, especially if aged for 4–8 years; Blanchots Dessus, Caillerets, Romanée, Grandes Ruchottes and Morgeots are among the best. Ordinary white Chassagne-Montrachet is usually enjoyable; the red is a little earthy, peppery and plummy and can be an acquired taste. Best Premiers Crus for reds include Clos de la Boudriotte, Clos St-Jean and Clos de la Chapelle. Best producers: (whites) Blain-Gagnard★★, Coffinet-Duvernay★, B COLIN★, M COLIN★★, P COLIN★★, P-Y COLIN-MOREY★★, J-N GAGNARD★★, V GIRARDIN★, B Moreau★★, M MOREY★, T MOREY★, V MOREY★★, M Niellon★★, J & J-M Pillot★★, P Pillot★, RAMONET★★; (reds) V GIRARDIN★, B Moreau★★, V MOREY★★, RAMONET★★. Best years: (whites) (2013) 12 11 09 **08 07 06 05 02**; (reds) (2013) 12 11 09 **08 07 06 05 03 02 99**.

CHARDONNAY

Chardonnay is at a real crossroads. From being lauded as the world's greatest white grape, it has suffered an astonishing fall from grace; so much so that I have conducted tastings where no one admitted to liking Chardonnay. Dear oh dear. It is still one of the world's star grapes, as numerous examples from Burgundy, California, Australia, South Africa, New Zealand and Chile demonstrate. But the world has suffered an avalanche of cheap sugary junk sadly bearing the name Chardonnay, which has massacred Chardonnay's reputation, especially among the new generation of wine enthusiasts. There is now a move toward more balanced, less oaky and even oak-free Chardonnay at all levels, from cheap to expensive, but too much commercial Chardonnay is still lifeless and flat. Luckily, excellent affordable Chardonnays are starting to appear in southern France and the New World, and at higher levels the wines are increasingly elegant and irresistible. But the consumer has yet to be convinced. Courage! Quality will out in the end.

WINE STYLES

Using oak The reason for Chardonnay's wonderful versatility lies in its susceptibility to the winemaker's aspirations and skills. The most important manipulation is the use of the oak barrel for fermenting and aging the wine. Chardonnay is the grape of the great white Burgundies and these are fermented and matured on their creamy lees in oak (not necessarily new oak); the effect is to give a marvellous round, nutty richness to a wine that is yet savoury and dry.

The New World winemakers sought to emulate the great Burgundies, planting Chardonnay and employing thousands of oak barrels (mostly new), and their success has caused winemakers everywhere else to see Chardonnay as the perfect variety – easy to grow, easy to turn into wine and easy to sell to an adoring public. But, as in all things, familiarity can breed contempt.

France Although a relatively neutral variety if left alone (this is what makes it so suitable as a base wine for Champagne-method sparkling wine), the grape can ripen in a surprising range of conditions, developing a subtle gradation of flavours going from the sharp apple-core greenness of Chardonnay grown in Champagne or the Loire Valley, through the exciting, bone-dry yet succulent flavours of white Burgundy, to sheer minerality in the Jura or a round, tropical flavour in Languedoc-Roussillon.

Other regions The most significant move currently is to reduce oak influence to the bare minimum or, indeed, none. Italy produces Chardonnay that can be bone dry and lean, or fat, spicy and lush. Spain does much the same. California and Australia virtually created their reputations on great, viscous, almost syrupy, tropical fruits and spice-flavoured Chardonnays, but both are re-focusing on top-quality full-bodied, oatmealy styles or unoaked versions. Some of the best New World Chardonnays, dry but ripe, fresh and subtly oaked, or fruit-led and unoaked, are coming from South Africa. New Zealand is producing beautifully balanced Chardonnays, their fragrant fruit only subtly oaked, while Chile and Argentina, in their different ways, have rapidly learned how to make fine Chardonnay, oaked and unoaked. Add Germany, Austria, Canada, New York State, Oregon, Greece, Portugal, Croatia, Slovenia, Moldova, Romania, England (for sparkling), Belgium, even China, and you'll see it can perform almost anywhere.

BEST PRODUCERS

France *Chablis* Billaud-Simon, DAUVISSAT, Droin, W Fèvre, Louis Michel, C Moreau, RAVENEAU; *Côte d'Or* H Boillot, J-M Boillot, Bonneau du Martray, BOUCHARD, CARILLON, COCHE-DURY, M COLIN, COLIN-MOREY, DROUHIN, A Ente, J-N GAGNARD, JADOT, A Jobard, LAFON, H Lamy, Dom. LEFLAIVE, MOREY, M Niellon, RAMONET, ROULOT, SAUZET; *Mâconnais* D & M Barraud, Bret, Ferret, Merlin, Saumaize-Michelin, J Thévenet.

Other European Chardonnays
Austria BRÜNDLMAYER, TEMENT, VELICH, WIENINGER; *Germany* HUBER, Johner, KNIPSER, REBHOLZ, WITTMANN; *Italy* BELLAVISTA, CA' DEL BOSCO, GAJA, ISOLE E OLENA, LAGEDER, Lis Neris, Castello della Sala (Cervaro), TIEFENBRUNNER (Linticlarus), Vie di Romans; *Spain* CHIVITE, Enate, Manuel Manzaneque, Muñoz, TORRES.

New World Chardonnays
Australia BANNOCKBURN, Bindi (Quartz), Brookland Valley, CAPE MENTELLE, COLDSTREAM HILLS, CULLEN, Curly Flat, Diamond Valley, GIACONDA, GROSSET, HOWARD PARK, LEEUWIN, Moorooduc, OAKRIDGE (864), PENFOLDS, PIERRO, Savaterre, SHAW & SMITH, TAPANAPPA, TARRAWARRA, TYRRELL'S, VASSE FELIX, VOYAGER, Woodlands, YABBY LAKE.

New Zealand ATA RANGI, BABICH, Bell Hill, BRANCOTT, CHURCH ROAD, CLOUDY BAY, CRAGGY RANGE, Dog Point, DRY RIVER, Escarpment, FELTON ROAD, FROMM, KUMEU RIVER, MATUA VALLEY, NEUDORF, NGATARAWA, PALLISER, Peregrine, SAINT CLAIR, SERESIN, TE MATA, TerraVin, TRINITY HILL, VAVASOUR, Vidal.

USA AU BON CLIMAT, CALERA, Chateau St Jean, DOMAINE DROUHIN OREGON, DOMAINE SERENE, DUTTON GOLDFIELD, EVENING LAND, Gary FARRELL, FLOWERS, HANZELL, HdV, IRON HORSE, KISTLER, Littorai, MARCASSIN, MERRYVALE, Peter MICHAEL, RAMEY, RIDGE, SAINTSBURY, SANFORD, SHAFER, STONY HILL, TALBOTT.

Canada Le CLOS JORDANNE, Closson Chase, Flat Rock, Joie Farm, Norman Hardie, Pearl Morissette, Quails' Gate, TAWSE.

South Africa Ataraxia, BOUCHARD FINLAYSON, CHAMONIX, Paul CLUVER, Crystallum, HAMILTON RUSSELL, JORDAN, MULDERBOSCH, THELEMA, VERGELEGEN.

Chile, Argentina Aquitania (Sol de Sol), CATENA, COBOS, CONCHA Y TORO, DE MARTINO, ERRÁZURIZ, LEYDA, Maycas del Limarí, MONTES, TABALÍ, TAPIZ.

CHASSELAS Chasselas is considered a table grape worldwide. Only in BADEN (where it is called Gutedel), Switzerland (as FENDANT in VALAIS) and SAVOIE does it make decent light, dry wines with a slight prickle. A few Swiss examples, notably from CHABLAIS and Dézaley, rise above this.

CH. CHASSE-SPLEEN★ *Moulis AC, Haut-Médoc, Bordeaux, France* Chasse-Spleen is not a Classed Growth, but during the 1980s it built a tremendous reputation for ripe, concentrated and powerful wines under the late proprietor, Bernadette Villars. The château has been run by Villars' daughter Céline since 2000, and recent vintages are starting to show the form of the old days. Second wine: l'Ermitage de Chasse-Spleen. Best years: 2012 11 10 **09 08 07 06 05 04 03 02 01 00**.

CHÂTEAU-CHALON AC *Jura, France* The most prized – and pricey – *vin jaune*. But beware – the flavour will shock your taste buds like no other French wine. Made from the Savagnin grape and aged like sherry under a yeast *flor*, but in old barrels, it is not released until at least 6 years after the vintage and can be kept for decades. Best producers: Baud★, Berthet-Bondet★★, Bourdy★, Butin★★, Chevassu-Fassenet, Courbet, Macle★★, Mossu★. Best years: 2007 **06 05 04 03 02 00 99 98 97 96 95**.

CHÂTEAU-GRILLET AC★★ *Rhône Valley, France* This rare and expensive RHÔNE white, made from Viognier and aged in young oak, has magic wisps of orchard fruit and harvest bloom when young. Now owned by Bordeaux's Ch. LATOUR, it is being made for early drinking, although until 2010 it was best drunk after 5 years. More tight and reserved than CONDRIEU. Best years: 2013 12 11 10 09 **08 07 06 05 04 03 01 00 98 95**.

CHATEAU MONTELENA *Napa Valley AVA, California, USA* Classic California Chardonnay★★ and an Estate Cabernet★★ that are impressive, if slow to develop. The Napa Valley Cabernet★ and Zinfandel are gentle and delightful. Best years: (Chardonnay) (2013) (12) 11 **10 09 08 07 06 05 04 03 02 01**; (Cabernet) 2010 09 **08 07 06 05 03 02 01 00 99 98 91 90**.

CHATEAU MUSAR *Ghazir, Lebanon* Ch. Musar★★ is a blend of Cabernet Sauvignon, old-vine Carignan and Cinsaut. A wine of real, if wildly exotic, character, with sweet dried fruits, which shows best when aged for a minimum of 10 years. Part classic Bordeaux and part spicy Rhône, it maintains its uniqueness in a world of standardization. White Ch. Musar★ is a slightly oxidized old-style wine made from indigenous Obaideh (like Chardonnay) and Merwah (similar to Semillon). Hochar Père & Fils and the younger Musar Cuvée are less complex, but more fruit-forward. Best years: (red) 2006 05 04 **03 02 00 99 98 97 95 94**.

CHATEAU STE MICHELLE *Washington State, USA* Pioneering winery with an enormous range, including several attractive vineyard-designated Chardonnays★ (some ★★), Cabernet Sauvignons★ and Merlots★ (Cold Creek Vineyard★★, Indian Wells★★). Good Riesling, both dry and sweet, and increasingly interesting red Meritage★ and Syrah★. Partnership with Italy's ANTINORI and Germany's Ernst LOOSEN has produced dark, powerful Tuscan-style Cabernet Col Solare★★, attractive Riesling Eroica★ and a thrilling sweet version, Single Berry Select★★★, made in tiny quantities. Best years: (premium reds) (2012) 11 10 **09**.

CHÂTEAUNEUF-DU-PAPE AC *Rhône Valley, France* A large (3200ha/ 7900-acre) vineyard area between Orange and Avignon. The sweetly red-fruited, aromatic red wine is based on Grenache, plus Syrah and Mourvèdre (10 other red and white varieties are also allowed). Heady and powerful, it should also be balanced and succulent, a picture of ripe, rounded elegance. Always choose Châteauneuf from a single estate, denoted by the papal coat of arms or mitre embossed on the bottle neck. Top reds, particularly old-vine cuvées, will age for 10 years or more, but don't feel you have to pay extra for 'prestige' cuvées: from a good estate, the normal release will be far cheaper, less dense and often more easily enjoyable. Only 5% of Châteauneuf is white; made mainly from Grenache Blanc, Bourboulenc, Clairette and Roussanne, these wines are great with Mediterranean herb and garlic dishes. Many whites are best young. **Best producers: (reds)** J Barrot★, L Barrot★, BEAUCASTEL★★, Beaurenard★★, Bois de Boursan★★, H Bonneau★★, Bosquet des Papes★★, les Cailloux★★, Chante-Perdrix★, CHAPOUTIER★, la Charbonnière★★, Charvin★, Clos du Caillou★, Clos du Mont Olivet★★, CLOS DES PAPES★★★, Clos St-Jean★, Cristia★, Cros de la Mûre★★, Font du Loup★, FONT DE MICHELLE★★, Fortia★, Gardine★★, Gigognan★, Giraud★, Grand Tinel★, Grand Veneur★, la Janasse★★★, Marcoux★★, Mas de Boislauzon★, Mathieu★, Mont-Redon★, la Mordorée★★, la Nerthe★, Ogier★, Pégaü★★, RAYAS★★★, Roger Sabon★★, St-Préfert★, St-Siffrein, Sénéchaux★, Solitude★★, Tardieu-Laurent★, P Usseglio★★, Vaudieu★, Vieille Julienne★★, Le Vieux Donjon★★, VIEUX TÉLÉGRAPHE★★; **(whites)** BEAUCASTEL★★★, la Charbonnière, CLOS DES PAPES★★, Clos St-Michel, FONT DE MICHELLE★★, Gardine★, Grand Veneur★, Marcoux★★, Mont-Redon★, RAYAS★★, Vaudieu, VIEUX TÉLÉGRAPHE★. **Best years: (reds)** 2012 10 09 **07** 06 05 04 03 01 00 99 98 96 95 90 89 88.

CHAUME See COTEAUX DU LAYON AC.

JEAN-LOUIS CHAVE *Rhône Valley, France* Chave's red HERMITAGE★★★ is one of the world's great wines, a supreme Syrah, surpassed only by the cellar-selected Cathelin★★★, produced occasionally (2009, 03, 00, 1998, 95, 91, 90). His complex white Hermitage★★★ (Marsanne with some Roussanne) sometimes outlasts the reds, as it evolves toward its honeyed, nutty, vertiginous peak. Also excellent *terroir*-speaking red ST-JOSEPH★★ and occasional stunning sweet Vin de Paille★★. Expensive, but worth the money. *Négociant* business makes sound red and white Hermitage, and lively, fruit-rich CÔTES DU RHÔNE Mon Coeur and St-Joseph Offerus. **Best years: (reds)** (2013) 12 11 10 09 **07** 06 05 04 03 01 00 99 98 97 96 95 **94** 92 91 90 89 88 86 85 83 82 79 78; **(whites)** 2013 12 11 10 09 08 07 06 05 04 03 01 00 99 98 97 96 95 94 93 92 91 90 89 88 85 83.

CHÉNAS AC *Beaujolais, Burgundy, France* The smallest BEAUJOLAIS Cru. Styles range from light and elegant to austere and needing time to develop Burgundian tones. **Best producers:** Ch. Bonnet (Vieilles Vignes★), des Brureaux, DUBOEUF, H Lapierre (Vieilles Vignes★), B Santé★. **Best years: (2013)** 11.

CHENIN BLANC One of the most underrated and versatile white wine grapes in the world. In the LOIRE VALLEY, where it is also called Pineau de la Loire, it is responsible for sweet, medium, dry and sparkling wines. The great sweet wines of COTEAUX DU LAYON, QUARTS DE CHAUME, BONNEZEAUX and VOUVRAY are some of the longest-lived of all wines. There is an increasing emphasis on barrel-fermented and aged dry wines, especially in ANJOU and now in TOURAINE, the best of which are a revelation. In South Africa, old vines are providing wines of tremendous individuality. Styles range from sparkling, through easy-drinking, dryish wines and modern barrel-fermented versions, to botrytized dessert wines (Alheit, Beaumont, Botanica, Jean Daneel, DeMorgenzon, Ken Forrester, Kleine Zalze, MULLINEUX, SADIE FAMILY, The Winery of Good Hope). Chenin is also influential in quality white blends. New Zealand

and Australia have produced good varietal examples, and it is also grown in California (DRY CREEK VINEYARD, Graziano), Argentina and Spain (Can Ràfols dels Caus, Escoda Sanahuja).

LARRY CHERUBINO Western Australia Since 2003, Larry Cherubino, former chief winemaker at HOUGHTON, has made wine for his family company; the wines are regarded as among Australia's finest. Wines change from year to year, particularly in the good-value Ad Hoc range (Wall Flower Riesling★★); The Yard label (Riesling★, Shiraz★★) is for single-vineyard wines. Look for new Laissez Faire label (especially Fiano★ and Syrah★★) and premium Cherubino range which includes Margaret River Cabernet★★, Frankland River Shiraz★★ and Cabernet★★, Pemberton Sauvignon Blanc★★ and Porongurup Riesling★★.

CH. CHEVAL BLANC★★★ St-Émilion Grand Cru AC, 1er Grand Cru Classé, Bordeaux, France Along with AUSONE, the leading ST-ÉMILION estate. Right on the border with POMEROL, it seems to share some of its sturdy richness, but with an extra spice and purity of fruit that is impressively, recognizably unique. An unusually high percentage (60%) of Cabernet Franc is often used in the blend. Gorgeous when young, yet with a remarkable ability to age. Second wine: Le Petit Cheval. Best years: 2012 11 10 09 08 **07 06 05 04 03 02 01 00 99 98 96 95 90 89**.

DOM. DE CHEVALIER Pessac-Léognan AC, Cru Classé de Graves, Bordeaux, France Some of Bordeaux's finest wines. The red★★ starts out firm and reserved, but over 10–20 years gains heavenly cedar, tobacco and blackcurrant flavour. As vineyards have matured, recent vintages have greater purity of fruit. The brilliant white★★★ is both fermented and aged in oak barrels; in the best vintages it will still be improving at 15–20 years. Best years: (reds) 2012 11 10 09 **08 07 06 05 04 03 02 01 00 99 98 96**; (whites) 2012 11 10 09 08 **07 06 05 04 02 01 00 99 98 96**.

CHEVALIER-MONTRACHET AC See MONTRACHET AC.

CHEVERNY AC Loire Valley, France The local speciality is the white Romorantin grape, which makes a bone-dry wine under the AC Cour-Cheverny, but the best whites are from Chardonnay. Also pleasant Sauvignon, Pinot Noir, Gamay and bracing CRÉMANT DE LOIRE. Drink young. Best producers: Cazin★★, Cheverny co-op, Clos du Tue-Boeuf★, la Désoucherie, la Gaudronnière, Gendrier/Huards★, Maison, H Marionnet, de Montcy★, du Moulin, Luc Percher★, Salvard★, F Saumon, Veilloux★.

CHIANTI DOCG Tuscany, Italy It may be the best-known name in Italian wine, but plain Chianti has recently slid so far down the price ladder that the best one could say of it is that it is cheap and cheerful – and therefore probably ought not to be categorized DOCG, supposedly reserved for Italy's finest. 'Chianti', when followed with a zonal name, such as Rufina, Colli Aretini, Colli Fiorentini or Colli Senesi, can be altogether superior, but don't bet on it. Chianti must be composed 75–100% of Sangiovese, the optional 25% being made up of Tuscan varieties like Canaiolo or Colorino, or (for more expensive but usually atypical examples) of varieties like Cabernet, Merlot and Syrah. Best producers: (Chianti Colli Fiorentini) Il Corno, Corzano e Paterno, Malenchini, Pasolini dall'Onda, Castello di Poppiano★, La Querce; (Chianti Colli Senesi) Campriano★, Casale-Falchini★, Castello di Farnetella★, Pietraserena. See also CHIANTI RUFINA.

CHIANTI CLASSICO DOCG *Tuscany, Italy* The historic CHIANTI zone, in the hills between Florence and Siena; in the 1930s it acquired the epithet 'Classico'; in 1996 it gained legal separation from Chianti, yet at the same time confusion was created by allowing Chianti Classico to be either 100% Sangiovese or a minimum of 80% Sangiovese with 20% other/international red varieties, thus opening the floodgates to a bewildering range of styles. Recent developments suggest there is a return to a more traditional expression of Chianti Classico. The finest Riserva wines can improve for decades, a fact that is gradually being accepted as proof of Chianti Classico's pre-eminent position as Tuscany's finest red wine. White grapes were finally banned from the blend in 2006 (although given the change in climatic conditions, perhaps this should be reconsidered). Best producers (Riserva or top cru): Castello di Ama★, ANTINORI★ (Riserva★★), BADIA A COLTIBUONO★★★, BIBBIANO★★, Il Borghetto★★, Brancaia★, Cacchiano★, Capaccia★★, Carpineto★, Casalose★, Castellare★, Castell'in Villa★, Collelungo★★, Colombaio di Cencio★★, Casa Emma★, FELSINA★★, Fonteruloti, FONTODI★★, ISOLE E OLENA★★★, Il Mandorlo★★, MONSANTO★★, Il Palazzino★★, Paneretta★★, Panzanello★★, Poggerino★★, Poggio al Sole (Casasilia★★), Poggiopiano★★, Querceto★, QUERCIABELLA★★, Castello dei RAMPOLLA★, RICASOLI (Castello di Brolio★), Riecine★★, Rignana★, Rocca di Castagnoli★★, San Felice★, San Giusto a Rentennano★★★, San Polo in Rosso★, Casa Sola★★, Terrabianca★, Vecchie Terre di Montefili★★, Vignamaggio★, Villa Cafaggio★★, Villa Calcinaia★★, Villa Rosa★. Best years: (2011) **10 09 08 07 06 04 01 99 97 95 90 89 88 85 83**.

CHIANTI RUFINA DOCG *Tuscany, Italy* CHIANTI sub-zone in the Apennine foothills east of Florence, where wines were noted for exceptional structure and longevity long before they joined the ranks of Chianti. Pomino DOC is a higher zone, almost entirely surrounded by Chianti Rufina; dominated by Frescobaldi, it makes greater use of French varieties such as Merlot, Cabernet and Chardonnay. Best producers: (Riserva) Basciano★, Tenuta di Bossi★, Colognole★, Frascole★, FRESCO-BALDI★★, Grati/Villa di Vetrice★, Grignano★, Lavacchio★, SELVAPIANA★★★, Castello del Trebbio★. Best years: (2011) **10 09 08 07 06 04 03 01**.

FRANÇOIS CHIDAINE *Montlouis-sur-Loire AC, Vouvray AC, Loire Valley, France* Along with Jacky BLOT, François Chidaine has inspired a new generation of vignerons with wines of wonderful purity, precision and length, differentiated by soil type and aspect, including, since 2006, VOUVRAY from Prince Poniatowski's famous vineyard, Le Clos Baudoin. 80% of the wines are dry. Montlouis Les Lys★★, a *moelleux* Sélection de Grains Nobles, is made only in exceptional vintages. Biodynamic since 1999. Best years: (sec/demi-sec) (2013) **12 11 09 08 07 06**; (moelleux) **2011 09 03 97**.

CHIMNEY ROCK *Stags Leap District AVA, California, USA* Powerful yet elegantly sculpted Cabernet Sauvignon★★ and a meritage blend called Elevage★★. There's also an ageworthy Elevage Blanc★ (a blend of Sauvignons Blanc and Gris) and a tangy Fumé Blanc★. Best years: (Elevage) (2010) **09 08 07 06 05 04 03 02 01 00 99 98 97**.

CHINON AC *Loire Valley, France* Lovely light reds full of raspberry fruit and fresh summer earth to drink young (from gravelly soils), and heavyweights for keeping (from clay and limestone slopes); it is always worth buying a single-estate wine. Made mainly from Cabernet Franc. Small amount of white (from Chenin Blanc). Best producers: P Alliet★★, B BAUDRY★★, Baudry-Dutour★, la Bonnelière★, P Breton★, Coulaine★, Couly-Dutheil★, DRUET★, C Joguet★★, A & J Lenoir★, la Noblaie★, de

Pallus★★, Dom. de l'R★, P Sourdais★, S & B Sourdais/Logis de la Bouchardière★. Best years: 2013 **11 10 09 08 06 05 04**.

CHIROUBLES AC *Beaujolais, Burgundy, France* Light, fragrant, delicious wine from the highest in altitude of the BEAUJOLAIS Crus. Best producers: la Combe au Loup★, D Coquelet★, D Desvignes★, la Grosse Pierre★, des Marrans★. Best years: (2013) **11**.

CHIVITE *Navarra DO, Navarra, Spain* After a family feud, new chairman Julián Chivite has split the holding into two separate companies, Gran Feudo for less expensive easy drinkers (red★, rosé★, unoaked Chardonnay★) and Chivite Family Estates for the top range, Colección 125, which includes a red Reserva★ (sometimes ★★), classy white Blanco★★ (barrel-fermented Chardonnay) and sweet Vendimia Tardía★★ (Muscat). Chivite's northerly estate, Pago de Arínzano★★, has its own appellation since 2008.

CHOREY-LÈS-BEAUNE AC *Côte de Beaune, Burgundy, France* Village that makes good, if not great, Burgundy at prices most of us can afford. No Premiers Crus but some interesting single-vineyard wines. Best producers: Arnoux★, DROUHIN★, Maillard★, TOLLOT-BEAUT. Best years: 2012 **11 10 09 08 05**.

CHURCH ROAD *Hawkes Bay, North Island, New Zealand* Premium-wine project owned by Pernod Ricard. Reserve Chardonnay★ is now one of the country's best. Reserve Syrah★ is also very good. Flagship label Tom makes outstanding Cabernet-Merlot★★ and Chardonnay★★ only in top vintages. Best years: (reds) 2013 **10 09 08 07 05 02**.

CHURCHILL'S *Port DOC, Douro, Portugal* Established in 1981, it was the first new PORT shipper for 50 years. The wines can be good, notably Vintage★, LBV★, Crusted★, single-quinta Gricha★ and a well-aged, nutty dry white port★. Churchill Estates★ and Quinta da Gricha★★ are also made as unfortified DOURO reds. Best years: (Vintage) 2011 **07 03 00 97 94 91 85**; (Quinta da Gricha) 2009 **07 03 01 99**.

CINSAUT Also spelt Cinsault. Found mainly in France's southern RHÔNE, PROVENCE and LANGUEDOC-ROUSSILLON. Ideal for rosé wine. In blends, Cinsaut's low alcohol calms high-degree Grenache and freshens the wine. Its early 1950s vines add intensity to the fabled CÔTES DU RHÔNE Ch. de Fonsalette red from the Ch. RAYAS family. Rare as a single varietal, but CLOS CENTEILLES, Mas des Chimères and Dom. d'Aupilhac, among others, make fine examples in Languedoc. Mainstay of the blend for Lebanon's CHATEAU MUSAR. Popular as a bulk blender in South Africa, enthusiasts of the Rhône style are bringing out serious quality, especially from old vines. California has some fine old vines, and there is resurgence in Chile, with Itata producing some stunning examples.

CIRÒ DOC *Calabria, Italy* Cirò Rosso, a slender, Gaglioppo-based wine of ancient pedigree, has improved notably since 2005, with the rise of artisan producers. Also a dry rosé and a dry white from Greco. Best producers: À Vita★★, Sergio Arcuri★, Caparra & Siciliani★, Librandi★ (Riserva★★), San Francesco★. Best years: (reds) (2012) **11 10 09 08 07 06 05**.

BRUNO CLAIR *Marsannay, Côte de Nuits, Burgundy, France* Top producer from MARSANNAY with several single-vineyard cuvées there, and an impressive range from other top vineyards including CHAMBERTIN Clos de Bèze★★ and Gevrey-Chambertin Clos St-Jacques★★. Also good-value SAVIGNY La Dominode★★ and a delicious Marsannay rosé★. Best years: (top reds) (2013) **12 11 10 09 08 07 06 05 03 02 99 98 96 90**.

CLAIRETTE DE DIE AC *Rhône Valley, France* Underrated sparkling wine (at least 75% Muscat), grown in beautiful high sub-Alpine vineyards: off-dry, with a creamy bubble and a honeyed, grapy, orchard-fresh fragrance. Drink young. Best producers: Achard-Vincent★, Clairette de Die co-op, D Cornillon, Jacques Faure, Poulet★, J-C Raspail★. See also CRÉMANT DE DIE.

A CLAPE *Cornas AC, Rhône Valley, France* The maestro estate in CORNAS, with 5ha (12 acres). Dense, tannic wines that reward patient cellaring, full of rich, roasted fruit – though occasionally, as in 2004 and 2006, scented and sublime – consistently excellent and often ★★★. Younger vine Renaissance★ is good lower-key Cornas. Also fine red CÔTES DU RHÔNE★ and authentic, tangy ST-PÉRAY★. Best years: (Cornas) 2013 12 11 10 09 **08 07 06 05 04 03 02 01 00 99 98 97 96 95 94 91 90 89 88 85 83 78**.

LA CLAPE AC *Languedoc, France* Mountainside vineyards on the coast south-east of Narbonne, with strong maritime influence. Some excellent whites from Bourboulenc and Clairette, and fine, herb-scented reds and rosés, mainly from Grenache, Syrah and Mourvèdre. Whites and reds can age. Best producers: d'Anglès★, Camplazens★, l'Hospitalet★/BERTRAND, Mas du Soleilla★, Mire l'Étang, Moyau★, La Négly★, Pech Redon★, Ricardelle★. Best years: (reds) (2013) 12 **11** 10 **09** 08 07 06 05.

CLARE VALLEY *South Australia* This historic upland region to the north of Adelaide has a deceptively moderate climate and is able to grow both warm-climate and cool-climate grapes successfully, including fine, aromatic Riesling, marvellously textured Semillon, scented Viognier, rich, robust Shiraz and Cabernet blends, and peppery but voluptuous Grenache. Best producers: (whites) Tim ADAMS★★, Jim BARRY★★, Wolf BLASS (Gold Label★), Leo Buring (Leonay★★), Crabtree★, GROSSET★★★, Kilikanoon★, KNAPPSTEIN★★, KT★★, Leasingham★, Mitchell★, MOUNT HORROCKS★★, O'Leary Walker★★, PETALUMA★★, Pikes★, Skillogalee★, Taylors/Wakefield★; (reds) Tim ADAMS★★, Jim BARRY★★, GROSSET★★★, Kilikanoon★, KNAPPSTEIN★, Leasingham★, Mitchell★, MOUNT HORROCKS★, O'Leary Walker★, Pikes★, Skillogalee★, Taylors/Wakefield, WENDOUREE★★. Best years: (Shiraz) 2013 12 10 09 08 **06 05 04 03 02 01 99 98 97 96 94 92 91 90**; (Riesling) 2013 12 **11** 10 **09 08 06 05 04 03 02 01 99 98 97**.

CH. CLARKE *Listrac-Médoc AC, Bordeaux, France* This property had millions spent on it by the late Baron Edmond de Rothschild during the late 1970s, and from the 1998 vintage leading Bordeaux winemaker Michel Rolland has been consultant enologist. The wines can have an attractive blackcurrant fruit and now a lot more Merlot (70%) is giving them more ripeness and polish. There is also a small production of dry white wine, le Merle Blanc★. Best years: 2012 **11** 10 **09 08 07 06 05 04 03 01**.

CLIFF LEDE *Stags Leap District AVA, California, USA* Known for its STAGS LEAP Cabernet Sauvignon and Sauvignon Blanc wines; elegant, long-aging Poetry Cabernet Sauvignon★★ is especially impressive. Also owns Breggo Cellars, which specializes in ripe, full-bodied Pinot Noir★ from the ANDERSON VALLEY. Best years: (Poetry) 2009 **07 05 04 01**.

CH. CLIMENS ★★★ *Barsac AC, 1er Cru Classé, Bordeaux, France* Leading estate in BARSAC, with fabulous, sensuous wines: rich and succulent, yet streaked with lively lemon acidity. Easy to drink at 5 years, but a good vintage will be richer and more satisfying after 10–15 years. Second wine: les Cyprès. Best years: 2012 **11** 10 **09 07 06 05 04 03 02 01 00 99 98 97 96 95**.

CLONAKILLA *Canberra, Australia* Tim Kirk is clearly one of the country's finest winemakers and his flagship Shiraz-Viognier★★★ is the benchmark for the style in Australia: elegant, lavender-scented, fleshily textured and complex, with the structure to age beautifully. Also sublime Viognier★, increasingly impressive Riesling★ and Semillon-Sauvignon Blanc. More modestly priced O'Riada Shiraz★, HILLTOPS Shiraz and a classy Syrah made from the estate's old vines. Best years: (Shiraz-Viognier) (2013) 12 11 10 09 08 07 **06 05 04 02 01 00 99 98 97 95 94 93 92.**

CLOS DE L'ANHEL *Corbières AC, Languedoc, France* Organic since 2003, Sophie Guiraudon and Philippe Mathias produce remarkable wines with a power and elegance unusual even for the CORBIÈRES. Top wine is smooth, rich Les Dimanches★★; also Les Terrassettes★, Les Autres and Le Lolo de l'Anhel. Best years: (Les Dimanches) (2013) 12 **11 10 09 08 07 06 05 04.**

CLOS DU BOIS *Alexander Valley AVA, Sonoma County, California, USA* I've always been partial to the house style here: gentle, fruit-dominated SONOMA Chardonnay, Merlot and Cabernet. Top cuvées can be quite impressive: Calcaire Chardonnay★★, rich, strong Briarcrest Cabernet Sauvignon★★ and Marlstone★★, a red BORDEAUX-style blend. Unoaked Chardonnay is a welcome addition. Now owned by Constellation; let's hope the quality stays up. Best years: (reds) 2012 11 10 **09 08 07 06 05 04 03 02 01 00 99 97.**

CLOS CANARELLI *Figari AC, Corsica, France* Yves Canarelli vinifies using stainless steel tanks, terracotta amphorae and egg-shaped cement tanks, with yeast from his biodynamic vineyard. The reds, which include Carcaghjolu Neru★ (a local grape that he has replanted) and Tarra d'Orasi★ from 140-year-old, pre-phylloxera vines, are still a bit rustic. White★★ (Vermentino) and rosé★★ (Nielluccio-Sciaccarello-Grenache) are fresh, complex and aromatic. Best years: (2013) **12 11 10 09 08.**

CLOS CENTEILLES *Minervois AC, Languedoc, France* Excellent MINERVOIS and Minervois La Livinière. Clos Centeilles★★ is the top wine; Capitelle de Centeilles★ and Carignanissime★ are 100% Cinsaut and 100% Carignan respectively; Campagne de Centeilles is also predominantly Cinsaut. Innovative red and white IGPs, C de Centeilles, revive long-lost grape varieties. Best years: (reds) (2013) 12 **11 10 09 08 07 06 05.**

CLOS ERASMUS★★★ *Priorat DOCa, Cataluña, Spain* Profound and personal PRIORAT from Daphne Glorian's tiny estate. Convincing second wine, Laurel★. Best years: (2011) 10 **09 08 07 05 04 03 02 01 00 99 98 97 96.**

CLOS DE GAMOT *Cahors AOP, South-West France* The Jouffreau family, proud of their 400-year heritage, produce benchmark CAHORS★★ (Clos St-Jean★★★). The wines need aging to develop ever-increasing subtlety and complexity. A cuvée from centenarian vines★★ is made in the best vintages. Best years: (2012) (11) 10 09 **08 06 05 04 02 01 98.**

LE CLOS JORDANNE *Niagara Peninsula VQA, Ontario, Canada* The intention is to make BURGUNDY-style Pinot Noir and Chardonnay. Le Grand Clos Pinot Noir faintly echoes Burgundy's Grand Cru; actually, the echo is too faint. Pinot isn't working here, but there are some delightful – and, if you like, Burgundian – Chardonnays: Le Clos Jordanne★, Le Grand Clos★. All organic.

CLOS D'UN JOUR *Cahors AOP, South-West France* Véronique and Stéphane Azémar, now officially organic, continue their climb toward the top of the CAHORS tree. Le Clos d'un Jour★ is exceptional value for money; a third of their grapes are vinified in clay vats, but their Un Jour★ is 100% Malbec and aged in oak. Best years: (2012) (11) 10 09 **08 06 05.**

CLOS DES LAMBRAYS AC *Grand Cru, Côte de Nuits, Burgundy, France* This 8.8ha (22-acre) Grand Cru vineyard in MOREY-ST-DENIS is almost entirely owned by the domaine of the same name, though Taupenot-Merme also has a few rows – not quite enough to make a barrel a year. Thierry

Brouin, manager at the Dom. des Lambrays★★★, favours early picking and the use of stems to make a vibrant, spicy style of wine. **Best years:** (2013) 12 11 10 09 **06 05 03 02 00.**

CLOS MARIE *Pic St-Loup AC, Languedoc, France* Powerful, Syrah-dominated reds: Glorieuses★, Métairies du Clos★, Simon★ and L'Olivette★. Also white cuvée Manon. **Best years:** (2013) 12 11 **10 09 08 07 06 05.**

CLOS MOGADOR★★★ *Priorat DOCa, Cataluña, Spain* René Barbier Ferrer was one of the pioneers who relaunched the reputation of PRIORAT in the 1980s. The wine is a ripe, intense, brooding monster built to age. **Best years:** (2011) 10 09 08 **07 06 05 04 03 01 00 99 98 97.**

DOM. DU CLOS NAUDIN *Vouvray AC, Loire Valley, France* Philippe Foreau runs this first-rate 11.5ha (28-acre) VOUVRAY domaine. Depending on the vintage, he produces a range of styles: Sec (dry)★★, Demi-Sec (medium-dry)★★ and Moelleux (sweet)★★ (rare Moelleux Réserve)★★, as well as a sparkling Mousseux★★ that accounts for 40% of production. The wines are supremely ageworthy. **Best years:** (Moelleux Réserve) (2013) **11 09 05 03 97 96 95 90 89.**

CLOS DES PAPES *Châteauneuf-du-Pape AC, Rhône Valley, France* The red CHÂTEAUNEUF-DU-PAPE★★★ has 20% Mourvèdre, which gives structure, length, complexity and extra longevity. More ample, fleshy and heady recently – a stylistic change – with enough very ripe Grenache to make the wine approachable in its youth and provide an initial gush of coated fruit. The marvellous, refined, long-lived white★★ takes on the nutty, complex character of aged Burgundy after 5 or 6 years. **Best years:** (red) (2013) 12 11 10 09 **08 07 06 05 04 03 01 00 99 98 97 96 95 94 90 89 88.**

CLOS DE LA ROCHE AC *Grand Cru, Côte de Nuits, Burgundy, France* The biggest and often best of the 5 MOREY-ST-DENIS Grands Crus. The wine has a lovely, bright, red-fruits flavour when young, and should become richly chocolaty or gamy with age. **Best producers:** BOISSET★★, Castagnier★★, DROUHIN★★★, DUJAC★★★, HOSPICES DE BEAUNE★★, Dom. LEROY★★★, H Lignier★★, Perrot-Minot★★, Ponsot★★★, Chantal Remy★★, ROUSSEAU★★★. **Best years:** (2013) 12 11 10 09 **08 07 06 05 03 02 01 99 98 96 95 93 90.**

CLOS ST-DENIS AC *Grand Cru, Côte de Nuits, Burgundy, France* This small (6.5ha/16-acre) Grand Cru, which gave its name to the village of MOREY-ST-DENIS, produces wines that are headier than CLOS DE LA ROCHE in youth, becoming wonderfully silky, with the texture that only great Burgundy can regularly achieve. Best after 10 years or more. **Best producers:** Arlaud★★, P Charlopin★★, DUJAC★★★, JADOT★★, Jouan★★, Ponsot★★★. **Best years:** (2013) 12 11 10 09 **08 07 06 05 03 02 01 99 98 96 95 90.**

CLOS DE LOS SIETE *Mendoza, Argentina* Under the guidance of Bordeaux enologist Michel Rolland, in 1998 a group of 7 (*siete* in Spanish) French producers selected vineyards in the heart of the UCO VALLEY and contributed grapes to Clos de los Siete★★, a rich Malbec-based blend. Under the label Cuvelier Los Andes the owners of Ch. LÉOVILLE-POYFERRÉ produce profound wines such as Colección★, a

Malbec-based blend exhibiting indulgent, violet-scented fruit (also Malbec, Cabernet and Merlot bottlings). The Grand Vin★★ is an opulent, layered and ageworthy blend, while Grand Malbec★★ is intense and perfumed – both need time but repay the wait. Ultra-modern

Bodega Diamandes is owned by Bordeaux's MALARTIC-LAGRAVIÈRE. Its Gran Reserva★★ Malbec-based blend turns heads; also elegant Chardonnay and Viognier★, and classy, value-for-money Perlita (Malbec-Syrah).

CLOS DE TART AC *Grand Cru, Côte de Nuits, Burgundy, France* 7.5ha (18-acre) Grand Cru (monopoly of the Mommessin family). Intense, concentrated wines made by traditional methods with a modern result. Exceptional quality★★★ – and price! Second wine La Forge du Tart in most vintages. Best years: (2013) 12 11 10 09 08 **07 06** 05 **03 02 01 00 99 96 95 90**.

CLOS TRIGUEDINA *Cahors AOP, South-West France* Jean-Luc Baldès makes some of the best-known and admired CAHORS★; top cuvée Probus★★ manages to combine tradition and modernity. The 'New Black Wine' revives a historical tradition for cooked and fortified wine perhaps best forgotten. Best years: (2012) (11) 10 09 **08 06 05 02 01** 98.

CLOS DU VAL *Napa Valley AVA, California, USA* Elegant Cabernet Sauvignon★ (STAGS LEAP DISTRICT★★), Chardonnay★, Merlot★, Pinot Noir★ and Zinfandel★. Reserve Cabernet★ ages well. Best years: (Reserve Cabernet) (2012) (10) **09 08 07** 06 05 04 03 02 01 00 99 97 96 95 94.

CLOS DE VOUGEOT AC *Grand Cru, Côte de Nuits, Burgundy, France* Enclosed by Cistercian monks in the 14th century, and today a tourist attraction, this large (50ha/125-acre) vineyard is now divided among 80+ owners. As a result, Clos de Vougeot is one of the less reliable Grands Crus; better wine should come from the upper and middle parts. But the best results come from the producers who know what they are doing, regardless of site. When it is good it is wonderfully fleshy, turning deep and exotic after 10 years or more. Best producers: H Boillot★, Chopin★★, J-J Confuron★★★, Eugénie★★★, FAIVELEY★, GRIVOT★★, Anne GROS★★★, JADOT★★, F Lamarche★★, Dom. LEROY★★★, T LIGER-BELAIR★★, MEO-CAMUZET★★★, Millot★★, Denis MORTET★★★, MUGNERET-Gibourg★★★, Ch. de la Tour★★ (Vieilles Vignes★★★), VOUGERAIE★★. Best years: (2013) 12 11 10 09 **08 07** 06 05 **03 02 01 00 99 98 96 95 93 90**.

CLOT DE L'OUM *Côtes du Roussillon-Villages AC, Roussillon, France* Powerful, dense wines from organic vineyards: Numéro Uno★★ (Syrah with a little Carignan), Saint Bart Vieilles Vignes★, La Compagnie des Papillons★.

CLOUDY BAY *Marlborough, South Island, New Zealand* Cloudy Bay achieved cult status with the first release of its zesty, herbaceous Sauvignon Blanc in 1985. After a dip in the early 2000s, the winery is getting back on form despite high production levels. Sauvignon Blanc★★ has regained a lot of its leafy zest. Sauvignon Blanc Te Koko★★ is very different: rich, creamy, oak-matured and bottle-aged. Cloudy Bay also makes Chardonnay★★, superb ALSACE-style Gewurztraminer★★ and Riesling★★ (late-harvest Riesling sometimes ★★★) and very good Pinot Noir★★. Vintage Pelorus★★ is a high-quality old-style CHAMPAGNE-method fizz and non-vintage Pelorus★★ is excellent too. Cloudy Bay recently ventured out of Marlborough to produce a fine CENTRAL OTAGO Pinot Noir Te Wahi★★ Best years: (Sauvignon Blanc) **2013** 12 11 10 09 08.

PAUL CLUVER *Elgin WO, South Africa* Trail-blazing ELGIN winery, now making its best wines yet. Cool-loving varieties respond well here: minerally, refined Sauvignon Blanc★; compact, layered Chardonnay★★; subtle scented Gewurztraminer★★; vibrant, dryish Rieslings★★ and thrilling Noble Late Harvest★★★ botrytis dessert version. Standard Pinot Noir★ is silky and refreshing; the ethereal charm of single-vineyard Seven Flags★★ belies its complexity and ageworthiness. Best years: (whites) 2013 **12 11 10 09 08 07**.

COATES & SEELY *Hampshire, England* Established in 2009 at the Wooldings vineyard (planted in 1989); now with almost 50ha (123 acres) planted in various parts of Hampshire. All 3 sparkling wines have piercing fruit married with biscuity softness.

COBB WINES *Sonoma Coast AVA, California, USA* Small, prestigious Pinot Noir producer in one of the coolest areas of SONOMA COUNTY. Most wines are light in colour, but brilliantly scented and structured (Diane Cobb★★, Emmaline Ann★★). Best years: (2012) (11) **10 09 08 07 06 05**.

COBOS *Mendoza, Argentina* Small Argentine-American operation. Top-of-the-range Volturno★★★ (previously called uNico), an intense, dramatic Cabernet-based blend, showcases old-vine fruit from the Marchiori vineyard in the Perdriel district of MENDOZA. The Marchiori vineyard is also the source of Malbec★★, Cabernet★★ and rich, exotic Chardonnay★★ under the Bramare label. UCO VALLEY Bramare Malbec★★ is also excellent. The Felino★ range offers dazzling purity of fruit and great quality for the price. Best years: (uNico): (2011) 10 09 **08** 06.

J-F COCHE-DURY *Meursault, Côte de Beaune, Burgundy, France* Jean-François Coche-Dury and son Raphaël are modest superstars, quietly turning out some of the finest wines on the CÔTE DE BEAUNE. Top wines are CORTON-CHARLEMAGNE★★★ and MEURSAULT Perrières★★★, but even the BOURGOGNE Blanc★★ is excellent. Reds, from VOLNAY★★ and MONTHELIE★, are delicious even when young. Best years: (whites) (2013) 12 11 10 09 **08 07 06 05 04 02 01 00 99 95**.

COCKBURN'S *Port DOC, Douro, Portugal* Big improvements already from the Symington family since they bought Cockburn's in 2010, aiming to recapture past glories. Best known for Special Reserve ruby port. Also stylish Vintage★ and Quinta dos Canais★. Best years: (Vintage) 2011 **07 03 00 97 94 91 70 63 60 55**; (dos Canais) 2010 09 08 **07 03 01 00 95**.

CODORNÍU *Cava DO, Cataluña, Spain* The biggest CHAMPAGNE-method sparkling wine company in the world. Anna de Codorníu★ and Jaume Codorníu★ are especially good, but all the sparklers are better than the CAVA average. Drink young for freshness. Codorníu also owns an extensive portfolio of wineries in Spain and elsewhere.

COLCHAGUA *Rapel, Chile* RAPEL sub-region and home to several exciting estates, such as the Apalta hillside vineyard, where LAPOSTOLLE, MONTES, SANTA RITA, VENTISQUERO and others have plantings. Syrah and Carmenère do very well here. Chimbarongo and Los Lingues to the east are cooler due to the influence of the Andes. New vineyards toward the coast in Marchíhüe, Lolol and Pumanque are delivering exciting reds and whites, especially Syrah and Viognier. New coastal region Paredones is showing great promise for salty Sauvignon Blancs and juicy, refreshing Pinot Noirs. Best producers: CASA SILVA★, CONO SUR★★, EMILIANA★★, Hacienda Araucano/Lurton★, Koyle★, LAPOSTOLLE★★, Los Vascos, LUIS FELIPE EDWARDS★, MONTES★★, MontGras, Neyen★★, VENTISQUERO★ (Pangea★★), Viu Manent★.

COLDSTREAM HILLS *Yarra Valley, Victoria, Australia* Founded by Australian wine guru James Halliday; now owned by Treasury. Chardonnay★ (Reserve★★) is subtle and delicate, but with real depth. Pinot Noir★ is usually good: sappy and smoky with cherry fruit. Reserve Cabernet★ can be very good when ripe; Merlot★★ ripens more successfully. Best years: (Reserve Chardonnay) 2013 12 11 **10 07 06 05 03**.

COLIN *Chassagne-Montrachet, Côte de Beaune, Burgundy, France* Extended family in ST-AUBIN and neighbouring CHASSAGNE-MONTRACHET, producing much fine white Burgundy. Michel Colin-Deleger's Chassagne domaine is now split between sons Bruno★ and Philippe★. Marc Colin★★ has handed over to three of his children, while his eldest, Pierre-Yves Colin-Morey★★, who has set up on his own, is the one to watch.

COLLI ORIENTALI DEL FRIULI DOC *Friuli-Venezia Giulia, Italy* Many Italian denominations begin with 'Colli' (hills). This one, on the Slovenian border, covers 20 varietal types of wine. Potentially the most exciting are the reds from the indigenous Refosco and Schioppettino and dry whites from Friulano, Ribolla Gialla, Sauvignon Blanc and Malvasia Istriana. Best producers: Ca' Ronesca★, Dario Coos★, Dorigo★, Le Due Terre★★, Livio FELLUGA★★, Walter Filiputti★, Adriano Gigante★, Livon★, Meroi★, Miani★★, Davide Moschioni★★, Rocca Bernarda★, Rodaro★, Ronchi di Cialla★, Ronchi di Manzano★★, Ronco del Gnemiz★★, Scubla★, Sirch★★, Specogna★, Le Vigne di Zamò★★, Zof★. Best years: (whites) (2013) 12 11 10 09 08 07 06 04.

COLLI PIACENTINI DOC *Emilia-Romagna, Italy* Wines from the hills of Piacenza. The best-known red, sometimes frothing, is Gutturnio, a Barbera-Bonarda blend. Other wines from the Pinot family, Cabernet and oddballs Ortrugo and Trebbianino. With the exception of the more serious Gutturnios, most wines best drunk young. Best producers: Luretta★, Lusenti, Castello di Luzzano★, Il Poggiarello★, La Stoppa★, Torre Fornello★, La Tosa (Cabernet Sauvignon★).

COLLINE TERAMANE DOCG *Abruzzo, Italy* A subzone in the northern half of ABRUZZO, where the distance between the notably sandy hills, vines and the Adriatic sea is at its narrowest, yielding the region's most refined expression of Montepulciano d'Abruzzo. Best producers: Faraone★, Illuminati★★, Masciarelli★, Nicodemi, Emidio Pepe★★.

COLLINES RHODANIENNES, IGP DES *Rhône Valley, France* Exciting granite/schist hillside region between Vienne and Valence includes new vineyard of Seyssuel, with flinty, long-lived Syrahs. Also a few juicy Merlots and Gamays, and Viogniers with CONDRIEU-like finesse. Best producers: les Alexandrins, Barou (Viognier), P & C Bonnefond★, COLOMBO★, P Gaillard★, J-M Gérin (Viognier), JAMET★★, Pascal Jamet, P Jasmin, Monteillet, S Ogier★, A PERRET★, Pichat, C Pichon, J Pilon (Marsanne), G Vernay★, P-J Villa, Vins de Vienne★ (Sotanum★★). Best years: (reds) 2013 12 11 10 09 07 05.

COLLIO DOC *Friuli-Venezia Giulia, Italy* Some of Italy's most expensive and controversial dry white wines are from these hills on the Slovenian border. There are 19 types of wine, from local Friulano and Malvasia Istriana to international varieties. However, it's the white grapes vinified as though they were being made into red wines – so-called 'natural wines' or 'orange wines' – that are causing a stir, notably from the likes of GRAVNER and Podversic. Best producers: Borgo Conventi★, Borgo del Tiglio★★, La Castellada★, Damijan★, Livio FELLUGA★★, Marco Felluga★, Fiegl★, GRAVNER★★, Jermann★, Edi Keber★, Renato Keber★★, Livon★, Podversic★, Primosic★, Princic★, Puiatti★, Roncùs★★, Russiz Superiore★, Schiopetto★, Matijaz Tercic★★, Venica & Venica★★, Villa Russiz★★, Villanova★, Zuani★★. Best years: (whites) (2013) 12 11 10 09 08 07 06.

COLLIOURE AC *Roussillon, France* Fishing port in the Pyrenean foothills. The red wine can age for a decade but is marvellously rip-roaring when young. Best producers: (reds) Abbé Rous, Baillaury★, CAZES★, Clos de Paulilles★, MAS BLANC★★, la Rectorie★★, la Tour Vieille★, Vial Magnères★. Best years: (2013) 12 11 10 09 08 07 06 05.

COLOMBARD In France, Colombard traditionally has been distilled to make Armagnac and Cognac, but has now emerged as a table wine grape in its own right, notably as a mainstay of CÔTES DE GASCOGNE. At its best, it has a lovely, crisp acidity and fresh, aromatic fruit. The largest plantings are in California, where it generally produces rather less distinguished wines, although French winemaker Yannick Rousseau makes a superb version from old vines in RUSSIAN RIVER VALLEY. In South Africa it can produce attractive refreshing wines. Australia also has some bright-eyed examples (especially PRIMO ESTATE).

JEAN-LUC COLOMBO *Cornas AC, Rhône Valley, France* Colombo is a media-hungry, unashamed modernist. The domaine has been lifted by presence of daughter Laure. His rich CORNAS is more opulent and less tannic than most; top cuvées are les Ruchets★★ and the lush old-vines la Louvée★★. Among his *négociant* wines, CONDRIEU Amour de Dieu★★, CHÂTEAUNEUF-DU-PAPE les Bartavelles★ and red and white HERMITAGE le Rouet★ stand out, although some offerings don't always seem fully ripe. Also fragrant, improving ST-PÉRAY la Belle de Mai★ (sometimes ★★), plus good red and white CÔTES DU RHÔNE★ and COLLINES RHODANIENNES★. Best years: (Cornas) 2013 12 11 10 **09 07 06 05 04 03 01 00 99 98**.

COLOMÉ *Salta, Argentina* Established in the early 19th century, Colomé is one of the oldest, most remote and beautiful wineries in South America. Swiss billionaire owner Donald Hess has invested in a state-of-the-art winery and has been renovating and planting vineyards. Altura Maxima, at 3111m (10,200ft) above sea level, is the world's highest commercial vineyard, and is biodynamic. The Estate Malbec★★ is an aromatic, wild, herby wine. Reserva Malbec★★ is impressively plush, dense with blue fruit and alcohol. Torrontés★★ is thrillingly lush and scented. Bodegas Amalaya★ is a nearby Hess-owned independent project, specializing in Malbec and Torrontés blends. Best years: (top reds) 2011 10 09 **08**.

COLORADO *USA* With their high altitudes, many regions in the Rocky Mountains seem perfect to grow wine grapes, but arid conditions, soil anomalies and cold winters make much of Colorado unsuitable. As a result, 90% of the fruit used by Colorado's 100+ wineries comes from one of the two appellations: the warmer Grand Valley AVA and the slightly cooler (and higher in altitude) West Elks AVA. Most vineyards are at 1200–2100m (4000–7000ft). Riesling and Gewürztraminer do well here, with reds from Cabernets Franc and Sauvignon. Best producers: Balistreri, BookCliff Vineyards★, Boulder Creek★, Canyon Wind★★, Carlson, Colorado Cellars, Guy Drew★, Alfred Eames Cellars★, Garfield Estates★, Infinite Monkey Theorem, Jack Rabbit Hill★, Plum Creek★, Sutcliffe★, Terror Creek★, Two Rivers★, Winery at Holy Cross Abbey★.

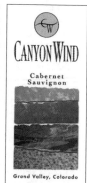

Grand Valley, Colorado

COLUMBIA CREST *Washington State, USA* An offshoot of CHATEAU STE MICHELLE, and now the largest winery in Washington State, producing top-calibre wines at everyday prices. Two Vines budget label is good. Grand Estates Shiraz★, Cabernet Sauvignon★ and Chardonnay★ are strong suits, as is the H3★ label for Horse Heaven Hills fruit; these are good young but will age for several years. Reserve Syrah★ can be heavily oaked but has impressive style. Best years: (reds) (2012) 11 10 **09**.

COLUMBIA VALLEY AVA *Washington State, USA* The largest of WASHINGTON's viticultural regions, covering a third of the state's landmass and encompassing both the YAKIMA VALLEY and WALLA WALLA VALLEY, as well as the newer AVAs of Red Mountain, Wahluke Slope, Rattlesnake Hills, Horse Heaven Hills, Snipes Mountain, Columbia Gorge, Naches Heights, Ancient Lakes and Lake Chelan. It produces 99% of the state's wine grapes: Merlot, Cabernet Sauvignon and Chardonnay are the most widely planted varieties. **Best producers:** Airfield★, ANDREW WILL★★, BETZ★, CADENCE★★, CHATEAU STE MICHELLE★, COLUMBIA CREST★, CORLISS ESTATES★★, DELILLE CELLARS★★, DUNHAM★, Goose Ridge, GRAMERCY★, HEDGES★, JANUIK★, L'ECOLE NO 41★★, LONG SHADOWS★★, Matthews Cellars★★, OWEN ROE★, QUILCEDA CREEK★★★, Mark RYAN★, SYNCLINE★, WOODWARD CANYON★★. **Best years:** (reds) (2012) 11 10 **09 08 07 06**.

COMMANDARIA *Cyprus* A wine of tradition, dating back to the Crusades. The world's oldest wine brand. Made from sun-dried, usually Xynisteri, grapes. Some are disappointing, but Etko Centurion, Keo St John and Sodap St Barnabas can be rich and complex. Liquid history in a bottle.

CONCHA Y TORO *Maipo, Chile* Chile's biggest wine company, with around 10,500 ha (26,000 acres) of vineyards. Casillero del Diablo is best for oddballs like Pinot Grigio and Malbec, less good for Cabernet, Merlot and Carmenère. Stepping up, Trio★, Marqués de Casa Concha★ and Terrunyo★★ are good reds and, especially, whites. Amelia★★ is the top Chardonnay. Cabernet Sauvignon-based Don Melchor★★★ is impressively velvety and complex in recent releases. Exciting Ucúquer cool-climate development at the mouth of Rapel River. The related Maycas del Limarí winery offers crisp Sauvignon Blanc★, tangy, mineral Chardonnay★★ (especially Quebrada Seca★★) and ripe, scented yet dense Syrah★★. Palo Alto winery is in MAULE. Trivento★ is an important Argentinian project. See also ALMAVIVA, CONO SUR.

CONDRIEU AC *Rhône Valley, France* The home of Viognier, fragrant but expensive wine from mainly granite soils. Ranges from scented, full and opulent to sweet, late-harvested. The best have a clear mineral streak: more of this style have been made recently. Quality varies, so stick to top names. Best drunk young, though Vernay's Coteau de Vernon can live for 20 years. **Best producers:** G Barge★, P Benetière★, P & C Bonnefond★★, CHAPOUTIER★, du Chêne★, L Chèze★, Clusel-Roch★, COLOMBO★★, CUILLERON★★★, DELAS★★, C Facchin★, Faury★★, P Gaillard★★, Y Gangloff★★, J-M Gérin★, GUIGAL★★, F Merlin★★, Monteillet★★, Mouton★, R Niero★★, A Paret★★, A PERRET★★, C Pichon★, J Pilon★, ROSTAING★★, St-Cosme★★, G Vernay★★★, F Villard★★.

CONERO DOCG *Marche, Italy* Denomination now split between Conero DOCG and Rosso Conero DOC. Conero (with lower yields) has a minimum of 85% Montepulciano and a maximum of 15% Sangiovese; Rosso Conero may include 15% international varieties. **Best producers:** Garofoli★★, Leopardi Dittajuti★, Mecella★, Monte Schiavo★★, Moroder★★, Le Terrazze★, Umani Ronchi★★. **Best years:** (2011) 10 09 08 07 06 04.

CONO SUR *Colchagua, Chile* Dynamic sister winery to CONCHA Y TORO, and now the largest Pinot producer in the world. Top-of-the-range Ocio★ is positively unctuous, yet refreshing; CASABLANCA-sourced 20 Barrels Pinot Noir★★ is rich and perfumed. Minerally, crunchy 20 Barrels Sauvignon Blanc★★ is from one of Casablanca's coolest sites. Chardonnay★★, Merlot★★ and Cabernet Sauvignon★★ under 20 Barrels and Single Vineyard labels are excellent, as are Reserva Especial

Riesling★★, Gewürztraminer★ and Viognier★. Basic releases have lost a little character recently.

CH. LA CONSEILLANTE★★ *Pomerol AC, Bordeaux, France* Elegant, exotic, velvety wine that blossoms beautifully after 5–6 years but can age much longer. Second wine: Duo de Conseillante (from 2007). **Best years:** 2012 11 10 09 **08 07 06 05 04 03 02 01 00 99 98 96 95**.

CONSTANTIA WO *South Africa* The historic heart of South African wine, covering much of Simon van der Stel's original 1685 land grant. Today 10 properties stretch along the Constantiaberg, from STEENBERG in the south to Beau Constantia in the north. Sauvignon Blanc thrust this cool-climate area into the limelight, and the increasing trend for Semillon-Sauvignon blends is realized in Constantia Uitsig's elegant, flavoursome Constantia White★ and Groot Constantia's poised, persistent Reserve White★. Wines such as Eagles' Nest Shiraz★★, STEENBERG's Merlot and BORDEAUX blend Constantia Glen Five★★ show reds have a promising future. Also popular Cap Classique sparkling wines. **Best producers:** Beau Constantia, BUITENVERWACHTING★, Constantia Glen★, Constantia Uitsig★, Eagles' Nest★★, Groot Constantia★, High Constantia, KLEIN CONSTANTIA★★, STEENBERG★★. **Best years:** (whites) 2013 **12 11 10 09 08 07 06** 0

BODEGA CONTADOR *Rioja DOCa, La Rioja, Spain* ARTADI's former winemaker Benjamín Romeo launched his own estate with a collection of tiny old vineyards, and caused a sensation. He makes wines in an increasingly elegant, less superripe style: Contador★★★, La Viña de Andrés Romeo★★ and La Cueva del Contador★★, and the refreshing Qué Bonito Cacareaba★ white; also tasty Macizo★ white from CATALUÑA. **Best years:** (2011) 10 09 **08 07 06** 05 **04 03 02 01** 00.5.

ALDO CONTERNO *Barolo DOCG, Piedmont, Italy* One of BAROLO's more important producers; Aldo's children have deviated from their late father's traditional route, choosing to make mostly modern, concentrated wines from tiny yields aged in new oak. Various Barolos, from their prime Bussia vineyard: Colonnello★, Cicala★, Romirasco★ and, in top vintages, Granbussia★★. Also well-made BARBERA D'ALBA Conca Tre Pile★, LANGHE Nebbiolo Il Favot★★ and two Langhe Chardonnays. **Best years:** (Barolo) (2011) (10) 09 08 **07 06 04** 01 99 98 97 96 95 90 89 88.

GIACOMO CONTERNO *Barolo DOCG, Piedmont, Italy* Roberto Conterno has succeeded his father Giovanni (Aldo's brother), continuing to make traditional BAROLO at their Monforte cantina from Serralunga fruit, but now vinifying his Barolo entirely in large (Austrian) wood. The flagship wine is Barolo Monfortino★★★ (only released after some 5 or 6 years in oak barrels), but Barolo Cascina Francia★★★ is also very good, as is the BARBERA D'ALBA★★ and LANGHE Nebbiolo★★. **Best years:** (Monfortino) (2011) (10) (09) (08) **07** 06 04 02 01 00 99 98 97 96 95 90 89 88 85 82 71.

CONTINO *Rioja DOCa, Rioja, Spain* An estate on some of the finest RIOJA land, half-owned by CVNE but run with passion and skill as a boutique operation. Beautifully balanced Reserva★★, a scented single-vineyard Viña del Olivo★★ (sometimes ★★★) and a remarkable, piercing Graciano★★ – all age beautifully. Also white Rioja★. **Best years:** (Reserva) (2010) 09 **08 07 06 05 04 03 02 01 00 99 98** 95 94 86 85.

COONAWARRA *South Australia* A cigar-shaped ridge of terra rossa soil over limestone, Coonawarra can produce sublime Cabernet with leafy blackcurrant flavours yet real inky depth, and spicy Shiraz that can age for years. Riesling, Sauvignon and Merlot can be good too. Massive expansion outside the terra rossa strip has caused inconsistency and many poor wines bearing the Coonawarra label, but this has spurred the owners of the terra rossa land to redouble their efforts to produce some of Australia's best wine. Best producers: BALNAVES★★, Bowen, BRAND'S★★, Hollick★, Katnook★★, Ladbroke Grove, Leconfield★, LINDEMAN'S★★, MAJELLA★★★, PARKER★★, PENLEY★★, PETALUMA★, ST HUGO★★, WYNNS★★★, Zema★. Best years: (Cabernet Sauvignon) (2013) 12 10 09 08 **06 05 04 03 02 01 99 98 97 96 94 91 90**.

COOPERS CREEK *Auckland, North Island, New Zealand* Successful HAWKES BAY Swamp Reserve Chardonnay★ and tangy MARLBOROUGH Sauvignon Blanc★. GISBORNE Arneis★ and Albariño★, Marlborough Riesling★ and Late Harvest Riesling★ are also good. A smart range of Reserve reds from Hawkes Bay includes powerful Syrah★ and complex Merlot★ and Cabernet Sauvignon blends★. Best years: (Chardonnay) (2013) **10 09 07**.

FRANCIS FORD COPPOLA *Rutherford AVA, California, USA* Movie director Francis Ford Coppola splits his winemaking activities between luxury and lifestyle brands, with volume approaching 1 million cases. He purchased the historic Inglenook Niebaum winery in 1975, and in 2011 finally acquired the trademarked Inglenook name. Rubicon★, a BORDEAUX blend, is still a bit thick-set for my taste. However, beginning with the 2011 there are hints in the young wines that Coppola is serious about restoring a more balanced classic Napa style Cabernet as well as restoring the historic winery. Also noteworthy are Cask Cabernet★★, Edizione Pennino★ (Zinfandel), RC Reserve Syrah★ and tiny amounts of Merlot★★ and Cabernet Franc★★, as well as white blend Blancaneaux★. The Francis Ford Coppola Winery in Sonoma County is an elaborate tourist destination, where brands include Sofia bubblies and good-value Coppola Diamond Collection varietals. Best years: (Rubicon) (2013) (12) (11) 10 **09 08 07 06 05 04 03 02 01 00 99 97 96 95 94 91**.

CORBIÈRES AC *Languedoc, France* Huge region of mixed quality. It can, especially its cru of Boutenac, produce some of LANGUEDOC's best reds, with juicy fruit and a whiff of wild hillside herbs. Excellent young, but the best can age for years. White Corbières can be tasty; drink young. Best producers: Baillat★, La Baronne★, Bel-Evêque★, Caraguilhes★, Cascadais★, CLOS DE L'ANHEL★, Clos Perdus★, Embrès-et-Castelmaure★, Étang des Colombes★, Fontsainte★, Grand Crès★, Grand Moulin★, Haut-Gléon★, Hélène★, l'Ille★, Lastours★, Mansenoble★, Ollieux-Romanis★, les Palais★, St-Auriol★, Voulte-Gasparets★. Best years: (reds) (2013) 12 **11 10 09 08 07 06 05**.

CORISON *Napa Valley AVA, California, USA* Cathy Corison is one of NAPA VALLEY's best Cabernet producers, steering clear of the heavily oaked, over-extracted style favoured by many Napa newcomers. The straight Cabernet★★★ and Kronos Vineyard Cabernet★★★ are

CORISON
KRONOS VINEYARD
NAPA VALLEY
CABERNET
SAUVIGNON

gorgeous, ageworthy wines. She also makes ANDERSON VALLEY Gewurztraminer★. Best years: (Kronos) (2012) (11) 10 **09 08 07 06 05 04 03 01 00 99 95 91 90**.

CORLISS ESTATES *Columbia Valley AVA, Washington State, USA* Michael and Lauri Corliss produce a bold mineral Syrah★★, a complex BORDEAUX-style red★★, and an ageworthy Cabernet Sauvignon★★ that ranks with the top in Washington. Wines are released after significant bottle-aging, adding complexity and balance. Best years: (2012) (11) (10) 09 **08 07 06 05**.

CORNAS AC *Rhône Valley, France* Pure Syrah wines with clearer, racier fruit and balance in the past 10 years, including some remarkable 2010s; compelling alternatives to pricey neighbours HERMITAGE and CÔTE-RÔTIE. When young, the wines are dark red, with brooding dark fruit aromas; the fruit comes with a mineral tang. Best producers: ALLEMAND★★★, F Balthazar★★, CLAPE★★★, COLOMBO★★, du Coulet★, Courbis★★, DELAS★, E & J Durand★★, Equis, G Gilles★, JABOULET, J Lemenicier★, P Lionnet★, J Michel★, V Paris★★, Cave de TAIN★, Tardieu-Laurent★, Tunnel★, A Voge★★. Best years: 2013 12 11 10 09 **07 06 05 04 03 01 00 99 98 97 96 95 94 91 90 89 88 85**.

CORSE AC, VIN DE *Corsica, France* Overall AC for CORSICA with 5 superior sub-regions: Calvi, Coteaux du Cap Corse, Figari, Porto Vecchio and Sartène. Ajaccio and Patrimonio are entitled to their own ACs. The most distinctive wines, mainly red, come from local grapes: Nielluccio and Sciaccarello for reds, Vermentino (known locally as Vermentinu or Malvasia) for whites. There are some rich sweet Muscats, especially from Muscat du Cap Corse AC. Best producers: Alzipratu★, ARENA★, Clos d'Alzeto★, CLOS CANARELLI★, Clos Capitoro, Clos Culombu★, Clos Landry★, Clos Nicrosi★, Gentile, Yves Leccia★, Maestracci★, Comte Peraldi★, Renucci★, Saparale, Signadore, Torraccia★.

CORSICA *France* This Mediterranean island has continued its trend toward quality, reaping the benefits of investment in equipment, replanting native grape varieties and working the vines organically to best express the site and *terroir*. Syrah, Merlot, Cabernet Sauvignon and Mourvèdre for reds, and Chardonnay and Sauvignon Blanc for whites, are used to complement the local reds (Nielluccio, Sciaccarello and Aleatico) and whites (Barbarossa, Bianco Gentile and Vermentino). Whites and rosés are pleasant for drinking young; reds are more exciting and can age for 3–4 years. See also CORSE AC.

CORTES DE CIMA *Alentejo, Portugal* Good modern Portuguese reds. Blends of Aragonez (Tempranillo) and Syrah with Portuguese grapes such as Trincadeira and Touriga Nacional are used for spicy, fruity Chaminé, oaked red Cortes de Cima★ and a splendid dark, smoky Reserva★★. Also aromatic varietal Touriga Nacional★★ and Incógnito★★, a gutsy, black-fruited blockbuster Syrah. Best years: **2010 09 08 05 04 03**.

CORTESE White grape variety of south-eastern PIEDMONT in Italy; it can produce good, zesty, fairly acidic, dry whites. Sometimes labelled simply as Cortese Piemonte DOC, its main purpose is as the sole grape in GAVI.

CORTON AC *Grand Cru, Côte de Beaune, Burgundy, France* The only red Grand Cru in the CÔTE DE BEAUNE; the best examples have some of the perfumed class of fine CÔTE DE NUITS. Too much land was classified as Grand Cru and some does not deserve it. Best wines are from Bressandes, Clos du Roi, Le Corton and Le Rognet. New excitement with participation of Dom. de la ROMANÉE-CONTI from 2009. Very little white Corton. Best producers: B Ambroise★★, d'Ardhuy★★, Bonneau du Martray★★, CHANDON DE BRIAILLES★★, Croix★★, Dubreuil-Fontaine★★, FAIVELEY★★★, Follin-Arbelet★, Camille Giroud★★, Guyon★★, JADOT★★★, Dom. LEROY★★, MEO-CAMUZET★★★, Dom. du Pavillon/Bichot★★, J Prieur★★, Dom. de la ROMANÉE-CONTI (from 2009), Senard★, TOLLOT-BEAUT★, VOUGERAIE★★. Best years: (reds) (2013) 12 11 10 09 **08 07 06** 05 **03 02 01** 99 98 96 95 90.

CORTON-CHARLEMAGNE AC *Grand Cru, Côte de Beaune, Burgundy, France*
Corton-Charlemagne, on the west and south-west flanks and at the top of the famous CORTON hill, is the largest of Burgundy's white Grands Crus. It can produce some of the most impressive white Burgundies – richly textured yet with a fine mineral quality. The best should show their real worth only at 10 years or more. Best producers: H Boillot★, Bonneau du Martray★★★, BOUCHARD PÈRE ET FILS★★, Champy★★, COCHE-DURY★★★, DROUHIN★★, FAIVELEY★★, V GIRARDIN★★, JADOT★★★, P Javillier★★, Louis LATOUR★★, J Prieur★★, Rapet★★, M Rollin★★, ROUMIER★★, TOLLOT-BEAUT★★, VOUGERAIE★★. Best years: 2012 11 10 09 08 **07 06 05 04 02 00**.

CORVINA Indigenous grape of VENETO, the basis of all VALPOLICELLA (AMARONE, RECIOTO and *ripasso*). Traditionally blended with Rondinella and Molinara, it is nowadays more often partnered with Croatina and the fashionable Oseleta and makes some exciting IGT Veronese reds.

CH. COS D'ESTOURNEL★★★ *St-Estèphe AC, 2ème Cru Classé, Haut-Médoc, Bordeaux, France* One of the leading châteaux of BORDEAUX. The wine is classically made for aging, needing 10 years to show really well. Used to have a high proportion of Merlot (around 40%) but from 2007 Cabernet Sauvignon has been on the increase (65–85%). Recent vintages have been dark, brooding and powerful. Small production of white from 2005 and new state-of-the-art winery in 2008. Second wine: les Pagodes de Cos. Best years: 2012 11 10 09 08 **07 06 05** 04 03 02 01 00 96 95 90 89.

DOM. COSSE-MAISONNEUVE *Cahors AOP, South-West France* Cult bio-dynamic producer of CAHORS; experience has tamed their initially prodigal use of new wood. From the fruity Le Combal★, move up through Le Petit Sid★★ to Les Laquets★★ and finally Le Sid★★, which reflects the iron that underlies the soil. Best years: (2012) 11 10 09 **08 06 05** 04 01.

COSTANTI *Brunello di Montalcino DOCG, Tuscany, Italy* One of the original Montalcino estates, making fine BRUNELLO★★ (Riserva★★) and ROSSO DI MONTALCINO★, as well as Vermiglio★, a partially barrique-aged Sangiovese, and 'international' style Merlot-Cabernet blend Calbello★. Best years: (Brunello) (2011) (10) (09) (08) **07 06 04 01** 99 97 95 90 88 85 82.

COSTERS DEL SEGRE DO *Cataluña, Spain* DO in western CATALUÑA, with an array of grape varieties, generally good quality and moderate prices. Best producers: Castell del Remei★, Celler de Cérvoles★, Tomàs Cusiné★, RAÏMAT★. Best years: (reds) 2010 **09 08 07 06 05 04** 03 01.

COSTIÈRES DE NÎMES AC *Rhône Valley, France* Region west of Avignon. Reds are bright, spicy, chewy, perfumed, the best substantial; rosés are nicely full young gluggers; whites are tasty, rich versions of Marsanne and Roussanne. Best producers: l'Amarine★, Amphoux, Grande Cassagne★, Lamargue, Mas des Bressades★, Mas Carlot★, Mas Neuf, Mourgues du Grès★, Nages★, d'Or et de Gueules★, la Patience, Roubaud★, Tardieu-Laurent, la Tour de Beraud★, la Tuilerie, Vieux-Relais★. Best years: 2012 11 10 09 07.

CÔTE DE BEAUNE *Côte d'Or, Burgundy, France* Southern part of the CÔTE D'OR: beginning at the hill of CORTON, north of the town of BEAUNE, the Côte de Beaune progresses south as far as MARANGES. Mostly red, but whites dominate MEURSAULT, ST ROMAIN, ST AUBIN, PULIGNY and CHASSAGNE.

CÔTE DE BEAUNE AC *Côte de Beaune, Burgundy, France* Small AC, high on the hill above the town of Beaune, named to ensure confusion with the title of the region. Lean but attractive reds and whites. Best producers: DROUHIN★, Giboulot★, VOUGERAIE★. Best years: (red) 2012 11 10 09 05.

CÔTE DE BEAUNE-VILLAGES AC *Côte de Beaune, Burgundy, France* Red wine AC covering 16 villages, such as LADOIX, MARANGES and MEURSAULT. Blends from several villages are sold as Côte de Beaune-Villages. Best producers: DROUHIN★, JADOT★, LAFARGE★. Best years: 2012 11 10 09 05.

CÔTE DE BROUILLY AC *Beaujolais, Burgundy, France* Wine from the slopes of Mont Brouilly, a small, abrupt volcanic mountain in the south of the BEAUJOLAIS Crus area. The wine is deeper in colour and fruit and has more intensity than that of BROUILLY. Best producers: G Chetaille★, J Duport, Lagneau (Vieilles Vignes★), Ch. Thivin★★. Best years: (2013) 11.

CÔTE CHALONNAISE See BOURGOGNE-CÔTE CHALONNAISE.

CÔTE DE NUITS *Côte d'Or, Burgundy, France* The northern part of the CÔTE D'OR and *not* an AC. Almost entirely red wine country, the vineyards start in the southern suburbs of Dijon and continue south in a narrow swathe to below the town of NUITS-ST-GEORGES. Some of the greatest wine names in the world – GEVREY-CHAMBERTIN, VOUGEOT and VOSNE-ROMANÉE etc.

CÔTE DE NUITS-VILLAGES AC *Côte de Nuits, Burgundy, France* The wines (mostly red) are often good, sourced from lesser villages north of GEVREY and south of NUITS – not very deep in colour but with a nice cherry fruit. Best producers: (reds) l'Arlot, D BACHELET, BELLENE, Chopin-Groffier★, David Clark★, J-J Confuron, de la Douaix★, Gille★, JADOT, G Jourdan★, Loichet, Millot★. Best years: (reds) (2013) 12 **11** 10 09 08 05.

CÔTE D'OR *Burgundy, France* Europe's most northerly great red wine area, and also the home of some of the world's best dry white wines. The name, meaning 'golden slope', refers to a 48km (30-mile) stretch between Dijon and Chagny, which divides into the CÔTE DE NUITS in the north and the CÔTE DE BEAUNE in the south.

CÔTE ROANNAISE AC *Loire Valley, France* Small, improving AC in the upper LOIRE producing Gamay reds and rosés; the best are of BEAUJOLAIS-VILLAGES standard. Vin de pays whites can be good. Best producers: A Baillon, V Giraudon, de la Paroisse, M Piat, R Sérol★.

CÔTE-RÔTIE AC *Rhône Valley, France* The Côte-Rôtie, or 'roasted slope', produces one of France's finest, most intriguing red wines. Stylistically, this is where Rhône meets Burgundy – unless it has been over-oaked. On its steep slopes, the Syrah balances full aromatic ripeness with freshness, and the small amount of white Viognier sometimes included adds exotic or violet fragrance. Lovely young, it is better aged for 5–8 years. Best producers: G Barge★★, Bernard★, Billon★, P & C Bonnefond★, Bonserine★★, B Burgaud★, J Champet★, CHAPOUTIER★★, Clusel-Roch★★, CUILLERON★★, DELAS★★, Duclaux★★, Garon★, X Gérard, J-M Gérin★★, GUIGAL★★, JAMET★★★, P Jasmin★★, Levet★, Monteillet★, R Niéro★, S Ogier★★, Pichat, Rosiers★, ROSTAING★★, J-M Stéphan★, Tardieu-Laurent★★, VIDAL-FLEURY★, F Villard★★, Vins de Vienne★. Best years: 2013 12 11 10 09 07 06 05 04 03 01 00 99 98 95 94 91 90 89 85.

COTEAUX D'AIX-EN-PROVENCE AC *Provence, France* The first AC in the south to allow Cabernet Sauvignon to enhance the traditional local grape varieties Grenache, Cinsaut, Mourvèdre, Syrah and Carignan. The reds can age. Some decent fresh rosé. The whites, mostly traditionally made, are merely pleasant. Best producers: Ch. Bas★, les Bastides★, les Béates★★, Beaupré★, Calissanne★, d'EOLE★, Fonscolombe, Revelette★, Valdition, Vignelaure★. Best years: (reds) (2013) 12 11 10 **09 08 07 06 05**.

COTEAUX DE L'ARDÈCHE, VIN DE PAYS DES *Rhône Valley, France* Increasingly good, lively red wines made from Cabernet Sauvignon, Syrah, Merlot or Gamay, and dry, fresh whites from Chardonnay,

Viognier or Sauvignon Blanc. Best producers: Vignerons Ardéchois, Colombier, DUBOEUF, G Farge (white), G Flacher, Grangeon, Louis LATOUR★, Mas de Libian (Viognier), Notre Dame de Cousignac, Pradel, Romaneaux-Destezet★, St-Désirat★, Vigier.

COTEAUX DE L'AUBANCE AC *Loire Valley, France* Smallish AC north of COTEAUX DU LAYON AC for sweet or semi-sweet white wines made from Chenin Blanc. Top sweet wines are labelled Sélection de Grains Nobles. Best producers: Bablut★★/Daviau, Dittière, Giraudières, Haute Perche★, Montgilet★★, Princé, Richou★★, Rochelles★/J-Y Lebreton. Best years: 2011 **10 09 07 06 05 04 03 02 01 97 96**.

COTEAUX BOURGUIGNONS AC *Burgundy, France* New AC has replaced BOURGOGNE Grand Ordinaire from 2011. Expect a load of reclassified cheap BEAUJOLAIS which may be easier to market under this spurious name.

COTEAUX CHAMPENOIS AC *Champagne, France* Still wines from Champagne, notably from Bouzy, Aÿ and Hautvillers. Usually fairly acid. The best age for 5 years or more. Best producers: Paul Bara★, BOLLINGER★, Egly-Ouriet★, Geoffroy★, H Goutorbe, Benoît Lahaye★, LAURENT-PERRIER, Joseph PERRIER, Ch. de Saran★/MOËT & CHANDON. Best years: (2012) 09 08 **07 04**.

COTEAUX DU GIENNOIS AC *Loire Valley, France* AC near SANCERRE for Sauvignon Blanc white wines, reds and rosés from Pinot Noir or Gamay. Best producers: E Balland★, C&F Berthier★, J-M Berthier★★, H BOURGEOIS★, M Langlois, J Mellot★, de Montbenoit★, Quintin, Florian Roblin, Thibault, Villargeau.

COTEAUX DU LANGUEDOC AC *Languedoc, France* Large region between Nîmes and Narbonne, producing around 51 million bottles of beefy red, tasty rosé and surprisingly characterful whites. Quality is improving year by year. Gradually being replaced by the larger LANGUEDOC AC, which covers Roussillon as well. A number of 'crus' are in the process of being delineated by climate and soil type – among the best of these are La CLAPE, PIC ST-LOUP and TERRASSES DU LARZAC – some of which have been granted their own appellations. All is in a state of flux. See also LANGUEDOC-ROUSSILLON. Best producers: d'Aupilhac★, les Aurelles★, Clavel★, la Coste★, Lacroix-Vanel★, Mas Cal Demoura★, Mas des Chimères★, Mas Jullien★, Mas de Martin, Montcalmès, Peyre Rose★, Poujol★, PRIEURE DE ST-JEAN DE BÉBIAN★★, Puech-Haut★, St-Martin de la Garrigue★, Terre Megère★. Best years: (2013) 12 **11 10 09 08 07 06 05**.

COTEAUX DU LAYON AC *Loire Valley, France* Sweet wine from the Layon Valley, south of Angers. The wine is made from Chenin Blanc grapes that, ideally, are attacked by noble rot or, for intense but fresher styles, dried by warm, autumnal breezes that concentrate grape sugars. In great years like 2007, and from a talented grower, this can be one of the world's exceptional sweet wines. Six villages are entitled to use the Coteaux du Layon-Villages AC, which requires lower yields; the village name appears on the label. Three sub-areas, BONNEZEAUX, QUARTS DE CHAUME and Chaume, have their own ACs. Best producers: P Aguilas★★, P Baudouin★★, Baumard★★, Bergerie★★, Cady★★, P Delesvaux★★, Dom. F L, Forges★, de Juchepie★, OGEREAU★★, Passavant★, PIERRE-BISE★★★, Pithon-Paillé★, Quarres★, J Renou★★, Roulerie★★, Sablonnettes★★, Sauveroy★, Soucherie★★. Best years: 2011 **10 09 07 06 05 04 03 02 01 97 96 95 90**.

COTEAUX DU LOIR AC See JASNIÈRES AC.

COTEAUX DU LYONNAIS AC *Beaujolais, Burgundy, France* Good, light, BEAUJOLAIS-style reds and a few whites and rosés from scattered vineyards between Villefranche and Lyon. Drink young.

COTEAUX DU QUERCY AOP *South-West France* Cabernet Franc-based area south of CAHORS. Fruity food-friendly wines, best kept for 3–4 years. Best producers: d'Ariès, Ganapes, la Garde, Merchien★ (IGP wines). Best years: (2012) 11 **10 09** 08 06 05.

COTEAUX VAROIS-EN-PROVENCE AC *Provence, France* Improving area north of Toulon and stretching inland, where it is notably cooler than the coast, with new plantings of classic grapes. Best producers: Alysses★, Calisse★, Deffends★, Duvivier, Fontlade, Garbelle, Gayolle, Margüi★, Miraval★, Routas★, St-Estève, St-Jean-le-Vieux, Triennes★. Best years: (2013) 12 11 **10 09**.

CÔTES DE BERGERAC AOP See BERGERAC.

CÔTES DE BORDEAUX AC See BLAYE, CADILLAC, CASTILLON, FRANCS.

CÔTES DE BOURG AC *Bordeaux, France* Earthy but blackcurranty reds which can age for 6–10 years. A little dry but dull white. Best producers: Brulesécaille★, Bujan★, Civrac, FALFAS★, Fougas (Maldoror★), Grand-Maison★, Grave (Nectar★), Guerry★, Haut-Guiraud★, Haut-Macô★, Haut-Mondésir★, Mercier★, Nodoz★, ROC DE CAMBES★★. Best years: 2012 **10 09** 08 05 03.

CÔTES DU BRULHOIS AOP *South-West France* A handful of rapidly improving winemakers clustered round the city of Agen. The reds will age. Best producers: La Bastide, Bois de Simon, Coujetou-Peyret, Pountet, des Thermes, Vignerons du Brulhois co-op. Best years: (2012) 11 **10 09** 08.

CÔTES CATALANES, IGP DES *Roussillon, France* Covering much the same area as the CÔTES DU ROUSSILLON AC; co-ops dominate production but there is a growing number of talented individual producers, especially in the Fenouillèdes hills, benefiting from outside investment. Warm, rich, spicy reds, often from old-vines Grenache Noir and Carignan, plus Syrah; full-bodied minerally whites from Grenache Blanc and Gris, and Macabeo. Best producers: CASENOVE★, CAZES★, l'Horizon, Jones★, Matassa, Pertuisane, Olivier Pithon, Préceptorie de Centenach, le Soula★★/GAUBY, Soulanes.

CÔTES DE DURAS AOP *South-West France* South of BERGERAC, and currently the hottest of the Bordeaux satellites, home to many organic growers. The vanguard is led by domaines Haut Lavigne★, Hauts de Riquets★, Mont Ramé★, Mouthes-le-Bihan★★ and Petit Malromé★. More traditional estates include des Allegrets, Chater★, Condom-Perceval (sweet white★★) and Laulan★. Best years: (reds) 2012 11 **10 09** 08.

CÔTES DE GASCOGNE, IGP DES *South-West France* Tangy-fresh, fruity, mostly white, wine-bar-style wines that outsell everything else from the South-West put together. Drink young. Best producers: Arton, Brumont★, Cassagnoles, Chiroulet★, Haut Campagnau★, de Joÿ, Lauroux, Ménard, Millet★, Pellehaut★, PLAIMONT★, San de Guilhem★, Sédouprat, TARIQUET★.

CÔTES DU JURA AC *Jura, France* This AC includes a variety of ageworthy wines, including specialities *vin jaune* and *vin de paille*. Savagnin makes strong-tasting whites, often sherry-like; some Chardonnay is made in this style, while others are dry and mineral, reminiscent of good CÔTE CHALONNAISE. Very light, distinctive reds and rosés from local Poulsard and Trousseau and also from Pinot Noir. Newly confident Jura producers are now being seen far more in export markets. See also CRÉMANT DU JURA AC. Best producers: Badoz★, Baud, Berthet-Bondet★, Bourdy★, Buronfosse, Ganevat★★, Labet★★, Macle★, Marnes-Blanches, Pignier★★, Reverchon, Rijckaert★, A & M Tissot★. Best years: 2012 11 **10 09**.

CÔTES DU MARMANDAIS AOP *South-West France* Gascony's northern gateway. Abouriou, Cot, Fer Servadou, Gamay and Syrah give the reds a southern twist. Best producers: Beaulieu★, Beyssac★, Bonnet, ELIAN DA ROS★★, Lassolle, Cave du Marmandais. Best years: (reds) 2012 11 **10 09** 08 06 05.

CÔTES DE PROVENCE AC *Provence, France* Large AC mainly for fruity reds and rosés to drink young. Whites have improved. Three new sub-appellations show that producers are taking regional differences more seriously: Côtes de Provence-Ste Victoire, producing wines with fresh minerality and good aging ability; Côtes de Provence-La Londe, for wines with salty-mineral acidity, mainly rosés but also rich, fruity reds; and Côtes de Provence-Pierrefeu. Best producers: l'Arnaude, Barbanau★, la Bernarde★, Clos d'Alari, Clos de la Procure, Commanderie de Peyrassol★, la Courtade★, Coussin Ste-Victoire★, Cressonnière★, la Croix★, d'ESCLANS, Féraud★, Ferme des Lices, Galoupet, Gavoty★, Houchart, Jale, Malherbe, Mas de Cadenet, Mauvanne★, Minuty★, Ott★, Pourcieux, Réal Martin★, RICHEAUME★, Rimauresq★★, Roquefort★, St-Albert, St-André de Figuière, Ste Marguerite, Sarrins★, SORIN★, Élie Sumeire★, les Valentines.

CÔTES DU RHÔNE AC *Rhône Valley, France* AC for the whole RHÔNE VALLEY. Over 90% is red and rosé, mainly Grenache, with some Cinsaut, Syrah, Carignan and Mourvèdre. Modern winemaking has improved many wines, which are generally juicy, spicy and easy to drink, ideally within 5 years. Most wine is made by co-ops, some improving. Best producers: (reds) Amouriers★, d'Andézon★, les Aphillanthes★, l'Aure, A Brunel★, Camille Cayran, Chamfort, D Charavin★, Charvin★★, CLAPE★, Clos des Grillons, Co Ho La, COLOMBO★, Coteaux des Travers, Coudoulet de BEAUCASTEL★, Cros de la Mûre★★, Dauvergne Ranvier, DELAS, Espiers★, Fonsalette★★, FONT DE MICHELLE★, Gramenon★★, Grand Moulas★, Grand Prébois★, GUIGAL★★, Haut-Musiel, Hugues★, JABOULET★, JAMET★★, la Janasse★★, Lombard★, la Manarine, Mas de Libian★, Montfaucon★, la Mordorée★, la RÉMÉJEANNE★★, M Richaud★, Romarins, Rouge Garance, St-Estève d'Uchaux, St-Etienne, ST GAYAN, Ste-Anne★, Santa Duc★, la Soumade★, Tardieu-Laurent★, Texier (Brézème★), Tours★, Trapadis★, Vieille Julienne★, Vieux-Chêne★; (whites) Cassan, Coudoulet de BEAUCASTEL★, Estézargues co-op★, P Gaillard★, GUIGAL★★, Mas de Sainte Croix, la RÉMÉJEANNE★, Saint-Amant★, Ste-Anne★, Texier★★, Trapadis★. Best years: (reds) **2012 11 10**.

CÔTES DU RHÔNE-VILLAGES AC *Rhône Valley, France* AC covering 18 villages in the southern CÔTES DU RHÔNE that have traditionally made superior wine (especially CAIRANNE, Laudun, Massif d'Uchaux, Séguret, Valréas, Sablet, Visan – and from 2012, Gadagne). Some exciting, good value wines. Best are spicy, food-friendly reds that can age well, notably in 2010. Best producers: Achiary★, Beaurenard★, Boissan★, de Bord, Bramadou, Brugalière, de Cabasse★, Cabotte★, Chapoton★, Chaume-Arnaud★, Clos des Mourres, Combe★, Coriançon★, Coste Chaude, Cros de la Mûre★, J David★, Durieu, Echevin, Espigouette★, Estézargues co-op★, Florane, Fourmente★, Gramenon★, Grand Veneur★, la Janasse★★, Jérôme★, Lucena, Mourchon★, Pélaquié★, Piaugier★, Pique Basse★, Rabasse-Charavin★, Rasteau co-op★, la RÉMÉJEANNE★, Roche-Audran, Cave St-Maurice, St-Pierre, St-Siffrein, Saladin, Val des Rois, Valériane, Viret★. Best years: (reds) **2012 11 10 09 07**.

CÔTES DU ROUSSILLON AC/CÔTES DU ROUSSILLON-VILLAGES AC *Roussillon, France* ROUSSILLON's catch-all AC, dominated by co-ops. It's a hot area, but there's a lively bunch of estates making exciting reds and doing surprisingly good things with whites. Red wines from the best (northern) sites may use the Côtes du Roussillon-Villages AC, and villages Caramany, Latour-de-France, Lesquerde and Tautavel may add their own name. Best producers: (reds) Calvet-Thunevin, CAZES★, Chênes★, Clos des Fées★, CLOT DE L'OUM★, Ferrer-Ribière★, Fontanel★, Força Réal, Gardiés★, GAUBY★★, Jau, Joliette, Laporte★, Mas Amiel★, Mas Crémat★, Mossé, Piquemal, Olivier Pithon★, Réveille, Rivesaltes co-op, Roc des Anges★, Sarda-Malet★, Schistes★. Best years: (2013) 12 11 10 09 08 07 06 05.

CÔTES DE THONGUE, IGP DES *Languedoc, France* Zone north-east of Béziers, where some dynamic estates are producing excellent results, with intriguing blends as well as varietal wines. Best producers: l'Arjolle★, les Chemins de Bassac, La Croix Belle, Monplézy.

QUINTA DO CÔTTO *Douro DOC and Port DOC, Douro, Portugal* Quinta do Côtto DOURO red and creamy Paço de Teixeró white are good, and Grande Escolha★★ can be excellent: initially powerful, rich and cedary when mature. Best years: (Grande Escolha) 2011 10 08 07 01 00 97 95 94 90.

VIGNOBLES DE LA COULÉE-DE-SERRANT *Savennières AC, Loire Valley, France* Nicolas Joly is biodynamics' most vocal proponent and, with his winemaker daughter Virginie, produces powerfully concentrated, ageworthy SAVENNIÈRES wines with atypically high alcohol. Top cuvée hails from monopole Clos de la Coulée de Serrant★★, a steep, walled 7ha (17-acre) vineyard with its own sub-appellation. Also impressive Savennières Clos de la Bergerie★★ and Les Vieux Clos★. Best years: (2012) 09 08 07 06 05 04 03 02 01 00 97 96 95 90 89.

PIERRE COURSODON *St-Joseph AC, Rhône Valley, France* Family-owned 16ha (40-acre) domaine producing rocking, fruit-laden, rich ST-JOSEPH★ from old vines. Reds need up to 4 years to show their magnificent cassis, truffle and violet richness, especially La Sensonne★★, aged in new oak, and le Paradis St Pierre★★. Food-friendly whites, especially Paradis St Pierre★ from Marsanne. Best years: (reds) 2013 12 11 10 09 07 06 05 03 01 99 98.

COUSIÑO MACUL *Maipo, Chile* Sixth-generation Cousiño family winery. The old Macul winery near Santiago city is a draw for tourists, but wines are now made in a modern facility further south. Best known for Antiguas Reservas★ and premium wines such as Lota★ and Finis Terrae★.

CH. COUTET★★ *Barsac AC, 1er Cru Classé, Bordeaux, France* BARSAC's largest Classed Growth property; on great form in recent years, and with its finesse and balance it is once again a classic Barsac. Extraordinarily intense Cuvée Madame★★ is made in exceptional years. Best years: 2012 11 10 09 07 06 05 04 03 02 01 00 99 98 97 96 95.

CRAGGY RANGE *Hawkes Bay and Martinborough, North Island, New Zealand* Ambitious winery; style becomes more attractive with each vintage. HAWKES BAY wines include bold, Cabernet-based The Quarry★★, a rich, butch Merlot blend called Sophia★★ and Le Sol Syrah★★ (sometimes ★★★). Also elegant Gimblett Gravels Syrah★★, Merlot★ and Chardonnay★; fine Te Muna Road (MARTINBOROUGH) Pinot Noir★★, Sauvignon Blanc and Riesling★; restrained yet intense Avery Sauvignon Blanc★ from MARLBOROUGH. Best years: (Syrah) (2013) 11 10 09 08 07 06 04.

QUINTA DO CRASTO *Douro DOC and Port DOC, Douro, Portugal* Well-situated property with good Vintage★ PORT, massively enjoyable juicy reds Crasto★ and Crasto Superior★, complex Reserva Old Vines★★★, oaky but excellent Touriga Nacional★★ and Tinta Roriz★★, and flagship reds Vinha da Ponte★★★ and Maria Teresa★★★. Austere Xisto★ red is a venture with Jean-Michel Cazes of Ch. LYNCH-BAGES. Pleasant spicy Crasto white★. Best years: (Vintage port) 2011 10 07 04 03 00 99 97 95 94; (Ponte) 2010 07 04 00; (Maria Teresa) 2011 09 07 05 03 01 98.

CRÉMANT D'ALSACE AC *Alsace, France* Good traditional-method sparkling wine from ALSACE, usually made from Pinot Blanc and/or Pinot Gris. Reasonable quality, if not great value for money. Best producers: J-B Adam★, P Blanck★, Dirler-Cadé★, Dopff au Moulin★, A Dussourt★, J Gross★, Mittnacht Frères, MURÉ★, OSTERTAG★★, Pfaffenheim co-op, E Rentz, A Stoffel★, TURCKHEIM co-op.

CRÉMANT DE BOURGOGNE AC *Burgundy, France* Most Burgundian Crémant is white and is made either from Chardonnay alone or blended with Pinot Noir. Gamay, Aligoté, Pinot Blanc, Pinot Gris, Melon de Bourgogne and Sacy are also allowed in small measure. The result, especially in ripe years, can be full, soft, almost honey-flavoured – but needs 2–3 years' aging for mellowness to develop. Best producers: L Bouillot, A Delorme, L Loron, Simonnet-Febvre, A Sounit, Veuve Ambal; (co-ops) Bailly (rosé★), Hautes-Côtes, Lugny★, St-Gengoux-de-Scissé, Viré★.

CRÉMANT DE DIE AC *Rhône Valley, France* Traditional-method fizz made entirely from the Clairette Blanche grape. Crisper, more steely and less aromatic than CLAIRETTE DE DIE. Best producers: Jacques Faure, J-C Raspail★.

CRÉMANT DU JURA AC *Jura, France* AC for fizz from all over Jura, which accounts for a quarter of the region's production. Largely Chardonnay-based; Poulsard, a pale red grape, is dominant in the pinks. Best producers: Fruitière Vinicole d'Arbois, Baud★, Champ Divin, Grand★, La Maison du Vigneron (Marcel Cabelier), Montbourgeau★, Rolet★, A & M Tissot★★.

CRÉMANT DE LIMOUX AC *Languedoc, France* Sparkling wine made from a blend of Chardonnay, Chenin Blanc, Mauzac and Pinot Noir; the wines generally have more complexity than BLANQUETTE DE LIMOUX. Drink young. Best producers: l'Aigle★, Antech, Delmas, DENOIS, Fourn, Guinot, J Laurens★, Martinolles★, Rives-Blanques, SIEUR D'ARQUES.

CRÉMANT DE LOIRE AC *Loire Valley, France* Traditional-method sparkling wine from grapes from Anjou, Saumur and Touraine. Aged for at least 12 months, wines are generally finer than those of VOUVRAY and SAUMUR MOUSSEUX; increasingly Chardonnay is added to Loire stalwarts Chenin Blanc and Cabernet Franc, giving fresh, elegant fruit. Drink young. Best producers: l'Aulée, Baumard★, Bouvet-Ladubay★, Brizé★, Fardeau★, Gratien & Meyer, Langlois-Château★, des Liards★/Berger, Michaud★, Nerleux★, Passavant★, Richou, St-Just★, Varinelles★.

CRIOTS-BÂTARD-MONTRACHET AC See BÂTARD-MONTRACHET AC.

CROFT *Port DOC, Douro, Portugal* Owned by the Fladgate Partnership (along with TAYLOR'S and FONSECA), these wines are showing distinct improvement, especially at basic level. Vintage ports★★ have traditionally been elegant, rather than thunderous. Single-quinta Quinta da Roêda★ is pretty good. Also pioneering pink. Best years: (Vintage) 2011 09 **07 04 03 00 94 91 77 70 66 63 55**; (Roêda) 2008 **05 04 97 95**.

CROZES-HERMITAGE AC *Rhône Valley, France* The largest of the northern Rhône ACs, a mix of plains and hills. Ideally, the pure Syrah reds should have a strong, clear, black fruit flavour. You can drink them young (from the plains), but in ripe vintages the more red-fruited granite hill wines improve greatly for 2–5 years. In lesser years, too much clumsy oak on the more expensive wines can obscure the fruit. The best whites (2010 for instance) can age for 3–5 years. Best producers: (reds) A Belle★★, Bruyères★★, CHAPOUTIER★, Y Chave★, Colombier★ (Cuvée Gaby★★), Combier★ (Clos des Grives★★), E Darnaud★★, DELAS★ (Le Clos★★, Dom. des Grands Chemins★★), O Dumaine★, Entrefaux★, Fayolle Fils & Fille★★, Ferraton★, GRAILLOT★★, Paul JABOULET, P & V Jaboulet★, Lises★, Michelas St

Jemms, Murinais★, Pavillon-Mercurol★, Pochon★, Remizières★★, G Robin★★, Rousset (Picaudières★★), Cave de TAIN, Tardieu-Laurent★, Vins de Vienne★; (whites) Y Chave★, Colombier★, Combier★, Dard & Ribo★★, DELAS, O Dumaine★, Entrefaux★ (Les Pends★), Fayolle Fils & Fille★, Ferraton★, GRAILLOT★, Habrard★, Mucyn★, Pochon★ (Ch. Curson★★), Remizières★, M Sorrel★★. Best years: (reds) 2013 **12 11 10** 09 07 06 05 03 01 99.

YVES CUILLERON *Condrieu AC, Rhône Valley, France* Yves Cuilleron has a master touch with CONDRIEU's Viognier grape. Les Chaillets★★★, from old vines, is rich and sensual, with perfumed honey and apricot aromas. La Petite Côte★★ and 18-month-aged Vertige★★ are also exceptional, and the late-harvest Ayguets★★★ is a compelling, extraordinary sweet whirl of dried apricots, honey and barley sugar. Cuilleron also makes red and white ST-JOSEPH★★, ST-PÉRAY★★ and limited amounts of ripe, dark, oaked, spicy CÔTE-RÔTIE★★. A joint venture, les Vins de Vienne, with Pierre Gaillard and François Villard, produces COLLINES RHODANIENNES Sotanum★★ (100% Syrah) and Taburnin★★ (100% Viognier). Best years: (Condrieu) 2013 12 11 **10** 09 08 07 06 05 04.

CULLEN *Margaret River, Western Australia* One of the original MARGARET RIVER vineyards, now run on biodynamic principles by Vanya Cullen. Kevin John Chardonnay★★★ is complex and satisfying; Sauvignon-Semillon★★ marries nectarines with melon and nuts. Diana Madeline Cabernet Sauvignon-Merlot★★★ is gloriously soft, deep and scented. Mangan Malbec-Petit Verdot-Merlot★★ is wild and delicious. Best years: (Cabernet Sauvignon-Merlot) (2013) 12 11 10 09 08 **07** 05 04 03 02 01 00 99 98 97 96 95 94.

CURICÓ *Chile* Most of the big producers here have planted Cabernet Sauvignon, Merlot, Carmenère, Chardonnay and Sauvignon Blanc. It's a bit warm for whites, except in the east by the Andes, but the long growing season provides good fruit concentration for reds. Best producers: Echeverría★, SAN PEDRO★, Miguel TORRES★★, VALDIVIESO★.

CVNE *Rioja DOCa, Rioja, Spain* Compañía Vinícola del Norte de España is the full name of this firm, usually known as 'coonay'. Viña Real Reserva★★ and Gran Reserva★★ reds can be rich and meaty, and easily surpass the more commercial Crianzas. Imperial Reserva★★ is balanced and delightful; Gran Reserva★★★ is long-lived and impressive. Top of the range is red Real de Asúa★★★. Best years: (Reservas) (2009) 08 **07** 05 04 03 02 01 98 96 95 94 91 90 89 87 86 85.

DIDIER DAGUENEAU *Pouilly-Fumé AC, Loire Valley, France* This much-needed innovator died in 2008 and was succeeded by his son, Louis-Benjamin. The range starts with Blanc Fumé★★ and moves up through flinty Buisson Renard★★ to barrel-fermented Silex★★ and Pur Sang★★ to Asteroïde★★, which is made in tiny quantities from ungrafted vines. Also a SANCERRE★★ from the precipitous Les Monts Damnés. Wines benefit from 4–5 years' aging. Also makes Jurançon Les JARDINS DE BABYLONE★. Best years: (2013) 12 11 **10** 09 08.

ROMANO DAL FORNO *Valpolicella DOC, Veneto, Italy* VALPOLICELLA Superiore★★ from Monte Lodoletta vineyard, outside the Valpolicella Classico area, is a model of power and grace; AMARONE★★★ and Vigna Seré★★★ (RECIOTO DELLA VALPOLICELLA) are even more voluptuous. Best years: (Amarone) (2011) **10** 09 08 07 06 04 03 01 00 97 96 95.

DALLA VALLE *Napa Valley AVA, California, USA* Stunning hillside winery, producing some of NAPA's most irresistible Cabernets. Maya★★★ is a magnificent blend of Cabernet Sauvignon and Cabernet Franc; the straight Cabernet Sauvignon★★★ is almost as rich and brilliantly balanced. The wines drink well at 10 years, but will keep for 20 or more.

DÃO DOC *Beiras, Portugal* With steep slopes and a great climate for local grape varieties, Dão is now producing characterful, scented, austerely satisfying red and white wines. Best producers: (reds) ALIANCA (Quinta da Garrida★), Quinta de Cabriz★, Julia Kemper★, Quinta das Maias★, Quinta do Mondego (Munda★), Pape★★, Quinta da Pellada★★, Quinta dos ROQUES★★, Quinta de Sães★, Caves SÃO JOÃO★, SOGRAPE★ (Quinta dos Carvalhais★), Quinta da Vegia★★; (whites) Quinta das Maias★, Quinta dos ROQUES★, Quinta de Sães★, SOGRAPE★. Best years: (reds) (2012) 11 09 **08 05 04 03 01 00 99 97 96 95**.

D'ARENBERG *McLaren Vale, South Australia*
At his 100-year-old family winery, Chester Osborn makes blockbuster Dead Arm Shiraz★★, Ironstone Pressings Grenache-Shiraz-Mourvèdre★★, Coppermine Road Cabernet Sauvignon★★, Custodian Grenache★ and numerous other blends from low-yielding old vines. These are big,

brash, character-filled wines, and are continually being joined by new ideas. In difficult times, Osborn steadily bought up plots of ancient vines around the Vale. Stellar but expensive single-vineyard Grenache (Beautiful View★★, Blewitt Springs★★, The Derelict Vineyard★★). Don't overlook the whites: Money Spider★ (Roussanne) and Hermit Crab★★ (Viognier-Marsanne) are lush and waxy. Best years: (Dead Arm Shiraz) (2013) 12 10 08 **06 05 04 03 02 01 00 97 96 95**.

VINCENT DAUVISSAT *Chablis, Burgundy, France* Refreshing, seductive and beautifully structured CHABLIS, with the fruit balancing the subtle influence of mostly older oak. Look for La Forest★★, the more aromatic Vaillons★★★ and the powerful Les Clos★★★. Also a red IRANCY★. Best years: (top crus) (2013) 12 11 **10 09 08 07 06 05 02 00 99**.

MARCO DE BARTOLI *Sicily, Italy* The winery is most noted for a dry, unfortified MARSALA-style wine called Vecchio Samperi – the late Marco De Bartoli's idea of what Marsala was before the English merchant John Woodhouse first fortified it for export. Particularly fine is the 20-year-old Ventennale★★: dry, intense and redolent of candied citrus peel, dates and raisins. Also excellent MOSCATO PASSITO DI PANTELLERIA Bukkuram★★.

DE BORTOLI *Riverina, New South Wales/Yarra, Victoria, Australia* Family-owned company producing large amounts of good-quality quaffing wine as well as some starry stuff, including YARRA VALLEY Chardonnay★★, Sauvignon★, Syrah★★, Pinot Noir★, Cabernet★ and three Melba★ Cabernet blends. The RIVERINA winery first gained prominence for its world-class botrytized Semillon (Noble One★★★), but is now equally well known for the quality of its budget labels – Sacred Hill, Deen and Montage. VICTORIA-based Sero, Windy Peak and Gulf Station quaffers can be good too. Best years: (Noble One) 2011 **10 08 07 06 04 03 02 00 98 96 95 94 93 90**.

DE LOACH *Russian River Valley AVA, California, USA* Revitalized under owner BOISSET of France, this property makes an array of stylish Pinot Noirs★★ and soft nutty Chardonnays★ from estate fruit. The winery recently released its first wines (three Pinot Noirs and a Chardonnay) from the cool Marin County AVA. Best years: (Pinot Noir) (2013) (12) (11) **10 09 08 07 06 05 04 03**.

DE MARTINO *Maipo, Chile* Old-established winery producing primarily robust but not over-concentrated red wines. Single Vineyard wines such as Alto de Piedras Carmenère★★ (from MAIPO), El León Carignan★★ from old vines in MAULE and Quebrada Seca Chardonnay★★ from LIMARÍ are among Chile's best examples of these grapes; Cabernet Sauvignon-based Familia★★ is dense and complex. Viejas Tinajas★★★ from Itata include a magnificent scented red from unirrigated old-vine Cinsault, and a captivating, floral white from dry-farmed Muscat, both vinified in the traditional Chilean way, in old earthenware amphorae (*tinajas*).

DE TRAFFORD *Stellenbosch WO, South Africa* David Trafford's barrel-fermented Chenin Blanc★, from venerable Helderberg vines, is rich and ageworthy; the Straw Wine★★ is honey-tinged and succulent. Spicy-rich yet elegant Syrah 393★★ heads the reds. Cabernet Sauvignon★ and Merlot★, alone and with Shiraz in Elevation 393★, are classically styled and built to age. Sijnn, a new venture at the mouth of the Breede River, shows much promise. Best years: (reds) 2012 **11** 10 09 08 07 06 05 04 03.

DEHLINGER *Russian River Valley AVA, California, USA* Outstanding Pinot Noir★★★ from vineyards in the cool RUSSIAN RIVER VALLEY, best at 5–10 years old. Also mouthfilling Chardonnay★★ and bold, peppery Syrah★★. Recent vintages of Cabernet Sauvignon★★ reflect a surge in quality. Best years: (Pinot Noir) (2011) 10 **09** 08 07 06 05 04 03 02.

MARCEL DEISS *Alsace AC, Alsace, France* Jean-Michel Deiss is fanatical about *terroir* and, controversially for ALSACE, his top wines are now blends, named according to the vineyard – Grands Crus Altenberg, Mambourg and Schoenenbourg are all ★★★. These are outstanding wines of huge character, often with some residual sugar. Pinot Noir Burlenburg★★ is vibrant and delicious. Basic Riesling and Pinot Blanc are delightful. Best years: (Grand Cru blends) (2013) (12) **11** 10 09 08 07 05 04 03 02 01.

DELAS FRÈRES *Rhône Valley, France* Upmarket, reliable merchant (owned by ROEDERER) selling wines from the whole RHÔNE VALLEY, but with its own vineyards in the northern Rhône. Single-vineyard wines include dense, powerful red HERMITAGE (Dom. des Tourettes★★, Les Bessards★★★), which needs a decade or more to reach its peak, perfumed CÔTE-RÔTIE La Landonne★★ and complex, *terroir*-specific ST-JOSEPH Ste-Épine★★; CROZES-HERMITAGE Le Clos★★ is good, too. Classy, aromatic CONDRIEU Clos Boucher★★ and good-value GRIGNAN-LES-ADHÉMAR red★, VACQUEYRAS★, VENTOUX red★ and TAVEL rosé. Best years: (premium reds) 2013 12 11 10 09 **07** 06 05 04 03 01 00 **99** 98 97 96 95 91 90 89 78.

DELEGAT *Henderson, Auckland, North Island, New Zealand* Family-run winery, getting larger by the second through Oyster Bay's massive expansion (Sauvignon Blanc, delicate Chardonnay, gently fruity Pinot Noir, soft-textured HAWKES BAY Merlot, sparkling wines from MARLBOROUGH). Chardonnay Reserve★, Merlot Reserve★ and Cabernet from Hawkes Bay.

DELILLE CELLARS *Columbia Valley AVA, Washington State, USA* Wines from some of the best YAKIMA vineyards. Chaleur Estate red★★ is a powerful, ageworthy Cabernet-Merlot BORDEAUX-style blend. Chaleur Estate Blanc★★ (Semillon-Sauvignon Blanc) has a GRAVES-like character. Doyenne is the RHÔNE-style label: Syrah★★ is serious, as are Métier★ and Aix★. D2 is an early-drinking red. Best years: (Chaleur Estate red) (2012) **11** 10 **09** 08 07 06.

DENBIES *Surrey, England* Impressive single vineyard with 107ha (265 acres) of vines planted on chalky slopes outside Dorking. Wines improving now with veteran Australian John Worontschak in charge of winemaking.

Sweet botrytis-influenced Noble Harvest, Greenfields fizz and medium-dry Chalk Ridge Rosé are the best wines.

JEAN-LOUIS DENOIS *Pays d'Oc IGP, Languedoc, France* Maverick producer based in LIMOUX; continually experimenting. His Chloé★ is made from Merlot, mixing the flavour of BORDEAUX with a bit of southern warmth. Also red and white Limoux★ and some good fizz★.

DEUTZ *Champagne AC, Champagne, France* This small company has been owned by Rouzaud family (who run ROEDERER) since 1993. The non-vintage Brut★★ is now regularly one of the best in CHAMPAGNE, sometimes boasting a cedary scent, while the top wines are the classic Blanc de Blancs★★, the weightier Cuvée William Deutz★★ and the de luxe vintage blanc de blancs Amour de Deutz★★. Pernod Ricard New Zealand produces Deutz Marlborough Cuvée★ under licence from Deutz. Best years: (2008) 07 06 05 **04 02 00 99 98 96 95 90 89 88**.

DEVIL'S LAIR *Margaret River, Western Australia* Former PENFOLDS white wine maker Oliver Crawford has made an impact with 9th Chamber Chardonnay★★★. The long-established Chardonnay★★ and Cabernet Sauvignon★★ and the Fifth Leg easy-drinkers have never been better, while the modestly priced Hidden Cave range – Chardonnay★, Sauvignon-Semillon★ and Cabernet-Shiraz★ – is turning heads.

D F J VINHOS *Portugal* Owned by one of Portugal's most innovative wine-makers, José Neiva. The large range includes off-dry Pink Elephant rosé, Segada red and white from LISBOA and Pedras do Monte from PENÍNSULA DE SETÚBAL. At the top end are the Grand'Arte reds, including fruity, peppery Trincadeira★ and beefy Alicante Bouschet★, the DFJ range (Alvarinho-Chardonnay★, Tinta Roriz-Merlot, Touriga Nacional-Touriga Franca★) and prestige wines from the DOURO (Escada★), ALENQUER (Francos Reserva) and LISBOA (Consensus).

DIAMOND CREEK *Diamond Mountain AVA, Napa County, California, USA* Small estate making only Cabernet Sauvignon, from 3 vineyards: Gravelly Meadow★★, Red Rock Terrace★★, Volcanic Hill★★★. Traditionally huge, tannic wines taking a decade to come around: now showing less tannin, and wonderful perfume and balance even when young. Best years: (2012) (10) **09 08 07 06 05** 04 03 02 01 00 99 98 97 96 95 94 92.

SCHLOSSGUT DIEL *Burg Layen, Nahe, Germany* Armin Diel excels at all styles of Riesling: sparkling, dry, and classic Auslese. From Dorsheim's top sites (Burgberg, Goldloch, Pittermännchen), these wines are generally ★★. Good Sekt★ too. Best years: (2013) 12 11 **10 09 08 07 05 04**.

DISTELL *Stellenbosch, South Africa* South Africa's largest wine company; wineries include consistent performers such as Neethlingshof, Durbanville Hills★ and Lomond★, near Cape Agulhas. The Fleur du Cap★ range is improving; Noble Late Harvest★★ botrytized dessert wine stands out. Two wineries in PAARL, Nederburg★ and Plaisir de Merle★, are run separately. There has been admirable progress across Nederburg's wide range; Ingenuity White★★ is a harmonious blend of 8 varieties; the Red★ is a vibrant mix of Sangiovese and Barbera with Nebbiolo. Botrytized Edelkeur★ is sold only through an annual auction.

DOGLIANI DOCG *Piedmont, Italy* Regarded as the finest source of Dolcetto, thanks to poor calcareous soils, altitude, sunny sites and proximity to the Maritime Alps. Dogliani can be aged in bottle (unlike most Dolcetto) when from the best producers. Best producers: M & E Abbona★, Ca' Viola, Chionetti★★, Donadei-Fabiani★★, Luigi Einaudi★, Pecchenino★, San Fereolo★★. Best years: 2013 12 11 10 09 08 07.

CH. DOISY-DAËNE★★ *Sauternes AC, 2ème Cru Classé, Bordeaux, France*
Owned by enologist Denis Dubourdieu (see Ch. REYNON), a consistently good property in BARSAC (although it uses the SAUTERNES AC). Principally Sémillon, with a splash of Sauvignon Blanc. It ages well for 10 years or more. The extra-rich Extravagant★★★ is produced in exceptional years. Doisy-Daëne Sec★ is a perfumed, barrel-fermented dry white; drink young. Best years: (sweet) 2012 11 **10 09 07 06 05 04 03 02 01 99 98.**

CH. DOISY-VÉDRINES★★ *Sauternes AC, 2ème Cru Classé, Bordeaux, France*
Next door to DOISY-DAËNE (and also using the SAUTERNES AC), Doisy-Védrines is a richly botrytized wine, fatter and more syrupy than most BARSAC. Best years: (sweet) 2012 11 **10 09 07 05 04 03 01 99 98 97 96 95 90.**

DOLCETTO Variety generally producing purple wines bursting with fruit. Virtually exclusive to PIEDMONT and LIGURIA, it boasts several DOCs and 3 DOCGs in Piemonte, with styles ranging from intense and rich in Alba, Ovada and Diano d'Alba, to lighter, more perfumed in Acqui and Asti. Many of the most serious wines are from Alba. Usually best drunk within 1–2 years, a few traditionally vinified wines can last 10 years. A tiny bit in California and Australia. Best producers: (Alba) Alario★★, ALTARE★★, Boglietti★★, Bongiovanni★★, Bricco Maiolica★, Bricco Rosso★, Brovia★, Elvio Cogno★★, Conterno-Fantino★★, GIACOSA★, B Marcarini★, B MASCARELLO★, G MASCARELLO★★, Paitin★, Pelissero★★, G RINALDI★★★, ROAGNA★★, Albino Rocca★★, Sandrone★, Vajra★★, Vietti★, Gianni Voerzio★, Roberto VOERZIO★. See also DOGLIANI.

DÔLE *Valais, Switzerland* Red wine from the VALAIS made from at least 51% Pinot Noir, the rest being Gamay. Dôle is generally a light wine. Most should be drunk young and lightly chilled. Best producers: G Clavien, Faye, Jean-René Germanier, A Mathier, Provins, G Raymond.

DOMAINE CARNEROS *Carneros AVA, California, USA* Very successful TAITTINGER-owned sparkling wine house. The vintage Brut might match Taittinger's Champagne if it were made a little drier. Far classier are vintage Le Rêve★★ (100% Chardonnay) and attractive Pinot Noirs★★. The winery also makes a small amount of a white from Pinot Noir grapes.

DOMAINE CHANDON *Yarra Valley, Victoria, Australia* MOËT & CHANDON's Aussie offshoot makes fine Pinot Noir-Chardonnay fizz: non-vintage Brut★ and Cuvée Riche, vintage Brut★★, Rosé★★, Blanc de Blancs★, Blanc de Noirs★, ZD★★ (Zero Dosage), YARRA VALLEY Brut★★ and a Tasmanian Cuvée★★, plus sparkling red Pinot-Shiraz★. Table wines under the Green Point label often of ★★ quality. The Green Point name is also used on fizz for export markets.

DOMAINE CHANDON *Napa Valley AVA, California, USA* California's first French-owned (MOËT & CHANDON) sparkling wine producer majors in reasonable price, but doesn't match the quality of Moët's subsidiaries in Australia or Argentina. Reserve bottlings can be rich and creamy. Étoile★ is an aged de luxe wine, also made as a flavourful Rosé★.

DOMAINE DROUHIN OREGON *Willamette Valley AVA, Oregon, USA* Burgundy wine merchant Robert DROUHIN bought 40ha (100 acres) in OREGON in 1987. In 2013 the family acquired the Roserock vineyard in the Eola-Amity Hills AVA, a property planted to 45ha (111 acres) of Pinot Noir and 4.5ha (11 acres) of Chardonnay, greatly expanding their estate production. The regular Pinot Noir★ (can be ★★) is lean but can be delightfully scented. The de luxe Pinot Noir Laurène★★ (can be

★★★) is supple and voluptuous when not over-oaked. Pinot Noir Louise★★ is a selection of the finest barrels in the winery. Also very good Chardonnay Arthur★★. Best years: (Pinot Noir) (2012) 11 10 **09 08 07**.

DOMAINE SERENE *Willamette Valley AVA, Oregon,* USA Full-bodied Pinot Noir Evenstad Reserve★★ is aged in French oak and has striking black cherry and currant flavours. Single-vineyard Pinot Noirs are a focus of the winery (Mark Bradford Vineyard★★, Jerusalem Hill★). The Chardonnay Clos du Soleil★★ and Evenstad Reserve★★ have a rich apple and hazelnut character. Best years: (Pinot Noir) (2012) 11 10 **09 08 07**.

DOMINIO DEL PLATA *Mendoza, Argentina* Superstar winemaker Susana Balbo crafts exquisite wines in the shadow of the Andes. Top wine Nosotros★★ is a lush blockbuster Malbec, but not typical of the estate. Susana Balbo Signature Malbec★★ is elegant and delicious; Brioso★★, a BORDEAUX-style blend, is structured and pure. BenMarco Malbec★ and Cabernet Sauvignon★ are extremely good, as is Zohar Fiano★. The lower-priced Crios range (Torrontés★) is exceptional value for money, including a new Salta Tannat★★. Susana Balbo also shares her expertise with neighbour Finca La Anita (Malbec★★, Syrah★, Petit Verdot★, Semillon★, Tocai Friulano★). Best years: 2012 11 10 **09** 07.

DOMINUS★★ *Napa Valley AVA, California, USA* Owned by Christian MOUEIX, director of Bordeaux superstar PÉTRUS. Wines are based on Cabernet Sauvignon, with leavenings of Merlot and Cabernet Franc. Early releases were excessively tannic, but recent wines are mellow and delicious. Best years: (2012) (10) **09 08 07** 06 05 04 03 02 01 00 99 97 96 95 94 91 90.

DOÑA PAULA *Mendoza, Argentina* Doña Paula performs brilliantly with both red and white wines. The top wine, Selección de Bodega Malbec★★, continues to beat the drum for the estate. The Estate Malbec★ exhibits beautiful violet-edged fruit; also intense, tropical Estate Sauvignon Blanc★. Further down the ladder, the Paula range is great value, especially the sharp, fresh Sauvignon Blanc★. The addition of a stunning range of single-vineyard wines from Luján de Cuyo and Gualtallary (Alluvia Parcel★★) is gathering plaudits.

DÖNNHOFF *Oberhausen, Nahe, Germany* Helmut Dönnhoff is the quiet winemaking genius of the NAHE, conjuring from 25ha (62 acres) in top sites some of the most mineral dry and naturally sweet Rieslings in the world. The very best are the subtle, long-lived wines from the Niederhäuser Hermannshöhle★★★ and Oberhäuser Brücke★★★ vineyards. Eiswein★★★ is equally exciting. Best years: (Hermannshöhle Grosses Gewächs) (2013) 12 11 10 **09 08 07** 05.

DOUBLEBACK *Walla Walla Valley AVA, Washington State, USA* A collaboration between former NFL quarterback Drew Bledsoe and Chris Figgins of LEONETTI CELLAR. The Cabernet Sauvignon★★ is a powerful, cassis- and currant-scented wine that is sourced from five different WALLA WALLA VALLEY vineyards. Best years: (2012) 11 10 **09 08**.

DOURO DOC *Douro, Portugal* Most of Portugal's best reds now come from the Douro. And prices of the top wines have soared. Quality can be superb when the lush, scented fruit is not smothered by new oak. Reds may improve for 10 years or more. Whites from higher-altitude vineyards have improved hugely, and are best drunk young. Best producers: (reds) ALIANÇA

(Quinta dos Cuatro Ventos★), Altano (Reserva★), Maria Doroteia Serôdio Borges (Fojo★★), Casal de Loivos★★, Chryseia★★, Quinta do CÔTTO, Quinta do CRASTO★★, Casa Ferreirinha/FERREIRA, Quinta da Gaivosa★ (Abandonado★★★, Vinha de Lordelo★★), Quinta de Macedos★, Quinta da Manoella★ (Vinhas Velhas★★★), NIEPOORT★★, Quinta do NOVAL★★, Quinta da Padrela★, Quinta do Passadouro★ (Reserva★★), Pintas★★, Poeira★★★, Quinta do Portal★, RAMOS PINTO★, Quinta da Romaneira★, Quinta de la ROSA★, Quinta do Vale Dona Maria★★, Quinta do Vale Meão★★★, Quinta do Vallado (Reserva Field Blend★★★), Quinta de VESÚVIO★★, Xisto★. Best years: (reds) (2012) 11 **10 09 08 07 05 04 03 01 00 97**.

DOW'S *Port DOC, Douro, Portugal* The grapes for Dow's Vintage PORT★★ come mostly from the Quinta do Bomfim – also the name of the excellent single quinta★★. Dow's ports are relatively dry compared with GRAHAM's and WARRE's (also owned by Symingtons). Good Crusted★ and some excellent aged tawnies★★. Quinta Senhora da Ribeira★★ has made impressive ports since 1998, released 'en primeur'. Best years: (Vintage) 2011 07 03 00 97 94 91 85 83 80 77 70 66 63 60 55; (Bomfim) (2010) (09) **06 01 99 98 95 92 87 86**; (Senhora da Ribeira) 2010 **09 08 06 05 04 99 98**.

JOSEPH DROUHIN *Beaune, Burgundy, France* Beaune-based merchant with substantial holdings in CHABLIS as well as DOMAINE DROUHIN OREGON. Flagship CÔTE D'OR whites include BEAUNE Clos des Mouches★★★ and MONTRACHET Marquis de Laguiche★★★. Finer still are the graceful perfumed reds such as CHAMBOLLE-MUSIGNY Premier Cru★★ and Grands Crus Grands-ÉCHÉZEAUX★★★, MUSIGNY★★★, etc. Good-value cheaper wines too. Best years: (top reds) (2013) 12 11 10 09 08 07 05 02 99 96 95.

PIERRE-JACQUES DRUET *Bourgueil AC, Loire Valley, France* Druet's BOURGUEILS les Cent Boisselées★, Grand Mont★★ and Vaumoreau★★ are subtly different, spicy expressions of Cabernet Franc that attain wonderful purity with age – keep for at least 3–5 years. Also small amounts of CHINON (Clos de Danzay★★). Best years: (top cuvées) (2013) 11 **10 09 08 07 06 05 04 03**.

DRY CREEK VALLEY AVA *Sonoma, California, USA* Best known for Sauvignon Blanc, Zinfandel and Cabernet Sauvignon, this valley runs parallel and west of ALEXANDER VALLEY AVA, and similarly becomes hotter moving northward. Best producers: DRY CREEK VINEYARD★, Duxoup★, FERRARI-CARANO★, Lambert Bridge★, Michel-Schlumberger★, NALLE★★, Pezzi King★, Preston★, Quivira★, Rafanelli (Zinfandel★★), RIDGE (Lytton Springs★★★), SEGHESIO★. Best years: (reds) (2012) **10 09 08 07 06 05 03 02 01 00**.

DRY CREEK VINEYARD *Dry Creek Valley AVA, California, USA* An early advocate of Fumé Blanc★, Dry Creek remains faithful to the brisk racy style. Fumé Blanc DCV3★ (sometimes ★★) is from the original (1972) Dry Creek Valley vineyard and displays subtle notes of fig and herb. A drink-young Chardonnay (Reserve★) is attractive, but the stars here are a superb Dry Chenin Blanc★★, red Meritage★, Merlot★ and Old Vine Zinfandel★★. Mother Clone Zinfandel★★ a recent and welcome entry. Best years: (Old Vine Zin) (2012) **10 09 08 07 06 05 03 02 01 00**.

DRY RIVER *Martinborough, North Island, New Zealand* Low yields and an uncompromising attitude to quality at this tiny winery have created some of the country's top Gewurztraminer★★★, Pinot Gris★★, powerful, long-lived Craighall Riesling★★★, sleek Chardonnay★★ and intense, ultra-ripe yet mineral Pinot Noir★★★. Excellent Syrah★★ is made in tiny quantities. Best years: (Craighall Riesling) (2013) 11 **10 09 08 06**; (Pinot Noir) 2012 11 **10 09 08 07 06 03**.

151

GEORGES DUBOEUF *Beaujolais, Burgundy, France* Duboeuf is responsible for more than 10% of the wine produced in BEAUJOLAIS. Given the size of his operation, the quality of the wines is reasonable. His BEAUJOLAIS NOUVEAU is usually reliable, but his top wines are those he bottles for independent growers, particularly Jean Descombes★ in MORGON, and Clos des Quatre Vents★ and la Madone★ in FLEURIE. Duboeuf also makes wine from the MÂCONNAIS, the southern RHÔNE VALLEY and the LANGUEDOC.

DUCKHORN *Napa Valley AVA, California, USA* Duckhorn's focus is on Merlot★★ and Cabernet★ – and there's some tasty Sauvignon Blanc. Paraduxx★ blends Zinfandel and Cabernet; Decoy is the budget line. Goldeneye, based in ANDERSON VALLEY, specializes in Pinot Noir★; Migration has a range of cool-climate Pinot Noirs and Chardonnays. Best years: (Merlot) (2012) **10 09 08 07 06 05 03**.

CH. DUCRU-BEAUCAILLOU★★★ *St-Julien AC, 2ème Cru Classé, Haut-Médoc, Bordeaux, France* Traditionally the epitome of ST-JULIEN, mixing charm and austerity, fruit and firm tannins. Flawed from mid-1980s to 1990; back on form since 95, more luscious since 03. Second wine: la Croix de Beaucaillou. Best years: 2012 11 10 09 **08 07 06 05 04 03 02 01 00 99 98**.

CH. DUHART-MILON★★ *Pauillac AC, 4ème Cru Classé, Haut-Médoc, Bordeaux, France* Property adjacent to and owned by LAFITE-ROTHSCHILD. A healthy portion of Merlot (35%) adds flesh to the steely Pauillac character. Rising quality since 2005. Prices have risen on the back of Asian interest in Lafite. Best years: 2012 11 10 09 **08 07 06 05 04 03 02 01**.

DUJAC *Morey-St-Denis, Côte de Nuits, Burgundy, France* The Seysses family estate is based in MOREY-ST-DENIS. Perfumed, elegant wines, including a small quantity of white Morey-St-Denis★, but the outstanding bottlings are the Grands Crus – ÉCHÉZEAUX★★★, CLOS DE LA ROCHE★★★, BONNES-MARES★★★ and CLOS ST-DENIS★★★, with CHAMBERTIN★★★ and ROMANEE-ST-VIVANT★★★ since 2005. All need to age for a decade or more. Son Jeremy makes *négociant* cuvées under Dujac Fils et Père label. Best years: (Grands Crus) (2013) 12 11 10 09 08 06 05 03 02 01 00 **99 98 96 95 90 89**.

DUNHAM CELLARS *Columbia Valley AVA, Washington State, USA* Family-owned winery in a remodelled airplane hangar near the Walla Walla airport. Wines are powerful and extracted, including Cabernet Sauvignon★★, Syrah★, Lewis Vineyard Syrah★★, Trutina★ (BORDEAUX-style blend), Three Legged Red (named after a much-loved winery dog) and 'Shirley Mays' Chardonnay. Best years: (reds) (2012) 11 10 09 08.

DUNN VINEYARDS *Howell Mountain AVA, California, USA* Austere, concentrated, hauntingly perfumed, long-lived Cabernet Sauvignon★★★ from HOWELL MOUNTAIN; NAPA VALLEY Cabernets★★ are less powerful but still scented. Randy Dunn keeps his alcohol levels reasonable, and the reward is wines that age superbly. Best years: (2012) (10) 09 **08 07 06 05 03 01 00 99 97 96 95 94 93 92 91 90 88 87**.

DURBANVILLE WO *South Africa* Durbanville borders Cape Town's northern suburbs. Cool breezes from both the Atlantic Ocean and False Bay give Sauvignon Blanc invigorating minerality. Semillon also does well. Merlot shows promise both on its own and blended with Cabernet Sauvignon, though the latter sometimes struggles to ripen. Best producers: De Grendel★, Diemersdal★, Durbanville Hills★, Meerendal, Nitida★.

DURIF See PETITE SIRAH.

DUTTON GOLDFIELD *Russian River Valley AVA, California, USA* Racy, elegant and deeply flavoured Chardonnays★, Pinot Noirs★★, Zinfandels★★ and a superb cool-climate Syrah★★ from long-time cool-climate winemaker

Dan Goldfield. Most of the fruit, grown by Steve Dutton, is from the RUSSIAN RIVER VALLEY. The superb Freestone Hill Pinot Noir★★★ is from one of the coldest parts of SONOMA COUNTY. Goldfield also makes wine from fruit grown in even-cooler Marin County. Most wines take years to reach their peak. Best years: (Pinot Noir) 2010 09 08 07 06 05 04 01 99.

JOHN DUVAL *Barossa Valley, South Australia* John Duval was the winemaker for Penfolds GRANGE from 1986 to 2002. He started his family label in 2003, specializing in Shiraz and blends sourced from old-vine BAROSSA fruit. Shiraz-Grenache-Mourvèdre blend Plexus★★ is plush, vibrant, deeply flavoured and approachable; white Plexus★★ is a round, waxy RHÔNE-style blend with wonderful fruit purity; Entity Shiraz★★ combines elegance, finesse and approachability with concentrated flavour and power; ultra-concentrated Eligo Shiraz★★ is made from the best parcels from the vintage. He also consults in WASHINGTON STATE, Chile and elsewhere in Australia.

DUVAL-LEROY *Champagne AC, Champagne, France* One of the largest family-owned producers in CHAMPAGNE, with 170ha (420 acres) of vineyards. Non-vintage Fleur de Champagne is crisp and fresh; vintage★ wines (★★ in 2004), de luxe Femme de Champagne★★ and the Authentis★ label are increasingly good. Best years: 2006 05 04 03 02 99 96 95.

ÉCHÉZEAUX AC *Grand Cru, Côte de Nuits, Burgundy, France* The Grands Crus of Échézeaux and the smaller and more prestigious Grands-Échézeaux are sandwiched between the world-famous CLOS DE VOUGEOT and VOSNE-ROMANÉE. Look for subtlety, intricacy, delicacy from Échézeaux and a little more weight, with a sumptuous dark fruit overlay, from the 'Grands' version. Best producers: Arnoux-Lachaux★★, BOUCHARD PÈRE & FILS★★, Cacheux-Sirugue★★, Clos Frantin/Bichot★★, DROUHIN★★, D Duband★★, DUJAC★★★, Eugénie★★, GRIVOT★★★, A-F GROS★★★, Jayer-Gilles★★, F Lamarche★★, LIGER-BELAIR★★★, MUGNERET-Gibourg★★★, Perdrix★★, J Prieur★★, Dom. de la ROMANÉE-CONTI★★★, E Rouget★★★. Best years: (2013) 12 11 10 09 08 07 06 05 03 02 01 99 98 96 95 93 90.

EDEN VALLEY See BAROSSA, pages 76–7.

CH. L'ÉGLISE-CLINET★★★ *Pomerol AC, Bordeaux, France* A tiny 5.5ha (13-acre) domaine with a very old vineyard – one of the reasons for the depth and elegance of the wines. The other is the winemaking ability of owner Denis Durantou. The wine can be enjoyed young, though the best vintages should be cellared for 10 years or more. Second wine: La Petite Église. Best years: 2012 11 10 09 08 07 06 05 04 03 02 01 00 99 98 96 95.

EL ESTECO *Salta, Argentina* One of the oldest wineries in Cafayate, formerly known as Michel Torino (wines are still sold under that name in the UK). Excellent value, with the Don David★ range offering complexity and easy drinking at the same time (the Torrontés★ is benchmark SALTA). Altimus★ red blend tops the range.

EL PORVENIR DE CAFAYATE *Salta, Argentina* The arrival of Paul Hobbs as consultant winemaker has added a dash of class to this great little winery. The Laborum Torrontés★, Syrah★, Cabernet Sauvignon and Malbec★ are powerful and intense, but the Tannat★ leads the way. Reasonably priced blends under the Amauta label.

ELGIN WO *South Africa* High-lying district where summer cloud helps to keep temperatures reasonable, creating good conditions for pure-fruited, structured and fresh Sauvignon Blanc, Chardonnay, Riesling and Pinot Noir. Best producers: Almenkerk, Paul CLUVER★★, Neil ELLIS★, Iona★★, Catherine Marshall★, Oak Valley★, Shannon★★, Spioenkop, THELEMA★.

DOM. ELIAN DA ROS *Côtes du Marmandais AOP, South-West France* Elian's eclectic wines show influences from ALSACE, BURGUNDY and the LOIRE (with his use of Cabernet Franc). Top wines are Chante Coucou★ and Clos Baquey★★; they need aging. Also a varietal from the Abouriou grape★. Best years: (2012) (11) (10) **09 08 06 05 04**.

ELIM WO *South Africa* Vineyards at the southernmost tip of the continent of Africa with 150ha (370 acres) under vine; wind and birds are the main hazards. Sauvignon Blancs, citrous and leafy, solo and blended with Semillon, punch above their weight. Pinot Noir and Shiraz show promise. Elim wines can be South Africa's snappiest, freshest styles, so long as the winemakers are not seduced by oak and overripeness. Best producers: The Berrio★, Black Oystercatcher★, Cederberg Ghost Corner★★, Strandveld★, Zoetendal★.

ELK COVE *Willamette Valley AVA, Oregon, USA* Back in 1974, Elk Cove was one of the pioneers in the WILLAMETTE VALLEY. Today the Campbell family produces Pinot Gris★, Pinot Blanc★, Riesling and a Riesling-based dessert wine called Ultima. Basic Pinot Noir★★ frequently outclasses the more expensive single-vineyard Pinot Noirs (Roosevelt, Windhill★, La Bohème★). Best years: (Pinot Noir) (2012) 11 10 **09 08**.

NEIL ELLIS *Stellenbosch WO, South Africa* Winemaker and *négociant*, renowned for invigorating Groenekloof Sauvignon Blanc★★ and STELLENBOSCH reds (blackcurranty Cabernet Sauvignon★, supple Cabernet-Merlot★). Single-vineyard Syrah★ and Cabernet★, old-vine Grenache, and a subtly delicious Chardonnay★ from cool ELGIN confirm his versatility. Best years: (Cabernet) 2011 **10 09 08 07 06 05 04 03**.

ELQUI *Chile* Chile's northernmost wine region (though the nascent Huasco and Copiapó are even further north), close to the Atacama desert, with steep, arid valleys, cooling winds and exceptional clarity of light (some of the world's finest space observatories are located here), and high-altitude vineyards, some as high as 2000m (6500ft) above sea level. Syrah, in an elegant, fragrant style, excels, along with crisp Sauvignon Blanc and fresh Chardonnay. Best producers: Chono★, FALERNIA★ (reds★★), Mayu★ (reds★★), SAN PEDRO★ (Castillo de Molina Sauvignon Blanc★).

ERNIE ELS *Stellenbosch WO, South Africa* Golfer Ernie Els's property lies on the prime red wine slopes of the Helderberg. Winemaker Louis Strydom crafts a powerful, polished range headed by flagships Ernie Els Signature★★, a dark, serious BORDEAUX blend, rich, international-style Proprietor's Blend★, combining the Bordeaux grapes with Shiraz, and Proprietor's Cabernet Sauvignon★★. Two whites are made from bought-in fruit. Best years: (Signature) 2011 **10 09 08 07 06 05 04 03**.

EMILIA-ROMAGNA *Italy* Emilia and Romagna are two parts of a very heterogeneous wine region. Romagna, from Bologna east to the Adriatic, closely follows the Tuscan pattern of wines, with reds from Sangiovese and Trebbiano whites. Emilia, while producing some serious still wines, makes a speciality of frothing reds (and whites), not just LAMBRUSCO but also Barbera, Bonarda, Malvasia and others. See also COLLI PIACENTINI, ROMAGNA.

EMILIANA *Colchagua, Chile* Winemaker Alvaro Espinoza takes a biodynamic and organic approach. Entry-level Adobe range is good; Novas★★ range is significantly better. Red blend Coyam★★ (sometimes ★★★) is one of Chile's most fascinating wines. Gê★★, a 'Super Coyam', is dense, powerful and ageworthy. Best years: (Coyam) 2011 10 09 **08 07 06 05 03 01**.

EMRICH-SCHÖNLEBER *Monzingen, Nahe, Germany* Although Monzingen is not the most prestigious of NAHE villages, Werner Schönleber has steadily brought his 18ha (45-acre) property into the front ranks. His vigorous, spicy Rieslings are consistently ★★ to ★★★ and his Eisweins are ★★★. Best years: (2013) 12 11 **10 09 08 07 06 05**.

ENTRAYGUES-ET-DU-FEL AOP, ESTAING AOP *South-West France* Two diminutive ACs in the hills above the Lot Valley. Notable for tingling crisp dry whites from Chenin Blanc (Dom. Méjanassère★) and tangy reds from Dom. Laurent Mousset★. Note also wines from nearby Nicolas Carmarans and Patrick Rols. Drink young.

ENTRE-DEUX-MERS AC *Bordeaux, France* Large AC between the rivers Garonne and Dordogne, producing some of the freshest, snappiest dry white wine in France. In general, drink the latest vintage, though better wines will last a year or two. Most of Bordeaux's basic red wine under the BORDEAUX AC comes from here too. Sweet wines are sold as PREMIÈRES CÔTES DE BORDEAUX, CADILLAC, LOUPIAC and STE-CROIX-DU-MONT. Best producers: Beauregard-Ducourt, BONNET★, Castenet

Greffier, de Fontenille★, Landereau★, Marjosse★, Nardique la Gravière★, Ste-Marie★, Tour de Mirambeau★, Toutigeac★, Turcaud★.

DOM. D'EOLE *Coteaux d'Aix-en-Provence AC, Provence, France* Organic estate with rosé Cuvée Caprice★ and red Cuvée Léa★★, a powerful 50:50 blend of Syrah and Grenache. Best years: (2013) 12 11 **10 09 08 07 06**.

ERBACH *Rheingau, Germany* Erbach's famous Marcobrunn vineyard is one of the top spots for Riesling along the Rhine. The village wines are elegant, while those from Marcobrunn are more powerful. Best producers: Jakob Jung★, Knyphausen, Langwerth von Simmern★, SCHLOSS REINHARTS-HAUSEN★★, Schloss Schönborn★★. Best years: (2013) 12 11 10 **09 08 07 06 05**.

ERDEN *Mosel, Germany* Middle MOSEL village with the superb Prälat and Treppchen vineyards. Wines are rich and succulent with a strong mineral character. Best producers: Christoffel★★, Erbes, Dr Hermann★, Dr LOOSEN★★★, Meulenhof, MOLITOR★, Mönchhof, Pauly-Bergweiler★, Dr Weins-Prüm★. Best years: (2013) 12 11 **10 09 08 07 06 05**.

ERRÁZURIZ *Aconcagua, Chile* Old family-run winery, rapidly modernizing under dynamic Eduardo Chadwick. Its portfolio includes the Arboleda range, Seña★★, a ripe, dense Cabernet-based blend from western ACONCAGUA, and Viñedo Chadwick★★★, a single-vineyard Cabernet Sauvignon from Puente Alto, a high-quality area of MAIPO. The classic label is Don Maximiano Founder's Reserve★★ (sometimes ★★★), a Cabernet Sauvignon-based red from Aconcagua, also the source of La Cumbre Syrah★★, rich, perfumed Kai Carmenère★ and dense red The Blend★. Also very good Wild Ferment Chardonnay★★ and Pinot Noir★★ from CASABLANCA. New cool-climate Manzanar vineyard in coastal Aconcagua is exciting, especially for Sauvignon Blanc★★ and Syrah★★. Best years: (reds) 2011 10 09 **08 07 06 05 04 03 01**.

CH. D'ESCLANS *Côtes de Provence AC, Provence, France* Sacha Lichine claims that Garrus★, a wood-aged blend of old-vine Grenache and Rolle, is the 'most expensive rosé in the world'. For lesser mortals, there are Les Clans★, Esclans★★, Whispering Angel★ and a red, Déesse. Sacha won't thank me for saying this, but I think his best wine is the powerful, exotic white Déesse Astrée★★. Best years: (2013) 12 11 **10**.

ESPORÃO *Alentejo DOC, Portugal* Huge estate in the heart of the ALENTEJO, where Australian David Baverstock makes some delightful varietals, including Touriga Nacional★, Syrah★, Alicante Bouschet★ and Verdelho★, and Esporão red★ and white★ Reservas. Good new DOURO wines from Quinta dos Murças. Best years: (reds) 2011 **08 07 05 04 01 00**.

ESTAING AOP See ENTRAYGUES-ET-DU-FEL.

CH. DES ESTANILLES *Faugères AC, Languedoc, France* The best site is the Clos du Fou★★, with its steep schistous slope planted with Syrah. Raison d'Être★ and L'Impertinent★ reds are Syrah-dominant; L'Impertinent★ white is a blend of Marsanne and Roussanne with some Viognier. Inverso★ is an oak-aged white blend. Best years: (reds) (2013) 12 **11 10**.

ETNA DOC *Sicily, Italy* Sicily's still-active volcano is clad with vines (Nerello Mascalese and Nerello Cappuccio for reds, Catarratto and Carricante for whites) for half of its circumference and up to 1000m (3300ft). In the 19th century the red wines were much in demand for their perfume and elegance, shipped across Europe to be blended with the famous wines of Barolo and Burgundy, but in the 20th century demand fell away, leaving empty terraces. Since 2000 they have been revived, making a storming comeback, and are being likened to – guess what? – fine Barolo (or Burgundy). Best producers: Benanti★★, Il Cantante★, Frank Cornelissen★★, Cottanera★, Graci★★, Nicosia, Passopisciaro, Russo★, Terre Nere★★, Barone di Villagrande. Best years: (2013) 12 **11 10 09 08 07 06 04 01**.

L'ÉTOILE AC *Jura, France* A tiny area within the CÔTES DU JURA that has its own AC for whites, mainly Chardonnay with some Savagnin, and for *vin jaune* and *vin de paille*. Best producers: Cartaux-Bougaud, Geneletti★, Montbourgeau★, P Vandelle★. Best years: 2012 **11 10 09**.

CH. L'ÉVANGILE★★ *Pomerol AC, Bordeaux, France* A neighbour to PÉTRUS and CHEVAL BLANC, this estate has been wholly owned and managed by the Rothschilds of LAFITE-ROTHSCHILD since 1999. The wine is quintessential POMEROL – rich, fat and exotic. Recent vintages have been very good (2009 and 2010 were ★★★), but expect further improvement as the Rothschild effect intensifies. Second wine: Blason de l'Évangile. Best years: 2012 11 10 09 08 **07 06 05 04 03 02 01 00 99 98 95 90**.

EVENING LAND *Willamette Valley AVA, Oregon, USA* Ambitious project, with respected vineyards in California, Oregon and Burgundy, and Dominique LAFON to oversee winemaking. Complex WILLAMETTE VALLEY Blue Label Pinot Noir★, excellent vineyard-specific Gold Label Pinot Noirs★★, and elegant, nutty Gold Label Chardonnay★★. Also good Gamay Noir★. Best years: (Pinot Noir) (2012) 11 10 **09 08**.

BODEGAS FABRE *Mendoza and Patagonia, Argentina* Owned by French couple Hervé and Diane Joyaux Fabre, in an old area of MENDOZA called Vistalba in Luján de Cuyo. Famous for Malbec under various labels, including Phebus and Fabre Montmayou. Dense damson and plum Grand Vin★★ is impressive. Gran Reserva single-vineyard wines include Gran Malbec★★. Viñalba★ wines are some of Argentina's best value for money, with remarkable purity of fruit and freshness; Gran Reservado can be ★★. A PATAGONIA winery produces attractive wines under the same labels, the Fabre Montmayou Barrel Selection Malbec★★ being particularly good.

FAIRVIEW *Paarl WO, South Africa* Owner Charles Back believes South Africa' strength, especially in warmer areas, lies with Rhône varieties. These ar expressed in the 'Goats' range: Goat-Roti★, Goats do Roam★, etc. Fine Shiraz★★ (Eenzaamheid★★, The Beacon★★, Jakkalsfontein★★)

Pinotage★ (Primo★★), Pegleg Carignan★, Merlot★ and Cabernet Sauvignon★. Good whites include Oom Pagel Semillon★★, Viognier★ and complex Nurok★★, a white blend based on Rhône varieties. Outstanding sweet wine La Beryl★★★. Back also owns Spice Route. Best years: (Shiraz) 2012 11 10 09 08 07 06 05 04 03.

JOSEPH FAIVELEY *Nuits-St-Georges, Côte de Nuits, Burgundy, France* There's been a revolution in this famous house since Erwan Faiveley took the helm in 2005. Gone are the dry-as-dust tannic reds, replaced by vibrant fruit and a great sense of *terroir* from vineyards such as CORTON★★★, CHAMBERTIN-Clos-de-Bèze★★★ and Mazis-Chambertin★★, as well as a range of less expensive wines from MERCUREY★, among others. Recent expansion into the CÔTE DE BEAUNE in PULIGNY★★ – with the acquisition of more than 1ha (2.5 acres) of Grand Cru – and MEURSAULT★. Best years: (top reds) (2013) 12 11 10 09 08 07; (whites) (2013) 12 11 10 09 08 07.

FALERNIA *Elqui, Chile* Established in 1998 when Italian immigrants Aldo Olivier and his brother-in-law Giorgio Flessati forsook Piedmont for the stunning ELQUI valley and swiftly made a name for themselves with Alta Tierra Reserva Syrah★★ from vines at up to 2000m (6500ft). Carmenère★★ also excellent. Mayu★ wines are from the same stable.

FALESCO *Lazio, Italy* Property of the famous winemaking Cotarella brothers. Their Poggio dei Gelsi★ is considered the best of the Est! Est!! Est!!! wines, but they are better known for their Merlot Montiano, the essence of smooth if somewhat soulless modernity. Best years: (Montiano) (2012) 11 10 09 08 07 06 04 01 00.

CH. FALFAS★ *Côtes de Bourg AC, Bordeaux, France* Biodynamic estate making concentrated, structured wine that needs 4–5 years to soften. Le Chevalier★ is an old-vines cuvée. Best years: 2012 10 09 08 06 05 04.

FALUA See João Portugal RAMOS.

CH. DE FARGUES★★ *Sauternes AC, Bordeaux, France* Property run by the Lur-Saluces family, who until 1999 also owned Ch. d'YQUEM. Their continued commitment to high quality shows in this fine, rich wine. Best years: 2011 10 09 07 06 05 04 03 02 01 99 98 97 96 95 90 89.

BY FARR *Geelong, Victoria, Australia* Nick Farr makes wine from the 4.8ha (12-acre) family vineyard. Three single-vineyard Pinot Noirs express their different soils and aspects: Farrside★★ is complex yet ethereal; Sangreal★★ shows elegance with power; the close-planted Tout Pres★★★ is dense, fleshy and ageworthy. The Shiraz★★ is meaty, minerally, dry and firm; Viognier★ is heady, complex and alluring; Chardonnay★ is austere yet tangy and elegant. More moderately priced wines under the Farr Rising label, including classy Chardonnay, dry Saignée (a Pinot rosé), and Pinot Noirs from GEELONG★ and MORNINGTON.

GARY FARRELL *Russian River Valley AVA, California, USA* Pioneering producer of fine Pinot Noir★ and Chardonnay★★ from the RUSSIAN RIVER VALLEY, along with very tasty Zinfandel★★. New owners are focusing on small-lot, single-vineyard wines. Farrell now has his own high-quality Alysian★★ project, also in Russian River. Best years: (Pinot Noir) (2012) 10 09 08 07 06 05 04 03 02 01 00.

FAUGÈRES AC *Languedoc, France* The schistous hills north of Béziers produce red wines whose ripe, plummy flavour marks them out from other LANGUEDOC reds. Best producers: Alézon★, Jean-Michel ALQUIER★, l'Ancienne Mercerie, Léon Barral★, Cébène★, Chenaie★, Clos Fantine, ESTANILLES★, Les Fusionels, Haut Lignières, la Liquière★, Ollier-Taillefer (Castel Fossibus★), Saint-Antonin, Trinités. Best years: (2013) 12 11 10 09 08 07 06 05.

FAUSTINO *Rioja DOCa, País Vasco and Rioja, and Cava DO, Spain* Family-owned and technically very well equipped, but they should try harder. Fair Reserva V and Gran Reserva I red Riojas, as well as a more modern, oak-aged red, Faustino de Autor, fruit-driven Faustino Crianza and top-end Faustino 9 Mil★.

FEILER-ARTINGER *Rust, Neusiedlersee, Burgenland, Austria* Kurt Feiler makes sumptuous Ausbruch dessert wines★★: the finest are labelled Essenz★★★. Also Solitaire★★, a suave blend of Blaufränkisch with Merlot and Cabernet Sauvignon. Best years: (sweet whites) (2013) (12) 11 **10** 09 08 07 06 05 04; (Solitaire) (2013) (12) (11) **10** 09 08 07 06.

LIVIO FELLUGA *Colli Orientali del Friuli DOC, Friuli-Venezia Giulia, Italy* Important, reliable source of good to very good FRIULI wines. Top billing goes to Sossó★★, a blend of native Refosco and Pignolo with Merlot. Terre Alte★★ is a white blend (Friulano-Pinot Bianco-Sauvignon) at a similar level. Illivio★ is a tasty blend of Pinot Bianco, Chardonnay and Picolit; well-made varietals include Pinot Grigio, Sauvignon and Friulano.

FÈLSINA *Chianti Classico DOCG, Tuscany, Italy* Full, chunky CHIANTI CLASSICO★★ wines which improve with several years' bottle age. Quality is good to outstanding; most notable are the single-vineyard Riserva Rancia★★ and (under the regional IGT Toscana) Sangiovese Fontalloro★★. Also good Cabernet Maestro Raro★ and Chardonnay I Sistri★. Best years: (Fontalloro) (2011) 10 **09 08 07 06 04 01 99.**

FELTON ROAD *Central Otago, South Island, New Zealand* Runaway success with biodynamic vineyards in the old goldfields of Bannockburn. Intensely fruity, seductive Pinot Noir★★ is surpassed only by very limited quantities of concentrated, complex Block 3★★★ and Block 5★★★. Intense and spicy Calvert★★★ and fleshy, scented Cornish Point★★ are from separate vineyards. Three classy Rieslings (all ★★) range from dry (sometimes ★★★) to sweet. Mineral, citrus unoaked Elms Chardonnay★★ can be one of New Zealand's best; barrel-fermented Chardonnay★★ is funky and delicious; limited edition Block 2★★★ is sensational. Best years: (Pinot Noir) (2013) 12 **10** 09 08 07 06 05 03 02.

FENDANT *Valais, Switzerland* Chasselas wine from the steep slopes of the VALAIS. It should be slightly *spritzig*, with a nutty character, but many are thin and virtually characterless. Drink very young. Best producers: Chappaz, Jean-René Germanier, A Mathier, Simon Maye, D Mercier, Dom des Muses.

FERNGROVE *Great Southern, Western Australia* Ambitious winery – now almost wholly owned by Chinese interests – showing the great quality potential of sunny yet cool Frankland River. Top labels are on song: plush, brambly Majestic Cabernet★★ is often one of the state's finest, King Malbec★★ is scented and lush, Cossack Riesling★★ and Diamond Chardonnay★★ are also very good. Sauvignon-Semillon★ is tangy and Cabernet-Merlot★ rich and eucalyptusy. The flagship Stirlings Shiraz-Cabernet blend★ is pretty good, though I'd like less oak.

FERRARI *Trento DOC, Trentino, Italy* Founded in 1902, the firm is a leader for *metodo classico* sparkling wine. Consistent, classy wines include Ferrari Brut★, Maximum Brut★, Perlé★, Rosé★ and vintage Giulio Ferrari Riserva del Fondatore★★, aged 8 years on its lees and an Italian classic.

FERRARI-CARANO *Dry Creek Valley AVA, California, USA* Full-bodied regular Chardonnay★ has apple-spice fruit; the Reserve★ is deeply flavoured, with more obvious oak. Attractive Fumé Blanc★. Red wines include Trésor★★ (a BORDEAUX blend), Siena★★ (based on Sangiovese), Syrah★, Merlot★ and Zinfandel★, plus a new line of premium reds called PreVail (Back Forty Cabernet★★). Best years: (reds) 2010 09 08 07 06 05 03 02 01 00 99.

FERREIRA *Port DOC and Douro DOC, Douro, Portugal* Old PORT house owned by SOGRAPE. Best known for excellent tawny ports: creamy, nutty Quinta do Porto 10-year-old★ and Duque de Bragança 20-year-old★★. The Vintage★★ is increasingly good. Ferreira's unfortified wine operation, Casa Ferreirinha, produces Portugal's most sought-after red, Barca Velha★★★ (sometimes); made from DOURO grape varieties (mainly Tinta Roriz), it is produced only in the finest years – just 17 vintages since 1952. Marginally less good years are sold as Reserva Especial★. Quinta da Leda reds★★ are also fine. Best years: (Vintage) 2011 07 03 00 97 95 94 91 85 83 82 78 77 70 66 63; (Barca Velha) 2004 00 99 95 91 85 83 82.

CH. FERRIÈRE★★ *Margaux AC, 3ème Cru Classé, Haut-Médoc, Bordeaux, France* MARGAUX's smallest Classed Growth. Same owners as Ch. CHASSE-SPLEEN, and managed by Claire Villars. The ripe, rich and perfumed wines are among the best in MARGAUX AC. Best years: 2012 10 09 08 06 05 04 03 02 01 00 99 98 96.

FETZER *Mendocino County, California, USA* Important winery that has never fulfilled its potential. Locals swear by the quality of the cellar door releases, but we never see these in the outside world. Basic wines are OK, with tasty Gewürztraminer, Riesling and Syrah★. Bargain-priced Valley Oaks line is decent value. A leader in organic viticulture with improving Bonterra range: Chardonnay, Viognier, Roussanne, Merlot, Zinfandel, Cabernet Sauvignon and Sangiovese. Sold in 2011 to Chile's CONCHA Y TORO, but I'm still waiting for the sea change.

FIANO Exciting, distinctive, low-yielding southern Italian white grape variety originating in CAMPANIA and spreading now to BASILICATA, PUGLIA and SICILY – and Australia. Best producers: (Campania) Colli di Lapio★, Feudi di San Gregorio, La Guardiense★, L Maffini (Kràtos★), MASTROBERARDINO★, Ciro Picariello★, Terredora di Paolo★, Vadiaperti★, Villa Diamante★★; (Puglia) Polvanera★; (Sicily) PLANETA (Cometa★★), Settesoli (Inycon★); (Australia) Coriole, Fox Gordon★, Oliver's Taranga, Rutherglen Estates, Witches Falls; (Argentina) DOMINIO DEL PLATA.

CH. DE FIEUZAL *Pessac-Léognan AC, Cru Classé de Graves, Bordeaux, France* Fieuzal, with advice from the owner of ANGÉLUS, can be the most exotic and lush of all PESSAC-LÉOGNANS. The red★ is juicy and drinkable almost immediately, but ages well. The white★★, gorgeous, perfumed (and ageworthy), is the star performer. Second wine (red and white): l'Abeille de Fieuzal. Best years: (reds) 2012 11 10 09 08 07 06 01 00 98 96 95; (whites) 2012 11 10 09 08 07 06 05.

CH. FIGEAC★★ *St-Émilion Grand Cru AC, 1er Grand Cru Classé, Bordeaux, France* The wine traditionally has a delightful fragrance and gentleness of texture. An unusually high percentage (70%) of Cabernets Franc and Sauvignon make it more structured than other ST-ÉMILIONS. Somewhat erratic in the late 1980s, but since 1996 is again the lovely Figeac of old: consistent in style and quality and sometimes ★★★. Controversially,

Figeac was not promoted to Premier Grand Cru Classé 'A' in 2012 while more boisterous neighbours were. The consequences have been a change of management and Michel Rolland hired as consultant winemaker. I just pray the style won't change. Second wine: la Grange Neuve de Figeac. Best years: 2012 11 10 09 **08 07** 06 05 04 03 02 01 00 99 98 96 95.

FIGGINS *Walla Walla Valley AVA, Washington State, USA* Winemaker Chris Figgins (LEONETTI CELLAR) planted new vineyards in the WALLA WALLA VALLEY. Figgins Estate Red★★ is a Bordeaux-style blend; he also makes a small amount of Riesling★. Best years: (2012) 11 10 **09**.

FINCA DECERO *Mendoza, Argentina* Decero means 'from scratch', this being a new winery in Agrelo, with a distinctly hand-crafted approach. Malbec★, Cabernet Sauvignon★ and Petit Verdot★★ from the Remolinos vineyard are the stand-out varietals. The jasmine-perfumed Amano★★ (a blend of Malbec, Cabernet, Petit Verdot and Tannat) gets better with each vintage. Best years: 2011 10 **09 07** 06.

FINGER LAKES AVA *New York State, USA* Cool region in upstate NEW YORK STATE, where some winemakers are establishing a regional style for dry (and sweet) Riesling. Chardonnay and sparkling wines also star. Pinot Noir and Cabernet Franc are the best reds, but encouraging experiments with Blaufränkisch, Teroldego and even Syrah and Saperavi add variety and excitement. Wineries around Seneca and Cayuga lakes can now use those smaller designations on their labels. Best producers: ANTHONY ROAD★, Casa Larga (Ice Wine), Chateau Lafayette Reneau★, FOX RUN★, Dr Konstantin FRANK★, Heron Hill, King Ferry, LAMOREAUX LANDING★, Martini-Reinhardt, Ravines★, Red Newt, Sheldrake Point★, Swedish Hill, TIERCE★, Wagner, Hermann J WIEMER★.

FITOU AC *Languedoc, France* Enclave in CORBIÈRES hills, a great place for dark, herb-scented reds. Best producers: Abelanet, Bertrand-Bergé★★, Lerys★, Maria Fita, Milles Vignes, Nouvelles★, Rochelière, Rolland, Roudène★, Wiala. Best years: (2013) 12 **11** 10 09 08 07 06 05.

FIXIN AC *Côte de Nuits, Burgundy, France* Although it's next door to GEVREY-CHAMBERTIN, Fixin tends to have a more rustic touch. The best Premiers Crus such as Clos de la Perrière and les Arvelets can age well. Best producers: P Charlopin★, Coillot, Galeyrand★, Pierre Gelin★★, Alain Guyard★, Joliet/Clos de la Perrière★★, MORTET★. Best years: (reds) (2013) 12 11 10 **09** 08 07 06 05 03 02 99.

LA FLEUR DE BOÜARD★ *Lalande-de-Pomerol AC, Bordeaux, France* Hubert de Boüard (of ANGÉLUS) acquired this property in 1998. The wines are as rich and sensuous as good POMEROL. A super-cuvée, Le Plus★, aged in new oak barrels for 33 months, is both challenging and expensive. I'd like less oak. Best years: 2012 11 10 **09** 08 07 06 05 04 02.

CH. LA FLEUR-PÉTRUS★★ *Pomerol AC, Bordeaux, France* Like the better-known PÉTRUS and TROTANOY, this is owned by the dynamic MOUEIX family. Unlike its stablemates, it is situated entirely on gravel soil and tends to produce tighter wines with less immediate fruit but considerable elegance and cellar potential. Among POMEROL's top dozen properties. Best years: 2012 11 10 09 08 **06** 05 04 03 02 01 00 99 98 96 95 90.

FLEURIE AC *Beaujolais, Burgundy, France* The best-known BEAUJOLAIS Cru, Fleurie can reveal heady perfumes and a delightful juicy fruit. But demand has meant that many wines are overpriced and dull. Best producers: Ch. de Beauregard (Poncié★), M Chignard (Moriers★), DUBOEUF (la Madone★, Clos des Quatre Vents★), la Madone/Despres★, Y Métras★, B Métrat★, J Sunier★, Villa Ponciago★. Best years: (**2013**) 11.

FLORA SPRINGS *Napa Valley AVA, California, USA* Best known for red wines such as BORDEAUX-blend Trilogy★★, Merlot★★, Cabernet Sauvignon★★. Barrel-fermented Chardonnay★★ and Soliloquy Vineyard Sauvignon Blanc★ top the whites. Also Italian varieties, including weighty Pinot Grigio★ and lightly spiced Sangiovese★, available only at the winery. Best years: (Trilogy) (2012) 11 **10 09 08 07 06 05 04 03 02 01 00 99**.

FLOWERS *Sonoma Coast AVA, California, USA* Small producer whose estate vineyard a few miles from the Pacific yields delicate yet intense wines. Camp Meeting Ridge Pinot Noir★★★ and Chardonnay★★ offer beautifully restrained, subtly balanced aromas and flavours. Also SONOMA COAST★★ wines from purchased fruit. Best years: (Chardonnay) (2013) (12) 11 **10 09 08 07 06 05 04 03** 01; (Pinot Noir) (2012) **10 09 08 07 06 05 04 03 01 00 99**.

AMBROGIO & GIOVANNI FOLONARI *Tuscany, Italy* Father and son team with various properties/brands, including Cabreo (Sangiovese-Cabernet Il Borgo, Chardonnay La Pietra) and Nozzole (powerful Cabernet Il Pareto★★) in CHIANTI CLASSICO, plus VINO NOBILE estate TorCalvano-Gracciano, Campo al Mare in BOLGHERI and BRUNELLO producer La Fuga.

FONSECA *Port DOC, Douro, Portugal* Owned by the same group as TAYLOR'S (Fladgate Partnership), Fonseca makes ports in a rich, densely plummy style. Vintage★★★ is magnificent, the aged tawnies★★ superb. Guimaraens★★ is the 'off-vintage' wine. Crusted★ and Late Bottled Vintage★★ are among the best examples of their styles, as is the Terra Prima★ organic port. Quinta do Panascal★ is the single-quinta vintage. Best years: (Vintage) 2011 **09 07 03 00 97 94 92 85 83 77 75 70 66 63 55**.

JOSÉ MARIA DA FONSECA *Península de Setúbal, Portugal* A huge range of wines, from fizzy Lancers Rosé to serious reds. Best include Hexagon★★, FSF★★ (Syrah-Trincadeira-Tannat), Domingos Soares Franco Private Collection★, and Garrafeiras with codenames like TE★★. Periquita is the mainstay, with Clássico★ made only in the best years. Also SETÚBAL made mainly from the Moscatel grape: 5-year-old★ and 20-year-old★★. Older vintage-dated Setúbals are rare but superb.

DOM. FONT DE MICHELLE *Châteauneuf-du-Pape AC, Rhône Valley, France* CHÂTEAUNEUF-DU-PAPE reds★★, in particular Cuvée Étienne Gonnet★★, with richness and southern herb fragrance – and great value for money. Fresh, accomplished, aromatic whites★★. Successful new Gonnet Pères & Fils range (VENTOUX red★). Best years: (Étienne Gonnet red) 2012 11 10 09 **07 06 05 04 03 01 00 99 98 95 90**.

FONTODI *Chianti Classico DOCG, Tuscany, Italy* Superbly sited estate, with modern-style CHIANTI CLASSICO★★ and Riserva Vigna del Sorbo★★. Flaccianello della Pieve★★★ (100% Sangiovese), from a selection of best bunches, remains IGT. Pinot Nero and Syrah★★ are made under the Case Via label. Best years: (Flaccianello) (2011) **10 09 08 07 06 04 01**.

FORADORI *Teroldego Rotaliano DOC, Trentino, Italy* Producer of dark, spicy, berry-fruited wines from Teroldego grapes, including TEROLDEGO ROTALIANO★ and a couple of crus, Morei★★ and Sgarzon★★. Best years: (Sgarzon) (2011) **10 09 08 07 06 04**.

FORST *Pfalz, Germany* Village with outstanding vineyard sites, including the Ungeheuer or 'Monster', which can show marvellous mineral intensity and richness. Equally good are the Kirchenstück, Jesuitengarten, Freundstück and Pechstein. Best producers: Acham-Magin, BASSERMANN-JORDAN★★, von BUHL★★, BÜRKLIN-WOLF★★, MOSBACHER★★, E Müller, von Winning★, Wolf★★. Best years: (2013) 12 11 **10 09 08 07 06 05 04**.

O FOURNIER *Argentina, Chile, Spain* Exciting Tempranillo and Malbec from old vines in the La Consulta area of Mendoza's UCO VALLEY. Alfa Crux★★ (a Tempranillo-Malbec-Merlot blend) is top of the line, while Alfa Crux Malbec★★ is an excellent, juicy expression of Argentina's flagship red grape. Also very good Syrah★. B Crux★ is the lighter, but delicious, second label. An operation in Chile produces excellent Centauri Sauvignon Blanc★★ from the Leyda Valley and Centauri★★ red blend, plus other exciting MAULE reds. Also a venture in RIBERA DEL DUERO, Spain, with O Fournier★, Alfa Spiga★ and less oaky Spiga★★ cuvées.

FOX RUN *Finger Lakes AVA, New York State, USA* A leader in dry Riesling★, Fox Run also produces elegant Reserve Chardonnay★, spicy, attractive Pinot Noir, Merlot and Cabernet Franc★, and a complex, fruit-forward red Meritage. Also collaborates on TIERCE.

FRAMINGHAM *Marlborough, South Island, New Zealand* Small winery owned by SOGRAPE. Much of Framingham's success is thanks to the thoughtful and uncompromising approach of English winemaker Dr Andrew Hedley. Aromatic grape varieties do well, particularly Riesling: Select★★, off-dry Classic★ and Dry★. Pure, spicy Gewürztraminer★★ with its ALSACE-style big brother F-Series★★, and sleek, ethereal Pinot Gris★★ are among New Zealand's best. In favourable years sweet wines★★★ can be truly outstanding. **Best years:** (Riesling) 2013 **12 11 10 09 07 06**.

VIN DE FRANCE In 2010, France's former Vin de Table category was transformed into Vin de France. Although the classification encompasses mainly entry-level wines, sometimes made from multi-regional blends, it is also being used by innovative quality-driven producers. The latter have generally chosen to opt out of the formal classification system in order to explore unusual blends, areas outside of the traditional AOP or IGP classifications, or unconventional vinification techniques. **Best producers:** (Beaujolais) M Lapierre; (Languedoc-Roussillon) Le Casot des Mailloles★, Hautes Terres, Mas Coutelou, Thierry Navarre, Rosemary★★, Terre Inconnue★, Turner-Pageot; (Loire) P Archambault, C Courtois★, J Courtois★★, Lionel Gosseaume★; (Provence) Henri Milan★.

FRANCIACORTA DOCG *Lombardy, Italy* *Metodo classico* fizz made from Pinot and Chardonnay grapes. Recognized as a DOCG in 1996, when the styles 'Franciacorta' and 'Satèn' were trademarked. Innovatively, the disgorgement date (*sboccatura*) has to be shown on the label. The region also makes still wines under the DOC Curtefranca. **Best producers:** Giovanni Arcari★★, BELLAVISTA★★, Fratelli Berlucchi★, Guido Berlucchi★, Biondelli★, CA' DEL BOSCO★★, Castellino★, Cavalleri★★, La Ferghettina★, Enrico Gatti★, Monte Rossa★, Il Mosnel★, Ricci Curbastro★, San Cristoforo★, Uberti★, Villa★.

FRANCISCAN *Napa Valley AVA, California, USA* Consistently good wines at fair prices: the Cuvée Sauvage Chardonnay★★ is a blockbusting, savoury mouthful, and the Cabernet Sauvignon-based meritage Magnificat★ is very attractive. Part of Constellation.

FRANCS-CÔTES DE BORDEAUX AC *Bordeaux, France* Tiny area east of ST-ÉMILION for reds and a little white; the top wines are good value. The Thienpont family (Ch. Puygueraud) is the driving force. **Best producers:** les Charmes-Godard★, Franc-Cardinal, Francs★, Laclaverie★, Marsau★, Nardou, Pelan★, la Prade★, le Priolat, Puygueraud★★, Vieux Saule. **Best years:** 2012 **10 09 08 05**.

DR KONSTANTIN FRANK *Finger Lakes AVA, New York State, USA* The good doctor was a pioneer of *vinifera* grapes in the FINGER LAKES region in the

1960s. Now run by his grandson Fred, the winery continues to spotlight the area's talent with Riesling★ and Rkatsiteli★, an obscure but delightful Georgian white grape. Also some nice Chateau Frank fizz.

FRANKEN *Germany* 6100ha (15,070-acre) wine region specializing in dry wines – recognizable by their squat Bocksbeutel bottles (familiar because of the Portuguese wine Mateus Rosé). Silvaner is the traditional variety, although Müller-Thurgau is more widely planted. The most famous vineyards are on slopes around WÜRZBURG, RANDERSACKER, IPHOFEN and Escherndorf.

FRANSCHHOEK WO *South Africa* Huguenot refugees settled in this picturesque valley, encircled by breathtaking mountain peaks, in the 17th century. Many wineries and other landmarks still bear French names. The valley is recognized for its whites – Semillon is a local speciality (a few vines are over 100 years old) – though reds are establishing a reputation. Best producers: BOEKENHOUTSKLOOF★, CHAMONIX★★, Colmant★★, La Motte★, La Petite Ferme, Landau du Val, L'Ormarins, Solms-Delta★, Stony Brook. Best years: (reds) 2012 11 10 09 08 07 06 05.

FRASCATI DOC *Lazio, Italy* Rome's quaffing wine. It may be made from Trebbiano or Malvasia or blends thereof; better examples have a higher proportion of Malvasia. Mostly mediocre, but Frascati Superiore DOCG is good, as is sweet Cannellino DOCG. Other light, dry Frascati-like wines come from neighbouring DOCs in the hills of the Castelli Romani and Colli Albani, including Marino, Montecompatri, Velletri and Zagarolo. Best producers: Casale Marchese★, Castel de Paolis★, Colli di Catone★, Piero Costantini/Villa Simone★, Fontana Candida★, Zandotti★.

FREIXENET *Cava DO, Cataluña, Spain* The second-biggest Spanish sparkling wine company (after CODORNÍU) makes the famous Cordon Negro Brut CAVA in a vast network of cellars in Sant Sadurní d'Anoia. Freixenet owns other Cava brands (including Castellblanch and Segura Viudas) plus international interests in France, California, Australia and Argentina.

FRESCOBALDI *Tuscany, Italy* Ancient Florentine company selling large quantities of blended CHIANTI, but from its own vineyards (some 1000ha/ 2470 acres in Tuscany) it produces good commercial wines at Castello di Nipozzano (CHIANTI RUFINA Nipozzano Riserva★★, Montesodi★★ and the BORDEAUX-blend Mormoreto★★), Castello di Pomino (Benefizio Chardonnay★) and Castelgiocondo (BRUNELLO DI MONTALCINO★), where Sangiovese for Brunello and Merlot for the 'super-Tuscan' Luce are grown. Frescobaldi owns several other estates in Tuscany including, since 2005, a

majority stake in the famous Bolgheri estate, ORNELLAIA. Best years: (premium reds) (2011) **10 09 08 07 06 04 01**.

FREYCINET *Tasmania, Australia* Claudio Radenti and Lindy Bull's tiny winery on TASMANIA's east coast has been a pioneer of the Tasmanian industry since her parents established the property in 1979. Radenti's fastidious attention to detail and minimalist intervention showcase the Freycinet vineyard, whether it be with the sublime, ageworthy Pinot Noir★★★, alluring lean Chardonnay★★, or pure, tight Riesling★. Also one of Australia's finest bubblies, Radenti★★★.

FRIULI ISONZO DOC *Friuli-Venezia Giulia, Italy* Superior zone of white and red wine production on former riverbed flats. The DOC covers numerous styles, the best being whites: Chardonnay, Pinot Grigio and Sauvignon. There are some decent reds too (Merlot does well). Best producers: (Isonzo DOC) Borgo San Daniele★, Colmello di Grotta★, Sergio & Mauro Drius★★, Lis Neris★★, Masùt da Rive★, Pierpaolo Pecorari★★, Giovanni Puiatti★, Ronco del Gelso★★, Vie di Romans★★, Villanova★. Best years: (whites) (2013) **12 11 10** 09 08 07 06.

FRIULI-VENEZIA GIULIA *Italy* North-east Italian region bordering Austria and Slovenia. The hilly DOC zones of COLLIO and COLLI ORIENTALI produce some of Italy's finest whites, notably from Friulano, Ribolla Gialla, Malvasia Istriana, Sauvignon Blanc and Chardonnay, and good reds mainly from Cabernet, Merlot and Refosco. Good-value wines from the DOCs of Friuli Aquileia, FRIULI ISONZO, Friuli Latisana and Friuli Grave, in the rolling hills and plains. CARSO DOC is an emerging source of fine, salty white wines.

FROG'S LEAP *Rutherford AVA, Napa Valley, California, USA* John Williams, a leader in the organic/biodynamic movement, makes supple, ageworthy Cabernet Sauvignon★★, minerally Sauvignon Blanc★★ and a fine Zinfandel★★. Best years: (reds) (2012) **11 10 09 08 07 05** 01.

FROMM *Marlborough, South Island, New Zealand* Small winery where low-yielding vines and intensively managed vineyards are the secret behind a string of winning white wines – including fine Clayvin Vineyard Chardonnay★★, Riesling Spätlese★ and Riesling Auslese★★ – and intense, long-lived reds, including Clayvin Vineyard Pinot Noir★★★, Fromm Vineyard Pinot Noir★★, Brancott Valley★ and scented, peppery Syrah★★. Best years: (Pinot Noir) (2013) 12 11 **10** 09 07 06 05 04 03.

FRONSAC AC *Bordeaux, France* Small area west of POMEROL making good-value Merlot-based wines. The top producers have taken note of the feeding frenzy in neighbouring Pomerol and sharpened up their act accordingly, with finely structured wines, occasionally perfumed, and better with at least 5 years' age. Best producers: Carles (Haut-Carles★), Chadenne, Dalem★, la Dauphine★, Fontenil★, la Grave, Haut-Ballet, Mayne-Vieil (Cuvée Aliénor★), Moulin Haut-Laroque★, Richelieu★, la Rivière★, la Rousselle★, Tour du Moulin, les Trois Croix★, la Vieille Cure★, Villars★. Best years: 2012 11 **10 09 08** 06 05 03 01.

FRONTON AOP *South-West France* From north of Toulouse, some of the most distinctive and improving reds – silky, with hints of violets and licorice – of South-West France. Négrette is the chief grape (often 100%) but producers often blend in Cabernet and/or Syrah. Best producers: Baudare★, Bellevue-la-Forêt★, Bouissel★, Boujac★, Caze★, Laurou, PLAISANCE★, le Roc★, Viguerie de Belaygues★. Best years: (2012) **11 10** 09.

FUMÉ BLANC See SAUVIGNON BLANC, pages 284–5.

FURLEIGH ESTATE *Dorset, England* Newcomer winning awards with both still and sparkling wines. Excellent still Bacchus Fumé★★, plus sparkling Blanc de Blancs★★, Blanc de Noirs★★ and Classic Cuvée★.

FÜRST *Bürgstadt, Franken, Germany* Paul Fürst goes from strength to strength: his dry Rieslings★★ are unusually elegant, while Burgundian-style Spätburgunder (Pinot Noir) reds★★ and barrel-fermented Weissburgunder (Pinot Blanc) whites★★ are some of Germany's best. Sensual, intellectual wines with excellent aging potential. Best years: (dry Riesling) (2013) 12 11 **10 09 08 07** 05; (reds) (2013) (12) 11 **10 09 08 07**.

JEAN-NOËL GAGNARD *Chassagne-Montrachet, Côte de Beaune, Burgundy, France*
Run by Gagnard's daughter Caroline Lestimé, who consistently makes some of the best wines of CHASSAGNE-MONTRACHET, particularly Premiers Crus Caillerets★★★ and Morgeot★★. Top wine is rich, toasty BÂTARD-MONTRACHET★★★. All are capable of extended cellaring. Reds★ are good, but not in the same class. Also cousins Blain-Gagnard and Fontaine-Gagnard. **Best years:** (whites) (2013) 12 11 10 **09 08 06 05 04 02 00 99**.

GAILLAC AOP *South-West France* A huge variety of wines: whites, mainly from Mauzac and Len de l'El, range from dry to ultra-sweet; reds and rosés are from local grapes too – Braucol, Duras – and sometimes Syrah. Some reds are matured in wood and can be kept. Sparkling Gaillac has no added yeasts or sugar. **Best producers:** Bourguet, Brin, CAUSSE MARINES★★, Escausses★, Labarthe, Stéphane Lucas★, Mas Pignou, du Moulin, Palvié★, PEYRES ROSES★★, Pialentou, PLAGEOLES★★, la RAMAYE★★, Rotier★. **Best years:** (reds) 2012 11 10 09; (sweet whites) 2012 11 10 09 07.

GAJA *Barbaresco DOCG, Piedmont, Italy* Angelo Gaja, an influential if controversial figure, was instrumental in changing the perception of PIEDMONT from an old-fashioned region to a world-class area of sophistication and high price, drawing attention to the then less-known BARBARESCO zone. Into this fiercely conservative area, full of fascinating grape varieties but proudest of the native Nebbiolo, he introduced French grapes like Cabernet Sauvignon (Darmagi★★), Sauvignon Blanc (Alteni di Brassica★) and Chardonnay (Gaia & Rey★★). When his efforts to change the BAROLO and Barbaresco regulations (to allow other varieties besides Nebbiolo) were thwarted, Gaja renounced the DOCG and reclassified his top wines as LANGHE Nebbiolo (Sori San Lorenzo★★, Sori Tildin★★ and Costa Russi★★). However, economic reality has meant that he continues to produce a traditional Barbaresco and has re-introduced a Barolo★ (his Langhe Nebbiolos 'Conteisa'★★ and 'Sperss'★★ are from the La Morra Cerequio vineyard and a prime Serralunga plot). Gaja has also invested in BRUNELLO DI MONTALCINO (Pieve Santa Restituta) and BOLGHERI (Ca' Marcanda). **Best years:** (Barbaresco) (2011) (10) **09 08 07 06 04 01 99 98 97 96**.

GALICIA *Spain* Up in Spain's hilly, verdant north-west, Galicia is renowned for its Albariño whites. There are 5 DOs: RÍAS BAIXAS can make excellent, fragrant Albariño, with modern equipment and serious wine-making; Ribeiro DO has also invested heavily in new equipment, and better local white grapes such as Treixadura are now being used; it's a similar story with the Godello grape in the mountainous Valdeorras DO, where producers such as the young Rafael Palacios, from the ubiquitous Rioja-based family, are reaching new heights for ageworthy, individual whites. Some ambitious reds from the Mencía grape are also made there and in the Ribeira Sacra DO, and various other native red varieties are being rediscovered throughout the region. Monterrei DO has found a showcase estate in Quinta da Muradella★★, with Raúl PÉREZ as the consulting winemaker. An increasing number of ageworthy whites and reds are now produced.

GALLO *Central Valley, California, USA* Gallo, the world's largest family-owned wine company – and for generations a byword for cheap, drab wines – has made a massive effort to change its reputation since the mid-1990s, beginning with the release of Chardonnay and Cabernet Sauvignon from their Sonoma Estate. The new upscale Signature Series focuses on

Chardonnay and Pinot Noir. New SONOMA COAST vineyards are in a very cool area, with stylish single-vineyard Two Rock Chardonnay. Vineyards in RUSSIAN RIVER VALLEY and the SONOMA COAST have been planted to Pinot Noir and Pinot Gris. Even so, Gallo continues to produce oceans of ordinary wine. Turning Leaf isn't going to turn many heads, but Rancho Zabaco and Dancing Bull (Sauvignon Blanc★, Zinfandel★) brands are a notch up. Gallo also owns Louis M MARTINI, Frei Brothers, William Hill, Mirassou and CENTRAL COAST's Bridlewood, top-selling Barefoot Cellars, plus Covey Run and Columbia Winery in WASHINGTON.

GAMAY The only grape allowed for red BEAUJOLAIS. In general Gamay wine is rather rough-edged and quite high in raspy acidity, but in Beaujolais, so long as the yield is not too high, it can achieve a wonderful, juicy-fruit gluggability. Elsewhere in France, it is successful in the Ardèche, where there are some vines from the 1950s, Auvergne, Savoie and the Loire (sometimes blended with Pinot Noir) and less so in the Mâconnais. In Switzerland it is blended with Pinot Noir to create DÔLE and Goron. Also found in Canada, Oregon, Brazil, New Zealand, Australia, South Africa, England and Italy.

GANTENBEIN *Fläsch, Graubünden, Switzerland* Since 1982 Daniel Gantenbein has focused on producing intense and powerful versions of the Burgundian varieties, and has won a fine reputation above all for his Pinot Noir★★, as well as Chardonnay★★ and Riesling★. Best years: (Pinot Noir) (2013) (12) 11 **10 09 08 07 05.**

GARD, IGP DU *Languedoc, France* Mainly reds and rosés from the western side of the RHÔNE delta. Most red is light, spicy and attractive. Some fresh young rosés and whites have been improved by modern winemaking. Best producers: des Aveylans★, Cantarelles, Coste Plane, Grande Cassagne★, Guiot★, Mas des Bressades★.

GARNACHA BLANCA See GRENACHE BLANC.

GARNACHA TINTA See GRENACHE NOIR.

GATTINARA DOCG *Piedmont, Italy* 100% Nebbiolo red wine from a volcanic zone in northern PIEDMONT. In neighbouring DOCs of Lessona, Bramaterra, Boca, Ghemme, Fara and Carema, Nebbiolo may be blended with other varieties. Best producers: Antoniolo★, Mauro Franchino★★, Paride Iaretti★★, Nervi★, Travaglini★, Antonio Vallana. Best years: (2011) (10) 09 **08 07 06 04 03 01 00 99 98.**

DOM. GAUBY *Côtes du Roussillon-Villages AC, Roussillon, France* Marvellously concentrated but balanced wines. Highlights include powerful CÔTES DU ROUSSILLON-VILLAGES Vieilles Vignes★★, Muntada★★, red and white les Calcinaires★★, as well as a gorgeously seductive white CÔTES CATALANES Coume Gineste★. Some imaginative experimental cuvées. Also involved in excellent red and white le Soula★★ (Côtes Catalanes). Best years: (reds): (2013) 12 11 **10 09 08 07 06 05.**

GAVI DOCG *Piedmont, Italy* Though officially Piedmontese, Gavi lies on the border with LIGURIA, and is very much influenced by this coastal province. From just over 1000ha (2470 acres) over 11 communes along the Lemme Valley, the Cortese grape gives wines of either lemony, lean structure or, sometimes, a white flower scent. Ideally unoaked. Some sparkling is made. Best producers: Battistina★, Bergaglio★, Broglia★, La Caplana★★, La Chiara★, Chiarlo★, Fontanafredda, La Giustiniana★★, Pio Cesare, San Pietro★, Roberto Sarotto★★, La Scolca★, Tassarolo★, Villa Sparina.

CH. GAZIN★★ *Pomerol AC, Bordeaux, France* Large château in POMEROL, situated next to the legendary PÉTRUS. The wine, traditionally a succulent, sweet-textured Pomerol, seemed to lose its way in the 1980s but has now got much of its character back under owner Nicolas de Bailliencourt. Best years: 2012 11 10 09 **08 07 06 05 04 03 02 01 00 99 98 96 95**.

GEELONG *Victoria, Australia* Cool-climate, maritime-influenced region, but not quite as cool as MORNINGTON PENINSULA across Port Phillip Bay. Impressive Pinot Noir, Chardonnay, Riesling, Sauvignon and Shiraz. Best producers: Austin's★, BANNOCKBURN★★, Clyde Park, By FARR★★, Lethbridge★, Scotchmans Hill★, Terindah.

GEMTREE *McLaren Vale, South Australia* Investment from a Chinese entrepreneur has led to a dramatic expansion of the Buttery family business without any loss of quality. 130ha (320 acres) are farmed biodynamically. Reds are the prime focus and range from the fruity, youthful Luna Temprana★ and richer, darker Luna Roja★★ Tempranillos through several classy Shiraz, including the profound, brambly Obsidian★★ and fascinating White Lees★★. Also tangy, adult Moonstone Savagnin★.

GEROVASSILIOU *Macedonia AO, Greece* Bordeaux-trained Evángelos Gerovassiliou has 40ha (100 acres) of vineyards and a modern winery in Epanomi in northern Greece. High-quality fruit results in Syrah-dominated Gerovassiliou red★ and some fresh, modern whites, including fabulously scented Malagousia★★, Viognier★, barrel-fermented Chardonnay, Fumé, and Assyrtiko-Malagousia blend Gerovassiliou★ white.

GEVREY-CHAMBERTIN AC *Côte de Nuits, Burgundy, France* A new generation of growers has restored the reputation of Gevrey as a source of well-coloured, firmly structured, powerful, perfumed wines that become rich yet savoury with age. Village wines should be kept for at least 5 years, Premiers Crus and the 9 Grands Crus for 10 years or more, especially CHAMBERTIN and Clos-de-Bèze. The Premier Cru Clos St-Jacques is worthy of promotion to Grand Cru, with Cazetiers and Combottes not far behind. Best producers: D BACHELET★★, Louis Boillot★, A Burguet★★, P Charlopin★, B CLAIR★★, Confuron-Cotetidot★, P Damoy★★, DROUHIN★, C Dugat★★★, B Dugat-Py★★, Durocé★★, S Esmonin★, FAIVELEY★★, J-M Fourrier★★, Geantet-Pansiot★★, Harmand-Geoffroy★, JADOT★★, Denis MORTET★★★, Perrot-Minot★, Rossignol-Trapet★★, J Roty★★, ROUSSEAU★★★, Sérafin★, J & J-L Trapet★★, C Tremblay★★, VOUGERAIE★. Best years: (2013) 12 11 10 09 **08 07 06** 05 **03 02** 01 99 98 96 95 93 90.

GEWÜRZTRAMINER *Gewürz* means spice, and typically the wine is spicy, exotically perfumed with rose petals and lychees, and low in acidity. It may have originated in France's Jura or in the Italian village of Tramin. Frequently labelled Traminer. It makes an appearance in many wine-producing countries; quality is mixed and styles vary enormously, from the fresh, light, florally perfumed wines produced in Italy's ALTO ADIGE to the rich, luscious, late-harvest ALSACE Vendange Tardive. Best in Alsace and also good in Austria's Styria (STEIERMARK), southern Germany, Croatia, California, Chile and New Zealand. Small amounts in Canada, South Africa and Australia.

GIACONDA *Beechworth, Victoria, Australia* In spite of (or perhaps because of) Giaconda's tiny production, Rick Kinzbrunner is one of Australia's most influential winemakers. Following on from his success, BEECHWORTH has become one of the country's most exciting viticultural regions. His tightly structured, minerally, savoury Chardonnay★★★ is one of Australia's best – as are both the serious and beautiful Pinot Noir★★★ (a Beechworth-YARRA blend) and the deep, gamy, HERMITAGE-style Warner Vineyard Shiraz★★★. Look for the Estate Vineyard Shiraz★ and joint venture with CHAPOUTIER, Ergo Sum Shiraz★. Best years: (Chardonnay) (2013) (12) 11 10 08 07 **06 05 04 02 00 99 98 96 93**.

BRUNO GIACOSA *Barbaresco DOCG, Piedmont, Italy* One of the great winemakers of the LANGHE hills, indeed of Italy; still a traditionalist, he has reduced maturation time for his BARBARESCOS and BAROLOS to a maximum of 4 years. Superb Barbarescos (Asili★★★, Santo Stefano★★★, Rabajà★★★) and Barolos (Rocche del Falletto★★★, Falletto★★). Excellent BARBERA D'ALBA★, Dolcetto d'Alba★, Roero ARNEIS★ and sparkling Extra Brut★★. Setback in 2006 when Bruno suffered a stroke, leading to the sale of that (promising) vintage in bulk. Best years: (2011) (10) 09 08 **04 01 00 99 98 97 96 95 90 89 88 85 82**.

GIANT STEPS *Yarra Valley, Victoria, Australia* Entrepreneur/master brewer/founder of DEVIL'S LAIR Phil Sexton and cheesemaker/chef/winemaker Steve Flamsteed make a dynamic duo whose careful study of *terroir* has led to outstanding single-vineyard Chardonnays (Tarraford★★, Sexton★★) and Pinots (Tarraford★★, Applejack★★★). The purchase of the outstanding Applejack vineyard will take the enterprise to the next level. Modestly priced Innocent Bystander range impresses, and includes Australia's best Moscato fizz.

GIGONDAS AC *Rhône Valley, France* Gigondas red wines are mainly Grenache, plus Syrah and, increasingly, Mourvèdre. They offer big, spiced southern flavours, ideally with some cool, mineral touches, and are good value; most drink well with 5 years' age, but will happily age for much longer. Best producers: P Amadieu★★, la Bouïssière★★, Brusset★★, Cassan★, Cayron★, Clos des Cazaux★★, Clos du Joncuas★, Cros de la Mûre★★, Espiers★★, Font-Sane★, la Fourmone★, les Goubert★, Gour de Chaulé★, Grand Bourjassot, Grand Montmirail, Grapillon d'Or★★, GUIGAL★, Longue-Toque★, Mas des Restanques, Montvac★★, Moulin de la Gardette★★, Paillère & Pied-Gû, les Pallières★★, Famille Perrin★, Pesquier★★, Piaugier★, Raspail★, Raspail-Ay★★, Redortier★, Roubine★★, St-Cosme★★, ST GAYAN★★, Santa Duc★★, Tardieu-Laurent★★, la Tourade★, Tourelles★★, Trignon★. Best years: 2012 **11 10 09 08 07 06 05 04 03 01 00 99 98 95**.

CH. GILETTE★★ *Sauternes AC, Bordeaux, France* These astonishing wines are stored in concrete vats as opposed to the more normal wooden barrels. This virtually precludes any oxygen contact, and it is oxygen that ages a wine. Consequently, when released at up to 20 years old, they are bursting with life and lusciousness. Best years: **1990 89 88 86 85 83 82 81 79 78 76 75 71 70 67 61 59 55 53 49**.

GIPPSLAND *Victoria, Australia* Diverse wineries along the southern VICTORIA coast, all tiny but with massive potential. Results are erratic, occasionally brilliant. Nicholson River's exotic, hedonistic Chardonnay sometimes hits ★★, Shiraz can be ★★★. Bass Phillip Pinot Noirs (Reserve★★★, Premium★) are among the best in Australia, with a cult following. McAlister★ is a tasty red BORDEAUX blend. Best producers: Bass Phillip★★★, William Downie★★, Philippa Farr, McAlister★, Nicholson River★★.

VINCENT GIRARDIN *Santenay, Côte de Beaune, Burgundy, France* This successful MEURSAULT-based merchant surprised us all by selling up to BOISSET and going off to Picardy to farm cereals. However, the label and the winemaking team continue. Best known for well-crafted whites, such as CHASSAGNE (Cailleret★★). Best years: (whites) (2013) 12 11 10 09 08 07.

GISBORNE *North Island, New Zealand* Gisborne, with its hot, humid climate and fertile soils, delivers both quality and quantity. New Zealand's third largest region in terms of wine production and fourth by vineyard area. Christened (by local growers) 'The Chardonnay Capital of New Zealand', although the focus is shifting to Pinot Gris, while Gewürztraminer and Chenin Blanc are also a success. Good reds, however, are hard to find. Best producers: COOPERS CREEK★, MILLTON★★, Spade Oak, Vinoptima★★. Best years: (Chardonnay) (2013) 10 09 07 05.

GIVRY AC *Côte Chalonnaise, Burgundy, France* Important CÔTE CHALONNAISE village. The reds have an intensity of fruit and ability to age that are unusual in the region. There are some attractive, fairly full, nutty whites, too. Best producers: Bourgeon★, Chofflet-Valdenaire★, Clos Salomon★, Joblot★★, F Lumpp★★, Masse, Ragot★, Sarrazin★. Best years: (reds) (2013) 12 11 10 09; (whites) (2013) 12 11 10 09.

GLAETZER *Barossa Valley, South Australia* Colin Glaetzer, one of the BAROSSA VALLEY's most enthusiastic and successful winemakers, started his family label in 1995; his son Ben now makes a range of rip-roaring Barossa wines. There is fleshy Wallace Shiraz-Grenache★, rich, superripe Bishop Shiraz★★ (from 30–60-year-old vines), the opulent, succulent and velvety Amon-Ra Shiraz★★ and Anaperenna★★, a deep, dense Shiraz-Cabernet blend. Ben also makes reds and whites for the Heartland label using fruit from vineyards in Langhorne Creek and LIMESTONE COAST; look for the Dolcetto & Lagrein red blend. Best years: (Bishop Shiraz) 2013 12 10 08 06 05 04 02 01 99 98 96.

GLEN CARLOU *Paarl WO, South Africa* Long-time winemaker Arco Laarman is bringing more restraint to the range at this property owned by Californian businessman Donald Hess. Whites are led by a trio of Chardonnays: characterful Unwooded Chardonnay★, rich but elegant regular Chardonnay★ and single-vineyard Quartz Stone★★. There are also three modern Cabernets: well-fruited regular; concentrated Gravel Quarry★★; and Grand Classique★, a Cabernet-based BORDEAUX blend with good aging potential. Best years: (Chardonnay) 2013 12 11 10 09 08 07 06 05 04 03.

GLERA When you're drinking PROSECCO, the name of the grape it's made from is Glera. Prosecco is the name of a village that produced fizz and gave its name to the grape and the wine – but the grape has been officially renamed Glera. You will start to see the name Glera on bottles of fizz made outside the designated Prosecco area.

CH. GLORIA★ *St-Julien AC, Haut-Médoc, Bordeaux, France* An interesting property, created out of tiny plots of Classed Growth land scattered all round ST-JULIEN. Generally very soft and sweet-centred, the wine nonetheless ages well. Same owner as Ch. ST-PIERRE. Second wine: Peymartin. Best years: 2012 11 10 09 08 07 06 05 04 03 01 00 98 95.

GODELLO See VERDELHO.

169

GONZÁLEZ BYASS *Jerez y Manzanilla DO, Andalucía, Spain* Tío Pepe★ fino is the world's biggest-selling sherry. The old sherries are superb: intense, dry Amontillado del Duque★★★; rich, complex, sweet Oloroso Matusalem★★ and Palo Cortado Apóstoles★★; treacly Noé Pedro Ximénez★★★. One step down is the Alfonso Dry Oloroso★. The firm pioneered the rediscovery of single-vintage (non-solera) dry olorosos★★ and palos cortados★★. Outstanding new Palmas★★★ range of three unfiltered ('en rama') finos and an amontillado.

GOSSET *Champagne AC, Champagne, France* Gosset is the oldest wine producer in CHAMPAGNE, based in Aÿ. Complex, rich Grande Réserve Brut★★ is a three-vintage blend that has 5 years' aging before release; intense non-vintage Blanc de Blancs★★. Smoky, developed Grand Millésime★★ and more austere Celebris★★ (rosé★★), needing extra time to shine. Best years: 2007 04 03 02 **00 99 98 96 95 90**.

GRAACH *Mosel, Germany* Important Middle MOSEL wine village with 4 vineyard sites, the most famous being Domprobst (also the best) and Himmelreich. The wines have an attractive fullness to balance their steely acidity, and great aging potential. Best producers: Kees-Kieren★, von Kesselstatt★, Dr LOOSEN★★, MOLITOR★★, Philipps-Eckstein, J J PRÜM★★, S A Prüm★, M F RICHTER★, Willi SCHAEFER★★★, SELBACH-OSTER★★, Dr Weins-Prüm★. Best years: (2013) 12 11 **10 09 08 07 06 05 04 02 01**.

GRACIANO Rare, low-yielding but excellent Spanish grape, traditional in RIOJA, NAVARRA and Extremadura. It makes dense, well structured, fragrant reds, and its high acidity adds life when blended with low-acid Tempranillo. In Portugal it is called Tinta Miúda. Grown by BROWN BROTHERS, ROSEMOUNT and others in Australia. Small amounts in LODI, California.

GRAHAM'S *Port DOC, Douro, Portugal* Part of the Symington empire, making rich, florally scented Vintage Port★★★, sweeter than DOW's and WARRE's, but with the backbone to age. In non-declared years makes a fine vintage wine called Malvedos★★. Six Grapes is one of the best premium rubies, and Crusted★★ and 10-years★★, 20-years★★, 30-years★★★ and single-harvest tawnies★★★ are consistently excellent. Best years: (Vintage) 2011 **07 03 00 97 94 91 85 83 80 77 75 70 66 63 60**; (Malvedos) (2011) (10) **09 05 01 99 98 95 92 90**.

ALAIN GRAILLOT *Crozes-Hermitage AC, Rhône Valley, France* Excellent family estate producing concentrated, rich, fruity Syrah reds. The top wine is the classy, long-lived CROZES-HERMITAGE la Guiraude★★; the regular Crozes-Hermitage★★ is wonderful too, and great for early drinking, as are the ST-JOSEPH★ and a fragrant white Crozes-Hermitage. Keep top reds for at least 5 years. Son Max has promising Dom. des Lises★ estate and Equis brand (also CORNAS, St-Joseph). Best years: (la Guiraude) 2013 12 11 **10 09 07 06 05 04 03 01 00 99 95**.

GRAMERCY CELLARS *Walla Walla Valley AVA, Washington State, USA* Fine Syrah Lagniappe★★ with mineral notes, and a version from Walla Walla Valley★★. The Cabernet Sauvignon★★ ranks among the top in the state. Also Tempranillo 'Inigo Montoya'★ and Mourvèdre-based L'Idiot du Village★★. Best years: (2012) 11 10 **09 08**.

GRAMPIANS AND PYRENEES *Victoria, Australia* Two cool-climate regions in central western VICTORIA, producing some of Australia's most characterful Shiraz and Riesling, savoury Chardonnay and subtle Pinot Gris. Best producers: BEST'S★★, Blue Pyrenees, Dalwhinnie★★, JAMSHEED★★, MOUNT LANGI

GHIRAN★★, Redbank★, SEPPELT★★, The Story★★, Summerfield★, Taltarni★. Best years: (Shiraz) (2013) 12 10 09 07 **06 05 04 03 02 01 99 98 97 96 94**.

CH. GRAND-PUY-DUCASSE★ *Pauillac AC, 5ème Cru Classé, Haut-Médoc, Bordeaux, France* Form recovered after 1995; greater regularity since 2005. Approachable after 5 years, but the best vintages can improve for considerably longer. Second wine: Prélude à Grand-Puy-Ducasse. Best years: 2012 11 10 09 08 **07 06 05 04 02 00 96**.

CH. GRAND-PUY-LACOSTE★★ *Pauillac AC, 5ème Cru Classé, Haut-Médoc, Bordeaux, France* Classic PAUILLAC, with lots of blackcurrant and cigar-box perfume. It begins fairly dense, but as the wine develops, the flavours mingle with the sweetness of new oak to become one of Pauillac's most memorable taste sensations. Second wine: Lacoste-Borie. Best years: 2012 11 10 09 08 **07 06 05 04 03 02 01 00 99 98 96 95 90 89**.

GRANDS-ÉCHÉZEAUX AC See ÉCHÉZEAUX AC.

GRANGE★★★ *Barossa Valley, South Australia* In 1950, Max Schubert, chief winemaker at PENFOLDS, visited Europe and came back determined to make a wine that could match the great BORDEAUX reds. Undeterred by a lack of Cabernet Sauvignon grapes and French oak barrels, he set to work with BAROSSA Shiraz and barrels made from the more pungent American oak. Schubert eventually achieved global recognition for his stupendously complex, thrillingly rich wine, which only begins to reveal its magnificence after 10 years in bottle – but is even better after 20 – and never tastes remotely like Bordeaux. Best years: (2013) (12) (10) 08 06 05 04 **02 01 99 98 96 94 92 91 90 88 86 84 83 80 76 71 66 62 53**.

DOM. DE LA GRANGE DES PÈRES *IGP de l'Hérault, Languedoc, France* Meticulously crafted unfiltered red★★, a blend of Syrah, Mourvèdre and Cabernet Sauvignon; only 500 cases produced each year. The white★★, based on Roussanne with Marsanne and Chardonnay, is made in even smaller quantities. Best years: (red) (2013) 12 11 **10 09 08 07 06 05**.

GRANGEHURST *Stellenbosch WO, South Africa* Boutique winery known for classically styled BORDEAUX-style blends: Cabernet-led Grangehurst★★ and Cabernet-Merlot★★, Cabernet Reserve★, Shiraz-Cabernet Reserve★. Also modern Pinotage★ and Nikela★, a polished blend of Pinotage with Cabernet, Merlot and Shiraz. All mature well for several years and are deliberately held back with later-than-normal release times. Best years: **2008 07 06 05 04 03 01 00**.

GRANS-FASSIAN *Leiwen, Mosel, Germany* LEIWEN owed its reputation initially to Gerhard Grans. Both sweet and dry Rieslings have gained in sophistication over the years: Spätlese★★ and Auslese★★ from TRITTENHEIMER Apotheke are particularly impressive. Eiswein is ★★★ in good vintages. Best years: (2013) 12 11 **10 09 08 07 06 05**.

ALFRED GRATIEN *Champagne AC, Champagne, France* This small company makes some of my favourite CHAMPAGNE. Its wines are made in wooden casks, which is very rare nowadays. The non-vintage★★ blend is usually 4 years old when sold, rather than the normal 3 years, and can age further. The vintage★★★ is deliciously balanced and toasty when released, but can age for another 10 years. New vintage Blanc de Blancs★. The prestige cuvée, Cuvée Paradis★★, is non-vintage. Best years: (2002) **00 99 98 97 96 95 91 90 89 88 85 83**.

GRAVES AC *Bordeaux, France* The Graves region covers the area south of the city of Bordeaux to Langon, but the villages in the northern half broke away in 1987 to form the PESSAC-LÉOGNAN AC. In the southern Graves, a new wave of winemaking has produced plenty of clean, bone-dry white wines with lots of snappy freshness, as well as more complex soft, nutty, barrel-aged whites, and some juicy, quick-drinking reds. Sweet white wines take the Graves Supérieures AC; the best make a decent substitute for the more expensive SAUTERNES. Best producers: Archambeau★, Ardennes★, Brondelle★, Chantegrive★, Clos Floridène★★, Crabitey★, Ferrande, Fougères★, Haura★, l'Hospital, Léhoul★, Magence, Magneau★, Rahoul★, Respide (Callipyge★), Respide-Médeville★, St-Robert (Cuvée Poncet Deville★), Seuil, Toumilon, Tourteau-Chollet★, Venus, Vieux-Ch.-Gaubert★, Villa Bel-Air★; (sweet) Brondelle, Léhoul. Best years: (reds) 2012 **11** 10 09 08 05 04 01; (dry whites) 2012 **11** 10 09 08 07 06 05.

GRAVNER *Friuli-Venezia Giulia, Italy* 'Natural wine' guru Josko Gravner is seen as a revolutionary or a fanatic – his wines brilliant or undrinkable. In recent years he has fermented his white wines in amphorae dug into the winery floor, leaving them exposed to oxygen to ferment, macerate and clarify, with no intervention for months. Gravner is phasing out all white grapes except Ribolla Gialla. On the red side he limits himself to the indigenous Pignolo, which is not released for 10 years post-production.

GREAT SOUTHERN *Western Australia* A vast, cool-climate, mostly dry region encompassing the sub-regions of Frankland River, Denmark, Mount Barker, Albany and Porongurup. Frankland River is particularly successful with Riesling, Shiraz and Cabernet; Denmark with Chardonnay and Pinot Noir; Mount Barker with Riesling and Shiraz; Albany with Pinot Noir; Porongurup with Riesling and Pinot Noir. Plantings have boomed in recent years, especially in Frankland River, as water issues are resolved. Best producers: Alkoomi★, Castelli★, Castle Rock★★, CHERUBINO★★, FERNGROVE★, Forest Hill★, Frankland Estate★★★, Gilberts★, HAREWOOD★★, HOUGHTON★★, HOWARD PARK★★, Lake House, Marchand & Burch★★, Plantagenet★, Rockcliffe (formerly Matilda's Estate), Singlefile★★, Three Drops★, West Cape Howe★★, Wignalls, Willoughby Park.

PATRICIA GREEN CELLARS *Willamette Valley AVA, Oregon, USA* Various bottlings of Pinot Noir (Croft Vineyard★★, Eason Vineyard★, Balcombe Vineyard★, Notorious★★, Reserve★) from vineyards in Ribbon Ridge, Dundee Hills, Chehalem Mountains and Eola Hills. Also fine Sauvignon Blanc★. Best years: (Pinot Noir) 2012 11 10 **09** 08.

GRENACHE BLANC An underrated white grape in the south of France, with a rapidly growing band of admirers. It can make light anise and pear-scented young whites, or heroically dense, oily mouth-fillers. Low-yield examples take surprisingly well to oak. Generally best within a year of the vintage, although the odd old-vine example can age impressively (Château RAYAS is half Grenache Blanc). Grown as Garnacha Blanca in Spain, where it's now producing some stunning examples in PRIORAT, Terra Alta, Méntrida and RIOJA. A few old vines are contributing to some characterful blends and varietal wines in South Africa and California.

GRENACHE NOIR Among the world's most widely planted red grapes – the bulk of it in Spain, where it is called Garnacha Tinta. It is a hot-climate grape and in France it reaches its peak in the southern RHÔNE, especially in CHÂTEAUNEUF-DU-PAPE, where it combines great alcoholic strength with rich yet refined raspberry fruit and a sensuous perfume from the herb-strewn hills. It is generally blended with Syrah, Mourvèdre, Cinsaut or other southern French grapes. With Cinsaut, it can make wonderful rosé in TAVEL, LIRAC and CÔTES DE PROVENCE, as well as in NAVARRA in Spain. Throughout Spain, Garnacha is making an impressive comeback as young growers rediscover old vineyards. In addition to Aragón's CALATAYUD, CAMPO DE BORJA and CARIÑENA, CATALUÑA's PRIORAT and Montsant, and RIOJA, the movement is particularly spectacular in the Gredos mountains west of MADRID, and also in MANCHUELA and JUMILLA. Grenache is also the basis for the *vins doux naturels* of RASTEAU in the southern Rhône and BANYULS and MAURY in the ROUSSILLON. In SARDINIA, as Cannonau, it produces deep, tannic reds and lighter, modern wines, although traditional sweet and fortified styles can still be found. Produced in VENETO's Colli Berici DOC as Tai (was Tocai) Rosso. Also grown in CALIFORNIA and SOUTH AUSTRALIA, where it is finally being accorded respect as imaginative winemakers realize there is a great resource of century-old vines capable of making wild and massively enjoyable reds, either alone or with Syrah and/or Mourvèdre. More is being planted in WASHINGTON STATE, and in South Africa, where it is a popular component in Rhône-style wines.

GRÈS DE MONTPELLIER *Languedoc AC, France* A subzone of the LANGUEDOC AC covering vineyards all round Montpellier. Lacks a true identity, but includes some good producers, including: Blanville, Clavel★, l'Engarran★, Saumarez, Valmagne. Best years: (2013) 12 11 10 09 08 07 06 05.

GRGICH HILLS ESTATE *Rutherford AVA, California, USA* Classic NAPA VALLEY Chardonnay★★, which can age for at least a decade. Also tasty Fumé Blanc★, ripe, rich Cabernet★, plummy Merlot★ and a huge, old-style Zinfandel★. Best years: (Chardonnay) (2012) 11 10 09 08 07 06 05 04 03.

GRIGNAN-LES-ADHÉMAR AC *Rhône Valley, France* Mid-Rhône region with sometimes full, spice-pepper and herbs reds and rosés with juicy fruit. Nutty dry white. Drink young, though best such as Grangeneuve last well. Best producers: Décelle, DELAS★, Grangeneuve★, Lônes, Montine★, St-Luc★, Vieux Micocoulier. Best years: 2012 11 10 09.

GRIOTTE-CHAMBERTIN AC See CHAMBERTIN AC.

JEAN GRIVOT *Vosne-Romanée, Côte de Nuits, Burgundy, France* Étienne Grivot settled into a successful stride from 1995 and then raised his game from 2004 with increasingly ripe yet always fine and complex wines from a host of VOSNE-ROMANÉE Premiers Crus (Beaux Monts★★★) as well as fine CLOS DE VOUGEOT★★★, ÉCHÉZEAUX★★★ and RICHEBOURG★★★. Best years: (2013) 12 11 10 09 08 07 06 05 04 03 02 01 99 98 96 95.

GROS *Côte de Nuits, Burgundy, France* Brilliant wines from various members of the family, especially Anne Gros, Michel Gros, Gros Frère et Soeur and Anne-Françoise Gros. Look out for CLOS DE VOUGEOT★★★, ÉCHÉZEAUX★★★ and RICHEBOURG★★★ as well as good-value HAUTES-CÔTES DE NUITS★. Best years: (2013) 12 11 10 09 08 07 06 05 03 02 99 96.

GROSSET *Clare Valley, South Australia* Jeffrey Grosset is a perfectionist, crafting tiny quantities of hand-made wines. A Riesling specialist, he sources single-vineyard Watervale★★★ and Polish Hill★★★ from his own properties; both are supremely good and age well. Thrilling Alea Off-dry Riesling★ from a vineyard at Watervale's highest altitude. Cabernet blend Gaia★★ is smooth and seamless. Also outstanding ADELAIDE HILLS wines: Piccadilly Chardonnay★★★, very fine Pinot

Noir★★ and one of Australia's finest, tautest Semillon-Sauvignon★★★. Best years: (Riesling) 2013 12 11 10 **09 06 05 04 03 02 01 00 99**.

CH. GRUAUD-LAROSE★★ *St-Julien AC, 2ème Cru Classé, Haut-Médoc, Bordeaux, France* One of the largest ST-JULIEN estates. Until the 1970s the wines were classic, cedary St-Juliens; from the early 80s, they became darker, richer and coated with new oak, yet inclined to exhibit an unnerving feral quality. Recent vintages have mostly combined considerable power with finesse, despite disappointments in 2002 and 03. On great form since 2008 and still relatively good value. Second wine: Sarget de Gruaud-Larose. Best years: 2012 11 10 09 08 **07 06 05 04 01 00 99 98 96**.

GRÜNER VELTLINER Austrian grape, also grown in the Czech Republic, Slovakia, Hungary, Italy, New Zealand and California. It is at its best in Austria's KAMPTAL, KREMSTAL and the WACHAU, and in ALTO ADIGE'S Eisacktal, where the soil and cool climate bring out all the lentilly, white-peppery aromas. Styles vary from light and tart to savoury, mouthfilling yet appetizing wines equalling the best in Europe.

GUIGAL *Côte-Rôtie AC, Rhône Valley, France* Internationally famous name, producing big, oaked wines from a wide spread of vineyards in CÔTE-RÔTIE, which includes the Ch. d'Ampuis★★ label as well as Dom. de Bonserine★ (La Garde★★, La Viallière★), VIDAL-FLEURY (La Chatillonne★★) and the Guigal range from domaine and purchased grapes. Côte-Rôtie Brune et Blonde is ★★. The big-flavoured La Mouline, La Turque and La Landonne all rate ★★★ in most critics' opinions – and sometimes in mine. CONDRIEU★★ (la Doriane, sometimes ★★★) is big, obvious, opulent and fragrant. Red and white HERMITAGE★★ and Ermitage Ex-Voto★★ are also good to excellent. Good-value ST-JOSEPH★ (red and white), CÔTES DU RHÔNE★, chunky GIGONDAS★ and bright, full TAVEL★ rosé. Best years: (top reds) 2013 12 11 10 09 08 07 **06 05 04 03 01 00 99 98 97 95 94 91 90 89 88 85 83 82 78**.

CH. GUIRAUD★★ *Sauternes AC, 1er Cru Classé, Bordeaux, France* High price reflects the fact that fermentation takes place in 100% new oak barrels, but the lush, rich texture of the wine can take the wood. Keep best vintages for 10 years or more. Second wine: Petit Guiraud (from 2005). Also dry white G de Guiraud. Best years: 2011 10 **09 07 06 05 04 03 02 01 99 98 97 96 95 90 89 88**.

GUSBOURNE *Kent, England* Set to become one of the major UK sparkling wine producers. Blanc de Blancs★★, Rosé★ and Brut Reserve★★ are all very good. Still wines are made in very limited quantities, but the 2011 Guinevere★★ (Chardonnay) and Pinot Noir★★ may be the best still wines ever produced in the UK from these two varieties.

FRITZ HAAG *Brauneberg, Mosel, Germany* MOSEL grower with vineyards in the BRAUNEBERGER Juffer and Juffer Sonnenuhr. Pure, elegant Rieslings, at least ★★ quality, with Auslese and above often reaching ★★★. Best years: (2013) 12 11 10 **09 08 07 06 05 04 02**.

REINHOLD HAART *Piesport, Mosel, Germany* Theo Haart produces sensational Rieslings – with blackcurrant, peach and citrus aromas – from the great PIESPORTer Goldtröpfchen vineyard. Ausleses are often ★★★. Best years: (2013) 12 11 **10 09 08 07 06 05 04 02**.

HAMILTON RUSSELL VINEYARDS *Hemel en Aarde Valley WO, South Africa* A pioneer in the WALKER BAY region. Delicately scented Pinot Noir★★ has an uninterrupted history since 1981, the taut, minerally Chardonnay★★

(often ★★★) since 1983. Under the Ashbourne label, intriguing Pinotage-based red★ and impressive Sauvignon Blanc-based Sandstone★★, fermented in amphoras. Under Southern Right label, more Pinot-like Pinotage★ and zingy, easy-drinking Sauvignon Blanc★. Best years: (Pinot Noir) 2012 **11 10 09 08 07 06 05 04**; (Chardonnay) 2013 **12 11 10 09 08 07 06 05 04 03**.

HAMILTON RUSSELL VINEYARDS
Pinot noir
ESTATE WINE OF ORIGIN HEMEL-EN-AARDE VALLEY
GROWN, MADE, MATURED AND BOTTLED ON THE HAMILTON RUSSELL VINEYARDS ESTATE
HEMEL-EN-AARDE VALLEY, HERMANUS, CAPE OF GOOD HOPE
WINE OF SOUTH AFRICA
750ml   Alc.13.5%Vol.

HANDLEY *Anderson Valley AVA, Mendocino County, California, USA* Serious producer of sparkling wines, including one of California's best Brut Rosés★. Aromatic Gewürztraminer★★ and Riesling★★, and two bottlings of Chardonnay (DRY CREEK VALLEY★ and ANDERSON VALLEY★), are worth seeking out. The Anderson Valley estate Pinot Noirs (regular★, Reserve★★) are in a lighter, more subtle style. Syrah★ is excellent.

HANZELL *Sonoma Valley, California, USA* Pioneering producer of crisp, minerally Chardonnay★★ and ageworthy Pinot Noir★★. Estate-grown Ambassador's 1953 Vineyard Chardonnay★★ is made from some of the oldest Chardonnay vines in California.

HARAS DE PIRQUE *Maipo, Chile* Located in Pirque, a sub-region of MAIPO in the foothills of the Andes. Dense, spicy Elegance Cabernet Sauvignon★★ leads the portfolio; Cabernet-based Character★★ is equally impressive, and more approachable. Savoury Cabernet-Carmenère blend Albis★★ is a joint venture with Italy's ANTINORI.

HARDYS *McLaren Vale, South Australia* Owned by Accolade (formerly Constellation), the basic wines under the Hardy labels do no honour to the great family tradition. Varietals (especially Shiraz and Grenache) under the Nottage Hill label are more reliable. Top of the tree are the Eileen Hardy Shiraz★★ and Thomas Hardy Cabernet★★, both dense reds for hedonists. Eileen Hardy Chardonnay★★ is more elegant, tightly structured and focused than it used to be. Eileen Hardy Pinot Noir★★ from TASMANIA could be interesting. New mid-price William Hardy range offers reasonable quality regional varietals at fair prices. Best years: (Eileen Hardy Shiraz) (2013) (12) 10 08 **06 05 04 03 02 01 00 98 97 96 95 93**.

HAREWOOD ESTATE *Great Southern, Western Australia* One of Denmark's finest vineyards, owned by James Kellie (ex-HOWARD PARK). The portfolio demonstrates Kellie's skill and knowledge of the GREAT SOUTHERN, especially with powerful Cabernet Sauvignon★, gutsy yet silky smooth Frankland River Shiraz★, intense, zesty Riesling★★, tangy Sauvignon-Semillon and elegant single-vineyard Denmark Chardonnay★★.

HARLAN ESTATE★★★ *Oakville AVA, California, USA* One of California's most sought-after reds, a full-bodied and robustly tannic BORDEAUX blend offering layers of ripe black fruits and heaps of new French oak. Dense but thrilling upon release, the wine is built to develop for 10 years. Bond★ is a cheaper label from small NAPA VALLEY hillside vineyards.

HARTENBERG ESTATE *Stellenbosch WO, South Africa* Shiraz is the prime performer here: fleshy and accessible regular Shiraz★, The Stork★★ and single-vineyard Gravel Hill★★. Merlot and Cabernet also perform well, topped by The Mackenzie★★ Bordeaux-style blend. Also fine Chardonnay★ (refined, complex The Eleanor★), off-dry Riesling★ and crunchy Sauvignon. Best years: (top reds) 2011 **10 09 08 07 06 05 04 03**.

HARTFORD FAMILY *Russian River Valley AVA, California, USA* Chardonnays and Pinot Noirs from RUSSIAN RIVER and SONOMA COAST bear the Hartford Court label: most have textbook cool-climate intensity and acidity. Pinot Noirs include Arrendell Vineyard★★, Land's Edge★★, Fog Dance★★, Far Coast★, Seascape★; Chardonnays include Seascape★★, Four Hearts★, Stone Côte★. Hartford old-vine Zinfandels include Fanucchi-Wood Road★★ and Highwire★★. Owned by Jackson Family Wines.

HARTWELL *Stags Leap District AVA, Napa Valley, California, USA* Gloriously fruity and elegant Cabernet Sauvignon★★ from a small vineyard in the STAGS LEAP DISTRICT. There's an equally supple Merlot★★ and lower-priced Misté Hill Cabernet Sauvignon★. Best years: (Cabernet Sauvignon) (2012) 10 09 08 07 06 05 03 02 01 00 99 98 97.

HATTENHEIM *Rheingau, Germany* Village with 13 vineyard sites, including Steinberg, a monopoly of Kloster Eberbach★. Best producers: Barth★, Lang, Langwerth von Simmern★, G Müller★, Ress★, SCHLOSS REINHARTSHAUSEN★★, Schloss Schönborn★★. Best years: (2013) 12 11 10 09 08 07 06 05.

CH. HAUT-BAGES-LIBÉRAL★ *Pauillac AC, 5ème Cru Classé, Haut-Médoc, Bordeaux, France* PAUILLAC property that has quietly been gathering plaudits for some years: loads of unbridled delicious fruit, a positively hedonistic style but underpinned by tannin – and its lack of renown keeps the price just about reasonable. The wines age well. Best years: 2012 11 10 09 08 06 05 04 03 02 01 00 98 96 95.

CH. HAUT-BAILLY★★ *Pessac-Léognan AC, Cru Classé de Graves, Bordeaux, France* Traditionally one of the softest and most charming of the PESSAC-LÉOGNAN Classed Growths, and on good form during the 1990s. New ownership from 1998 has gradually returned Haut-Bailly to a leading role, no longer always soft and silky, but increasingly full of personality and style. On a winning streak since 2005. Second wine: la Parde-de-Haut-Bailly. Best years: 2012 11 10 09 08 07 06 05 04 02 01 00 98 96 95 90 89.

CH. HAUT-BATAILLEY★ *Pauillac AC, 5ème Cru Classé, Haut-Médoc, Bordeaux, France* This estate has produced too many wines that are light, attractively spicy, but rarely memorable. Owner François-Xavier Borie of GRAND-PUY-LACOSTE is changing this and from 2005 the wines have shown much improvement, becoming distinctly more substantial. Best years: 2012 11 10 09 08 07 06 05 04 03 02 01 00 98.

CH. HAUT-BRION *Pessac-Léognan AC, 1er Cru Classé, Graves, Bordeaux, France* This property's excellent gravel-based vineyard is now part of Bordeaux's suburbs. The red wine★★★ is one of Bordeaux's most subtle, with a magical ability to age. There is a small amount of white★★★ which, at its best, is memorably rich yet marvellously dry, blossoming over 5–10 years. Second wine: (red) le Clarence de Haut-Brion (from 2007), previously Bahans-Haut-Brion. Best years: (red) 2012 11 10 09 08 07 06 05 04 03 02 01 00 99 98 96 95 90; (white) 2012 11 10 09 08 07 06 05 04 03.

CH. HAUT-MARBUZET★★ *St-Estèphe AC, Haut-Médoc, Bordeaux, France* Impressive ST-ESTÈPHE wine worthy of classification, with great, rich, mouthfilling blasts of flavour and lots of new oak. Best years: 2012 11 10 09 08 06 05 04 03 02 01 00 98 96 95.

HAUT-MÉDOC AC *Bordeaux, France* The finest gravelly soil is here in the southern half of the MÉDOC peninsula; this AC covers all the decent vineyard land not included in the 6 village ACs (MARGAUX, MOULIS, LISTRAC, ST-JULIEN, PAUILLAC and ST-ESTÈPHE). Wines vary in quality and style. Best producers: d'Agassac★, Belgrave★, Belle-Vue★, Bernadotte★, Cambon la Pelouse★, Camensac, CANTEMERLE★, Charmail★, Cissac★, Citran★, Coufran, la

LAGUNE★, Lanessan★, Malescasse★, Maucamps★, Peyrabon★, Sénéjac★, SOCIANDO-MALLET★★, la Tour-Carnet★, Tour-du-Haut-Moulin★, Villegeorge. Best years: 2012 11 10 **09 08 06 05 04 03 02 01**.

HAUTES-CÔTES DE BEAUNE AC See BOURGOGNE-HAUTES-CÔTES DE BEAUNE AC.
HAUTES-CÔTES DE NUITS AC See BOURGOGNE-HAUTES-CÔTES DE NUITS AC.

HAWKES BAY *North Island, New Zealand* New Zealand's second largest and one of its most prestigious wine regions. Plenty of sunshine, moderately predictable weather during ripening and a complex array of soils make it ideal for a range of wine styles. Traditionally known for Cabernet Sauvignon and, particularly, Merlot, it now also makes some superb Syrah. Whites can be very good too, especially Chardonnay. Free-draining Gimblett Gravels is the outstanding area. **Best producers:** Alpha Domus★, Bilancia★★, CHURCH ROAD★★, Clearview★, COOPERS CREEK★, CRAGGY RANGE★★, Elephant Hill★★, Esk Valley★★★, MATUA VALLEY★, Mission★, Moana Park★, MORTON ESTATE★, Newton Forrest★ (Cornerstone★★), NGATARAWA★★, C J PASK★, Sacred Hill★★, Stonecroft★, Te Awa★, TE MATA★★, TRINITY HILL★★, Unison★, Vidal★★, VILLA MARIA★★. **Best years:** (top reds) (2013) 10 09 08 07 06 04.

HdV *Carneros AVA, California, USA* A joint venture between Hyde Vineyards of Napa Valley and Aubert and Pamela de Villaine of Burgundy. Known for its minerally, Burgundian-style Chardonnays★★, the winery also makes small amounts of Cabernet Sauvignon, Syrah and BORDEAUX-blend Belle Cousine★. **Best years:** (Chardonnay) 2011 10 **09 08** 07 06 05 04 03 02.

HEATHCOTE *Central Victoria, Australia* This wine region's unique feature is the deep russet Cambrian soil, formed more than 600 million years ago, which is found on the best sites and is proving ideal for Shiraz. BROWN BROTHERS and TYRRELL'S have extensive recent plantings. **Best producers:** BROWN BROTHERS★★, Foster e Rocco, Greenstone, Heathcote Estate★★, Heathcote Winery★★, Jasper Hill★★★, Red Edge★, Sanguine★★, Shelmerdine, TYRRELL'S★ (Rufus Stone★★), Wild Duck Creek★. **Best years:** (Shiraz) (2013) 12 10 09 **08 06 05 04 03 02 01 00 97 96 95 94 91 90**.

HEDGES FAMILY ESTATE *Columbia Valley AVA, Washington State, USA* Top wines are Cabernet-Merlot blends using fruit from prime Red Mountain AVA vineyards: Hedges Family Estate Red Mountain★ is powerful and ageworthy, tannic but full of cassis fruit, and La Haute Cuvée★★ is restrained and scented. Excellent Bel'Villa Syrah★★. Red CMS★ (Cabernet-Merlot-Syrah) and crisp white CMS (Sauvignon-Chardonnay-Marsanne) are the biggest sellers. **Best years:** (top reds) (2012) 11 10 **09 08**.

DR HEGER *Ihringen, Baden, Germany* Joachim Heger specializes in powerful, dry Weissburgunder (Pinot Blanc)★★ and Spätburgunder (Pinot Noir)★★. Winklerberg Grauburgunder★★ is also serious stuff, while his ancient Yellow Muscat vines deliver powerful dry wines★ and rare but fabulous TBAs★★. **Best years:** (whites) (2013) 12 **11 10 09 08 07 05**.

CHARLES HEIDSIECK *Champagne AC, Champagne, France* Charles Heidsieck is the most consistently fine of all the major houses, with vintage★★★ Champagne declared only in the very best years. The non-vintage★★ is regularly of vintage quality; these age well for at least 5 years. **Best years:** (2002) **00 96 95 90 89 88 85 82**.

HEITZ CELLAR *Napa Valley AVA, California, USA* Star attraction here is the Martha's Vineyard Cabernet Sauvignon★★. Many believe that early bottlings of Martha's Vineyard are among the best wines ever produced in CALIFORNIA. Heitz also produces Trailside Vineyard Cabernet★, Bella Oaks Vineyard Cabernet★ and a NAPA Cabernet★, as well as scented Sauvignon Blanc★. Dry Grignolino Rosé★ is a snappy picnic delight. Best years: (Martha's Vineyard) (2010) (09) **08 07 06 05 04 03 02 97 96 92 91.**

HENNERS *East Sussex, England* Planted in 2007, this newcomer is making some excellent sparkling wines – Brut★★, Brut Reserve and Rosé – using the classic CHAMPAGNE grape varieties.

HENRIOT *Champagne AC, Champagne, France* In 1994 Joseph Henriot bought back the name of his old-established family company. Henriot CHAMPAGNEs have a limpid clarity; the range includes non-vintage Brut Souverain★, Blanc de Blancs★★ and Rosé Brut★; vintage Brut★★ and Rosé; and de luxe Cuvée des Enchanteleurs★★. Best years: 2006 05 **03 02 00 98 96 95 90 89 88 85.**

HENRIQUES & HENRIQUES *Madeira DOC, Madeira, Portugal* The wines to look for are the 15-year-old★★ and 20-year-old★★ versions of the classic varieties. Vibrant Sercial and Verdelho, and rich Malmsey and Bual are all fine examples of their styles. Henriques & Henriques also has vintage Madeiras★★★ of extraordinary quality.

HENRY OF PELHAM *Niagara Peninsula VQA, Ontario, Canada* A pioneer of *vinifera* wines in the Niagara Peninsula. Best are Riesling Icewine★, Speck Family Reserve Riesling★, Chardonnay★, Cabernet-Merlot and Cuvée Catharine fizz.

HENSCHKE *Eden Valley, South Australia*

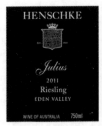

Winemaker Stephen Henschke and his viticulturist wife Prue make some of Australia's grandest reds from old vines: stunning HILL OF GRACE★★★, Mount Edelstone Shiraz★★★, Tappa Pass Shiraz★★, Cyril Henschke Cabernet★★ (sometimes★★★), Johann's Garden Grenache★, and Shiraz blends Henry's Seven★ and Euphonium★★ (formerly Keyneton Estate). Whites are led by perfumed Julius Riesling★★ and toasty yet fruity Louis Semillon★★ (both can be ★★★). ADELAIDE HILLS plantings at Lenswood yield waxy, toasty Croft Chardonnay★, scented Giles Pinot Noir★★ and impressive Abbotts Prayer Merlot-Cabernet★★. Best years: (Mount Edelstone) (2013) 10 08 07 06 05 **04 02 01** 99 96 94 92 91 90 88 86.

HÉRAULT, IGP DE L' *Languedoc, France* A huge region, covering the entire Hérault *département*. The better-known OC is often used in preference to Hérault. Red wines predominate, based on Carignan, Grenache and Cinsaut, and most of the wine is sold in bulk. But things are changing. There are lots of hilly vineyards with great potential, and MAS DE DAUMAS GASSAC followed by GRANGE DES PÈRES have made waves internationally. Whites are improving, too. Best producers: GRANGE DES PÈRES★★, Magellan, Marfée, Mas Conscience, MAS DE DAUMAS GASSAC★, Mas Gabriel, Poujol.

HERMITAGE AC *Rhône Valley, France* Hermitage, from a steep, largely granite vineyard above the town of Tain l'Hermitage in the northern RHÔNE, is revered throughout the world as a rare, rich red wine – expensive, memorable and classic. The best growers, with mature Syrah vines, can create superbly original wine, needing 5–10 years' aging even in a light year and a minimum of 15 years in a ripe, very sunny vintage. White Hermitage, from Marsanne plus Roussanne, is less famous, but the best – wonderfully rich wines, made by traditionalists – can outlive the reds, sometimes aging for as long as 40 years into an exotic, complex fullness. **Best producers:** A Belle★, CHAPOUTIER★★, J-L CHAVE★★★, Y Chave★, Colombier★★, COLOMBO★, DELAS★★, B Faurie★★, Fayolle Fils & Fille★, Ferraton★, GUIGAL★★, Paul JABOULET★, P & V Jaboulet, Nicolas Perrin, Remizières★, J-M Sorrel★, M Sorrel★★★, Cave de TAIN★, Tardieu-Laurent★★, les Vins de Vienne★. **Best years:** (reds) 2013 12 11 10 09 07 06 05 04 03 01 00 99 98 97 96 95 94 91 90 89 88 85 83 78.

HESSISCHE BERGSTRASSE *Germany* A small (448ha/1006-acre), warm region near Darmstadt. Riesling occupies over half the vineyards. Lovely Eiswein★★ is made by the Domäne Bergstrasse. Simon-Bürkle★ is reliable too.

HEWITSON *Barossa Valley, Adelaide Hills, South Australia* The pride of Dean Hewitson's portfolio is in the glorious old vine-growers' vineyards (such as Old Garden, planted to Mourvèdre in 1853). Hewitson makes fine, delicate whites and complex, expressive reds sourced from small parcels of grapes sourced from the regions near Adelaide. Grenache-based Miss Harry★ is floral and plush; Mad Hatter Shiraz★★ powerful and ultra-concentrated; Old Garden★★★ is brambly, fleshy and awesome, while Baby Bush Mourvèdre★ is vibrant and enticing.

HEYMANN-LÖWENSTEIN *Winningen, Mosel, Germany* A leading estate in WINNINGEN in the Lower MOSEL. Its dry Rieslings are unusually full-bodied for the region; those from the Röttgen and Uhlen sites often reach ★★. Also powerful Auslese★★. **Best years:** (2013) 12 11 **10 09 08 07 05**.

HIDALGO *Jerez y Manzanilla DO, Andalucia, Spain* Hidalgo's Manzanilla La Gitana★★ is deservedly one of the best-selling manzanillas in Spain. Hidalgo is family-owned, and only uses grapes from its own vineyards. Brands include Amontillado Napoleon★★, Jerez Cortado Wellington★★ and rich but dry Oloroso Viejo★★.

HIDDEN BENCH *Niagara Peninsula VQA, Ontario, Canada* Consistently good red and white meritage blends, Riesling and Pinot Noir. Felseck Vineyard label is their best for whites.

HILL OF GRACE★★★ *Eden Valley, South Australia* This stunning Shiraz celebrated its 50th vintage in 2012. It is regarded by many as sharing the pinnacle of Australian winemaking with Penfolds GRANGE. It is made by HENSCHKE from a single vineyard which stands opposite the Gnadenberg (or Hill of Grace) Lutheran Church. The vineyard was first planted in the 1860s, and the old vines produce a powerful, structured wine with superb ripe black fruit, chocolate, coffee, earth, leather and a whole lot more. Can be cellared for 20 years or more. **Best years:** (2013) (12) 10 08 07 06 05 04 **02 01 99 98 97 96 95 94 93 92 91 90 88 86**.

HILLTOP *Neszmély, Hungary* Winemaker Akos Kamocsay produces fresh, bright wines, especially white. Indigenous varieties such as Irsai Olivér and Cserszegi Füszeres line up with Gewürztraminer, Sauvignon Blanc★, Pinot Gris and Chardonnay. Good but controversial TOKAJI.

HILLTOPS *New South Wales, Australia* High-altitude cherry-growing region with a small but fast-growing area of vineyards around the town of Young. Good potential for reds from Cabernet Sauvignon and Shiraz, plus bright, tangy Riesling. Moppity's budget-priced Lock & Key range offers some of the best value in the country. **Best producers:** Chalkers Crossing★★, Freeman★, Grove Estate, MCWILLIAM'S/Barwang★, Moppity★, Woodonga Hill.

FRANZ HIRTZBERGER *Wachau, Niederösterreich, Austria*   Superlative quality. The finest wines are the concentrated, elegant Smaragd Rieslings from Singerriedel★★★ and Hochrain★★★. The best Grüner Veltliner comes from Honivogl★★★. Best years: (Riesling Smaragd) (2013) 12 11 **10 09 08 07 06 05 04 03 02.**

HOCHHEIM *Rheingau, Germany*   Village best known for having given the English language the word 'Hock' for Rhine wine, but it has good individual vineyard sites, especially Domdchaney, Hölle (hell!) and Kirchenstück. Best producers: Flick★, KUNSTLER★★, Werner★. Best years: (2013) 12 11 **10 09 08 07 06 05 04.**

HOPE FAMILY WINES *Paso Robles AVA, California, USA*   The Hope Family began farming in PASO ROBLES more than three decades ago, and helped build its reputation as a premium winegrowing region. Today Hope Family makes solid wines under 5 labels: Liberty School (Cabernet Sauvignon, Chardonnay, and Syrah-based Cuvee), Treana★ (red and white RHÔNE-style blends), Candor★ (Merlot and Zin), Austin Hope (Syrah★★ and Grenache★) and Troublemaker★ (Rhône-style red blend).

HORTON VINEYARDS *Virginia, USA*   Horton's Viognier★ established VIRGINIA's potential as a wine region and ignited a rush of wineries wanting to make the next CONDRIEU. Innovations include a sparkling Viognier and varietals such as Tannat, Petit Manseng and Rkatsiteli. The Cabernet Franc★ is among the best value red wines of the eastern US.

DOM. DE L'HORTUS *Pic St-Loup AC, Languedoc, France*   One of PIC ST-LOUP's pioneering estates. The red Bergerie de l'Hortus★, a ready-to-drink unoaked Syrah-Mourvèdre-Grenache blend, has delightful flavours of herbs, plums and cherries. Big brother Grande Cuvée★★ needs time for the fruit and oak to come into harmony. The white Grande Cuvée★ is a Chardonnay-Viognier-Roussanne blend. Best years: (Grande Cuvée red) (2013) 12 11 **10 09 08 07 06 05.**

HOSPICES DE BEAUNE *Côte de Beaune, Burgundy, France*   Scene of a theatrical auction on the third Sunday in November each year, now under the auspices of Christie's, the Hospices is an historic foundation which sells the wine of the new vintage from its holdings in the CÔTE D'OR to finance its charitable works. Pricing reflects charitable status rather than common sense, but the auction trend is regarded as an indicator of which way the market is heading. Much depends on the Hospices' winemaking, which has been variable but is becoming more reliable, as well as on the maturation and bottling, which are in the hands of the purchaser of each lot.

HOUGHTON *Swan District, Western Australia*   WESTERN AUSTRALIA's biggest winery. The budget-priced 'Stripe' range includes the flavoursome White Classic★. Moondah Brook Cabernet Sauvignon★ and Shiraz★ are a step up in quality. The regional Wisdom range has a MARGARET RIVER Cabernet★★, as well as sublime funky Chardonnay★★ and pure, taut Sauvignon Blanc★★ from PEMBERTON. Opulent, dense yet elegant Gladstones Cabernet★★ from Margaret River and powerful, lush Jack Mann Cabernet Sauvignon★★ from Frankland River.

HOWARD PARK *Margaret River, Western Australia*   Howard Park has vineyards in MARGARET RIVER and GREAT SOUTHERN. Top-quality Abercrombie Cabernet Sauvignon (sometimes ★★★), plus zesty, floral Riesling★★ and classy Chardonnay★★. Good Scotsdale Shiraz★★ and Leston Cabernet★. Affordable MadFish label is good for Riesling★, Shiraz, Sauvignon-Semillon★ and unwooded Chardonnay★. Marchand &

Burch label has exquisite Chardonnay★★, Pinot Noir★★ (rare Gibraltar Rock★★★) and Shiraz★, as well as tiny quantities of Burgundy (yes, French Burgundy). Best years: (Cabernet) (2013) 12 11 10 09 08 07 **05 04 03 02 01 99 96 94 92 91 90 88 86**; (Riesling) 2013 12 11 10 09 **08 06 05 04 03 02 01 97 95 92 91 89**.

HOWELL MOUNTAIN AVA *Napa Valley, California, USA* NAPA's north-eastern corner is noted for powerhouse Cabernet Sauvignon and Zinfandel, as well as exotic, full-flavoured Merlot. Best producers: BERINGER (Merlot★★), Cade★, CAKEBREAD★, DUNN★★★, La Jota★★, Ladera★★, Liparita★, O'Shaughnessy★, PINE RIDGE (Cabernet Sauvignon★), VIADER★★, White Cottage★. Best years: (reds) (2012) 10 **09 08 07 06 05 03 02 01 00 99 98 97 96 95 94 91 90**.

HUBER *Malterdingen, Baden, Germany* For two decades Bernhard Huber has been crafting full-bodied Chardonnay★★ and increasingly sophisticated Pinot Noir★★. Over-oaked in the past, now more fleshy and balanced. Charming Muskateller★. Best years: (red) (2013) (12) 11 **10 09 08 07 05**.

HUET *Vouvray AC, Loire Valley, France* The highly respected Noël Pinguet handed over the winemaking reins to Benjamin Joliveau in 2012, a tricky year, like 2013, so it's not yet easy to judge the new team. Huet traditionally produces complex, traditional VOUVRAY that can age for decades. Biodynamic methods are bringing into even sharper focus the individual traits of its 3 excellent sites – le Haut-Lieu, Clos du Bourg and le Mont. These yield dry★★, medium-dry★★★ or sweet★★★ and Pétillant★★ or Mousseux★★ sparkling wines, depending on the vintage. Cuvée Constance *liquoreux*, made in exceptional years, is a blend of parcels. Best years: (sec, demi-sec) (2013) 11 **10 07 06**; (moelleux) 2011 10 **09 05 04 03 02 01 00 99 98 97 96 90 89**.

HUGEL *Alsace AC, Alsace, France* Basic Gentil cuvée is gluggable but fairly featureless, but Jubilee Riesling is a reliable ★★. Best sweet wines are Vendange Tardive★★ and Sélection de Grains Nobles★★★. Despite owning some Grand Cru land, Hugel continues to ignore the system for labelling purposes. Patriarch Jean Hugel died in 2009, but quality has actually improved under the leadership of his nephew Etienne. Best years: (Jubilee dry Riesling) (2013) (12) 11 **10 09 08 07 05 03 01**.

HUNTER VALLEY *New South Wales, Australia* NEW SOUTH WALES' oldest wine zone overcomes a tricky climate to make fascinating, ageworthy Semillon and rich, buttery Chardonnay. Shiraz is the mainstay for reds, aging well but nowadays fresh and drinkable young; Cabernet is occasionally successful. Premium region is the Lower Hunter Valley; the Upper Hunter has few wineries but extensive vineyards in between the coal mines. Best producers: Allandale★, Audrey Wilkinson, BROKENWOOD★★★, De Iuliis★, Harkham★, Hope★, Lake's Folly★, Margan Family★, Mount Pleasant★★/MCWILLIAM'S, MEEREA PARK★, Oakvale, Scarborough, THOMAS★★, Tower★, Tulloch, Keith Tulloch★, TYRRELL'S★★. Best years: (Shiraz) (2013) 11 10 09 07 **06 04 03 02 00 99 98 97 96 94 91**.

HUNTER'S *Marlborough, South Island, New Zealand* One of MARLBOROUGH's stars, with fine, if austere, Sauvignon★, savoury Burgundian Chardonnay★, vibrant long-lived Riesling★ and sophisticated Pinot Noir★. Attractive Miru Miru fizz★. Best years: (Chardonnay) (2013) **12 10 09 07 06 05**.

CH. DU HUREAU *Saumur-Champigny AC, Loire Valley, France* Philippe Vatan barely uses oak; his SAUMUR-CHAMPIGNYs are particularly lifted and silky. The basic red, Tuffe★, is bright and fruity; Fours à Chaux★ shows elegant structure, while cuvées Lisagathe★★ and Fevettes★★ need a bit of time. Jasmine-scented white SAUMUR★ is exceptional in top years, and dry white Foudre★ is rich and complex. Decent fizz and occasional sweet Coteaux de Saumur. Best years: (top reds) 2013 11 **10 09 08 06 05 04 03**.

INGLENOOK See Francis Ford COPPOLA.

INNISKILLIN *Niagara Peninsula VQA, Ontario, Canada* One of Canada's leading wineries, with good Pinot Noir★ and Cabernet Franc, well-rounded Chardonnay★ and rich Vidal Icewine★★, Riesling Icewine★ and Sparkling Vidal Icewine★. Also in the OKANAGAN VALLEY in British Columbia. Best years: (Vidal Icewine) **2013 12 10 09 08 07 05 04 03 02 00**.

IPHOFEN *Franken, Germany* Important wine town in FRANKEN for dry Riesling and Silvaner. Both are powerful, with a pronounced earthiness. Top site: Julius-Echter-Berg. Best producers: JULIUSSPITAL★, Johann Ruck★, Hans Wirsching★. Best years: (2013) 12 **11 09 08 07 06 05 04 02**.

IRANCY AC *Burgundy, France* This northern outpost of vineyards, just south-west of CHABLIS, is an unlikely champion of the clear, pure flavours of the Pinot Noir grape. But red Irancy can be delicate, lightly touched by the ripeness of plums and strawberries, and can age well. Best producers: Colinot, DAUVISSAT★, Goisot★, Richoux★. Best years: (2013) 12 11 **10 09 06 05**.

IRON HORSE VINEYARDS *Sonoma County, California, USA* A pioneer of the Green Valley AVA, part of the RUSSIAN RIVER VALLEY. Outstanding sparkling wines, with vintage Brut★★ and Blanc de Blancs★★ delicious on release but highly suitable for aging. The Brut LD★★★ (Late Disgorged) is a heavenly mouthful – yeasty and complex. Also Wedding Cuvée★ (blanc de noirs), Brut Rosé★, Ultra Brut★ and Joy!★★, which is aged for 10–15 years before release. Still wines include lovely Pinot Noir★★, stunningly fresh, crisp Rued Clone Chardonnay★★ and a delicious unoaked Chardonnay★.

IROULÉGUY AOP *South-West France* The only French Basque wines. Tannat, usually blended with Cabernet Franc, gives fascinating, robust reds that are softer than MADIRAN. Whites are mainly from Petit Courbu. Best producers: Ameztia★, ARRETXEA★★, Brana★, Ilarria★, Irouléguy co-op (red Mignaberry★, dry white Xuri d'Ansa★), Mourguy★. Best years: (reds) (2012) 11 **10 09 08 06 05**.

ISOLE E OLENA *Chianti Classico DOCG, Tuscany, Italy* Piemontese Paolo De Marchi has long been one of the pacesetters in CHIANTI CLASSICO. His Chianti Classico★★, characterized by clean, elegant and spicily perfumed fruit, excels in every vintage. The thrilling Cepparello★★★, made from 100% Sangiovese, is the top wine. Excellent Syrah★★, Cabernet Sauvignon★★★, Chardonnay★★ and VIN SANTO★★★. Best years: (Cepparello) (2011) **10 09 08 07 06 04 03 01 99 98 97 95 90 88**.

CH. D'ISSAN★★ *Margaux AC, 3ème Cru Classé, Haut-Médoc, Bordeaux, France* This lovely moated property pulled its socks up in the 1990s. When successful (there's been a rising crescendo through the 2000s), the wine can be one of the most delicate and scented in the MARGAUX AC. Best years: 2012 11 10 09 **08 07 06 05 04 03 02 01 00 98 96 95**.

ITATA See BÍO BÍO.

J VINEYARDS *Sonoma County, California, USA* Established as a sparkling wine house by Judy Jordan. The J★ Brut is an attractive mouthful, as is the more complex Vintage Brut★★; J also makes a series of top-notch RUSSIAN RIVER Pinot Noirs★★ including excellent vineyard designates, as well as a small amount of tasty Pinotage★.

PAUL JABOULET AÎNÉ *Rhône Valley, France* During the 1970s, Jaboulet led the way in raising the world's awareness of the great quality of RHÔNE wines. Although some of the wines are still good, they are no longer the star in any appellation. Best wines are top red HERMITAGE La Chapelle (this was a ★★★ wine in its heyday) and whites La Chapelle★ and Chevalier de Stérimberg★. Also CROZES-HERMITAGE Dom. de Thalabert and Dom. de Roure★, attractive CORNAS Dom. de St-Pierre★, ST-JOSEPH Le Grand Pompée★, reliable CÔTES DU RHONE Parallèle 45, good-value VENTOUX Les Traverses★ and sweet, perfumed MUSCAT DE BEAUMES-DE-VENISE★★. In 2006, Jaboulet was bought by Swiss financier Jean-Jacques Frey, owner of Ch. la LAGUNE, causing an internationalization of style; a return to Rhône roots would be welcome. Best years: (La Chapelle) 2013 12 11 10 09 **07 05 01 99 98 97 96 95 94 91 90 89 88 78**.

JACKSON ESTATE *Marlborough, South Island, New Zealand* Sauvignon Blanc is showing much more traditional zip after a couple of sweaty vintages; barrel-fermented Grey Ghost Sauvignon Blanc★★ can improve with a little age. Restrained Chardonnay and powerful Vintage Widow Pinot Noir★. Best years: (Pinot Noir) (2013) **12 10 07 06 05 04**.

JACKSON-TRIGGS *Okanagan Valley VQA, British Columbia, Canada* Top-flight reds include Gold Series Merlot★ and single-vineyard Sun Rock Shiraz★. Also good Riesling Icewine and Entourage★ fizz. Osoyoos Larose★★ is a BORDEAUX blend made for the French Groupe Taillan. Also in NIAGARA PENINSULA: Delaine Syrah★ is potentially excellent.

JACOB'S CREEK *Barossa Valley, South Australia*
Australia's leading export brand, more consistent than its rivals, especially its Riesling★, Grenache-Shiraz★ and Blanc de Blancs fizz★. Also showing imagination with new wines like Fiano★ and Sangiovese★. Reserve and Limited Release wines can be ★★. Top-end wines include Steingarten Riesling★★★ and

Centenary Hill Shiraz★★ from the BAROSSA, plus Orlando Jacaranda Ridge Cabernet Sauvignon★ from COONAWARRA and Orlando Lawson's Shiraz★★ from PADTHAWAY. New super-premiums Johann Shiraz-Cabernet★★ and Reeves Point Chardonnay★★ are very impressive. Best years: (Steingarten Riesling) 2013 12 11 10 07 06 **05 04 03 02 01 97**.

JACQUESSON *Champagne AC, Champagne, France* The non-vintage is an austerely-styled one-off that changes each year to produce the best possible blend. Cuvée No. 737★★ (the tenth version made), based on the 2009 harvest, was released at the end of 2013. Also superb single-vineyard, single-cru and single grape variety Champagnes from Avize Champ Caïn★★ (Chardonnay), Aÿ Vauzelle Terme★★ (Pinot Noir) and Dizy Corne Bautray★★ (Chardonnay), and a saignée pink fizz, Dizy Terres Rouges Rosé★★. Best years: (2005) 04 **02 00 97 96 95 93 90 89 88 85**.

LOUIS JADOT *Beaune, Côte de Beaune, Burgundy, France* Ambitious merchant which has been expanding southward, especially in MOULIN-A-VENT (Ch. des Jacques★) and POUILLY-FUISSÉ. Top domaine whites from the CÔTE D'OR include PULIGNY-MONTRACHET Folatières★★ and CHEVALIER-MONTRACHET les Demoiselles★★★, while the relatively meaty reds range from attractive BEAUNE Premiers Crus★★ through to sumptuous BONNES MARES★★★ and MUSIGNY★★★. Best years: (top reds) (2013) 12 11 10 09 **08 07 06** 05 03 99 90; (whites) (2013) 12 11 **10 09 08 06 05 04**.

JEREZ Y MANZANILLA DO/SHERRY

Andalucía, Spain

The Spanish now own the name outright – at least in the EU, where the only wines that can be sold as sherry come from the triangle of vineyard land between the Andalusian towns of Jerez de la Frontera (inland), and Sanlúcar de Barrameda and Puerto de Santa María (by the sea). Australia, South Africa and California have traditionally made fortified sherry-style wines; South Africa has agreed to drop the label term 'sherry' and Australia is replacing the term 'sherry' with 'apera', but California has yet to reach agreement with the EU and producers may still use the term 'sherry' for wines sold locally.

The best sherries can be spectacular. Three main factors contribute to the high-quality potential of wines from this region: the chalky-spongy albariza soil where the best vines grow, the Palomino Fino grape – unexciting table wines but potentially great once transformed by the sherry-making processes – and a natural yeast called *flor*. All sherry must be a minimum of 3 years old, but fine sherries age in barrel for much longer. Sherries must be blended through a solera system. About a third of the wine from the oldest barrels is bottled, and the barrels topped up with slightly younger wine from another set of barrels and so on, for a minimum of 3 sets of barrels. The idea is that the younger wine takes on the character of older wine, as well as keeping the blend refreshed.

MAIN SHERRY STYLES

Fino and manzanilla Fino sherries derive their extraordinary, tangy, pungent flavours from *flor*. Young, newly fermented wines destined for these styles of sherry are deliberately fortified very sparingly to just 15–15.5% alcohol before being put in barrels for their minimum of 3 years' maturation. The thin, soft, oatmeal-coloured mush of *flor* grows on the surface of the wines, protecting them from the air (and thereby keeping them pale) and giving them a characteristic sharp, pungent tang. The addition of younger wine each year feeds the *flor*, maintaining an even layer. Manzanillas are fino-style wines that have matured in the cooler seaside conditions of Sanlúcar de Barrameda, where the *flor* grows thickest and the fine, salty tang is most accentuated.

Amontillado True amontillados are fino sherries that have continued to age after the *flor* has died (after about 5 years) and so finish their aging period in contact with air. These should all be bone dry and taste of raisins and buttered brazils. Medium-sweet amontillados are concoctions in which the dry sherry is sweetened with mistela, a blend of grape juice and alcohol.

Oloroso This type of sherry is strongly fortified after fermentation to deter the growth of *flor*. Olorosos, therefore, mature in barrel in contact with the air, which gradually darkens them while they remain dry, but develop rich, intense, nutty and raisiny flavours.

Other styles Manzanilla pasada is aged manzanilla, with greater depth and nuttiness. Palo cortado is an unusual, deliciously nutty, dry style somewhere in between amontillado and oloroso. Sweet oloroso creams and pale creams are almost without exception enriched solely for the export market. Sweet, syrupy varietal wines are made from sun-dried Pedro Ximénez or Moscatel grapes.

See also individual producers.

BEST PRODUCERS AND WINES

Argüeso (Manzanilla San León, Manzanilla Las Medallas).

BARBADILLO (Manzanilla Eva, Manzanilla En Rama, Manzanilla Solear, Amontillado Príncipe, Amontillado de Sanlúcar, Palo Cortado Obispo Gascón, Oloroso Seco Cuco).

Delgado Zuleta (Manzanilla Pasada La Goya).

El Maestro Sierra.

Equipo Navazos (La Bota de...)

Fernando de Castilla.

Garvey (Amontillado Tio Guillermo, Palo Cortado, Pedro Ximénez Gran Orden).

GONZÁLEZ BYASS (Tio Pepe Fino, Palmas range, Amontillado del Duque, Apóstoles Palo Cortado, Matusalem Oloroso, Vintage Oloroso, Noé Pedro Ximénez).

HIDALGO (Manzanilla La Gitana, Manzanilla Pasada Pastrana, Amontillado Napoleon, Jerez Cortado Wellington, Oloroso Viejo).

LUSTAU (Almacenista single-producer wines, Puerto Fino, Fino La Ina, East India Solera).

OSBORNE (Fino Quinta, Amontillado 51-1A, Amontillado Coquinero, Oloroso Bailén, Oloroso Sibarita, Oloroso Solera India, Pedro Ximénez).

Sánchez Romate (Pedro Ximénez Cardenal Cisneros).

Tradición.

VALDESPINO (Fino Inocente, Amontillado Coliseo, Amontillado Tio Diego, Palo Cortado Cardenal, Oloroso Don Gonzalo, Pedro Ximénez Niños).

Valdivia (Sacromonte).

Williams & Humbert (Alegría Manzanilla, Palo Cortado).

JAMET★★★ *Côte-Rôtie AC, Rhône Valley, France* For years, a top-class domaine. In 2013 the two brothers Jean-Paul and Jean-Luc split the business: Jean-Paul and Corinne Jamet run the main domaine, which continues to give wines of wonderful style. The full-bodied, intricate reds, led by the marvellous Côte Brune★★★, age beautifully for well over a decade. Superb CÔTES DU RHÔNE★★ and COLLINES RHODANIENNES Syrah★★. Best years: 2013 12 11 10 09 **08 07 06 05 04 03 01 99 98 97 96 95 91 90 89 88**.

JAMSHEED *Victoria, Australia* Two years working with Paul Draper at California's RIDGE set winemaker Gary Mills on the adventure of his life in wine. His wines are sourced from the YARRA VALLEY, BEECHWORTH and CENTRAL VICTORIA, with 5 different expressions of Syrah (Garden Gully★★, Seville★), key ingredients being minimal intervention and the use of older oak. Entry-level Harem wines are favourites of sommeliers.

JANUIK *Columbia Valley AVA, Washington State, USA* Experience as head winemaker at CHATEAU STE MICHELLE allows Mike Januik to source fruit from exceptional sites. His Cold Creek Chardonnay★★ is among the top in the state. Lewis Vineyard Syrah★★ is rich, earthy and bold, and Cabernet Sauvignons (Champoux Vineyard★★, Ciel du Cheval★★) are chocolaty, complex and ageworthy. Best years: (reds) (2012) 11 10 09 08.

JARDIN See JORDAN, South Africa.

JARDINS DE BABYLONE *Jurançon AOP, South-West France* Exquisitely elegant, understated wines from Louis-Benjamin DAGUENEAU's micro-vineyard: sweet★★★ from Gros Manseng and dry★★ blend that includes rare Camaralet and Lauzet grapes. Best years: (sweet) 2010 **09 08 07 04**.

JASNIÈRES AC *Loire Valley, France* Tiny AC north of Tours. Reputation for long-lived, bone-dry whites from Chenin Blanc, though new movers and shakers here and in neighbouring appellation Coteaux du Loir (which additionally makes delicate Pineau d'Aunis and Gamay reds) are picking Chenin riper. Sweet wine may be made in good years. Best producers: Bellivière★★, le Briseau★, J Gigou★★, Les Maisons Rouges★, J P Robinot★. Best years: (2013) 12 11 **10 09 08 07 05 04**.

JEREZ Y MANZANILLA DO/SHERRY See pages 184–5.

JOHANNISBERG *Rheingau, Germany* Probably the best known of all the Rhine wine villages, with 10 vineyard sites, including the famous Schloss Johannisberg. Best producers: Prinz von Hessen★, Johannishof★★, SCHLOSS JOHANNISBERG★★, Trenz. Best years: (2013) 12 11 **10 09 08 07 05 04**.

JORDAN *Alexander Valley AVA, Sonoma County, California, USA* Ripe, fruity Cabernet Sauvignon★★ with a cedar character rare in California, and with aging potential. The winery has recently moved toward greater use of mountain-grown Cabernet. Chardonnay★ from RUSSIAN RIVER VALLEY fruit is nicely balanced. Best years: (Cabernet) (2012) (10) **09 08 07 06 02 01 97 95 94**.

JORDAN *Stellenbosch WO, South Africa* Meticulous attention to detail ensures consistent quality. Chardonnays (creamy/limy regular★★; dense, nutty, balanced Nine Yards★★) and delicious peppery Chenin★★ head a strong white range. Syrah★★, Cabernet Sauvignon★, Merlot★ and BORDEAUX-blend Cobblers Hill★★ are beautifully balanced for aging. Sophia★★, a barrel selection of Cobblers Hill, is sold only at auction. Sold under the Jardin label in the USA. Best years: (Chardonnay) 2013 12 11 **10 09 08 07 06 05 04 03**; (Cobblers Hill) 2011 **10 09 08 07 06 05 04**.

JOSMEYER *Alsace AC, Alsace, France* Family-owned Josmeyer produces wines from biodynamic vineyards, 3.5ha (8.5 acres) of which are in the Hengst and Brand Grands Crus. Pure, rather delicate wines without much residual sugar are the order of the day, although Vendange Tardive★★ and Sélection de Grains Nobles★★ wines are made when conditions are favourable. Various blends, for example Gri-Gris★, are intriguing and food-friendly, while entry-level Artist series★ wines are consistent. Creamy-textured Pinot Auxerrois 'H' Vieilles Vignes★★, incisive Rieslings from Hengst★★ and Brand★★ and the potent Gewurztraminer Brand★★ are worth seeking out. Best years: (Hengst Riesling) (2013) 12 11 10 09 **08 05 04 02 00**.

TONI JOST *Bacharach, Mittelrhein, Germany*   Peter Jost was the grower who put the MITTELRHEIN on the map. From the Bacharacher Hahn site come some delicious, racy Rieslings★; Auslese★★ adds creaminess without losing that pine-needle scent. Best years: (2013) 12 11 **10 09 08 07 06 05**.

JULIÉNAS AC *Beaujolais, Burgundy, France*   Juliénas is attractive, 'serious' BEAUJOLAIS, which can be big and tannic enough to develop in bottle. Best producers: B Broyer★, Coquard★, D Desvignes★, DUBOEUF (Ch. des Capitans★), Ch. de Juliénas★, Matray (Vieilles Vignes★), Pelletier★, B Santé★, M Tête★. Best years: (**2013**) 11 10.

JULIUSSPITAL *Würzburg, Franken, Germany*   A 16th-century charitable foundation, with 172ha (425 acres) of vineyards, known for its dry wines – especially from IPHOFEN and WÜRZBURG. Look out for the Würzburger Stein wines, especially the grapefruity Silvaners★★ and petrolly Rieslings★★. Best years: (2013) 12 **11 09 08 07 05**.

JUMILLA DO *Murcia and Castilla-La Mancha, Spain*   Jumilla's reputation is for brutal alcoholic reds, but dense, serious yet balanced reds from Monastrell (Mourvèdre) show the region's potential. A few interesting dry Muscats. Best producers: Carchelo, Casa Castillo★★, Casa de la Ermita, Juan Gil★, Luzón★, El Nido★. Best years: 2012 11 **10** 09 **08 07 06 05 04 01**.

JURA See ARBOIS, CHÂTEAU-CHALON, CÔTES DU JURA, CRÉMANT DU JURA, l'ÉTOILE.

JURANÇON AOP *South-West France*   The sweet white wine made from late-harvested grapes can be heavenly, with floral, spicy, apricot-quince and pineapple flavours and citrus acidity. The lemony dry wine can be just as ageworthy. Best producers: Bellegarde★, Bordenave★, Camin Larredya★, Castera★, CAUHAPÉ★★, Clos Guirouilh★, Clos Thou★, Guirardel, JARDINS DE BABYLONE★★★, LAPEYRE★★, SOUCH★★, Uroulat★★. Best years: (sweet) (2012) 11 10 **09 07 05 04 01 00 97**.

KAIKEN *Mendoza, Argentina*   Owned by Chilean Viña MONTES, this winery concentrates on Malbec and Cabernet Sauvignon. The straightforward Reserva line is great value for money and the Ultra line offers powerful, plush, violet-scented Malbec★★ and Cabernet Sauvignon★★. Kaiken Mai★ super-premium Malbec tops an impressive range.

KAISERSTUHL *Baden, Germany*   A 4000ha (10,000-acre) volcanic stump rising to 555m (1820ft) and overlooking the Rhine plain. Pinot varieties excel. Best producers: BERCHER★★, Gleichenstein★, Dr HEGER★★, Karl H Johner★, Franz Keller★★, Knab★, Salwey★★, Schneider★★. Best years: (dry whites) (2013) 12 11 **10 09 08 07 06**.

KAMPTAL *Niederösterreich, Austria*   3800ha (9400-acre) wine region centred on the town of Langenlois, making some impressive dry Riesling and Grüner Veltliner. Best producers: BRÜNDLMAYER★★★, Ehn★, Eichinger★, Hiedler★, Hirsch★, Jurtschitsch★★, Fred Loimer★★, SCHLOSS GOBELSBURG★★, Topf. Best years: (2013) 12 11 **10 09 08 07 06**.

KANONKOP *Stellenbosch WO, South Africa*   Pinotage and Kanonkop are synonymous: the black label Pinotage★★★ is made in minuscule quantities from one of the oldest blocks in South Africa, planted in 1953;

standard Pinotage★★, from younger vines, is equally stylish. Muscular, savoury BORDEAUX-blend Paul Sauer★★ matures for 10 years or more. A straight Cabernet Sauvignon★★ (sometimes ★★★) is very good too. Best years: (Paul Sauer) 2011 **10 09 08 07 06 05 04 03 02 01 00 99 98**.

KARTHÄUSERHOF *Trier, Mosel, Germany* Christoff Tyrell's Ruwer estate was at the top of its game when sold to his cousin in 2013. Rieslings combine aromatic extravagance with racy brilliance. Most wines, including some dry styles, are now ★★, some Auslese and Eiswein ★★★. Best years: (2013) 12 11 10 **09 08 07 06 05 04 02**.

KÉKFRANKOS See BLAUFRÄNKISCH.

KELLER *Flörsheim-Dalsheim, Rheinhessen, Germany* Klaus Keller and son Klaus-Peter are the leading winemakers in the hill country of RHEINHESSEN, away from the Rhine riverbank. They produce a stunning range of varietal dry wines and naturally sweet Rieslings, as well as extra-special dry Grosses Gewächs Rieslings★★★ from 3 sites. Astonishing TBA★★★ from Riesling and Rieslaner. Best years: (2013) 12 11 10 **09 08 07 06 05 04**.

KENDALL-JACKSON *Sonoma County, California, USA* The late Jess Jackson founded KJ in 1982; it now produces about 5 million cases under the Jackson Family Estates umbrella. KJ's volume leader, Vintner's Reserve Chardonnay (2 million cases) is made entirely from estate-grown fruit. Now joined by a fresh, neutral-oaked Chardonnay called Avant. Higher levels of quality are found in the Grand Reserve reds and whites, the vineyard-based Highland Estates★ series and the top-of-the-range red BORDEAUX-blend Stature★★. See also page 336.

KENWOOD *Sonoma Valley AVA, California, USA* This winery – bought by BANFI in 2012 – has always represented very good quality at reasonable prices. The Sauvignon Blanc★ has floral and melon flavours with a slightly earthy finish. Long-lived Artist Series Cabernet Sauvignon★★ is the flagship, Jack London Zinfandel★★ is impressive, and RUSSIAN RIVER VALLEY Pinot Noir★ is fine value. Best years: (Zinfandel) (2012) **10 09 08 07 06 05 04**.

KIEDRICH *Rheingau, Germany* Top vineyard here is the Gräfenberg, for long-lived, mineral Rieslings. Sandgrub and Wasseros are other good sites. Best producer: WEIL★★. Best years: (2013) 12 11 10 **09 08 07 06 05**.

KING ESTATE *Oregon, USA* Over 400ha (1000 acres) are certified organic at the King Estate vineyard in Lorane, far south of the more popular WILLAMETTE VALLEY. The Pinot Gris★ is first-rate. The Pinot Noirs have taken time to perfect, but the Signature Collection Pinot Noir★ is a powerful currant- and cassis-flavoured wine, and the Domaine★ is a good example of Oregon Pinot Noir. Best years: (reds) (2012) 11 10 **09 08**.

CH. KIRWAN★ *Margaux AC, 3ème Cru Classé, Haut-Médoc, Bordeaux, France* This MARGAUX estate has shown considerable improvement since the mid-1990s. Wines now have greater depth and power (can be ★★), but less perfume. Now working on bringing the elegance back. Second wine: Les Charmes de Kirwan. Best years: 2012 11 10 09 **08 07 06 05 04 02 01 00 99 98 96**.

KISTLER *Sonoma Valley AVA, California, USA* One of California's trail-blazing Chardonnay producers, with wines from individual vineyards: Kistler Vineyard, Durell Vineyard and Dutton Ranch can be ★★★; McCrea Vineyard and ultra-cool-climate Camp Meeting Ridge Vineyard★★. All possess great complexity with good aging potential. Also a number of single-vineyard Pinot Noirs (some ★★) that go from good to very good. Best years: (Kistler Vineyard Chardonnay) (2012) **10 09 08 07 06 05 04**.

KLEIN CONSTANTIA *Constantia WO, South Africa* Bordeaux luminaries Hubert de Boüard and Bruno Prats are now minority shareholders in this showpiece estate, known for crisp Sauvignon Blanc★ (occasional vibrant Perdeblokke★★), piquant dry Riesling★, excellent barrel-fermented white blend Madame Marlbrook★★, bright Cabernet-led BORDEAUX-blend Marlbrook, and Vin de Constance★ (recent vintages ★★★), a thrilling Muscat dessert wine based on the 18th-century Constantia. Best years: (Vin de Constance) 2009 **08 07** 06 05 04 02 01 99 97 96 95.

KNAPPSTEIN *Clare Valley, South Australia* Three outstanding single-vineyard wines from mature vines: Ackland Riesling★★, Enterprise Cabernet★★ and Yertabulti Shiraz★★. The regular Riesling★★ is reliably good and Three★ intriguingly combines Gewürztraminer with Riesling and Pinot Gris. The Enterprise Brewery (established 1878) has been re-opened with refreshing results. Best years: (Enterprise Cabernet Sauvignon) (2013) 12 10 09 08 06 **05** 04 03 02 01 00 99 98.

KNIPSER *Laumersheim, Pfalz, Germany* The Knipsers produce a wide range of wines, including rarities (for Germany) such as Sauvignon Gris and Syrah. Their most convincing wines, though, are dry Rieslings★★, perfumed Spätburgunder★★ (Pinot Noir) and Chardonnay★★. Best years: (2013) 12 11 **10** 09 08 07 06.

EMMERICH KNOLL *Wachau, Niederösterreich, Austria* Some of Austria's greatest dry white wines. Rich, complex Riesling and Grüner Veltliner are packed with fruit and invariably ★★, with versions from Loibenberg, Kellerberg and Schütt sites often ★★★. They repay keeping for 5 years or more. Best years: (Riesling Smaragd) (2013) 12 11 **10** 09 08 07 06 05 04 02 01.

KOEHLER-RUPRECHT *Kallstadt, Pfalz, Germany* Powerful, concentrated, long-lived dry Rieslings★★★ from the Kallstadter Saumagen site, oak-aged botrytized Elysium★ and Burgundian-style Spätburgunder (Pinot Noir)★. Best years: (Saumagen Riesling) (2013) 12 11 **10** 09 08 07 06 05 04 03.

KOLLWENTZ *Neusiedlersee-Hügelland, Burgenland, Austria* Expert in both white and red wines. Fine Chardonnays★★ and Sauvignon Blanc★ are matched by Austria's best Cabernet Sauvignon★, single-vineyard Blaufränkisch★★ and spicy red blends such as Steinzeiler★★ (mostly Blaufränkisch, with Cabernet and Zweigelt) and Eichkogel★ (Blaufränkisch-Zweigelt). Best years: (reds) (2013) (12) 11 **10** 09 08 07 06.

KONGSGAARD *Napa Valley AVA, California, USA* High-end producer of excellent Chardonnays★★ celebrated for their elegance and complexity; The Judge★★, with its rich pear-apple character, is particularly impressive. The winery also makes a blockbuster Syrah★★ that is rich, dark and brooding. Best years: (Chardonnay) **2010** 09 08 03 01.

KOOYONG *Mornington Peninsula, Victoria, Australia* Under the same ownership as the nearby Port Phillip Estate. Wines include single-vineyard Pinot Noirs (Haven★★★, Ferrous★★, Meres★) and Chardonnays (Faultline★★, Farrago★★). The Kooyong Estate Chardonnay★★ is structured, complex and restrained and the Estate Pinot Noir★★ needs time to show its seductive best. Entry-level Clonale Chardonnay★★ and Massale Pinot Noir★ show real personality and pure varietal character.

ALOIS KRACHER *Illmitz, Burgenland, Austria* Austria's greatest sweet wine maker until his untimely death in 2007. Son Gerhard is following ably in his footsteps. Nouvelle Vague wines are aged in new barriques, while Zwischen den Seen wines are aged in steel tanks. The Grande Cuvée and TBAs from Scheurebe, Welschriesling and Chardonnay are all ★★★. Best years: (sweet whites) (2013) (12) 11 **10** 09 08 07 06 05 04 02.

KREMSTAL *Niederösterreich, Austria* 2243ha (5540-acre) wine region around Krems, producing some of Austria's best whites, from Riesling and Grüner Veltliner. Best producers: Malat★★, Mantlerhof★, Sepp Moser★, NIGL★★, NIKOLAIHOF★★, Proidl★, Salomon★★, Stadt Krems★. Best years: (2013) 12 11 **10 09 08 07 06**.

KRUG *Champagne AC, Champagne, France* Owned by luxury goods behemoth LVMH, this serious CHAMPAGNE house makes seriously expensive wines. The non-vintage Grande Cuvée★★ is deservedly regarded as one of the leading de luxe super-brands, though recent releases have become a little more international in style. Also an impressive vintage★★, rosé★★ and an ethereal, outrageously expensive, single-vineyard Clos du Mesnil★★★ Blanc de Blancs. Single-vineyard Clos d'Ambonnay is for millionaires only. Best years: 2003 (02) **00 98 96 95 90 89 88 85 82 81 79**.

KRUTZLER *Deutsch-Schützen, Südburgenland, Austria* Perwolff★★, one of Austria's most ageworthy red wines, is a generously oaked Blaufränkisch-based blend with a little Cabernet Sauvignon. The Blaufränkisch Reserve★ is almost as fine. Best years: (2013) (12) 11 **10 09 08 07 06 05**.

PETER JAKOB KÜHN *Oestrich, Rheingau, Germany* A brilliant biodynamic grower and winemaker, Kühn makes substantial dry Rieslings and thrilling nobly sweet wines, occasionally★★★. Best years: (2013) 12 11 **10 09 07 06 05**.

KUMEU/HUAPAI *Auckland, North Island, New Zealand* A small but significant viticultural area north-west of Auckland. The 11 wineries profit from their proximity to New Zealand's largest city, but most make little or no wine from grapes grown in their home region due to the heavy clay soils and erratic weather patterns. Best producers: COOPERS CREEK★, KUMEU RIVER★★, MATUA VALLEY★, West Brook. Best years: (Chardonnay) (2013) **10 09 07 06 05**.

KUMEU RIVER *Kumeu, Auckland, North Island, New Zealand* Family winery with adventurous, high-quality wines: a big, complex Chardonnay★★★ and three single-vineyard Chardonnays – Maté's★★★, Coddington★★ and Hunting Hill★★ – plus a fruity oak-aged Pinot Gris★. Pinot Noir is still a bit of a struggle. Best years: (Chardonnay) (2013) **10 09 07 06 05**.

KÜNSTLER *Hochheim, Rheingau, Germany* Gunter Künstler makes some of the best dry Rieslings★★ in the RHEINGAU – powerful, mineral wines. Also earthy and pricey Pinot Noir. Best years: (2013) 12 11 **10 09 08 07 06 05**.

KWV *Paarl WO, South Africa* Continued improvement at this industry giant, mainly from new The Mentors range (Semillon★★, Grenache Blanc★, Cabernet Franc★) which focuses on *terroir*. The huge range includes the flagship Cathedral Cellar range, led by bright-fruited, well-oaked Cabernet-based Triptych★ and full-flavoured, oaked Chenin Blanc★. New flagship Perold Tributum★★ blends Pinotage (the variety developed by Professor Abraham Perold), Cabernet and Shiraz into a polished whole. PORT-style and Muscadel fortifieds remain superb value.

DOM. LABRANCHE-LAFFONT *Madiran AOP, South-West France* Christine Dupuy is a rare female vigneronne in this appellation. Fine MADIRAN★ (Vieilles Vignes★★) and excellent PACHERENC★★ (both sweet and dry). Best years: (red) (2012) 11 **10 09 08 06 05**; (sweet white) (2012) 11 **10 09 06 05**.

LADOIX AC *Côte de Beaune, Burgundy, France* Most northerly village in the CÔTE DE BEAUNE. The best vineyards are included in Grands Crus CORTON and CORTON-CHARLEMAGNE, but otherwise most used to be sold off as CÔTE DE BEAUNE-VILLAGES. That's starting to change with some decent Ladoix reds and exotic whites. Best producers: (reds) Cachat-Ocquidant★, Chevalier★, E Cornu★, M Mallard★ (Les Joyeuses★★); (whites) R & R Jacob★, S Loichet★. Best years: (reds) (2013) 12 11 10 **09 08 07 05 03 02.**

MICHEL LAFARGE *Volnay, Côte de Beaune, Burgundy, France* These are not easy wines to understand, and I've been disappointed as often as I've been thrilled. Some outstanding red wines, notably VOLNAY Clos des Chênes★★, Volnay Clos du Château des Ducs★★ (a monopole) and less fashionable BEAUNE Grèves★★. BOURGOGNE Rouge★ is good value. Top wines start out lean, but should blossom after 10 years or more aging. Best years: (top reds) (2013) 12 11 10 09 08 **07 06 05 03 02 99 98 97 96 95 91 90.**

CH. LAFAURIE-PEYRAGUEY★★ *Sauternes AC, 1er Cru Classé, Bordeaux, France* Took off in the 1980s and is now one of the most consistent SAUTERNES properties: sumptuous and rich when young, and marvellously deep and satisfying with age. Occasionally close to YQUEM in body and flavour. Best years: 2011 10 **09 07 06 05 04 03 02 01 99 98 97 96 95 90 89 88 86.**

CH. LAFITE-ROTHSCHILD★★★ *Pauillac AC, 1er Cru Classé, Haut-Médoc, Bordeaux, France* This property was bought by the Rothschild banking family in 1868 and they still own it today. Lafite is frequently cited as the epitome of elegance, indulgence and expense (the Chinese are certainly doing their bit to ensure the latter!). Since the late 1990s vintages have been superb, with added depth and body to match the wine's traditional finesse. Second wine: les Carruades de Lafite-Rothschild. Best years: 2012 11 10 09 08 **07 06 05 04 03 02 01 00 99 98 96 95 94 90 89 88 86 85 82.**

CH. LAFLEUR★★★ *Pomerol AC, Bordeaux, France* Using some of POMEROL's most traditional winemaking, this tiny estate can seriously rival the great PÉTRUS for texture, flavour and aroma. But a high percentage (50%) of Cabernet Franc makes this a more elegant wine. Second wine: Pensées de Lafleur. Best years: 2012 11 10 09 08 **07 06 05 04 03 02 01 00 99 98 96 95.**

LAFON *Meursault, Côte de Beaune, Burgundy, France* One of Burgundy's current superstars, with prices to match. Early exponent of biodynamics for brilliant MEURSAULT (Clos de la Barre★★, Charmes★★★, Perrières★★★), le MONTRACHET★★★ and exciting long-lived reds from VOLNAY (Santenots-du-Milieu★★★, Champans★★). Also Héritiers Lafon★ in the Maconnais (Clos du Four★, Clos de la Crochette★, VIRÉ-CLESSÉ★) and from 2008 Dominique Lafon label for Meursault, Beaune, Volnay, Puligny Champsgains★★. Best years: (whites) (2013) 12 11 10 09 08 **07 06 05 04 02;** (reds) (2013) 12 11 10 09 08 **07 06 05 03 02 99 98 96 90.**

CH. LAFON-ROCHET★ *St-Estèphe AC, 4ème Cru Classé, Haut-Médoc, Bordeaux, France* Good-value, affordable Classed Growth claret. Nowadays an increase in the amount of Merlot makes the wine less austere but still structured. Delicious and blackcurranty after 10 years. Best years: 2012 11 10 09 **08 06 05 04 03 02 01 00 99 98 96 95.**

ALOIS LAGEDER *Alto Adige DOC, Trentino-Alto Adige, Italy* Among the leading independents in ALTO ADIGE, making good, medium-priced varietals and pricey estate and single-vineyard wines such as Löwengang Cabernet★ and Chardonnay★★, Sauvignon Lehen★★, Cabernet Cor Römigberg★, Pinot Noir Krafuss★, Pinot Bianco Haberle★ and Pinot Grigio Benefizium Porer★. White Casòn★★ is based on Pinot Grigio and Chardonnay with Viognier; the red Casòn★★ is Merlot-Cabernet based.

CH. LAGRANGE★★ *St-Julien AC, 3ème Cru Classé, Haut-Médoc, Bordeaux, France*
Good fruit and perfume, meticulous winemaking and consistently fine quality mark out this large estate owned by Japanese company Suntory, an occasional surfeit of tannin being the only cautionary note. Dry white les Arums de Lagrange. Second wine: les Fiefs de Lagrange. **Best years:** 2012 11 10 09 **08 06 05 04 03 02 01 00 98 96 95 90**.

LAGREIN Black grape of ALTO ADIGE, producing deep-coloured, brambly, chocolaty reds and full-bodied, attractively scented rosés. Brazil and Australia produce a bit. **Best producers:** Colterenzio co-op (Cornell★), Glögglhof, Gries co-op★, Hofstätter★, LAGEDER★, Laimburg★, Muri-Gries★, J Niedermayr, I Niedriest★, Plattner-Waldgries★, Hans Rottensteiner★, Terlano co-op★★, Thurnhof★★, TIEFENBRUNNER★★, Zemmer★.

CH. LA LAGUNE★ *Haut-Médoc AC, 3ème Cru Classé, Haut-Médoc, Bordeaux, France* The closest MÉDOC Classed Growth to Bordeaux city. The soils are sandy-gravel and the wines round and elegant in style. Took a dip in the late 1990s but new investment from 2000 (same ownership as Paul JABOULET AÎNÉ) has improved things without adding any real personality. **Best years:** 2011 10 **09 08 06 05 04 03 02 00 98 96 95**.

LALANDE-DE-POMEROL AC *Bordeaux, France* To the north of its more famous neighbour POMEROL, this AC produces ripe, plummy wines with an unmistakable mineral edge that are very attractive at 4–5 years old, but age reasonably well too. Even though they lack the concentration of top Pomerols, the wines are not particularly cheap. **Best producers:** Annereaux★, Bertineau St-Vincent★, Chambrun★, la Croix des Moines★, la Croix-St-André★, les Cruzelles★, La FLEUR DE BOÜARD★, Garraud★, Grand Ormeau★, Haut-Chaigneau, les Hauts Conseillants, Jean de Gué★, Laborderie-Mondésir★, Perron (La Fleur★), Sabines★, Sergant, la Sergue★, Siaurac★, Tournefeuille★. **Best years:** 2012 11 **10 09 08 06 05 04 01 00**.

LAMBRUSCO *Emilia-Romagna, Italy* 'Lambrusco' refers to a heterogeneous family of black grape varieties, grown in 3 DOC zones on the plains of EMILIA and 1 in LOMBARDY. Today the cheap and cheerful stuff of the 1980s is all but forgotten, but there is genuine quality Lambrusco (especially Lambrusco di Sorbara and Grasparossa di Castelvetro), frothing, acidic and dry or off-dry, ideal as a partner to the rich local foods. **Best producers:** Barbieri, Barbolini, F Bellei★, Casali, Cavicchioli★, Chiarli, Vittorio Graziano★, Oreste Lini, Stefano Spezia, Venturini Baldini.

LAMOREAUX LANDING *Finger Lakes AVA, New York State, USA* Consistently good winery. Its Chardonnay Reserve★ is a regular medal winner, and the Pinot Noir★ is arguably the region's best. Also attractive Merlot★, Cabernet Franc★, Dry Riesling★ and some single-vineyard Rieslings.

LANDMARK *Sonoma County, California, USA* Chardonnays include Overlook★★ and the oakier Damaris Reserve★★ and Lorenzo★★. Tropical-fruited Courtyard Chardonnay★ is lower-priced. Pinot Noir from Kastania Vineyard★★ (SONOMA COAST) is beautifully focused. The winery has replanted its estate vineyard to Rhône varieties, and first sightings of Grenache and Syrah are impressive.

LANGHE DOC *Piedmont, Italy* Catch-all DOC covering 8 different wine styles, of which the most important is Langhe Nebbiolo: the early-drinking fruity wine that BAROLO and BARBARESCO producers make from either declassified wine or from Nebbiolo fruit from outside the Barolo and Barbaresco zones. Unlike NEBBIOLO D'ALBA there's no minimum aging and up to 15% of other red grapes can be added. Should represent good value for money and age for up to 10 years in bottle. Best producers: (reds) ALTARE★, Boglietti (Buio★★), Silvano Bolmida★, Bongiovanni (Falletto★★), Cascina Fontana★★, Clerico★, Aldo CONTERNO★, Giacomo CONTERNO★★, Conterno-Fantino (Monprà★★), GAJA★★, Marchesi di Gresy (Virtus★★), Bartolo MASCARELLO★★, Giuseppe MASCARELLO★★, F Nada (Seifile★★), Vigneti Luigi Oddero★★, Parusso (Bricco Rovella★★), Punset★★, G RINALDI★★★, ROAGNA★★, Giovanni ROSSO★★, Trediberri★, Vajra★, Roberto VOERZIO★★. Best years: (Nebbiolo) 2012 11 10 09 08 07 06 04 01 99 98 97.

CH. LANGOA-BARTON★★ *St-Julien AC, 3ème Cru Classé, Haut-Médoc, Bordeaux, France* Owned by the Barton family since 1821, the impressive and well-priced Langoa-Barton is usually less scented and elegant though often richer than its ST-JULIEN stablemate LÉOVILLE-BARTON. It will usually improve for 15–20 years. Second wine: Réserve de Léoville-Barton (a blend from the young vines of both Barton properties). Best years: 2012 11 10 09 08 07 06 05 04 03 02 01 00 99 98 96 95.

LANGUEDOC AC *Languedoc-Roussillon, France* New AC, gradually replacing COTEAUX DU LANGUEDOC and covering the entire LANGUEDOC-ROUSSILLON region. Reds and rosés mainly from Grenache Noir, Syrah and Mourvèdre, with Cinsaut and Carignan; whites from Grenache Blanc, Roussanne, Rolle and a handful of others. Quality across this vast area ranges from simple to sublime.

LANGUEDOC-ROUSSILLON *France* This vast area of southern France, running from Nîmes to the Spanish border and covering the *départements* of the GARD, HÉRAULT, Aude and Pyrénées-Orientales, is still a source of undistinguished cheap wine, but is also one of France's most exciting wine regions. The transformation is the result of reviving ancient vineyards, better grape varieties, modern winemaking and ambitious producers, from the heights of GRANGE DES PÈRES to very good local co-ops. The best wines are the reds, particularly those from CORBIÈRES, MINERVOIS, FAUGÈRES, ST-CHINIAN, TERRASSES DU LARZAC and PIC ST-LOUP, some revivals of ancient grape varieties, and some new-wave Cabernets, Merlots and Syrahs, as well as the more traditional *vins doux naturels* such as BANYULS, MAURY and MUSCAT DE RIVESALTES; but we are now seeing exciting whites as well, particularly as new plantings of Chardonnay, Marsanne, Roussanne, Viognier, Vermentino (Rolle) and Sauvignon Blanc mature and growers begin to appreciate the old traditional varieties. An all-embracing appellation, LANGUEDOC AC, was agreed in 2007. See also BLANQUETTE DE LIMOUX, CABARDÈS, COLLIOURE, COTEAUX DU LANGUEDOC, CÔTES DU ROUSSILLON, CÔTES CATALANES, CÔTES DE THONGUE, FITOU, GRÈS DE MONTPELLIER, LIMOUX, MUSCAT DE FRONTIGNAN, MUSCAT DE ST-JEAN-DE-MINERVOIS, OC, PÉZENAS, PICPOUL DE PINET, RIVESALTES.

LANSON *Champagne AC, Champagne, France* Non-vintage Lanson Black Label★ is reliably tasty and, like the rosé★ and vintage★★ wines, especially de luxe Noble Cuvée★★, improves greatly with aging. Also three new Extra Age multi-vintage blends in rosé, regular★ and Blanc de Blancs★ styles. Best years: 2004 02 99 98 97 96 95 93 90 89 88 85 83 82.

LAPEYRE *Jurançon AOP, South-West France* Jean-Bernard Larrieu, fiercely organic, produces a fine range of JURANÇON wines, ranging from dry, especially from older vines (Vitatge Vielh★, Mandoulem★★), through to ever sweeter gems such as Magendia★ and Vent Balaguer★★. Both sweet and dry wines age well. Best years: (sweet) 2011 10 09 07 05 04 03.

L LAPOSTOLLE

LAPOSTOLLE *Rapel, Chile* Owned by Marnier-Lapostolle of France, with consultancy from BORDEAUX winemaker Michel Rolland. Cuvée Alexandre Merlot★★, from the acclaimed Apalta area in COLCHAGUA, was its first hit back in 1994, now eclipsed by red blend Clos Apalta★★★. Even so, Cuvée Alexandre Cabernet★★ and Syrah★★ are tremendously tasty. Good Pinot Noir★, rich, creamy Chardonnay★ and delightful, juicy Casa Carmenère★. Parts of the Apalta estate are now biodynamic.

DOM. LAROCHE *Chablis, Burgundy, France* Significant CHABLIS domaine with associated *négociant*, plus interests in Languedoc, Chile and South Africa; merged in 2009 with larger Jeanjean operation, retaining minority share. Should not change wine styles noticeably.

LAS MORAS *San Juan, Argentina* Successful winery in SAN JUAN, producing consistently attractive wines at all price levels, from a wide range of grape varieties. Famed for its spicy 3 Valleys Gran Shiraz★; plummy Pedernal Malbec★ and Mora Negra★, an aromatic Malbec-Bonarda blend, are also classy.

CH. LASCOMBES★ *Margaux AC, 2ème Cru Classé, Haut-Médoc, Bordeaux, France* One of the great underachievers in the MARGAUX AC and little worth drinking in the 1980s and 90s, but new American ownership and investment and the advice of consultant enologist Michel Rolland have begun to make an occasional difference; the 2005 and 2009 are the best for a generation, 2008 and 2010 weren't. Now owned by a French insurance company (since 2011). Best years: 2012 11 09 **07 06 05 04 00**.

CH. LATOUR★★★ *Pauillac AC, 1er Cru Classé, Haut-Médoc, Bordeaux, France* Latour's reputation is based on powerful, long-lasting wines. Strangely, in the early 1980s there was an attempt to make lighter, more fashionable wines, with mixed results. The late 80s saw a return to classic Latour, much to my relief. Its reputation for making fine wine in less successful vintages is well deserved. Recently, and controversially, decided to store its wine until ready to drink. Second wine: les Forts de Latour. Best years: 2012 11 10 09 08 **07** 06 05 **04 03 02 01** 00 99 98 97 96 95 94 90 89.

LOUIS LATOUR *Beaune, Burgundy, France* Merchant almost as well known for his COTEAUX DE L'ARDÈCHE Chardonnays as for his Burgundies. Latour's white Burgundies are much better than the reds, although the red CORTON-Grancey★★ can be very good. Latour's oaky CORTON-CHARLEMAGNE★★, from his own vineyard, is his top wine, but there is also good CHEVALIER-MONTRACHET★★, BÂTARD-MONTRACHET★★ and le MONTRACHET★★. Best years: (top whites) (2013) 12 11 10 **09 08 07 06 05 02**.

CH. LATOUR-MARTILLAC *Pessac-Léognan AC, Cru Classé de Graves, Bordeaux, France* The vineyard here is strictly organic, and has many ancient vines. The deep, dark, well-structured reds★ have been fairly consistent since the late 1990s. Whites★ are thoroughly modern and of good quality. Good value as well. Best years: (reds) 2012 11 10 09 **08 06 05 04 03 02 01** 00 98 96 95; (whites) 2012 11 10 09 08 07 06 05 04 02.

CH. LATOUR-À-POMEROL *Pomerol AC, Bordeaux, France* Directed by Christian MOUEIX of PÉTRUS fame, this property makes luscious wines with loads of gorgeous fruit and enough tannin to age well. Best years: 2012 11 10 09 **08 07 06 05** 04 02 01 00 99 98 95 90.

LATRICIÈRES-CHAMBERTIN AC See CHAMBERTIN AC.

LAUREL GLEN *Sonoma Mountain AVA, California, USA* Cabernet-only mountain-top winery, famous for restrained, cedary, ageworthy wines. Laurel Glen★★ is ripe but dry, with deep fruit flavours, aging after 6–10 years to a perfumed, complex BORDEAUX style. Counterpoint★ is an excellent second label. Sold in 2011 to a group headed by wine industry veteran Bettina Sichel. Best years: (2012) (10) **09 08 06 05 02 01 99 98 97 96 95 94**.

LAURENT-PERRIER *Champagne AC, Champagne, France* Large, family-owned CHAMPAGNE house, offering flavour and quality at reasonable prices. Non-vintage is light and savoury; the vintage★ is good, and the top wine, Grand Siècle★★ (sometimes★★★) can be among the finest Champagnes of all. Non-vintage rosé★ is good; vintage Alexandra Rosé★★★ is excellent. Best years: **2004 02 00 99 97 96 95 90 88 85 82**.

L'AVENIR *Stellenbosch WO, South Africa* The refined range is headed by Chenin Blanc (Provenance★, Single Block★★) and Pinotage (cheerfully fruity Far & Near, well-oaked Provenance, ageworthy Single Block★★). Promising Cabernet★ and BORDEAUX-blend Stellenbosch Classic★. Best years: (Pinotage) 2012 **11 10 09 08 07 06 05 04**.

CH. LAVILLE-HAUT-BRION★★★ *Pessac-Léognan AC, Cru Classé de Graves, Bordeaux, France* One of the finest white PESSAC-LÉOGNANS, with a price tag to match. Fermented in barrel, it needs 10 years or more to reach its savoury but luscious peak. Renamed La MISSION HAUT-BRION *blanc* from the 2009 vintage. Best years: **2008 07 06 05 04 03 02 01 00 96 95 94**.

DOMAINE COSTA LAZARIDI *Drama, Greece* State-of-the-art, Bordeaux-inspired winery making good use of indigenous and international varieties. Fresh gooseberry Amethystos white★ (Sauvignon Blanc, Sémillon and Assyrtiko); a fascinatingly intense Viognier★ with a stunning, oily, peach kernel finish; tasty Château Julia Chardonnay★; and fine Amethystos Cava★, an oak-aged Cabernet from very low yields.

LAZIO *Italy* The nation's political centre is not famous for wine, being able to boast not much more than glugging whites based on Trebbiano and Malvasia, such as Est! Est!! Est!!! di Montefiascone and FRASCATI. The region's most interesting wines are reds based on Cesanese, an up-and-coming variety. Best producers: Casale del Giglio★, Castel de Paolis (Quattro Mori★★), Cerveteri co-op (Tertium★), FALESCO, Giuliani Marcella★, Paola di Mauro (Vigna del Vassallo★★), l'Olivella★, Pietra Pinta★, Trappolini★, Villa Santa★.

L'ECOLE No 41 *Walla Walla Valley AVA, Washington State, USA* Velvety and deeply flavoured Seven Hills Vineyard Merlot★, good Cabernet Sauvignon★ and lush Syrah★★; a BORDEAUX blend called Apogee★ from the Pepper Bridge vineyard in WALLA WALLA VALLEY is dark and challenging, neighbouring Ferguson★ richer, more feral. Best wines are the barrel-fermented Semillons: a nutty COLUMBIA VALLEY★★ version and Luminesce Seven Hills Vineyard★★. Chenin Blanc★ is honeyed, Chardonnay★ is attractive and oatmealy. Best years: (top reds) (2012) 11 10 **09**.

LEEUWIN ESTATE *Margaret River, Western Australia* MARGARET RIVER'S perennial high flier, with pricey, supremely balanced Art Series Chardonnay★★★ – richer than it was, but wonderfully savoury. Art Series Cabernet Sauvignon★★ (sometimes ★★★) exhibits superb blackcurrant and cedar balance. Art Series Riesling★ is complex and fine, Shiraz★★ is exceptional. Prelude (Chardonnay★★) and Siblings (Sauvignon Blanc-Semillon★) give Leeuwin pleasure at lower prices. Best years: (Art Series Chardonnay) (2013) (12) 11 10 09 08 **07 06 05 04 02 01 00 99 98 97**.

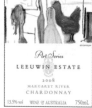

195

DOM. LEFLAIVE *Puligny-Montrachet, Côte de Beaune, Burgundy, France* Famous
white Burgundy producer with extensive holdings in some of the greatest
vineyards of PULIGNY-MONTRACHET (les Pucelles★★★), Chevalier-
MONTRACHET★★★, BÂTARD-MONTRACHET★★★ and a tiny slice of le
MONTRACHET★★★. Anne-Claude Leflaive has taken the family domaine
right back to the top using biodynamic methods. The wines are
understandably expensive, and in common with others from the region
should be drunk a little earlier than used to be the case. More reasonably
priced Mâcon-Verzé★. Best years: (2013) 12 11 10 **09 08 07 05**.

OLIVIER LEFLAIVE *Puligny-Montrachet, Côte de Beaune, Burgundy, France*
Négociant Olivier Leflaive specializes in crisp, modern white wines from
the CÔTE D'OR and the CÔTE CHALONNAISE, mostly for early drinking. Lesser
ACs – ST-ROMAIN★, MONTAGNY★, MERCUREY★, ST-AUBIN★, RULLY★ – offer
good value, but the rich, oaky BÂTARD-MONTRACHET★★ is the star turn.
Best years: (top whites) (2013) 12 11 10 **09 08** 07.

PETER LEHMANN *Barossa Valley, South Australia* BAROSSA doyen Lehmann
died in 2013, but the company continues to buy grapes from many local
growers and owns the superb Stonewell vineyard, which gives its name to
a great Shiraz★★★. The 1885 Shiraz★★★ from the Ebenezer vineyard is
another stunner. Juicy, fruit-packed reds include 8 Songs Shiraz★★ and
Mentor Cabernet★★. The top whites have been consistently sublime in
recent years: impeccably balanced Wigan Eden Valley Riesling★★★ and
rich, pure, zesty, unwooded Margaret Semillon★★★ from Barossa
Valley old vines. Also lemony Semillon★★ and Chenin★, and dry, long-
lived Eden Valley Riesling★★. Befuddling array of budget lines – but the
quality is holding up. Best years: (Stonewell Shiraz) (2013) (12) (11) 10 09 08
06 05 04 03 02 01 99 98 96 94 93 90 89.

LEITZ *Rüdesheim, Rheingau, Germany* Some of the RHEINGAU's best dry and off-
dry Rieslings, especially from the Berg Rottland★★ and Berg
Schlossberg★★ sites, whose recent vintages go from strength to strength.
Best years: (2013) 12 11 10 **09 08 07 06 05**.

LEIWEN *Mosel, Germany* In the 1990s this village became a hotbed of
MOSEL Riesling revolution, and it is still a source of excellent, reasonably
priced Rieslings. Best producers: GRANS-FASSIAN★★, Carl Loewen★★, Josef
Rosch★, ST URBANS-HOF★★. Best years: (2013) 12 11 10 **09 08** 07 05.

LEMBERGER See BLAUFRÄNKISCH.

LENZ WINERY *Long Island, New York State, USA* A leading LONG ISLAND winery
focused on BORDEAUX varietal reds: the Estate Merlot★★ is elegant and
powerful with soft, balanced tannins. Dry Gewürztraminer★ is spicy and
tasty; Chardonnay★ can be good, as can sparkling wines.

LEONETTI CELLAR *Walla Walla Valley AVA, Washington State, USA* WALLA WALLA
VALLEY's first winery opened in 1977. Today it produces highly sought-
after, rich and velvety Cabernet Sauvignon★★ and Merlot★★ aged in a
combination of French and American oak; dense and powerful
Reserve★★★. Sangiovese★★ has very fine texture and lots of new wood.
Most of the fruit is now estate grown. Best years: (2012) 11 10 **09 08** 07.

CH. LÉOVILLE-BARTON★★★ *St-Julien AC, 2ème Cru Classé, Haut-Médoc,*
Bordeaux, France A traditionalist's delight, made by Anthony Barton,
whose family has run this ST-JULIEN property since 1826. Dark, dry and
tannic, and not overly oaked, the wines are often underestimated, but
over 10–20 years they achieve a lean yet sensitively proportioned beauty
rarely equalled in Bordeaux. Second wine: Réserve de Léoville-Barton.
Best years: 2012 11 10 09 08 **07 06 05 04 03 02 01 00 99 98 96 95 94 90 89**.

CH. LÉOVILLE-LAS-CASES★★★ *St-Julien AC, 2ème Cru Classé, Haut-Médoc, Bordeaux, France* The largest of the three Léoville properties, making wines of startlingly deep, dark concentration. I now find them so dense and thick in texture that it is difficult to identify them as ST-JULIEN, but they still achieve the highest of all the St-Julien prices. Second wine: Le Petit Lion (since 2007), previously Clos du Marquis. Best years: 2012 11 10 09 08 **07** 06 **05** 04 03 02 01 00 99 98 96 95 94 93 90 89.

CH. LÉOVILLE-POYFERRÉ★★★ *St-Julien AC, 2ème Cru Classé, Haut-Médoc, Bordeaux, France* Since 1986 the wine has gradually increased in richness without wavering from its reserved and elegant style. A string of excellent wines in the 90s and 00s frequently show more classic ST-JULIEN style than those of neighbour LÉOVILLE-LAS-CASES and have resulted in a considerable increase in popularity and reputation. Second wine: Moulin-Riche. Best years: 2012 11 10 09 08 **07** 06 **05** 04 03 02 01 00 99 98 96 95 90 89.

DOM. LEROY *Vosne-Romanée, Côte de Nuits, Burgundy, France* In 1988 Lalou Bize-Leroy bought the former Dom. Charles Noëllat in VOSNE-ROMANÉE, renaming it Domaine Leroy. Here she produces fiendishly expensive, fabulously concentrated wines with biodynamic methods and ludicrously low yields from vineyards such as CHAMBERTIN★★★, CLOS DE VOUGEOT★★★, MUSIGNY★★★, RICHEBOURG★★★ and ROMANÉE-ST-VIVANT★★★. Not to be confused with her *négociant* house, Maison Leroy, which contains stocks of great mature vintages, or her personal estate, Dom. d'Auvenay. Best years: (top reds) (2013) 12 11 10 09 08 **07** 06 05 **03** 02 01 00 99 96 90 89.

LEYDA See SAN ANTONIO.

VIÑA LEYDA *San Antonio, Chile* Pioneering winery founded in 1997 that led to the creation of the exciting coastal appellation Leyda Valley in 2002. Famed for its Pinot Noirs (Cahuil★★, Las Brisas★★, Lot 21★★) and Sauvignon Blanc★★ from the Garuma vineyard. Also makes lovely unoaked Chardonnay★★, Riesling★, Sauvignon Gris★, Pinot Noir Rosé★ and a thrilling, scented Syrah Reserva★.

COMTE LIGER-BELAIR *Côte de Nuits, Burgundy, France* Louis-Michel Liger-Belair makes stylish, perfumed wines in VOSNE-ROMANÉE, including serious aux Reignots★★, scented ECHÉZEAUX★★★ and the monopoly of la ROMANÉE itself. The domaine keeps growing, with NUITS-ST-GEORGES Clos des Grandes Vignes (monopole) the latest addition. Best years: (2013) 12 11 10 09 08 **07** 06 05 **03** 02.

THIBAULT LIGER-BELAIR *Côte de Nuits, Burgundy, France* Thibault Liger-Belair makes rich, plump wines from his NUITS-ST-GEORGES base, including Premier Cru les St-Georges★★ and Grands Crus RICHEBOURG★★ and CLOS DE VOUGEOT★★. There are some terrific MOULIN-À-VENT offerings too. Best years: (2013) 12 11 10 09 08 **07** 06 05 **02**.

LIGURIA *Italy* Thin coastal strip of north-west Italy, running from the French border at Ventimiglia to the Tuscan border. Best grapes: Vermentino or its aromatic cousin Pigato; try Lambruschi★ and Cascina Feipu dei Massaretti★. Best wines, mostly drunk by natives or tourists, are the Cinqueterre, Colli di Luna, Riviera Ligure di Ponente and Gamay-esque Rossese di Dolceacqua DOCs.

LIMARÍ *Chile* During the past decade this valley – 400km (250 miles) north of Santiago – has shown that its cold ocean influence, long sunshine hours and chalky/clay soils can produce world-class wines. Chardonnay and Syrah are the top performers, both expressing fresh, vibrant flavours and subtle yet clear minerality. Also some salty Sauvignons from the coastal region. Best producers: DE MARTINO★, Maycas del Limarí★/CONCHA Y TORO, TABALÍ★, TAMAYA★.

LIMESTONE COAST *South Australia* Zone for south-east of South Australia, with more limestone than anywhere else in Australia. Wine areas include COONAWARRA, PADTHAWAY, Mount Benson, Robe, Wrattonbully and Mount Gambier. New vineyards in this far-flung area have Coonawarra-like terra rossa soil over limestone, with great potential for reds and whites, especially as climate change starts to affect warmer sites.

LIMOUX AC *Languedoc, France* The first AC in the LANGUEDOC to allow Chardonnay and Chenin Blanc, which must be vinified in oak. Production is dominated by the SIEUR D'ARQUES co-op. Red Limoux is made from Merlot and Cabernet with local varieties. Best producers: d'ANTUGNAC★, Bégude★, Mouscaillo, Rives-Blanques★, SIEUR D'ARQUES. See also BLANQUETTE DE LIMOUX, CRÉMANT DE LIMOUX.

LINDEMAN'S *Murray Darling, Victoria, Australia* Large, historic company, part of Treasury Wine Estates. Now a 'global' brand, sourcing wines from wherever they choose. The 'Bin' and Cawarra range showed some signs of revival but this seems to have petered out. Traditionally strong in COONAWARRA (minerally St George Cabernet★★, spicy Limestone Ridge Shiraz-Cabernet★★ and red BORDEAUX-blend Pyrus★★). Best years: (Coonawarra reds) 2013 12 10 09 08 **06 05 04 01 99 98 96 94 91 90**.

LINDEN *Virginia, USA* For three decades, Jim Law has quietly farmed a hillside vineyard about an hour's drive west of Washington DC; many of northern Virginia's new star winemakers learned their craft at Linden. Law believes steep slopes will provide Virginia's best new vineyard sites. He crafts European-styled wines of impressive concentration and finesse, including Hardscrabble red blend★ of BORDEAUX varieties, Hardscrabble Chardonnay★ and minerally Sauvignon Blanc.

LIRAC AC *Rhône Valley, France* Underrated AC between TAVEL and CHÂTEAUNEUF-DU-PAPE. Reds can run with lively, spiced but dry fruit and robust tannins, and are helped by Mourvèdre. They age over 8–10 years but are good, if stony, young. Châteauneuf owners with Lirac vineyards are raising quality. Refreshing rosé has lovely strawberry fruit; whites can be very good, with the body to accompany full southern flavours. Best producers: Aquéria, Beaumont★, Boucarut★, Bouchassy★, Carabiniers★, Clos des Sources, Corne-Loup, Duseigneur★, la Genestière★, Alain Jaume★, Joncier★, Lafond-Roc-Épine★★, Lorentine★, Maby★, Mas Isabelle★, Mont-Redon★, la Mordorée★★, Pélaquié★, Roger Sabon★★, St-Roch★, Ségriès, Tavel co-op★. Best years: (reds) **2012 11 10 09 07 06 05**.

LISBOA *Portugal* This used to be called Estremadura, and is Portugal's most productive region, occupying the western coastal strip, with an increasing number of clean, characterful wines. The leading area is ALENQUER DOC and there are eight other DOC regions; however, much of the region's best wine is simply labelled as Vinho Regional Lisboa. Spicy, perfumed reds are often based on Castelão, but Tinta Roriz (Tempranillo), Cabernet Sauvignon, Syrah and Touriga Nacional contribute to top examples, which can benefit from 4 or 5 years' aging. Top producers also make fresh, aromatic whites. Best producers: Quinta de Chocapalha★, Quinta da Cortezia★, D F J VINHOS, Quinta dos Loridos (Loridos Chardonnay Extra Brut★), Quinta do Monte d'Oiro★★, Companhia Agricola do Sanguinhal, Quinta de Sant'Ana, Casa SANTOS LIMA★. See also BUCELAS. Best years: (reds) 2011 **08 07 05 04 03 01 00**.

LISINI *Brunello di Montalcino DOCG, Tuscany, Italy* Historic estate owned by the Lisini-Clementi family, producing consistently excellent quality with potential to age in bottle: San Biagio IGT★, ROSSO DI MONTALCINO★★, BRUNELLO DI MONTALCINO★★★, Riserva★★★ and Ugolaia★★★. Best years: (2012) 11 10 09 06 **04 01** 99 98 97 96 94 90 89 88 86.

LISTRAC-MÉDOC AC *Haut-Médoc, Bordeaux, France* Set back from the Gironde and away from the best HAUT-MÉDOC gravel ridges, Listrac wines can be good but never thrilling, and are marked by solid fruit, a slightly coarse tannin and an earthy flavour. More Merlot and warmer vintages are now producing softer wines. Best producers: Cap Léon Veyrin, Clos des Demoiselles, CLARKE★, Ducluzeau, Fonréaud★, Fourcas-Borie★, Fourcas-Dupré★, Fourcas-Hosten★, Mayne-Lalande★, Reverdi★, Saransot-Dupré★. Best years: 2012 11 10 09 08 06 05 03 01.

LLANO ESTACADO *Texas High Plains AVA, Texas, USA* Texas' largest premium winery, in the western part of the state. Llano produces a wide array of wines at consistent quality and reasonable prices. Nice unoaked Chardonnay and exotically perfumed white blend Viviana★.

LODI AVA *California, USA* No longer California's best-kept wine secret. Located in the northern part of the CENTRAL VALLEY AVA, vineyard planting in the past decade has expanded to around 40,470ha (100,000 acres), making Lodi the value-for-money quality leader for a variety of styles – mainstreamers like Merlot and Cabernet, but more excitingly old-vine Zinfandel, Carignan, Cinsaut and outsiders like Petite Sirah, Tannat, Teroldego and Vermentino. Lately there has been a promising move toward Spanish varieties, including Tempranillo and Albariño. If California wants an experimental hothouse, Lodi could fit the bill. Best producers: Bokisch★, Ironstone★, Jessie's Grove★, McManis★, Mettler Family★, Michael-David★, Old Ghost★, Peirano Estate★, RAVENSWOOD★, Woodbridge/MONDAVI.

LOIRE VALLEY *France* The Loire river cuts right through the heart of France. The middle reaches are the home of world-famous SANCERRE and POUILLY-FUMÉ. The region of TOURAINE makes good Sauvignon Blanc and Gamay, while at VOUVRAY and MONTLOUIS-SUR-LOIRE Chenin Blanc makes some pretty good fizz and scintillatingly fresh, minerally still whites, ranging from sweet to very dry. The Loire's best reds are made in CHINON, BOURGUEIL, ST-NICOLAS-DE-BOURGUEIL and SAUMUR-CHAMPIGNY, mainly from Cabernet Franc, with ANJOU-VILLAGES improving fast. Anjou is famous for rosé, but the best wines are white Chenin Blanc, either sweet from the Layon Valley or dry from SAVENNIÈRES and ANJOU, where a new generation of producers is making richer, barrel-fermented and aged wines. Near the mouth of the river around Nantes is MUSCADET. See also BONNEZEAUX, CABERNET D'ANJOU, CHEVERNY, CÔTE ROANNAISE, COTEAUX DE L'AUBANCE, COTEAUX DU GIENNOIS, COTEAUX DU LAYON, CRÉMANT DE LOIRE, JASNIÈRES, MENETOU-SALON, POUILLY-SUR-LOIRE, QUARTS DE CHAUME, QUINCY, REUILLY, ROSÉ DE LOIRE, SAUMUR, SAUMUR MOUSSEUX, VAL DE LOIRE.

LOMA LARGA *Casablanca, Chile* One of Chile's leaders in cool-climate reds, specializing in crunchy Cabernet Franc★, Malbec★, Pinot Noir★ and Syrah★ made by a French winemaker hailing from the Loire region. Whites are also good. Excellent second label, Lomas del Valle.

LOMBARDY *Italy* Lombardy, whose capital is Milan, is a larger consumer than producer, though OLTREPÒ PAVESE does produce a lot of grapes, many of them used in Italy's *spumante* industry. There are some interesting wines from Oltrepò; also from VALTELLINA, Valcalepio and Garda's LUGANA. FRANCIACORTA makes top-quality sparklers.

LONG ISLAND *New York State, USA*   Long Island encompasses 3 AVAs: the Hamptons, North Fork, and the broader Long Island AVA. People have likened growing conditions to BORDEAUX, and the long growing season, combined with a maritime influence, does produce similarities. Certainly Merlot and Cabernet Franc are the best reds, with Chardonnay the best white. Best producers: BEDELL★, CHANNING DAUGHTERS★, LENZ★, Macari, Martha Clara, Palmer★, Paumanok★, Pellegrini★, Pindar, Raphael, SHINN ESTATE, WÖLFFER★. Best years: (reds) 2012 10 **09 08 07 06 02 01**.

LONG MEADOW RANCH *Napa Valley AVA, California, USA*   A Napa rising star with serious, impressive Cabernet Sauvignon★★ and a gravelly Sauvignon Blanc.

LONG SHADOWS *Columbia Valley AVA, Washington State, USA*   A series of partnerships, led by Allen Shoup. It includes Pedestal★★ with Michel Rolland, Feather★ with Randy DUNN, Poet's Leap★★ with Armin Diel of Schlossgut DIEL, Saggi★ with Ambrogio and Giovanni FOLONARI, Sequel★★ with John DUVAL, and Chester-Kidder★ with Allen Shoup and Gilles Nicault, the group's head winemaker. Also Gilles' own RHÔNE-style red, Côte Nicault★. Best years: (reds) (2012) 11 10 **09 08**.

DR LOOSEN *Bernkastel, Mosel, Germany*   Loosen's estate has portions of some of the MOSEL's most famous vineyards: Treppchen and Prälat in ERDEN, Würzgarten in ÜRZIG, Sonnenuhr in WEHLEN, Himmelreich in GRAACH and Lay in BERNKASTEL. Most of the wines achieve ★★, and the sweeter styles frequently ★★★. Even the most basic Rieslings are excellent, year in year out, and the dry Rieslings are growing in stature. A joint venture with CHATEAU STE MICHELLE in Washington revolutionized Riesling production in that state. Best years: (2013) 12 11 **09 08 07 06 05 04**.

LÓPEZ DE HEREDIA *Rioja DOCa, Rioja, Spain*   Family-owned RIOJA company, still aging wines in old oak casks. Younger red wines are called Viña Cubillo★, and mature wines Viña Tondonia★★ and Viña Bosconia★★. Good, oaky whites, including Viña Gravonia★★. Gran Reserva red and white wines are a different world, often ★★★ in their idiosyncratic way. Best years: (Viña Tondonia Reserva) **2002 01 00 99 98 96 95 94 93 91 87 86 85**.

LOUPIAC AC *Bordeaux, France*   A sweet wine area across the Garonne river from BARSAC. The wines are attractively sweet without being gooey. Drink young in general, though the best can age. Best producers: Clos Jean★, Cros, Dauphiné-Rondillon★, Loupiac-Gaudiet, Noble★, Ricaud, les Roques★. Best years: **2011 10 09 07 05 03**.

CH. LA LOUVIÈRE *Pessac-Léognan AC, Bordeaux, France*   The star of PESSAC-LÉOGNAN's non-classified estates, its reputation almost entirely due to owner André Lurton's determination. Well-structured reds★ and fresh, Sauvignon-based whites★★ are excellent value. Best years: (reds) 2012 11 10 09 **08 06 05 04 02 01 00**; (whites) **2012 11 10 09 08 07 06 05 04 02**.

LUBÉRON AC *Rhône Valley, France*   AC east of Avignon. Production is dominated by co-ops; their light wines drink young. Domaine wines (Grenache, Syrah) have more body. Whites are often oaked. Best producers: Bonnieux co-op, la Canorgue, la Citadelle★, Fontenille★, de l'Isolette★, La Vieille Ferme (white), St-Estève de Néri★, la Tour-d'Aigues co-op, des Tourettes, Val Joanis★, la Verrerie. Best years: **2012 10**.

STEFANO LUBIANA *Tasmania, Australia*   One of the stars of the Tasmanian wine scene, proudly showing off a new cellar door facility. Vintage★★, non-vintage★ and Prestige★ (10 years on lees) sparkling wines rank with the best in Australia. Chardonnay★ is restrained and elegant, Sauvignon Blanc★ shows greengage and passionfruit characters, while the Pinot Noir★ has weight, concentration and a velvety texture. Entry-level 'Primavera' Pinot Noir is pretty tasty.

LUGANA DOC *Lombardy, Italy*   Dry white (occasionally sparkling) from the Trebbiano di Lugana grape (aka Verdicchio) grown on the southern shores of Lake Garda. Well-structured wines from the better producers can develop excitingly over a few years. Best producers: Ca' dei Frati★★, Ottella★, Provenza★, Visconti★, Zenato★, Zeni.

LUIGI BOSCA *Mendoza, Argentina*   Old family-owned winery that constantly delights with the unexpected. The La Linda★ range offers excellent value for everyday drinking. At estate level the Malbec★, sparkling Brut Nature★, Pinot Noir and Riesling are the pick of the bunch. At the top end, the white blend Gala 3★★ is among Argentina's best whites, and Icono★★, a Malbec-Cabernet Sauvignon blend, is a hedonist's dream. Seriously old-vine field blends plus old-vine Chardonnay under the Los Nobles★ label are gorgeous. Side project Viña Alicia★★ for exceptional, tiny production reds, mainly Malbec but also Nebbiolo, Petit Verdot and Cabernet Sauvignon, and the wonderful Tiara★★ blend of Riesling, Savagnin and Albariño.

LUIS FELIPE EDWARDS *Colchagua, Chile*   Family-owned winery that combines commercial winemaking with innovation and investment in new locations. The LFE900 project is a stunning series of vineyards at up to 900m (3000ft) above the Colchagua Valley floor, planted to Cabernet, Syrah, Malbec, Carmenère and others. Also good Gran Reserva★ reds, Cabernet-dominant Doña Bernarda★ and Marea de Leyda range (Sauvignon Blanc★★, Pinot Noir★).

DOM. LUNEAU-PAPIN *Muscadet Sèvre-et-Maine, Loire Valley, France*   Pierre Luneau-Papin and his son, Pierre-Marie, make a thrilling range of 7 'cru' Muscadets from the region's rich smörgåsbord of soils: micaschist (Pierre de La Grange★, Clos des Allées★, Excelsior★★), schist (Pueri Solis★★), serpentite (Terre de Pierre★), gneiss (Les Pierres Blanches★), granite (Le L d'Or★★). With age, Excelsior, Pueri Solis and Le L d'Or take on a Burgundian complexity. Best years (Le L d'Or): (2013) **10 09 07 05 03 99**.

LUSSAC-ST-ÉMILION AC *Bordeaux, France*   Much of the wine from this AC, which tastes like a lighter ST-ÉMILION, is made by the first-rate local co-op and should be drunk within 4 years of the vintage; certain properties are worth seeking out. Best producers: Barbe-Blanche★, Bel-Air, Bellevue★, Courlat★, la Grenière, Lussac★, Lyonnat★, Mayne Blanc, Le Rival★, La Rose Perrière. Best years: **2012 10 09 08 05**.

LUSTAU *Jerez y Manzanilla DO, Andalucía, Spain*   Specializes in supplying 'own-label' wines to supermarkets, often of very good quality. Look out for the Almacenista★★ range: very individual sherries from small, private producers. Lustau acquired the La Ina Fino★ brand in 2008.

CH. LYNCH-BAGES *Pauillac AC, 5ème Cru Classé, Haut-Médoc, Bordeaux, France*   I am a great fan of Lynch-Bages red★★★, with its almost succulent richness, its gentle texture and its starburst of flavours: all butter, blackcurrants and mint – and it is now one of PAUILLAC's most popular wines. Sadly, its price is rapidly approaching the stratospheric. Impressive at 5 years, beautiful at 10 and irresistible at 20. Second wine:

Echo de Lynch-Bages (since 2008), previously Haut-Bages-Averous. Also a small amount of white wine, Blanc de Lynch-Bages★. Best years: (reds) 2012 11 10 09 **08 07 06 05 04 03 02 01 00 99 98 96 95 90**.

FRÉDÉRIC MABILEAU *St-Nicolas-de-Bourgueil*
AC, Loire Valley, France Meticulous attention to detail yields ST-NICOLAS-DE-BOURGUEIL (Les Rouillères★, Les Coutures★★, Éclipse★★) and BOURGUEIL (Racines★) of startling fruit purity and finesse. A white SAUMUR★★ and ANJOU BLANC attest to Frédéric's passion for

Chenin Blanc. Also ANJOU Cabernet Sauvignon. Certified organic from 2009. Best years: (top reds) (2013) **11 10 09** 08 07 06 05 04 03.

LE MACCHIOLE *Bolgheri, Tuscany, Italy* One of the leading quality estates of the new Tuscany. Mainstay is Paleo Rosso★★, a pure Cabernet Franc. Best-known wine is the Merlot Messorio★★, while Scrio★★ is one of the best Syrahs in Italy. Best years: (2011) **10 09 08 07 06 04 03 01 00 99**.

MÂCON AC *Mâconnais, Burgundy, France* The basic Mâconnais AC, but most whites are labelled under the superior MÂCON-VILLAGES AC. Rarely exciting. Mâcon Blanc is a rather expensive basic quaffer. Drink young.

MÂCON-VILLAGES AC *Mâconnais, Burgundy, France* Appellation covering 26 villages. Co-ops still dominate production, making wines from modest to excellent. A handful of growers make more exciting wines from individually named villages such as Mâcon-Lugny and Mâcon la Roche Vineuse. Best villages: Bussières, Chaintré, Chardonnay, Charnay, Clessé, Cruzille, Davayé, Igé, Lugny, Prissé, la Roche Vineuse, Uchizy, Verzy. Best producers: D & M Barraud★★, A Bonhomme★★, Bret Brothers★★, Deux Roches★, la Greffière★★, Guffens-Heynen★★, A & J Guillot★★, Guillot-Broux★★, LAFON★, Maillet★, Jean Manciat★, Merlin★★, Michel★, Pauget★, Rijckaert★, Robert-Denogent★★, Saumaize-Michelin★, Valette★, Verget★★, J-J Vincent★. Best years: (2013) **12 11 10 09**. See also VIRÉ-CLESSÉ.

MACPHAIL *Sonoma Coast AVA, California, USA* Pinot Noir★ (SONOMA COAST★★, Wildcat Vineyard★★) and Chardonany★ from cool-climate vineyards show great intensity and depth.

MADEIRA DOC *Madeira, Portugal* The holiday island of Madeira seems an unlikely place to find a serious wine. However, Madeiras are very serious wines indeed and the best can survive to a great age. Traditionally made from 4 'noble' white grape varieties: Malvasia (or Malmsey), Boal (or Bual), Verdelho and Sercial. Many vineyards have been replanted to the red Tinta Negra Mole, but also to some white grapes, including the rare, high-acid Terrantez. Inexpensive Madeira is heated in huge vats (*estufagem*); modern controls give better flavours than used to be possible. The best wines are wood-aged naturally in the subtropical warmth. All except dry wines are fortified early on and may be sweetened with fortified grape juice before bottling. Basic 3-year-old Madeira is made mainly from Tinta Negra Mole, whereas higher-quality 10-year-old, 15-year-old and vintage wines (from a single year, aged in cask for at least 20 years) tend to be made from one of the 'noble' grapes. Colheita (or Single Harvest) is early-bottled vintage Madeira, which can be released after 5 years in wood (7 years for Sercial). Best producers: BARBEITO★★, Barros e Souza, H M Borges, HENRIQUES & HENRIQUES★★, Justino's Madeira Wines★, MADEIRA WINE COMPANY★, Pereira d'Oliveira.

MADEIRA WINE COMPANY *Madeira DOC, Madeira, Portugal* This company (now back under the control of the Blandy family) ships more than half of all Madeira exported in bottle, under brand names such as Blandy's, Cossart Gordon, Leacock's. Big improvements have taken place in 5-, 10- and 15-year-old wines, including a tasty 5-year-old (a blend of Malvasia and Bual) called Alvada★. Vintage wines★★★ are superb. Specially blended 'early release' single-harvest wines are tangy.

MADIRAN AOP *South-West France* Current production is divided between the high-extraction, all-new-oak, tough, macho wines that need keeping, and a newer, lighter style in response to marketing demands. Best producers: AYDIE★★, Barréjat★, BERTHOUMIEU★★, Bouscassé★★, Capmartin★★, Chapelle Lenclos★★, Clos Basté★★, du Crampilh★, Damiens★★, LABRANCHE-LAFFONT★★, Laffitte-Teston★, MONTUS★★, Pichard★, PLAIMONT, Viella★. Best years: (2012) 11 **10** 09 **08** 06 05 04 02 01.

VINOS DE MADRID DO *Madrid region, Spain* The southern part of the Madrid region has sprung to life with some well-equipped wineries that have pioneered the rediscovery of unappreciated old vineyards, particularly on the granite soils of the Gredos mountains to the west, with Garnacha and the white Albillo Real grapes, but also on the limestone hills to the east, with Garnacha and the white Malvar. Best producers: 4 Monos, Vinos Ambiz★, Ricardo Benito, Bernabeleva★, Comando G★, Jeromín★, Licinia, Marañones★★, El Regajal★, El Rincón★, Tagonius.

CH. MAGDELAINE★ *St-Émilion Grand Cru AC, 1er Grand Cru Classé, Bordeaux, France* Dark, rich, aggressive wines, yet with a load of luscious fruit and oaky spice. In lighter years the wine has a gushing, easy, tender fruit and can be enjoyed at 5–10 years. 2011 was the last vintage of this wine; owner MOUEIX has now amalgamated the estate with BELAIR-MONANGE. Best years: 2011 10 09 08 **06** 05 04 03 01 00 99 98 96 95.

MAIPO *Chile* Historic heart of the Chilean wine industry; increasingly encroached upon by Chile's capital, Santiago. Cabernet is king and many premium-priced reds come from here, but warming conditions are pushing vineyards higher into the Cordilleras. Best producers: ALMAVIVA★★★, Antiyal★★, CARMEN★★, CONCHA Y TORO★★, COUSIÑO MACUL★, DE MARTINO★★, Domus Aurea (Peñalolén★), HARAS DE PIRQUE★★, PÉREZ CRUZ★, SANTA CAROLINA★, SANTA RITA★, UNDURRAGA★, Viñedo Chadwick★★★/ERRÁZURIZ.

MAJELLA *Coonawarra, South Australia* A trademark lush, sweet vanillin oakiness to the reds is always balanced by dense, opulent fruit. The profound Malleea★★★ (Cabernet-Shiraz) is the flagship, while the Cabernet Sauvignon★★★ (a succulent, fleshy cassis bomb) and Shiraz★★ are almost as good and very reasonably priced; the Musician★★ (Cabernet-Shiraz) is rich but deliciously drinkable.

MÁLAGA DO *Andalucía, Spain* A curious blend of sweet wine, alcohol and juices; production is dwindling. The best are intensely nutty, raisiny and caramelly. A 'sister' appellation, Sierras de Málaga, includes non-fortified wines. Best producers: Cortijo Los Aguilares★, Gomara★, López Hermanos★, Jorge Ordóñez★★, Telmo RODRIGUEZ★, Friedrich Schatz★.

CH. MALARTIC-LAGRAVIÈRE★★ *Pessac-Léognan AC, Cru Classé de Graves, Bordeaux, France* Now one of Pessac-Léognan's most reliable properties. Reds are serious but approachable; the tiny amount of white★★ is made from a majority of Sauvignon Blanc (80%) and is immediately delicious, and softens after 3–4 years into a lovely nutty wine. Best years: (reds) 2012 11 10 09 08 **07** 06 05 04 03 02 01 00; (whites) **2012** 11 **10** 09 08 **07** 06 05.

MALBEC A red grape, rich in tannin and flavour, from South-West France. The major ingredient in CAHORS wines, where it is also known as Auxerrois or Cot; it is also planted in the LOIRE, as Cot. It's making small inroads in Spain. Successful in Chile and especially in Argentina, where it produces lush-textured, ripe, perfumed, damsony reds. In California and New Zealand it sometimes appears in BORDEAUX-style blends. In South Africa and Australia it is used in blends and for varietal wines.

CH. MALESCOT ST-EXUPÉRY★★ *Margaux AC, 3ème Cru Classé, Haut-Médoc, Bordeaux, France* Once one of the most scented, exotic reds in Bordeaux, and since 2000 it has rediscovered that glorious cassis and violet perfume which makes it one of Bordeaux's most delightful reds. Best years: 2012 11 10 09 **08 07 06 05 04 03 02 01 00**.

HERDADE DA MALHADINHA NOVA *Alentejo DOC, Portugal* Ultra-modern winery and wines: Monte da Peceguina red★, white and rosé, and top wines, Malhadinha Tinto★★ (red), Malhadinha Branco★ (white) and Marias da Malhadinha★★.

MALLECO *Chile* The southernmost appellation in Chile – though there are vineyards further south – Malleco has a tricky climate for winemaking (cold and wet) but a dry Pacific wind results in racy wines with character. Pioneered by Viña Aquitania, most plantings are Chardonnay and Pinot Noir. Best producers: Viña Aquitania (Sol de Sol), William Fèvre.

MALVASIA This grape, of Greek origin, is widely planted, especially in Italy, and is found in many guises, both white and red. In Friuli and in Croatia, as Malvasia Istriana, it produces light, mildly fragrant wines of considerable youthful charm, while in TUSCANY, UMBRIA and the rest of central Italy it is widely used to make innocuous dry and sweet whites. On the islands, Malvasia is used in rich dry or sweet wines in Bosa and Cagliari (in SARDINIA), and in Lipari off the coast of SICILY to make really tasty, apricotty sweet wines. As a black grape, Malvasia Nera is blended with Negroamaro in PUGLIA and occasionally with Sangiovese in CHIANTI. Variants of Malvasia grow in Spain's CATALUÑA and CANARY ISLANDS and mainland Portugal. On the island of MADEIRA it produces sweet fortified wine, sometimes known by its English name, Malmsey.

MAN O'WAR *Waiheke Island, Auckland, North Island, New Zealand* The largest vineyard on WAIHEKE. After a slow start there are now some cracking wines, including tangy, salty Sauvignon★★, Gravestone★★ (Sauvignon-Semillon), heroic Valhalla Chardonnay★★ and even more powerful Ironclad Cabernet★★, plus strong, spicy Dreadnought Syrah★★ (sometimes ★★★). Best years: (reds) (2013) **10 09 08 07**.

LA MANCHA DO *Castilla-La Mancha, Spain* Spain's vast central plateau is Europe's biggest delimited wine area. Since 1995, non-native grape varieties have been introduced, including Macabeo (Viura), Verdejo, Chardonnay, Cabernet Sauvignon, Petit Verdot, Merlot and Syrah. Whites are rarely exciting but are often fresh and attractive (see AIRÉN). Reds can be light and fruity, or richer. Best producers: Ayuso, Campos Reales★, Vinícola de Castilla (Castillo de Alhambra, Señorío de Guadianeja), Finca Antigua★, Fontana★, Muñoz (Blas Muñoz★).

MANCHUELA DO *Castilla-La Mancha, Spain* Higher, hillier, cooler than its huge neighbour La MANCHA. The international recognition gained since 2000 by Finca Sandoval has helped a small band of private producers and quality-conscious co-ops to get a foothold in foreign markets. Best producers: Altolandón★, Cien y Pico★, Finca Sandoval★★, Monegrillo, Ponce★★, San Antonio Abad, Vega Tolosa, Vitivinos.

DOM. ALBERT MANN *Alsace AC, Alsace, France* Powerful, flavoursome and ageworthy wines from Grand Cru vineyards, including intense, mineral Rieslings from Furstentum★★ and Schlossberg★★ and rich Furstentum Gewurztraminer★★. Impressive range of Pinot Gris includes astonishing Sélections de Grains Nobles★★★. Basic wines are stylish and reliable. Best years: (Grand Cru Riesling) (2013) 12 11 10 09 08 07 05 01.

MANOS NEGRAS *Mendoza, Argentina* Good Torrontés★ from SAN JUAN, Pinot Noir from PATAGONIA and Malbec★ from the oh-so-trendy Altamira in the UCO VALLEY. Soil-focused wines highlight a new trend to show the impact of the many soil types in Argentina, the Malbec Stone Soil Select★ being the best. Also a series of wines from Chile.

MANZANILLA See Jerez y Manzanilla.

MARANGES AC *Côte de Beaune, Burgundy, France* AC right at the southern tip of the CÔTE DE BEAUNE. Slightly tough red wines of medium depth, which are rightly mainly sold as CÔTE DE BEAUNE-VILLAGES. Some growers are beginning to show their mettle. Less than 5% of production is white. Best producers: BACHELET-Monnot★, Chevrot★, Contat-Grangé★, Cyrot-Buthiau★, DROUHIN. Best years: (reds) (2013) 12 11 10 09 08 07 05 03 02.

MARCASSIN *Sonoma County, California, USA* Helen Turley focuses on cool-climate Chardonnay and Pinot Noir of incredible depth and restrained power. Single-vineyard Chardonnays and Pinot Noirs are very difficult to obtain but can rank ★★★.

MARCHE *Italy* Adriatic region best known for VERDICCHIO but producing increasingly good reds from Montepulciano and Sangiovese, led by CONERO and ROSSO PICENO, and also from the delightfully aromatic, indigenous Lacrima di Morro d'Alba. Good international varietals such as Cabernet, Chardonnay and Merlot under the Marche IGT or Esino DOC, as well as blends with the native grapes. Best of the whites are Il Coroncino★★, La Monacesca★★, Villa Bucci★★. Best of the reds are Boccadigabbia's Akronte★ (Cabernet), La Monacesca's Camerte★ (Sangiovese-Merlot), Monte Schiavo's Adeodato★★ (Montepulciano), Oasi degli Angeli's Kurni★ (Montepulciano), Le Terrazze's Chaos★ (Montepulciano-Merlot-Syrah) and Umani Ronchi's Pelago★ (Montepulciano-Cabernet-Merlot).

MARCILLAC AOP *South-West France* Currants, dry red wines (and a little rosé). The reds are rustic but full of soft fruit flavour and should be drunk at 2–5 years old. Best producers: l'Albinie★, Costes★, Cros/Philippe Teulier★, Marcillac-Vallon co-op, Jean-Luc Matha★.

MARGARET RIVER *Western Australia* This coastal region quickly established its name as a leading area for Cabernet, with marvellously deep, BORDEAUX-like structured reds. Now Chardonnay, concentrated and opulent, vies with Cabernet for top spot, but there is also fine leafy Semillon, often blended with citrus-zest Sauvignon. Increasingly popular Shiraz provides the occasional gem. Best producers: Amelia Park, Arlewood, Ashbrook, Brookland Valley★★, CAPE MENTELLE★★, Chapman Grove★, Larry CHERUBINO★★, CULLEN★★★, DEVIL'S LAIR★★, Edwards, Evans & Tate★★, Fermoy Estate★, Flametree★, Fraser Gallop★★, Gralyn★, HOWARD PARK★★, Juniper Estate★★, LEEUWIN ESTATE★★★, Lenton Brae★, McHenry Hohnen★, MOSS WOOD★★, PIERRO★★, Sandalford★★, Snake & Herring, Stella Bella★★,

Umamu★, VASSE FELIX★★★, VOYAGER ESTATE★★, Watershed★, Woodlands★★, Xanadu★★★. Best years: (Cabernet-based reds) 2013 12 11 10 09 **08 07 05 04 03 01 00 99 98 96 95**.

MARGAUX AC *Haut-Médoc, Bordeaux, France* AC centred on the village of Margaux. Gravel banks dotted through the vineyards mean the wines are rarely heavy and should have a divine perfume after 7–12 years. Best producers: (Classed Growths) Boyd-Cantenac★, BRANE-CANTENAC★★, Cantenac Brown★, Dauzac★, FERRIÈRE★★, Giscours★, ISSAN★★, KIRWAN★, MALESCOT ST-EXUPÉRY★★, MARGAUX★★★, PALMER★★★, PRIEURÉ-LICHINE★, RAUZAN-SÉGLA★, Tertre★; (others) ANGLUDET★, Eyrins★, la Gurgue★, Labégorce★, Monbrison★, SIRAN★. Best years: 2012 11 10 09 **08 06 05 04 02 01 00.**

CH. MARGAUX★★★ *Margaux AC, 1er Cru Classé, Haut-Médoc, Bordeaux, France* Frequently the most seamless, flawless wine in the Médoc, so much so that I occasionally pine for a few faults to add a little frisson of unpredictability. Also delicious white Pavillon Blanc★★, from Sauvignon Blanc (100%), but it must be the most expensive BORDEAUX AC wine by a mile. Second wine: Pavillon Rouge★★. Best years: (reds) 2012 11 10 09 08 **07 06 05 04 03 02 01 00 99 98 96 95 90 89**; (whites) **2012 11 10 09 08 07 06 05 04.**

MARIMAR ESTATE *Sonoma County, California, USA* The sister of Spanish winemaker Miguel TORRES has established her own winery in the cool Green Valley region of RUSSIAN RIVER VALLEY. Excellent Chardonnay and Pinot Noir, particularly from Don Miguel Vineyard: the Chardonnay★★ (sometimes ★★★) is intense but restrained in a European way, and likely to age gracefully at 10 years old. Acero★★ is a fine, minerally, unoaked version. Recent vintages of full-flavoured Pinot Noir★★★ are the best yet. Best years: (Pinot Noir) **2012 10 09 08 07 06 05 03 02 01.**

MARLBOROUGH *South Island, New Zealand* This spectacularly successful wine region only planted its first commercial vines in 1973. Marlborough is now home to well over half the country's vines. Its three main vineyard areas are Southern Valleys, Wairau Valley and AWATERE VALLEY, and its long, cool and relatively dry ripening season, cool nights and free-draining stony soils are the major assets. Its snappy, aromatic Sauvignon Blanc first brought the region fame worldwide. Fine-flavoured Chardonnay, steely Riesling, elegant traditional-method fizz and luscious botrytized wines are other successes. Pinot Noir is now establishing a strong regional identity and Syrah is showing real scented form. Best producers: ASTROLABE★★, BRANCOTT★, Churton★, Clos Marguerite★, CLOUDY BAY★★, The Crossings★, Delta, Dog Point★, Forrest★, Foxes Island★, FRAMINGHAM★★, FROMM★★, Greywacke★★, HUNTER'S★, JACKSON ESTATE★, Lawson's Dry Hills★, Mahi★, Marisco★, MORTON ESTATE★, Mount Riley★, Mud House★, Nautilus★, SAINT CLAIR★, SERESIN★, Stoneleigh★, Jules Taylor★, Te Whare Ra★, TerraVin★★, Tinpot Hut★, Tohu★, VILLA MARIA★★, WITHER HILLS, YEALANDS★. Best years: (Chardonnay) (2013) **12 10 09 07 06**; (Pinot Noir) (2013) **12 10 07 06 05**; (Sauvignon Blanc) 2013 **12 11 10 09**. See also AWATERE VALLEY.

MARQUÉS DE CÁCERES *Rioja DOCa, Rioja, Spain* Crisp, aromatic, modern whites★ and rosés★, and fleshy, fruity reds (Reservas★). There is also a luxury red, Gaudium★. Best years: (reds) (2011) **10 09 08 07 06 05 04 03 01 99 98 96 95 94 92.**

MARQUÉS DE GRIÑÓN *Castilla-La Mancha, Spain* Estate of Carlos Falcó (the eponymous Marqués), near Toledo, with its own Dominio de Valdepusa DO. Good but sometimes overripe wines: basic Caliza, Summa Varietalis★, Dominio de Valdepusa Cabernet Sauvignon★, Petit Verdot★, Syrah★ and Eméritus★★, a blend of the 3 varieties. Top wine AAA★ is based on Petit Verdot. Best years: (Eméritus) 2008 05 **04 03 02 01 00 99 98**.

MARQUÉS DE MURRIETA *Rioja DOCa, Rioja, Spain* This RIOJA bodega faithfully preserves the traditional style of long aging, but typical time in barrel has been reduced by a third. The ornately labelled Castillo Ygay Gran Reserva★★ (sometimes ★★★) is less forbidding, more fascinating, than in the past. There's a more international-styled, oaky cuvée, Dalmau★★. Whites★★ (can be★★★) are dauntingly oaky but age brilliantly; reds are packed with savoury mulberry fruit. Best years: (reds) 2009 **07 06 05 04 03 01 00 99 96 95 94 92 91 89 87 85**.

MARQUÉS DE RISCAL *Rioja DOCa, País Vasco and Rueda DO, Castilla y León, Spain* A producer that has restored its reputation for classic pungent RIOJA reds (Reserva, Gran Reserva★★). Expensive Barón de Chirel★★, with significant Cabernet content, is made only in selected years. Aromatic RUEDA whites★. Best years: (Barón de Chirel) (2011) (10) **06 03 01 96 95 94**.

MARSALA DOC *Sicily, Italy* Fortified wines, once as esteemed as sherry or Madeira. A taste of an old Vergine (unsweetened) Marsala, fine and complex, will show why. Today most is sweetened and used for cooking, though some are fighting back, notably DE BARTOLI★★, Florio (Baglio Florio★, Terre Arse★), Pellegrino (Soleras★, Riserva 1962★).

MARSANNAY AC *Côte de Nuits, Burgundy, France* Village originally known for its pleasant if austere rosé, but now the reds are much more interesting, perfumed and sometimes surprisingly plush. Whites mostly dull. Best producers: Audoin★, P Charlopin★★, B CLAIR★★, Fournier★★, Geantet-Pansiot★, JADOT★, MÉO-CAMUZET★, D MORTET★★, Pataille★★, J & J-L Trapet★. Best years: (reds) (2013) 12 **11 10 09 08 05**.

MARSANNE Undervalued white grape yielding rich, honeysuckle-scented, nutty wines in the northern Rhône (notably HERMITAGE, CROZES-HERMITAGE, ST-JOSEPH and ST-PÉRAY), often with the more scented, lively Roussanne. Generally drink young, except the Hermitage, which can take on complexity and mature for decades. Also increasingly successful in southern Rhône and LANGUEDOC blends, and performs well in California and Australia. As Ermitage, it produces some good wines, sweet as well as dry, in Swiss VALAIS. It is now being planted in South Africa.

MARTINBOROUGH/WAIRARAPA *North Island, New Zealand* A cool, dry climate, free-draining soil and a passion for quality are this region's greatest assets. Mild autumn weather promotes intense flavours balanced by good acidity: top Pinot Noir and complex Chardonnay, intense Cabernet blends in favourable years, full Sauvignon Blanc and honeyed Riesling. Best producers: (Martinborough) ATA RANGI★★★, CRAGGY RANGE★★, DRY RIVER★★★, Escarpment★★, Gladstone★★, Kusuda★★, MARTINBOROUGH VINEYARD★★, Murdoch James★, Nga Waka★, PALLISER ESTATE★★; (Wairarapa) Johner★★, Matahiwi★, Schubert★★, Urlar★. Best years: (Pinot Noir) (2013) 12 **11 10 09 08 07 06**.

MARTINBOROUGH VINEYARD *Martinborough, North Island, New Zealand* Famous for Pinot Noir★★ but also makes impressive Chardonnay★, spicy Riesling★, creamy Pinot Gris★ and luscious botrytized styles★★

when vintage conditions allow. Good vineyard sites and sensitive winemaking have produced a string of very elegant wines. Best years: (Pinot Noir) (2013) 12 11 10 09 08 07 06.

MARTÍNEZ BUJANDA *Rioja DOCa, País Vasco, Spain* This family-owned firm produces some of the best modern RIOJA. It was split in two in 2007: Jesús Martínez-Bujanda keeps the Valdemar winery in Rioja, while Carlos and Pilar Martínez-Bujanda retain the Finca Valpiedra and Finca Antigua estates and the Cosecheros y Criadores wine company. Valpiedra wines are revitalized since 2006 vintage, with crisp whites and rosés, lush young-vines red Cantos★ and scented, refined Reserva★★.

LOUIS M MARTINI *Napa Valley AVA, California, USA* Historic Napa jewel making a strong comeback since purchase by E&J GALLO in 2002. Winemaker Mike Martini has turned the quality around with fine Cabernets from the famed Monte Rosso★ vineyard and ALEXANDER VALLEY.

MARYLAND *USA* Maryland's Boordy Vineyards was the pioneer in French hybrid varieties, but the state fell behind its neighbour VIRGINIA in growth and quality, despite sharing a similar moderate climate and benefits of the Blue Ridge Mountains. However, things have improved dramatically since the turn of the century as new wineries have implemented rigorous vineyard standards. Boordy replanted nearly 20ha (50 acres) of vines in a move to boost quality – the first fruits of this effort were harvested in 2010 and are already adding excitement to a booming state wine industry, with more than 65 wineries. Best producers: Basignani, Black Ankle, Boordy, Knob Hill, Slack, Sugarloaf Mountain.

DOMAINES PAUL MAS *Languedoc, France* Large, dynamic, family-owned producer near PÉZENAS, and also in LIMOUX, with one of the best ranges in the south of France, from basic varietals up to single-estate wines, under various labels, including The Arrogant Frog, La Forge, Mas des Tannes. Also owns Dom. Astruc, Dom. de Martinolles and Crès Ricards.

DOM. DU MAS BLANC *Banyuls AC, Roussillon, France* Run by the Parcé family, this estate makes great traditional BANYULS, specializing in the *rimage* (early-bottled vintage) style (La Coume★★). Also Banyuls Hors d'Age★★ from a solera laid down in 1955, plus a range of Jean-Michel Parcé COLLIOURES★★. Best years: (2013) 12 11 10 09 08 07 06 05.

MAS BRUGUIÈRE *Pic St-Loup AC, Languedoc, France* L'Arbouse★ has rich, spicy Syrah character, while La Grenadière★★ develops buckets of black fruit and spice after 3 years. Super-cuvée Le Septième★★ (seventh generation) blends Mourvèdre with some Syrah. Calcadiz is an easy-drinking red; aromatic, fruity, refreshing white Les Mûriers★ is based on Roussanne. Best years: (reds) (2013) 12 11 10 09 08 07 06 05.

MAS LA CHEVALIÈRE *IGP Pays d'Oc, Languedoc, France* State-of-the-art winery created by LAROCHE in the early 1990s. Wines include La Croix Chevalière★ (Syrah-Merlot-Grenache) and Mas la Chevalière Rouge★ from the estate vineyard. Best years: (2013) 12 11 10 09 08 07 06 05.

MAS DE DAUMAS GASSAC *IGP de l'Hérault, Languedoc, France* Aimé Guibert and his son Samuel have proved over 30 years that the HÉRAULT, once associated with cheap table wine, can produce fine, ageworthy wines. Cabernet Sauvignon-based red★ is firm and tannic; Cuvée Emile Peynaud★★ is more concentrated. Best of all is the lush, scented white★★ (Viognier-Chardonnay-Petit Manseng-Chenin). Sweet Vin de Laurence★★ can be delectable. Best years: (reds) 2013 12 11 10 09 08 07 06 05.

MAS DOIX *Priorat DOCa, Cataluña, Spain* The Doix and Llagostera families own some extraordinary old Garnacha and Cariñena vineyards, which provide the grapes for some equally impressive wines. Doix Vinyes Velles★★ is probably the first of the new generation PRIORATs to reach the heights of the pioneers such as CLOS ERASMUS, CLOS MOGADOR and Alvaro PALACIOS' L'Ermita. Best years: (2012) 11 **10 09 08 07 06 05 04 03 02 01**.

BARTOLO MASCARELLO *Barolo DOCG, Piedmont, Italy* Run by Maria Teresa, Bartolo's daughter, since his death in 2005. Remains true to its traditional roots laid down at the cantina's birth in 1919, if with more attention to detail. The BAROLO★★★ is a blend of 4 vineyards: Rué, San Lorenzo, Cannubi and Rocche dell'Annunziata. The BARBERA D'ALBA★, Dolcetto d'Alba★ and Freisa★ can need a little time to soften. Also a small amount of LANGHE Nebbiolo. Best years: (Barolo) (2011) 10 09 08 06 **05 04 01 00 99 98 96 95 91 90 89 88 86 85 82 78 76 71 69 67 64 58 55**.

GIUSEPPE MASCARELLO *Barolo DOCG, Piedmont, Italy* Traditional BAROLO cantina. Top-flight Barolo 'crus' Villero★★, Santo Stefano di Perno★★, Monprivato★★★ and Monprivato Riserva Cà d'Morissio★★★. Also extremely good Dolcetto d'Alba (Scudetto★★), BARBERA D'ALBA (Santo Stefano di Perno★★) and LANGHE Nebbiolo★★. Best years: (Barolo) (2011) 10 09 08 07 06 **04 03 01 00 99 98 97 96 95 91 90 89 88 86 85 82**.

MASI *Veneto, Italy* Large private firm, one of the driving forces in VALPOLICELLA. Campofiorin★ (effectively if not legally a *ripasso* Valpolicella) is worth looking out for, as is AMARONE (Mazzano★★, Campolongo di Torbe★★). Valpolicella's Corvina grape is also used in red blend Toar★; Osar★ is made from a local grape, Oseleta, rediscovered by Masi. The wines of Serègo Alighieri★ are also produced by Masi. Best years: (Amarone) (2011) **10 09 08 07 06 04 03 01 00 97**.

MASTROBERARDINO *Campania, Italy* For many years this family firm flew the quality flag almost alone in CAMPANIA in southern Italy. Best known for red TAURASI★★ and white Greco di Tufo★ and Fiano di Avellino★. Best years: (Taurasi Radici) (2011) 10 **09 08 07 06 05 04 01 99 97 96 95**.

MATETIC VINEYARDS *San Antonio, Chile* Matetic makes high-quality organic wines – especially under the EQ label. The estate is in the warmer part of SAN ANTONIO, which explains exceptional, concentrated and scented Syrah★★, but there's also fleshy Pinot Noir★, juicy Sauvignon Blanc★, refreshing Coastal Sauvignon★ and tasty Cab Franc-driven Winemaker's Blend★. Cheaper Corralillo★ range also very good.

MATUA VALLEY *Auckland, North Island, New Zealand* Once exciting winery; more commercial since becoming part of Foster's (now Treasury Wine Estates). Even so, top wines have dramatically improved with the release of classy Single Vineyard Wairau Sauvignon Blanc★ from MARLBOROUGH, Dartmoor Chardonnay★★ and Matheson Merlot★, Cabernet Sauvignon★ and Grenache-Syrah-Viognier★ from HAWKES BAY, Cromwell and Bannockburn Pinot Noir★ from CENTRAL OTAGO. Second label: Shingle Peak. Best years: (Hawkes Bay reds) (2013) 10 **09 08 07 04**.

CH. MAUCAILLOU★ *Moulis AC, Haut-Médoc, Bordeaux, France* Maucaillou shows that you don't have to be a Classed Growth to make high-quality claret. Expertly made by the Dourthe family, it is soft but classically flavoured, accessible early on but ages well for 10–12 years. Best years: 2012 11 **10 09 08 06 05 04 03 02 00 98**.

MAULE *Chile* The most southerly region of Chile's CENTRAL VALLEY, with wet winters and a large day/night temperature difference. Almost 30% of Chile's vines are planted here, with nearly 10,000ha (25,000 acres) of

Cabernet Sauvignon alone. Merlot does well on the cool clay soils, and there is some tasty Carmenère, Cabernet Franc and Syrah. Whites are mostly Chardonnay and Sauvignon Blanc. A new community of producers has recently been redefining the region's identity, especially using old-vine Carignan in the Cauquenes sub-region, and there's a general feeling that Maule has some of Chile's best mature vineyards, just waiting to be discovered. Best producers: Apaltagua★, J Bouchon, Casa Donoso★, CONCHA Y TORO★, DE MARTINO★★, O FOURNIER★★, Gillmore★★, La Reserva de Caliboro★★, Odfjell★, Palo Alto, TORRES★★, VALDIVIESO★.

MAURICIO LORCA *Mendoza, Argentina* Groundbreaking, frequently oak-free wines. The Opalo★ (can be ★★) range, all unoaked, are intensely pure *terroir* expressions. The Fantasía★ range includes a fresh, perfumed Malbec. The pioneering Malbrontes★ blends Malbec with Torrontés into a scented fruit bomb.

MAURO *Castilla y León, Spain* Mariano García made his name as VEGA SICILIA's winemaker for 30 years and now successfully leads his family's estate. Wines include Crianza★★, Vendimia Seleccionada★★ and Terreus★★★. Best years: (2012) 11 **10** 09 **08 07** 06 05 04 03 02 01 00 99 98 97 96 95.

MAURY AC *Roussillon, France* A *vin doux naturel*, mainly from Grenache Noir. It can be made in either a young, fresh style (vintage) or the locally revered and delicious old *rancio* style. You can occasionally find examples at 30, 40, 50 years old, and more. Maury Sec is a new appellation for red table wines. Best producers: la Coume du Roy/Maurydoré★, Mas Amiel★★, Maury co-op★, Pla del Fount★★, la Pléiade★.

MAUZAC The traditional basis of white GAILLAC and BLANQUETTE DE LIMOUX. Fresh and green-appley when picked early, it loses its acidity on the vine and can then produce luscious sweet wines.

MAXIMIN GRÜNHAUS *Mertesdorf, Mosel, Germany* Great wine estate, with two top vineyards, Abtsberg and Herrenberg, both of monastic origin. Dr Carl von Schubert makes chiefly dry and medium-dry wines of great subtlety. In good vintages the Ausleses and other top wines are ★★★ and are among the most long-lived white wines in the world. Best years: (2013) 12 11 10 **09 08 07** 06 05 04 03 02 **99** 97 95.

MAZIS-CHAMBERTIN, MAZOYÈRES-CHAMBERTIN See CHAMBERTIN AC.

McLAREN VALE *South Australia* Sunny maritime region south of Adelaide, producing superb full-bodied wines from Shiraz, Grenache and Cabernet, plus experimental successes like Nero d'Avola, Primitivo, Nebbiolo, Montepulciano, Graciano, Tempranillo and Touriga Nacional. White Fiano, Savagnin, Marsanne, Roussanne and Viognier are now making their mark, along with chubby Chardonnay. This innovative move toward warmer-climate grapes is going to play a crucial part in Australia's future as conditions get relentlessly hotter. Best producers: Battle of Bosworth, Cascabel, CHAPEL HILL★★, Clarendon Hills★, Coriole★, D'ARENBERG★★, Fox Creek★★, GEMTREE★★, HARDYS★★, Kangarilla Road★, Maxwell★, Geoff MERRILL★, Ministry of Clouds★, Mitolo, Noon★★, Oliver's Taranga★★, S C PANNELL★★, Paxton, Pirramimma, PRIMO ESTATE★★, RockBare, ROSEMOUNT★, Scarpantoni, Shingleback★, Tatachilla★, Ulithorne★, Willunga 100★, WIRRA WIRRA★★, Woodstock, Yangarra.

McPHERSON CELLARS *Texas, USA* Kim McPherson is leading Texas winemakers toward Rhône varieties for white wines and Spanish and Italian grapes for reds. Consistently good wines, including Rhône-style white blend Les Copains and red La Herencia, a blend of spicy Tempranillo and earthy Monastrell.

McWILLIAM'S *Riverina, New South Wales, Australia* Large family winery, with interests right across Australia. HUNTER VALLEY offers classic bottle-aged Mount Pleasant Semillons (Elizabeth★★, Lovedale★★★), buttery Chardonnays★ and Shiraz from Rosehill★, Old Paddock & Old Hill★★ and Maurice O'Shea (★★★ in best years). Classy sweet Morning Light Botrytis Semillon★★ and Liqueur Muscat★★ from RIVERINA, and good table wines from HILLTOPS Barwang★ vineyard. McWilliam's also owns Lillydale in the YARRA VALLEY (Chardonnay★★), BRAND'S in COONAWARRA, and Evans & Tate in MARGARET RIVER. Best years: (Lovedale Semillon) (2013) (12) (10) **09 08 07 06 05 04 03 02 01 00 99 98 97 96 95 94 87 86 84 83**.

MÉDOC *AC Bordeaux, France* The Médoc peninsula north of Bordeaux on the left bank of the Gironde river produces a good fistful of the world's most famous reds. These are all situated in the HAUT-MÉDOC, the southern, more gravelly half of the area. The Médoc AC, for reds only, covers the northern part. The best vineyards are on gravel outcrops from the ever-present clay and are producing increasingly attractive, earthy but juicy wines. Best at 3–5 years old.

Best producers: Bournac★, Cardonne, Escurac★, Goulée★, les Grands Chênes★, Greysac★, L'Inclassable★, Labadie, Loudenne, Lousteauneuf★, les Ormes-Sorbet★, Patache d'Aux★, Poitevin★, POTENSAC★★, Preuillac★, Ramafort★, Rollan de By★, la Tour de By★, la Tour Haut-Caussan★, Tour St-Bonnet★, Vieux-Robin★. Best years: **2011 10 09 08 06 05 04 03**.

MEEREA PARK *Hunter Valley, New South Wales, Australia* Brothers Rhys and Garth Eather specialize in single-vineyard, old-vine HUNTER VALLEY Semillon and Shiraz; they are helping breathe new life into the region. Hell Hole Semillon★★ is vibrant, lemony and restrained when young, gently toasty, mineral and delicious with age. The flagship red, Alexander Munro Shiraz★★, seamlessly integrates fruit, oak and tannins, and pure brambly flavours.

MEERLUST *Stellenbosch WO, South Africa* Venerable estate back to its best. Cabernet★★ is supple yet vibrant, Merlot★ plush and finely textured; together with Cabernet Franc they achieve harmony and complexity in Rubicon★★, one of the Cape's first BORDEAUX blends. Also pure, silky Pinot Noir★ and elegant, fresh Chardonnay★★. Best years: (Rubicon) **2010 09 08 07 06 05 04**; (Chardonnay) **2013 12 11 10 09 08 07 06**.

ALPHONSE MELLOT *Sancerre AC, Loire Valley, France* Biodynamic producer with an equal focus on white and red SANCERRE. Other than white cuvée La Moussière★, wines come exclusively from old vines and show a fine balance of fruit and oak. Satellite★★ is from 60-year-old vines. White Edmond★★ and red and white Génération XIX★★ are outstanding and reward keeping. Also makes IGP Les Pénitents: aromatic, fruity but fine Chardonnay and increasingly serious Pinot Noir★. Best years: (Edmond white) (2013) **12 11 10 09 08**.

CHARLES MELTON *Barossa Valley, South Australia* Leading light in hand-crafted Shiraz, Grenache and Mourvèdre in the BAROSSA. Fruity Grenache rosé Rose of Virginia★★ is arguably Australia's best; RHÔNE-blend Nine Popes★★ (sometimes ★★★), heady, sumptuous

Grenache★★, smoky Shiraz★★ and Sparkling Red★★ have all attained cult status. Cabernet Sauvignon can be ★★. Two single-site Shiraz: fleshy, blackberry-pastille Grains of Paradise★★ from the Barossa Valley, and fragrant, elegant, brambly Voices of Angels★★ from the Eden Valley. Best years: (Nine Popes) (2013) 12 10 09 **05 04 03 02 01 99 98 96 95 94 91 90**.

MENCÍA Known as Jaen in Portugal's DÃO, this Iberian grape gives characterful, intensely fruity, dense, attractively funky red wines, when not overoaked, in Spain's emerging BIERZO, Ribeira Sacra and Valdeorras (GALICIA) regions. Best producers: (Spain) Castro Ventosa, Dominio do Bibei, Estefanía, Guímaro, Mengoba, Descendientes de J Palacios, Raúl PÉREZ, Picos de Cabariezo, Ponte da Boga, Dominio de Tares, Tilenus, D Ventura; (Portugal) Quinta das Maias.

MENDEL *Mendoza, Argentina* The core of this estate is an 80-year-old 25ha (60-acre) vineyard planted to Malbec, Cabernet Sauvignon and Petit Verdot; non-estate fruit is sourced for some cuvées. Malbec★★ is deep, fresh and perfumed; Finca Remota★★ Malbec (can be ★★★) seamlessly combines power and elegance; the top cuvée Unus★★ (Cabernet Sauvignon-Malbec) is fine boned, glossy and intense. An old-vine Semillon★ is magical and intriguing. Best years: (reds) 2011 **10** 09.

MENDOCINO COUNTY *California, USA* Northernmost county of the North Coast AVA. It includes cool-climate ANDERSON VALLEY, excellent for sparkling wines and Pinot Noir, warmer Redwood Valley AVA, with good Zinfandel and Cabernet, and high-altitude Mendocino Ridge AVA. Coro is a Zinfandel-based blend made by numerous wineries. Best producers: Black Kite★, Brutocao★, Claudia Springs★, FETZER, Goldeneye★, Graziano, HANDLEY★★, Husch, Lazy Creek★, Littorai★★, Mariah★, McDowell Valley★, NAVARRO★★, Pax★, ROEDERER ESTATE★★, Saracina★, SCHARFFENBERGER CELLARS★★. Best years: (reds) 2012 **10 09 07 06 05 04 03 01 00**.

MENDOZA *Argentina* The most important wine province in Argentina, accounting for around 80% of the country's wine. Situated in the eastern foothills of the Andes, Mendoza's bone-dry climate produces powerful, high-alcohol reds. The region is complex and vast. Altitude is the key: the higher the vineyards, the higher the quality, so the UCO VALLEY has the freshest whites and the raciest reds. Ancient areas to the south and west of Mendoza city, including Vistalba, Agrelo, Perdriel, Luján de Cuyo and Las Compuertas, are famed for profound, intense, structured reds. Best producers: ACHAVAL FERRER★★, Alpamanta★, ALTA VISTA★, ALTOS LAS HORMIGAS★★, Anduluna★, BENEGAS★, Bressia★★, CATENA★★, Clos de Chacras★, COBOS★★, DOMINIO DEL PLATA★★, DOÑA PAULA★★, FABRE MONTMAYOU★, FINCA DECERO★, Finca Sophenia★, KAIKEN★, LUIGI BOSCA★, Lurton★, MANOS NEGRAS★, MAURICIO LORCA★, MENDEL★★, NORTON★, PASCUAL TOSO★, PULENTA★, RICCITELLI★, TAPIZ★, TERRAZAS DE LOS ANDES★★, TRAPICHE★★, ZUCCARDI★. See also UCO VALLEY.

MENETOU-SALON AC *Loire Valley, France* Chalky-clean Sauvignon whites and cherry-fresh Pinot Noir reds and rosés from west of SANCERRE. Best producers: R Champault, Chatenoy★, Chavet★, J-P Gilbert★, N Girard, P Jacolin, J Mellot, H Pellé★, J-M Roger★, J Teiller★, Tour St-Martin★.

MÉO-CAMUZET *Vosne-Romanée, Côte de Nuits, Burgundy, France* Super-quality estate. New oak barrels and luscious, rich fruit combine in superb wines, which age well. CLOS DE VOUGEOT★★★, RICHEBOURG★★★ and

CORTON★★ are grandest, along with the VOSNE-ROMANÉE Premiers Crus (aux Brulées★★★, Cros Parantoux★★★, les Chaumes★★). Fine NUITS-ST-GEORGES (aux Boudots★★, aux Murgers★★). Also less expensive *négociant* wines. Best years: (2013) 12 11 10 09 08 **07 06** 05 **03 02 01** 99 96 95 91.

MERCUREY AC *Côte Chalonnaise, Burgundy, France*   The red from this village
🍷 is usually pleasant and strawberry-flavoured, sometimes rustic, and can take some aging. Not much white, but I like its buttery, even spicy, taste. Best at 3–4 years old. Best producers: (reds) FAIVELEY★, Hasard★, M Juillot★, Lorenzon★★, F Raquillet★, Rodet★, de Suremain★★, Theulot-Juillot★, de Villaine★★; (whites) Ch. de Chamirey★, FAIVELEY (Clos Rochette★), M Juillot★, O LEFLAIVE★. Best years: (reds) (2013) 12 **11 10 09 08 05**.

MERLOT See pages 214–15.

GEOFF MERRILL *McLaren Vale, South Australia*   High-profile winemaker,
🍷🍷 with a nicely judged bottle-aged Reserve Cabernet★ in a light, early-picked style, Reserve Shiraz★ (Henley★★), Chardonnay★ (Reserve★★) and moreish unoaked, yet ageworthy, Bush Vine Grenache★★. Also makes tasty 'BMW'★ reds and whites with English cricket legends Ian Botham and Bob Willis.

MERRYVALE *Napa Valley AVA, California, USA*   A Chardonnay powerhouse
🍷 (Silhouette★★, CARNEROS★★, Starmont★★), but reds are not far behind, with BORDEAUX-blend Profile★★ and juicy NAPA VALLEY Merlot★★. Best years: (Chardonnay) (2012) **10 09 08 07** 06 05 04 03 02 01.

MEURSAULT AC *Côte de Beaune, Burgundy, France*   The biggest and most
🍷 popular white wine village in the CÔTE D'OR. There are no Grands Crus, but a whole cluster of Premiers Crus, of which Perrières, Charmes and Genevrières stand out. The general standard is better than in neighbouring PULIGNY and village Meursault from named vineyard sites (such as Tesson, Tillets) is particularly exciting and good value. These pale gold wines are lovely to drink young, but ought to age for 5–8 years. Virtually no Meursault red is now made. Best producers: M Ampeau★★, P Boisson★, BOUCHARD PÈRE & FILS★, M Bouzereau★, V Bouzereau★, Boyer-Martenot★★, Coche-Bizouard★★, COCHE-DURY★★★, Darnat★, Deux MONTILLE★, DROUHIN★★, A Ente★★★, J-P Fichet★★, Henri Germain★, GIRARDIN★★, Grux★, JADOT★★, P Javillier★★, Antoine Jobard★★, Rémi Jobard★★, LAFON★★★, Latour-Labille★, Matrot★★, Mikulski★★, P MOREY★★, Pernot-Belicard★★, J Prieur★★, ROULOT★★★. Best years: (2013) 12 11 **10 09 08 07 06 05 04 02**.

MEYER-NÄKEL *Dernau, Ahr, Germany*   Of the handful of top growers in the
🍷🍷 AHR, Werner Näkel has the best track record for structured yet elegant Spätburgunder (Pinot Noir)★★ from 3 Grosses Gewächs sites. Consistent if pricey wines. Best years: (2013) (12) 11 **10 09 08** 07 06 04.

CH. MEYNEY★ *St-Estèphe AC, Haut-Médoc, Bordeaux, France*   One of the most
🍷 reliable ST-ESTÈPHES, producing broad-flavoured wine with dark, plummy fruit. Second wine: Prieur de Meyney. Best years: 2012 11 10 09 **08 06 05 04** 03 02 01 00 98 96.

PETER MICHAEL WINERY *Sonoma County, California, USA*   British-born Sir
🍷 Peter Michael has turned a country retreat into an impressive winery known for its very expensive small-batch wines. Les Pavots★★ is the estate red BORDEAUX blend (L'Espirit des Pavots★★ is also good). Top Chardonnays include Mon Plaisir★★, Cuvée Indigène★, Ma Belle-Fille★★ and La Carrière★. Also Le Caprice Pinot Noir★. Best years: (Les Pavots) **2010** 09 08 07 06 05 04 03 02 01 00 99 97 96 95 94 91.

MERLOT

Red wine without tears. That's the reason Merlot has vaulted from being merely Bordeaux's red wine support act, well behind Cabernet Sauvignon in terms of class, to being the red wine drinker's darling, planted like fury all over the world. It is able to claim some seriousness and pedigree, but – crucially – can make wine of a fat, juicy character, mercifully low in tannic bitterness, which can be glugged with gay abandon almost as soon as the juice has squirted from the press. Yet this doesn't mean that Merlot is the jelly baby of red wine grapes. Far from it. Some of Bordeaux's greatest wines are based on it.

WINE STYLES

Bordeaux Merlot The great wines of Pomerol and St-Émilion, on the right bank of the Dordogne, are largely based on Merlot and the best of these – for example, Château Pétrus, which is virtually 100% Merlot – can mature for 20–30 years. In fact, there is more Merlot than Cabernet Sauvignon planted throughout Bordeaux, and I doubt if there is a single red wine property that does not have some growing, because the variety ripens early, can cope with cool conditions and is able to bear a heavy crop of fruit. In a cool, damp area like Bordeaux, Cabernet Sauvignon cannot always ripen, so the soft, mellow character of Merlot is a fundamental component of the blend, even in the best Cabernet-dominated Médoc estates, imparting a supple richness and approachability to the wines. Go-ahead areas like Blaye and Castillon depend on it.

Other European regions The south of France has briskly adopted the variety, producing easy-drinking, fruit-driven wines, but in the hot Languedoc the grape often ripens too fast to express its full personality and can seem a little simple, even raw-edged, unless handled well. Italy has long used very high-crop Merlot to produce light quaffers in the north, particularly in the Veneto, though today Friuli and Alto Adige make fuller styles. There are some impressive examples from Tuscany, and it can be found as far south as Sicily. The Swiss canton of Ticino is often unjustly overlooked for its intensely fruity, oak-aged versions. Eastern Europe has the potential to provide fertile pastures for Merlot: so far the most convincing, juicy styles have come from Croatia, Hungary and Bulgaria; the younger examples are almost invariably better than the old. In Spain, Merlot only really succeeds in cool sites.

New World Youth is also important in the New World, nowhere more so than in Chile. Chilean Merlot, often blended with Carmenère, has leapt to the front of the pack of New World examples with gorgeous garnet-red wines of unbelievable crunchy-fruit richness that cry out to be drunk virtually in their infancy. California Merlots often have more serious pretensions, but the nature of the grape is such that its soft, juicy quality still shines through. Cooler sites in Washington State have produced some impressive wines, and the east coast of the US has good examples from places such as Long Island. In South Africa, Merlot on the right sites is showing improvement, and in New Zealand the warm, dry conditions of Hawkes Bay and Waiheke Island are producing classic styles. Australia seems to find Merlot problematic (winemakers believe things will improve as better clones become more widespread), but there are some fine exceptions from cooler areas, including some surprisingly good fizzes – red fizzes, that is!

BEST PRODUCERS

France

Bordeaux (St-Émilion) ANGÉLUS, BEAU-SÉJOUR BÉCOT, CANON, Clos Fourtet, La Mondotte, PAVIE, PAVIE-MACQUIN, TERTRE-RÔTEBOEUF, TROPLONG-MONDOT, VALANDRAUD; *(Pomerol)* le BON PASTEUR, Clinet, la CONSEILLANTE, l'ÉGLISE-CLINET, l'ÉVANGILE, la FLEUR-PÉTRUS, GAZIN, Hosanna, LATOUR-À-POMEROL, PETRUS, le PIN, TROTANOY.

Other European Merlots

Italy (Friuli) Livio FELLUGA; *(Tuscany)* Castello di Ama (l'Apparita), Castelgiocondo (Lamaione), Le MACCHIOLE (Messorio), ORNELLAIA (Masseto), Petrolo, San Giusto a Rentennano, Tua Rita (Redigaffi); *(Lazio)* FALESCO; *(Sicily)* PLANETA.

Spain (Vino de la Tierra de Castilla) Pago del Ama.

Switzerland Brivio, Daniel Huber, Stucky, Tamborini, Christian Zündel.

New World Merlots

USA (California) Arrowood, BERINGER, Buccella, Chateau St Jean, MERRYVALE, NEWTON, Pahlmeyer, SHAFER; *(Washington)* ANDREW WILL, LEONETTI, LONG SHADOWS (Pedestal), WOODWARD CANYON; *(New York)* BEDELL, LENZ, SHINN ESTATE, WOLFFER.

Australia BRAND'S, COLDSTREAM HILLS, Elderton, Fermoy Estate, Irvine, PARKER COONAWARRA ESTATE, TAPANAPPA, Tatachilla, YALUMBA (Heggies).

New Zealand CRAGGY RANGE, Esk Valley, FROMM, C J PASK, Sacred Hill (Broken Stone), TRINITY HILL, VILLA MARIA.

South Africa Bein, Eagles' Nest, Laibach, Shannon, THELEMA, VERGELEGEN.

Chile CARMEN, CASABLANCA (Nimbus Estate), CONCHA Y TORO, CONO SUR (20 Barrels), Gillmore, LAPOSTOLLE (Cuvée Alexandre).

215

MICHIGAN *USA* If you think of Michigan's Lower Peninsula as the palm of your right hand, then the tip of your pinky finger is prime wine country. Here one finds the Leelanau and Old Mission peninsulas, which are shielded from the worst effects of the northern climate by Lake Michigan. Look for cool-climate *vinifera* varieties such as Riesling, Pinot Blanc and Gewurztraminer, as well as hybrids developed especially for harsh northern winters (Frontenac, Marquette). The Lake Michigan Shore area in southwestern Michigan also produces noteworthy wines. Best producers: Black Star Farms, Chateau Grand Traverse, Left Foot Charley, L Mawby.

MILLTON *Gisborne, North Island, New Zealand* Biodynamic vineyard whose top wines include the powerful Clos de Ste Anne Chardonnay★, lush Riverpoint Viognier★, Opou Vineyard Riesling★ and complex barrel-fermented Chenin Blanc★★. Chardonnays and Rieslings both age well. Deliciously savoury Syrah★★ and good, gentle Pinot Noir★. Excellent Clos Samuel sweet Viognier★★. Best years: (whites) 2013 **10 09 07**.

MINER FAMILY *Oakville AVA, California, USA* Dave Miner has 32ha (80 acres) planted on a ranch 300m (1000ft) above the OAKVILLE valley floor. Highlights include yeasty, full-bodied Chardonnay★ (Oakville Ranch★★, Wild Yeast★★) as well as intense Merlot★★ and Cabernet Sauvignon★★ that demand a decade of aging. Also a stylish Viognier★★ and a striking Rosé★ from purchased fruit.

MINERVOIS AC *Languedoc, France* Attractive, mostly red wines from north-east of Carcassonne, made mainly from Syrah, Carignan and Grenache. The local co-ops produce good, juicy, quaffing wine, but the best wines are made by the estates: full of ripe, red fruit and pine-dust perfume, for drinking young. It can age, especially if a little new oak has been used. The cru of La Livinière can be particularly scented and fine. Overripening, however, is a concern. Best producers: (reds) Aires Hautes★, Ch. Bonhomme★, Borie de Maurel★, CLOS CENTEILLES★, la Croix Martelle, Pierre Cros★, Fabas★, la Grave, Maris, Massamier la Mignarde, Oupia, Oustal Blanc★, Primo Palatum, Pujol, St-Jacques d'Albas, Ste-Eulalie★, Senat★, TOUR BOISEE★, Villermbert-Julien★. Best years: (2013) 12 **11 10** 09 08 07 06 05.

CH. LA MISSION HAUT-BRION★★★ *Pessac-Léognan AC, Cru Classé de Graves, Bordeaux, France* In the past I have often found the wine long on power but short on grace, but when the owners laid on a tasting reaching way back into the 1920s and the general quality level was majestic, with the vintages since 1990 actually outshining the admittedly beautiful earlier wines, I finally accepted La Mission's true brilliance. Muscularity and richness combined with depth and fragrance is quite a challenge, but La Mission meets it triumphantly. Best years: (reds) 2012 11 10 09 08 **07 06 05 04 03 02 01 00 98 96 95 94 90 89 88**; (whites) **2012 11 10 09** (formerly LAVILLE-HAUT-BRION).

MISSION HILL *Okanagan Valley VQA, British Columbia, Canada* Kiwi winemaker John Simes – with consultant enologist Michel Rolland – crafts a range of noteworthy wines. Excellent Perpetua Chardonnay★★, SLC Sauvignon Blanc★ and Reserve Pinot Blanc★; reds include BORDEAUX-style blend Oculus★★, Martin's Lane Pinot Noir★★, SLC Merlot★ and Reserve Cabernet Sauvignon and Shiraz★.

MITTELRHEIN *Germany* Small (460ha/1135-acre) wine region, adjoining the RHEINGAU. Seventy percent of the wine is Riesling, but the vineyard area is shrinking as the sites are steep and difficult to work. The best growers (such as Toni JOST★, Müller★★, Ratzenberger★ and Weingart★★), clustered around Bacharach and Boppard, make wines of a striking mineral tang and dry, fruity intensity. Best years: (2013) 12 11 **10 09 08 07.**

MOËT & CHANDON *Champagne AC, Champagne, France* Owned by LVMH, Moët & Chandon dominates the CHAMPAGNE market (more than 25 million bottles a year), and has become a major producer of sparkling wine in California, Argentina, Brazil and Australia too. China is next. Non-vintage is becoming more consistent and has been good in magnum for some time. The vintage rosé★★ can show a rare Pinot Noir floral fragrance. The de luxe cuvée, Dom Pérignon★★★, can be one of the greatest Champagnes of all, but you've got to age it for a number of years after release or you're wasting your money; but, of course, most of the people who drink it have a different view of money to you or me. Best years: 2006 04 **03 02** 00 99 98 96 95 90 88 86 85 82.

MARKUS MOLITOR *Bernkastel-Wehlen, Mosel, Germany* Dynamic estate with fine vineyards throughout Middle MOSEL. Brilliant Riesling Auslesen, often ★★★, and probably the best, if costly, Spätburgunder (Pinot Noir)★ from the Mosel. Best years: (2013) 12 11 **10 09 08 07** 06 05 04.

MONBAZILLAC AOP *South-West France* BERGERAC's best-known sweet wine, nowadays vastly improved and seriously rivalling all but the best SAUTERNES at a fraction of the price. The best will age for 10 years and more. Best producers: l'ANCIENNE CURE★★, Bélingard (Blanche de Bosredon★), Grande Maison★★, Haut-Bernasse★, Haut-Montlong (Grande Cuvée), les Hauts de Caillevel★★, Pécoula, La Rayre, Theulet★, TIRECUL LA GRAVIÈRE★★★, VERDOTS★★. Best years: (2012) 11 **10 07** 06 05 03 00.

CH. MONBOUSQUET★ *St-Émilion Grand Cru AC, Grand Cru Classé, Bordeaux, France* Gérard Perse, owner of Ch. PAVIE, transformed this struggling estate into one of ST-ÉMILION's 'super-crus'. The reward was promotion to Grand Cru Classé in 2006. Rich, voluptuous and very expensive, the wine is drinkable from 3–4 years but will last much longer. Also a plush white Monbousquet★ (BORDEAUX AC). Best years: 2012 11 10 **09 08 07** 06 05 04 03 02 01 00.

ROBERT MONDAVI *Napa Valley, California, USA* A Californian institution, best known for regular Cabernet Sauvignon, Reserve Cabernet★ and dense, gravelly To Kalon★★ Cabernet. Regular★ and Reserve★★ Pinot Noir are velvety smooth, supple wines. Whites include Fumé Blanc★ (Sauvignon Blanc) and Chardonnay★ (Reserve★★). Now part of Constellation's Icon Estates portfolio; Mondavi's lower-priced 'lifestyle' lines, Private Selection and Woodbridge (from LODI in the Central Valley), are promoted separately. Best years: (Cabernet Sauvignon Reserve) **2010 09 08 07** 06 05 04 03 02 01 00 99 98 97 96.

MONSANTO *Chianti Classico DOCG, Tuscany, Italy* Sangiovese-based wines topped by the CHIANTI CLASSICO Riserva Il Poggio★★★, a traditional-style single-vineyard cru, remarkable for its discreet austerity and need of bottle age. Chianti Classico Riserva★★★ is equally excellent. Best years: (2011) (10) **09 08 07** 06 04 01 99.

MONTAGNE-ST-ÉMILION AC *Bordeaux, France* A ST-ÉMILION satellite with rather good red wines. The wines are normally ready to drink in 4 years but age quite well in their slightly earthy way. Best producers: Beauséjour★, Calon★, La Couronne, Croix Beauséjour★, Faizeau★, Gachon★, Haut Bonneau, Maison Blanche★, Montaiguillon★, Rocher Corbin★, Roudier, Teyssier, Vieux-Ch.-St-André★. Best years: **2012 10 09 08** 05.

MONTAGNY AC *Côte Chalonnaise, Burgundy, France* Wines from this CÔTE CHALONNAISE village can be rather lean, but are greatly improved now that some producers are giving their wines a touch of new oak. Generally best with 2–3 years' bottle age. **Best producers:** S Aladame★, BOUCHARD PÈRE ET FILS★, BUXY★, Davenay★, FAIVELEY, Louis LATOUR★, O LEFLAIVE★, A Roy★, J Vachet★. **Best years:** (2013) 12 11 10.

MONTANA See BRANCOTT.

MONTECUCCO DOC *Tuscany, Italy* Emerging source of fine Sangiovese-based wines in its own right, rather than simply as a source of fruit for its more famous neighbour BRUNELLO DI MONTALCINO, with whom it shares a similarity of style. The DOC also covers a Vermentino and a white blend. **Best producers:** (reds) Amiata★, Campinuovi★.

MONTEFALCO DOC *Umbria, Italy* Good Sangiovese-based Montefalco Rosso is outclassed by dense, enveloping Sagrantino di Montefalco DOCG (dry) and glorious sweet red Sagrantino Passito from dried grapes. **Best producers:** Adanti★, Antonelli★, Caprai★★ (25 Anni★★★), Colpetrone★, Fontecolle★, Milziade Antano★★, Perticaia★, Scacciadiavoli★. **Best years:** (Sagrantino) (2011) 10 09 **08 07 06 04 01 00 99 98.**

MONTEPULCIANO Grape grown mostly in eastern Italy (unconnected with TUSCANY's Sangiovese-based wine VINO NOBILE DI MONTEPULCIANO). In ABRUZZO, can produce deep-coloured, fleshy, brambly, spicy wines with moderate tannin and acidity, which also helps to keep the rosé wines (called Cerasuolo) fresh. Besides Montepulciano d'Abruzzo DOC (with subzone COLLINE TERAMANE), it is used in CONERO DOCG and ROSSO PICENO DOC in the MARCHE and also in UMBRIA, Molise and PUGLIA. **Best producers:** (Montepulciano d'Abruzzo) Cataldi Madonna★, Contesa★★, Cornacchia★, Filomusi Guelfi★, Illuminati★★, Marramiero★★, Masciarelli★, Montori★, Emidio Pepe★★, Umani Ronchi★, La Valentina★, VALENTINI★★★. **Best years:** (2011) 10 **09 07 06 04 01.**

MONTEREY COUNTY *California, USA* Large CENTRAL COAST county south of San Francisco, including the Salinas Valley, boasting a mix of small estates and vast plantations. The most important AVAs are Monterey, Arroyo Seco, Chalone, Carmel Valley and Santa Lucia Highlands. Best grapes are Chardonnay, Riesling and Pinot Blanc, with some good Cabernet Sauvignon and Merlot in Carmel Valley and superb Pinot Noir in the Santa Lucia Highlands. **Best producers:** Belle Glos★★, Bernardus★★, Capiaux★, Chalone★, Estancia★, Jekel★, Joullian★★, Mer Soleil★, MORGAN★★, Roar★, TALBOTT★★, Testarossa★, Ventana★★.

MONTES *Colchagua, Chile* One of Chile's pioneering wineries in the modern era, notable for development of top-quality vineyard land on the steep Apalta slopes of COLCHAGUA and the virgin country of Marchíhue out toward the Pacific. Chardonnay★ (Alpha★★) and Sauvignon Blanc★ (Leyda★★) are tasty and fruit-led; all the reds are more austere and need bottle age. Cabernet-based Montes Alpha M★★ is consistently good and newly released top-of-the-range Taita★★ blend is promising (and set records as Chile's most expensive wine). Other impressive reds are Montes Alpha Syrah★★, Montes Folly★★ and a vibrant, scented Carmenère called Purple Angel★★. The Outer Limits range includes Sauvignon Blanc★★ and Pinot Noir★ from cool-climate Zapallar on the ACONCAGUA coast, Outer Limits CGM (Carignan-Grenache-Mourvèdre) from Apalta in Colchagua and Cinsault★★ from Itata.

MONTEVERTINE *Tuscany, Italy* Based in the heart of CHIANTI CLASSICO, Montevertine is famous for its non-DOC wines, particularly Le Pergole Torte★★★. This was among the first of the so-called 'super-Tuscans' made solely with Sangiovese, and it remains one of the best. A little Canaiolo is included in the fine Montevertine Riserva★★. Best years: (Le Pergole Torte) (2011) 10 **09 08 07 06 04 01 00 99 97 95**.

MONTHELIE AC *Côte de Beaune, Burgundy, France* Mainly red wine village lying behind MEURSAULT and VOLNAY on the CÔTE DE BEAUNE. The wines generally have a lovely cherry fruit and make pleasant drinking at a good price. Best producers: BOUCHARD PÈRE ET FILS, COCHE-DURY★, Darviot-Perrin★, Florent Garaudet★, R Jobard★, LAFON★★, G ROULOT★★, de Suremain★. Best years: (reds) (2013) 12 11 **10 09 07 06 05**.

MONTILLA-MORILES DO *Andalucía, Spain* Sherry-style wines that used to be sold almost entirely as lower-priced sherry substitutes. However, the wines *can* be superb, particularly the top dry amontillado, oloroso and rich Pedro Ximénez styles. Best producers: Alvear★★, Aragón, Gracia Hermanos, Pérez Barquero★★, Toro Albalá★★.

DOM. DE MONTILLE *Côte de Beaune, Burgundy, France* Consistently stylish VOLNAY (Champans★★, Taillepieds★★), POMMARD (Pezerolles★★, Rugiens★★) and BEAUNE (Grèves★), which demand aging. From 2005 brilliant VOSNE-ROMANÉE Malconsorts★★★. Also top PULIGNY-MONTRACHET Le Cailleret★★★. Expensive. *Négociant* business called Deux Montille★. Best years: (reds) (2013) 12 11 10 09 **08 07** 05 **03 02 99 96 90**.

MONTLOUIS-SUR-LOIRE AC *Loire Valley, France* On the opposite bank of the Loire to VOUVRAY, Montlouis makes similar styles (dry, medium, sweet and traditional-method fizz). New blood is injecting a healthy dose of ambition. Non-dosage gently sparkling *pétillant originel* wines are well worth seeking out. Still wines ideally need 3–5 years, particularly the sweet *moelleux*. Best producers: Alex-Mathur★, L Chanson, L Chatenay★, F CHIDAINE★★, L & B Jousset★, des Liards★/Berger, Le Rocher des Violettes★, F Saumon★, Taille aux Loups★★/BLOT. Best years: (sec) (2013) **12 11 10 08 07**; (moelleux) **2011 09 05 04 03 02 01 99 97 96**.

MONTRACHET AC *Côte de Beaune, Burgundy, France* This world-famous Grand Cru straddles the boundary between the villages of CHASSAGNE-MONTRACHET and PULIGNY-MONTRACHET. Wines have a unique combination of concentration, finesse and perfume: white Burgundy at its most sublime. Chevalier-Montrachet, immediately above it on

the slope, yields slightly leaner wine that is less explosive in its youth, but good examples become ever more fascinating with age. Best producers: BOUCHARD★★★, M COLIN★★★, DROUHIN (Laguiche)★★★, LAFON★★★, Louis LATOUR★★, Dom. LEFLAIVE★★★, LEROY★★★, Prieur★★★, RAMONET★★★, Dom. de la ROMANÉE-CONTI★★★, SAUZET★★, Thénard★★. Best years: (2013) 12 11 10 09 08 07 **06** 05 **04 02 00 99 95 92 90 89**.

MONTRAVEL AOP *South-West France* Adjoining Bordeaux, the wines here have something of the same style: crisp and dry whites, medium-sweet from Côtes de Montravel AOP and ultra-sweet from Haut-Montravel AOP. Montravel reds are in a modern oak-aged style, while less ambitious reds are sold as BERGERAC or Côtes de Bergerac. Best producers: du Bloy★★, Jonc Blanc★★, Laulerie, Libarde, Mallevieille, Masburel★, Moulin

Caresse★, Pique-Sègue, Puy-Servain★★, le Raz. Best years: (sweet) 2012 11 10 09 07 05 04 03 00; (red) (2012) (11) 10 **09 08 06 05 04 02**.

CH. MONTROSE★★ *St-Estèphe AC, 2ème Cru Classé, Haut-Médoc, Bordeaux, France* Leading ST-ESTÈPHE property, once famous for dark, brooding wine that would take around 30 years to reach its prime. Montrose has now returned to a powerful style, though softer than before. Recent vintages have been extremely good, with heroic 2005 and 2009 (both ★★★). Sold in 2006; lots of investment and greater precision in the wines. Second wine: la Dame de Montrose. Best years: 2012 11 10 09 08 **07** 06 05 04 03 02 01 00 98 96.

CH. MONTUS *Madiran AOP, South-West France* Alain Brumont clings to a precarious lead in MADIRAN, largely because of his media flair, his keen ambition and his ability to dodge all manner of financial disasters. His all-Tannat, hefty oak-aged reds Montus (Prestige★★) and Bouscassé (Vieilles Vignes★★) have white counterparts: PACHERENC DU VIC-BILH★★, dry and in varying degrees of sweetness. Best years: (red) (2012) (11) 10 09 **07** 06 05 04 02 01 00; (sweet white) (2012) 11 **10** 09 07 06 05.

MORELLINO DI SCANSANO DOCG *Tuscany, Italy* Morellino is the local name for Sangiovese in south-west TUSCANY. The wines, traditionally agreeable gluggers, are becoming more serious under DOCG, not necessarily to their advantage. Best producers: E Banti★, Belguardo★, Cecchi★, Lohsa★/POLIZIANO, Il Macereto★, Mantellassi★, Massi di Mandorlaia★, Morellino di Scansano co-op★, Moris Farms★★, Podere 414★, Poggio Argentiera★★, Le Pupille★★. Best years: **2012** 11 10 09 08 07 06 04 01 00.

MOREY *Chassagne-Montrachet, Côte de Beaune, Burgundy, France* Albert, Bernard, Jean-Marc, Marc, Michel Morey-Coffinet, Thomas and Vincent – how do you sort them out? Try CHASSAGNE-MONTRACHET Premiers Crus Baudines (Thomas), Embrazées (Vincent), Chenevottes (Jean-Marc) or Virondot (Marc), all ★★. There's also Pierre Morey for excellent MEURSAULT★★ and Pierre-Yves COLIN-Morey.

MOREY-ST-DENIS AC *Côte de Nuits, Burgundy, France* Morey has 5 Grands Crus (CLOS DES LAMBRAYS, CLOS DE LA ROCHE, CLOS ST-DENIS, CLOS DE TART and a share of BONNES-MARES) as well as some very good Premiers Crus. Basic village wine is sometimes unexciting, but from a quality grower the wine has good fruit and acquires an attractive depth as it ages. A tiny amount of startling nutty white wine is also made, especially Premier Cru Monts Luisants. Best producers: Pierre Amiot★, Arlaud★★, Dom. des Beaumont★, Castagnier★, CLAIR★★, David Clark★(until 2012), DUJAC★★★, A Jeanniard★★, Dom. des Lambrays★★, H Lignier★★★, Lignier-Michelot★★, H Perrot-Minot★, Ponsot★★, ROUMIER★★, Sérafin★★, Taupenot-Merme★★. Best years: (2013) 12 11 10 09 08 07 06 05 03 02 00 99 98 96 90.

MORGAN *Monterey County AVA, California, USA* This Santa Lucia Highlands pioneer specializes in Pinot Noir and Chardonnay. The single-vineyard Pinots from the Double L★★, Rosella's★★ and Garys'★★ vineyards combine ripe fruit, structure and elegance. Also a fresh, appealing unoaked Chardonnay called Metallico★. Best years: (Pinot Noir) 2012 10 09 08 07 06 05 04.

MORGON AC *Beaujolais, Burgundy, France* The longest-lasting of BEAUJOLAIS Crus, wines that – at their best – have delightful cherry fruit and the structure to age. Named sub-zones like Côte du Py and Javernières are considered to be the source of many of the best Morgons. There are, however, many more Morgons, made in a commercial style for early drinking, which are nothing more than a pleasant, fruity – and pricey –

drink. Best producers: J-P Brun/Terres Dorées★, G Descombes★, D Desvignes★, L-C Desvignes (Côte du Py★★, Voûte St Vincent★), DUBOEUF (Jean Descombes★), J Foillard★★, M Lapierre★★. Best years: (2013) 11 10.

MORNINGTON PENINSULA *Victoria, Australia* Exciting cool-climate maritime region dotted with small vineyards. Chardonnay runs the gamut from honeyed to leafy, but increasing numbers are oatmealy, minerally and scented; Pinot Noir can be very stylish in warm years, especially from vineyards in the cooler Red Hill subzones. Best producers: Crittenden★, Dexter, Eldridge, Hurley★, KOOYONG★★, Main Ridge★★, Montalto★, Moorooduc★★, Ocean Eight★, Paradigm Hill★, PARINGA ESTATE★★, Port Phillip Estate★, Quealy, Scorpo, Stonier★★, TEN MINUTES BY TRACTOR★★, T'Gallant★, Tuck's Ridge, Willow Creek★, YABBY LAKE★★. Best years: (Pinot Noir) 2013 12 10 09 08 07 06 05 04 03 02 01 00 99 98 97 95.

MORRIS *Rutherglen, Victoria, Australia* Historic winery with outstanding fortified wines. David Morris is the custodian of a store of aged fortifieds that have been with his family since 1859. Old favourites include Liqueur Muscat★★ and Tokay★★ (Old Premium★★★), 'ports' and 'sherries'.

DENIS MORTET *Gevrey-Chambertin, Côte de Nuits, Burgundy, France* Before his untimely death in 2006, Denis Mortet had built a brilliant reputation for his GEVREY-CHAMBERTIN (various cuvées, all ★★★) and tiny amounts of CHAMBERTIN★★★. Early vintages are deep coloured and powerful; recent years show increased finesse, a trend being continued by his talented son Arnaud. Best years: (2013) 12 11 10 09 **08 07 06** 05 **03 02 96 95 93**.

MORTON ESTATE *Marlborough, Hawkes Bay, Bay of Plenty, Auckland, New Zealand* Founded in 1983, this is one of the country's larger wineries, making wine from all major regions. Top-of-the-line Black Label wines can be very good and include a full-bodied Chardonnay★★ and Merlot-Cabernet★ from HAWKES BAY, plus a stylish MARLBOROUGH Sauvignon Blanc★ and a rich, complex, vintage-dated sparkling wine. White Label wines offer excellent value, particularly Chardonnay and Pinot Gris★. Best years: (Chardonnay) (2013) 10 **09 07 06**.

GEORG MOSBACHER *Forst, Pfalz, Germany* This 20ha (50-acre) estate makes mostly dry white wines in FORST. Best of all are the dry Rieslings★★ from the Forster Ungeheuer site, which are among the lushest in Germany. Delicious young, but worth cellaring. Best years: (2013) 12 11 **10 09 08 07 06 05**.

MOSCATO D'ASTI DOCG *Piedmont, Italy* Delicately scented, gently bubbling wine, made from Moscato Bianco grapes grown in the hills between Acqui Terme, Asti and Alba in north-west Italy. The DOCG is the same as for ASTI, but only select grapes go into this wine, which is frizzante (semi-sparkling) rather than fully sparkling. Drink while they're bubbling with youthful fragrance. Best producers: Araldica/Alasia★, Ascheri★, Bera★★, Braida★, Cascina Castlèt★, Cascina Fonda★, Cascina Pian d'Or★, La Caudrina★★, Cerutti★, Michele Chiarlo, Giuseppe Contratto★, Coppo★, Forteto della Luja★, Bruno GIACOSA★★, Icardi★, Marenco★, Beppe Marino★, La Morandina★, Marco Negri★, Perrone★★, Saracco★★, Scagliola★, La Spinetta★★, I Vignaioli di Santo Stefano★, Gianni Voerzio★.

MOSCATO PASSITO DI PANTELLERIA DOC *Sicily, Italy* Powerful dessert wine made from the Muscat of Alexandria, or Zibibbo, grape. Pantelleria is a small island south-west of SICILY, closer to Africa than it is to Italy. The grapes are picked in mid-August and laid out in the hot sun to shrivel for a couple of weeks. They are then crushed and fermented to give an amber-coloured, intensely flavoured sweet Muscat. Drink within

5–7 years. Best producers: Benanti★, D'Ancona★, DE BARTOLI★★, Donnafugata (Ben Ryé★), Murana★, Nuova Agricoltura co-op★, Pellegrino.

MOSEL *Germany* A collection of vineyard areas on the Mosel and its tributaries, the Saar and the Ruwer, amounting to 8,765ha (21,660 acres). The Mosel river rises in the French Vosges before forming the border between Germany and Luxembourg. In its first German incarnation in the Upper Mosel, the light, tart Elbling grape holds sway, but with the Middle Mosel begins a series of villages responsible for some of the world's very best Riesling wines: LEIWEN, TRITTENHEIM, PIESPORT, BRAUNEBERG, BERNKASTEL, GRAACH, WEHLEN, ÜRZIG and ERDEN. The wines have tremendous slatiness and an ability to blend the greenness of citrus leaves and fruits with the golden warmth of honey. Great wines are rarer between Erden and Koblenz, although WINNINGEN and Pünderich are islands of excellence. The Saar can produce wonderful, piercing wines in villages such as Serrig, Ayl, Ockfen and Wiltingen. Ruwer wines are slightly softer yet equally long-lived; the estates of MAXIMIN GRÜNHAUS and KARTHÄUSERHOF are world class. Since 2007 only the name 'Mosel' is permitted on labels in place of the region's former name Mosel-Saar-Ruwer.

MOSHIN VINEYARDS *Russian River Valley, California, USA* Retired mathematics professor Rick Moshin has a strong, almost cultish, following for his brilliant Pinot Noirs★★ and a handful of other wines (Zinfandel★, Petite Sirah★, Merlot★) made in small quantities. Best years: (Pinot Noir) **2010** 09 08 07 06 05 04 03.

MOSS WOOD *Margaret River, Western Australia* Seminal MARGARET RIVER winery. From its home vineyard comes heavenly scented Cabernet★★★ needing at least 5 years to blossom, classy Chardonnay★★, pale, fragrant Pinot Noir★ and crisp, fruity but ageworthy Semillon★★. Excellent Ribbon Vale★★ wines come from a nearby single vineyard. There's also very good Cabernet-based Amy's★. Best years: (Cabernet) (2013) 11 10 09 08 07 05 04 03 01 00 99 98 96 95 94 91 90 85.

J P MOUEIX *Bordeaux, France* The Moueix family runs a thriving merchant business specializing in the wines of the Right Bank, particularly POMEROL and ST-ÉMILION. Generally high quality. Also owns PÉTRUS, la FLEUR-PÉTRUS, BELAIR-MONANGE, LATOUR-À-POMEROL, TROTANOY, Hosanna and others.

MOULIN-À-VENT AC *Beaujolais, Burgundy, France* Potentially the greatest of the BEAUJOLAIS Crus – so long as you want your Beaujolais to be dark and powerful – which takes its name from an ancient windmill that stands above Romanèche-Thorins. The granitic soil yields a majestic wine that with time can transform into a rich Burgundian style more characteristic of the Pinot Noir than the Gamay. Best producers: J-P Brun/Terres Dorées, DUBOEUF, Ch. des Jacques★/JADOT, L Lardy (Thorins), Thibault LIGER-BELAIR (Vieilles Vignes★★), Ch. du Moulin à Vent★ (Champ de Cour★★), Richard Rottiers (Climat Champ de Cour★), La Tour du Bief★/V GIRARDIN. Best years (2013) 11 10.

MOULIS AC *Haut-Médoc, Bordeaux, France* Small AC within the HAUT-MÉDOC. Much of the wine is excellent – delicious at 5–6 years old, though good examples can age 10–20 years – and not overpriced. Best producers: Anthonic, Biston-Brillette★, Branas-Grand-Poujeaux★, Brillette★, CHASSE-SPLEEN★, Duplessis, Dutruch-Grand-Poujeaux, Gressier-Grand-Poujeaux, MAUCAILLOU★, Moulin-à-Vent, POUJEAUX★. Best years: 2012 11 10 **09 08 06 05** 03 02 01 00.

MOUNT HORROCKS *Clare Valley, South Australia* Stephanie Toole has transformed this label into one of the CLARE VALLEY's best, with minerally, limy yet gentle Riesling★★ from a single vineyard in Watervale; waxy, cedary Semillon★★; complex, savoury Shiraz★; velvety-textured Cabernet★ with a pure core of blackcurrant; and one of Australia's most delicious stickies (dessert wine), the Cordon Cut Riesling★★, which shows zingy fruit character with a satisfying lush texture.

MOUNT LANGI GHIRAN *Grampians, Victoria, Australia* Quintessential cool-climate Shiraz★★★ with remarkable dark plum, blackberry, chocolate and pepper spice and perfumes of eucalyptus and violet. Dark, intriguing Cabernet Sauvignon★★, delightful Riesling★ and honeyed Pinot Gris★. Less expensive Cliff Edge★ and Billi Billi★. Best years: (Shiraz) (2013) 12 10 09 08 07 **06 05 04 03 99 98 97 96 95 94** 93.

MOUNT MARY *Yarra Valley, Victoria, Australia* Classic YARRA VALLEY property, using only estate-grown grapes. Dry white Triolet★★ is blended from Sauvignon, Semillon and Muscadelle; red Quintet★★ (★★★ for keen Francophiles), from Cabernet Sauvignon and Franc, Merlot, Malbec and Petit Verdot, ages beautifully. The Pinot Noir★★ is equally as good. Best years: (Quintet) (2013) 12 10 08 07 **06 05 03 01 00 99 98 97 96 95 94 93 92** 91 90 88 86.

MOUNT VEEDER AVA *Napa Valley, California, USA* Small south-west NAPA AVA with impressive, rough-hewn Cabernet Sauvignon and Zinfandel, frequently from mountainside vineyards. Best producers: Chateau Potelle★, Robert Craig★★, Hess Collection★★, Lagier Meredith★★, Lokoya★★, Mayacamas Vineyards★, Mount Veeder Winery★, Rubissow★★. Best years: (Cabernet) **2010 09 08 07 06 05 04 02 01**.

MOURVÈDRE The variety originated in Spain, where it is called Monastrell. It dominates the JUMILLA DO and also Alicante, Bullas and Yecla. It needs lots of sunshine to ripen, which is why it performs well on the Mediterranean coast of France at BANDOL. It is increasingly important as a source of body and tarry, pine-needle flavour in the wines of CHÂTEAUNEUF-DU-PAPE, GIGONDAS and parts of LANGUEDOC-ROUSSILLON. It is making quite a reputation in CALIFORNIA (J Lohr Gesture and Villicana in PASO ROBLES) and Australia – where it is sometimes known as Mataro and can develop a tremendous black fruit and licorice richness (Caillard, HEWITSON, SPINIFEX, Teusner) – and is also starting to make its presence felt in South Africa and Chile. Best producers: (Spain) Bernabé Navarro, Rafael Cambra, Castaño, Casa Castillo, Los Frailes, Juan Gil, Enrique Mendoza, El Nido, Bruno Prats, El Sequé.

MOUTON-CADET *Bordeaux AC, Bordeaux, France* The most widely sold red BORDEAUX in the world was created by Baron Philippe de Rothschild in the 1930s. Blended from the entire Bordeaux region, the wine has always been undistinguished – well, I once had a rather good 1966 – and never cheap, but I have to admit quality is on the up. Also a bright breezy white, rosé, and Réserve GRAVES, MÉDOC, ST-ÉMILION and SAUTERNES.

CH. MOUTON-ROTHSCHILD★★★ *Pauillac AC, 1er Cru Classé, Haut-Médoc, Bordeaux, France* Baron Philippe de Rothschild died in 1988, having raised Mouton from a run-down Second Growth to its promotion to First Growth in 1973, and a reputation as one of the greatest wines in the world. It can still be the most magnificently opulent of the great MÉDOC reds, but inexcusable inconsistency frequently made me want to downgrade it. Recent vintages (since 2004) have been back on top form. When young, it is rich and indulgent on the palate, aging after 15–20 years to a complex bouquet of blackcurrant and cigar box. There is also a white wine, Aile d'Argent. Second wine: Le Petit Mouton. Best years: (red) 2012 11 10 09 08 **07** 06 **05** 04 03 02 01 00 99 98 97 96 95 90.

MUDGEE *New South Wales, Australia* Small region neighbouring HUNTER VALLEY, with a higher altitude and marginally cooler temperatures. Carefully-sited new plantings are giving it a fresh lease of life and producers are beginning to make the best use of very good fruit. Best producers: Abercorn, Farmer's Daughter, Logan, Lowe Family, Miramar, Oatley★, Robert Stein★.

MUGA *Rioja DOCa, Rioja, Spain* Traditional family winery making high quality, rich red RIOJA★ (Gran Reserva Prado Enea★★★). It is the only bodega in Rioja where every step of red winemaking is still carried out in oak containers. The modern Torre Muga Reserva★★ marks a major stylistic change. Top cuvée is Aro★★. Whites★★ are excellent and rosés★ are good. Best years: (Torre Muga Reserva) (2010) 09 **06** 05 04 03 0₁ 99 98 96 95.

MUGNERET *Vosne-Romanée, Côte de Nuits, Burgundy, France* Distinguished family winery in VOSNE-ROMANÉE, led by the sisters at Mugneret-Gibourg: great ECHÉZEAUX★★★, Ruchottes-CHAMBERTIN★★ and various NUITS cuvées, especially les Chaignots★★. Then there's Gérard Mugneret and cousin Denis Mugneret, both sound producers with bright and juicy reds. Best years (M-Gibourg): (2013) 12 11 10 09 08 **07** 06 05 03 02 99.

J-F MUGNIER *Chambolle-Musigny, Côte de Nuits, Burgundy, France* Frédéric Mugnier produces beautifully crafted wines at the Ch. de Chambolle-Musigny, especially les Amoureuses★★ and Grand Cru MUSIGNY★★★. In 2004 the 9ha (23-acre) NUITS-ST-GEORGES Clos de la Maréchale★★ vineyard came back under his control; now delivering very stylish wines; a small section has been grafted over to white wine production. Best years: (2013) 12 11 10 09 08 **07** 06 05 02 01 00 99 98 96 93 90.

MULDERBOSCH *Stellenbosch WO, South Africa* New owner Charles Bank (former owner of California cult winery SCREAMING EAGLE) has hired winemaker Adam Mason, ex-KLEIN CONSTANTIA. Various Chenin Blancs – notably 3 single-vineyard wines, all ★★, and oak-brushed, concentrated Steen op Hout★★. Sauvignon Blanc★ is now enriched with Semillon; new barrel-fermented Blanc Fumé★★ has delicious crunchy blackcurrant/passionfruit character. Chardonnay (regular★, barrel fermented★) is following a classic, drier style. Faithful Hound★ red BORDEAUX-style blend is well-structured but recently more supple. Cabernet Sauvignon Rosé accounts for half the total production. Best years: (barrel-fermented Chardonnay) 2013 **12 11 10** 09 08 07 06 05 04 03.

MÜLLER-CATOIR *Neustadt-Haardt, Pfalz, Germany* This PFALZ producer makes wine of a piercing fruit flavour and powerful structure rarely surpassed in Germany, including Riesling, Scheurebe, Rieslaner, Gewürztraminer, Muskateller and Pinot Noir – all ★★. BA and TBA are invariably ★★★. Best years: (2013) 12 11 **10** 09 08 **07** 06 05 04 02.

EGON MÜLLER-SCHARZHOF *Scharzhofberg, Mosel, Germany* Some of the world's most exquisite – and most expensive – sweet Rieslings are this perfectionist estate's Auslese, Beerenauslese, Trockenbeerenauslese and Eiswein: all usually ★★★. Regular Kabinett and Spätlese wines are pricey but classic. Best years: (2013) (12) 11 10 09 **08 07 06 05 04 03 02 01 99**.

MULLINEUX *Swartland WO, South Africa* Chris and Andrea Mullineux are a South African/American husband-and-wife team, founder-members of the SWARTLAND Independent. The Schist Syrah★★ (sometimes ★★★), rich and structured, and fresh, expressive Granite Syrah★★ (sometimes ★★★) really do reflect their different soils; the restrained, elegant Syrah★★ is a blend of both. A Schist Chenin★★, from 35-year old vines, is understated yet focused. Intense, honeyed Straw Wine★★ is also from Chenin, and exciting White★★ is Chenin based.

G H MUMM *Champagne AC, Champagne, France* Mumm's non-vintage brand, Cordon Rouge, disappointing in the 1990s, has improved. Elegant de luxe Cuvée R Lalou★ and traditionally excellent Blanc de Blancs Mumm de Cramant★ have been joined by fine Blanc de Noirs Mumm de Verzenay★. Best years: 2006 **04 02 99 98 96 95 90 89 88 85 82**.

MUMM NAPA *Napa Valley AVA, California, US* The California offshoot of Champagne house MUMM has always made good bubbly, and after a slight dip is now back on form. Brut Prestige★ is a fair drink; Brut Rosé★ is better than most pink Champagnes. Elegant vintage-dated Blanc de Blancs★★ and flagship DVX★★. Part of Pernod Ricard.

RENÉ MURÉ *Alsace AC, Alsace, France* The pride and joy of this domaine's fine vineyards is the Clos St-Landelin, a parcel within the Grand Cru Vorbourg. The Clos is the source of lush, concentrated wines, with particularly fine Riesling★★ and Pinot Gris★★. The Muscat Vendange Tardive★★ is rare and remarkable, as is the opulent old-vine Sylvaner Cuvée Oscar★. The Vendange Tardive★★ and Sélection de Grains Nobles★★★ wines are among the best in Alsace. Best years: (Clos St-Landelin Riesling) (2013) (12) 11 10 09 08 07 06 05 04 02 01.

ANDREW MURRAY VINEYARDS *Santa Barbara County, California, USA* Working with RHÔNE varieties, Andrew Murray has created an impressive array of wines. Rich, aromatic Viognier★ and Roussanne★★ whites, as well as several Syrahs (Roasted Slope★★, Hillside Reserve★★). Espérance★ is a spicy blend patterned after a serious CÔTES DU RHÔNE. Best years: (Syrah) (2012) **10 09 08 07 06 05 04 03 02**.

MUSCADET AC *Loire Valley, France* AC for the region around Nantes in north-west France; the simplest wines are best drunk young and fresh as an apéritif or with the local seafood. Wines from 3 better-quality zones (Muscadet Coteaux de la Loire, Muscadet Côtes de Grand-Lieu and Muscadet Sèvre-et-Maine) are typically labelled *sur lie*. They must be matured on the lees for a maximum of 12 months and show greater depth of flavour and more fruit. The new *crus communaux* are from vineyards planted in some of the region's best soils (granite, gneiss, quartz, sandstone and schist), but are not permitted to use a 'sur lie' label, despite a minimum of 17 months' lees aging. The rich flavours of aged styles can partner white meats as well as fish and shellfish. Best producers: Bonhomme★, Bonnet-Huteau★, de la Chauvinière/J Huchet★, Chéreau-Carré★ (Chasseloir, l'Oiselinière), Choblet/Herbauges★, Clisson, Coing de St Fiacre, Bruno Cormerais★, Dorices★, l'Ecu★, Gadais★, Jacques Guindon★, Landrons★, LUNEAU-PAPIN★, Metaireau★, le Pallet, la Pépière, RAGOTIÈRE★, Sauvion★, la Touche★. Best years: (sur lie) 2013 11 **10 08 07**.

225

MUSCAT

It's strange, but there's hardly a wine grape in the world which makes wine that actually tastes of the grape itself. Yet there's one variety that is so joyously, exultantly grapy that it more than makes up for all the others – the Muscat, generally thought to be the original wine vine. In fact, there seem to be about 200 different branches of the Muscat family worldwide, but the noblest of these and the one that always makes the most exciting wine is called Muscat Blanc à Petits Grains (the Muscat with the small berries). These berries can be crunchily green, golden yellow, pink or even brown – as a result Muscat has a large number of synonyms. The wines they make may be pale and dry, rich and golden, sparkling or still, subtly aromatic or as dark and sweet as treacle.

WINE STYLES

France Muscat is grown from the far north-east right down to the Spanish border, yet is rarely accorded great respect in France. This is a pity, because the dry, light, hauntingly grapy Muscats of Alsace are some of France's most delicately beautiful wines. It pops up sporadically in the Rhône Valley, especially in the sparkling wine enclave of Die. Mixed with Clairette, the Clairette de Die Tradition is a fragrant, grapy, honest fizz that deserves to be better known. Muscat de Beaumes-de-Venise is a delicious manifestation of the grape, this time fortified, musky and sweet. Its success has encouraged the traditional fortified winemakers of Languedoc-Roussillon to make fresher, more perfumed wines as well as unfortified late-harvest wines and, especially around Rivesaltes, dry vins de pays/IGPs. Some aromatic off-dry aperitif styles in Provence.

Italy Various types of Muscat are grown in Italy. In the north-west, especially Piedmont, Moscato Bianco/Moscato di Canelli makes the fragrantly sweet sparklers called Asti or (less bubbly) Moscato d'Asti; the same grape makes Tuscany's Moscadello di Montalcino. Orange Muscat (Moscato Giallo/Goldmuskateller) is used in the north-east for making passito-style dessert (or occasionally dry) wines, while Muscat of Alexandria prevails in the south, especially in relation to the great passitos of Pantelleria. Italy also has red varieties: Moscato Nero for rare sweet wines in Lazio, Lombardy and Piedmont; Moscato Rosa/Rosenmuskateller for delicately sweet wines in Trentino-Alto Adige and Friuli-Venezia Giulia.

Other regions Elsewhere in Europe, Muscat is a component of some Tokajis in Hungary, Crimea has shown how good it can be in the Massandra fortified wines, and the rich golden Muscats of Samos and Patras are among Greece's finest wines. As Muskateller in Austria and Germany, it makes primarily dry, subtly aromatic wines. In Spain, Moscatel de Valencia is sweet, light and great value, Moscatel de Gran Menudo is on the resurgence in Navarra and Castilla-La Mancha and i has also been introduced in Mallorca. The little-known, old, solera-aged Moscatels from Jerez can be sensational. Portugal's Moscatel de Setúba is also wonderfully rich and complex. California grows Muscat, ofte calling it Muscat Canelli (and the Muscat category is one of the fastest growing in the US), but South Africa and Australia make better use of i With darker berries, and called Muscadel in South Africa and Brow Muscat in Australia, it makes some of the world's sweetest and mo luscious fortified wines, especially in the north-east Victoria regions of Rutherglen and Glenrowan in Australia.

BEST PRODUCERS

Sparkling Muscat
France (*Clairette de Die*) Achard-Vincent, Clairette de Die co-op, Poulet & Fils, Jean-Claude Raspail.

Italy (*Asti*) G Contratto, Gancia; (*Moscato d'Asti*) Bera, Braida, Cascina Fonda, La Caudrina, Perrone, Saracco, La Spinetta, Gianni Voerzio.

Brazil Courmayeur, Monte Paschoal, Salton.

Dry Muscat
Austria (*Muskateller*) Gross, POLZ, Sattlerhof, TEMENT.

France (*Alsace*) J-M Bernhard, Dirler-Cadé, Kientzler, Kuentz-Bas, OSTERTAG, Rolly Gassmann, SCHOFFIT, Bruno Sorg, TRIMBACH, WEINBACH, ZIND-HUMBRECHT.

Germany (*Muskateller*) BERCHER, Dr HEGER, HUBER, MÜLLER-CATOIR, REBHOLZ.

Spain (*Alicante*) Bocopa co-op; (*Jumilla*) Juan Gil; (*Málaga*) Jorge Ordóñez; (*Penedès*) TORRES (Viña Esmeralda).

Italy (*Goldmuskateller*) LAGEDER.

Sweet Muscat
Australia (*Liqueur Muscat*) All Saints, Baileys of Glenrowan, BROWN BROTHERS, Buller, Campbells, CHAMBERS, John Kosovich, MCWILLIAM'S, MORRIS, Pfeiffer, Seppeltsfield, Stanton & Killeen, Talijancich, YALUMBA.

Austria KRACHER, Opitz, H TSCHIDA.

France (*Alsace*) Ernest Burn, René MURÉ, Rolly Gassmann, SCHOFFIT; (*Beaumes-de-Venise*) Bernardins, Durban, Paul JABOULET, Pigeade; (*Frontignan*) la Peyrade; (*Rivesaltes*) CAZES, Jau.

Greece SAMOS co-op.

Italy (*Goldmuskateller*) Viticoltori Caldaro, Thurnhof; (*Moscato Passito di Pantelleria*) DE BARTOLI, Murana.

Portugal (*Moscatel de Setúbal*) BACALHÔA, J M da FONSECA.

South Africa KLEIN CONSTANTIA.

Spain (*Alicante*) Gutiérrez de la Vega, Enrique Mendoza, Primitivo Quiles; (*Jerez*) VALDESPINO; (*Jumilla*) Silvano García; (*Navarra*) Camilo Castilla, CHIVITE; (*Sierras de Málaga*) Jorge Ordóñez, Telmo RODRÍGUEZ; (*Valencia*) Gandía.

227

MUSCAT OF ALEXANDRIA This grape rarely shines in its own right but performs a useful job worldwide, adding sultry perfume and fleshy fruit to what would otherwise be dull, neutral white wines. It is common for sweet and fortified wines throughout the Mediterranean basin (in Sicily it is called Zibibbo) and in South Africa (where it is also known as Hanepoot), as well as being a fruity, perfumed bulk producer there and in Australia, where it is also known as Gordo Blanco or Lexia.

MUSCAT DE BEAUMES-DE-VENISE AC *Rhône Valley, France* *Vin doux naturel* (fortified) from the southern Rhône. Irresistible grapy perfume and bright honeyed fruit plus a little spirit bite when young – perfect as an aperitif wine. Becomes very rich and concentrated when aged, for example Bernardins and Durban. Best producers: Beaumalric★, Beaumes-de-Venise co-op★, Bernardins★★, DELAS★, Durban★★, Fenouillet★, Pau JABOULET★★, La Ligière, Pigeade★★, VIDAL-FLEURY★.

MUSCAT DE FRONTIGNAN AC *Languedoc, France* Muscat *vin doux naturel* on the Mediterranean coast. Quite impressive but can be a bit cloying. Muscat de Mireval AC, a little further inland, can have a touch more acid freshness and quite an alcoholic kick. Also Muscat de Lunel further east. Best producers: (Frontignan) Mas Rouge, la Peyrade★, Stony; (Lunel) Mas des Pigeonniers, Moulinas; (Mireval) Rencontre.

MUSCAT DE LUNEL, MUSCAT DE MIREVAL See MUSCAT DE FRONTIGNAN

MUSCAT DE RIVESALTES AC *Roussillon, France* Made from both Muscat Blanc à Petits Grains and Muscat of Alexandria, the wine can be very good from go-ahead producers who keep the aromatic skins in the juice for longer periods to gain extra perfume and fruit. Most delicious when young. Best producers: Baixas co-op (Dom. Brial★, Ch. les Pins★), CASENOVE★, CAZES★★, Chênes★, Corneilla, Fontanel★, Força Réal★, l'Heritier, Jau★ Laporte★, de Nouvelles★, Piquemal★, des Vents.

MUSCAT DE ST-JEAN-DE-MINERVOIS AC *Languedoc, France* AC in the remote Minervois hills for fortified Muscat. Less cloying, more tangerine and floral than some Muscats from the plains. Best producers: Barroubio, Clos Bagatelle, Clos du Gravillas, Vignerons de Septimanie.

MUSIGNY AC *Grand Cru, Côte de Nuits, Burgundy, France* One of a handful of truly great Grands Crus, combining power with an exceptional depth of fruit and lacy elegance – an iron fist in a velvet glove. Best producers: DROUHIN★★★, JADOT★★★, Dom. LEROY★★★, J-F MUGNIER★★★, J Prieur★★, ROUMIER★★★, VOGÜÉ★★★, VOUGERAIE★★★. Best years: (2013) 11 10 09 08 07 06 05 **03 02 01 00** 99 98 96 95 93 90.

Joseph Drouhin

PROPRIÉTÉ DE LA FAMILLE DROUHIN

MUSIGNY
GRAND CRU

NAHE *Germany* 4172ha (10,300-acre) wine region named after the River Nahe, which joins the Rhine by BINGEN, opposite RÜDESHEIM in the RHEINGAU. The Rieslings from this geologically complex region are often among Germany's best. The finest vineyards are those of Niederhausen and SCHLOSSBÖCKELHEIM, as well as Dorsheim and Münster in the lower Nahe. Stylistically, the wines fall midway between the Mosel and the Rheingau.

CH. NAIRAC★★ *Barsac AC, 2ème Cru Classé, Bordeaux, France* An established name in BARSAC which, by dint of enormous effort, produces a sweet wine sometimes on a par with the First Growths. The influence of aging new oak casks, adding spice and even a little tannin, means this can age for 10–15 years. Best years: 2011 **10 09 07 06 05 04 03 02 01 99 98 97**.

NALLE *Dry Creek Valley AVA, California, USA* This family-owned winery specializes in juicy, spicy, berryish Zinfandels★★ with refreshingly low alcohol levels. The wines are delicious when young, but they can improve with age. Best years: 2012 **10 09 08 07 06 05**.

NAPA VALLEY AVA *California, USA* An AVA that covers virtually all the wines made in Napa County and one that is strenuously promoted as California's premier wine region by a highly efficient trade organization, the Napa Valley Vintners. Sub-AVAs have been and are being created. There are a significant number that, over a generation or so, have proved that their wines do have a particular personality; among them, I'd include CARNEROS, STAGS LEAP, HOWELL MOUNTAIN, Diamond Mountain, SPRING MOUNTAIN, MOUNT VEEDER, OAKVILLE and RUTHERFORD. See also pages 230–1.

NAVARRA DO *Navarra, Spain* Vineyards planted to Cabernet Sauvignon, Merlot, Tempranillo, Garnacha, Chardonnay and Moscatel (Muscat), producing juicy reds, barrel-fermented whites and modern sweet Muscats, but quality is haphazard. Best producers: Artazu★, Azul y Garanza★, Camino del Villar★, Camilo Castilla (Capricho de Goya Muscat★★), CHIVITE★ (Arínzano★★), Iñaki Núñez★, Inurrieta★, Lezaun★, Lupier★★, Castillo de Monjardín, Nekeas co-op★, Ochoa, Señorío de Sarria, Emilio Valerio★★. Best years: 2011 **10 09 08 07 06 05 04 03 01**.

NAVARRO VINEYARDS *Anderson Valley AVA, California, USA* Small, family-owned producer of sensational Gewürztraminer★★★, Pinot Gris★★, Riesling★★, Dry Muscat★★ and late-harvest Riesling★★★, perfectly balanced Pinot Noir★★ and a dozen other stellar wines.

NEBBIOLO The grape variety responsible for the majestic wines of BAROLO and BARBARESCO. Its name may derive from the Italian for fog, *nebbia*, because it ripens late when the hills are shrouded in autumn mists. It needs a thick skin to withstand this fog, so often gives very tannic wines that need years to soften. When grown in the limestone soils of the Langhe hills around Alba, Nebbiolo produces wines that are only moderately deep in colour but have a wonderful array of perfumes and an ability to develop great complexity with age. The variety is used for NEBBIOLO D'ALBA and ROERO, and for barrique-aged blends, often with Barbera and/or Cabernet, sold under the LANGHE DOC. Nebbiolo is also the principal grape for reds of Carema DOC on the VALLE D'AOSTA border as well as of northern PIEDMONT's GATTINARA and Ghemme, where it is called Spanna. In LOMBARDY it is known as Chiavennasca and is used in the Valtellina DOC and VALTELLINA SUPERIORE DOCG wines. Outside Italy, rare examples are made in Australia (S C PANNELL is outstanding; Arrivo, Joseph/PRIMO ESTATE, Longview, Luke Lambert, Pizzini, Solita, Tar & Roses and Thick as Thieves are very good), California, Virginia (BARBOURSVILLE and Breaux), Brazil, Argentina and South Africa.

NEBBIOLO D'ALBA DOC *Piedmont, Italy* 100% Nebbiolo wine from vines grown in the hills around Alba, excluding the BAROLO and BARBARESCO zones; aged for 12 months before release. Style varies between the fruitier wines from the ROERO and the more earthy examples from elsewhere. Best producers: Alario★, Brezza★★, Bricco Maiolica★, Brovia★★, Burlotto★★, Cascina Chicco★, Ceretto★, Correggia★, GIACOSA★★, Pio Cesare★, Renato Ratti★, Sandrone★, Vietti★. Best years: (2012) **11 10 09 08 07 06 04**.

NAPA VALLEY

California, USA

From the earliest days of California wine, and through all its ups and downs, the Napa Valley has been the standard-bearer for the whole industry and the driving force behind quality and progress. The magical Napa name – derived from an Indian word for plenty – applies to the fertile valley itself, the county in which it is found and the AVA for the overall area, but the region is so viticulturally diverse that the appellation is virtually meaningless.

The valley was first settled by immigrants in the 1830s, and by the late 19th century Napa, and in particular the area around the communities of Rutherford and Oakville, had gained a reputation for exciting Cabernet Sauvignon. Despite the long, dark years of Prohibition, this reputation survived and when the US interest in wine revived during the 1970s, Napa was ready to lead the charge.

GRAPE VARIETIES

Most of the classic French grapes are grown, but Cabernet is the one that sells best and is most widely recognized. In Napa, Cabernet is king, and Napa's strongest reputation is for varietal Cabernet and Bordeaux-style (or meritage) blends, usually Cabernet-Merlot. Pinot Noir and Chardonnay, for both still and sparkling wines, do best in the south, from Yountville down to Carneros. Zinfandel is grown mostly at the north end of the valley. Syrah, Viognier, Sangiovese and Malbec are relatively new here.

SUB-REGIONS

The most significant vine-growing area is the valley floor running from Calistoga in the north down to Carneros, below which the Napa River flows out into San Pablo Bay. It has been said that there are more soil types in Napa than in the whole of France, but much of the soil in the valley is heavy, clayish, over-fertile, difficult to drain and really not fit to make great wine. Some of the best vineyards are tucked into the mountain slopes at the valley sides or in selected spots at higher altitudes.

There is as much as a 10°C temperature difference between torrid Calistoga and Carneros at the mouth of the valley, cooled by Pacific fog and a benchmark for US Pinot Noir and cool-climate Chardonnay. A dozen or more major sub-areas have been identified along the valley floor and in the mountains, although there is much debate over how many have a real claim to individuality. Rutherford, Oakville and Yountville in the mid-valley produce Cabernet redolent of dust, dried sage and ultra-ripe blackcurrants. A bit to the north the St Helena AVA produces more elegant wines, capable of long aging. Softer flavours come from Stags Leap to the east. The higher-altitude vineyards of Diamond Mountain, Spring Mountain and Mount Veeder along the Mayacamas mountain range to the west produce deep Cabernets, while Howell Mountain in the north-east also has stunning Zinfandel and Merlot.

See also CARNEROS AVA, HOWELL MOUNTAIN AVA, MOUNT VEEDER AVA, NAPA VALLEY AVA, OAKVILLE AVA, RUTHERFORD AVA, SPRING MOUNTAIN AVA, STAGS LEAP DISTRICT AVA; and individual producers.

**2012 10 09 08 07 06 05 04
01 99 95 94 91 90**

BEST PRODUCERS

**Cabernet Sauvignon and
meritage blends**

Altamura, Anderson's Conn Valley, ARAUJO, Barnett (Rattlesnake Hill), Bennett Lane, BERINGER, Bryant Family, Buccella, Burgess Cellars, Cafaro, Cain, CAKEBREAD, CAYMUS, Chappellet, CHATEAU MONTELENA, Chateau Potelle (VGS), CHIMNEY ROCK, CLIFF LEDE, Clos Pegase, CLOS DU VAL, Colgin, COPPOLA (Rubicon), CORISON, Cosentino, Robert Craig, DALLA VALLE, Darioush, Del Dotto, DIAMOND CREEK, DOMINUS, Dunn, Eisele, Elyse, Envy, Far Niente, FLORA SPRINGS, Forman, Freemark Abbey, FROG'S LEAP, Grace Family, Groth, HARLAN ESTATE, HARTWELL, HEITZ, Honig, Jarvis, Jones Family, Leo Joseph, Krupp Brothers, Ladera, La Jota, KONGSGAARD, Lang & Reed, Lewis Cellars, Livingston Moffett, Lokoya, LONG MEADOW RANCH, Long Vineyards, Markham, Louis M MARTINI, Mayacamas Vineyards, MERRYVALE, Peter MICHAEL, MINER, MONDAVI, Monticello, Mount Veeder Winery, NEWTON, Oakville Ranch, OPUS ONE, O'Shaughnessy, Pahlmeyer, Palladian, Paradigm, Robert Pecota, PHELPS, PINE RIDGE, Pride, QUINTESSA, Raymond, Rubissow, Rudd Estate, Saddleback, St Clement, ST SUPÉRY, SCREAMING EAGLE, Seavey, SHAFER, SILVER OAK, SILVERADO, SPOTTSWOODE, Staglin Family, STAG'S LEAP WINE CELLARS, Sterling, Swanson, Terra Valentine, The Terraces, Titus, Turnbull, VIADER, Villa Mt Eden, Vine Cliff, Vineyard 29, Von Strasser, Whitehall Lane, ZD.

NEGROAMARO Together with Primitivo, Negroamaro is one of PUGLIA's most important black grapes, indigenous to the heel-like Salento peninsula, responsible for the increasingly good Salento Rosato (rosé) as well as stony SALICE SALENTINO DOC and other red wines.

NELSON *South Island, New Zealand* Nelson is made up of small hills and valleys with a wide range of mesoclimates, separated from MARLBOROUGH by mountains at the northern end of South Island. Pinot Noir, Chardonnay, Riesling and Sauvignon Blanc do well. Best producers: Brightwater★, Greenhough★★, Himmelsfeld, Kina Beach, NEUDORF★★★, Rimu Grove★, Seifried★, Waimea★, Woollaston★. Best years: (whites) (2013) **12 11 10 09 07**.

NERELLO MASCALESE Along with 'cousin' Nerello Cappuccio, it is responsible for Sicily's ETNA ROSSO DOC. It is grown at 400–1000m (1300–3300ft) above sea level on the north- and east-facing rich lava slopes of Mount Etna.

NERO D'AVOLA SICILY's great red grape is now planted all over the island. Its deep colour, high sugars and acidity make it useful for blending, especially with the lower-acid Nerello Mascalese, but also with Cabernet, Merlot and Syrah. On its own, and from the right soils, it can be brilliant, with a soft, ripe, spicy blackberry and damson character. Examples range from simple quaffers to many of Sicily's top reds. Some now in Australia.

NEUCHÂTEL *Switzerland* Swiss canton with 600ha (1480 acres) of high-altitude vineyards, mainly Chasselas whites and Pinot Noir reds and rosé. Best producers: Ch. d'Auvernier, Chambleau, Châtenay-Bouvier, Gerber.

NEUDORF *Nelson, South Island, New Zealand* Some of New Zealand's most stylish wines, including gorgeous, creamily textured Chardonnay★★★, rich but scented Pinot Noir★★ (sometimes ★★★), Sauvignon Blanc★★, Riesling★★ and Pinot Gris★. Best years: (Chardonnay) (2013) **12 11 10 09 08 06 05**; (Pinot Noir) (2013) **12 10 09 07 06 05**.

NEW HALL *Essex, England* Planted in 1969, this is one of the UK's oldest vineyards and at 63ha (156 acres), one of the largest. Supplies many wineries with grapes, particularly Pinot Noir, and now starting to make its own decent wines, especially Bacchus★.

NEW SOUTH WALES *Australia* Australia's most populous state is responsible for about 29% of the country's grape production. The largest centres of production are the irrigated areas of RIVERINA, and Murray Darling, Swan Hill and Perricoota on the Murray River, where better viticultural and winemaking practices and lower yields have led to significant quality improvement. Smaller premium-quality regions include the old-established HUNTER VALLEY – which is undergoing a revival as younger winemakers appear on the scene – Cowra, higher-altitude MUDGEE and, especially, ORANGE and HILLTOPS. CANBERRA is an area of tiny vineyards and great potential at chilly altitudes, as is Tumbarumba at the base of the Snowy Mountains.

NEW YORK STATE *USA* Wine grapes were first planted on Manhattan Island in the mid-17th century, but it wasn't until the early 1950s that a serious wine industry began to develop in the state as *vinifera* grapes were planted to replace natives such as *Vitis labrusca*. Weather conditions, particularly in the north, can be challenging, but improved viticulture makes a good vintage possible in most years. The most important region is the FINGER LAKES in the north of the state, which is enjoying a surge of consumer interest in Riesling, but can also shine with other whites, and some reds. LONG ISLAND produces serious BORDEAUX-style reds and good Chardonnay. Hudson River Region has a couple of good producers and a few upstarts are producing noteworthy wines amid the ocean of plonk along the shores of Lake Erie.

NEWTON *Napa Valley AVA, California, USA* Spectacular winery and steep vineyards high above St Helena, owned by French luxury giant LVMH. Cabernet Sauvignon★★, Merlot★★ and Claret★ are some of California's most pleasurable examples. Even better is the challenging, intellectual, single-vineyard Cabernet Sauvignon-based The Puzzle★★★. Newton pioneered the unfiltered Chardonnay★★ style, but the cheaper Red Label Chardonnay★ is also very attractive. Best years: (Cabernet Sauvignon) 2012 **10 09 08 07 06 05 03 02 01 00 99 97 96 95 94.**

NEWTON JOHNSON *Upper Hemel-en-Aarde Valley WO, Walker Bay, South Africa* Family-owned winery specializing in Pinot Noir and Chardonnay. Well-structured yet supple Family Vineyards Pinot Noir★★ is a blend of 3 distinctive sites, which are also bottled individually (Windansea★★, Block 6★★, Mrs M★★). Family Vineyards Chardonnay★★ has classic restraint and precision. Equally characterful are Resonance★ (Sauvignon Blanc-Semillon) and Shiraz-based Full Stop Rock★. Best years (Family Vineyards Pinot Noir): **2013 12 11 10 09 08.**

NGATARAWA *Hawkes Bay, North Island, New Zealand* Increasingly impressive Chardonnay★★, botrytized Riesling★ and Merlot-Cabernet★ under the premium Alwyn label. The Glazebrook range includes attractive Chardonnay★ and Cabernet-Merlot★, both of which are best drunk within 5 years. Best years: (reds) (2013) **10 09 07 06.**

NIAGARA PENINSULA *Ontario, Canada* Sandwiched between lakes Erie and Ontario, the Niagara Peninsula benefits from regular breezes off Lake Ontario, buffered by the Niagara escarpment. Icewine, from Riesling and Vidal, is the showstopper, with international acclaim. Chardonnay and Riesling lead the dry whites, with promising reds from Pinot Noir, Merlot and Cabernet Franc. Best producers: 13th Street, Charles Baker, Cave Spring, Château des Charmes, Le CLOS JORDANNE★, Colaneri★, Coyote's Run, Creekside★, Fielding, Flat Rock★, HENRY OF PELHAM★, HIDDEN BENCH★, INNISKILLIN★, Lailey, Malivoire★, Pearl Morissette★, Ravine, Reif, Rosewood★, Southbrook★, Stratus★, TAWSE★★, THIRTY BENCH★, Vineland Estates★. Best years: (Icewine) **2010 09 08 07 05 04 03 02 00 99.**

NIEPOORT *Port DOC and Douro DOC, Douro, Portugal* Remarkable small wine and PORT producer of Dutch origin. Outstanding Vintage ports★★★, old tawnies★★★ and colheitas★★★. Complex, unfiltered LBVs★★ are among the best in their class. The Vintage port second label is Secundum★★. Niepoort also produces fine red, white and rosé DOURO Redoma★, white Tiara★★, and red Vertente★, Batuta★★★ and Charme★★. Best years: (Vintage) 2011 09 08 **07 05 03 00 97 94 92 91 87 85 82 80 77 70 66 63.**

NIERSTEIN *Rheinhessen, Germany* The name of both a small town and a large Bereich, which includes the infamous Grosslage Gutes Domtal. The top vineyard sites (Pettenthal, Brudersberg, Hipping, Oelberg and Orbel) are some of the best in the Rhine Valley. Best producers: Gunderloch★, Heyl zu Herrnsheim, Kühling-Gillot★★, St Antony★, Schätzel, Schneider, Seebrich. Best years: (2013) **12 11 10 09 08 07 05.**

NIGL *Senftenberg, Kremstal, Austria* Consistently fine and crystalline Riesling and Grüner Veltliner from this organic estate. Top vineyard is called Piri★ but each year Martin Nigl releases his best wines under the Privat★★ label. Best years: (2013) 12 11 **10 09 08 07 06**.

NIKOLAIHOF *Wachau, Niederösterreich, Austria* Biodynamic estate making some of the best wines in the WACHAU as well as in nearby Krems-Stein in KREMSTAL, including steely, intense Rieslings from the famous Steiner Hund vineyard, always ★★. Best years: (2013) 12 11 **10 09 08 07 06**.

DOM. DE NIZAS *Pézenas, Languedoc AC, France* Same ownership as NAPA-based CLOS DU VAL. Intense red PÉZENAS★ (Mourvèdre-Carignan-Grenache), a spicy red LANGUEDOC, and a white from Roussanne, Rolle (Vermentino) and a drop of Viognier. Entry-level Le Mazet de Sallèlles, both red and white. Best years: 2013 12 **11 10 09 08 07 06**.

NK'MIP *Okanagan Valley VQA, British Columbia, Canada* North America's first aboriginal-owned winery, situated in Canada's only desert, near the town of Osoyoos. Top-flight Syrah★★, Pinot Noir★ and Riesling Icewine★★.

NOBILO *Kumeu/Huapai, Auckland, North Island, New Zealand* Restrained Sauvignon Blanc and a vibrant Chardonnay★ from MARLBOROUGH, but most wines have a sweetish edge. Owns Selaks in AUCKLAND and Drylands in Marlborough (intense Sauvignon Blanc★, Chardonnay★, Riesling★). Best years: (Chardonnay) (2013) 12 **10 09 07**.

NOËLLAT *Côte de Nuits, Burgundy, France* None of this family's domaines in VOSNE-ROMANÉE were thrilling in the past, but Georges Noëllat – in the hands of Maxime Cheurlin since 2010 – is now stunning. Michel Noëllat less thrilling; okay but oaky. Down the road in VOUGEOT, Hudelot-Noëllat is also looking great these days, with fine, perfumed wines.

NOEMÍA *Patagonia, Argentina* The partnership between Noemi Cinzano (owner of Argiano in Tuscany) and famed winemaker Hans Vinding-Diers discovered these precious few hectares of near-derelict, ancient Malbec vineyards. Now one of the world's top Malbec producers. Noemía★★★ is elegant, complex, ageworthy – and expensive. Second wine J Alberto★★ is exceptional and its sibling, A Lisa★, is glorious on release. Vinding-Diers has also realized his dream of producing a 'Grand Vin' in the BORDEAUX tradition – layered, precise Noemía '2'★★ (a Cabernet-Merlot blend). Best years: (Noemía) 2011 10 09 08 07 **06** 04 01.

NORTON *Mendoza, Argentina* A Mendoza institution with an impressive range, reds outshining whites. Enjoyable everyday wines under the Norton Reserva label. Norton Privada★, a lush, chocolaty blend of Malbec, Cabernet and Merlot, has been consistently fine and good value. Finca Perdriel★ blend is dense with old-vine fruit, Quorum★ is a multi-vintage, multi-varietal red, and the icon wine, Gernot Langhes★, is from low-yielding old vines. Torrontés★ is best of the whites.

QUINTA DO NOVAL *Port DOC and Douro DOC, Douro, Portugal* Owned by AXA-Millésimes, this property is the source of extraordinary Quinta do Noval Nacional★★★, made from ungrafted vines – virtually unobtainable except at auction. Other Noval ports are excellent too (Quinta do Noval Vintage★★★, Silval★, Colheita★★, stunning 40-year-old tawny★★★). Also DOURO red, Quinta do Noval Tinto★★. Best years: (Nacional) 2011 **07 03 00 97 94 87 85 70 66 63 62 60 31**; (Vintage) 2011 08 **07 04 03 00 97 95 94 91 87 85 70 66 63 60 31**.

NUITS-ST-GEORGES AC *Côte de Nuits, Burgundy, France* This large AC is one of the few reliable 'village' names in Burgundy. Although it has no Grands Crus, many of its Premiers Crus (it has 38!) are extremely good. The red can be rather slow to open out, often needing at least 5 years, but it ages to a delicious, chocolaty, deep figs-and-prune fruit. Minuscule amounts of white are made by l'Arlot★, Chevillon, Henri Gouges★ and RION. Best producers: l'Arlot★, Arnoux-Lachaux★★, BELLENE★,

S CATHIARD★★, J Chauvenet★★, R Chevillon★★, J-J Confuron★★, FAIVELEY★★, H Gouges★, GRIVOT★★, Jayer-Gilles★★, Lechenaut★★, Comte LIGER-BELAIR★★, T LIGER-BELAIR★★, B Leroux★★, MEO-CAMUZET★★, A Michelot★, MUGNERET-Gibourg★★, J-F MUGNIER★★, Perrot-Minot★★, RION★★, VOUGERAIE★★. Best years: (reds) (2013) 12 11 10 09 **08 07 06** 05 03 02 99 98 96 95 90.

NYETIMBER *West Sussex, England* The UK's largest sparkling producer with 151ha (373 acres) planted on eight sites, including 58ha (143 acres) on chalk downland in Hampshire. They produce four wines: Classic Cuvée★★★, Blanc de Blancs★★, Rosé★★ and newcomer sweetish Demi-Sec. Poor weather meant that no grapes were harvested in 2012.

OAKRIDGE *Yarra Valley, Victoria, Australia* Outstanding boutique winery, showcasing the YARRA's strengths. Single-vineyard wines are the focus. The 864 range includes complex, oatmealy Chardonnay★★★, impressive Pinot Noir★★, lush, structured Cabernet-Merlot★★ and seamless Syrah★★. The Local Vineyard Series (Chardonnay★, Pinot Noir★, Shiraz★) and budget-priced Over the Shoulder range are excellent value.

OAKVILLE AVA *Napa Valley, California, USA* This region is cooler than RUTHERFORD, which lies immediately to the north. Planted primarily to Cabernet Sauvignon, the area contains some of NAPA's best vineyards, both on the valley floor (MONDAVI, OPUS ONE, Paradigm) and hillsides (DALLA VALLE, HARLAN ESTATE, Oakville Ranch), producing wines that display lush, ripe black fruits and firm tannins. Best years: (Cabernet Sauvignon) 2012 10 09 08 07 06 05 04 03 02 01 00 99 95 94 91 90.

OC, IGP DU PAYS D' *Languedoc-Roussillon, France* Important IGP/vin de pays covering LANGUEDOC-ROUSSILLON. Overproduction has not helped its reputation, but an increasing number of fine reds and whites show what can be done. Best producers: l'Aigle★, Gérard BERTRAND★, Clovallon (Viognier★), Condamine Bertrand, Croix de St-Jean, DENOIS★, J & F Lurton★, MAS LA CHEVALIÈRE, Laurent Miquel (Viognier★★), Ormesson★, Pech-Céleyran, Quatre Sous★.

DOM. OGEREAU *Coteaux du Layon AC, Loire Valley, France* Vincent Ogereau's wines are sybaritic in concentration and purity of fruit, especially COTEAUX DU LAYON Clos des Bonnes Blanches★★★. The modestly priced ANJOU-VILLAGES★ (Cabernet Franc) drinks young but develops beautifully over 15 years or more in great vintages. The leaner Côte la Houssaye Anjou-Villages★ (Cabernet Sauvignon) takes 5 years to blossom. Also Clos le Grand Beaupréau SAVENNIÈRES and Tutti Frutti, a botrytized Cabernet Sauvignon. Best years: (sweet) 2011 10 09 07 05 03 02 01 97 96 95 90 89.

OKANAGAN VALLEY *British Columbia, Canada* The most important wine region of British Columbia and first home of Canada's Icewine. The Okanagan Lake helps temper the bitterly cold nights, but October frosts can be a problem. Chardonnay, Pinot Blanc, Pinot Gris and Pinot Noir are the top performers. South of the lake, Cabernet, Merlot and Syrah are having some success in Canada's only desert. Adjacent Similkameen Valley has promising BORDEAUX blends and Syrah. Best producers: Blue Mountain★, Burrowing Owl★, CedarCreek★, Church & State★, INNISKILLIN,

JACKSON-TRIGGS★, Joie Farm★, LaStella★, Meyer Family★, MISSION HILL★, Moon Curser★, NK'MIP CELLARS★, Painted Rock★, Pentâge, Quails' Gate★, Sandhill, Sperling Vineyards★, SUMAC RIDGE★, Summerhill★, Le Vieux Pin★. Best years: (reds) 2011 **10 09 08**.

OLTREPÒ PAVESE DOC *Lombardy, Italy* Italy's main source of Pinot Nero, used mainly for sparkling wines, upgraded to DOCG when made by the traditional method. The DOC covers still or frothing reds from Barbera and Bonarda, Pinot Nero red or blanc de noir, and whites from Pinot Bianco, Pinot Grigio, Riesling and Chardonnay, among others. Best producers: Cà di Frara★, Le Fracce★, Frecciarossa★, Castello di Luzzano, Mazzolino★, Monsupello★, Montelio★, Vercesi del Castellazzo★, Bruno Verdi★. Best years: (2012) **11 10 09 08 07 06 04**.

OPUS ONE *Oakville AVA, California, USA* BORDEAUX-blend wine, a joint venture initially between Robert MONDAVI and Baron Philippe de Rothschild of MOUTON-ROTHSCHILD, now Constellation-owned. Most Opus bottlings have been in the ★★ range, some achieving ★★★, in a beautifully cedary, minty manner whose balance and elegance can be a delight in modern-day NAPA. Best years: (2012) **10 09 08 07 06 05 04 99 98 97 96 95 94 93 92**.

ORANGE *New South Wales, Australia* Relatively small, wonderfully picturesque vineyard region. Uniquely in Australia, it is defined by altitude: its grapes must be grown more than 600m (1900ft) above sea level. Sauvignon Blanc, Chardonnay, Viognier and Riesling are most impressive so far. Pinot Noir has made the most exciting reds, although Cabernet Sauvignon and Shiraz have enormous potential. Best producers: Angullong, Bloodwood★, Cumulus, Logan★, Printhie, Philip SHAW★, Word of Mouth.

DOM. ORATOIRE ST-MARTIN *Côtes du Rhône-Villages AC, Rhône Valley, France* Careful fruit selection in a mature, high-terraced vineyard is the secret of Frédéric and François Alary's intense CAIRANNE reds and whites. Haut-Coustias white★ has peach and spice aromas, while the red★★ is a luscious mouthful of raspberries, herbs, liquorice and spice. Top red Cuvée Prestige★★, from 100-year-old Grenache and Mourvèdre vines, is deep and intense, with dark, spicy fruit. Best years: (Cuvée Prestige) 2012 **11 10 09 07 06 05**.

OREGON *USA* Oregon shot to stardom in the early 1980s following some perhaps overly generous praise of its Pinot Noir, but it is only with the release of a succession of fine recent vintages and some soul-searching by the winemakers about what style they should be pursuing that we can now begin to accept that some of the hype was deserved. Consistency is still a problem, however, with surprisingly warm weather now offering challenges along with the traditional ones of overcast skies and unwelcome rain. Chardonnay is undergoing a revival and beginning to show exciting form. Pinot Gris can be surprisingly complex. Pinot Blanc and Riesling are gaining momentum. The WILLAMETTE VALLEY is considered the best growing region, with Eola-Amity Hills the coolest zone and Dundee Hills the most densely planted. The warmer Umpqua and Rogue Valleys can produce good Cabernet Sauvignon, Cabernet Franc and Merlot, along with Viognier, Albariño, Tempranillo and Syrah. Best producers: (Rogue, Umpqua) ABACELA★, Bridgeview, Cliff Creek, Cowhorn, Foris★, Henry Estate, Irvine★, Kriselle, Quady North, Valley View.

TENUTA DELL'ORNELLAIA *Bolgheri, Tuscany, Italy* This beautiful property is now owned by FRESCOBALDI-controlled Tenute di Toscana Ornellaia★★, a Cabernet-Merlot blend, doesn't quite have the class of neighbouring SASSICAIA, but it is more lush; Masseto★★★ (Merlot) is superb. Second wine: Le Serre Nuove di Ornellaia★. Best years: (Ornellaia) (2011) **10 09 08 07 06 05 04 03 01 00 99 98 97 96 95**.

ORTENAU *Baden, Germany* A chain of granitic hills south of Baden-Baden, which produce elegant, generally dry Rieslings, and fragrant, medium-bodied Spätburgunder (Pinot Noir) reds. Best producers: Franckenstein★, Laible★★, Nägelsförst, Schloss Neuweier★★, Wolff Metternich★.

ORVIETO DOC *Umbria, Italy* Traditionally a lightly sweet white wine made from a blend of grapes including Procanico (Trebbiano) and Umbria's native Grechetto, basic Orvieto is today usually dry. In the Classico zone, however, richer, more complex wines exist, especially in the Superiore category. Also some very good botrytis-affected sweet wines. Best producers: Barberani★ (dry Castagnolo★★, sweet Calcaia★★), La Carraia★, Decugnano dei Barbi★, Palazzone★ (dry Campo del Guardiano★, sweet Muffa Nobilis★★), Castello della Sala★, Salviano★, Conte Vaselli★, Le Velette★.

OSBORNE *Jerez y Manzanilla DO, Andalucia, Spain* Spain's biggest drinks company. Osborne's sherry arm in Puerto de Santa María specializes in light Fino Quinta★. Amontillado Coquinero★, intense Bailén Oloroso★★ and Solera India Oloroso★★ are very good. It acquired Amontillado 51-1A★★★, Sibarita★★ and Venerable★★ soleras from defunct Domecq. Also a large estate at Malpica de Tajo in CASTILLA-LA MANCHA.

DOM. OSTERTAG *Alsace AC, Alsace, France* A biodynamic estate whose output is 50% Riesling, but which is more remarkable for Pinot Gris and Pinot Noir. The former is made in a Burgundian mode, using new oak barriques. This was such anathema to Alsace that the authorities declassified their wines for their atypicality! The A360P Pinot Gris★★★ has 50% new oak, and is stylish and rich. Fronholz Pinot Noir★★ is fragrant and complex but also ageworthy and serious. Best years: (A360p Pinot Gris) (2013) (12) **11 10 09 08 07 05 04 02 01**.

OWEN ROE *Columbia Valley AVA, Washington State, USA* David O'Reilly produces a broad range of wines in Washington and Oregon. Cabernet Sauvignon DuBrul Vineyard★★ is dense and powerful; Cabernet Sauvignon Red Willow 1973 Block★★ is made with fruit from one of the oldest vineyards in Washington State. Three single-vineyard BORDEAUX-style red blends from YAKIMA VALLEY fruit – Union Gap Vineyard, Red Willow Vineyard★ and DuBrul Vineyard★. Expressive Syrahs (Chapel Block★★, Ex Umbris★) rank among the best in the state. Best years: (Cabernet Sauvignon) (2012) **11 10 09 08**.

PAARL WO *South Africa* A great diversity of soil and climate favour every-thing from Cap Classique sparkling wines to sherry styles, but the fact that Paarl was famous for sherry tells you that it's fairly hot, and it is now big reds that are setting the quality pace, especially Shiraz. Viognier, solo and in white blends, is also performing well. Wellington, previously a ward within Paarl, is now a district in its own right. Best producers: Boschendal, DISTELL (Nederburg★, Plaisir de Merle★), FAIRVIEW★★, GLEN CARLOU★, KWV (The Mentors★), Rupert & Rothschild★, Scali★, Veenwouden★, Vilafonté★; Vondeling★; (Wellington) Diemersfontein★, Mont du Toit★. Best years: (premium reds) 2011 **10 09 08 07 06 05 04 03**.

PACHERENC DU VIC-BILH AOP *South-West France* MADIRAN's white wines, ranging from dry to sweet late-harvest styles. Best producers: AYDIE★, Barréjat, BERTHOUMIEU★★, Brumont (Bouscassé★, MONTUS★★), Capmartin★★, du Crampilh★, Damiens★★, LABRANCHE-LAFFONT★★, Laffitte-Teston★★, PLAIMONT. Best years: (sweet) (2012) **11 10 09 07 06 05**.

PADTHAWAY *South Australia* This wine region has always been the alter ego of nearby COONAWARRA, growing whites to complement Coonawarra's reds: Chardonnay has been particularly successful. Nowadays there are some excellent reds: Orlando's premium Lawson's Shiraz★★ is 100% Padthaway; even GRANGE has included Padthaway grapes. Best producers: Browns of Padthaway, Henry's Drive, Orlando★★/JACOB'S CREEK, Padthaway Estate.

BRUNO PAILLARD *Champagne AC, Champagne, France* CHAMPAGNE house created in the late 20th century by hands-on Bruno Paillard. Non-vintage Première Cuvée★ is lemony and crisp; Réserve Privée★ is a blanc de blancs; vintage Brut★★ is a serious wine. De luxe cuvée N.P.U. (Nec Plus Ultra)★★ is a barrel-fermented blend of Grands Crus made in top vintages. Best years: 2004 02 99 96 95 90 89 88.

PAÍS Once the most planted grape in Chile, and probably the same as Argentina's Criolla Chica and California's Mission, this rustic variety is still used for table wine in BÍO BÍO and MAULE. Old, dry-farmed vines are being used for finer wines and Miguel TORRES does a good sparkling País rosé.

ALVARO PALACIOS *Priorat DOCa, Cataluña, Spain* Alvaro Palacios is one of the driving forces of PRIORAT's rebirth, with his boutique winery founded in the late 1980s. His red wines (super-expensive, highly concentrated L'Ermita★★★, Finca Dofí★★ Les Terrasses Vinyes Velles★★, Gratallops Vi de la Vila★★ and affordable Camins del Priorat★) from old Garnacha vines and a dollop of Cabernet Sauvignon, Merlot, Cariñena and Syrah have won a cult following. Best years: (2011) 10 09 08 07 06 05 04 03 01 00 99 98 97 96 95.

PALETTE AC *Provence, France* Tiny AC just east of Aix-en-Provence. Even though the local market pays high prices, I find the reds and rosés rather tough and charmless. However, Ch. Simone manages to achieve a white wine of some flavour. Best producers: Crémade, Ch. Simone★.

PALLISER ESTATE *Martinborough, North Island, New Zealand* Winery producing some of New Zealand's best Sauvignon Blanc★★, as well as Riesling★, delightful Chardonnay★★ and Pinot Gris★, and impressive, rich-textured Pinot Noir★★. Good Méthode Traditionelle★ fizz, and exciting botrytized dessert wines in favourable vintages. Pencarrow is the tasty second label. Best years: (Pinot Noir) (2013) 12 11 10 09 08 07 06.

CH. PALMER★★★ *Margaux AC, 3ème Cru Classé, Haut-Médoc, Bordeaux, France* One of the leading properties in MARGAUX AC. The wine is wonderfully perfumed, with irresistible plump fruit, and recent vintages have been some of the finest ever. The very best vintages can age for 30 years or more. Second wine: Alter Ego★ (usually an excellent, scented red). Best years: 2012 11 10 09 08 07 06 05 04 03 02 01 00 99 98 96 95 90 89 88 86.

S C PANNELL *McLaren Vale, South Australia* Steve Pannell enjoyed corporate success as BRL HARDYS' chief red wine maker. He started without vineyards or a winery but in November 2012 he purchased an idyllic, long-sought-after Blewitt Springs vineyard. Pannell specializes in MCLAREN VALE Shiraz and Grenache, and he has had equal success with ADELAIDE HILLS Sauvignon★ and Pinot Gris★. Lavishly concentrated Shiraz-Grenache★★ and complex Shiraz★★ show the restraint and rich yet elegant fruit that is becoming more common locally. Excellent Touriga Nacional and Tempranillo – and Nebbiolo★★ (from Adelaide Hills) that is some of the best you'll find outside BAROLO.

CH. PAPE-CLÉMENT *Pessac-Léognan AC, Cru Classé de Graves, Bordeaux, France*
The expensive red wine★ became more consistent during the 1990s with the introduction of a deeper, darker style of wine: impressive, but difficult to recognize as PESSAC-LÉOGNAN. Recent vintages are more aromatic, but still very oaky, and may blossom to ★★ with a decade of aging. Also a small amount of fine, aromatic white wine★★. Second wine: (red) Clémentin. Best years: (reds) 2012 11 10 09 08 07 06 05 04 03 02 01 00 99 98 96 95 90; (white) 2012 11 10 09 08 07 06 05 04.

PARINGA ESTATE *Mornington Peninsula, Victoria, Australia* Teacher-turned-winemaker Lindsay McCall planted his suntrap site at Red Hill South in 1985. A rare Riesling★★ and excellent Estate Chardonnay★ are matched by Pinot Noir (entry-level Peninsula label, Estate★ and The Paringa★★), the best of which are ethereal with silky smooth texture, depth, power and finesse. Also multi-layered, intense, cool-climate Shiraz★★.

PARKER COONAWARRA ESTATE *Coonawarra, South Australia* The top label, cheekily named First Growth★★ (sometimes ★★★) in imitation of illustrious BORDEAUX reds, is regularly one of COONAWARRA's most impressively balanced yet profound reds. It is released only in better years. Second-label Terra Rossa Cabernet Sauvignon★ is lighter and leafier. Merlot★★ is among Australia's best. Best years: (First Growth) (2013) 12 11 08 07 06 05 04 01 99 98 96 93 91 90.

PASCUAL TOSO *Mendoza, Argentina* Californian consultant Paul Hobbs has transformed Toso into a leading Malbec producer. The rich Selected Vines Malbec★ and Cabernet★ set the house style. Alta Reserva Malbec★★ (also Syrah★) is concentrated and floral, inky deep Finca Pedregal★★ is magical, and top cuvée Magdalena Toso★★ is powerful, dense and long lived. Best years: (2012) 11 10 09 08 07 06 05.

C J PASK *Hawkes Bay, North Island, New Zealand* Chris Pask made the first wine in the now-famous Gimblett Gravels area of HAWKES BAY. Flagship Declaration label includes oaky Syrah★, rich Merlot, powerful Cabernet-Merlot-Malbec blend and classy Chardonnay★. Mid-range wines under the Gimblett Road label. Best years: (reds) (2013) 10 09 08 07 06.

PASO ROBLES AVA *California, USA* A large AVA at the northern end of SAN LUIS OBISPO COUNTY. Most famous for high-volume Cabernet and heady Zinfandel, there has been an influx of energetic, creative winemakers keen on Rhône varieties, led by the Perrin Brothers at TABLAS CREEK. The white and red Rhône varieties (Roussanne, Marsanne, Grenache, Syrah, Mourvèdre) are really proving their worth, along with old-timers like Petite

EBERLE

2006
PASO ROBLES
Côtes-du-Robles
RED WINE

Sirah and newcomers like Sangiovese, Tannat, Tempranillo, Aglianico, Vermentino and even Pinot Noir. Serious Bordeaux blends include Petit Verdot and Malbec. Expect fireworks. Best producers: Adelaida★, Alta Colina★, Ancient Peaks★, Clavo★, Clayhouse★, Cypher★, Daou★, Eberle★, Eos★, Four Vines★★, Halter Ranch★, Hearst Ranch★★, HOPE FAMILY★, Justin★★, J Lohr★, Minassian-Young★, Niner★, Peachy Canyon★★, TABLAS CREEK★★, Villicana★, Vina Robles★, Wild Horse★.

PASSIONATE WINE *Mendoza, Argentina* Matias Michelini leads a group of geniune mavericks in this new project that is causing a stir in Argentina. The MalBon★★ (Malbec-Bonarda) is beautifully rich and elegant, while the Demente★★ (Malbec-Cabernet Franc) is elegant and cedary. The

Via Revolucionaria (known in some markets as Inéditos) unfiltered Semillon 'Hulk'★ and Bonarda★ are very pure; red blend Montesco★ is delightful, Agua de Roca★★ Sauvignon Blanc is fresh and aromatic.

PATAGONIA *Argentina* Two main wine regions: Río Negro, with a 100-year history of wine production, and Neuquén, to the west. Both have extreme day/night temperature differences and relentless southerlies, resulting in deeply coloured, intense wines. Racy Pinot Noirs, graphite-edged Malbecs, pure, round Merlot and tasty sparkling wines. Also plantings in the Desierto project in La Pampa, north of Neuquén on the Colorado river, and in Chabut further south. Best producers: (Río Negro) Humberto Canale★, CHACRA★, FABRE MONTMAYOU★, NOEMÍA★★; (Neuquén) Fin del Mundo, NQN★, Familia Schroeder★, Universo Austral.

LUÍS PATO *Beiras, Portugal* Leading modernist, passionately convinced of the Baga grape's ability to make great reds on chalky-clay soil. Wines such as the Vinhas Velhas★, Vinha Barrosa★★, Vinha Pan★★ and the flagship Quinta do Ribeirinho Pé Franco★★ (from ungrafted vines) rank among Portugal's finest modern reds: some can reach ★★★ with age. Good white, Vinha Formal★, is 100% Bical. Also good fizz. Daughter Filipa makes delightful reds and whites under Nossa Calcário★★ and FP★ labels. Best years: (reds) (2012) 11 **09 05 04 03 01 00** 97 96 95 92.

PAUILLAC AC *Haut-Médoc, Bordeaux, France* The deep gravel banks around the town of Pauillac in the HAUT-MÉDOC are the heartland of Cabernet Sauvignon. For many wine lovers, the king of red wine grapes finds its ultimate expression in the 3 Pauillac First Growths (LATOUR, LAFITE-ROTHSCHILD and MOUTON-ROTHSCHILD). The large AC also contains 15 other Classed Growths. The uniting characteristic of Pauillac wines is their intense blackcurrant fruit flavour, pencil-shavings perfume and undertone of graphite. These are the longest-lived of BORDEAUX's great red wines. Best producers: Armailhac★, BATAILLEY★, Bellegrave, Clerc-Milon★, DUHART-MILON★, Fonbadet, GRAND-PUY-DUCASSE★★, GRAND-PUY-LACOSTE★★, HAUT-BAGES-LIBERAL★, HAUT-BATAILLEY★, LAFITE-ROTHSCHILD★★★, LATOUR★★★, LYNCH-BAGES★★★, Lynch-Moussas, MOUTON-ROTHSCHILD★★★, Pibran★, PICHON-LONGUEVILLE★★★, PICHON-LONGUEVILLE-LALANDE★★★, PONTET-CANET★★. Best years: 2012 11 10 09 08 **06 05 04 03 02 01 00 96 95 90** 89.

CH. PAVIE★★ *St-Émilion Grand Cru AC, 1er Grand Cru Classé, Bordeaux, France* Controversial style of wine – dense, rich, succulent – but there's no doubting the progress made since Gérard Perse acquired the property in 1998. So much so that (along with ANGÉLUS) it has now joined AUSONE and CHEVAL BLANC as a Premier Grand Cru Classé 'A' (2012 ST-ÉMILION classification). Best years: 2012 11 10 09 08 **07 06 05 04 03 02 01 00** 99.

CH. PAVIE-MACQUIN★★ *St-Émilion Grand Cru AC, 1er Grand Cru Classé, Bordeaux, France* This has become one of the stars of the ST-ÉMILION GRAND CRU since the 1990s, with promotion to Premier Grand Cru Classé in 2006. Rich, firm and reserved, the wines need 7–8 years and will age longer. Best years: 2012 11 10 09 08 **07 06 05 04 03 02 01 00** 99 98.

PÉCHARMANT AOP *Bergerac, South-West France* The iron-rich soil in this BERGERAC sub-appellation gives the wines their distinctive minerally style and aging qualities. Best producers: Bertranoux★, Chemins d'Orient★, Clos les Côtes★, Grand Jaure, Haut-Pécharmant★★, La Métairie★, Terre Vieille★, la Tilleraie, Tiregand★★. Best years: (2012) (11) 10 **09 06 05 04 01 00**.

PECORINO Relatively recently rescued from near-extinction, this is ABRUZZO's most fashionable white grape, capable (also in Le MARCHE) of making dry, generously alcoholic, punchy whites, likened to Viognier. Best producers: Cataldi Madonna★, Citra★, Contesa★★, Marramiero★, Montori★, Pasetti★, San Lorenzo★, Terra d'Aligi★, Tiberio★★, La Valentina★★.

PEGASUS BAY *Canterbury, South Island, New Zealand* Lush, mouthfilling Chardonnay★★, an almost chewy Pinot Noir★★ and its even richer big sister Prima Donna Pinot Noir★★ (can be ★★★), powerful, idiosyncratic Sauvignon Blanc-Semillon★★, all kinds of very stylish Riesling★★ (sometimes ★★★) and an occasional heavenly Gewurztraminer★★★. These are some of the most original wines in New Zealand, and all will age well. Best years: (Pinot Noir) (2013) (12) 11 09 08 07 06.

PEMBERTON *Western Australia* Exciting emergent humid but cool-climate region, deep in the Karri forests of the south-west. So far, white varieties have done best on the fertile soils, especially taut, tangy Sauvignon Blanc and thrilling, minerally Chardonnay. Occasional superb examples of Riesling, Viognier, Semillon, Pinot Grigio and Marsanne, as well as distinguished sparkling wine. Best of the reds so far is Pinot Noir, with good Shiraz in warm vintages, and occasional BORDEAUX blends. HOUGHTON leads the way with Wisdom range. Best producers: Bellarmine★, CHERUBINO★, HOUGHTON★★, Lillian, Pemberley★★, Picardy★, Salitage.

PENEDÈS DO *Cataluña, Spain* The booming CAVA industry is based in Penedès, and the majority of the still wines are white, made from the Cava trio of Parellada, Macabeo and Xarel-lo, clean and fresh when young, but seldom exciting, although the newfound interest in low-yield Xarel-lo opens new avenues. The reds are variable, the best made from Cabernet Sauvignon and/or Tempranillo and Merlot. Best producers: Albet i Noya★, Can Feixes★, Can Ràfols dels Caus★★, Cavas Hill, Colet★, Gramona★, Jané Ventura★, Jean León★, Marques de Monistrol, Masía Bach★, Albert Milá i Mallofré, Puig & Roca★, Raventós i Blanc★, Sot Lefriec★, TORRES★★, Vallformosa.

PENFOLDS *Barossa Valley, South Australia* The jewel in the crown for Treasury group, with a stellar reputation in the Chinese market. Penfolds makes the country's most famous red wine, GRANGE★★★, and other superb reds such as RWT Shiraz★★★, Magill Estate Shiraz★★, St Henri Shiraz★, Bin 707 Cabernet★★ (sometimes★★★), Bin 389 Cabernet-Shiraz★★, Bin 407 Cabernet, Bin 28 Kalimna Shiraz★ and Bin 128 Coonawarra Shiraz. A new addition to the luxury range, Bin 169 Coonawarra Cabernet is breathtakingly elegant. Cellar Reserve wines are difficult to find but outstanding, and occasional releases of Special Bin reds are among Australia's best. Whites are led by expensive but excellent Yattarna Chardonnay★★★, stunningly good Reserve Bin A Chardonnay★★★ and impressive cool-climate Bin 311 Chardonnay★★; there's also citrous Bin 51 Eden Valley Riesling★. Thomas Hyland Cabernet, Shiraz and Chardonnay are pretty good, but previously reliable wines like Koonunga Hill show a dispiriting blandness. Best years: (top reds) 2013 12 10 08 06 04 02 99 98 96 94 91 90.

PENÍNSULA DE SETÚBAL *Portugal* Warm, maritime area south of Lisbon. Vinho Regional has decent whites and good reds; the best reds are from old Castelão vines, often under the Palmela DOC. SETÚBAL DOC produces sweet fortified wine. Best producers: (reds) BACALHÔA★, Herdade da Comporta, D F J VINHOS★, Ermelinda Freitas★, José Maria da FONSECA★, Pegões co-op, Pegos Claros★, Soberanas. Best years: 2012 11 08 07 05 04 03 01 00 99 97 96 95.

PENLEY ESTATE *Coonawarra, South Australia* Kym Tolley, a member of the PENFOLD family, launched Penley in 1991. Cabernet Sauvignon★★★ is outstanding. Chardonnay and Hyland Shiraz can reach ★★; Gryphon Merlot★ and fizz★ are good, too. Best years: (Cabernet Reserve) (2013) (12) 10 09 08 **07 06 05 04 02 00 99 98 96 94 93 92 91**.

PENNSYLVANIA *USA* Pennsylvania has seen its wine industry blossom over the last two decades, to about 165 wineries today. The state boasts the two highest elevation vineyards in the US east of the Rocky Mountains. Native and French hybrid grapes are common, with *vinifera* making inroads. Best producers: Allegro, CHADDSFORD, Presque Isle, Stargazers.

PEPPER BRIDGE WINERY *Walla Walla Valley AVA, Washington State, USA* This estate's vineyards, Pepper Bridge and Seven Hills, are two of WASHINGTON STATE's best. The Cabernet Sauvignon★ is powerful and requires aging to show its potential; Merlot★ is a muscular version of the variety; BORDEAUX-style blend Reserve★ is produced in very small amounts. Best years: (2012) 11 10 **09 08**.

RAÚL PÉREZ *Bierzo DO, Castilla y León and Ribeira Sacra DO, Galicia, Spain* The affable, BIERZO-born Pérez has taken the wine world by storm with his ultra-natural, elegant wines – not only those he produces here in north-western Spain (Ultreia de Valtuille★★★, El Pecado★★★), but also those from wineries where he consults elsewhere in the country.

PÉREZ CRUZ *Maipo, Chile* Modern winery in the Alto Maipo, close to the Andes foothills. Noted for minty Cabernet Sauvignon★, Syrah★, Cot★ (Malbec) and Liguai★★ (Syrah-Cabernet Sauvignon-Carmenère).

PERNAND-VERGELESSES AC *Côte de Beaune, Burgundy, France* The little-known village of Pernand-Vergelesses contains a decent chunk of the great Corton hill, including much of the best white CORTON-CHARLEMAGNE Grand Cru vineyard. As no one ever links Pernand with the heady heights of Corton-

DOMAINE CHANDON DE BRIAILLES
MISE DU   DOMAINE
PERNAND-VERGELESSES
PREMIER CRU
ÎLE DES VERGELESSES
APPELLATION PERNAND-VERGELESSES 1ER CRU CONTRÔLÉE
MISE EN BOUTEILLE AU
DOMAINE CHANDON DE BRIAILLES
VITICULTEUR A SAVIGNY-LES-BEAUNE, CÔTE-D'OR, FRANCE
ALCOOL 12.5 % BY VOLUME • PRODUCT OF FRANCE • 750 ML • CONTAINS SULFITES

Charlemagne, the whites sold under the village name can be a bargain. The wines can be a bit lean and dry to start with but fatten up beautifully after 2–4 years in bottle. The red wines sold under the village name are attractive when young, with a nice raspberry pastille fruit and a slight earthiness, and will age for 6–10 years. Best vineyard: Île des Vergelesses. Best producers: (reds) Champy★, CHANDON DE BRIAILLES★★, C Cornu★, Denis Père et Fils★, Dubreuil-Fontaine★; (whites) Dubreuil-Fontaine★, A Guyon, JADOT★, J-M Pavelot★, Rapet★, Rollin★. Best years: (reds) (2013) 12 11 10 09 **08 07** 05 03 02 99; (whites) (2013) 12 11 **10 09 08 07**.

ANDRÉ PERRET *Condrieu AC, Rhône Valley, France* A top CONDRIEU grower, with 2 standout cuvées: Clos Chanson★★ is mineral and dashing; Chéry★★★ is gloriously musky, floral and rich. Impressive, invigorating white and red ST-JOSEPH★★ (Les Grisières★★ from old Syrah vines). Very good COLLINES RHODANIENNES Syrah★ and Marsanne★. Best years: (Condrieu Chéry) **2013** 12 11 11 09 08 05.

JOSEPH PERRIER *Champagne AC, Champagne, France* The vintage Blanc de Blancs★★ and vintage Rosé★★ are classy and the NV Cuvée Royale★ is biscuity and creamy. Prestige Cuvée Josephine★★ has length and complexity, but the much cheaper Cuvée Royale Vintage★★ is the best deal. Best years: 2004 **02 99 98 96 95 90 89 88 85 82**.

PERRIER-JOUËT *Champagne AC, Champagne, France* After having 3 owners in 10 years, latest proprietors Pernod Ricard have definitely improved things (since the dire 1990s). Certainly the non-vintage is now a rather good drink once more, the Blason Rosé★ is charming and the de luxe vintage cuvée Belle Époque★ (known as Fleur de Champagne in the US) is pretty classy. Best years: 2007 06 **04 02 99 98 96 95 90 89 85 82**.

PESQUERA *Ribera del Duero DO, Castilla y León, Spain* Tinto Pesquera reds, 100% Tempranillo, richly coloured, firm, fragrant, have long been among Spain's best. Sold as Crianza★ and Reserva★; Gran Reserva★★ and Janus★★★ are made in the best years. The firm owns another RIBERA DEL DUERO estate, Condado de Haza★ (Alenza★★), plus ventures in Zamora (Dehesa La Granja★) and La MANCHA (Vínculo). Best years: (Pesquera Crianza) 2010 **09 07 06 05 04 01 99 96 95 94 93 92 91**.

PESSAC-LÉOGNAN AC *Bordeaux, France* AC for the northern (best) part of the GRAVES and including all the Classed Growths. The supremely gravelly soil tends to favour red wines. Thanks to cool fermentation and the use of new oak barrels, this is also one of the most exciting areas of France for top-class white wines. Best producers: (reds) Carbonnieux★, les Carmes Haut-Brion★, Dom. de CHEVALIER★★, Couhins-Lurton★, FIEUZAL★, HAUT-BAILLY★★, HAUT-BRION★★★, Larrivet-Haut-Brion★, LATOUR-MARTILLAC★, la LOUVIÈRE★, MALARTIC-LAGRAVIÈRE★★, la MISSION-HAUT-BRION★★★, PAPE-CLÉMENT★, SMITH-HAUT-LAFITTE★★; (whites) Brown★, Carbonnieux★, Dom. de CHEVALIER★★★, Couhins-Lurton★★, FIEUZAL★★, la Garde★, HAUT-BRION★★★, LATOUR-MARTILLAC★, LAVILLE-HAUT-BRION★★★, la LOUVIÈRE★★, MALARTIC-LAGRAVIÈRE★★, la MISSION-HAUT-BRION★★★, PAPE-CLÉMENT★★, Rochemorin★, SMITH-HAUT-LAFITTE★★. Best years: (reds) 2012 11 10 09 **08 06 05 04 02 01 00**; (whites) **2012 11 10 09** 08 07 06 05 04.

PETALUMA *Adelaide Hills, South Australia* Founded by Brian Croser, one of Australia's most influential winemakers (see TAPANAPPA) – now owned by brewer Lion Nathan. CHAMPAGNE-style Croser★ is stylish and fruitier than before. COONAWARRA★ (Cabernet-Merlot) and Chardonnay★ are consistently good and Hanlin Hill Riesling★★ from the CLARE VALLEY is at the fuller end of the spectrum and matures well. Best years: (Coonawarra) (2013) 12 10 09 08 **07 06 05 04 03 02 01 00 99 97 94 91 90**.

PETIT MANSENG Petit and Gros Manseng are an increasingly important pair of grapes in the far south-west of France. Left late to overripen naturally on the vines (their skins are too thick to allow development of noble rot), the sweetness of the juice is balanced by a refreshing acidity, the hallmark of JURANÇON and PACHERENC. Petit Manseng has found a hospitable home in Virginia, where it shines in dry, off-dry and sweet wines. Trialling in New Zealand.

PETIT VERDOT A rich, tannic variety, grown mainly in Bordeaux's HAUT-MÉDOC to add depth, colour and violet fragrance to top wines. Late ripening and erratic yield limit its popularity, but warmer-climate plantings in Australia, California, Virginia, Washington State, South Africa, Chile, Argentina, Israel, Spain, Portugal and Italy are giving exciting results, often from including only a few per cent in blends. Increasingly, varietal Petit Verdot wines are made in Spain and Argentina.

CH. PETIT-VILLAGE★ *Pomerol AC, Bordeaux, France*   This POMEROL used to be rather dry and dense, but has considerably softened up in recent vintages. New cellar and even better quality from 2006. Generally worth aging for 8–10 years. Best years: 2012 11 10 09 08 **07 06 05 04 03 02 01 00 99**.

PETITE ARVINE   A Swiss grape variety from the VALAIS, Petite Arvine has a bouquet of peach and apricot, and develops a spicy, honeyed character. Dry, medium or sweet, the wines have good aging potential. Also found in VALLE D'AOSTA in Italy. Best producers: Chappaz★, R Favre, A Mathier★, Maye, Dom. du Mont d'Or★, Rouvinez★, Varone.

PETITE SIRAH   Sometimes bottled under its other name, Durif (an obscure Rhône variety). Some 500 or more California wineries now make a varietal Petite Sirah. At its best, it is almost black but surprisingly scented and sweet-fruited, though it can be tannic and unfriendly. Australian, Mexican and Israeli examples are generally softer though still hefty, and can also occasionally develop a floral scent and blackberry fruit. It has a limited presence in South Africa. Best producers: (California) Alta Colina★★, Clayhouse, Cypher★★, Foppiano★, Jessie's Grove, J Lohr★, Loma Linda★, RAVENSWOOD★, RIDGE★★, Ripken★, Rosenblum, Stags' Leap Winery★★, TURLEY★★; (Australia) CALABRIA★, Campbells, DE BORTOLI, Stanton & Killeen; (Mexico) L A CETTO★.

CH. PÉTRUS★★★ *Pomerol AC, Bordeaux, France*   The powerful, concentrated wine (one of the most expensive red wines in the world) is the result of the caring genius of Pétrus' owners, the MOUEIX family, who have maximized the potential of the vineyard of almost solid clay, although the impressive average age of the vines has been much reduced by recent replantings. Drinkable for its astonishingly rich, dizzying blend of fruit and spice flavours after a decade, but top years will age for much longer, developing exotic scents of tobacco and chocolate and truffles. Best years: 2012 11 10 09 08 **07 06 05 04 03 02 01 00 99 98 96 95 90 89**.

DOM. PEYRES ROSES *Gaillac AOP, South-West France*   Astrid and Olivier Bonnafont, biodynamic growers, have joined the top rank of GAILLAC producers, with two dry whites (one unoaked★, and the oaked Cuvée Armand★) and three reds, including a remarkable Vieilles Vignes★★ and the oak-aged Cuvée Charles★. Finish with the luscious dessert wine, Cuvée Louis★★. Best years: (reds) 2012 11 10 08 05.

CH. DE PEZ★ *St-Estèphe AC, Haut-Médoc, Bordeaux, France*   One of ST-ESTÈPHE's leading non-Classed Growths, de Pez makes mouthfilling, satisfying claret with sturdy fruit. Slow to evolve, good vintages often need 10 years or more. Owned by Champagne house ROEDERER. Best years: 2012 11 10 09 08 07 06 05 04 03 02 01 00 98 96 95 90.

PÉZENAS *Languedoc AC, Languedoc, France*   From vineyards around the town of Pézenas, mainly from Syrah, Grenache and Mourvèdre. White and pink wines are COTEAUX DU LANGUEDOC or LANGUEDOC AC. Best producers: Aurelles★, Conte des Floris★, Magellan, NIZAS★, PRIEURÉ DE ST-JEAN DE BÉBIAN★★, Ste-Cecile du Parc★, Trinités, Villa Tempora. Best years: (reds) (2013) 12 11 10 09 08 07 06 05.

PFALZ *Germany*   This immense, 23,500ha (58,045-acre) wine region makes a lot of mediocre wine, but the quality estates can match the best that Germany has to offer. The northern area (the Mittelhaardt) can produce profound full-bodied Riesling, especially round the villages of Bad Dürkheim, WACHENHEIM, FORST and Deidesheim; Freinsheim, Kallstadt, Ungstein, Ruppertsberg, Gimmeldingen and Haardt also produce fine Riesling as well as Scheurebe, Rieslaner and Pinot Gris. In the Südliche Weinstrasse, the warm climate makes the area ideal for Spät-, Weiss- and Grauburgunder (aka Pinots Noir, Blanc and Gris), as well as Chardonnay, Gewürztraminer, Scheurebe, Muscat and red Dornfelder, the last often dark and tannic, sometimes with oak influence.

JOSEPH PHELPS *Napa Valley and Sonoma Coast, California, USA* Phelps' BORDEAUX-blend Insignia★★★ is usually one of California's top reds, strongly fruit-driven with a lively spicy background. Cabernets include Napa Valley★ and huge Backus Vineyard★★, beautifully balanced with solid ripe fruit. The Napa Merlot★ is ripe and elegant, with layers of fruit. Phelps was the first California winery to successfully major on RHÔNE varietals, and makes an intense Viognier★ and complex Syrah★. A more recent project has been the development of Freestone Vineyards: 40ha (100 acres) of Pinot Noir and Chardonnay on the SONOMA COAST. The first releases were in 2006 and the lushness of the Chardonnay★★ and the rich yet scented fruit of the Pinot Noir★ made an immediate impact. Top Chardonnay Ovation★★ and good second label Fogdog★. Best years: (Napa Cabernet) 2011 **10 09 08 07 06 05 04 02 01 00** 99 96 95 94 91.

PHILIPPONNAT *Champagne AC, Champagne, France* Much improved quality over the whole range. The non-vintage★ is (now) one of the best in Champagne, vintage★ is very good too, while single-vineyard Clos des Goisses★★★, from an extremely steep, south-facing vineyard, is some of the purest, ripest and longest-lasting wine in the whole of Champagne. Best years: (2007) 06 05 04 **02 00** 99 98 96 95 90.

CH. DE PIBARNON *Bandol AC, Provence, France* One of BANDOL's leading properties, with excellently located vineyards. The reds★★, extremely attractive when young, develop a truffly, wild herb character with age. Ripe, strawberryish rosé. Best years: (reds) (2013) 12 11 10 09 **08 07 06 05**.

PIC ST-LOUP *Languedoc AC, Languedoc, France* One of the coolest growing zones in the Midi, to the north of Montpellier; along with la CLAPE and the TERRASSES DU LARZAC it produces some of the best reds in the Languedoc. Syrah is the dominant variety, along with Grenache and Mourvèdre. Whites, usually IGP, from Marsanne, Roussanne and Rolle are showing promise. Best producers: Cazeneuve★, CLOS MARIE★, Ermitage du Pic St-Loup, l'Euzière★, l'HORTUS★, Lancyre★, Lascaux★, Lavabre★, MAS BRUGUIERE★, Mas de Mortiès★, Valflaunès. Best years: (reds) (2013) 12 **11 10 09** 08 07 06 05.

FRANZ X PICHLER *Wachau, Niederösterreich, Austria* One of Austria's most famous producers of dry wines; 'FX', as he is known, has handed the reins to his son Lucas. Grüner Veltliner and Riesling 'M'★★★ (for monumental) and Riesling Unendlich★★★ (endless) – alcoholically potent but balanced – are amazing. So are the Riesling Steinertal★★★ and the Grüner Veltliner Kellerberg★★★. Best years: (2013) 12 11 **10 09 08 07 06 05 04**.

RUDI PICHLER *Wachau, Niederösterreich, Austria* For some years Pichler has secured his place in the top tier of WACHAU producers. Riesling Achleiten and Grüner Veltliner Kollmütz and Hochrain are regularly ★★. Best years: (2013) 12 11 **10 09 08 07 06 05**.

CH. PICHON-LONGUEVILLE★★★ *Pauillac AC, 2ème Cru Classé, Haut-Médoc,*
Bordeaux, France Despite its superb vineyards, Pichon-Longueville
(called Pichon-Baron until 1988) wines were 'also-rans' for a long time.
In 1987 the property was bought by AXA and Jean-Michel Cazes of
LYNCH-BAGES took over the management. The improvement was
immediate and thrilling. Cazes is long gone, but many recent vintages
have been of First Growth standard, with firm tannic structure and rich
dark fruit. Cellar for at least 10 years, although it is likely to keep for 30.
Second wine: les Tourelles de Longueville. **Best years:** 2012 11 10 09 08 **07
06 05 04 03 02 01 00 99 98 96 95 91 90 89.**

CH. PICHON-LONGUEVILLE-LALANDE★★★ *Pauillac AC, 2ème Cru Classé,*
Haut-Médoc, Bordeaux, France The inspirational figure of May de
Lencquesaing forged the modern reputation of this property. It's now
(since 2007) controlled by Champagne house ROEDERER. Divinely scented
and lush at 6–7 years, the wines usually stay gorgeous for 20 at least.
Recent years contain a higher percentage of Cabernet Sauvignon and
have been excellent, although a little sturdier at the outset. Second wine:
Réserve de la Comtesse. **Best years:** 2012 11 10 09 08 **07 06 05 04 03 02 01
00 99 98 96 95 91 90 89.**

PICPOUL DE PINET AC *Languedoc, France* Fresh, salty, lemon-pithy white
wine made from Picpoul Blanc grown around the village of Pinet near
the Etang de Thau. Drink as young as possible. Quality has greatly
improved in recent vintages as co-ops get better and single estates
emerge. **Best producers:** Félines-Jourdan★, Mas Autanel★, Pinet co-op,
Pomerols co-op, St Martin de la Garrigue★.

PIEDMONT *Italy* The most important Italian region for the tradition of
quality wines. In the north, there is the Alto Piemonte volcanic zone
encompassing DOCs Carema, Bramaterra, Boca, Ghemme, Fara and
DOCG GATTINARA. To the south, in the LANGHE hills, there's BAROLO and
BARBARESCO, both masterful examples of the Nebbiolo grape, and other wines
from Dolcetto and Barbera grapes. In the Monferrato hills, in the provinces
of Asti and Alessandria, the Barbera, Moscato and Cortese grapes hold sway.
The broad DOCs of Langhe and Monferrato, backed by the region-wide
Piemonte DOC (the region does not admit IGT at all), are designed to
classify all wines of quality from a great range of grape varieties. See also ASTI,
GAVI, MOSCATO D'ASTI, NEBBIOLO D'ALBA, ROERO.

PIEROPAN *Veneto, Italy* The estate that single-handedly preserved SOAVE's
reputation for quality for many years still produces very good Soave
Classico★ and, from 2 single vineyards, Calvarino★★ and La
Rocca★★★. Excellent RECIOTO DI SOAVE Le Colombare★★ and opulent
Passito della Rocca★★. a barrique-aged blend of Sauvignon, Riesling
Italico (Welschriesling) and Trebbiano di Soave. Single-vineyard Soaves
can improve for 5 years or more, as can the sweet styles.

CH. PIERRE-BISE *Coteaux du Layon AC, Loire Valley, France* Claude Papin's
COTEAUX DU LAYON vineyard is divided into over 20 mini parcels based on
factors like soil depth, topography, and wind and sun exposure, that help
him analyse optimum ripeness. And the results are sublime: rich, yet
pure-fruited and precise Coteaux du Layon★★★ and QUARTS DE
CHAUME★★★ with a mineral undertow. Very good dry ANJOU BLANC★,
SAVENNIÈRES★, ANJOU Gamay★ and ANJOU-VILLAGES★★. **Best years:** (sweet)
2011 **10 09 07 05 03 02 01 97 96 95 90 89.**

PIERRO *Margaret River, Western Australia* Mike Peterkin doesn't make much Chardonnay★★★, yet it is a masterpiece of elegance and complexity. The Semillon-Sauvignon LTC★★ is full with just a hint of leafiness, balanced by refreshing acidity that gives it a surprising ability to age. The Pinot Noir★ will hopefully approach ★★ as the vines mature. Dark, dense Cabernet Sauvignon-Merlot Reserve★★ is the serious, BORDEAUX-like member of the family, while LTCf★ is more approachable, with a little touch of Cabernet Franc. The estate's Fire Gully★ vineyard is consistently good. Best years: (Chardonnay) (2013) 12 11 **10 09 08 06 05 04 03 02**.

PIESPORT *Mosel, Germany* Generic Piesporter Michelsberg wines, soft, sweet, forgettable, have nothing to do with the excellent Rieslings from the top Goldtröpfchen site. With intense peach and blackcurrant aromas they are unique among MOSEL wines. Best producers: GRANS-FASSIAN★★, J Haart★, Reinhold HAART★★, Hain★, von Kesselstatt★, Lehnert-Veit, ST URBANS-HOF★★. Best years: (2013) 12 11 **10 09 08 07 06 05 04**.

CH. LE PIN★★★ *Pomerol AC, Bordeaux, France* Now one of the most expensive wines in the world. The first vintage was 1979 and the wines, which are concentrated but elegant, sumptuous yet refined, are produced from 100% Merlot. The tiny 2.8ha (7-acre) vineyard lies close to those of TROTANOY and VIEUX-CHÂTEAU-CERTAN. Best years: 2012 11 10 09 08 **07 06 05 04 02 01 00 99 98 96 95 94 90 89 88**.

PINE RIDGE *Stags Leap District AVA, California, USA* Wines come from several NAPA AVAs, but its flagship Cabernet remains the supple, plummy STAGS LEAP DISTRICT★★. Andrus Reserve★★, a BORDEAUX blend, has more richness and power, while the HOWELL MOUNTAIN Cabernet★ offers intense fruit and structure for long aging. CARNEROS Merlot★ is spicy and cherry fruited, and Carneros Chardonnay★ looks good. Also a nice Chenin Blanc-Viognier. Best years: (Stags Leap Cabernet) (2012) **10 09 08 07 06 05 03 02 01 00 99 97 96 95**.

DOMINIO DE PINGUS *Ribera del Duero DO, Castilla y León, Spain* Since 1995, Peter Sisseck's tiny vineyards and winery have produced Pingus★★★, a cult wine of extraordinary depth and character. Second wine Flor de Pingus★★ and third wine Psi★★ are also super. Best years: (Pingus) (2011) 10 09 **08 07 06 05 04 03 00 99 96 95**.

PINOT BIANCO See PINOT BLANC.

PINOT BLANC Wines have a clear, yeasty, appley taste, and good examples can age to a delicious honeyed fullness. In ALSACE it is the mainstay of most CRÉMANT D'ALSACE. Important in northern Italy as Pinot Bianco and especially in ALTO ADIGE, where it reaches elevated levels of purity, complexity and longevity. Taken seriously in southern Germany and Austria (as Weissburgunder), producing imposing wines with ripe pear and peach fruit and a distinct nutty character. Also successful in Hungary, Slovakia, Slovenia and the Czech Republic and promising in California (notably from Robert Sinskey), Oregon's WILLAMETTE VALLEY, British Columbia in Canada, and England.

PINOT GRIGIO See PINOT GRIS.

PINOT NOIR

There's this myth about Pinot Noir that I think I'd better lay to rest. It goes something like this. Pinot Noir is an incredibly tricky grape to grow and an even more difficult grape to vinify; in fact Pinot Noir is such a difficult customer that the only place that regularly achieves magical results is the thin stretch of land known as the Côte d'Or, between Dijon and Chagny in France, where mesoclimate, soil conditions and 2000 years of experience weave an inimitable web of pleasure.

This just isn't so. The thin-skinned, early-ripening Pinot Noir is undoubtedly more difficult to grow than other great varieties like Cabernet or Chardonnay, but that doesn't mean that it's impossible to grow elsewhere – you just have to work at it with more sensitivity and seek out the right growing conditions. And although great red Burgundy is a hauntingly beautiful wine, it is not the only brilliant interpretation of this remarkable grape variety. The glorious thing about places like New Zealand, California, Oregon, Chile, Australia, Germany and South Africa is that we are seeing an ever-increasing number of wines that are thrillingly different from anything produced in Burgundy, yet with flavours that are unique to Pinot Noir.

WINE STYLES

France All France's great Pinot Noir wines come from Burgundy's Côte d'Or. Rarely deep in colour, they should nonetheless possess a wonderful fruit quality when young – raspberry, strawberry, cherry or plum – that becomes more scented and exotic with age, the plums turning to figs and prunes, and the richness of chocolate mingling perilously with truffles and well-hung game. Strange, challenging, hedonistic. France's other Pinots – in north and south Burgundy, the Loire, Jura, Savoie, Alsace and now occasionally in the south of France – are lighter and milder, and in Champagne its pale, thin wine is used to make sparkling wine.

Other European regions Since the 1990s, helped by good vintages, German winemakers have had considerable success in producing serious Pinot Noir (generally called Spätburgunder). Switzerland, where it is also called Blauburgunder, and Italy (as Pinot Nero) both have fair success, especially in Alto Adige. Austria and Spain have a couple of good examples and England has small amounts of increasingly enjoyable light styles. Romania, the Czech Republic and Hungary produce significant amounts of Pinot Noir, though of generally low quality.

New World Oregon is shedding its reputation as 'another Burgundy' and beginning to produce wines of excitingly different personalities from cool sub-regions Eola-Amity Hills, Dundee Hills and Chehalem Mountains. California offers ripe, stylish Russian River Valley examples; exotically scented wines of Carneros, Anderson Valley and Sonoma Coast; startlingly original offerings from Santa Barbara County (notably Sta. Rita Hills) and Santa Lucia Highlands in Monterey County.

New Zealand produces wines of thrilling fruit and individuality, most notably from Martinborough, Nelson, Marlborough, Canterbury's Waipara and Central Otago. Cooler regions of Australia – including Yarra Valley, Mornington Peninsula, Geelong, Beechworth, Adelaide Hills and Tasmania – are equally good. New Burgundian clones are gaining ground and quality in cooler spots in South Africa. Chile's San Antonio/Leyda, Casablanca and Bío Bío areas are beginning to shine.

BEST PRODUCERS

France *Burgundy* d'ANGERVILLE, Comte Armand, D BACHELET, G Barthod, J-M Boillot, BOUCHARD, CATHIARD, CHANDON DE BRIAILLES, R Chevillon, CLAIR, J-J Confuron, DROUHIN, C Dugat, B Dugat-Py, DUJAC, FAIVELEY, GRIVOT, Anne GROS, JADOT, LAFARGE, LAFON, Dom. LEROY, LIGER-BELAIR, H Lignier, MÉO-CAMUZET, de MONTILLE, MORTET, MUGNERET-GIBOURG, J-F MUGNIER, Ponsot, RION, Dom. de la ROMANÉE-CONTI, E Rouget, ROUMIER, ROUSSEAU, de VOGÜÉ, VOUGERAIE.

Other European Pinot Noirs
Germany Becker, BERCHER, FÜRST, HUBER, Johner, KELLER, Kesseler, KNIPSER, MEYER-NÄKEL, MOLITOR, REBHOLZ, SCHNAITMANN, STODDEN.

Italy CA' DEL BOSCO, Franz Haas, Haderburg, Hofstätter, Nals-Margreid.

Switzerland Adank, GANTENBEIN, Mathier.

New World Pinot Noirs
USA (California) Ancien, AU BON CLIMAT, CALERA, DEHLINGER, DUTTON GOLDFIELD, Merry Edwards, Gary FARRELL, FLOWERS, KISTLER, LANDMARK, Littorai, MARCASSIN, MORGAN, NAVARRO, Patz & Hall, RASMUSSEN, ROCHIOLI, SAINTSBURY, SANFORD, SEA SMOKE, Siduri, Talley, WILLIAMS SELYEM; *(Oregon)* ARGYLE, BEAUX FRERES, Cristom, DOMAINE DROUHIN, DOMAINE SERENE, Ken WRIGHT.

Canada (British Columbia) Blue Mountain, CedarCreek, MISSION HILL; *(Ontario)* Norman Hardie, INNISKILLIN, TAWSE.

Australia Ashton Hills, BANNOCKBURN, Bass Phillip, BAY OF FIRES, Bindi, Castle Rock, COLDSTREAM HILLS, Curly Flat, DE BORTOLI, Diamond Valley, William Downie, By FARR, FREYCINET, Gembrook Hill, GIACONDA, GIANT STEPS, GROSSET, Hurley, KOOYONG, Stefano LUBIANA, Marchand & Burch, Moorooduc, OAKRIDGE, Paradigm Hill, PARINGA, Stonier, Tamar Ridge, TARRAWARRA, TEN MINUTES BY TRACTOR, YABBY LAKE.

New Zealand ATA RANGI, Blind River, CLOUDY BAY, CRAGGY RANGE, Dog Point, DRY RIVER, Escarpment, FELTON ROAD, Foxes Island, FROMM, Kusuda, MARTINBOROUGH VINEYARD, NEUDORF, PALLISER ESTATE, PEGASUS BAY, Peregrine, QUARTZ REEF, Rippon, SAINT CLAIR, Schubert, SERESIN, Valli, VAVASOUR.

South Africa BOUCHARD FINLAYSON, CHAMONIX, Paul CLUVER, Crystallum, HAMILTON RUSSELL, NEWTON JOHNSON, The Winery of Good Hope.

Chile ANAKENA, CASA MARÍN, CASAS DEL BOSQUE, CONO SUR (Ocio), Viña LEYDA, Maycas del Limarí.

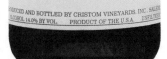

PINOT GRIS At its finest in ALSACE: with lowish acidity and a deep colour, the grape produces fat, rich dry wines that somehow mature wonderfully. It is very occasionally used in BURGUNDY (as Pinot Beurot) to add fatness to a wine. Italian Pinot Grigio, often boring, occasionally delicious, is currently so popular worldwide that New World producers are tending to use the Italian name in preference to the French version, but in general 'Grigio' implies a lighter, milder style. Also successful in Austria and Germany as Ruländer or Grauburgunder, and as Malvoisie in the Swiss VALAIS. There are good Romanian, Croatian and Czech examples, as well as spirited ones in Hungary (where it may appear as Szürkebarát). In a crisp style, it can be successful in Oregon and is showing promise in California, Virginia and OKANAGAN VALLEY in Canada. Now fashionable in New Zealand and cooler regions of Australia in a spicy pear style. Starting to appear in Chile and England.

PINOT MEUNIER An important ingredient in CHAMPAGNE and English sparkling wine, along with Pinot Noir and Chardonnay. Occasionally found in the LOIRE and OREGON and also grown in Germany under the name of Schwarzriesling.

PINOT NERO See PINOT NOIR.
PINOT NOIR See pages 248–9.

PINOTAGE A Pinot Noir x Cinsaut cross, conceived in South Africa in 1925. DeWaal's Top of the Hill is the oldest, planted in 1950 and still bearing. Highly versatile; classic versions are full-bodied and well-oaked with ripe plum, spice and maybe some mineral, redcurrant, banana or marshmallow flavours, but fresh, unoaked styles are good too. New Zealand, Australia and Israel (Barkan) have interesting examples, as does California: Graziano in MENDOCINO, Fort Ross in the SONOMA COAST and J VINEYARDS in RUSSIAN RIVER VALLEY make stylish versions. **Best producers:** (South Africa) Ashbourne★, BEYERSKLOOF★★, CHAMONIX★★, DeWaal★ (Top of the Hill★★), Diemersfontein★, FAIRVIEW★ (Primo★★), GRANGEHURST★, Kaapzicht★, KANONKOP★★, Laibach★, L'AVENIR★, Simonsig★★, Southern Right/HAMILTON RUSSELL★; (New Zealand) Muddy Water★, Te Awa★.

PIPER-HEIDSIECK *Champagne AC, Champagne, France* Piper's non-vintage★ is now gentle and biscuity, and the vintage★★ is showing real class. Also a plethora of new cuvées: Sublime (demi-sec), Divin (blanc de blancs), Rosé Sauvage and Rare★★, a de luxe blend available in 2002, 1999, 98, 88 and 79 vintages. **Best years:** 2006 04 **02 00 96 95 90 89 85 82**.

DOM. PLAGEOLES *Gaillac AOP, South-West France* Traditionalist-and-modernizer Bernard Plageoles has perpetuated his father's passion for 14 ancient Gaillac grape varieties, including Prunelart, Verdanel and the rare Ondenc, which goes into the lusciously sweet Vin d'Autan★★★, one of France's great stickies. Dry wines include a range from the Mauzac grape★ and bone-dry Mauzac Nature★ fizz. Reds include a remarkable varietal from the Duras★★ grape.

PRODUCTEURS PLAIMONT *Madiran AOP, St-Mont AOP and IGP des Côtes de Gascogne, South-West France* The largest, most reliable and most successful co-op in South-West France. The whites★, full of crisp fruit, are reasonably priced and are best drunk young. The reds, especially the very good Ch. de Sabazan★, are at their best after 5 years or so.

CH. PLAISANCE *Fronton AOP, South-West France* Marc Pénavayre's range (now organic) includes a fruity quaffer named after the château★ and a lightly oaked cuvée Thibaut★★ named after his son. Perhaps most interesting is Alabets★★, a 100% varietal from the Négrette grape. Best years: (2013) 12 11 10.

PLANETA *Sicily, Italy* Dynamic Sicilian estate. Chardonnay★ is one of the best in southern Italy; impressive Cabernet Sauvignon Burdese★★ and Merlot★★ and stellar, rich, spicy Santa Cecilia★★ (Nero d'Avola). The white Cometa★★ is a fascinating Sicilian version of FIANO. Marvellously fruity La Segreta red★ and white★ blends and Cerasuolo di Vittoria★.

PLUMPTON COLLEGE *East Sussex, England* The UK's only teaching establishment that covers vine growing and winemaking produces both still and sparkling wines. Best are sparklers The Dean Brut★ and The Dean Blush Brut★.

POL ROGER *Champagne AC, Champagne, France* Non-vintage Brut Réserve★ (formerly known as White Foil) is biscuity and dependable rather than thrilling. New ultra-dry wine called Pure★. Pol Roger also produces a vintage★★, a vintage rosé★★ and a vintage Chardonnay★★. Its top Champagne, the Pinot-dominated Cuvée Sir Winston Churchill★★, is a deliciously refined drink. All vintage wines will improve with at least 5 years' keeping. Best years: 2004 02 **00** 99 98 96 95 **90 89** 88 85 82.

POLIZIANO *Vino Nobile di Montepulciano DOCG, Tuscany, Italy* A leading light in Montepulciano. VINO NOBILE★ is smoother if more international than average, especially the Riserva Asinone★★. Le Stanze★★ (Cabernet Sauvignon-Merlot) can be outstanding – the fruit in part coming from owner Federico Carletti's other estate, Lohsa, in MORELLINO DI SCANSANO. Best years: (Vino Nobile) (2011) **10** 09 08 07 06 04 01.

POLZ *Steiermark, Austria* Aromatic dry white wines, mostly★, while Morillon (Chardonnay), Muskateller and Sauvignon Blanc frequently deserve ★★ for their combination of intensity and elegance. Best years: (2013) 12 11 **10 09** 08 07.

POMEROL AC *Bordeaux, France* This AC includes some of the world's most sought-after red wines. Pomerol's unique quality lies in its deep clay (though gravel also plays a part in some vineyards) in which the Merlot grape flourishes. The result is seductively rich, almost creamy wine with wonderful mouthfilling fruit flavours: often plummy, but with blackcurrants, raisins and chocolate, too, and mint and minerals to freshen it up. Best producers: Beauregard★, le BON PASTEUR★★, Bonalgue, Certan-de-May★, Clinet★★, Clos l'Église★★, Clos René, la CONSEILLANTE★★, l'ÉGLISE-CLINET★★★, l'ÉVANGILE★★, Feytit-Clinet★, la FLEUR-PÉTRUS★★, GAZIN★★, Hosanna★★, LAFLEUR★★★, LATOUR-À-POMEROL★, Montviel, Nénin★, PETIT-VILLAGE★, PÉTRUS★★★, Le PIN★★★, Rouget★, TROTANOY★★, VIEUX-CHÂTEAU-CERTAN★★. Best years: 2012 11 10 09 **08** 06 05 04 01 00 98 96 95.

POMINO DOC See CHIANTI RUFINA.

POMMARD AC *Côte de Beaune, Burgundy, France* The first village south of Beaune. At their best, the wines should have full, round, beefy flavours, and plenty of tannins. Can age well, often for 10 years or more. There are no Grands Crus, but Premiers Crus les Rugiens Bas and les Épenots are the best sites. There's even talk of promoting them. Best producers: Aleth-Girardin★, Comte Armand★★★, J-M Boillot★★, de Courcel★★, M Gaunoux★, V GIRARDIN★, Huber-Verdereau★★, Lejeune★, de MONTILLE★★, Parent★, Dom. du Pavillon/Bichot★, Ch. de Pommard★, Pothier-Rieusset★, Violot-Guillemard★★. Best years: 2012 11 10 09 08 **07** 06 05 **03** 02 99 98 96 90.

PORT DOC

Douro, Portugal

 The Douro region in northern Portugal, where the grapes for port are grown, is wild and beautiful, and part is classified as a World Heritage Site. Steep hills covered in vineyard terraces plunge dramatically down to the Douro river. Grapes are one of the few crops that will grow in the inhospitable climate, which gets progressively drier the further inland you travel. But not all the Douro's grapes qualify to be made into fortified port. A quota is established every year, and the rest are made into increasingly good unfortified Douro wines.

Red port grapes include Touriga Franca, Tinta Roriz, Touriga Nacional, Tinta Barroca, Tinta Cão, Tinta Amarela and Sousão. Grapes for white port include Côdega, Gouveio, Malvasia Fina, Rabigato and Viosinho. The grapes are partially fermented, and then *aguardente* (grape spirit) is added, which fortifies the wine and stops the fermentation, leaving sweet, unfermented grape sugar in the finished port.

PORT STYLES

Vintage Finest of the ports matured in bottle, made from grapes from the best vineyards. Vintage port is not 'declared' every year (usually there are 3 or 4 declarations per decade), and only during the second calendar year in cask if the shipper thinks the standard is high enough. It is bottled after 2 years, and may be consumed soon afterwards, as is not uncommon in the USA; at this stage it packs quite a punch. The British custom of aging for 20 years or more can yield exceptional mellowness. Vintage port throws a thick sediment, so requires decanting.

Single quinta (Vintage) A single-quinta port comes from an individual estate; many shippers sell a vintage port under a quinta name in years which are not declared as a vintage. It is quite possible for these 'off vintage' ports to equal or even surpass the vintage wines from the same house.

Aged tawny Matured in cask for 10, 20, 30 or even 40 years before bottling, older tawnies have delicious nut and fig flavours. The age is stated on the label.

Colheita Tawny from a single vintage, matured in cask for at least 7 years – potentially the finest of the aged tawnies.

Late Bottled (Vintage) (LBV) Port matured for 4–6 years in cask and vat, then usually filtered to avoid sediment forming in the bottle. Traditional unfiltered LBV has much more flavour and requires decanting; it can generally be aged for another 5 years or more.

Crusted This is a blend of good ports from 2–3 vintages, bottled without filtration after 3–4 years in cask. A deposit (crust) forms in the bottle and the wine should be decanted. A gentler, junior type of 'vintage' flavour.

Reserve (most can be categorized as Premium Ruby) has an average of 3–5 years' age. A handful represent good value.

Ruby The youngest red port with only 1–3 years' age. Ruby port should be bursting with young, almost peppery, fruit, and there has been an improvement in quality of late, except at the cheapest level.

Tawny Basic tawny is either an emaciated ruby, or a blend of ruby and white port, and is usually best avoided.

Rosé New category since 2008, usually very sweet, best served over ice or used in cocktails.

White Only the best taste dry and nutty from wood-aging; most are coarse and alcoholic, and best with tonic water and a slice of lemon.

POMMERY *Champagne AC, Champagne, France*   High-quality CHAMPAGNE house with a wide range of non-vintage cuvées. Along with Brut Royal and Apanage★, there are Summertime blanc de blancs, Wintertime blanc de noirs and Springtime rosé. Austere vintage Brut★ is tasty with maturity; prestige cuvée Louise, white★ and rosé★, is elegant when on form, but erratic. Best years: 2004 **02 00 99 98 96 95 92 90 89 88 85 82**.

CH. PONTET-CANET★★ *Pauillac AC, 5ème Cru Classé, Haut-Médoc, Bordeaux, France*   This property's vineyards are near those of MOUTON-ROTHSCHILD and are run biodynamically. Since 2000 the wine has been on fine form: typically big, chewy, intense PAUILLAC that develops a beautiful blackcurrant fruit. It's one of the wines of the vintage in 2004, 2005 and 2009 – and that's saying something. Used to be great value but prices have soared. Best years: 2012 11 10 09 08 **07 06 05 04 03 02 01 00 99 98 96 95 90**.

PONZI VINEYARDS *Willamette Valley AVA, Oregon, USA*   Luisa Ponzi crafts fine Pinot Gris★, Pinot Blanc★ and Chardonnay★ – juicy whites for early drinking. The Pinot Noirs★ are developing in complexity and profile. Best years: (reds) (2012) 11 10 **09 08**.

PORT See pages 252–3.

NICOLAS POTEL *Burgundy, France*   The eponymous Nicolas left the company in 2009 (see BELLENE). Inexpensive wines still being offered under the Nicolas Potel label, though without the man himself involved.

CH. POTENSAC★★ *Médoc AC, Bordeaux, France*   Owned and run by the Delon family, of LÉOVILLE-LAS-CASES, Potensac's fabulous success is based on a rich, sturdy personality, consistency and value for money. The wine can be drunk at 4–5 years, but fine vintages will improve for between 10 and 20 years. Best years: 2012 11 10 09 **08 07 06 05 04 03 02 00 98**.

POUILLY-FUISSÉ AC *Mâconnais, Burgundy, France*   The sexiest name in the MÂCONNAIS sometimes lives up to its billing for heady white Burgundy. But there is quite a difference in style from producers who vinify their wines simply in stainless steel to those who age them for up to 18 months in oak. The AC covers 5 villages: the richest wines come from Fuissé, the most mineral from Vergisson. Plans are afoot to designate Premier Cru vineyards. Best producers: D & M Barraud★★, Ch. de Beauregard★★, Bret Brothers★★, Cordier★★, Corsin★★, C & T Drouin★, J-A Ferret★★, Ch. Fuissé★★, Guffens-Heynen★★, R Lassarat★★, R Luquet★, O Merlin★★, Ch. des Rontets★★, J & N Saumaize★★, Saumaize-Michelin★★, Valette★★, Verget★★. Best years: (2013) 12 **11 10 09 08 07**.

POUILLY-FUMÉ AC *Loire Valley, France*   Sauvignon Blanc wines with an extra smokiness which supposedly comes from a flinty soil called silex. Fumé means 'smoked' in French. With a few notable exceptions, lacks something of the energy and ambition of SANCERRE. Best producers: F Blanchet★, Henri BOURGEOIS★, A Cailbourdin★, J-C Chatelain★, Chauveau★, Didier DAGUENEAU★★, Serge Dagueneau★, A Figeat★, Fouassière★, Ladoucette★, Landrat-Guyollot★, Masson-Blondelet★, R Minet★, M Redde★, Tinel-Blondelet★, Ch. de Tracy★. Best years: 2013 12 11 **11 10 09**.

POUILLY-LOCHÉ AC See POUILLY-VINZELLES AC.

POUILLY-SUR-LOIRE AC *Loire Valley, France*   Light appley wines from the tiny plantings (40ha/100 acres) of the Chasselas grape around Pouilly-sur-Loire, the town that gave its name to POUILLY-FUMÉ. Drink as young as possible. Best producers: Serge Dagueneau★; Landrat-Guyollot★.

POUILLY-VINZELLES AC *Mâconnais, Burgundy, France*   With its neighbour Pouilly-Loché, this AC lies somewhat in the shadow of POUILLY-FUISSÉ. Most wines come through the co-op, but there are some good domaines.

Best vineyard is Les Quarts. Best producers: Clos des Rocs★, DROUHIN★, Cave des Grands Crus Blancs★, la Soufrandière★★, Tripoz★, Valette★. Best years: (2013) 12 11 10 09.

CH. POUJEAUX★ *Moulis AC, Haut-Médoc, Bordeaux, France* Frequently Poujeaux is the epitome of MOULIS – beautifully balanced, gentle ripe fruit jostled by stony dryness – but just lacking that something extra to propel it to a higher plane. Attractive at 5–6 years old, good vintages can easily last for 10–20 years. Since 2007 same ownership as Clos Fourtet★★ in ST-ÉMILION. Best years: 2012 11 10 09 **08 06 05 04 03 01 00 98 96 95**.

PRAGER *Wachau, Niederösterreich, Austria* Toni Bodenstein is one of the pioneers of the WACHAU, producing the elegant high-elevation Riesling Wachstum★★★, other Rieslings from the Achleiten and Klaus vineyards (often ★★★) and excellent Grüner Veltliners from Achleiten★★★. Best years: (2013) 12 11 **10 09 08 07 06 05 04**.

PREMIÈRES CÔTES DE BORDEAUX AC *Bordeaux, France* Part of the hilly region opposite GRAVES and SAUTERNES (see CADILLAC-CÔTES DE BORDEAUX). As of 2008 this AC designation is for sweet white wines only. Mildly sweet in style; drink young. Best producers: Crabitan-Bellevue★, Fayau★, du Juge, Suau. Best years: **2011 10 09**.

CH. PRIEURÉ-LICHINE★ *Margaux AC, 4ème Cru Classé, Haut-Médoc, Bordeaux, France* Right Bank specialist Stéphane Derenoncourt (PAVIE-MACQUIN, CANON-LA-GAFFELIÈRE) is consultant winemaker, and some vintages now have more fruit, finesse and perfume, especially the 2009 and 2011. Best years: 2012 11 10 09 **08 07 06 05 04 03 01 00 99 98**.

PRIEURÉ DE ST-JEAN DE BÉBIAN *Pézenas-Languedoc AC, Languedoc, France* Pioneering LANGUEDOC estate, now Russian-owned with a talented Australian winemaker, producing an intense, spicy, generous red★★, second wine La Chapelle de Bébian, a barrel-fermented white★ and pink Bébian en rose. Best years: (reds) (2013) 12 11 **10 09 08 07 06 03 04**.

PRIMITIVO PUGLIA's leading black grape, producing rich, alcoholic wines. It came from Croatia during the 18th century and has been enjoying a renaissance since it was found to be identical to California's Zinfandel. Grown on the sandy soils of PRIMITIVO DI MANDURIA DOC and the chalky slopes of Gioia del Colle DOC, giving two very different red wines: the former full and pulpy, the latter lighter and minerally. It is also grown along the Salento peninsula as good Primitivo del Tarantino IGT and quaffable Salento Rosso DOC.

PRIMITIVO DI MANDURIA DOC *Puglia, Italy* Historically the most important appellation for PUGLIA's Primitivo grape, it is now being compromised by expansion and the permitted addition of 15% other grapes. Best producers: Felline★★, Morella★★, Pervini★, Giovanni Soloperto. Best years: (2012) 11 10 09 08 07 06 05 04.

PRIMO ESTATE *McLaren Vale, South Australia* Joe Grilli is one of Australia's most thoughtful – and chatty – winemakers; quality has climbed even higher as he sources better vineyards, primarily in MCLAREN VALE. For his premium label, Joseph, Grilli adapts the Italian AMARONE method for Moda Cabernet-Merlot★★ (★★★ with 10 years' age) and makes a dense, eye-popping, complex Joseph Red fizz★★. He also does a sensuous Botrytis Riesling La Magia★★, remarkably scented Angel Gully Shiraz★★ and fine, powerful Nebbiolo★★. Zesty dry white La Biondina Colombard★ and cherry-ripe Il Briccone Shiraz-Sangiovese★ are two of

Australia's best easy-drinkers. Also bright, velvety Merlesco Merlot. Best years: (Moda Cabernet-Merlot) (2012) 11 10 09 08 **07 06 05 04 02 01 00 99 98 97 96 95 94 93 91**.

PRINCE EDWARD COUNTY *Ontario, Canada* Newly designated viticultural area jutting into Lake Ontario, east of Toronto; 27 wineries have opened since 2000. Deep limestone makes the region ideal for Pinot Noir, Chardonnay and sparkling wine; the Chardonnays have positively Burgundian oatmeal texture. Best producers: Closson Chase★, Exultet Estates★, Norman Hardie★★, Hinterland★ (sparkling), Rosehall Run★.

PRIORAT DOCa *Cataluña, Spain* A hilly, isolated district with very low-yielding vineyards planted on precipitous slopes of deep slate soil. Old-style fortified *rancio* wines used to attract little attention. Then in the 1980s a group of young winemakers revolutionized the area, bringing in state-of-the-art winemaking methods and grape varieties such as Cabernet Sauvignon to back up the native Garnacha and Cariñena. Their rare, expensive wines have taken the world by storm. Ready at 5 years old, the best will last much, much longer. Best producers: Capafons-Ossó★, Cims de Porrera★★, CLOS ERASMUS★★★, CLOS MOGADOR★★★, Combier-Fischer-Gérin★★ (Trio Infernal 2/3★★), La Conreria d'Scala Dei★, Costers del Siurana (Clos de l'Obac★★), Ferrer Bobet★, Ithaca★, Les Cousins Marc & Adrià★, Mas Alta★★, MAS DOIX★★, Mas d'en Gil (Clos Fontà★★, Coma Vella★), Mas Martinet (Clos Martinet★★), Nin★, Alvaro PALACIOS★★★, Pasanau Germans (Finca la Planeta★), Saó del Coster★, TERROIR AL LIMÍT★★★, TORRES★★, VALL LLACH★★. Best years: (reds) (2011) 10 09 **08 07 05 04 03 01 00 99 98 96 95**.

PROSECCO DOC/DOCG *Veneto and Friuli-Venezia Giulia, Italy* Following years of misuse and abuse, the laws relating to this north-eastern Italian grape variety, and the slightly off-dry *spumante* or (less bubbly) *frizzante* wines derived from it, have been substantially revised. The grape has been renamed Glera. Prosecco is no longer a grape but a wine that may be produced only in designated areas of Veneto and Friuli, and only as DOCG or DOC. The DOCG applies only to the wines of the historic Veneto zones of Conegliano, Valdobbiadene (with Cartizze subzone) and Colli Asolani (or Asolo). Up to 15% of other grapes, including Chardonnay, may be used in addition to Glera. Most Prosecco is made by the Charmat (second fermentation in tank) method, but artisan producers are returning to higher-quality bottle-fermented Prosecco 'Colfòndo' (with sediment). Best producers: Adami★, Bele Casel★★, Biancavigna, Bisol★, Carpene Malvolti★, Casa Coste Piane★★, Le Colture★, Nino Franco★, Masottina★, La Riva dei Frati★, Ruggeri★, Vignarosa, Zardetto★.

PROVENCE *France* Provence is home to France's oldest vineyards, but is better known for its beaches and arts festivals than for its wines. However, even Provence is caught up in the revolution sweeping through the vineyards of southern France. Most of the wine comes from the CÔTES DE PROVENCE, COTEAUX VAROIS-EN-PROVENCE, Coteaux de Pierrevert and COTEAUX D'AIX-EN-PROVENCE. There are 5 smaller ACs (BANDOL, les BAUX-DE-PROVENCE, BELLET, CASSIS and PALETTE), and the BOUCHES-DU-RHÔNE, Alpilles, Alpes-Maritimes and Var IGPs are becoming increasingly important. Reds can be good. Two distinct rosé styles are emerging: lighter aperitif wine and a wood-aged 'gastronomic' style. Whites have a way to go, but top producers are making good wines from Rolle (Vermentino) and Viognier is beginning to appear.

J J PRÜM *Bernkastel, Mosel, Germany* There are a confusing number of Prüms in the MOSEL – this is the best estate, making some of Germany's most exquisite Riesling in sites like the Sonnenuhr★★★ in WEHLEN, Himmelreich★★ in GRAACH and Lay★★ and Badstube★★ in BERNKASTEL. Slow to develop but they all have great aging potential. Best years: (2013) (12) 11 **10 09 08 07 06 05 04 03 02 01 99 97**.

PUGLIA *Italy* This region was once a prolific source of blending wines, but an aspirational younger generation is producing more and better bottled examples, focused especially on the indigenous varieties of red Negroamaro, Primitivo and Uva di Troia, and white Bombino, Fiano, Greco and Malvasia. In the southern 'heel' of the region many wines are increasingly released under the simple Salento IGT, rather than risk losing the consumer in the myriad of tiny DOCs. That said, SALICE SALENTINO is one of the more reliable DOCs and the Uva di Troia grape is important in the CASTEL DEL MONTE DOC. The red Primitivo makes a big impact, but it is the Negroamaro grape grown on traditional bush-trained or *alberello* vines in the Salento peninsula that provides the best wines, whether red or the excellent *rosato* (pink). Best producers: L'Astore Masseria★★, Candido★, Duca Carlo Guarini★, Monaci★★, Morella★★, Taurino★★, Vallone★★.

PUISSEGUIN-ST-ÉMILION AC *Bordeaux, France* Small ST-ÉMILION satellite. The wines are generally fairly solid but with an attractive chunky fruit, for drinking at 3–5 years. Best producers: Bel-Air, Branda, Clarisse, Durand-Laplagne★, Fongaban, Guibeau-la-Fourvieille, Laurets, la Mauriane★, Producteurs Réunis, Soleil★. Best years: **2012 10 09 08 05**.

PULENTA ESTATE *Mendoza, Argentina* The altitude and proximity to the Andes ensure wines of purity, freshness and elegance. La Flor Malbec★ is juicy and full of fresh blue fruits; La Flor Sauvignon Blanc★ is a racy, tropical delight. The Estate range includes such oddities as Pinot Gris and late-harvest Cabernet Franc Tardío alongside supple, aromatic Malbec★ and Cabernet Sauvignon★. The sublime XI Gran Cabernet Franc★★ is packed with raspberry coulis richness and leafy freshness, and VII Gran Corte★★ red blend is dense and rich.

PULIGNY-MONTRACHET AC *Côte de Beaune, Burgundy, France* Puligny is one of the finest and most famous white wine villages in the world and adds the name of its greatest Grand Cru, le MONTRACHET, to its own. There are 3 other Grands Crus (BÂTARD-MONTRACHET, Bienvenues-BÂTARD-MONTRACHET and Chevalier-MONTRACHET) and 11 Premiers Crus. The flatter vineyards use the Puligny-Montrachet AC, whose standard is nowadays pretty good. Good vintages need 3-5 years' aging, while Premiers Crus and Grands Crus should last 10 years or more, but are often ready earlier. A few barrels of red wine are made. Best producers: BACHELET-Monnot★★, Blain-Gagnard★★, H Boillot★★, J-M Boillot★★, CARILLON★★★, Chartron★, Chavy★, Deux MONTILLE★, DROUHIN★★, B Ente★, FAIVELEY★★, JADOT★★, Louis LATOUR★, Dom. LEFLAIVE★★★, O LEFLAIVE★, Leroux★, P Pernot★★, Ch. de Puligny-Montrachet★★, SAUZET★★. Best years: (2013) 12 11 **10 09 08 07 06 05 04 02 00**.

PYRENEES See GRAMPIANS AND PYRENEES.

QUARTS DE CHAUME AC *Loire Valley, France* The Chenin Blanc grape finds one of its most rewarding mesoclimates in this 40ha (100-acre) AC within the larger COTEAUX DU LAYON AC; steep, sheltered, schistous slopes favour optimal ripening and noble rot. The result is intense, sweet wines with a mineral backbone, which can last for longer than almost any in the world – although many can be drunk after 5 years. Best producers: P Baudouin★, Baumard★★, Bellerive★★, Bergerie★★, Forges★, Laffourcade★, PIERRE-BISE★★★, Pithon-Paillé★, Plaisance★, Joseph Renou★★, Suronde★★, la Varière★. Best years: 2011 **10 09 07 06 05 03 02 01 97 96 95 90 89**.

QUARTZ REEF *Central Otago, South Island, New Zealand* Best known for powerful, serious Pinot Noir★★ (sometimes ★★★) and sleek bottle-fermented sparkling wine★ (vintage★★). Intensely flavoured, minerally, almost chewy Pinot Gris★ is one of their lesser-known stars. Best years: (Pinot Noir) (2013) **12 10 09 08 07 06**.

QUEENSLAND *Australia* The Queensland wine industry – closely linked to tourism – is expanding fast. About 60 wineries perch on rocky hills in the main region, the Granite Belt, near the NEW SOUTH WALES border. New areas South Burnett (north-west of Brisbane), Darling Downs (around the town of Toowoomba) and Mount Tamborine in the Gold Coast hinterland are showing promise. Alternative varieties such as Verdelho and Fiano are providing some inspiration. Best producers: Barambah, BOIREANN★★, Robert Channon★, Clovely Estate, Heritage, Lucas Estate, Preston Peak★, Pyramids Road, Robinsons Family, Sirromet, Summit Estate, Witches Falls★.

QUERCIABELLA *Chianti Classico DOCG, Tuscany, Italy* Modern Chianti producer with an extravagantly scented, rich-fruited CHIANTI CLASSICO★★. But the top wines are a tropical white Batàr★★ (Pinot Bianco-Chardonnay) and tobaccoey, spicy Camartina★★★ (Sangiovese-Cabernet). Mongrana★, a juicy, smooth-but-serious blend of Sangiovese, Merlot and Cabernet Sauvignon, is from a new estate in Maremma. Best years: (Camartina) (2011) **10 09 08 07 06 04 01 99**.

Querciabella
CHIANTI CLASSICO DOCG
2009
Agricola Querciabella

QUILCEDA CREEK *Washington State, USA* One of America's top Cabernet Sauvignons★★★, a wine with intense concentration and exceptional character. It benefits from cellaring for 7–10 years. A less expensive Columbia Valley Red★★ offers a tantalizing glimpse of the winemaking style. Best years: (2012) **11 10 09 08 07 06 05 04 03**.

QUINCY AC *Loire Valley, France* Appealingly racy, gooseberry-flavoured, dry white wine from Sauvignon Blanc vineyards west of Bourges. Can age for a year or two. Best producers: Ballandors★, H BOURGEOIS, Chevilly★, B & L Lecomte★, Mardon★, A Pigeat★, J C Roux★, J Rouzé★, Trotereau★.

QUINTARELLI *Valpolicella DOC, Veneto, Italy* The late Bepi Quintarelli was the great traditional winemaker of VALPOLICELLA; his daughter and family continue the tradition. The Classico Superiore★★ is left in cask for about 4 years and the famed AMARONE★★★ and RECIOTO★★ for up to 7 years before release. Alzero★★ is a spectacular Amarone-style wine made from Cabernets Franc and Sauvignon. The Garganega-based VENETO IGT Bianco Secco is a beautifully waxy thing. Best years: (Amarone) (2010) (09) (08) 07 **06 04 03 01 99 97 95 93 90 88 85 83**.

QUINTESSA *Rutherford AVA, California, USA* Silky, almost sensuously balanced BORDEAUX-blend red from impeccable organic vineyard. Unusually, Carmenère features in the blend. Best years: 2011 **10 09 07 05 01**.

QUPÉ *Santa Maria Valley AVA, California, USA* Qupé is focused on cooler-climate Syrahs and makes a savoury, tasty pepper- and violet-scented Bien Nacido Syrah★. The Reserve Chardonnay★ and Bien Nacido Cuvée★ (a Viognier-Chardonnay blend) have beguiling appley fruit and perfume. A leading exponent of red and white RHÔNE-style wines, including Viognier★, Marsanne★ and Roussanne★★. Best years: (Syrah) 2012 **10** 09 08 07 06 05 04 03 02 01 00 99 98.

CH. DE LA RAGOTIÈRE *Muscadet Sèvre-et-Maine, Loire Valley, France* The Couillaud brothers are pioneers. M★★ is an old-vines wine matured *sur lie* for more than 2 years. The standard Muscadet★ is elegant and built to last, too; lighter ones come from the Couillauds' other property, Ch. la Morinière. Vin de pays Chardonnay★ is a speciality and the Collection Privée label includes a late-harvest Petit Manseng, Sauvignon Gris★ and Viognier. Best years: (M) 2013 **10** 09 06 01 99.

RAÏMAT *Costers del Segre DO, Cataluña, Spain* Owned by CODORNÍU, this large, irrigated estate makes balanced wines from Tempranillo, Cabernet Sauvignon and Chardonnay. Also lively 100% Chardonnay CAVA.

DOM. DE LA RAMAYE *Gaillac AOP, South-West France* Individualistic wines: whites, mostly from Mauzac, include Les Cavaillés Bas★★, sweeter Sous-Bois de Rayssac★★ and, in great years, Quintessence★★★. Reds include La Combe d'Avès★★, a Duras-Braucol blend, and Prunelard-based Le Grand Tertre★★. Best years: (2012) (11) **10** 09 08 06 05 04.

RAMEY WINE CELLARS *Sonoma County, California, USA* David Ramey is one of the state's most creative winemakers (as well as a consultant for many other wineries) and his marvellously savoury, primarily CARNEROS and RUSSIAN RIVER-based Chardonnays★★ (Hyde★★, Ritchie★★★), NAPA-based Cabernet Sauvignons★★ and scented SONOMA-based Syrahs★★ are highly sought-after. Best years: (Cabernet) 2012 **10** 09 08 07 06 05 01.

RAMONET *Chassagne-Montrachet, Côte de Beaune, Burgundy, France* The Ramonets (Noël and Jean-Claude) produce some of the most complex of all white Burgundies from 3 Grands Crus (BÂTARD-MONTRACHET★★★, Bienvenues-BÂTARD-MONTRACHET★★★, le MONTRACHET★★★) and Premiers Crus (Ruchottes★★★, Caillerets★★★, Chaumées★★★, Boudriotte★★, Vergers★★, Morgeot★★). To spare your wallet, try the ST-AUBIN★ or the village CHASSAGNE-MONTRACHET★★. Red Clos de la Boudriotte★★ is excellent too. Best years: (whites) (2013) 12 11 **10** 09 **08** 07 06 05 02 00 99.

JOÃO PORTUGAL RAMOS *Alentejo, Portugal* João Portugal Ramos has built his ALENTEJO, TEJO (Falua) and DOURO (Duorum) empire from nothing. Excellent Vila Santa Trincadeira★, Aragonês (Tempranillo)★ and Syrah★, and intensely dark-fruited red blend Vila Santa Reserva★★. Good Marquês de Borba reds, with brilliant red Reserva★★. Tagus Creek is juicy and affordable. Best years: 2012 11 **08** 07 05 04 01 00 99 97.

RAMOS PINTO *Douro DOC and Port DOC, Douro, Portugal* Innovative company owned by ROEDERER. Full-bodied Late Bottled Vintage★ and tawny ports (10-year-old Quinta de Ervamoira★, 20-year-old Quinta do Bom Retiro★★). Vintage ports★★ are rich and early maturing. Consistently good Duas Quintas DOURO reds (Reserva★, Reserva Especial★★) and white (Branco Reserva★). Best years: (Vintage) 2011 **07** 04 03 00 97 95 94 83.

CASTELLO DEI RAMPOLLA *Chianti Classico DOCG, Tuscany, Italy* French-influenced CHIANTI CLASSICO★ plus IGTs Sammarco★★ (Cabernet Sauvignon-Sangiovese) and Vigna d'Alceo★★ (Cabernet Sauvignon-Petit Verdot). Best years: (Sammarco) (2011) (10) 09 **08** 07 06 04 01 00 99; (Vigna d'Alceo) (2011) **10** 09 08 07 06 04 01 00 99 98 97.

RANDERSACKER *Franken, Germany* Village near WÜRZBURG, producing excellent dry Riesling, dry Silvaner, spicy Traminer and piercingly intense Rieslaner. **Best producers:** Bürgerspital, JULIUSSPITAL★, Reiss, Schmitt's Kinder★, Störrlein★, Trockene Schmitts. **Best years:** (2013) 12 11 **10 09 08 07 06.**

RAPEL *Chile* One of Chile's most exciting red wine regions, the cradle of Chilean Carmenère, Rapel covers both the Cachapoal Valley in the north and the COLCHAGUA Valley in the south. New CONCHA Y TORO coastal development Ucúquer is promising thrilling cool flavours. **Best producers:** Altaïr★★/SAN PEDRO, ANAKENA★, CASA SILVA★, Clos des Fous★★, CONCHA Y TORO★★, CONO SUR★, EMILIANA★★, LAPOSTOLLE★★, Los Vascos, Misiones de Rengo★, MONTES★★, MontGras, Neyen★★, VENTISQUERO★, Viu Manent★.

KENT RASMUSSEN *Carneros AVA, California, USA* Delicious, oatmealy Chardonnay★★ capable of considerable aging and a fascinating juicy but also long-lasting Pinot Noir★★ are made by ultra-traditional methods. Ramsay is the second label, for Pinot Noir★, Cabernet Sauvignon and Merlot. **Best years:** (Pinot Noir) 2012 10 09 08 07 06 05 02 01 00 99 98.

RASTEAU *Rhône Valley, France* The AC is both for red wine and for *vin doux naturel*, fortified Grenache (red, white and a *rancio* version which is left in barrel for 2 or more years). The red, robust and spicy, delivers big flavours and does well in hot, dry vintages (2009). **Best producers:** E Balme, Beau Mistral★, Beaurenard★★, Coteaux des Travers, Escaravailles★, Gourt de Mautens★★ (until 2009, now IGP Vaucluse), Grand Nicolet★★, Ortas/Cave de Rasteau★, Famille Perrin★, Rabasse-Charavin, ST GAYAN, Santa Duc★, la Soumade★, Trapadis★. **Best years:** (reds) 2012 **11 10 09 07 06 05 04 03.**

RAUENTHAL *Rheingau, Germany* Only a few producers make the best of this village's great Baiken and Gehrn sites for intense, spicy Rieslings. **Best producers:** Georg BREUER★★, Langwerth von Simmern★, Staatsweingut (Kloster Eberbach)★. **Best years:** (2013) 12 11 **10 09 08 06 04.**

CH. RAUZAN-SÉGLA★★ *Margaux AC, 2ème Cru Classé, Haut-Médoc, Bordeaux, France* The purchase of the property by Chanel in 1994 followed by massive investment and astute management have propelled Rauzan-Ségla up the quality ladder. Now the wines have a rich plummy fruit, round, mellow texture, powerful woody spice and good concentration, though they rarely show typical MARGAUX scent. Second wine: Ségla. **Best years:** 2012 11 10 09 08 **07 06 05 04 03 02 01 00 98 96 95 90.**

DOM. RAVENEAU *Chablis, Burgundy, France* Beautifully nuanced CHABLIS from 3 Grands Crus (Blanchot★★★, les Clos★★★, Valmur★★★) and 4 Premiers Crus (Montée de Tonnerre★★★, Vaillons★★, Butteaux★★★, Chapelot★★), made using a combination of mostly old oak and stainless-steel fermentation. The wines can age for a decade or more. **Best years:** (top crus) (2013) 12 11 10 09 08 **07 06 05 02 00 99.**

RAVENSWOOD *Sonoma Valley AVA, California, USA* Zinfandel expert Joel Peterson established Ravenswood in 1976. Constellation bought the winery in 2001, but Peterson remains in evidence. Large-volume Vintners Blend★ has improved recently, and the old-vine Zinfandels (Sonoma★, Napa★, LODI★) are tasty and characterful. Single-vineyard wines like Teldeschi can be ★★. Super-premium Icon★★ is a blend of Carignan, Petite Sirah, Zinfandel and other grapes from ancient vines.

CH. RAYAS *Châteauneuf-du-Pape, Rhône Valley, France* Emmanuel Reynaud produces exotically fragrant, rich but subtle reds★★★ and whites★★ that age incredibly well. Methods are traditional, prices are high, but recent vintages are on top form – at its best Rayas is thrilling. The red is made entirely from low-yielding Grenache vines, while the white is a blend of

Clairette, Grenache Blanc and a drop or two (so rumour has it) of Chardonnay. Second-label Pignan can also be impressive. CÔTES DU RHÔNE Ch. de Fonsalette★★ is usually wonderful in the same style as Rayas, with a notable old-vine Syrah★★. Also fine VACQUEYRAS Ch. des Tours★. Best years: (Châteauneuf-du-Pape) (2013) 12 11 10 09 08 07 06 05 **04 03 01 99 98 96 95 94 91 90 89 88 86**; (whites) 2013 12 11 10 09 **08 07 06 05 04 03 01 00 99 98 97 96 95 94 91 90 89**.

RdV VINEYARDS *Virginia, USA* Former US Marine Rutger de Vink studied winemaking with Jim Law of LINDEN before establishing his own winery and steep sloping vineyard west of Washington DC. Generously financed and meticulously researched, RdV produces two BORDEAUX-style blends, Lost Mountain★★ and Rendezvous★. Launched in 2011, RdV immediately helped raise Virginia's national and international profile.

REBHOLZ *Siebeldingen, Pfalz, Germany* Crystalline Riesling★★, Weiss-burgunder★★ (Pinot Blanc) and Grauburgunder★ (Pinot Gris), with vibrant fruit aromas. Top of the range are intensely mineral dry Riesling★★★ from the Kastanienbusch and Sonnenschein vineyards, and extravagantly aromatic dry Muskateller★★. The sparkling wine★★ is among Germany's most elegant. Also fine Chardonnay★★ and serious Spätburgunder★★ (Pinot Noir) reds. Best years: (whites) (2013) 12 11 **10 09 08 07 06 05 04**; (reds) (2013) (12) 11 **10 09 08 07 06**.

RECIOTO DI SOAVE DOCG *Veneto, Italy* Sweet white wine made in the SOAVE zone from dried grapes. Garganega grapes give wonderfully delicate yet intense wines that age well for up to a decade. One of the best, ANSELMI's I Capitelli★★, is sold as IGT Veneto. Best producers: Cà Rugate★, La Cappuccina★★, Coffele★★, Gini★★, PIEROPAN★★, Prà★, Bruno Sartori★, Tamellini★★. Best years: (2011) **10 09 08 06 04**.

RECIOTO DELLA VALPOLICELLA DOCG *Veneto, Italy* The great sweet wine of VALPOLICELLA, made from grapes picked earlier than usual and left to dry on straw mats until February or March. The wines are deep in colour, with a rich, bitter-sweet cherryish fruit. Top wines age well for 10 years, but most are best drunk young. The Classico tag is important, though not essential. Best producers: Accordini★, ALLEGRINI★★, Bolla (Spumante★), Brigaldara★, BUSSOLA★★★, Michele Castellani★★, Corte Sant'Alda★★★, DAL FORNO★★★, MASI★, Novaia★, QUINTARELLI★★, Le Ragose★, Le Salette★, Serègo Alighieri★★, Speri★, Tommasi★, Villa Monteleone★★, Viviani★. Best years: (2011) 10 **09 08 06 05 04**.

RÉGNIÉ AC *Beaujolais, Burgundy, France* In good years this BEAUJOLAIS Cru is light, aromatic and enjoyable, but can be thin in lesser years. Best producers: J-M Burgaud★, DUBOEUF (Dom. des Buyats★), Rochette, Gilles Roux/de la Plaigne★, C Thevenet★. Best years: **(2013)** 11.

DOM. LA RÉMÉJEANNE *Côtes du Rhône AC, Rhône Valley, France* First-class property making a range of strikingly individual, punchy wines. Long-lived CÔTES DU RHÔNE les Genévriers★★ has the intensity, weight and texture of good CHÂTEAUNEUF-DU-PAPE, while CÔTES DU RHÔNE les Eglantiers★★ is superb. Both need at least 3–5 years' aging. Also good Côtes du Rhône les Chèvrefeuilles★ and les Arbousiers★ (good-value red and white). Best years: (les Genévriers) 2012 11 **10 09 07 06 05**.

REMELLURI *Rioja DOCa, País Vasco, Spain* Organic RIOJA estate producing red wines with far more fruit than usual and good concentration for aging – the best are ★★. There is also a delicate, barrel-fermented white★★. As of 2010, Telmo RODRÍGUEZ is at the helm again. Best years: (Reserva) (2010) 09 **07 06 05 04 03 02 01 99 98 96 95 94**.

REUILLY AC *Loire Valley, France* Dry but attractive Sauvignon from west of SANCERRE. Some pale Pinot Noir red and Pinot Gris rosé. **Best producers:** H Beurdin, G Bigonneau, D Jamain★, N & C Lafond, A Mabillot, J Rouzé, Les Demoiselles Tatin, J Vincent.

REYNEKE *Stellenbosch WO, South Africa* One of the Cape's first biodynamic wine farms. Natural ferment adds subtlety to vibrant Chenin Blanc★★ and cool, creamy yet precise Reserve White★★. Star reds are rounded, generous Syrah★ and spicy, herby Reserve Red★★ (Syrah-Cabernet Sauvignon); also perfumed Cornerstone BORDEAUX-style blend.

CH. REYNON *Cadillac-Côtes de Bordeaux AC, Bordeaux, France* Property of enology professor Denis Dubourdieu. Dry whites, particularly the fruity, minerally Sauvignon Blanc★, are delightful (drink the most recent vintage) and the red★ is good, too. The lovely white GRAVES Clos Floridène★★ is vinified at Reynon. **Best years:** (reds) **2012 11 10 09 08 06.**

RHEINGAU *Germany* 3145ha (7770-acre) wine region on a south-facing stretch of the Rhine flanking the city of Wiesbaden, planted mostly with Riesling and some Spätburgunder (Pinot Noir). At their best, the Rieslings are racy and slow-maturing. Famous names are no longer a guarantee of finest quality, as a new generation of winemakers is producing many of the best wines. See also ERBACH, HATTENHEIM, HOCHHEIM, JOHANNISBERG, KIEDRICH, RAUENTHAL, RÜDESHEIM. **Best years:** (2013) 12 11 **10 09 08 07 06 05.**

RHEINHESSEN *Germany* 26,500ha (65,480-acre) wine region with a number of famous top-quality estates, especially at river terrace villages Bodenheim, Nackenheim, NIERSTEIN and Oppenheim, and at BINGEN to the north-west. Further away from the river a few growers, such as KELLER, WITTMANN, Wagner-Stempel and Gutzler also make superlative wines. Weissburgunder (Pinot Blanc) is a rising star. **Best years:** (2013) 12 11 **10 09 08 07 05.**

RHÔNE VALLEY *France* The Rhône starts out as a river in Switzerland, cruising through Lake Geneva before hurtling westward into France. In the area south of Lyon, between Vienne and Avignon, the valley becomes one of France's great wine regions. In the northern part precipitous granite slopes overhang the river and the small amount of wine produced has remarkable individuality and great finesse. The Syrah grape reigns here in CÔTE-RÔTIE and on the great hill of HERMITAGE. ST-JOSEPH, CROZES-HERMITAGE and CORNAS also make excellent reds, while the white Viognier grape yields perfumed, musky wine at CONDRIEU and elegance at the tiny CHÂTEAU-GRILLET. In the southern part the steep slopes give way to hot, wide, alluvial plains, with hills both in the west and east. Most of these vineyards are either CÔTES DU RHONE or CÔTES DU RHÔNE-VILLAGES reds, whites and rosés, but there are also specific ACs, the best known being CHÂTEAUNEUF-DU-PAPE, GIGONDAS and the luscious golden dessert wine, MUSCAT DE BEAUMES-DE-VENISE. See also BEAUMES-DE-VENISE, CAIRANNE, CLAIRETTE DE DIE, COSTIÈRES DE NÎMES, COTEAUX DE L'ARDÈCHE, GRIGNAN-LES-ADHÉMAR, LIRAC, LUBÉRON, RASTEAU, ST-PÉRAY, TAVEL, VACQUEYRAS, VENTOUX, VINSOBRES.

RÍAS BAIXAS DO *Galicia, Spain* The best of GALICIA's DOs. The magic ingredient is the Albariño grape, making dry, fruity whites with a glorious fragrance and citrus tang. In general drink young, but there are now ageworthy whites and fragrant, Atlantic-cooled reds from native grape varieties. **Best producers:** Agro de Bazán★★, Castro Martín, Martín Códax★, Condes de Albarei★, Quinta de Couselo, Fillaboa★★, Forjas del

Salnés★★, Adegas Galegas★, Lagar de Besada★, Lagar de Fornelos★, La Val★, Gerardo Méndez★★, Viña Nora, Palacio de Fefiñanes★★, Pazo de Barrantes, Pazo de Señorans★★, Pazos de Lusco★, Santiago Ruiz★, Terras Gauda★★, Tricó★★, Valmiñor★, Zárate★★.

RIBERA DEL DUERO DO *Castilla y León, Spain* Dark, mouthfilling reds, ideally with delightful dry blackcurrant fruit, from Tinto Fino (Tempranillo), sometimes with a little Cabernet Sauvignon or Merlot – generally richer and more concentrated than those of RIOJA. But excessive expansion of vineyards, increase in yields and unrestrained use of oak may threaten its supremacy. Best producers: AALTO★★, Alión★★, Alonso del Yerro★★, Arroyo, Arzuaga★, Áster★, Los Astrales★, Dominio de Atauta, Balbás★, Briego, Casajús★★, Cillar de Silos★, Convento San Francisco★, O FOURNIER★, Goyo García Viadero★, Hacienda Monasterio★★, Hacienda Solano★, Matarromera★, Montecastro★★, Emilio Moro★★, Pago de los Capellanes★, Pago de Carraovejas★, Pedrosa/Pérez Pascuas★★, PESQUERA★★, PINGUS★★★, Protos★, Rodero★, Telmo RODRIGUEZ★, Hermanos Sastre★★, Tarsus★, TORRES (Celeste)★), Valduero★, Valtravieso, VEGA SICILIA★★★. Best years: (2011) 10 09 **05 04 03 01 00 99 96 95 94 91 90 89 86 85**.

BARONE RICASOLI *Chianti Classico DOCG, Tuscany, Italy* The largest estate in CHIANTI CLASSICO, complete with medieval castle. The flagship is Castello di Brolio★. Riserva Rocca Guicciarda★ is good value. Casalferro★★ (Merlot) is IGT. Best years: (Casalferro) (2011) **10 09 08 07 06 04 01**.

RICCITELLI *Mendoza, Argentina* Matías Riccitelli, son of Jorge Riccitelli (winemaker at NORTON), is making a name for himself with a beautiful little winery in Las Compueras and some stylish wines, concentrating on Malbec from different areas in Mendoza. Top wine is the impressive Republica del Malbec★★. Vineyard Selection Malbec★★ is intense and rich, while 'The Apple…' entry-level Malbec★★ is earthy and powerful.

DOM. RICHEAUME *Côtes de Provence AC, Provence, France* German-owned property, run on organic principles and producing impressively deep-coloured reds★; Les Terrasses★★ is from Syrah aged in new wood. Best years: (Terrasses) (2013) 12 11 10 09 08 07 **06**.

RICHEBOURG AC *Grand Cru, Côte de Nuits, Burgundy, France* Rich, fleshy wine from the northern end of VOSNE-ROMANÉE. Most domaine-bottlings are exceptional. All are fiendishly expensive. Best producers: GRIVOT★★★, Anne GROS★★★, A-F GROS★★★, Hudelot-NOËLLAT★★★, Dom. LEROY★★★, T LIGER-BELAIR★★, MÉO-CAMUZET★★★, Dom. de la ROMANÉE-CONTI★★★. Best years: (2013) 12 11 10 09 08 07 06 05 **03 02 01 00 99 98 96 95 93 91 90**.

MAX FERD RICHTER *Mülheim, Mosel, Germany* Modestly priced yet racy Rieslings from top sites, including WEHLENer Sonnenuhr★★, BRAUNEBERGER Juffer★★ and GRAACHER Domprobst★. Richter's Mülheimer Helenen-kloster vineyard produces a magical Eiswein★★★ virtually every year, unless wild boar eat the crop. Best years: (2013) 12 11 **10 09 08 07 06 05 04**.

RIDGE VINEYARDS *Santa Cruz Mountains AVA, California, USA* Trailblazing winery which produces some of California's most pleasing and original wines, with a particular emphasis on old-vine fruit. Paul Draper's Zinfandels★★★ have great intensity and age wonderfully, especially the Lytton Springs bottling from DRY CREEK VALLEY. Other reds, led by cool-climate Cabernet-based Monte Bello★★★, require years, if not decades, to come around. Geyserville★★ is a fascinating blend of Zinfandel with old-vine Carignan, Syrah and Petite Sirah which is good young but better old. There's fine Chardonnay★★, too. Best years: (Monte Bello) 2009 **08 07 06 05 03 02 01 00 99 98 97 95 94 93 92 91 90**.

RIESLING

 If you have tasted wines with names like Laski Riesling, Olasz Riesling, Welschriesling, Gray Riesling, Riesling Italico, Cape Riesling and the like and found them bland or unappetizing, do not blame the Riesling grape. These wines have filched Riesling's name, but have nothing whatsoever to do with the great grape itself.

Riesling is Germany's finest contribution to the world of wine – and herein lies the second problem. German wines fell to such a low level of general esteem through the proliferation of wines like Liebfraumilch during the 1980s that Riesling was dragged down with them.

So what is true Riesling? It is a very ancient German grape, probably the descendant of wild vines growing in the Rhine Valley. It certainly performs best in the cool vineyard regions of Germany's Rhine, Nahe and Mosel Valleys, and in Alsace and Austria. It also does well in Ontario in Canada, New Zealand and both warm and cool parts of Australia. Ironically, the Riesling revival is being led more by Australia than Germany. It is widely planted in Washington State and New York's Finger Lakes region.

Young Rieslings often show a delightful floral perfume, sometimes blended with the crispness of green apples, often lime, peach, nectarine or apricot, sometimes even raisin, honey or spice, depending upon the ripeness of the grapes. As the wines age, the lime often intensifies, and a flavour perhaps of slate, perhaps of petrol/kerosene, appears – or, in Australia, buttered toast! In general Rieslings may be drunk young, but top dry wines can improve for many years, and the truly sweet German styles can age for generations.

WINE STYLES

Germany These wines have a marvellous perfume and an ability to hold on to a piercing acidity, even at high ripeness levels, so long as the ripening period has been warm and gradual rather than broiling and rushed. German Rieslings can be bone dry, through to medium and lusciously sweet. Styles range from crisp elegant Mosels to riper, fuller wines from the Rheingau and Nahe, with rounder, fatter examples from the Pfalz and Baden regions in the south. The very sweet Trockenbeerenauslese (TBA) Rieslings are made from grapes affected by noble rot; for Eiswein (icewine), also intensely sweet, the grapes are picked and pressed while frozen.

Other regions France's Alsace gives generally austere, restrained wines, while the valleys of the Danube in Austria give stunning dry wines that combine richness with fragrance and elegance. The mountain vineyards of northern Italy and the cool vineyards of the Czech Republic and Slovakia can show a floral sharp style. Cool areas of South Australia, Tasmania, Victoria and Western Australia all offer superb – and different – examples typified by a citrus, mineral scent, and often challenging austerity. New Zealand's style is floral, fresh and frequently attractively off-dry, but with enough acidity to age. South Africa's best examples are sweet, but dry versions are appearing, with those from Elgin promising. Chile has some fragrant examples in San Antonio and Bío Bío. The USA has fragrant dry Rieslings from New York, mostly off-dry from the Pacific Northwest and often slightly sweet styles from California. Michigan and Ohio have excellent potential. Canada produces bone-dry Riesling to ultra-sweet Icewine.

BEST PRODUCERS

Germany

Dry BASSERMANN-JORDAN, G BREUER, BÜRKLIN-WOLF, BUSCH, Christmann, HEYMANN-LÖWENSTEIN, KELLER, KNIPSER, KOEHLER-RUPRECHT, KÜNSTLER, LEITZ, REBHOLZ, SAUER, WITTMANN.

Non-dry DIEL, DÖNNHOFF, HAAG, HAART, HEYMANN-LÖWENSTEIN, KARTHÄUSERHOF, Kesselstatt, KÜHN, KÜNSTLER, Dr LOOSEN, MAXIMIN GRÜNHAUS, MOLITOR, MÜLLER-CATOIR, MÜLLER-SCHARZHOF, J J PRÜM, ST URBANS-HOF, Willi SCHAEFER, SCHÄFER-FRÖHLICH, SCHLOSS LIESER, SELBACH-OSTER, WEIL, ZILLIKEN.

Austria

ALZINGER, BRÜNDLMAYER, Hiedler, HIRTZBERGER, J Högl, KNOLL, Loimer, Malat, NIGL, NIKOLAIHOF, F X PICHLER, Rudi PICHLER, PRAGER, SCHLOSS GOBELSBURG, Schmelz.

France

(Alsace) J-B Adam, Léon Beyer, P Blanck, A Boxler, DEISS, Dirler-Cadé, HUGEL, JOSMEYER, Kientzler, A MANN, MURÉ, OSTERTAG, SCHOFFIT, TRIMBACH, WEINBACH, ZIND-HUMBRECHT.

Australia

Tim ADAMS, Jim BARRY, Bloodwood, Leo Buring (Leonay), Castle Rock, Larry CHERUBINO, Crabtree, Eden Road, Forest Hill, Frankland Estate, FREYCINET, Frogmore Creek, Gilberts, GROSSET, Heggies, HENSCHKE, HOUGHTON, HOWARD PARK, JACOB'S CREEK (Steingarten), Kerrigan & Berry, Kilikanoon, KNAPPSTEIN, KT, Peter LEHMANN, Mesh, MOUNT HORROCKS, PETALUMA, Pewsey Vale, SEPPELT (Drumborg), Skillogalee, Three Drops.

Canada

(British Columbia) CedarCreek, Quails' Gate; *(Ontario)* Cave Spring, Château des Charmes (sweet), Flat Rock, TAWSE, THIRTY BENCH, Vineland Estates.

Chile CASA MARÎN, CONO SUR (Single Vineyard), Viña LEYDA.

New Zealand

Auburn, CLOUDY BAY, DRY RIVER, FELTON ROAD, Foxes Island, FRAMINGHAM, FROMM, Mt Difficulty, Mount Edward, NEUDORF, PEGASUS BAY, Te Whare Ra, VILLA MARIA.

South Africa Paul CLUVER (sweet).

USA

(Washington) CHATEAU STE MICHELLE (Eroica), LONG SHADOWS (Poet's Leap); *(New York)* ANTHONY ROAD, FOX RUN, Dr Konstantin FRANK, Ravines, Red Newt, Hermann J WIEMER.

265

RIDGEVIEW *West Sussex, England* The most consistent producer of stylish and good-value UK sparkling wines. Reasonable prices, good distribution plus exports mean that their wines tend to be released younger than some. Their Blanc de Blancs can match (and often beat) CHAMPAGNE. The range includes the traditional three-variety blends Cavendish★ and Bloomsbury★, Knightsbridge★ (blanc de noirs), Grosvenor★★★ (blanc de blancs), Fitzrovia★★, a Chardonnay-based rosé, and Victoria★★, a rosé from Pinots Noir and Meunier. Best years: **2011 10**.

RIESLANER One of the few German grape crossings of real merit, Rieslaner resembles Riesling, but with greater breadth and even higher acidity. This makes it an ideal sweet wine grape, as MÜLLER-CATOIR (Pfalz), KELLER (Rheinhessen) and some Franken growers have demonstrated.

RIESLING See pages 264–5.

CH. RIEUSSEC★★★ *Sauternes AC, 1er Cru Classé, Bordeaux, France* Apart from the peerless Ch. d'YQUEM, Rieussec is often the richest, most succulent wine of SAUTERNES. No Rieussec made in 2012. Dry white 'R' is nothing special. Second wine: Carmes de Rieussec. Owned by LAFITE-ROTHSCHILD. Best years: 2011 10 **09 07 06 05 04 03 02 01 99 98 97 96 95 90 89**.

RIGLOS *Mendoza, Argentina* This project is very specifically focused on high-altitude vineyards in Gualtallary in the UCO VALLEY. The Gran Cabernet★★, Gran Malbec★★ and red blend Gran Corte★★ are expertly crafted wines; exciting new Gran Cabernet Franc★★. More affordable Quinto Sauvignon Blanc and Malbec★ are also very good.

GIUSEPPE RINALDI *Barolo DOCG, Piedmont, Italy* Giuseppe Rinaldi BAROLOS are arguably the region's very finest, made naturally and carefully. A small, oversubscribed production of bottles from great vineyards: Barolo Brunate-Le Coste★★★, Barolo Cannubi San Lorenzo-Ravera★★★, LANGHE Nebbiolo★★★, Langhe Freisa★★★, BARBERA D'ALBA★★★, Dolcetto d'Alba★★★ and 'Rosae'★★ (from the Ruchè grape). Best years (Nebbiolo): (2011) 10 09 08 **07 06 05** 04 01 00 99 98 96 95 90 89 88 86 85.

RIOJA DOCa *Rioja, Navarra, País Vasco and Castilla y León, Spain* Rioja, in northern Spain, is not all oaky, creamy white wines and elegant, barrel-aged reds, combining oak flavours with wild strawberry and prune fruit. Over half Rioja's red wine is sold young, never having seen the inside of a barrel, and as such is one of Spain's best glugging reds; the white is increasingly tasty and fresh. Wine quality, as could be expected from such a large region with more than 400 producers, is inconsistent, but revitalized traditionalists, modernists who no longer favour over-extraction and over-oaking, and a new breed of 'terroirists' have relaunched the region in the right direction. Best producers: (reds) Alavesas, ALLENDE★★, Altos de Lanzaga★★/Telmo RODRÍGUEZ, ARTADI★★★, Baron de Ley★, Bodegas Bilbaínas, Campillo★, CAMPO VIEJO, CONTADOR★★, CONTINO★★, CVNE★★, DSG Vineyards★★, Exopto★, FAUSTINO, Viña Ijalba, LAN (Culmen★), LÓPEZ DE HEREDIA★★, MARQUES DE CÁCERES, MARQUES DE MURRIETA★★, MARQUES DE RISCAL★★, Marqués de Vargas★, MARTÍNEZ BUJANDA★, Abel Mendoza★★, Montecillo★, MUGA★★, Ostatu, Viñedos de Páganos★★, Palacios Remondo★★, REMELLURI★★, Fernando Remírez de Ganuza★★, La RIOJA ALTA★★, RIOJANAS, Olivier Rivière★★, Roda★★, Sierra Cantabria★★, Señorío de San Vicente★, Tobía, TORRES (Ibéricos★), Valdemar★, Valencio★, Valpiedra★★, Valsacro★; (whites) ALLENDE★★, CAMPO VIEJO, CONTINO★, DSG Vineyards★, LÓPEZ DE

HEREDIA★★, MARQUES DE CÁCERES, MARQUES DE MURRIETA★★, MUGA★★, REMELLURI★★, Olivier Rivière★, Valenciso★, Valsacro★. Best years: (reds) (2011) 10 09 **05 04 01 00 96 95 94 91 89 87 85**.

LA RIOJA *Argentina* Important region in Argentina. Producers specialize in excellent quality, value-for-money wines. La Rioja is also home to the largest FairTrade winery in South America. Best producers: Chañarmuyo, La Riojana co-op (FairTrade), San Huberto, Valle de la Puerta.

LA RIOJA ALTA *Rioja DOCa, Rioja, Spain* Fine, long-established RIOJA producer, making mainly Reservas and Gran Reservas. Its only Crianza, Viña Alberdi★, fulfils the minimum age requirements for a Reserva. Viña Arana★ and Viña Ardanza★★ Reservas age splendidly, and Gran Reservas 904★★★ and 890★★★ are among the very best of traditional Rioja. Torre de Oña★ and Áster★ (RIBERA DEL DUERO) are high-quality, modern, single-estate wines. Best years: (Gran Reserva 890) 2001 **98 95 94 89 87 85 82 81**.

BODEGAS RIOJANAS *Rioja DOCa, Rioja, Spain* A classic winery that has lately been content with producing larger amounts of lesser wines. The Reservas and Gran Reservas in 2 styles – elegant Viña Albina and richer Monte Real★ – plus refined Gran Albina. The Reservas can be kept for 5 years after release, Gran Reservas for 10 or more. Best years: (Monte Real Gran Reserva) 2001 **98 96 95 94 91 89 87 85**.

RION *Nuits-St-Georges, Côte de Nuits, Burgundy, France* Three related estates: Daniel, Armelle & Bernard, and the best-known, Michèle & Patrice. Patrice is noted for concentrated BOURGOGNE Rouge★, CHAMBOLLE-MUSIGNY les Cras★★ and NUITS-ST-GEORGES Clos des Argillières★★ and Clos St Marc★★. Best years: (top reds) (2013) 12 11 10 09 **08 07 06** 05 **03 02**.

RIVERINA *New South Wales, Australia* Centred on the town of Griffith and irrigated by the Murrumbidgee River, the Riverina is an important source of reliable quaffing wines. Many of Australia's best-known brands are based on wines from here. Locally based companies such as DE BORTOLI★ (Deen, Montage, Sacred Hill), Berton, Casella (YELLOWTAIL, Yendah), MCWILLIAM'S★ (Hanwood, Inheritance), Nugan Estate★ (Cookoothama, Talinga Park) and CALABRIA FAMILY★ (Richland) have lifted quality at budget prices. Remarkable sweet wines, led by Noble One Botrytis Semillon★★★ from De Bortoli; others from Calabria Family★, Cookoothama★★, Lillypilly and McWilliam's★★.

RIVERLAND *Australia* This important irrigated region, responsible for about 20% of the national grape crush, lies along the Murray River in SOUTH AUSTRALIA near the border with VICTORIA. Much goes to cheap quaffers but increased quality awareness has seen inferior varieties replaced. Here and there, wines of real character are emerging, including some remarkable reds from the Petit Verdot grape, but relentlessly warm conditions make it difficult to avoid a slight baked flatness in many of the wines. Although the 10-year drought was broken in 2011 by the most serious flooding in decades, there are concerns about long-term water supply and the area under vines is likely to continue to be reduced. Best producers: Angove, Banrock Station, Kingston Estate, YALUMBA (Oxford Landing).

RIVESALTES AC *Roussillon, France* Some of southern France's best fortified wines. Made from white Muscat (when it is called MUSCAT DE RIVESALTES) and Grenache Noir, Gris and Blanc. A *rancio* style ages beautifully. Best producers: Baixas co-op, CASENOVE★, CAZES★★, Chênes★, Las Collas, Fontanel★, Força Réal★, Joliette★, Laporte, Nouvelles★, Rivesaltes co-op, Sainte Barbe★★, Sarda-Malet★, Sisqueille★.

ROAGNA *Barbaresco and Barolo DOCG, Piedmont, Italy* Historic, traditional BARBARESCO cantina; the Roagna family also have a cantina and vineyards in BAROLO. Rich old-vine biodiversity through minimal viticultural intervention and long vinifications. Ethereal reds: Dolcetto d'Alba★★, LANGHE Rosso★★, stunning Barbarescos (Pajé★★★, Crichët Pajé★★★, Asili★★★, Montefico★★★) and Barolos (La Pira★★★). Whites are equally compelling, blends of Chardonnay and Nebbiolo: Langhe Bianco★★, Langhe Bianco 'Solea'★★★. Best years: (Nebbiolo) (2011) 10 09 **08 07** 06 **05** 04 **01 00 99 98 96 95**.

ROBERTSON WO *South Africa* Hot, dry inland area with lime-rich soils, uncommon in the Cape, that are ideal for vines. Chenin Blanc and Colombard are the major white varieties, though just over a quarter of all South Africa's Chardonnay also grows here, for both still and, increasingly, sparkling styles. Sauvignon can also be good. Muscadel (Muscat Blanc à Petits Grains) yields a benchmark fortified wine. Shiraz, Merlot and Cabernet are transforming the red scene. Best producers: Graham BECK★, Bon Courage, De Wetshof★, Quando, Robertson Winery, SPRINGFIELD ESTATE★, Van Loveren, Weltevrede.

ROC DE CAMBES★★ *Côtes de Bourg AC, Bordeaux, France* François Mitjavile of TERTRE-RÔTEBOEUF has applied diligence and genius to this property since he acquired it in 1988. The property is perfectly sited in an amphitheatre of tumbling limestone rock. Full and succulent, with ripe dark fruit, the wine takes the CÔTES DE BOURG appellation to new heights. Best years: 2012 11 10 09 **08 07** 06 05 04 03 02 01 00.

DOM. DES ROCHES NEUVES *Saumur-Champigny AC, Loire Valley, France* A shift to biodynamic methods and less new oak has elevated very good wines to a higher level. Fresh, pure and mineral, top cuvées Insolite SAUMUR★★ (Chenin Blanc) and Marginale SAUMUR-CHAMPIGNY★★ (Cabernet Franc) are excellent expressions of fruit and *terroir*. Generic Saumur-Champigny★ and Terres Chaudes★ are good value; Franc de Pied is from young, ungrafted vines. Bulles de Roche★ is a finely fruity sparkler. Best years: (Marginale) 2013 **11 09** 08 06 05 04 03.

ROCHIOLI *Russian River Valley AVA, California, USA* Well-known grape growers, the Rochioli family are equally good at winemaking, offering silky, black cherry Pinot Noir★★, richer, dramatic West Block Reserve Pinot★★, good Sauvignon Blanc and a range of cult Chardonnays★★. Best years: (Pinot Noir) **2010** 09 08 07 06 05 04 03 02 01 00.

ROCKFORD *Barossa Valley, South Australia* Outstanding winemaker Ben Radford has taken over as general manager; founder Robert O'Callaghan is never far away and his respect for old vines and antique machinery remains the winery's *raison d'être*. The wines retain their irresistible drinkability, depth of flavour and old-world charm. Masterful Basket

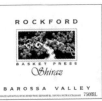

Press Shiraz★★, Riesling★★, slurpable Moppa Springs★ (Grenache-Shiraz-Mourvèdre), smoothly satisfying Rifle Range Cabernet★★ and Australia's best sparkling red, the Black Shiraz★★★. Best years: (Basket Press Shiraz) (2013) (12) 10 09 08 **06 05** 04 03 02 01 99 98 96 95 92 91 90.

TELMO RODRÍGUEZ *Spain* The son of REMELLURI's owner has formed a team of enologists and viticulturists that is active throughout Spain: it forms joint ventures with local growers and manages the winemaking.

Top wines: Molino Real★ (Sierras de MÁLAGA), Matallana★★ (RIBERA DEL DUERO), Las Beatas★★★ (RIOJA), Dehesa Gago Pago La Jara★★ (TORO), REMELLURI★★, Viña 105 (Cigales), Basa★ (RUEDA).

LOUIS ROEDERER *Champagne AC, Champagne, France* Some of the best, full-flavoured CHAMPAGNE around. Excellent non-vintage★★ and pale vintage rosé★★, big, exciting vintage★★, delicious vintage Blanc de Blancs★★ and the famous Roederer Cristal★★★ and Cristal Rosé★★★, de luxe cuvées which are nearly always magnificent, if slightly softer than before. Both the vintage and Cristal can usually be aged for 10 years or more; the non-vintage benefits from a bit of aging too. Best years: (2008) 06 05 04 **03 02 00 99 97 96 95 90 89 88 85**.

ROEDERER ESTATE *Anderson Valley AVA, California, USA* Offshoot of Louis ROEDERER, whose wines show how suitable the ANDERSON VALLEY is for fizz. Brut★★ (Quartet in the UK) is savoury and impressive, and will age beautifully; the top bottling, L'Ermitage★★★, is stunning. Lovely rosé★★. Best years: (L'Ermitage) 2008 07 06 05 04 03 02 00 99 97 96 94 92 91.

ROERO DOCG *Piedmont, Italy* The sand and limestone Roero hills lie across the Tanaro river from the LANGHE hills, home of BAROLO and BARBARESCO. Bright minerally whites from the Arneis grape. Nebbiolo reds are Roero DOCG and/or Roero Riserva DOCG after sometimes excessive wood aging; Nebbiolo is best bottled as a fresh early-drinking fruity wine (NEBBIOLO D'ALBA). Best producers: (Roero Arneis) Ca'Rossa★, Cornarea★★, GIACOSA★, Malvirà★, Marcarini★. Best years: 2012 11 10 09 08 07 06 04 01.

ROMAGNA *Emilia-Romagna, Italy* Historically a contender, with classic zones of Tuscany, for Italy's finest Sangiovese, Sangiovese di Romagna DOC (now simply Romagna DOC); in recent decades it has lost ground due to the industrialization of so much of the product. Producers have also followed the Tuscans down the misguided trail of allowing 'international' (French) grapes into their blend. On the white side, Trebbiano rules in terms of quantity, and Albana (Romagna Albana DOCG) supposedly for quality, though it only achieves excellence when sweet. Best producers: (Sangiovese) Castelluccio (IGT), Drei Donà★★, San Patrignano co-op/Terre del Cedro★ (Avi★★), Zerbina★★.

LA ROMANÉE AC★★★ *Grand Cru, Côte de Nuits, Burgundy, France* Tiny Grand Cru of the highest quality, owned and now made (since 2002) by Comte LIGER-BELAIR. Best years: (2013) 12 11 10 09 08 07 06 05 03 02.

LA ROMANÉE-CONTI AC★★★ *Grand Cru, Côte de Nuits, Burgundy, France* For many extremely wealthy wine lovers this is the pinnacle of red Burgundy. It is an incredibly complex wine with great structure and pure, clearly defined fruit flavour, but you've got to age it 15 years to see what all the fuss is about. The vineyard, wholly owned by Dom. de la ROMANÉE-CONTI, covers only 1.8ha (4.5 acres). Best years: (2013) 12 11 10 09 08 07 06 05 03 **02 00 99 98 97 96 95 93 90 89 88 85**.

DOM. DE LA ROMANÉE-CONTI *Vosne-Romanée, Côte de Nuits, Burgundy, France* This famous domaine owns a string of Grands Crus in VOSNE-ROMANÉE (la TÂCHE★★★, RICHEBOURG★★★, ROMANÉE-CONTI★★★, ROMANÉE-ST-VIVANT★★★, ÉCHÉZEAUX★★★ and Grands-Échézeaux★★★) as well as a small parcel of le MONTRACHET★★★. CORTON★★ since 2009. The wines are ludicrously expensive, especially at auction, but can be sublime: full of fruit when young, but capable of aging for 15 years or more to a marriage made in the heaven and hell of richness and decay. Best years: (reds) (2013) 12 11 10 09 07 06 05 03 **02 00 99 98 97 96 95 93 90 89 85 78**.

ROMANÉE-ST-VIVANT AC *Grand Cru, Côte de Nuits, Burgundy, France* The largest of VOSNE-ROMANÉE's 6 Grands Crus. At 10–15 years old the wines should reveal the keenly balanced brilliance of which the vineyard is capable, but a surly, rough edge sometimes gets in the way. Best producers: l'Arlot★, Arnoux-Lachaux★★★, S CATHIARD★★★, J-J Confuron★★★, DROUHIN★★★, Follin-Arbelet★★, Hudelot-NOËLLAT★★, JADOT★★★, LATOUR★★, Dom. LEROY★★★, Dom. de la ROMANÉE-CONTI★★★. Best years: (2013) 12 11 10 09 08 **07 06** 05 03 02 01 00 **99 98 96 95 93 90**.

CH. ROMANIN *Les Baux-de-Provence AC, Provence, France* Biodynamic vineyard owned by Jean-Louis Charmolüe, ex-owner of Ch. MONTROSE in Bordeaux. Top wine is Le Coeur de Romanin★★ from Syrah, Mourvèdre, Cabernet Sauvignon and Grenache. Also delightfully textured Château Romanin★★. Best years: (Le Coeur) (2013) 12 11 10 **09 08 07 06 05**.

QUINTA DOS ROQUES *Dão DOC, Beiras, Portugal* One of DÃO's finest producers, making wines from 2 quite different estates. Quinta dos Roques red★ is ripe and supple, while higher-altitude Quinta das Maias★ produces smoky, peppery reds. Top wines are the Roques Reserva★★, made from old vines and aged in 100% new oak, and Touriga Nacional★★. Both estates also have decent dry whites, especially Roques Encruzado★. Best years: (2012) 11 **10 09 08 07 05 04 03 01 00 97 96**.

QUINTA DE LA ROSA *Douro DOC and Port DOC, Douro, Portugal* The Bergqvist family have transformed this property into a small but serious producer of both PORT and unfortified DOURO (red★, white★, Reserva★★) wines. The Vintage Port★★ is excellent, as is unfiltered LBV★★; Finest Reserve and Tonel No. 12, a 10-year-old tawny, are also good. Passagem is a good DOURO red from their estate in the Upper Douro. Best years: (Vintage) 2011 **09 07 05 04 03 00 97 96 95 94 92 91**.

ROSÉ DE LOIRE AC *Loire Valley, France* Dry rosé from ANJOU, SAUMUR and TOURAINE. It can be lovely, full of red berry fruits, but drink as young as possible, chilled. It's far superior to Rosé d'Anjou AC, which is usually sweetish. Best producers: Hautes Ouches, F MABILEAU, OGEREAU, Passavant.

ROSÉ DES RICEYS AC *Champagne, France* Still, dark pink wine made from Pinot Noir grapes in the southern part of the CHAMPAGNE region. Best producers: Alexandre Bonnet★, Devaux★, Guy de Forez, Morel.

ROSEMOUNT *Hunter Valley, New South Wales, Australia* Rosemount virtually disappeared as a quality label, but they're back! With revitalized vineyards, a strong presence in MCLAREN VALE and the LIMESTONE COAST, and particular strength in Shiraz, Cabernet and Grenache. Their Nursery Project wines such as Fiano, Mataro and Graciano-Mataro-Grenache got everyone talking. Just as important is the evident improvement of Diamond Label Chardonnay★ and Shiraz★ and the release of crunchy fresh reds like Blends Shiraz-Cabernet★. If this improvement is not just a mirage, the wine drinkers of the world will thank you.

ROSETTE AOP *Bergerac, South-West France* A small BERGERAC region producing rather exquisite off-dry aperitif-style wines from Sémillon, which don't need the oak they sometimes get. Drink young. Best producers: de Coutancie★, Ch. Romain★.

ROSSO CONERO DOC See CONERO DOCG/ROSSO CONERO DOC.

ROSSO DI MONTALCINO DOC *Tuscany, Italy* BRUNELLO DI MONTALCINO must age for at least 4 years before release onto the market, so this wine was devised for quicker return on investment and a more approachable style. Like Brunello, Rosso di Montalcino must be 100% Sangiovese. Best producers as for Brunello. Best years: **2011 10 09 08 07 06**.

GIOVANNI ROSSO *Barolo DOCG, Piedmont, Italy* Davide Rosso makes some of Serralunga's most articulate BAROLOS: Vigna Rionda★★★, La Serra★★★, Cerretta★★★, Serralunga d'Alba★★★. Also BARBERA D'ALBA★★ and LANGHE Nebbiolo★★. Best years: 2011 10 09 08 07 06 05 04 01 00.

ROSSO DI MONTEPULCIANO DOC See VINO NOBILE DI MONTEPULCIANO DOCG.

ROSSO PICENO DOC *Marche, Italy* Often considered a poor relative of CONERO DOCG/ROSSO CONERO, but it can be rich and seductive when the full complement (70%) of Montepulciano is used, and also when it comes from the more restricted Superiore zone. Best producers: Boccadigabbia★ (Villamagna★★), Le Caniette★, Laurentina★, Monte Schiavo★, Saladini Pilastri★, Velenosi★. Best years: (2012) 11 10 09 08.

RENÉ ROSTAING *Côte-Rôtie AC, Rhône Valley, France* Modern, lightly oaked, enormously fine and aromatic wines with deep colour and – eventually – softly elegant fruit flavours, from some of the most coveted sites in CÔTE-RÔTIE: classic Côte-Rôtie★, Côte Blonde★★★ and la Landonne★★. Be patient. There's a very good CONDRIEU La Bonnette★★ too. Best years: (top crus) 2013 12 11 10 09 07 06 05 04 03 01 00 99 98 95 94 91 90 88.

DOM. ROULOT *Meursault, Côte de Beaune, Burgundy, France* Jean-Marc Roulot quietly outperforms in fine white Burgundy, from Bourgogne Blanc★, to village MEURSAULT such as Les Luchets★★ or the amazing Les Tessons Clos de Mon Plaisir★★, up to Premier Cru Clos des Bouchères★★ or Perrières★★★. Best years: (2013) 12 11 10 09 08 07 06 05 02 00.

GEORGES ROUMIER *Chambolle-Musigny, Côte de Nuits, Burgundy, France* Christophe Roumier is one of Burgundy's top winemakers, devoting as much attention to his vineyards as to cellar technique. Roumier rarely uses more than one-third new oak. His best wine is often BONNES-MARES★★★; other Grands Crus include MUSIGNY★★★, Ruchottes-Chambertin★★ and CORTON-CHARLEMAGNE★★. Best value are usually the village CHAMBOLLE★★ and an exclusively owned Premier Cru in MOREY-ST-DENIS, Clos de la Bussière★★. Best years: (reds) (2013) 12 11 10 09 08 07 05 03 02 01 99 98 96 95 90.

ROUSSANNE The RHÔNE VALLEY's best white grape, frequently blended with Marsanne to produce surprisingly fragrant, even salty, warm-climate whites. Roussanne is the more aromatic and elegant of the two, but growers usually prefer Marsanne due to its higher yields and lush personality. Old-vines Roussanne can be very refined, such as at CHATEAUNEUF-DU-PAPE. Now being planted in LANGUEDOC-ROUSSILLON and PROVENCE (Dom. Borrely-Martin makes a good example). Some interesting examples in SAVOIE (where it is called Bergeron) and Australia. Good potential in South Africa. While much of the Roussanne first planted in California has been identified as Viognier, a few true plantings produce fascinating, exotically fruited wines.

ARMAND ROUSSEAU *Gevrey-Chambertin, Côte de Nuits, Burgundy, France* Highly respected estate, with vineyards in CHAMBERTIN★★★, Clos-de-Bèze★★★, Mazis-Chambertin★★ and Charmes-Chambertin★★ as well as GEVREY-CHAMBERTIN Clos St-Jacques★★★ and CLOS DE LA ROCHE★★★. The long-lived wines are elegantly harmonious, elegant, yet rich. Best years: (2013) 12 11 10 09 08 07 06 05 03 02 99 96 93 91 90.

ROUSSETTE DE SAVOIE AC *Savoie, France* Fresh, floral, mineral white wines from the Altesse grape. Best producers: Dupasquier★★, E Jacquin★, Lupin, Prieuré St-Christophe★★, Saint-Germain★. Best years: 2013 12 11 09.

ROUSSILLON *France* The snow-covered peaks of the Pyrenees form a spectacular backdrop to the sun-baked, wind-swept ancient region of Roussillon, now the Pyrénées-Orientales *département*. The vineyards produce a wide range of fairly priced wines, mainly red, from the ripe, raisin-rich *vins doux naturels* to light, fruity-fresh vins de pays/IGPs. Once dominated by co-operatives, there are now some really exciting wines being made, both white and red, especially by individual estates. See also BANYULS, COLLIOURE, CÔTES CATALANES, CÔTES DU ROUSSILLON, CÔTES DU ROUSSILLON-VILLAGES, LANGUEDOC-ROUSSILLON, MAURY, MUSCAT DE RIVESALTES, RIVESALTES.

RUCHOTTES-CHAMBERTIN AC See CHAMBERTIN AC.

RÜDESHEIM *Rheingau, Germany* Village producing silky, aromatic wines from steep terraced vineyards high above the Rhine (Berg Schlossberg, Berg Rottland, Berg Roseneck and Bischofsberg). Best producers: Georg BREUER★★★, Johannishof★, Kesseler★★, LEITZ★★, Ress, Schloss Schönborn★, WEGELER★. Best years: (2013) 12 11 **10 09 08 07 06 05 04 02**.

RUEDA DO *Castilla y León, Spain* The RIOJA firm of MARQUES DE RISCAL launched the reputation of this region in the 1970s, first by rescuing the almost extinct Verdejo grape, then by introducing Sauvignon Blanc. Fresh young whites have been joined by barrel-fermented wines aiming for a longer life, particularly at Belondrade y Lurton, Castilla La Vieja and Ossian. Best producers: Alvarez y Diez, Antaño (Viña Mocén), Belondrade y Lurton★, Castelo de Medina★, Bodegas de Crianza Castilla La Vieja★, Cerrosol (Doña Beatriz), José Pariente★, Hermanos Lurton★★, MARQUES DE RISCAL★★, Naia★, Viñedos de Nieva, Ossian★, Palacio de Bornos★, Javier Sanz★, Vinos Sanz★, Sitios de Bodega★, Angel Rodríguez Vidal (Martinsancho★★).

RUFFINO *Tuscany, Italy* Huge operation, partly owned by American giant Constellation; production is still controlled by a branch of the Folonari family, and is increasingly oriented toward quality. Top wines include La Solatia★ (Chardonnay), Modus★ (Sangiovese-Cabernet-Merlot), Nero del Tondo★ (Pinot Noir) and Romitorio di Santedame★★ (Colorino-Merlot). Ruffino also owns VINO NOBILE estate Lodola Nuova, BRUNELLO Greppone Mazzi and Borgo Conventi in COLLIO.

RUINART *Champagne AC, Champagne, France* Ruinart has a surprisingly low profile given the quality of its wines. Non-vintage★ is very good, and better value than the Blanc de Blancs★, but the top wines here are the supremely classy Dom Ruinart Blanc de Blancs★★ and Dom Ruinart Rosé★★. Best years: (2007) 06 05 04 **02 00 98 96 95 90 88 85 83 82**.

RULLY AC *Côte Chalonnaise, Burgundy, France* Best known for white wines, often oak-aged. Reds are light, with a fleeting strawberry and cherry perfume. Most wines are reasonably priced. Best producers: (whites) d'Allaines★, J-C Brelière★, M Briday★, Devevey★, DROUHIN★, Dureuil-Janthial★★, Duvernay, FAIVELEY★, V GIRARDIN★, Hasard★, H & P Jacqueson★★, JADOT★, C Jobard★, O LEFLAIVE★, Rodet★, de Villaine★; (reds) Dureuil-Janthial★★, la Folie, H & P Jacqueson★. Best years: (whites) (2013) **12 10 09**; (reds) (2013) 12 **10 09**.

RUSSIAN RIVER VALLEY AVA *Sonoma County, California, USA* Beginning south of Healdsburg, this valley cools as it meanders toward the Pacific. In late 2011, the AVA was expanded by a whopping 5670ha (14,000 acres) in response to a controversial proposal by GALLO. Green Valley, a sub-AVA, is home to IRON HORSE, DUTTON GOLDFIELD and MARIMAR ESTATE. Along with SONOMA COAST and CARNEROS it is the leading producer of high-quality Pinot Noir and Chardonnay in North Coast California. Best producers: Alysian★, DE LOACH★★, DEHLINGER★★, DUTTON GOLDFIELD★★, Merry Edwards★★, Gary FARRELL★★, Foppiano★, HARTFORD★★, IRON HORSE★★, Kosta Browne★, MARIMAR ESTATE★★, MOSHIN★, Papapietro Perry★, Patz & Hall★, RAMEY★★, ROCHIOLI★★, Siduri★★, SONOMA-CUTRER★, Rodney Strong★, Joseph SWAN★, WILLIAMS SELYEM★★, WIND GAP★★. Best years: (Pinot Noir) 2010 09 08 07 06 05 04 03 02 01.

RUST EN VREDE *Stellenbosch WO, South Africa* Big bold, statement reds include Single Vineyard Syrah★ and 1694 Classification★ (a Cabernet-Shiraz blend named for the year the property was granted). Rust en Vrede★, a Cabernet-Shiraz-Merlot blend, reflects the farm's *terroir*; Shiraz★, Merlot and Cabernet all show fine, soft tannins and fresh fruit. The Guardian Peak reds are ripe and powerful in style. Best years: (Rust en Vrede estate wine) 2011 10 09 08 07 06 05 04 03.

RUSTENBERG *Stellenbosch WO, South Africa* Top-notch wines led by big but classically structured single-vineyard Cabernet Peter Barlow★★ and bold Five Soldiers★★ (Chardonnay). Standard Chardonnay★★ is more delicate, cheaper and equally good. There's also complex, layered BORDEAUX-style blend John X Merriman★ and R M Nicholson★, while RHÔNE-style wines are represented by a lean but scented Roussanne and intricate, refined Buzzard

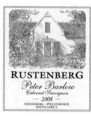

RUSTENBERG
Peter Barlow
Cabernet Sauvignon
2008
SIMONSBERG · STELLENBOSCH
SOUTH AFRICA

Kloof Syrah★★. Straw Wine★ is an occasional luscious 'sticky'. Best years: (Peter Barlow) (2009) 08 07 06 05 04 03 01; (Five Soldiers) 2012 11 10 09 08 07 06 05.

RUTHERFORD AVA *Napa Valley, California, USA* This viticultural area in mid-NAPA VALLEY has inspired endless argument over whether it has a distinct identity. The heart of the area, the Rutherford Bench, does seem to be a prime Cabernet Sauvignon zone, and many traditional Napa Cabernets come from here and exhibit the 'Rutherford dust' flavour. Best producers: Beaulieu (Private Reserve★), CAKEBREAD★, CAYMUS★★, COPPOLA★, FLORA SPRINGS★, Freemark Abbey★ (Bosché★★), FROG'S LEAP★, Hall★, PINE RIDGE★, QUINTESSA★, ST SUPÉRY★, Sequoia Grove★, Staglin★★. Best years: (Cabernet) 2010 09 08 07 06 05 04 03 02 01 00 99 95 94 93 91 90.

RUTHERGLEN *Victoria, Australia* This region is the home of heroic reds from Shiraz, Cabernet and Durif (Petite Sirah), and luscious, world-beating fortifieds from Muscat and Tokay (now called 'Topaque' – don't ask). These fortifieds are classified in quality terms from regional (Rutherglen) to Classic, Grand and Rare. Good sherry- and port-style wines. Best producers: (fortifieds) All Saints★★, Buller★★, Campbells★★, CHAMBERS★★★, Jones, MORRIS★★, Stanton & Killeen★★.

MARK RYAN WINERY *Columbia Valley AVA, Washington State USA* Mark Ryan McNeilly produces full-flavoured reds from vineyards in the YAKIMA VALLEY and Red Mountain AVAs. Bold Cabernet Sauvignons ('Lonely Heart'★★, 'Dead Horse'★★, 'Long Haul'★) and red blends, plus spice- and mineral-scented Syrahs ('Lost Soul'★, 'Wild Eyed'★). A lovely Viognier★ is crisp and refreshing. Best years: (2012) 11 10 09 08.

SAALE-UNSTRUT *Germany* Vines can only flourish in the folds of the river valleys in this bleak expanse of the former East Germany near Leipzig. This far north it is only just possible to ripen most grapes, yet 80 different varieties are now grown here, of which the most important are Riesling, Müller-Thurgau, Silvaner and Weissburgunder (Pinot Blanc). Only 765ha (1890 acres), mostly on limestone slopes, with a very dry, fragrant style being the most successful. Best producers: Böhme, Gussek★, Lützkendorf, Pawis★.

SACHSEN Germany 492ha (1215-acre) wine region centred on the cities of Meissen and Dresden along the Elbe Valley. At more than 50°N, grapes don't ripen easily, and frost is a constant hazard. Global warming is easing conditions, and some lovely, delicate dry Rieslings are beginning to appear, along with good Müller-Thurgau, Gewürztraminer, Silvaner and Weissburgunder (Pinot Blanc). Best producers: Schloss Proschwitz★, Vincenz Richter, Schwarz★, Klaus Zimmerling★.

SADIE FAMILY WINES Swartland WO, South Africa Eben Sadie's single-vineyard project focuses on specific sites of old vines (some over 100 years); the range has now expanded to 9 highly individual wines (all ★★ to ★★★) made with minimum intervention, in tiny quantities. He crafts just slightly larger quantities of Columella★★★ (Syrah with a little Mourvèdre and Grenache), which combines richness and power, and Palladius★★, a generously textured, multi-varietal dry white featuring Chenin Blanc. A separate venture, Sequillo, produces a mineral-fresh Syrah-based red★ and elegant barrel-fermented Chenin-based white★. Best years: (Columella) 2011 **10 09 08 07 06 05 04 03**.

SAGRANTINO High-quality, low-yielding, Umbrian black grape responsible in part for the medium-bodied MONTEFALCO Rosso (15% of the blend) and wholly for the full-bodied 100% Sagrantino di Montefalco (Secco and Passito) red wine styles.

ST-AMOUR AC Beaujolais, Burgundy, France The most northerly BEAUJOLAIS Cru, much in demand through the romantic connotation of its name. Wines with great intensity of colour that may be initially harsh, needing a few months to soften. Best producers: des Billards★, DUBOEUF★ (Dom. des Sablons★), des Duc★, Matray. Best years: (**2013**) **11 10**.

ST-AUBIN AC Côte de Beaune, Burgundy, France These days almost as good a source of white Burgundy (though in a less rich style) as its MONTRACHET neighbours, PULIGNY and CHASSAGNE, and much more affordable. En Remilly and Murgers Dents de Chien stand out as vineyards, along with Frionnes for pretty, perfumed Pinot Noir. Best producers: J-C BACHELET★★, F & D Clair★★, COLIN★★, P-Y COLIN-MOREY★★, Deux MONTILLE★, DROUHIN★, JADOT★, H Lamy★★, Lamy-Pillot★, Larue★, O LEFLAIVE★, B MOREY★, Prudhon★, RAMONET★★. Best years: (reds) (2013) 12 **11 10** 09 06 05; (whites) (2013) 12 **11 10** 09 08 07.

ST-BRIS AC Burgundy, France Appellation near CHABLIS for Sauvignon Blanc; drink young. Best producers: Clotilde Davenne, J-H Goisot★★, de Moor.

ST-CHINIAN AC Languedoc, France Large AC of hill villages, covering strong, spicy red wines with more personality and fruit than run-of-the-mill HÉRAULT, especially in crus Roquebrun and Berlou. Best producers: BORIE LA VITARÈLE★, Cazal-Viel★★, Clos Bagatelle★, la Dournie, Jougla, Madura★, Mas Champart★, Mas de Cynanque★, Maurel Fonsalade★, Milhau-Lacugue, Moulin de Ciffre, Moulinier, Navarre★, Rimbert★, Roquebrun co-op★, Tabatau (Lo Tabataire★), les Terrasses de Gabrielle★, Terres Falmet. Best years: (2013) 12 **11 10** 09 08 07 06 05.

SAINT CLAIR *Marlborough, South Island, New Zealand*★ Important player best known for its Sauvignon Blanc, usually made in a mouthfilling rather than snappy style. Wairau Reserve★★ is impressively intense; also single-vineyard Pioneer Block labels (tangy Bell★★). Excellent Reserve Chardonnay★★, tasty Gewürztraminer★ and Riesling. Various Pinot Noirs★ (Pioneer Block Doctor's Creek★★) and chocolaty Rapaura Reserve Merlot★ lead the reds. Vicar's Choice is the tasty entry-level label. Best years: (Sauvignon Blanc) 2013 **12 11 10 09 07**.

ST-ÉMILION AC *Bordeaux, France* The scenic Roman hill town of St-Émilion is the centre of Bordeaux's most historic wine region. The finest vineyards are on the plateau and *côtes*, or steep slopes, around the town, although an area to the west, called the *graves*, contains 2 famous properties, CHEVAL BLANC and FIGEAC. It is a region of smallholdings, with over 1000 properties, and consequently the co-operative plays an important part. The dominant early-ripening Merlot grape gives wines with a 'come-hither' softness and sweetness rare in red BORDEAUX. St-Émilion is the basic generic AC, with 4 'satellites' (LUSSAC, MONTAGNE, PUISSEGUIN, ST-GEORGES) allowed to annex their name to it. The best producers are found in the more tightly controlled ST-ÉMILION GRAND CRU AC category. Best years: **2012 10 09 08 05 01 00**.

ST-ÉMILION GRAND CRU AC *Bordeaux, France* ST-ÉMILION's top-quality AC, which includes the estates classified as Grand Cru Classé and Premier Grand Cru Classé (below). The classification is revised approximately every 10 years, most recently in 2012. This AC also includes many of the new wave of limited edition *vins de garage*. Best producers: (Grands Crus Classés) l'ARROSÉE★★, Balestard-la-Tonnelle★, Bellefont-Belcier★, Bellevue★, Clos de l'Oratoire★, la Dominique★, Faugères★, Fleur Cardinale★, Fombrauge★, Grand Corbin-Despagne★, Grand Mayne★, Grand Pontet★, Larmande★, MONBOUSQUET★, Pavie-Decesse★, Quinault l'Enclos★, Soutard★, la Tour Figeac★; (others) Boutisse, Gracia★, Mangot, Moulin St-Georges★, Rol Valentin★, TERTRE-RÔTEBOEUF★★, Teyssier★. Best years: 2012 11 10 **09 08 06 05 03 01 00 98 96 95**.

ST-ÉMILION PREMIER GRAND CRU CLASSÉ *Bordeaux, France* The St-Émilion élite level, divided into 2 categories – 'A' and 'B' – with (since 2012) ANGÉLUS and PAVIE joining CHEVAL BLANC and AUSONE in category 'A'. There are 14 'B' châteaux, with CANON-LA-GAFFELIÈRE, Larcis Ducasse and VALANDRAUD added from the 2012 classification. Best producers: ANGÉLUS★★★, AUSONE★★★, BEAU-SÉJOUR BÉCOT★★, Beauséjour★, BELAIR-MONANGE★★, CANON★★, CANON-LA-GAFFELIÈRE★★, CHEVAL BLANC★★★, Clos Fourtet★★, FIGEAC★★, la Gaffelière★, Larcis Ducasse★★, La Mondotte★★, PAVIE★★, PAVIE-MACQUIN★★, TROPLONG-MONDOT★, Trottevieille★, VALANDRAUD★★. Best years: 2012 11 10 **09 08 06 05 04 03 02 01 00 98 96 95**.

ST-ESTÈPHE AC *Haut-Médoc, Bordeaux, France* Large AC north of PAUILLAC with 5 Classed Growths. St-Estèphe wines have high tannin levels, and many start out with rather earthy textures, but given time (10–20 years) those sought-after flavours of blackcurrant and cedarwood do peek out. More Merlot has been planted to soften the wines and make them more accessible at an earlier age. As vintages get drier and hotter, these wines are coming into their own. Best producers: Le Boscq, CALON-SÉGUR★★, COS D'ESTOURNEL★★, Cos Labory★, Le Crock★, HAUT-MARBUZET★★, LAFON-ROCHET★, Lilian-Ladouys★, MEYNEY★, MONTROSE★★, Ormes de Pez★, PEZ★, Phélan Ségur★, Tronquoy-Lalande★. Best years: 2012 11 10 09 08 **06 05 04 03 02 01 00 96 95 90 89**.

DOM. SAINT GAYAN *Gigondas AC, Rhône Valley, France* The Meffre family work very old vines, making and maturing their wines in vat and large barrels. This is darkly fruited, chunky, really long-lived GIGONDAS★ (★★ in top years). Other reds, such as RASTEAU, are also good value. Best years: (Gigondas) 2012 11 10 **09 07 06 05 04 03 01 00 99 98 95 90**.

ST-GEORGES-ST-ÉMILION AC *Bordeaux, France* The smallest satellite of ST-ÉMILION, with lovely, soft wines that can nevertheless age for 6–10 years. Best producers: Calon, Macquin St-Georges★, St-André Corbin★, Ch. St-Georges★, Tour-du-Pas-St-Georges★, Vieux-Montaiguillon. Best years: 2012 **10 09 08 05**.

ST HALLETT *Barossa Valley, South Australia* Owned by brewer Lion Nathan. Excellent quaffers Poacher's Blend★ (Semillon-Sauvignon), Game-keeper's Shiraz-Grenache★ and delicious easy-drinking Gamekeeper's Shiraz★. These and the EDEN VALLEY Riesling★ are performing pretty well; venerable Old Block Shiraz★★ has regained top form and excellent Shiraz siblings Blackwell★ and Faith★ are deep and tasty. Best years: (Old Block) (2012) 10 09 08 **06 04 03 02 98 96 94 93 91 90**.

ST HUGO *Coonawarra and Barossa Valley, South Australia* This began life as Orlando's St Hugo, was known for a time as Jacob's Creek St Hugo, and now has its own label, with 3 slurpable siblings – Grenache-Shiraz-Mataro★ and seductive brambly Shiraz★★ from the BAROSSA and a South Australian Shiraz-Cabernet. But the main event is St Hugo COONAWARRA Cabernet Sauvignon★★, with its 30-year pedigree and concentrated blackcurrant fruit backed by fine tannins for long aging. A stunning Barossa Valley cellar door is promised. Best years: (Cabernet) (2013) 12 10 09 08 **05 04 03 02 01 00 99 98 96 93 91 90 88 86**.

ST INNOCENT *Willamette Valley AVA, Oregon, USA* St Innocent produces a number of *terroir*-driven single-vineyard Pinot Noirs (Justice Vineyard★★, Zenith Vineyard★) as well as a blended Villages Cuvée★. White wines include stylish Chardonnay (Freedom Hill Vineyard), Pinot Gris (Vitae Springs★, Freedom Hill) and crisp, apple-scented Pinot Blanc. Best years: (Pinot Noir) (2012) 11 10 **09 08**.

ST-JOSEPH AC *Rhône Valley, France* Long hillside AC, up and down the opposite bank of the Rhône to HERMITAGE, with some slopes as steep as Hermitage itself. Made from Syrah, the reds have mouthfilling, lively fruit with irresistible blackcurrant and hedgerow berries richness. Brilliant at 1–2 years, they can last for at least 10. The white

wines are pleasant and flowery to drink young, although an increasing number can age, as in 2010 and 2012. Best producers: (reds) CHAPOUTIER★, J-L CHAVE★★, Chêne★, L Chèze★, Courbis★, COURSODON★★, CUILLERON★★, Dard & Ribo★, DELAS★★, E & J Durand★★, Faury★, P Gaillard★★, Gonon★★, GRAILLOT★, B Gripa★★, GUIGAL★, Paul JABOULET★, P Jamet★, J-C Marsanne★, P Marthouret, Monier★, Monteillet★★, Mortier★★, Paret★, A PERRET★, C Pichon★, Richard (Nuelles★), Cave de TAIN★, Tardieu-Laurent★★, Vallet★, G Vernay★, P-J Villa★, F Villard★★; (whites) CHAPOUTIER★★, Chêne★★, L Chèze★, Courbis★ (Royes★★), COURSODON★, CUILLERON★★, DELAS★, Ferraton★, G Flacher★, P Gaillard★★, Gonon★, B Gripa★★, GUIGAL★, Monteillet★, A PERRET★★, J Pilon★, Villard★★. Best years: (reds) 2013 12 11 10 **09 07 06 05 03 01 00 99 98**; (whites) 2013 12 11 10 09 08 07 06 05.

ST-JULIEN AC *Haut-Médoc, Bordeaux, France* For many, St-Julien produces perfect claret, with an ideal balance between opulence and austerity and between the brashness of youth and the genius of maturity. It is the smallest of the principal HAUT-MÉDOC ACs but almost all is first-rate vineyard land and quality is high. Best producers: BEYCHEVELLE★★, BRANAIRE-DUCRU★★, DUCRU-BEAUCAILLOU★★★, GLORIA★, GRUAUD-LAROSE★★, LAGRANGE★★, LANGOA-BARTON★★, LÉOVILLE-BARTON★★★, LÉOVILLE-LAS-CASES★★★, LÉOVILLE-POYFERRÉ★★★, ST-PIERRE★★, TALBOT★. Best years: 2012 11 10 09 08 **06 05 04 03 02 01 00 98 96 95 90 89**.

ST-MONT AOP *South-West France* Best known for whites, though there are red and rosé wines too, all based on local grape varieties. Producteurs PLAIMONT★ have a near-monopoly.

ST-NICOLAS-DE-BOURGUEIL AC *Loire Valley, France* An enclave within the larger BOURGUEIL AC, and similarly producing light wines from vineyards toward the river, sturdier bottles from up the hill. Almost all the wine is red and with the same piercing red fruit flavours of Bourgueil, and much better after 7–10 years, especially in warm vintages. Best producers: Y Amirault★★, Clos des Quarterons★/T Amirault, la Cotelleraie/G Vallée★★, L & M Cognard-Taluau★, S David★★, F MABILEAU★★, J Taluau★. Best years: 2013 11 **10 09 08 06 05 04 03**.

ST-PÉRAY AC *Rhône Valley, France* Small, mainly granite-limestone, hilly area opposite Valence. Underrated white wines, mainly Marsanne, are ideally fragrant and mineral, but can be oaked and obviously rich. Also some rather hefty traditional-method fizz. Best producers: S Chaboud★, CHAPOUTIER★, CLAPE★, COLOMBO★, CUILLERON★, B Gripa★★, J Lemenicier★, J Pilon, Cave de TAIN★, Tardieu-Laurent★, J-L Thiers★, Tunnel★, Vins de Vienne, A Voge★ (Fleur de Crussol★★). Best years: 2013 12 11 **10 09 08 07**.

CH. ST-PIERRE★★ *St-Julien AC, 4ème Cru Classé, Haut-Médoc, Bordeaux, France* Small ST-JULIEN property making wines that have become a byword for ripe, lush fruit wrapped round with the spice of new oak. Drinkable early, but top vintages can improve for 20 years. Best years: 2012 11 10 09 08 **06 05 04 03 02 01 00 98 96 95 90 89**.

ST-ROMAIN AC *Côte de Beaune, Burgundy, France* Red wines with a firm, bitter-sweet cherrystone fruit and flinty-dry whites. Usually good value by Burgundian standards, but take a few years to open out. There's talk of introducing Premiers Crus for best vineyards such as Sous le Château. Best producers: (whites) Bazenet★, BELLENE★, H & G Buisson★, Chassorney★★, A Gras★★, O LEFLAIVE★, Verget★; (reds) A Gras★. Best years: (whites) (2013) 12 11 **10 09**; (reds) (2013) 12 11 **10 09 05**.

ST SUPÉRY *Napa Valley, California, USA* This French-owned property in RUTHERFORD gets most of its fruit from its Dollarhide Ranch in Pope Valley to the east. Tangy Sauvignon Blanc★, Merlot★ and ripe, juicy Cabernet Sauvignon★★, as well as an excellent white Meritage blend called Virtú★★, with a substantial amount of Semillon, and Cabernet-based red Élu★★. Best years: (Cabernet) (2012) **10 09 08 07 06 05 03 02 01**.

ST URBANS-HOF *Leiwen, Mosel, Germany* Nik Weis's dynamic estate has excellent vineyards in PIESPORT, and Ockfen and Wiltingen in the Saar. Crystalline Spätlese and Auslese are ★ to ★★, while Ockfener Bockstein TBA is always ★★★. Best years: (2013) 12 11 **10 09 08 07 05**.

ST-VÉRAN AC *Mâconnais, Burgundy, France* Often thought of as a POUILLY-FUISSÉ understudy, this is gentle, fairly fruity, normally unoaked Mâconnais Chardonnay. Overall quality is good and improving. Drink young. Best producers: D & M Barraud★, Cordier★, Corsin★★, Croix

Senaillet, Deux Roches★, DUBOEUF★, R Lassarat★, Merlin★, Poncetys★, Saumaize-Michelin★, Verget★, J-J Vincent★. Best years: (2013) **12 11 10 09**.

STE-CROIX-DU-MONT AC *Bordeaux, France* Best of the 3 sweet wine ACs that gaze jealously at SAUTERNES and BARSAC across the Garonne river (the others are CADILLAC and LOUPIAC). The wine is mellow and sweet rather than splendidly rich. Top wines can age for at least a decade. Best producers: Crabitan-Bellevue★, Loubens★, Lousteau-Vieil, Mailles, Mont, Pavillon★, la Rame★. Best years: **2011 10 09 07 05 03**.

SAINTSBURY *Carneros AVA, California, USA* Characterful winery whose Pinot Noirs★★ are brilliant examples of the perfume and fruit quality of CARNEROS; vineyard-designated Pinots, led by powerful Brown Ranch★★, are deeper and oakier, while Garnet★ is a delicious lighter style. Chardonnays★★ are impressive, best after 2–3 years, and new Syrah★ is tasty. Best years: (Pinot Noir) **2012 10 09 08 07 06 05 04 03 02 01 00**.

DUCA DI SALAPARUTA *Sicily, Italy* Corvo is the brand name for the basic range of Sicilian reds and whites, made from local grape varieties. There are superior whites, like Kados★★ from the Grillo grape, and fine reds like Duca Enrico★★ and Passo delle Mule★, both from Nero d'Avola, red blend Triskelè★, and Lavico★ from the Nerello Mascalese grape.

SALICE SALENTINO DOC *Puglia, Italy* One of the better DOCs in the Salento peninsula, using Negroamaro tempered with a dash of perfumed Malvasia Nera for ripe, chocolaty wines that acquire hints of roast chestnuts and prunes with age. Drink after 3–4 years, although they may last as long again. The DOCs of Alezio, Brindisi, Copertino, Leverano, Squinzano and others, plus various IGTs, are similar. Best producers: Candido★, Casale Bevagna★, Leone de Castris★, Due Palme★, Taurino★, Vallone★★, Conti Zecca. Best years: (reds) (2012) **11 10 09 08 06 04 01**.

SALTA *Argentina* The vineyards of Salta province, 700km (435 miles) north of MENDOZA, are concentrated along the Calchaquí Valley. Most of the traditional producers are located at Cafayate, at about 1750m (5750ft). Colomé, further up the valley, has been producing wine for nearly 200 years and its new vineyards, at over 3000m (10,000ft), are the highest in the world. High altitude, mostly sandy soils and almost no rain produce wines of intense colour and high alcohol content, with scented white Torrontés and lush inky Malbec, and Tannat promising much for the future of this region. Best producers: (Cafayate) Amalaya★, Domingo Hermanos, EL ESTECO/Michel Torino, EL PORVENIR DE CAFAYATE★, El Transito, Felix Lavaque, YACOCHUYA★; (Colomé) COLOMÉ★★.

SAMOS *Greece* The island of Samos has a centuries-old reputation for rich, sweet, Muscat-based wines. The Samos co-op's wines include deep gold, honeyed Samos Nectar★★, made from sun-dried grapes; apricotty Palaio★, aged for up to 20 years; and seductively complex Samos Anthemis★, fortified and cask-aged for up to 5 years.

SAN ANTONIO *Chile* A region that includes the sub-region of Leyda. Closeness to the icy Pacific Ocean decides whether you are best at snappy Sauvignon Blanc and fragrant Pinot Noir, or scented, juice-laden reds. There are half a dozen estates here, but big companies like CONCHA Y TORO, CONO SUR, SANTA RITA and MONTES are also making exciting wine from the region's fruit. Best producers: Amayna/Garcés Silva, CASA MARÍN★★, O FOURNIER★★, Viña LEYDA★★, LUIS FELIPE EDWARDS★, MATETIC★★, MONTES★.

SAN JUAN *Argentina* The second-largest wine region in Argentina, lying 2 hours' drive north of MENDOZA. Three transverse valleys, Pedernal, Tulum and the Zonda, make up the lunar landscape. It's hot and dry here, so it's no surprise to see varieties like Shiraz and Viognier performing well. Like most areas in Argentina, altitude is key to quality, with Pedernal (1400m/4600ft) leading the way. Best producers: Antigua, Callia, Casa Montes, Graffigna, LAS MORAS★, Xumek.

SAN LUIS OBISPO COUNTY *California, USA* CENTRAL COAST county best known for Chardonnay, Pinot Noir, a bit of old-vine Zinfandel, Syrah and Cabernet Sauvignon. Leading AVAs: Edna Valley, PASO ROBLES, SANTA MARIA VALLEY (shared with SANTA BARBARA COUNTY), Arroyo Grande Valley and York Mountain. Best producers: ALBAN★★, Claiborne & Churchill★, Edna Valley★★, Laetitia, Meridian★, Norman★, Saucelito Canyon★, Savannah-Chanelle★, Talley★★, Tolosa Estate. Best years: (reds) **2012 10 09 08 07 06 05 04 03 02 01 99 98 97 95 94.**

SAN PEDRO *Curicó, Chile* The group counts 10 wineries among its subsidiaries, including 2 in Argentina (Tamarí and Finca la Celia). Prominent among the Chilean operations is the quality-focused Viña LEYDA in SAN ANTONIO. Cachapoal-based Altaïr★★ is finding its stride. Under the San Pedro label, Castillo de Molina Reservas★★ are outstanding, especially the Sauvignon Blanc from ELQUI. Cabernet-based Cabo de Hornos★ is deep and concentrated. Also exciting reds from MAULE and Elqui, and single-vineyard wines under the 1865★★ label.

SANCERRE AC *Loire Valley, France* From a good grower, white Sancerre perfectly captures the bright green tang of the Sauvignon grape. Stony calcareous soils (*les caillottes*) produce the most forward, aromatic styles, while clay and limestone (*terre blanches*) and flint (*silex*) make for more ageworthy wines. Some growers produce a richer style using new oak. Pinot Noir reds from top producers are now a serious proposition, while Pinot Noir rosé is delicate and refreshingly dry. The wines are more consistent than those of neighbouring POUILLY. Prices reflect the appellation's popularity. Best producers: F & J Bailly-Reverdy★, G Boulay★★, H BOURGEOIS★★, H Brochard★, R Champault★, D Chotard★, F Cotat★★, F Crochet★, L Crochet★, Delaporte★, A Dezat★, Gitton★, A Gueneau, Serge Laloue★, Serge Laporte★, Y & P Martin★, A MELLOT★★, Mollet-Maudry★, G & P Morin★, H Natter★, V Pinard★, P Prieur★, J Reverdy★, P & N Reverdy★, C Riffault★, J-M Roger★, Thomas-Labaille★★, VACHERON★★, André Vatan★★. Best years: 2013 12 **11 10** 09.

SANDEMAN *Port DOC, Douro, Portugal, and Jerez y Manzanilla DO, Spain* The PORT operation is now owned by SOGRAPE and run by 7th-generation George Sandeman. Excellent aged tawnies: 20-year-old★ and 30-year-old★★. Vintage ports are better recently. Vau Vintage★ is good second label, for early drinking. Also a range of sherries. Best years: (Vintage) 2011 **07 03** 00 97 94 66 63 55.

SANFORD *Sta. Rita Hills AVA, California, USA* Richard Sanford planted the great Sanford & Benedict vineyard in the Santa Ynez Valley in 1971, thus establishing SANTA BARBARA as a potentially top-quality vineyard region. He subsequently planted an estate vineyard in the STA. RITA HILLS, an area that has burst onto the Pinot Noir scene with some spectacular wines (sharply focused, dark-fruited Pinot Noir★★, Chardonnay★★). Richard Sanford left in 2005 to found high-quality Alma Rosa label. Best years: (Pinot Noir) 2010 **09** 08 07 06 05 04 02 01 00 99.

DOM. LE SANG DES CAILLOUX *Vacqueyras AC, Rhône Valley, France* Top VACQUEYRAS estate with big, firmly fruited, peppery red wines. Cuvée de Lopy★★, from old-vine Grenache and Syrah, bursts with fruit over 10 or more years. The traditional cuvée★, restrained but full, is named Azalaïs,

Doucinello or Floureto, changing every vintage. Also intense, oaked, rich white Vacqueyras★. Best years: 2012 11 10 09 07 06 05 04 03 01 00 99 98.

SANGIOVESE Sangiovese, the most widely planted grape variety in Italy, reaches its greatest heights in central TUSCANY, especially in Montalcino, whose BRUNELLO is supposed to be 100% varietal. This grape has a wide range of sub-varieties, plus a growing number of 'improved' clones. Much care is taken when replanting, whether in CHIANTI CLASSICO, Brunello di Montalcino, VINO NOBILE DI MONTEPULCIANO or elsewhere. Styles range from pale, lively and cherryish, through vivacious mid-range Chiantis, to excellent Riservas and top Tuscan blends; the dense red fruit often has a sweet-sour streak, a whiff of herbs and the scratch of raw earth. Some fine examples in ROMAGNA. California producers including SEGHESIO are having a go; it does quite well in the SIERRA FOOTHILLS. Australia has good examples from Victoria's HEATHCOTE (Greenstone) and King Valley (Crittenden, Pizzini), MCLAREN VALE (CHAPEL HILL, Coriole), BAROSSA (PENFOLDS Cellar Reserve★) and MUDGEE (Oatley make snappy rosé). Also grown in Argentina, Chile, South Africa, Virginia, Washington State and New York.

SANTA BARBARA COUNTY *California, USA* CENTRAL COAST county, north-west of Los Angeles, known for Chardonnay, Riesling, Pinot Noir and Syrah. Main AVAs are STA. RITA HILLS, Santa Ynez Valley and most of SANTA MARIA VALLEY (the remainder is in SAN LUIS OBISPO COUNTY), all top areas for Pinot Noir. Best producers: AU BON CLIMAT★★, Babcock, BECKMEN★★, Brander★, Hitching Post★★, Longoria★, Melville★, Andrew MURRAY★★, Ojai★, Fess Parker★, QUPE★, Zaca Mesa★. Best years: (Pinot Noir) 2012 10 09 08 07 06 05 04 03 02 01 00.

SANTA CAROLINA *Maipo, Chile* One of Chile's oldest wineries, whose ancient cellars are within Santiago's urban sprawl; recognized as a National Monument in 1973, although much had to be rebuilt after the 2010 earthquake. This large and improving winery has vineyards in all of Chile's major wine regions, and an extensive range. Top wines are red blend VSC★★ and Herencia★★ (Carmenère).

SANTA CRUZ MOUNTAINS AVA *California, USA* A sub-region of the CENTRAL COAST AVA. Notable for long-lived Chardonnays and Cabernet Sauvignons, including the stunning Monte Bello from RIDGE. Also small amounts of robust Pinot Noir. Best producers: BONNY DOON★★, David Bruce★★, Clos La Chance★, Thomas Fogarty★, Kathryn Kennedy★★, Mount Eden Vineyards★★, RIDGE★★★, Santa Cruz Mountain Vineyard★.

SANTA MARIA VALLEY AVA *Santa Barbara County and San Luis Obispo County, California, USA* This cool valley is a prime source of Chardonnay, Pinot Noir and Syrah. Top vineyards are Bien Nacido and Sierra Madre. Best producers: AU BON CLIMAT★★, Belle Glos★★, Byron★★, Foxen★★.

SANTA RITA *Maipo, Chile* Long-established MAIPO giant. Red blends such as Triple C★★ (Cabernet Franc-Cabernet Sauvignon-Carmenère) show real flair. Floresta wines (Leyda Sauvignon Blanc★★ and Apalta Cabernet Sauvignon★) are tremendous. Expensive Cabernet-based Casa Real★★ is gradually modernizing itself and realizing its potential.

STA. RITA HILLS AVA *Santa Barbara County, California, USA* This small AVA lies at the western edge of the Santa Ynez Hills in SANTA BARBARA COUNTY. Fog and wind from the Pacific keep temperatures reasonably cool. Pinot Noir is the primary grape (along with small amounts of Syrah and

Chardonnay) and the wines have deeper colour, greater varietal intensity and higher acidity than others in the region – they have pretty high alcohols, too. **Best producers:** Babcock, Brewer-Clifton★★, Clos Pepe★★, Fiddlehead★★, Foley★★, Lafond★, Melville★, SANFORD★★, SEA SMOKE★★.

SANTENAY AC *Côte de Beaune, Burgundy, France*   Red Santenay wines often promise good ripe flavour, though they don't always deliver it, but are worth aging for 4–6 years in the hope that the wine will open out. Many of the best wines, both red and white, come from les Gravières Premier Cru on the border with CHASSAGNE-MONTRACHET. **Best producers:** (reds) R Belland★, Chevrot★, F & D Clair★, M COLIN★, J-N GAGNARD★, J Girardin★, V GIRARDIN★, Monnot★, D Moreau★, MOREY★★, L Muzard★★, Pousse d'Or★, J-M Vincent★★; (whites) V GIRARDIN★, Jaffelin, René Lequin-Colin★. **Best years:** (reds) (2013) 12 11 09 **07 05 02**.

CASA SANTOS LIMA *Alenquer DOC, Lisboa, Portugal*   A beautiful estate with a wide range: fruity, tasty Espiga reds and whites; spicy red★ and creamy, perfumed white Palha Canas; red and white Quinta das Setencostas★. Also varietal Touriga Nacional★, Touriga Franca★, Trincadeira★, Tinta Roriz★ and peachy, herby Chardonnay★.

CAVES SÃO JOÃO *Beira Atlântico, Portugal*   A pioneer of cool-fermented, white BAIRRADA, and makes rich, oaky Cabernet Sauvignon from its own vines. Rich, complex traditional reds and whites include outstanding Frei João★ (Reserva★★) from Bairrada and Porta dos Cavaleiros★★ from DÃO – they demand at least 10 years' age to show their quality.

SARDINIA *Italy*   Grapes of Spanish origin, like white Vermentino and Torbato and red Monica, Cannonau and Carignano, dominate production on this huge, hilly Mediterranean island, but they vie with a Malvasia of Greek origin and natives like Nuragus and Vernaccia. The cooler northern part (Gallura) favours Vermentino, while the southern and eastern parts are best suited to Cannonau and Monica reds, with Carignano dominating in the south-west. The wines used to be alcoholic monsters, but the current trend is for a lighter, modern, more international style. Frontrunners in pursuit of quality are ARGIOLAS, Capichera, Contini, Cantina Gallura, Alberto Loi, Santadi and Sella & Mosca. For authentic charm, try Giovanni Montisci's Cannonau di Sardegna DOC. See also CARIGNANO DEL SULCIS.

SASSICAIA DOC★★★ *Tuscany, Italy*   Legendary Cabernet Sauvignon-Cabernet Franc blend. Vines were planted in 1944 to satisfy the Marchese Mario Incisa della Rocchetta's thirst for fine red Bordeaux, which was in short supply during the war. First release was the 1968 vintage. Since then, Sassicaia's fame has increased as it proved itself to be one of the world's great Cabernets, combining a blackcurrant power of elegance and intensity with a heavenly scent of cigars. Since 1995 it has its own DOC within the BOLGHERI appellation. **Best years:** (2011) **10 08 07 06 04 01 99 98 97 95 90 88 85**.

HORST SAUER *Escherndorf, Franken, Germany*   Horst Sauer shot to stardom in the late 1990s and is a brilliant standard-bearer for FRANKEN. His dry Rieslings★★ and Silvaners★★ are unusually juicy and fresh for a region renowned for blunt, earthy wines. His late-harvest wines are frequently

★★★; they will easily live a decade, sometimes much more. Best years: (dry Riesling, Silvaner) (2013) 12 11 **10 09 08 07 06**.

SAUMUR AC *Loire Valley, France* Dry white wines, mainly from Chenin Blanc, with up to 20% Chardonnay; the best combine bright fruit with a mineral seam. The reds are lighter than those of SAUMUR-CHAMPIGNY and new Saumur Puy-Notre-Dame AC. Also dry to off-dry Cabernet rosé, and sweet Coteaux de Saumur in good years. Best producers: Château-Gaillard★, Clos Rougeard★★, Collier★, Filliatreau★, Fosse-Seche★, E Gastellier★, Guiberteau★, HUREAU★★, Langlois-Château★, R-N Legrand★, F MABILEAU★, la Paleine★, ROCHES NEUVES★★, St-Just★, Saumur co-op, Targé★, VILLENEUVE★★, Yvonne★★. Best years: (whites) 2013 **12 11 10 09 08 07**.

SAUMUR-CHAMPIGNY AC *Loire Valley, France* Saumur's best red wine. Cabernet Franc is the main grape and, on Saumur's soft limestone soils, produces among the Loire's most seductively perfumed, silky examples. Delicious young, it can age for 6–10 years, top cuvées even longer. Best producers: Clos des Cordeliers, Clos Cristal★, Clos Rougeard★★, de la Cune, B Dubois★, Filliatreau★, HUREAU★★, R-N Legrand★, Montguéret, Nerleux★, la Perruche★, Retiveau-Rétif★, ROCHES NEUVES★★, St-Vincent★, A Sanzay★, VILLENEUVE★★, Yvonne★. Best years: 2013 **11 10 09 08 06 05**.

SAUMUR MOUSSEUX AC *Loire Valley, France* Reasonable traditional-method sparkling wines, mainly from Chenin Blanc. Adding Chardonnay and Cabernet Franc makes the wine softer and more interesting. Usually non-vintage. Small quantities of rosé are also made. Best producers: Ch. de Beauregard, Bouvet-Ladubay★, Gratien & Meyer★, Grenelle★, la Paleine★, la Perruche★, Saumur co-op, Veuve Amiot.

SAUSSIGNAC AOP *Bergerac, South-West France* Slightly more mineral than the sweet wines of neighbouring MONBAZILLAC. Best after 3 years, but will age well. Best producers: Clos d'Yvigne★, La Maurigne★, Miaudoux★, Richard★.

SAUTERNES AC *Bordeaux, France* The name Sauternes is synonymous with the best sweet wines in the world. Sauternes and BARSAC both lie on the banks of the little river Ciron and are 2 of the very few areas in France where noble rot occurs naturally. Production of these intense, sweet, luscious wines from botrytized grapes is a risk-laden and extremely expensive affair, and the wines are never cheap. From good producers the wines are worth their high price – as well as 14% alcohol, they have a richness full of flavours of pineapples, peaches, syrup and spice. Good vintages should be aged for 5–10 years and can last two or three times as long. Best producers: Bastor-Lamontagne★, Clos Haut-Peyraguey★★, DOISY-DAËNE★★, DOISY-VÉDRINES★★, FARGUES★★, GILETTE★★, GUIRAUD★★, Haut-Bergeron★, les Justices★, LAFAURIE-PEYRAGUEY★★, Lamothe-Guignard★, Laville, Malle★, Rabaud-Promis★, Raymond-Lafon★, Rayne-Vigneau★, RIEUSSEC★★★, Sigalas Rabaud★★, SUDUIRAUT★★★, la TOUR BLANCHE★★, YQUEM★★★. Best years: 2011 **10 09 07 05 03 02 01 99 98 97 96 95 90 89 88**.

SAUVIGNON BLANC See pages 284–5.

SAUZET *Puligny-Montrachet, Côte de Beaune, Burgundy, France* Rich, full-flavoured white Burgundies, recently showing more classical restraint. Now biodynamic. Prime sites in PULIGNY-MONTRACHET★ with a great range of Premiers Crus, especially Combettes★★★, as well as small parcels of BÂTARD-MONTRACHET★★★ and Bienvenues-BÂTARD-MONTRACHET★★★. Best years: (2013) 12 11 10 **09 08 07 06 05 04 02**.

SAVENNIÈRES AC *Loire Valley, France* Wines from Chenin Blanc, produced on steep vineyards south of Anjou. Traditionally steely and dry, although some richer wines are being produced using new oak and malolactic fermentation. The top wines usually need at least 8 years, and can age for longer. Two vineyards have their own ACs: la Coulée de Serrant and Roche aux Moines. Best producers: Baumard★★, Closel★★, La COULÉE-DE-SERRANT★★, Épiré★★, Dom. F L★, Forges★, Damien Laureau★, aux Moines★, Eric Morgat★, OGEREAU, PIERRE-BISE★, Taillandier★. Best years: (2013) 12 11 09 08 07 06 05 04 03 02 01 99.

SAVIGNY-LÈS-BEAUNE AC *Côte de Beaune, Burgundy, France* Large village with reds dominating; usually dry and lean, they need 4–6 years to open out. Top Premiers Crus, such as Lavières, Peuillets and La Dominode, are more substantial. The white wines show a bit of dry, nutty class after 2–3 years. The wines are generally reasonably priced. Best producers: Belin★, BELLENE★, S Bize★, Camus-Bruchon★, Champy★, CHANDON DE BRIAILLES★, Chenu★, B CLAIR★★, Dublère★, M Écard★, J J Girard★, Guiton★, Guyon★, L Jacob★, Dom. LEROY★★, J-M Pavelot★. Best years: (reds) (2013) 12 11 10 09 08 05 02.

SAVOIE *France* Savoie's Alpine vineyards produce fresh, snappy white wines from the local Jacquère, Chasselas (to drink young), and the more interesting Altesse (see ROUSSETTE DE SAVOIE) and Bergeron grapes (aka Roussanne, grown only in Chignin). There are attractive light reds and rosés too, from Gamay or Pinot and some positively Rhône-like reds from the Mondeuse grape (related to Syrah) and the rare Persan. Good fizz is shortly to be Crémant de Savoie AC. The 16 best villages can add their own name to the label: these include Apremont, Abymes, Chignin and Arbin, near Chambéry, and Jongieux near Aix-les-Bains, along with Crépy and Ripaille growing Chasselas near Lac Léman (Geneva) and Ayse in the Arve Valley growing Gringet. Seyssel has its own AC for sparkling and dry whites. Two important producers, Domaine des Ardoisières and Domaine Gonin, are outside the AC area. Best producers: Belluard★★, A Berlioz★, G Berlioz★, Berthollier★, Dupasquier★, Giachino★, P Grisard★, l'Idylle★, E Jacquin★, Magnin★, Maillet, J Masson★, Prieuré St-Christophe★★, A & M Quenard★, J-P & J-F Quenard, P & A Quénard★, Saint-Germain★, Trosset★.

SAXENBURG *Stellenbosch WO, South Africa* In-demand red wines, led by dense, burly Private Collection Shiraz★★ and even richer, bigger Shiraz Select★★, plus excellent Cabernet★★ and Merlot★. Private Collection Sauvignon Blanc★★ and Chardonnay★ head the white range. Reds will improve for 5–8 years. Best years: (top reds) 2011 10 09 08 07 06 05 04.

WILLI SCHAEFER *Graach, Mosel, Germany* Classic MOSEL wines: Riesling Spätlese and Auslese from the GRAACHER Domprobst vineyard have a balance of piercing acidity and lavish fruit that is every bit as dramatic as Domprobst's precipitous slope. Extremely long-lived, they're frequently ★★★, as are the sensational Beerenauslese and Eiswein Schaefer produces in the ripest vintages. Best years: (2013) 12 11 10 09 08 07 06 05 04 02 01.

SCHÄFER-FRÖHLICH *Bockenau, Nahe, Germany* From vineyards in SCHLOSSBOCKELHEIM and the more obscure Bockenau, Tim Fröhlich produces racy dry Rieslings★★ and sumptuous nobly sweet wines★★★. Best years: (2013) 12 11 10 09 08 07 05.

SCHARFFENBERGER CELLARS *Anderson Valley AVA, California, USA* The quality trailblazer in the chilly ANDERSON VALLEY, now owned by top-performing neighbour ROEDERER. Non-vintage Brut★★, with lovely toasty depth, exuberant Rosé★★ and excellent vintage Blanc de Blancs★★.

SAUVIGNON BLANC

 Of all the world's grapes, the Sauvignon Blanc is leader of the 'love it or loathe it' pack. It veers from being wildly fashionable to totally out of favour, depending upon where it is grown and which country's wine writers are talking. But you, the consumers, love it – and so do I. Sauvignon is always at its best when full rein is allowed to its very particular talents, because this grape does give intense, sometimes shocking flavours, and doesn't take kindly to being put into a straitjacket. Periodically, producers lose confidence in its fantastic, brash, tangy personality and try to calm it down. Don't do it. Let it run free – it's that lip-smacking, in-yer-face nettles and lime zest and passionfruit attack that drinkers love. There's no more thirst-quenching wine than a snappy, crunchy young Sauvignon Blanc. Let's celebrate it.

WINE STYLES

Sancerre-style Sauvignon Although it had long been used as a blending grape in Bordeaux, where its characteristic green tang injected a bit of life into the blander, waxier Sémillon, Sauvignon first became trendy as the grape used for Sancerre, a bone-dry Loire white whose green gooseberry fruit and slightly smoky perfume inspired the winemakers of other countries to try to emulate, then often surpass, the original model.

The range of styles Sauvignon produces is as wide as, if less subtly nuanced than, those of Chardonnay. It is highly successful when picked slightly underripe, fermented cool in stainless steel, and bottled early. This is the New Zealand model and they in turn adapted and improved upon the Sancerre model from France. New Zealand is now regarded as the top Sauvignon country, and many new producers in places like Australia, South Africa, southern France, Hungary, Spain, Argentina and Chile are emulating this powerful mix of passionfruit, gooseberry and lime. South African and Chilean examples, from the coolest coastal regions, with tangy fruit and mineral depth, challenge New Zealand for quality.

Using oak Sauvignon also lends itself to fermentation in barrel and aging in new oak, though less happily than does Chardonnay. This is the model of the Graves region of Bordeaux, although generally here Sémillon would be blended in with Sauvignon to good effect.

New Zealand again excels at this style, and there are good examples from California (sometimes known as Fumé Blanc), Australia and northern Italy. The mix, usually led by Sémillon, is becoming a classy, ageworthy speciality of South Africa's coastal regions. In Austria, producers in southern Styria (Steiermark) make powerful, aromatic versions, sometimes with a touch of oak. In all these regions, the acidity that is Sauvignon's great strength should remain, with a nectarine fruit and a spicy, biscuity softness from the oak. These oaky styles are best drunk either within about a year, or after aging for 5 years or so, and can produce remarkable, strongly individual flavours.

Sweet wines Sauvignon is also a crucial ingredient in the great sweet wines of Sauternes and Barsac from Bordeaux, though it is less susceptible than its partner Sémillon to the sweetness-enhancing 'noble rot' fungus, botrytis.

Sweet Sauvignon-Semillon blends from elsewhere in the world range from the interesting to the outstanding – but the characteristic green tang of the Sauvignon should be found even at ultra-sweet levels.

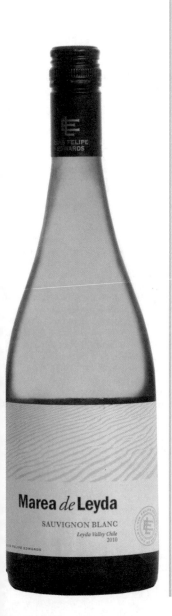

Marea *de* Leyda

SAUVIGNON BLANC

Leyda Valley Chile
2010

BEST PRODUCERS

France

Pouilly-Fumé J-C Chatelain, Didier DAGUENEAU, Ladoucette, Masson-Blondelet, de Tracy; *Sancerre* G Boulay, H BOURGEOIS, F Cotat, F Crochet, A MELLOT, VACHERON; *Pessac-Léognan* Dom. de CHEVALIER, Couhins-Lurton, FIEUZAL, HAUT-BRION, la LOUVIÉRE, MALARTIC-LAGRAVIERE, SMITH-HAUT-LAFITTE; *Graves* Clos Floridène; *Sauternes* GUIRAUD.

Other European Sauvignons

Austria Gross, Lackner-Tinnacher, Neumeister, POLZ, E Sabathi, Sattlerhof, TEMENT.

Italy Colterenzio, Peter Dipoli, Edi Kante, LAGEDER, Vie di Romans, Villa Russiz.

Spain (Rueda) Hermanos Lurton; MARQUES DE RISCAL, Palacio de Bornos, Javier Sanz, Sitios de Bodega; *(Penedès)* TORRES (Fransola).

New World Sauvignons

New Zealand ASTROLABE, Blind River, BRANCOTT, CLOUDY BAY, Dog Point, Gladstone, Greywacke, Lawson's Dry Hills, MATUA VALLEY, MAN O'WAR, NEUDORF, PALLISER, PEGASUS BAY, Sacred Hill, SAINT CLAIR, Stoneleigh, TE MATA, TerraVin. VAVASOUR, VILLA MARIA, YEALANDS.

Australia Angullong, BANNOCKBURN, Bird in Hand, Brookland Valley, Larry CHERUBINO, DE BORTOLI (Yarra Valley), Hanging Rock, HOUGHTON (Wisdom), Karribindi, Katnook Estate, Lenton Brae, Logan, Longview, Nepenthe, S C PANNELL, Philip Shaw, SHAW & SMITH, Stella Bella, Tamar Ridge, Word of Mouth.

USA ARAUJO, Brander, Coquerel, DRY CREEK (DCV3), FLORA SPRINGS (Soliloquy), GRGICH HILLS, HEITZ, Honig, KENWOOD, MONDAVI, ST SUPÉRY, SPOTTSWOODE.

Chile CASA MARÍN, CASAS DEL BOSQUE, CONCHA Y TORO (Terrunyo), CONO SUR (20 Barrels), ERRAZURIZ, O FOURNIER, Viña LEYDA, LUIS FELIPE EDWARDS, MONTES, SAN PEDRO (Castillo de Molina), SANTA RITA (Floresta), UNDURRAGA (T.H.).

South Africa Graham BECK (Pheasants' Run), CAPE POINT, Cedarberg Ghost Corner, Constantia Glen, Neil ELLIS, Flagstone, Fleur du Cap, Fryer's Cove, Hermanuspietersfontein, Iona, KLEIN CONSTANTIA, MULDERBOSCH, Oak Valley, Quoin Rock, SPRINGFIELD, STEENBERG, THELEMA, Tokara, VERGELEGEN.

285

SCHEUREBE   Silvaner x Riesling crossing found in Germany's PFALZ and RHEINHESSEN. In Austria it is sometimes labelled Sämling 88. At its best in Trockenbeerenauslese and Eiswein. When ripe, it has a marvellous flavour of honey, exotic fruits and the pinkest of pink grapefruit.

SCHILCHER Austria   Rosé and sparkling wine from the Blauer Wildbacher grape, a speciality of the West STEIERMARK. Its high acidity means you either love it or detest it. Best producer: Müller.

SCHLOSS GOBELSBURG Gobelsburg, Kamptal, Austria   This monastic estate, with vines in KAMPTAL's finest sites, was taken over by Michael Moosbrugger in 1996. Powerful but stunning Rieslings (Heiligenstein★★) and Grüner Veltliners (Lamm★★, Grub★★). Best years: (2013) 12 11 **10 09 08 07 06**.

SCHLOSS JOHANNISBERG Johannisberg, Rheingau, Germany   This historic 35ha (86-acre) estate has not always lived up to its reputation. Since 2005 a new director has greatly improved the winemaking. TBA★★★ has long been outstanding (and costly), but drier styles of Riesling (can be ★★) are now vigorous and spicy. Best years: (2013) 12 11 **10 09 08 07**.

SCHLOSS LIESER Lieser, Mosel, Germany   Top estate owned by Thomas Haag (son of Wilhelm, of the Fritz HAAG estate). MOSEL Rieslings★★, dry as well as sweet, marry richness with great elegance. Best years: (2013) 12 11 **10 09 08 07 06 05**.

SCHLOSS REINHARTSHAUSEN Erbach, Rheingau, Germany   Estate formerly owned by the Hohenzollern family, rulers of Prussia. Top sites include the great ERBACHer Marcobrunn. Good Rieslings★★ in all styles and Sekt★. Best years: (2013) 12 11 **10 09 08 07 06 05**.

SCHLOSSBÖCKELHEIM Nahe, Germany   This village's top sites are the Felsenberg and Kupfergrube; good wines also come from Mühlberg and Königsfels. Best producers: Dr Crusius★, DÖNNHOFF★★★, Gut Hermannsberg★★, SCHÄFER-FRÖHLICH★★. Best years: (2013) 12 11 **10 09 08 07 06 05**.

SCHNAITMANN Württemberg, Germany   A rising star, with reds and whites of equal excitement. Rainer Schnaitmann trained in New Zealand, and his Sauvignon Blanc★ is one of Germany's best. Fine Spätburgunder★★ (Pinot Noir) and Lemberger★. Best years: (2013) 12 11 **10 09 08 07**.

DOM. SCHOFFIT Alsace AC, Alsace, France   One of the two main owners of the outstanding Rangen Grand Cru vineyard, whose Clos St-Théobald wines are often ★★★: Gewurztraminer and Pinot Gris will improve for at least 5–6 years after release, Rieslings for even longer. The Cuvée Alexandre range is essentially declassified ALSACE Vendange Tardive. Irresistible Chasselas★★. Best years: (Clos St-Théobald Riesling) (2013) (12) (11) (10) **09 08 07 05 04 02 01 00 99 98 97**.

SCHRAMSBERG Napa Valley AVA, California, USA   The first California winery to make really excellent CHAMPAGNE-style sparklers from the classic grapes. These wines are generally among California's best, and as good as fine Champagne. The Crémant★ is an attractive, slightly sweetish sparkler; the Blanc de Noirs★★ and the Blanc de Blancs★★ are more classic. Bold, powerful J Schram★★ is rich and flavoursome and increasingly good. Top of the line is the Reserve Brut★★. Vintage-dated wines can be drunk with up to 10 years' age and can achieve ★★★ quality. A rosé sparkler★★ is a superb summer quaffer. The J Davies Cabernet Sauvignon★★, from Diamond Mountain, is named in honour of the late founder, Jack Davies. Also a line of vineyard-designated still Pinot Noir wines under the Davies Vineyards brand.

SCREAMING EAGLE *Oakville AVA, California, USA*   First made in 1992, in very limited quantities, Screaming Eagle★★ is one of California's most sought-after Cabernets each vintage – a huge, brooding wine that displays all the lush fruit of Oakville. The vineyard has been replanted and a new winery built, but a change in style is not expected.

SEA SMOKE *Sta. Rita Hills AVA, California, USA*   This boutique Pinot star is scaling back a bit on its rich, ripe style in favour of slightly lower alcohol levels. The Botella★ is the most approachable, followed by the more complex Southing★★ and blockbuster Ten★★. The winery makes just a splash of elegant 'Gratis' Chardonnay★. New fresh, low-dosage sparkler called Sea Spray. Best years: (Pinot Noir) 2010 09 08 07 05 04 03 02 01.

SEGHESIO *Sonoma County, California, USA*   Famous for Zinfandel, having been grape-growers in SONOMA COUNTY for a century. All bottlings, from Sonoma County★★ to the single-vineyard San Lorenzo★★ and Cortina★★, display textbook black fruit and peppery spice. Sangiovese★ from 1910 vines is one of the best in the state. Also look for fascinating Aglianico★ and crisp Italian whites such as Pinot Grigio★ and Arneis★.

SELBACH-OSTER *Zeltingen, Mosel, Germany*   Johannes Selbach is one of the MOSEL's new generation of stars, producing pure, elegant Riesling★★ from the Zeltinger Sonnenuhr site. Also fine wine from WEHLEN and GRAACH. Best years: (2013) 12 11 09 08 07 05.

SELVAPIANA *Chianti Rufina DOCG, Tuscany, Italy*   Since 1990 this estate has vaulted into the top rank of Tuscan estates, particularly with single-vineyard cru Bucerchiale CHIANTI RUFINA Riserva★★★ and 'super-Tuscan' IGT Fornace★★. Very good VIN SANTO★★. Best years: (Bucerchiale) (2012) 11 10 09 08 07 06 04 01 99 98 95 91 90 88 85.

SÉMILLON   Found mainly in South-West France, especially in the sweet wines of SAUTERNES, BARSAC, MONBAZILLAC and SAUSSIGNAC, because it is prone to noble rot (*Botrytis cinerea*). Also blended for its waxy texture with Sauvignon Blanc to make dry wine – almost all the great PESSAC-LÉOGNAN whites are based on this blend and exhibit vivid nectarine fruit and custardy softness. Good in Australia on its own (the accent over the é is dropped on New World labels) – aged Semillon from the HUNTER, BAROSSA and CLARE VALLEY can be wonderful: bone-dry, lime zesty yet toasty – or as a blender with Chardonnay. Semillon is also blended with Sauvignon in Western Australia, New Zealand, California (including ST SUPÉRY's Virtù★★), Washington State and in cooler regions of South Africa, where it is producing some outstanding results, often barrel-fermented (Cederberg's Ghost Corner★★ from ELIM, BOEKENHOUTSKLOOF★★ from Franschhoek vines).

SEPPELT *Grampians, Victoria, Australia*   From its GRAMPIANS base, Seppelt continues to excel with its flagship St Peters Shiraz★★, the definitive Show Sparkling Shiraz★★★ and the Original Sparkling Shiraz★. The Mount Ida Shiraz from HEATHCOTE is a welcome addition to the range. Drumborg Riesling★★ Chardonnay★, Pinot Gris★ and Pinot Noir★ from the super-cool Henty region of south-western VICTORIA stand out, and there are some excellent budget-priced table wines, notably The Victorians Shiraz.

SERESIN *Marlborough, South Island, New Zealand*   Film producer Michael Seresin's MARLBOROUGH winery, with a range of stylish organic/biodynamic wines. Intense Sauvignon Blanc★★ is full of youthful exuberance.

Creamy Reserve Chardonnay★★, succulent Pinot Gris★ and several rich, oaky Pinot Noirs★★ (some single-vineyard, the best of which will age for up to 7 years). Best years: (Pinot Noir) (2013) **12 11 10 09 07 06**.

SETÚBAL DOC *Portugal* Fortified wine from the Setúbal Peninsula south of Lisbon, called 'Moscatel de Setúbal' when made from at least 85% Moscatel, and 'Setúbal' when it's not. Best producers: BACALHÔA★★, José Maria da FONSECA★★.

SEYVAL BLANC Hybrid grape whose disease resistance and ability to ripen in a damp autumn make it a useful variety in England – for both still and sparkling wines – Quebec, NEW YORK STATE and other areas in the eastern US. Gives clean, sappy, grapefruit-edged wines that with age can sometimes give a very passable imitation of bone-dry CHABLIS.

SHAFER *Stags Leap District AVA, California, USA* One of the best NAPA wineries, run by the erudite and thoughtful Doug Shafer, and making unusually fruity One Point Five Cabernet★★ and stunning, focused Reserve-style Hillside Select★★★ that ages to a cedary beauty over a generation. Merlot★★ is also exciting. Relentless★ is made from estate-grown Syrah. Red Shoulder Ranch Chardonnay★ is classic full-bodied but scented CARNEROS style. Best years: (Hillside Select) **2010 09 08 07 06 05 04 03 02 01 00 99 98 97 96 95 94 93 91 90**.

SHARPHAM *Devon, England* Beautiful vineyard on a bend in the river Dart. Still wines include Bacchus★, Madeleine Angevine-based Estate Selection and Barrel Fermented. High-quality white and rosé sparklers★. Also makes great cheese.

PHILIP SHAW *Orange, New South Wales, Australia* Philip Shaw was at the winemaking helm of commercial giant ROSEMOUNT in the 1990s, and moved to Orange to build a family wine business around the picturesque Koomooloo vineyard, which he had planted in 1989. The No 19 Sauvignon Blanc★★ is tight and zesty; No 11 Chardonnay★ rich and minerally; the No 5 Cabernet Sauvignon★ fleshy, yet elegant.

SHAW & SMITH *Adelaide Hills, South Australia* Influential winery run by cousins Martin Shaw and Michael Hill Smith. Tangy Sauvignon Blanc★★ has been a runaway success since its first vintage in 1989; increasingly brilliant single-vineyard M3 Chardonnay★★★; and impressive, fleshy, cool-climate Shiraz★★. Delightful Riesling★ and Pinot Noir★ (expect these to be ★★ soon). The purchase of the 20ha (50-acre) Tolpuddle vineyard with its 25-year-old vines will transform Shaw & Smith into a major player in TASMANIA. Already impressive Chardonnay★★ and Pinot Noir★★ under the Tolpuddle label; expect stunning fizz next. Best years: (M3 Chardonnay) 2013 **12 10 09 08 07 06 05 04 03 02**.

SHERRY See JEREZ Y MANZANILLA DO, pages 184–5.

SHINN ESTATE *Long Island, New York State, USA* Former chef David Page and Barbara Shinn are the husband-and-wife team at this estate on LONG ISLAND's North Fork. They farm according to biodynamics, unusual on the US East Coast. Best wines are Sauvignon Blanc, Merlot★ and Cabernet Sauvignon★.

SHIRAZ See SYRAH, pages 300–1.

SHOBBROOK *Barossa Valley, South Australia* Five years working at Riecine in Tuscany proved formative, and since establishing his own winery Tom Shobbrook has turned himself into one of the BAROSSA's most lively and challenging personalities, pushing the limits of both biodynamic viticulture and natural winemaking. An old Eden Valley vineyard produces pure, minerally, zesty Riesling★★ fermented in ceramic jars. Thrilling Sauvignon★★ left on its skins for 6 weeks; enticingly rustic Carignan; Tommy Ruff Syrah-Mourvèdre★★ and Shobbrook Syrah★★, a Merlot he makes for his mum, and unbelievable Nebbiolo sherry are just a few of the brilliant beauties that his febrile brain ferments.

SICILY *Italy* The Mediterranean's largest island is a historically prolific producer of good wine, with sweet Malvasias from the Eolian islands and Zibibbos (see MOSCATO PASSITO DI PANTELLERIA) joining the fortified brews from MARSALA and tasty table wines from the Cataratto (white) and Perricone (black) varieties in the west, Nerello (black) and Carricante (white) in the north-east (ETNA and Messina's Faro), and powerful Nero d'Avolas and delicate Frappatos in the south-east. In the late 20th and early 21st centuries there has been a flurry of enological activity. Nero d'Avola has spread all over the island, varietally or blended, now with Frappato, now with Syrah. Co-ops like Settesoli – with attractive budget label Inycon and top-end Mandrarossa (often ★★) – are doing a tremendous job on the large-scale commercial front, and modern-thinking wineries, using both native and international grapes, are mushrooming. **Best producers:** Abbazia Santa Anastasia★★, Avide★, Benanti★★, Il Cantante★, Ceuso★, COS★★, Cottanera★, Cusumano★, Donnafugata★, Feudo Arancio★, Firriato★, Florio★, Graci★★, Gulfi★, Luna Sicana★, Morgante★★, Arianna Occhipinti★★, Palari★★, Pellegrino★, PLANETA★★ Rapitalà★, Duca di SALAPARUTA★, TASCA D'ALMERITA★★, Terrazze dell'Etna★, Vigneti Zabù★.

SIERRA FOOTHILLS AVA *California, USA* The key word here is foothills, since valley floor locations 130km (80 miles) east of San Francisco tend to be warmer and less likely to produce fine wine. Some of the state's oldest Zinfandel is here, and some old-vine Petite Sirahs are superb, long-lived brutes. The region also does well with Italian varieties like Sangiovese and Barbera. Look for wines from Shake Ridge Ranch vineyard. **Best producers:** AMADOR FOOTHILL★, Granite Springs★, Latcham, Lava Cap★, Perry Creek★, Sobon Estate, Twisted Oak★, Vino Noceto.

SIEUR D'ARQUES, LES VIGNERONS DU *Limoux AC, Languedoc, France* This modern co-op makes around 80% of the still and sparkling wines of LIMOUX. The BLANQUETTE DE LIMOUX and CRÉMANT DE LIMOUX are reliable, but the real excitement comes with the Toques et Clochers Chardonnays★. The co-op also makes a range of Pays d'OC wines.

SILVER OAK CELLARS *Napa Valley, California, USA*
Only Cabernet Sauvignon is made here, with bottlings from ALEXANDER VALLEY★★ and NAPA VALLEY★ grapes. Forward, generous, fruity wines, impossible not to enjoy young, yet with great staying power. Twomey is the owners' other winery, which started out making only Merlot but has expanded to include Pinot Noir from several AVAs as well as Sauvignon Blanc. **Best years:** (Napa Valley) **2010 09 08 07 06 05 04 03 02 01 00 99 97 96 95 94 93 92 91 90.**

SILVERADO VINEYARDS *Stags Leap District AVA, California, USA* The estate Cabernet Sauvignon★ has intense fruit and is drinkable fairly young; Limited Reserve★★ (not made every year) has more depth and is capable of aging; Solo★, from STAGS LEAP DISTRICT, displays the cherry fruit and supple tannins of this AVA. Also a fruity Merlot★, refreshing Sauvignon Blanc★, and Chardonnay★ with soft, inviting fruit and a silky finish. Best years: (Limited Reserve) **2009 05 02 01 99 95 94 91 90**.

CH. SIRAN★ *Margaux AC, Haut-Médoc, Bordeaux, France* Owned by the same family since 1848, this estate produces consistently good claret – increasingly characterful, approachable young, but with enough structure to last for as long as 20 years. Second wine: S de Siran. Best years: 2012 11 10 09 **08 07 06 05 04 03 02 01 00 98 96 95**.

CHARLES SMITH *Walla Walla Valley AVA, Washington State, USA* Charles Smith, ex-rock band manager, opened his first winery, K Vintners, in 2001, specializing in single-vineyard Syrah★ and Syrah blends, as well as good Merlot★. The Charles Smith label focuses on modern wines for early drinking, such as lemony Pinot Grigio, citrus and racy Kung Fu Girl Riesling★ and juicy Velvet Devil Merlot★. The best is yet to come from new developments and challenging single vineyards.

CH. SMITH-HAUT-LAFITTE *Pessac-Léognan AC, Cru Classé de Graves, Bordeaux, France* A change of ownership in 1990 heralded a decade of hard graft, resulting in massively improved quality. The reds, traditionally lean, now have much more fruit and perfume and can approach ★★. The white is a shining example of modern Bordeaux and at its best is ★★★. Second wine (red and white): Les Hauts de Smith. Also Cabernet Sauvignon-based Le Petit Haut Lafitte since 2007. Best years: (reds) 2012 11 10 09 08 **07 06 05 04 03 02 01 00 99 98 96**; (whites) **2012 11 10 09 08 07 06 05 04 02 01**.

SOAVE DOC *Veneto, Italy* In the hilly Soave Classico zone near Verona, the Garganega and Trebbiano di Soave (aka Verdicchio) grapes can produce smooth, nutty, scented wines. The blend may include 30% Chardonnay or Pinot Bianco, but while there are good examples of this style they tend to lack the personality of those made without resort to French grapes. Soave Superiore is DOCG, but the top private producers ignore it in protest at the anomalous rules governing the denomination: top wines nearly all remain Soave Classico DOC or, with screw cap, plain Soave DOC. Best producers: Bertani★, Ca' Rugate★, La Cappuccina★, Cecilia Beretta★, Coffele★, Fattori★, Gini★, Inama★, MASI★, PIEROPAN★★★, Portinari★, Prà★★, Suavia★★, Tamellini★. See also ANSELMI, RECIOTO DI SOAVE.

CH. SOCIANDO-MALLET★★ *Haut-Médoc AC, Haut-Médoc, Bordeaux, France* Consistently outshining many Classed Growths, the wines massively repay 10–20 years' aging, but exhibit classic flavours from as early as 5 years old. Best years: 2012 11 10 09 **08 06 05 04 03 02 01 00 98 96 95 90**.

SOGRAPE *Portugal* Portuguese giant; Mateus Rosé is still the company's golden egg, but Sogrape makes good VINHO VERDE (Quinta de Azevedo★), DOURO (Reserva Tinto★) and ALENTEJO (Vinha do Monte, Herdade do Peso★). A high-tech winery in DÃO produces the Quinta dos Carvalhais range, with promising varietal Encruzado★ (white) and Touriga Nacional★ (red); Reserva★★ and Único★★★ reds are further steps up. Casa Ferreirinha DOURO reds are always good. Callabriga★ reds from Douro, Alentejo and Dão are based on Aragonez (Tempranillo), blended with local varieties. Subsidiaries FERREIRA, SANDEMAN and Offley provide top-flight ports. Also owns Finca Flichman in Argentina, FRAMINGHAM in New Zealand, Ch. Los Boldos in Chile and Bodegas LAN in RIOJA.

SOLAIA★★ *Tuscany, Italy* One of ANTINORI's 'super-Tuscans', Solaia is a blend of Cabernet Sauvignon, Sangiovese and Cabernet Franc. Intense, with rich black fruit and classic structure. Not produced in every vintage. Best years: (2011) **10 09 08 07 06 04 01 99 98 97 95 94 93 91 90 88 86 85**.

SOMONTANO DO *Aragón, Spain* Erratic but eternally promising region in the Pyrenean foothills, with a mixture of international and local grapes. Chardonnay and Gewürztraminer are successful whites. Rosés are generally fresh and flavourful; reds, particularly from native Parraleta, Moristel or old-vine Garnacha, can be impressive. Less dependence on international varieties would be welcome. **Best producers:** Otto Bestué, Blecua★★, Enate★★, Fábregas, Irius★, Lalanne★, Laus★, Pirineos★, Viñas del Vero★ (Secastilla★). **Best years:** (reds) 2011 **10 09 07 05 04 03 01**.

SONOMA COAST AVA *California, USA* A huge appellation, defined on its western boundary by the Pacific Ocean, that attempts to bring together the coolest regions of SONOMA COUNTY. It encompasses the Sonoma part of CARNEROS and overlaps parts of SONOMA VALLEY and RUSSIAN RIVER. The heart of the appellation is the high coastal ridge only a few miles from the Pacific. Vintners and growers along the coastline have formed an association called the West Sonoma Coast Vintners to distinguish themselves from producers farther inland. Intense Chardonnays and Pinot Noirs are the focus. **Best producers:** Capiaux★, COBB★★, Donelan★, DUTTON GOLDFIELD★★, FLOWERS★★, Fort Ross★, HARTFORD FAMILY★★, KISTLER★★, Kosta Browne★, LANDMARK★, Littorai★, MacPhail★, MARCASSIN★★, Patz & Hall★, PHELPS★★, Siduri★★, W H Smith★★, Sonoma Coast Vineyards★★ (Balistreri Vineyard★★★), Sean Thackrey★, WIND GAP★★.

SONOMA COUNTY *California, USA* Sonoma's vine-growing area is big and sprawling – some 25,500ha (63,000 acres) – with dozens of soil types and mesoclimates, from the fairly warm SONOMA VALLEY and ALEXANDER VALLEY regions to the cool Green Valley, lower RUSSIAN RIVER VALLEY and SONOMA COAST. The best wines are from Chardonnay, Sauvignon Blanc, Cabernet Sauvignon, Pinot Noir and Zinfandel. Often the equal of rival NAPA in quality and originality of flavours. See also CARNEROS, DRY CREEK VALLEY.

SONOMA-CUTRER *Russian River Valley AVA, Sonoma County, California, USA* Rich, oaky, popular Chardonnays. Single-vineyard Les Pierres★★ is the most complex and richest; Cutrer★★ can also have a complexity worth waiting for; Founders Reserve★★ is made in very limited quantities; Russian River Ranches★ has improved in recent releases. Pinot Noir★ is tasty stuff. **Best years:** (Chardonnay) **2012 10 09 08 07 06 05 04 03 02**.

SONOMA VALLEY AVA *California, USA* The oldest wine region north of San Francisco, Sonoma Valley is on the western side of the Mayacamas Mountains, which separate it from NAPA VALLEY. Best varieties are Chardonnay and Zinfandel, with Cabernet and Merlot from hillside sites also good. **Best producers:** Arrowood★★, Chateau St-Jean★, B R Cohn, Fisher★, Gundlach Bundschu★★, HANZELL★★, KENWOOD★, Kunde★, LANDMARK★★, LAUREL GLEN★★, Matanzas Creek★, Moon Mountain★★, RAVENSWOOD★, St Francis★, Sebastiani, Three Sticks★. **Best years:** (Zinfandel) **2012 11 10 09 08 07 06 05 04 03 01**.

DOM. SORIN *Bandol AC, Provence, France* As well as red and rosé BANDOL★, Luc Sorin makes various CÔTES DE PROVENCE wines, including a mouthwatering white blend of Rolle and Sémillon★ and a crisp pink grapefruit- and cranberry-flavoured rosé Terra Amata★. **Best years:** (red Bandol) (2013) **12 11 10 09 08 07 06 05**.

SOTER VINEYARDS *Willamette Valley AVA, Oregon, USA* Moving from NAPA VALLEY, Tony Soter planted his first Oregon Pinot Noir in 2002. The Mineral Springs Pinot Noir★★ is outstanding, with *terroir*-driven flavours showing from a very young site. North Valley★ is the basic cuvée. Small amounts of sparkling wine★★. **Best years:** (2012) **11 10 09 08**.

SPARKLING WINES OF THE WORLD —

Made by the traditional (Champagne) method

Although Champagne is still the benchmark for top-class sparkling wines all over the world, the Champagne houses themselves have taken the message to California, Australia and New Zealand via wineries they've established in these regions. However, traditional-method fizz doesn't necessarily have to feature the traditional Champagne grape varieties (Chardonnay, Pinot Noir and Pinot Meunier), and this allows a host of other places to join the party. Strictly speaking only original Champagne from France is officially sanctioned to use the term 'Champagne method', but phrases such as Traditional or Classic Method indicate that these wines are painstakingly produced using the complex system of secondary fermentation in the bottle itself.

STYLES OF SPARKLING WINE

France The best examples have great finesse and include appley Crémant d'Alsace, produced from Riesling, Pinot Blanc and Pinot Gris, sometimes with a little Chardonnay; often inexpensive yet eminently drinkable Crémant de Bourgogne and Crémant du Jura, based mainly on Chardonnay; and some stylish Chenin-based examples from the Loire Valley, notably in Saumur, Montlouis-sur-Loire, Vouvray and Crémant de Loire. The Rhône has dry St-Péray and deliciously grapy Clairette de Die Tradition. Gaillac, and Blanquette and Crémant de Limoux are good dry sparklers. Limoux, Gaillac, Bugey and the Loire also make a little fizz by an older method using the unfinished primary fermentation to create bubbles in the bottle; this may be called *méthode ancestrale* or *gaillacoise* or, in the Loire, *pétillant originel.*

Rest of Europe Franciacorta DOCG is a recent success story for Italy. Most *metodo classico* sparkling wine is confined to the north, where ripening conditions are closer to those of Champagne, using similar grape varieties. Asti, Lambrusco and Prosecco are not usually Champagne-method wines. In Spain, Cava offers an affordable style for everyday drinking, while top producers are developing a new style of long-lived Cava based on the native Xarel-lo grape. German Sekt comes in two basic styles: one made from Riesling grapes, the other using Champagne varieties. Producers in Austria and Portugal are having increasing success with both local varieties and the classic Champagne grapes. The UK (England and Wales) is proving naturally suited to growing grapes for top-quality sparkling wine, with the best wines made from Chardonnay, Pinots Noir and Meunier, plus Seyval Blanc.

Other regions Australia has a wide range of styles, and regional characters are starting to emerge. Chilly Tasmania is the star performer, making some top fizz from Chardonnay and Pinot Noir. Red sparklers, notably those made from Shiraz, are an irresistible Australian curiosity with an alcoholic kick. Cool-climate New Zealand is now producing some world-class examples difficult to tell from good Champagne. Sparkling Sauvignon Blanc (mostly carbonated) is a recent development.

In California, some magnificent examples are produced – the best ones using grapes from Carneros or the Anderson Valley. Quality has been transformed by the efforts of French Champagne houses. Oregon is also a contender in the sparkling stakes, as is Canada.

Cap Classique is the South African name for the Champagne method; the best are very good. Israel, too, has some good examples. Brazil makes South America's best sparklers; Argentina and Chile have some good examples. Champagne house Moët has begun making fizz in China.

BEST PRODUCERS

Australia *white* Arras, BROWN BROTHERS, Cope-Williams, DOMAINE CHANDON (Green Point), FREYCINET, Hanging Rock, Heemskerk, Stefano LUBIANA, PETALUMA (Croser), Pipers Brook (Kreglinger), Taltarni (Clover Hill), YALUMBA (Jansz), Yarrabank, Yellowglen (Perle); *red* Peter LEHMANN (Black Queen), Charles MELTON, PRIMO ESTATE, ROCKFORD, SEPPELT, Ulithorne.

Canada *British Columbia* Blue Mountain, Sumac Ridge, Summerhill; *Ontario* 13th Street, Cave Spring, HENRY OF PELHAM, Hinterland; *Nova Scotia* L'Acadie, Benjamin Bridge.

France *Alsace* OSTERTAG, TURCKHEIM co-op; *Burgundy* Bailly co-op, Louis Bouillot, Lugny co-op, Albert Sounit; *Gaillac* PLAGEOLES; *Jura* A & M Tissot; *Limoux* J Laurens, Rives-Blanques; *Loire* Bouvet-Ladubay, CLOS NAUDIN, Gratien & Meyer, HUET, Langlois-Château; *St-Péray* Chaboud, J-L Thiers.

Germany *Nahe* DIEL; *Pfalz*, REBHOLZ, Wilhelmshof; *Rheingau* Barth, BREUER, Solter, WEGELER; *Rheinhessen* Raumland.

Italy *Franciacorta* BELLAVISTA, CA'DEL BOSCO, Cavalleri; *Friuli* Puiatti; *Piedmont* GIACOSA; *Sicily* TASCA D'ALMERITA; *Trento* FERRARI.

New Zealand CLOUDY BAY (Pelorus), Daniel le Brun, DEUTZ, HUNTER'S, No. 1 Family Estate, PALLISER, QUARTZ REEF.

South Africa Ambeloui, Graham BECK, Bon Courage, Colmant, High Constantia, Silverthorn, Simonsig, STEENBERG, Twee Jonge Gezellen, VERGELEGEN, VILLIERA.

Spain Can Ràfols dels Caus, CODORNÍU, Colet, FREIXENET, Gramona, Parxet, Recaredo, Signat, Agustí Torelló.

UK BALFOUR, BREAKY BOTTOM, CAMEL VALLEY, CHAPEL DOWN, COATES & SEELY, FURLEIGH ESTATE, GUSBOURNE, HENNERS, NYETIMBER, RIDGEVIEW, WISTON.

USA *California* DOMAINE CARNEROS, DOMAINE CHANDON, Gloria Ferrer, HANDLEY, IRON HORSE, J VINEYARDS, Laetitia, MUMM NAPA, ROEDERER ESTATE, SCHARFFEN-BERGER CELLARS, SCHRAMSBERG; *Oregon* ARGYLE, SOTER.

293

DOM. DE SOUCH *Jurançon AOP, South-West France* Legendary wines from veteran Yvonne Hégoburu, star of the film *Mondovino*. Fully organic, her range runs from dry through to ultra-sweet, including Cuvée Marie Kattalin★★, which, as it ages, develops unmistakable notes of black truffles. *Vivat regina*. Best years: (sweet) 2011 **09 08 07 05 03**.

SOUTH AUSTRALIA Australia's biggest grape-growing state, with some 70,000ha (173,000 acres) of vineyards and almost half the country's total production. Covers many wine styles, from bulk wines to the very best. Established regions are ADELAIDE HILLS, Adelaide Plains, CLARE, BAROSSA and Eden Valleys, MCLAREN VALE, Langhorne Creek, COONAWARRA, PADTHAWAY and RIVERLAND. Newer regions creating excitement include Mount Benson, Robe, Wrattonbully and Mount Gambier in the LIMESTONE COAST zone, Southern Flinders Ranges, Southern Fleurieu, Currency Creek and Kangaroo Island.

SOUTH-WEST FRANCE South-West France has many lesser-known and rapidly improving AOPs and IGPs, over 10 *départements* from the Massif Central to the Pyrenees. Bordeaux grapes (Cabernet Sauvignon, Merlot, Cabernet Franc for reds, Sauvignon Blanc, Sémillon, Muscadelle for whites) play their part in the various BERGERAC appellations, but away from there you will find interesting local varieties such as Fer Servadou, Tannat (in MADIRAN), Gros and Petit Manseng (in Gascony and JURANÇON), Mauzac, Duras and Len de l'El (in GAILLAC) and Négrette (in FRONTON). See also CAHORS, COTEAUX DU QUERCY, CÔTES DE DURAS, CÔTES DE GASCOGNE, CÔTES DU BRULHOIS, CÔTES DU MARMANDAIS, ENTRAYGUES-ET-DU-FEL, ESTAING, IROULÉGUY, MARCILLAC, MONBAZILLAC, MONTRAVEL, PACHERENC DU VIC-BILH, PECHARMANT, SAINT-MONT, TURSAN.

SPÄTBURGUNDER See PINOT NOIR.

SPINIFEX *Barossa Valley, South Australia* Focusing on Mediterranean varieties, the wines are restrained in oakiness, and have structure, fruit complexity and tannin density without astringency. Esprit★★ blends Mataro, Grenache, Shiraz, Carignan and Cinsault with elegance and finesse; La Maline Shiraz★ combines power, concentration and velvety texture; Indigene★★ showcases old-vine Mataro and Shiraz with opulence and tight structure.

SPOTTSWOODE *Napa Valley AVA, California, USA* Replanted in the mid-1990s, this beautifully situated 16ha (40-acre) vineyard west of St Helena has not missed a beat since the winery opened in 1982. Deep, blackberry- and cherry-fruited Cabernet Sauvignon★★★ is wonderful to drink early, but is best at 5–10 years. Sauvignon Blanc★★ (blended with a little Semillon and barrel fermented) is a sophisticated treat. Best years: (Cabernet) (2012) **10 09 08 07 06 05 04 03 02 01 00 99 98 97 96 95 94 91**.

SPRING MOUNTAIN AVA *Napa Valley, California, USA* Divided by the Mayacamas Mountain road that winds west, this rugged, forested area produces superb Cabernet Sauvignon and Chardonnay, as well as Sauvignon Blanc and Riesling. Best producers: Barnett, Cain★, NEWTON★★, Pride★, Smith-Madrone★, Spring Mountain Vineyard★, Terra Valentine★★.

SPRINGFIELD ESTATE *Robertson WO, South Africa* Abrie Bruwer's approach is strictly hands-off in his efforts to capture his vineyard's *terroir*. Méthode Ancienne Chardonnay★ is barrel fermented with vineyard yeasts and bottled without fining or filtration. Not every vintage makes it! Cabernet Sauvignon is also made as Méthode Ancienne★. The unwooded Wild Yeast Chardonnay★ and flinty, lively Life from Stone Sauvignon

Blanc★★ are also notably expressive. Work of Time★ is a Cabernet Franc-Merlot-based blend. Best years: (Sauvignon Blanc) 2013 12 11 10.

STAGS LEAP DISTRICT AVA *Napa County, California, USA* One of California's best-defined appellations. Located in south-eastern NAPA VALLEY, it is cooler than OAKVILLE or RUTHERFORD to the north, and the red wines have a recognizably mellow, balanced character. A little Sauvignon Blanc and Chardonnay are grown, but the true stars are Cabernet Sauvignon and Merlot. Best producers: Balducci★, CHIMNEY ROCK★★, CLIFF LEDE★, CLOS DU VAL★, HARTWELL★★, PINE RIDGE★★, SHAFER★★★, SILVERADO★, Robert Sinskey★, STAG'S LEAP WINE CELLARS★★, Stags' Leap Winery★.

STAG'S LEAP WINE CELLARS *Stags Leap District AVA, California, USA* Cabernet Sauvignon can be stunning: SLV from estate vineyards, Fay and Cask 23 (all ★★, sometimes★★★). Chardonnay★ (Arcadia Vineyard★★) is one of NAPA's most successful. Sauvignon Blanc★ (Rancho Chimiles★) is intensely flavoured, with brisk acidity. Sold in 2007 to CHATEAU STE MICHELLE and ANTINORI of Italy. Best years: (Cabernet) 2010 09 08 07 06 05 04 03 02 01 00 99 98 97 96 95 94 91 90.

STEENBERG *Constantia WO, South Africa* The oldest farm in CONSTANTIA, part of the Graham BECK stable, produces some of South Africa's best Sauvignon Blanc★★: straight Sauvignon★ is pure upfront fruit; more fruit-forward, vigorous Black Swan★★ (replaces Reserve) contains grapes from the extant part of the farm's oldest vineyard. Barrel-fermented Semillon★★ and complex, ageworthy Magna Carta★★ (Sauvignon Blanc-Semillon). Reds include Catharina★★ (Cabernet or Merlot-led), smoky Shiraz★★ and Merlot★★, and experimental Nebbiolo★. Steenberg Brut 1682★ Cap Classique fizz is elegant and biscuity. Best years: (whites) 2013 12 11 10 09 08 07 06 05 04.

STEIERMARK *Austria* 3870ha (9560-acre) region (Styria in English) in south-east Austria is divided into 3 areas: Südoststeiermark, Südsteiermark (the most important) and Weststeiermark. Technically the warmest of the Austrian wine regions, but the best vineyards are on cool, high-altitude slopes. The tastiest wines are Morillon (Chardonnay, often unoaked), Sauvignon Blanc and Gelber Muskateller (Muscat). For many growers, Steierische Klassik on the label indicates unoaked wines. Best producers: Gross★★, Lackner-Tinnacher★, Neumeister★, POLZ★★, E Sabathi★, H Sabathi★, Sattlerhof★★, Walter Skoff, TEMENT★★, Wohlmuth★.

STELLENBOSCH WO *South Africa* District with the greatest concentration of wineries in the Cape; the vineyards straddle valley floors and stretch up the mountain slopes. Climates, soils and wine styles are diverse; smaller units of origin – wards – are now being demarcated to more accurately reflect this diversity. The renowned reds, led by Cabernet Sauvignon, are matched by some excellent Sauvignon Blanc and Chardonnay, as well as modern Chenin Blanc and Semillon. Best producers: Bein★, BEYERSKLOOF★, De Toren★, DE TRAFFORD★★, Delaire Graff★★, DeMorgenzon★, DeWaal★, Edgebaston★, Neil ELLIS★, Ernie ELS★★, Ken Forrester★, The Foundry★★, GRANGEHURST★★, HARTENBERG★★, Haskell★, JORDAN★★, KANONKOP★★★, Kleine Zalze★, L'AVENIR★, Le Riche★★, MEERLUST★★, Meinert★, Morgenster★, MULDERBOSCH★, Quoin Rock★, REYNEKE★★, RUST EN VREDE★, RUSTENBERG★★, SAXENBURG★★, Spier★, Stark-Condé★★, THELEMA★★, Tokara★★, VERGELEGEN★★★, VILLIERA★, WARWICK★★, Waterford★★, Waterkloof★, The Winery of Good Hope★★.

SWEET WINES OF THE WORLD

Great sweet wines, which tend to cost a good deal, generally use the intense sweetness of their own grapes – rather than having any sweetness added. But it's not easy to grow grapes with enough sweetness. The classic way to gain sweetness is through 'noble rot' or botrytis.

Botrytis Traditionally there were only a very few areas of the world where good summers would ripen the grape and then as autumn set in a mixture of warm sunshine and fog or mists would cause the grapes to rot. Obviously rot will usually destroy crops, but there is a type of fungal infection called 'noble rot' that actually concentrates the sugars and acids in the grapes, so that the juice becomes more and more like a ridiculously sweet syrup. These grapes are then harvested late in the season, often berry by berry. They're so sweet that they have an enormous potential alcohol (alcohol is created by the transformation of sugar into alcohol by yeast action), but yeasts can only operate up to 15–16% alcohol, at which point they die. Any remaining sugar stays in the wine as sweetness.

Conditions for noble rot appear fairly regularly in Sauternes, Barsac and Monbazillac in South-West France, famous for luscious syrupy wines with intense flavours of peach and pineapple, barley sugar spices and beeswax honey. The main grape varieties are Sémillon and Sauvignon. Sauternes in particular has been taken as the model for ambitious winemakers around the world. Nearby parts of South-West France, such as Jurançon, make similar wines, often from locally specific grape varieties, without benefit of noble rot, but by leaving the grapes to shrivel naturally on the vine: a method called *passerillage*.

The Loire Valley is France's other main sweet wine area, getting noble rot in its Chenin Blanc, particularly in Bonnezeaux, Coteaux du Layon, Quarts de Chaume and Vouvray. Orvieto in Italy can make wines with *muffa nobile* (noble rot). Tokaji in Hungary also gets regular botrytis.

Germany also has a great sweet wine tradition: when conditions are right, the Riesling grape manages to combine high acidity with stratospheric sugar levels. The wines are normally labelled Beerenauslese or Trockenbeerenauslese. Austria makes similar, though weightier styles, while Alsace makes equivalents called Sélection de Grains Nobles from not just Riesling, but also Pinot Gris and Gewurztraminer.

Semillon, Sauvignon and Riesling grapes are used in parts of Australia, New Zealand, the USA and South Africa to make botrytized sweet wines.

Eiswein A German and, occasionally, Austrian rarity, made from frozen Riesling grapes picked in the depth of winter, which manages a thrilling marriage of fierce acidity and unctuous sweetness. Canada has made a speciality of Icewine (still and sparkling) using Riesling, Vidal, Cabernet Franc and other varietals, and China has released its first examples.

Muscat The Mediterranean countries – in particular France, Spain and Greece – as well as Portugal, Australia, South Africa and Israel have a variety of sweet Muscat wines, many of them fortified.

Late harvest Throughout the world, many fairly sweet wines are made from late-harvested (therefore very ripe) but not botrytis-infected grapes.

See also ALSACE, BARSAC, BANYULS, BORDEAUX WHITE WINES, COMMANDARIA, COTEAUX DU LAYON, GAILLAC, JEREZ/SHERRY, JURANÇON, MADEIRA, MÁLAGA, MARSALA, MAURY, MONBAZILLAC, MONTILLA-MORILES, MUSCAT, ORVIETO, PACHERENC-DU-VIC-BILH, PORT, RECIOTO DI SOAVE, RECIOTO DELLA VALPOLICELLA, SAINT MONT, SAUSSIGNAC, SAUTERNES, SETÚBAL, TOKAJI, VIN SANTO, VOUVRAY; and individual producers.

Château Suduiraut
PREMIER CRU CLASSÉ EN 1855

SAUTERNES

2007

BEST PRODUCERS

France *Alsace* HUGEL, WEINBACH, ZIND-HUMBRECHT; *Bordeaux* CLIMENS, Clos Haut-Peyraguey, COUTET, DOISY-DAËNE, DOISY-VÉDRINES, FARGUES, GILETTE, GUIRAUD, LAFAURIE-PEYRAGUEY, NAIRAC, Raymond-Lafon, RIEUSSEC, Sigalas-Rabaud, SUDUIRAUT, la TOUR BLANCHE, YQUEM; *Loire* Baumard, F CHIDAINE, CLOS NAUDIN, Fesles, HUET, OGEREAU, PIERRE-BISE, Taille aux Loups/BLOT; *South-West (Monbazillac)* l'ANCIENNE CURE, Grande Maison, TIRECUL LA GRAVIÈRE, VERDOTS; *(Saussignac)* Clos d'Yvigne; *(Jurançon)* CAUHAPÉ, JARDINS DE BABYLONE, LAPEYRE, de SOUCH; *(Pacherenc du Vic-Bilh)* AYDIE, BERTHOUMIEU, MONTUS; *(Gaillac)* PLAGEOLES, RAMAYE.

Italy ANSELMI, AVIGNONESI (Vin Santo), Barberani (ORVIETO Muffa Nobile), Dri (Ramandolo), Maculan (Torcolato), PIEROPAN.

Germany DÖNNHOFF, EMRICH-SCHÖNLEBER, KELLER, KÜHN, LOOSEN, MAXIMIN GRÜNHAUS, MÜLLER-CATOIR, MÜLLER-SCHARZHOF, J J PRÜM, H SAUER, Willi SCHAEFER, SCHÄFER-FRÖHLICH, SCHLOSS JOHANNISBERG, WEIL, ZILLIKEN.

Austria FEILER-ARTINGER, Haider, KRACHER, Opitz, Schröck, TSCHIDA, VELICH.

Hungary *Tokaji* Disznókö, Chateau Megyer, Chateau Pajzos, Royal Tokaji, Szepsy, Tokaj Kereskedöház.

Greece Argyros (*Santorini*), SAMOS.

Spain Alta Alella, Camilo Castilla, CHIVITE, Gutiérrez de la Vega, Heretat de Cesilia, Jorge Ordóñez, Telmo RODRÍGUEZ.

Portugal BACALHÔA, J M da FONSECA.

Australia BROWN BROTHERS (Noble Riesling), CALABRIA, Cookoothama, DE BORTOLI (Noble One), MCWILLIAM'S, MOUNT HORROCKS, PRIMO ESTATE.

New Zealand ATA RANGI, CLOUDY BAY, FELTON ROAD, Forrest, FRAMINGHAM, FROMM, Greywacke (Late Harvest Riesling), MARTINBOROUGH VINEYARD, PEGASUS BAY, TRINITY HILL, VILLA MARIA.

USA ANTHONY ROAD, BERINGER (Nightingale), Casa Larga (Ice Wine), Far Niente (Dolce), NAVARRO.

Canada Château des Charmes, HENRY OF PELHAM, INNISKILLIN, JACKSON-TRIGGS, NK'MIP, Reif.

South Africa Paul CLUVER, Delheim, Fleur du Cap, KLEIN CONSTANTIA, Nederburg.

297

JEAN STODDEN *Rech, Ahr, Germany* From less than 7ha (17 acres), the Stodden family produce a wide range of Spätburgunders (Pinot Noir), from light and fruity to powerful Grosses Gewächs★★ from 3 sites. Given long oak-aging, these are pricy but structured wines designed for cellaring. Best years: (2013) 12 11 **10 09 08 07 06**.

STONY HILL *Napa Valley AVA, California USA* Founded by Fred and Eleanor McCrea in 1953, this tiny rock-strewn hillside produces sublime, minerally Chardonnay★★, dry Riesling★ and Gewurztraminer★. The McCreas' son Peter and his wife Willinda now run the property with long-time winemaker Mike Chelini. Followers swear that the Chardonnays improve for decades. The first estate Cabernet Sauvignon was released from the 2008 vintage. Best years: (Chardonnay) 2010 **09 08 07 06 05 03 01 00.**

STONYRIDGE *Waiheke Island, Auckland, North Island, New Zealand* The leading winery on WAIHEKE ISLAND, Stonyridge specializes in reds. The top label, Larose★★★, is a remarkably BORDEAUX-like red of real intensity; Pilgrim★★ is a sexy, sultry CHÂTEAUNEUF-DU-PAPE lookalike. Best years: (Larose) (2013) **10 09 08 07 05 02.**

CH. SUDUIRAUT★★★ *Sauternes AC, 1er Cru Classé, Bordeaux, France* Together with RIEUSSEC, Suduiraut is regarded as a close runner-up to YQUEM. Although the wines are delicious at only a few years old, the richness and excitement increase enormously after a decade or so. Seemed to be under-performing in the 1980s and mid-90s, but owners AXA (see PICHON-LONGUEVILLE) have put it back on irresistible song. No Suduiraut was made in 2012. Best years: 2011 10 **09 07 06 05 04 03 02 01 99 98 97 96 95 90.**

SWAN DISTRICT *Western Australia* The original WESTERN AUSTRALIA wine region, spread along the fertile silty flats of Perth's Swan River. It used to specialize in fortified wines. Modern whites and reds are fresh and generous but unmemorable. Best producers: Paul Conti, Faber★, Heafod Glen, HOUGHTON★, John Kosovich, Lamont★, Mandoon★★, Oakover, Olive Farm, Pinelli, Sittella, Upper Reach★.

JOSEPH SWAN VINEYARDS *Russian River Valley AVA, California, USA* The late Joseph Swan made legendary Zinfandel in the 1970s and was one of the first to age Zinfandel★★ in French oak. In the 1980s he turned to Pinot Noir★ which is made in a rather old-fashioned but satisfying way. Also some old-style Syrah. Best years: (Zinfandel) **2010 09 08 07 06 05 02 01 00.**

SWARTLAND WO *South Africa* Warm inland district running up the west coast, and very much *the* wine area of the moment, partly because it is home to numerous patches of ancient bush vines. Most planted red varieties are Cabernet Sauvignon and Syrah, although the latter has greater association with the area; Chenin Blanc, much from old vines, leads the whites, but there are also plots of more obscure red and white varieties. The Swartland Independent comprises around a dozen cutting-edge producers, intent on expressing the Swartland in their wines. Great reds and whites are already making waves. Best producers: Badenhorst Family Wines★★, Lammershoek, MULLINEUX★★★, Porseleinberg★★, SADIE FAMILY★★★.

SYNCLINE *Columbia Valley AVA, Washington State, USA* The focus here is on Rhône-style wines. COLUMBIA VALLEY Syrah★ shows game and mineral flavours; single-vineyard McKinley Springs Syrah★★ has intriguing coffee bean and floral aromas; also earthy Mourvèdre★, dusty Cinsault★, chewy Grenache-Carignan, and crisp, refreshing Grenache Blanc★. Also pithy, fresh Grüner Veltliner★, delightful Pinot Noir★ and excellent Scintillation★★ fizz. Best years: (2012) 11 10 **09 08**.

SYRAH See pages 300–1.

TABALÍ *Limarí, Chile* Winery set up in 1993. Best wines are the Reserva Especial Syrah★★, Reserva Especial Chardonnay★★ and Reserva Especial Sauvignon Blanc★★ from Caliza vineyard near the ocean.

TABLAS CREEK VINEYARD *Paso Robles AVA, California, USA* This joint venture between the Perrin family (of Ch. de BEAUCASTEL in Châteauneuf-du-Pape) and the Haas Family of Vermont is putting Rhône varieties on the map in SAN LUIS OBISPO COUNTY. The elegant, cherry-scented red Esprit de Tablas★★ and the Côtes de Tablas★★ (red and white) are especially impressive. Best years: (reds) **2012** 10 09 08 07 06.

LA TÂCHE AC★★★ *Grand Cru, Côte de Nuits, Burgundy, France* Along with la ROMANÉE and la ROMANÉE-CONTI, the greatest of the great VOSNE-ROMANÉE Grands Crus. Owned by Dom. de la ROMANÉE-CONTI. The wine provides layer on layer of flavours; keep it for 10 years or you'll only experience a fraction of the pleasure you paid big money for. Best years: (2013) 12 11 10 09 07 06 05 03 **02 01 00** 99 **96 95 93 90**.

TAHBILK *Goulburn Valley, Central Victoria, Australia* Old-fashioned family company established in 1860, making big, chewy red wines, matured largely in old wood. 1860 Vines Shiraz★, Eric Stevens Purbrick Shiraz and Cabernet show the style, and need years of cellaring. Rich and perfumed Marsanne★★ and floral-scented Viognier★. Best years: (Eric Stevens Purbrick Shiraz) 2013 12 11 10 09 08 06 05 04 03 02 01 00 99 98 97 96 94.

CAVE DE TAIN *Hermitage, Rhône Valley, France* Large, progressive co-op offering good-value wines from the northern Rhône. Greatly improved quality. Impressive CROZES-HERMITAGE les Hauts du Fief★, fine CORNAS★, genuine red ST-JOSEPH★, white St-Joseph Terre d'Ivoire and HERMITAGE★. Topping the range are an old-vine red Hermitage Gambert de Loche★★, a classy white Hermitage Au Coeur des Siècles★★ and a deliciously rich Vin de Paille★★ from Marsanne. Also still and sparkling ST-PÉRAY★. Best years: (top reds) 2013 12 11 10 **09 07** 06 05 04 03 01 00 99 98 95.

TAITTINGER *Champagne AC, Champagne, France* The top wine, Comtes de Champagne Blanc de Blancs★★★, can be memorable for its creamy, foaming pleasures; the Comtes de Champagne rosé★★ is elegant and oozing class. Prélude is an attractive, fuller-bodied non-vintage style made from 4 Grands Crus and aged for 4 years before release. Non-vintage Les Folies de la Marquetterie is from a steeply sloping single vineyard. Best years: (2008) 06 05 **04 03 02 00** 99 98 96 95 90 89 88 85 82.

CH. TALBOT★ *St-Julien AC, 4ème Cru Classé, Haut-Médoc, Bordeaux, France* Chunky, soft-centred but sturdy, capable of aging well for 10–20 years and produced in abundance (100ha/250-acre vineyard). This isn't classic, cedary St-Julien but is consistently full-bodied and well priced. Also a tasty white wine, Caillou Blanc de Talbot★★. Second wine: Connétable de Talbot. Best years: 2012 11 10 09 **08 05** 04 03 02 01 00 98 96 95 90 89.

TALBOTT *Monterey County, California, USA* Estate known for its Chardonnays: Sleepy Hollow Vineyard★★ (from the Santa Lucia Highlands), Cuvée Cynthia★★ and Diamond T★★ are all packed with ripe tropical fruit and ample oak. Kali Hart Chardonnay★ gives a taste of the style on a budget. Also Chardonnay and Pinot Noir under the Logan label.

TAMAYA *Limarí, Chile* LIMARÍ estate started in 1997. Easy-drinking, unoaked Reserva Carmenère★ and top-grade T Limited Release Syrah★★ and Chardonnay★★.

SYRAH/SHIRAZ

Syrah now produces world-class wines in France, Australia – where as Shiraz it produces some of the New World's most remarkable reds – Chile, New Zealand, California and, increasingly, South Africa, Argentina and Washington State. And wherever it appears it trumpets a proud and wilful personality based on loads of flavour and unmistakable originality.

When Syrah is grown in the coolest, most marginal areas for full ripening, such as France's Côte-Rôtie or New Zealand, it produces scented, elegant, smoky, blackberryish wines. Syrah's heartland – Hermitage and Côte-Rôtie in the northern Rhône Valley – comprises a mere 365ha (900 acres) of steeply terraced, often granite, vineyards producing barely enough wine to spread the word to new drinkers. This may be one reason for its relatively slow uptake by growers in other countries, who simply had no idea as to what kind of flavour the Syrah grape produced, so didn't copy it. But Syrah's popularity in both the warm and the reasonably cool wine regions of the world becomes more evident with every vintage.

WINE STYLES

French Syrah Traditional Syrah had a savage, almost coarse, throaty roar of a flavour. And from the very low-yielding Hermitage vineyards, it sometimes took decades for the flavours to come together. But improved winemaking and a mix of scented new clones with the haughty old vines have revealed Syrah with a majestic depth of fruit – blackberry and damson, loganberry and plum – some quite strong tannin, occasionally bacon smoke and potato skins, but also a warm creamy aftertaste, and a promise of chocolate and occasionally a scent of violets. These characteristics have made Syrah popular throughout southern France as an 'improving' variety for traditional red wines, even though the hot climate tends to make its fruit jammy, and it is now a major red variety in Provence, often combined with Grenache and/or Mourvèdre.

Australian Shiraz Australia's most widely planted red grape has become, in many respects, its premium varietal – especially in the Barossa, Clare, Eden Valley and McLaren Vale regions of South Australia. A diverse range of high-quality examples is also coming from Victoria's high country and cool-climate vineyards, increasingly elegant examples from New South Wales' Hunter Valley, and exciting, more restrained styles from Western Australia, Victoria's Yarra Valley and South Australia's Adelaide Hills, as well as patches of Canberra, Tasmania and Queensland. Flavours range from rich, intense, thick sweet fruit coated with chocolate and seasoned with leather, herbs and spice, to fragrant, floral and flowing with damson and blackberry fruit.

Other regions Washington State is turning out superb Rhône-style blends and varietal Syrahs. California's Syrahs are mostly high-octane, though occasionally beautifully restrained. Canada makes two styles: lush and fruity in British Columbia's desert conditions, and northern Rhône-style in cooler Ontario. Chile's coastal and cool-climate regions produce a string of exciting new offerings every vintage, and warmer, spicy Syrah comes from inland plantings like Apalta. Elegant examples are emerging from South Africa's warmer and cooler regions. New Zealand's cool-climate offerings are thrillingly different – light yet lush, green-streaked, florally scented yet succulent. Italy, Spain, Portugal, Switzerland and Argentina are beginning to shine, as are Israel, Lebanon and Morocco.

BEST PRODUCERS

France
Rhône ALLEMAND, F Balthazar, G Barge, A Belle, CHAPOUTIER, J-L CHAVE, Y Chave, CLAPE, Clusel-Roch, Courbis, COURSODON, CUILLERON, DELAS, Duclaux, E & J Durand, B Faurie, P Gaillard, J-M Gérin, Gonon, GRAILLOT, Gripa, GUIGAL, JAMET, P Jasmin, S Ogier, V Paris, ROSTAING, M Sorrel, Tardieu-Laurent, G Vernay, F Villard; *Languedoc* Jean-Michel ALQUIER, ESTANILLES, GAUBY.

Other European Syrah
Italy (Piedmont) Bertelli; *(Tuscany)* Stefano Amerighi, d'Alessandro, FONTODI, ISOLE E OLENA, Le MACCHIOLE; *(Sicily)* Cottanera, PLANETA.
Portugal CORTES DE CIMA, Quinta do Monte d'Oiro.
Spain Abadía Retuerta, Casa Castillo, Finca Sandoval, Enrique Mendoza, Pago de Vallegarcía.

New World Syrah/Shiraz
Australia Tim ADAMS, Jim BARRY, BEST'S, Rolf BINDER, BROKENWOOD, Grant BURGE, CHAPEL HILL, CLONAKILLA, Craiglee, Dalwhinnie, D'ARENBERG, DE BORTOLI, Dutschke, John DUVAL, GEMTREE, HARDYS (Eileen Hardy), HENSCHKE, HEWITSON, Jasper Hill, Peter LEHMANN, MAJELLA, Charles MELTON, MOUNT LANGI GHIRAN, S C PANNELL, PENFOLDS, ROCKFORD, SEPPELT, SHAW & SMITH, TORBRECK, Turkey Flat, TYRRELL'S, WENDOUREE, The Willows, WIRRA WIRRA (RSW), YALUMBA, Yering Station (Reserve).

New Zealand Bilancia, CRAGGY RANGE, DRY RIVER, Esk Valley, FROMM, MAN O'WAR, MILLTON, Passage Rock, Stonecroft, Te Awa, TE MATA, Te Whare Ra, TRINITY HILL, Vidal, VILLA MARIA.

South Africa BOEKENHOUTSKLOOF, DE TRAFFORD, Eagles' Nest, FAIRVIEW, The Foundry, HARTENBERG, MULLINEUX, SADIE FAMILY, SAXENBURG.

USA (California) ALBAN, ARAUJO, BECKMEN, DEHLINGER, DUTTON GOLDFIELD, KONGSGAARD, Krupp Brothers, Lagier Meredith, Andrew MURRAY, Pax, QUPE, RAMEY, Sean Thackrey, Truchard; *(Washington)* BETZ, CAYUSE, GRAMERCY, SYNCLINE.

Canada (British Columbia) Church & State, JACKSON-TRIGGS, Painted Rock; *(Ontario)* Colaneri, Creekside.

Chile CASA MARÍN, DE MARTINO, ERRAZURIZ, FALERNIA, LAPOSTOLLE, LOMA LARGA, MATETIC, Maycas del Limarí, MONTES, TABALÍ, TAMAYA, UNDURRAGA (T.H.).

301

TANNAT Its name implies high tannic content, but when fully ripe it is dark and dense yet delightfully scented, especially in parts of California, Brazil, Argentina and Chile. It is widely planted in Uruguay owing to its thick skin's ability to withstand wet weather. Compulsory (either on its own or blended) in MADIRAN, TURSAN and IROULÉGUY in South-West France.

TAPANAPPA *Adelaide Hills, South Australia* The partnership of the families of Brian Croser (formerly of PETALUMA), Arnould d'Hautefeuille (BOLLINGER) and Jean-Michel Cazes (LYNCH-BAGES) explores the notion of *terroir*. Sublime Chardonnay from the Tiers Vineyard★★★ in the ADELAIDE HILLS; supremely elegant Cabernet-Shiraz and Merlot from the mature Whalebone Vineyard★★ at Wrattonbully; and increasingly ethereal Pinot Noir from Foggy Hill Vineyard★★ on the Southern Fleurieu Peninsula.

BODEGA TAPIZ *Mendoza, Argentina* Modern, high-tech winery with vineyards in MENDOZA and SALTA, delivering consistently good wines. Malbec★, Syrah★, Viognier★ and Torrontés★ are great value for money – soft and pure – while the reserve Chardonnay★ and Merlot★ accentuate the beauty of cool-climate UCO VALLEY vineyards. Jean Claude Berrouet, ex-Ch. PÉTRUS, is now involved.

TARIQUET *Côtes de Gascogne IGP, South-West France* Brand name of the Grassa family, who produce some of France's snappiest, fruitiest, affordable dry wines (e.g. Côté★, a Sauvignon-Chardonnay blend) on their 900ha (2200-acre) estate. Also oak-aged★ and late-harvest★ styles.

TARRAWARRA *Yarra Valley, Victoria, Australia* Meticulous attention to detail is the keynote at Tarrawarra. Twenty eight estate blocks are monitored for inclusion in the Reserve range: ageworthy Chardonnays★★ showing finesse, primal flavours and complex minerality and Pinot Noirs★★ with briary complexity, velvety texture and fine, tongue-coating tannins. These wines age marvellously. Under the Estate label there is an easy-drinking Chardonnay and a delightful Pinot Noir. The Single Block range includes a classy white Viognier-Marsanne-Roussanne and J-Block Shiraz. The rare flagship 'MDB' Chardonnay★★★ and 'MDB' Pinot Noir★★★, named for founder Marc Besen, are exquisite. Best years: (Pinot Noir) 2013 12 10 08 06 04 03 02 01 98 97 96.

TASCA D'ALMERITA *Sicily, Italy* Estate in the highlands of central SICILY. Native grape varieties give excellent Rosso del Conte★★ (based on Nero d'Avola) and white Nozze d'Oro★ (based on Inzolia), but there are also Chardonnay★★ and Cabernet Sauvignon★★ of extraordinary intensity and elegance. Almerita Brut★ (Chardonnay) is a fine traditional-method sparkler. Relatively simple Regaleali Bianco and Rosé are good value.

TASMANIA *Australia* Tasmania may be a minor state viticulturally, with around 1400ha (3460 acres) of vines, but the island has a diverse range of mesoclimates, with the north-east, east and south all offering completely different conditions. The generally cool climate has always attracted seekers of greatness in Pinot Noir and Chardonnay, and good results are becoming more consistent as the vines mature and viticultural know-how spreads. Riesling, Gewürztraminer and Pinot Gris perform well, but the real star is fabulous premium fizz. Best producers: Apsley Gorge, Arras★★★, BAY OF FIRES★★, Bream Creek, Domaine A, FREYCINET★★, Frogmore Creek★, Heemskerk★, Home Hill★, Jansz★★/YALUMBA, Stefano LUBIANA★, Moorilla★, Pipers Brook, Pirie★★, Pressing Matters★, Providence, Stoney Rise, Tolpuddle★★. Best years: (Pinot Noir) 2013 12 10 07 06 05 03 02 01 00 99 98 97 95 94.

TAURASI DOCG *Campania, Italy* Finally emerging as a source of brilliant red wine, Taurasi is underpinned by the soaring calcareous and volcanic hills of Irpinia and the magic of the Aglianico grape. Irpinia Campi Taurasini DOC provides an early-drinking version, while Taurasi is best drunk 10 years after the harvest, like BAROLO (with which it is frequently compared). Best producers: A Caggiano★★, Feudi di San Gregorio, Cantina Lonardo★★, MASTROBERARDINO★★, S Molettieri, Perillo★★, Quintodecimo★, Sabino Loffredo★, Struzziero, Luigi TECCE★★★, Terredora di Paolo★. Best years: (2012) 11 08 **07 06 04 01 00 99 98 97 96 95**.

TAVEL AC *Rhône Valley, France* Rosé from north-west of Avignon, in two styles: aromatic-aperitif, or chunky and heady, the traditional one. The latter style needs food – garlic, herbs or Chinese cuisine. Best producers: Pierre Amadieu, Aquéria, Genestière★, GUIGAL★, Lafond Roc-Épine★, Maby★, de Manissy, Montézargues★, la Mordorée★, Moulin-la-Viguerie★, Rocalière★, Vignerons de Tavel, Trinquevedel★★.

TAWSE WINERY *Niagara Peninsula VQA, Ontario, Canada* Voted Canada's top winery three years in a row. Top-notch Robyn's Block Chardonnay★★, Carly's Block Riesling★ and Cherry Avenue Pinot Noir★.

TAYLOR'S *Port DOC, Douro, Portugal* The aristocrat of the PORT industry, founded in 1692. Now part of the Fladgate Partnership, along with FONSECA and CROFT. Its Vintage★★★ (sold as Taylor Fladgate in the USA) is superb; Quinta de Vargellas★★ is an elegant, cedary, single-quinta vintage port made in the best of the 'off-vintages'. Quinta de Terra Feita★★, the other main component of Taylor's Vintage, is also often released as a single quinta. Taylor's 20-year-old★★ is a very fine aged tawny. First Estate is a successful premium ruby. Best years: (Vintage) 2011 09 **07 03 00 97 94 92 85 83 80 77 75 70 66 63 60 55 48 45 27**; (Vargellas) 2009 08 **05 04 01 99 98 96 95 91 88 87 82 67 64 61**.

TE MATA *Hawkes Bay, North Island, New Zealand* HAWKES BAY's glamour winery, best known for Coleraine★★★ and Awatea★, based on Cabernet Sauvignon with Merlot and Cabernet Franc. Also toasty Elston Chardonnay★★ (sometimes ★★★). All 3 wines can age for 5–10 years. Scented, peppery, elegant Bullnose Syrah★★, delicious Cape Crest Sauvignon Blanc★★ (can be ★★★) and Zara Viognier★★. Trailblazing Woodthorpe single-vineyard range includes fine Syrah★★ and gorgeous, crunchy Gamay★. Best years: (Coleraine) (2013) **10 09 08 07 06 04 02 00**.

LUIGI TECCE *Taurasi DOCG, Campania, Italy* Luigi Tecce grows high-altitude, ancient-vine Aglianico grapes that he makes into thrilling Satyricon Campi Taurasini DOC★★ and Poliphemo TAURASI★★★. He is trialling vinification in amphorae. Best years: (2012) 11 08 07 06 **04 03 01 00 99 98 97**.

TEJO *Portugal* Portugal's second-largest wine region straddles the river Tagus (Tejo). Hotter and drier than LISBOA to the west, vineyards in the fertile flood plain are being uprooted in favour of less vigorous soils away from the river. Best producers: (reds) Quinta da Alorna, Quinta do Alqueve, Casa Cadaval★, Quinta do Casal Branco★ (Falcoaria★), D F J VINHOS★, Caves Dom Teodósio, Quinta do Falcão, Falua/J P RAMOS (Reserva★), Quinta da Lagoalva da Cima★, Companhia das Lezírias, Rui Reguinga (Tributo★★), Quinta da Ribeirinha (Vale de Lobos).

TEMENT *Südsteiermark, Austria* Austria's best Sauvignon Blanc★★ (single-site Zieregg★★★) and Morillon★★ (Chardonnay). Both varieties are fermented and aged in oak, giving power, depth and subtle oak character. The Gelber Muskatellers are unusually racy – perfect aperitif wines. Red Arachon★★ is a joint venture with F X PICHLER and Szemes in BURGENLAND. Best years: (2013) 12 11 10 09 08 07.

TEMPRANILLO Spain's best native red grape can deliver wonderful wild strawberry and spicy, tobaccoey flavours. Important in RIOJA, PENEDÈS (as Ull de Llebre), RIBERA DEL DUERO (as Tinto Fino or Tinta del País), La MANCHA and VALDEPEÑAS (as Cencibel), TORO (as Tinta de Toro), NAVARRA, SOMONTANO and UTIEL-REQUENA. Portugal grows it in the ALENTEJO (as Aragonez) and in the DOURO, DÃO and LISBOA (as Tinta Roriz). Wines can be deliciously fruity for drinking young, but Tempranillo also matures well, and its flavours blend happily with oak. Good examples in Argentina (O FOURNIER), California (Bokisch, Justin, Twisted Oak, VIADER, Kenneth Volk), Oregon (ABACELA), Washington (CAYUSE), Australia (Tim ADAMS, GEMTREE, La Linea, Mayford, Nepenthe, Pondalowie, Running with Bulls/YALUMBA, Sanguine, Tar & Roses, Willunga 100), New Zealand (Elephant Hill, TRINITY HILL) and South Africa.

TEN MINUTES BY TRACTOR *Mornington Peninsula, Victoria, Australia* Three vineyards, just 10 minutes by tractor apart, produce various Chardonnays and Pinot Noirs, which include impressive, totally different single-vineyard wines (Judd★★, McCutcheon★★, Wallis★★) and the Estate blends. Regional varietals use the 10X label.

TEROLDEGO ROTALIANO DOC *Trentino-Alto Adige, Italy* Teroldego is a TRENTINO grape variety, producing mainly deep-coloured, leafy, blackberry-flavoured wine from gravel soils of the Rotaliano plain. Best producers: Barone de Cles★, M Donati★, Dorigati★, Endrizzi★, FORADORI★★, Conti Martini★, Mezzacorona (Riserva★), Cantina Rotaliana★, A & R Zeni★. Best years: 2011 10 **09 08 07** 06 04 01.

TERRASSES DU LARZAC *Languedoc AC, Languedoc, France* Northern part of the Languedoc, recognized for its cooler climate, higher altitudes and fresher wines. Best producers: Clos du Serres★, Ch. Jonquières, Mas Cal Demoura★, Mas des Chimères★, Mas de l'Ecriture★, Mas Jullien★, Mas de la Séranne★, Montcalmès★, Pas de l'Escalette★, La Pèira★, Réserve d'O, les Souls. Best years: (reds) (2013) 12 **11 10 09 08 07** 06 05.

TERRAZAS DE LOS ANDES *Mendoza, Argentina* Owned by LVMH. Reds and whites from high-altitude vineyards around Luján de Cuyo in MENDOZA. Top reds are single-vineyard Las Compuertas Malbec★★ and Cabernet Sauvignon★★. Cheval des Andes★★★, a stunning Cabernet Sauvignon-Malbec blend, is a joint venture with CHEVAL BLANC of ST-ÉMILION. Best years: (Cheval des Andes) 2008 **07 06 05 03 02 01**.

CASTELLO DEL TERRICCIO *Tuscany, Italy* Estate in the Pisan hills. Top red Lupicaia★★ (Cabernet-Merlot) and less pricey Tassinaia★★ (Sangiovese-Cabernet-Merlot). Syrah-based Castello del Terriccio can be scented and exciting, potentially ★★★. White wines are Rondinaia★★ (Chardonnay) and Con Vento★ (Sauvignon Blanc). Best years: (Lupicaia) (2011) 10 **09 08** 06 05 04 01 00 **98 97**.

TERROIR AL LÍMIT *Priorat DOCa, Cataluña, Spain* South Africa's Eben SADIE and German partner Dominik Huber revolutionized PRIORAT by making extraordinarily complex wines in a lighter, more elegant style than the norm, from old Garnacha and Cariñena vineyards. Top wines: Les Tosses★★, Les Manyes★★, Dits del Terra★★, Arbossar★★. They have now added a remarkable white, Pedra de Guix★★. Best years: (reds) 2011 10 09 **08 07 05 04**.

TERTRE-RÔTEBOEUF★★ *St-Émilion Grand Cru AC, Bordeaux, France*
ST-ÉMILION's most exceptional unclassified estate. The richly seductive, Merlot-based wines sell at the same price as the Premiers Grands Crus Classés – and so they should. Same ownership as the outstanding ROC DE CAMBES. Best years: 2012 11 10 09 **08 07 06 05 04 03 02 01 00 99 98 96 95**.

TEXAS *USA* Texas enjoyed tremendous wine industry growth in the first decade of this century, though the state government has slashed financial and marketing support. The state has 8 AVAs, with the Texas High Plains the most significant, and more than 200 wineries. Mediterranean grapes such as Grenache, Tempranillo, Syrah and Sangiovese have risen in favour over the traditional Cabernets and Chardonnay. Thunderstorms are capable of destroying entire crops in minutes. Best producers: Becker★, Fall Creek, Flat Creek, Haak, LLANO ESTACADO★, MCPHERSON★, Messina Hof.

THELEMA *Stellenbosch WO, South Africa* With over 30 years under their belt on this former fruit farm, the Webbs are making better wines than ever. New flagship Rabelais★★, a Cabernet Sauvignon-led blend, has greater power and structure than blackcurranty regular Cabernet Sauvignon★★ (occasionally ★★★) and self-descriptive The Mint★★. Also ripe fleshy Merlot★ (Reserve★★), spicy, accessible Shiraz★, barrel-fermented Chardonnay★★, vibrant Sauvignon Blanc★★ and citrussy Riesling★. Sutherland Vineyards in ELGIN are providing wines of character as vines mature – minerally Sauvignon★, oatmeal Chardonnay★ and intriguing, restrained Viognier-Roussanne★. Best years: (Cabernet Sauvignon) (2010) **09 08 07 06 05 04 03**; (Chardonnay) 2013 **12 11 10 09 08 07 06 05 04 03**.

THERMENREGION *Niederösterreich, Austria* Warm 2200ha (5435-acre) region south of Vienna, taking its name from the spa towns of Baden and Bad Vöslau. Gumpoldskirchen, near Vienna, has rich white wines from local varieties Zierfandler and Rotgipfler. The red wine area around Baden produces improving St Laurent, Pinot Noir and Cabernet. Best producers: Alphart★, Fischer★, Piriwe, Reinisch★, Stadlmann★, Zierer. Best years: (reds) (2013) (12) **11 10 09 08 07**.

THIRTY BENCH *Niagara Peninsula VQA, Ontario, Canada* Excellent Riesling★★, very good BORDEAUX-style red blends★ and a fine barrel-fermented Chardonnay★.

THOMAS *Hunter Valley, New South Wales, Australia* Andrew Thomas produces exemplary Semillon and Shiraz from individual vineyards: Braemore Semillon★★ is a traditional, ageworthy HUNTER white, while The OC Semillon★ is a delicious early-drinking style. Kiss Shiraz★★, from old vines, is ripe, powerful and velvety, and Shiraz from DJV, Motel Block and Sweetwater vineyards look set to enhance Thomas's cult status.

THREE CHOIRS *Gloucestershire, England* This 30ha (74-acre) estate makes a large range of good-value still and sparkling wines. Varietals Bacchus★ and Siegerrebe★, plus blends Coleridge Hill and Midsummer Hill are well worth buying. Excellent visitor facilities, including a small hotel.

TICINO *Switzerland* Italian-speaking canton. 85% of production is Merlot, usually soft and gluggable, but can be more serious with some oak barrel-aging. White Merlot has a local following. Best producers: Brivio★,

Delea★, Gialdi, Huber★, Werner Stucky★, Tamborini★, Terreni alla Maggia★, Valsangiacomo, Christian Zündel★.

TIEFENBRUNNER *Alto Adige DOC, Trentino-Alto Adige, Italy* Herbert Tiefenbrunner began his career at this castle (Schloss Turmhof) as a teenager in 1943. In his 80s, he still helps son Christof in the winery, producing 20-plus wines, mostly under the ALTO ADIGE DOC. Exceptionally pure, varietally focused whites are best, especially Chardonnay Linticlarus★★ and Müller-Thurgau Feldmarschall★★, grown at 1000m (3280ft). Best years: (Feldmarschall) 2012 11 10 09 08 07 06 04.

TIERCE *Finger Lakes AVA, New York State, USA* As the FINGER LAKES gained a reputation for exceptional Riesling, three winemakers – Peter Bell of FOX RUN, Johannes Reinhardt of ANTHONY ROAD and David Whiting of Red Newt – decided to collaborate on a single wine to help define a regional style for dry Riesling★. The winemakers contribute some of their best lots and the three determine the final blend together. They've now built a track record to show how good New York Riesling can be and how well it ages.

TIGNANELLO★★ *Tuscany, Italy* In the early 1970s, Piero ANTINORI employed the almost unheard-of practice of aging in small French oak barrels and used Cabernet Sauvignon (20%) in the blend with Sangiovese. The quality was superb, and Tignanello's success sparked off the 'super-Tuscan' movement. Best years: (2011) 10 09 08 07 06 04 01 00.

TINTA RORIZ See TEMPRANILLO.

CH. TIRECUL LA GRAVIÈRE *Monbazillac AOP, South-West France* Bruno Bilancini makes the best (and most expensive) of MONBAZILLAC wines, comparable with top SAUTERNES, with a high proportion of Muscadelle and unusually regular benefit from botrytization. The top wine, Cuvée Madame★★★, is world class. Best years: (2012) 11 10 09 07 05 04 03.

TOKAJI *Hungary* Hungary's classic, liquorous wine of historic reputation, with its unique, sweet-and-sour, sherry-like tang, comes from 28 villages on the Hungarian–Slovak border. Mists from the Bodrog river ensure that noble rot on the Furmint, Hárslevelü and Muscotaly (Muscat Ottonel) grapes is a fairly common occurrence. Degrees of sweetness are measured in *puttonyos*. Discussions continue about traditional oxidized styles versus fresher modern versions. Best producers: Disznókö★★, Château Megyer★★, Oremus★, Château Pajzos★★, Royal Tokaji★★, Istvan Szepsy★★, Tokaj Kereskedöház★. Best years: 2009 07 06 05 03 00 99 97 93.

TOLLOT-BEAUT *Chorey-lès-Beaune, Burgundy, France* Traditionally very fruity with seductive oak texture, I've recently noted an unwelcome aggressive oak style in many of them. The village-level ALOXE-CORTON★ is good, but the top BEAUNE Premier Crus★ are better. Whites are more variable, but at best delicious. Best years: (reds) (2013) 12 11 10 09 08 07 06 05 02 99.

TORBRECK *Barossa Valley, South Australia* A bitter ownership battle has left American billionaire Pete Kight in charge – continuing along the path that Dave Powell trod, specializing in opulent, massively structured reds from 60- to 120-year-old Shiraz, Grenache and Mataro (Mourvèdre) vines. Made in minute quantities, the flagship RunRig★★, single-vineyard Descendant★★ and Factor★★ are all richly concentrated, powerful Shiraz, while the stratospherically priced The Laird garners lofty points from American commentators. Easier-to-drink The Steading★

and unoaked Juveniles★★ are Grenache-Mataro-Shiraz blends; Wood-cutter's Semillon and Shiraz are lightly oaked, mouthfilling quaffers.

TORO DO *Castilla y León, Spain* This region has attracted a number of well-known winemakers from other Spanish regions and from France. Mainly robust red wines. The main grape, Tinta de Toro, is a local clone of Tempranillo, and there is some Garnacha. Best producers: Viña Bajoz, Dominio del Bendito★, Campo Eliseo★, Fariña, Frutos Villar (Muruve), Garanza, Matarredonda, Maurodos★★, Numanthia★★, Paydos★★, Pintia★★/ VEGA SICILIA, Telmo RODRIGUEZ★★, Sobreño, Teso La Monja★★, Toresanas/ Bodegas de Crianza Castilla La Vieja, Valpiculata★, Vega Saúco, Villaester.

TORRES *Penedès DO, Cataluña, Spain* Iconic family winery based in CATALUNA. White quaffer Viña Sol★, spicy Viña Esmeralda★, classic, barrel-fermented Fransola★★ (Sauvignon Blanc with some Parellada) and delicate Milmanda★ Chardonnay. Reds include oaky Gran Coronas★ (Tempranillo-Cabernet), perfumed Mas Borràs★ (Pinot Noir) and raisiny Atrium (Merlot). The top reds are Grans Muralles★★, from Catalan grapes, BORDEAUX-blend Reserva Real★★ and Mas La Plana★★ (Cabernet Sauvignon). A new PRIORAT winery produces distinguished red Perpetual★★ and juicy Salmos★. The family also owns wineries in RIBERA DEL DUERO (Celeste★), RIOJA (Ibéricos★), Chile and California (MARIMAR ESTATE). Best years: (Mas La Plana) (2010) 09 **07** 06 05 **04 03** 01 00 99 98 97.

MiGUEL TORRES *Curicó, Chile* TORRES' Chilean operation, which began in the early 1970s, is now producing its best ever wines, under the direction of Miguel Torres Junior: snappy Sauvignon Blanc★; grassy, fruity, organic Santa Digna Cabernet Sauvignon rosé★; exciting, sonorous old Carignan Cordillera★★; weighty, blackcurrant Manso de Velasco Cabernet★★; and Conde de Superunda★★, a tremendous, dense red blend based on Tempranillo and Cabernet Sauvignon. Also Santa Digna Estelado rosé, a sparkling wine made from the País grape. Best years: (Manso de Velasco) 2010 09 **08** 07 06 **05** 04 03 02 01.

TORRONTÉS Intensely aromatic white grape variety widely planted in Argentina – some 8500ha (21,000 acres). In recent years lower yields and cool fermentation in stainless steel have resulted in dry, fresh whites with lovely tropical fruit salad flavours, juicy acidity and a floral fragrance. The best wines tend to come from the northern province of SALTA. Best producers: (Salta): COLOMÉ, Domingo Hermanos, DOMINIO DEL PLATA, EL ESTECO/Michel Torino, EL PORVENIR DE CAFAYATE, Etchart; (Mendoza): Alta Vista, DOÑA PAULA, Monteviejo.

CH. LA TOUR BLANCHE★★ *Sauternes AC, 1er Cru Classé, Bordeaux, France* Full-bodied, rich and aromatic SAUTERNES, which now ranks with the best of the Classed Growths. Second wine: Les Charmilles de Tour Blanche. Best years: 2012 11 10 **09 07** 06 05 04 03 02 01 99 98 97 96 95 90 89.

DOM. TOUR BOISÉE *Minervois AC, Languedoc, France* Fine MINERVOIS, including red Jardin Secret★, Cuvée Marie-Claude★ (aged for 12 months in barrel), fruity Cuvée Marielle Frédérique, and white Cuvée Marie-Claude★ (Marsanne, Macabeo and a hint of Muscat à Petits Grains for added aroma). Best years: (reds) (2013) 12 **11 10** 09 08 07 06.

CH. TOUR DES GENDRES *Bergerac AOP, South-West France* Luc de Conti makes his modern BERGERAC with as much sophistication as top BORDEAUX. Generously fruity Moulin des Dames★ and the more serious la Gloire de Mon Père★★ reds are mostly Cabernet Sauvignon. Full, fruity and elegant Moulin des Dames★★ white is a blend of Sémillon, Sauvignon Blanc and Muscadelle. His entry-level range includes some of the best-value wines in Bergerac. Best years: (reds) 2012 11 10 09 06 05.

TOURAINE AC *Loire Valley, France* General AC in the central LOIRE; largely everyday wines to drink young, though an ambitious minority are making more ageworthy wines, many of which are labelled Vin de Pays du VAL DE LOIRE or even Vin de FRANCE. Most reds are from Gamay and, in hot years, can be juicy, rustic-fruited wines. There is a fair amount of red from Cabernets Sauvignon and Franc too, and some good Côt (Malbec). Best whites are Sauvignon Blanc, which can be a good substitute for SANCERRE at half the price, and the rare Romorantin; there's also decent Chenin and Chardonnay. White and rosé sparkling wines are made by the traditional method but rarely have the distinction of the best VOUVRAY and CRÉMANT DE LOIRE. Best producers: l'Aulée, La Chapinière, F CHIDAINE★, Clos de la Briderie★, Clos Roche Blanche★, Clos du Tue-Boeuf★, Corbillières★, J Delaunay★, X Frissant, de la Garrelière★, L Gosseaume★, J-C Mandard, Marcadet★, Henry & J-S Marionnet/la Charmoise★, J-F Merieau★, Michaud★, Octavie★, Pré Baron★, J Preys★, Puzelat-Bonhomme★, Ricard★. Best years: (reds) (2013) 11 10 09 08 06 05.

TOURIGA NACIONAL High-quality red Portuguese grape, rich in aroma and fruit. It contributes deep colour and tannin to PORT, and is rapidly increasing in importance for powerful black plum and violet-scented table wines throughout the country. Several producers in Spain have now planted it. Small but important plantings in South Africa enhance some of the impressive port styles emerging across the country. Australia, Brazil and California are starting to test its potential for scented dry reds.

TRAPICHE *Mendoza, Argentina* The fine wine arm of Peñaflor, Argentina's biggest wine producer. Medalla Cabernet Sauvignon★★ is dense and satisfying, Malbec-Cabernet Franc Iscay★★ is solid and rich, while the newer Syrah-Viognier Iscay★★ is a serious delight, and the annual trio of single-vineyard Malbecs (often ★★★) are stunning expressions of how good the grape can be. The Finca Las Palmas★ range introduces Trapiche's style at accessible prices, while the Trapiche varietal range offers impressive quality and great value for money.

TREBBIANO The most widely planted white Italian grape variety. As Trebbiano Toscano, it is the base for numerous neutral, dry white wines, as well as much VIN SANTO. Better grapes also masquerade under the Trebbiano name, notably the Trebbianos from SOAVE, LUGANA (Verdicchio) and ABRUZZO – grapes capable of full-bodied, fragrant wines. Called Ugni Blanc in France, where it is primarily used for distilling, but it makes decent CÔTES DE GASCOGNE whites and is used in small quantities (around 10%) to provide essential acidity for Rolle in Provençal whites. It can perform the same role in hot countries such as Australia.

TRENTINO *Italy* Wines from this northern Italian region rarely have the verve or perfume of ALTO ADIGE examples, but can make up for this with riper, softer flavours. The Trentino DOC covers numerous different styles of wine, including whites Pinot Bianco and Grigio, Chardonnay, Moscato Giallo, Müller-Thurgau and Nosiola, and reds Lagrein, Marzemino and Cabernet. Trento Classico is a DOC for traditional-method fizz. Best producers:

N Balter★, N Bolognani★, La Cadalora★, Castel Noarna★, Cavit co-op, Cesconi★★, De Tarczal★, Dorigati, FERRARI★★, Graziano Fontana★, FORADORI★★, Letrari★, Longariva★, Conti Martini★, Maso Cantanghel★★, Maso Furli★, Maso Roveri★, Mezzacorona, Pojer & Sandri★, Pravis★, San Leonardo★★, Simoncelli★, E Spagnolli★, Vallarom★, La Vis co-op. See also TEROLDEGO ROTALIANO.

DOM. DE TRÉVALLON *Provence, France* Iconoclastic Eloi Dürrbach makes brilliant reds★★ (at best ★★★) – a tradition-busting blend of Cabernet Sauvignon and Syrah, mixing herbal wildness with a sweetness of blackberry, blackcurrant and black, black plums – and a tiny quantity of white★★★. The reds age well, but are intriguingly drinkable in their youth. IGP des Alpilles from 2009. Best years: (reds) (2013) 12 11 10 09 **08 07 06 05.**

ERNST TRIEBAUMER *Rust, Neusiedlersee-Hügelland, Burgenland, Austria* Ernst's two sons produce wines in every conceivable style, including excellent Ausbruch★★, but the estate is justly celebrated for its Blaufränkisch. Long-lived Mariental is invariably ★★★, and Oberer Wald ★★. Best years (reds): (2013) (12) **11 10 09 08 07 06.**

TRIMBACH *Alsace AC, Alsace, France* An excellent grower/merchant whose trademark is beautifully structured, emphatically dry, subtly perfumed elegance. Top wines are Gewurztraminer Cuvée des Seigneurs de Ribeaupierre★★, Riesling Cuvée Frédéric Émile★★ and Riesling Clos Ste-Hune★★★. Also very good Vendange Tardive★★ and Sélection de Grains Nobles★★. Best years: (Clos Ste-Hune) (2013) (12) (11) (10) (09) (08) **07 05 04 03 02 01 00 99 98 97 96 95 93 92 90.**

TRINITY HILL *Hawkes Bay, North Island, New Zealand* Many top wines from the Gimblett Gravels area, including flagship Homage Syrah★★★ (co-fermented with a small amount of Viognier), an irresistibly soft yet peppery Syrah★★, impressive Merlot★★, gutsy long-lived Cabernet Sauvignon-Merlot blend The Gimblett★★, plus a big and complex Chardonnay★★. Trinity also makes a good job of less mainstream styles such as Montepulciano★, Tempranillo★★, Arneis and Viognier★★. Also sweet Noble Viognier★★. Best years: (reds) (2013) **10 09 08 07 06 04.**

TRITTENHEIM *Mosel, Germany* Important village with some excellent vineyard sites, notably the Apotheke (pharmacy) and Leiterchen (little ladder). Sleek wines, with crisp acidity and plenty of fruit. Best producers: A Clüsserath★, Clüsserath-Eifel, Clüsserath-Weiler, F-J Eifel★, GRANS-FASSIAN★★, Loersch, Josef Rosch★. Best years: (2013) 12 11 **10 09 08 07 05.**

CH. TROPLONG MONDOT★ *St-Émilion Grand Cru AC, 1er Grand Cru Classé, Bordeaux, France* The late Christine Valette produced dense, concentrated wines here since the mid-1980s. Her reward – elevation to Premier Grand Cru Classé in 2006. Typically, I have found the wines oaky and extractive, but they are certainly powerfully structured and mouthfillingly textured, and seem to have been easing up in recent vintages. Best years: 2012 11 10 09 **08 07 06 05 04 03 02 01 00 99 98 96 95 90.**

CH. TROTANOY★★ *Pomerol AC, Bordeaux, France* This POMEROL estate (like PÉTRUS and LATOUR-À-POMEROL) has benefited from the brilliant touch of the MOUEIX family. Had a dip in the mid-1980s (due to lots of replanting) but top form ever since. Best years: 2012 11 10 09 08 **07 06 05 04 03 02 01 00 98 96 95 90.**

HANS TSCHIDA *Illmitz, Neusiedlersee, Burgenland, Austria* Also known as Angerhof – because Illmitz is packed with different Tschidas – this property is renowned for its TBAs★★★ and Schilfwein★★ from dried rather than botrytized grapes. Sämling (Scheurebe) and Chardonnay give the finest results. **Best years (sweet whites):** (2013) (12) 11 10 09 08 07 06.

CAVE DE TURCKHEIM *Alsace AC, Alsace, France* Important co-op with good basics (Réserve★) in all varieties. Consistent CRÉMANT D'ALSACE★. Brand★ and Hengst★★ bottlings are rich and offer value for money. **Best years:** (Grand Cru Gewurztraminer) (2012) 11 10 09 07 05 04.

TURLEY *Napa Valley AVA, California, USA* Larry Turley's ultra-ripe Zinfandels★★, from a number of old vineyards, are either praised for their profound power and depth or damned for their tannic, high-alcohol, PORT-like nature. Petite Sirah★★ is similarly built. **Best years:** (Zins) 2011 10 09 08 07 06 05 04 03 02 01 00.

TURSAN AOP *South-West France* From vineyards between Bordeaux and the Spanish border. Reds are Tannat-based blends with the Cabernets. Crisp, refreshing whites, mainly from the local Baroque grape. All for drinking young. **Best producers:** Baron de Bachen★ (eclectic wines made by master chef Michel Guérard), Dulucq★, Tursan co-op.

TUSCANY *Italy* Tuscany's rolling hills, clad with vines, olive trees and cypresses, have produced wine since at least Etruscan times. Today, its many DOC/DOCGs are based on the red Sangiovese grape and are led by CHIANTI CLASSICO, BRUNELLO DI MONTALCINO and VINO NOBILE DI MONTEPULCIANO, as well as famous 'super-Tuscans' like ORNELLAIA and TIGNANELLO. The term super-Tuscan was coined in the 1980s by journalists, who applied it to wines that, despite their high quality and use of expensive equipment in the winery, did not satisfy the restrictive local DOC regulations (usually Chianti) and therefore had to be labelled Vino da Tavola. In the 1990s the wine laws changed and the majority of super-Tuscans are now sold under the regionwide IGT Toscana. The growth of international grapes, notably Merlot, across the region was by now endemic, threatening to compromise these Tuscan wines for ever. Since 2000 there has been a re-evaluation of these classic wine styles, with more attention being paid to the importance of Sangiovese and its unique ability to express Tuscany's *terroir* perfectly. Among white wines the salty dry VERNACCIA DI SAN GIMIGNANO and sumptuously sweet VIN SANTO, courtesy of the Trebbiano and Malvasia grapes, stand out. See also BOLGHERI, CARMIGNANO, MORELLINO DI SCANSANO, ROSSO DI MONTALCINO, SASSICAIA, SOLAIA.

TYRRELL'S *Hunter Valley, New South Wales, Australia* Top-notch family company with prime HUNTER vineyards celebrated its 150th anniversary in 2008. It is expanding into COONAWARRA, MCLAREN VALE and HEATHCOTE, with impressive results. Comprehensive range, from good-value quaffers (Old Winery★, Lost Block★) to excellent Vat 47 Chardonnay★★ and Vat 8 Shiraz★. Semillon is the speciality, with single-vineyard wines (all at least ★★) – Stevens, Belford and the rare HVD – and, best of all, the superb Vat 1★★★. **Best years:** (Vat 1 Semillon) (2013) (11) 10 09 07 05 04 03 02 99 98 97 96 95 94 93 92 91 90 89 87; (Vat 47 Chardonnay) 2013 11 10 09 08 07 06 05 04 03 02 00.

UCO VALLEY *Mendoza, Argentina* This valley, in the foothills of the Andes, is an old secret of Argentine viticulture, recently rediscovered: most vineyards are new, but there are precious old plantings too, for example in La Consulta. With vineyards at 1000–1500m (3200–4900ft) above sea level, it's Argentina's best spot for Chardonnays, especially from the Tupungato area (including Gualtallary). Reds are showing fascinating flavours – especially Malbec, Merlot, Syrah and Tempranillo. Best producers: Anduluna★, ATAMISQUE★★, CATENA★★, CLOS DE LOS SIETE★★, Cuvelier Los Andes★★, Diamandes★, DOÑA PAULA★★, O FOURNIER★★, PASSIONATE WINE★, RIGLOS★★, Salentein★, TAPIZ★, ZORZAL★.

UGNI BLANC See TREBBIANO.

UMATHUM *Frauenkirchen, Neusiedlersee, Burgenland, Austria* Biodynamic producer Josef Umathum emphasizes finesse and sheer drinkability and resists heavy use of oak. The single-vineyard Ried Hallebühl★★ and Blaufränkisch Kirschgarten★★ are usually his top wines, but St Laurent Vom Stein★ and Zweigelt-dominated Haideboden★ sometimes match them in quality. Best years: (reds) (2013) (12) 11 **10 09 08 07**.

UMBRIA *Italy* ORVIETO accounts for almost 70% of DOC wines in Umbria, but there are full-bodied reds from Torgiano DOC and MONTEFALCO DOC.

UNDURRAGA *Maipo, Chile* Long-established family winery; new management in 2008 brought an injection of quality. Wines in the T.H.★★ (Terroir Hunter) and Sibaris ranges are transforming the reputation of the winery, aided by the consultancy of Alvaro Espinoza. Considerable investment in sparkling wine production.

ÜRZIG *Mosel, Germany* Middle MOSEL village with the famous red slate Würzgarten (spice garden) vineyard tumbling spectacularly down to the river and producing marvellously spicy and long-lived Riesling. Best producers: J J Christoffel★, Jos. Christoffel★★, Erbes★, Dr LOOSEN★★★, MOLITOR★★, Mönchhof, Pauly-Bergweiler★, S A Prüm★, Weins-Prüm★. Best years: (2013) 12 11 **10 09 08 07 06 05 04**.

UTIEL-REQUENA DO *Valencia, Spain* Famous for rosés, mostly from the Bobal grape. Improving reds often complement Bobal with Tempranillo. Groundbreaking Mustiguillo★★ winery now has its own appellation, DO Terrerazo. Best producers: Cerrogallina★, Gandía, Bruno Murciano★, Murviedro, Palmera (L'Angelet★), Sierra Norte, Torre Oria, Dominio de la Vega.

DOM. VACHERON *Sancerre AC, Loire Valley, France* This biodynamic domaine is reputed for its elegant Pinot Noir SANCERRE, now benefiting from less extraction and no new oak. Flagship wines Belle Dame★★ red and the flinty Les Romains★★ white have been joined by two single-site whites, Le Paradis★★ and Les Grands Champs★★ from limestone soils. The basic Sancerres – a cherryish red★ and a grapefruity white★ – have reserves of complexity that set them above the crowd. Best years: (Belle Dame) (2013) 12 **09 08 07 06 05 04**.

VACQUEYRAS AC *Rhône Valley, France* Red wines, mainly Grenache, account for 95% of production; they have a warm, spicy bouquet and a rich deep flavour that seems infused with the herbs and pine dust of the south and its plateau vineyards. Lovely, if robust, to drink at 2–3 years, though good wines will age for 10 years. Best producers: Pierre Amadieu, Amouriers★, la Charbonnière★, Clos de Caveau, Clos des Cazaux★★, Couroulu★, DELAS★, Font de Papier★, Font Sarade, la Fourmone★, la Garrigue★, Paul JABOULET★, Alain Jaume, Monardière★★, Montirius★★, Montmirail★, Montvac★, Ondines, Famille Perrin, Roucas Toumba★, SANG DES CAILLOUX★★, Tardieu-Laurent★★, la Tourade★, Ch. des Tours★. Best years: **2012** 11 **10 09 07 06 05 04 03 01 99**.

VAL DE LOIRE, IGP *Loire Valley, France* Regional denomination that covers all 14 designated wine-producing regions of the LOIRE VALLEY – over 7,300ha (18,000 acres). Key whites are Sauvignon Blanc, Chardonnay and Chenin Blanc. The focus for reds is Gamay, Cabernets Franc and Sauvignon, with some Pinot Noir. It is increasingly a refuge for ambitious producers whose wines punch well above the weight of their appellation, especially in TOURAINE. Best producers: Ampelidae★, M Angeli/Sansonnière★★, S Bernaudeau, M Berneau-Marechal, l'Ecu★, La Grange aux Belles, Levin Wines (Le Vin de Levin★), H Marionnet★, A MELLOT★, J-F Merieau★, J Mourat/Moulin Blanc★, RAGOTIÈRE★★, Ricard, Robinot★.

VALAIS *Switzerland* Swiss canton flanking the Rhône. Between Martigny and Sierre the valley turns north-east, creating an Alpine suntrap, and this short stretch of terraced vineyards provides many of Switzerland's most individual wines from Fendant (Chasselas), Johannisberger (Silvaner), Pinot Noir and Gamay, and several stunning examples from Syrah, Chardonnay, Ermitage (Marsanne) and Petite Arvine. Best producers: Bonvin★, Chappaz★, Cina★, G Clavien★, Cottagnoud★, Dorsaz★, Jean-René Germanier★★, Chandra Kurt, Adrian Mathier★, S Maye★, Mercier★, Dom. du Mont d'Or★, Dom des Muses★, Provins, Rouvinez★, Valais Mundi★, M Zufferey★.

CH. VALANDRAUD★★ *St-Émilion Grand Cru AC, 1er Grand Cru Classé, Bordeaux, France* From progenitor of the 'garage wine' sensation in ST-ÉMILION in the early 1990s to Premier Grand Cru Classé in the 2012 classification. What a story! Originally a big, rich, extracted wine from low yields, from grapes mainly grown in different parcels around St-Émilion. Now the grapes come from a top-quality limestone-based site and the wines are rich, powerful and  firmly structured. Also a white Blanc de Valandraud★. Best years: 2012 11 10 09 08 07 06 05 04 03 02 01 00 99 98.

VALDEPEÑAS DO *Castilla-La Mancha, Spain* Valdepeñas offers some of Spain's best inexpensive oak-aged reds, but there is an increasing number of unoaked, fruit-forward reds as well. In fact, there are more whites than reds, at least some of them modern, fresh and fruity. Best producers: Miguel Calatayud, Los Llanos, Luís Megía, Real, Félix Solís, Casa de la Viña.

VALDESPINO *Jerez & Manzanilla DO, Andalucía, Spain* Owned by Grupo Estévez (Marqués del Real Tesoro, Tio Mateo), probably the quality leader in Jerez today. Fino Inocente★★ (can be ★★★), Palo Cortado Cardenal★★★, Pedro Ximénez Niños★★★ and dry Amontillado Coliseo★★★ are stunning examples of sherry's different styles. Minute amounts of sensational Toneles★★★ (sweet Moscatel).

VALDIVIESO *Curicó, Chile* Varietals are attractive and direct, Reservas from cooler regions a definite step up, and Single Vineyard Chardonnay★, Pinot Noir★ and Malbec★ are quite impressive. Multi-varietal, multi-vintage blend Caballo Loco★ (mad horse) is always fascinating and unpredictable. Éclat★★, based on old Carignan, is chewy and rich. Also Éclat Botrytis Semillon★★.

VALENCIA *Spain* The best-known wines from Valencia DO are the inexpensive, sweet, grapy Moscatels. Simple, fruity whites, reds and rosés are also good. Alicante DO to the south produces a little-known treasure, the

Fondillón dry or semi-dry fortified wine, as well as a cluster of wines made by a few quality-conscious modern wineries. Monastrell (Mourvèdre) is the main red grape variety. Best producers: (Valencia) J Belda, Rafael Cambra★, Enguera, Gandía, Los Frailes★★, Los Pinos★, Celler del Roure★; (Alicante) Bernabé Navarro★★, Bocopa★, Heretat de Cesilia★, Gutiérrez de la Vega (Casta Diva Muscat★★), El Sequé★, Enrique Mendoza★★, Salvador Poveda★, Bruno Prats★★, Primitivo Quiles★, Telmo RODRÍGUEZ (Al-Muvedre★) . See also UTIEL-REQUENA.

VALENTINI *Abruzzo, Italy* Excellent traditional Abruzzese estate in the heart of the COLLINE TERAMANE. The grapes are vinified in huge barrels. Trebbiano d'Abruzzo★★★ is one of Italy's finest white wines, combining poise, delicate fruit and deft minerality; equally exciting are the Cerasuolo d'Abruzzo★★★, more of an ethereal red than a *rosato* made from Montepulciano grapes, and the mighty – but rare – Montepulciano d'Abruzzo★★★: 2006 is the most recent release. Best years: (Trebbiano) (2011) 10 09 08 **07 06 05 04 03** 01; (Montepulciano) 2006 02 01 00 **97 95**.

VALL LLACH *Priorat DOCa, Spain* This tiny winery, owned by Catalan folk singer Lluís Llach, produces powerful reds★★ dominated by old-vine Cariñena. Best years: 2010 09 **08 07 06 05 04 03** 01 00 99 98.

VALLE D'AOSTA *Italy* Tiny Alpine valley sandwiched between PIEDMONT and the Alps in northern Italy. The regional DOC covers around 20 wine styles, referring either to a grape variety (like Gamay or Pinot Nero) or to a delimited region like Donnaz (light red from steep Nebbiolo vineyards). Best are the dry Petite Arvine and the sweet Chambave Moscato. Best producers: R Anselmet★, C Charrère/Les Crêtes★, La Crotta di Vegneron★, Grosjean, Institut Agricole Regional★, Onze Communes co-op, Ezio Voyat★.

VALLE CENTRAL See CENTRAL VALLEY, Chile.

VALPOLICELLA DOC *Veneto, Italy* Styles range from a light, cherryish red to dense, burly AMARONE and rich, PORT-like RECIOTO (both DOCG). Most of the better table wines are Valpolicella (Classico) Superiore from the hills north of Verona and are made predominantly from Corvina and Corvinone grapes, plus Rondinella. The most concentrated, ageworthy wines are made either from a particular vineyard, or by refermenting the wine on the skins and lees of the Amarone, a style called *ripasso*, or by using a portion of dried grapes. Best producers: Accordini★, ALLEGRINI★★, Bertani★, Brigaldara★, Brunelli★, BUSSOLA★★★, Michele Castellani★, Cecilia Beretta★, Corte Sant'Alda★★, Valentina Cubi★, DAL FORNO★, Guerrieri-Rizzardi★, Marion★★, MASI★, Mazzi★, Monte dei Ragni★★★, Morandina, C S Negrar★, Novaia★, QUINTARELLI★★, Le Ragose★, Le Salette★, Serègo Alighieri★, Speri★★, Villa Monteleone★, Viviani★, Zenato★, Zeni★. Best years: (Valpolicella Superiore) (2012) **11 10 09 08 06 04 01** 00.

VALTELLINA SUPERIORE DOCG *Lombardy, Italy* Red wine produced on the granitic Alpine slopes of northern LOMBARDY. There is a basic light Valtellina DOC red, made from at least 90% Nebbiolo (here called Chiavennasca), but the best wines are Valtellina Superiore DOCG from sub-zones like Grumello, Inferno, Sassella and Valgella. From top vintages the wines are attractively perfumed and approachable. Sfursat or Sforzato is a high-alcohol AMARONE-like red made from semi-dried grapes. Best producers: ArPePe (Arturo Pelizzatti Perego)★★, La Castellina★, Enologica Valtellinese★, Fay★, Nino Negri★, Nera★, Rainoldi★, Conti Sertoli Salis★, Triacca★. Best years: (2011) **10 09 08 07 06 04 01**.

VAN VOLXEM *Wiltingen, Mosel, Germany* Estate with old vines in Scharzhofberg and Wiltinger Gottesfuss. Off-dry and opulent style is atypical and controversial, but often ★★. Best years: (2013) 12 11 **10 09 08 07 05**.

CH. VANNIÈRES *Bandol AC, Provence, France* Leading BANDOL estate, owned by the Boisseaux family since the 1950s. Wines are bottled unfiltered, and Mourvèdre makes up to 90–95% of the red Bandol★★. Also CÔTES DE PROVENCE and IGP wines. Best years: (2013) 12 11 10 09 **08 07 06 05**.

VASSE FELIX *Margaret River, Western Australia* MARGARET RIVER's first vineyard and winery (planted in 1967). New vineyards have been added and the winery is clearly focused on what Margaret River does best: Cabernet, Chardonnay and Semillon-Sauvignon. The flagship Heytesbury Chardonnay★★★ is tighter, leaner and finer than before, while the powerful Cabernet-blend red Heytesbury★★★ shows greater elegance. There's a decadently rich Cabernet Sauvignon★★ and oak-led Shiraz★, and the regular Chardonnay★ is pleasurable drinking for a modest price. Best years: (Heytesbury red) (2013) 12 11 10 09 **08 07 05** 04 01 99 97 96 95.

VAUD *Switzerland* The Vaud's main vineyards border Lake Geneva (Lac Léman), with 4 sub-regions: la Côte, Lavaux, CHABLAIS, Côtes de l'Orbe-Bonvillars. Fresh light white wines are made from Chasselas; at Dézaley it gains depth. Reds from Gamay and Pinot Noir. Best producers: Henri Badoux, Bovard★, la Chenalettaz, Cidis, Conne, Cruchon, Dubois, Obrist, Pinget★, J & P Testuz★.

VAVASOUR *Marlborough, South Island, New Zealand* First winery in Marlborough's AWATERE VALLEY, making one of New Zealand's best Chardonnays★★, a fine, lush Pinot Noir★★ and palate-tingling, oak-tinged Sauvignon Blanc★★. Second-label Dashwood is also top stuff, particularly the tangy Sauvignon Blanc★★. Best years: (Sauvignon Blanc) (2013) 12 11 10 09.

VEGA SICILIA *Ribera del Duero DO, Castilla y León, Spain* Among Spain's most expensive wines – rich, fragrant, complex and very slow to mature, and by no means always easy to appreciate. The first estate in Spain to introduce French varieties: about one-fifth of the vines are now Cabernet Sauvignon, along with Tempranillo, Malbec and Merlot. Top wine Unico★★★ is aged in wood for 5 or 6 years. Second wine: Valbuena★★. A subsidiary winery makes the more modern Alión★. In TORO the Pintia winery makes unusually elegant wines, for the region. Good dry Furmint★ from Oremus winery in Hungary. Best years: (Unico) (2004) 02 00 99 **96 95 94 91 90 89 87 86 85 83 82 81 80 79 76 75 74 70 68**.

VELICH *Neusiedlersee, Burgenland, Austria* Heinz Velich makes Austria's most mineral and sophisticated Chardonnay★★ from old vines in the Tiglat vineyard. Also first-rate dessert wines★★. Best years: (Tiglat Chardonnay) (2013) (12) **11 10 09 08**; (sweet) (2013) (12) **11 10 09 08 07 06**.

VENETO *Italy* Usually the most prolific wine region in Italy, a major source of Pinot Grigio and the home of VALPOLICELLA, BARDOLINO and SOAVE as well as DOCs from Garda (e.g. BIANCO DI CUSTOZA) in the west, via BREGANZE and the PROSECCO zones of Conegliano and Valdobbiadene, to Piave on the border with FRIULI. Pretty well every wine style is covered, from a variety of native and international grapes. With its port of Venice and crossroads-cities like Verona linking it with points south and north, Veneto has become the most cosmopolitan of regions, though it retains more than its share of local peculiarities such as the dried-grape method of producing so-called *vini da meditazione*. See also AMARONE, RECIOTO DI SOAVE, RECIOTO DELLA VALPOLICELLA.

VENTISQUERO *Maipo, Chile* State-of-the-art, ecologically friendly winery. Flagship wines are the Grey label (Syrah★, Cabernet Sauvignon★, GCM★, Pinot Noir★). Reserva whites are also good. Also a rapidly improving range under the Yali label (Viognier★). Pangea★★, from the Apalta region of COLCHAGUA, is a joint venture wine with the Australian John DUVAL (who made Penfolds GRANGE famous). New ultra-northern Huasco Valley promises tingling whites and reds.

VENTOUX AC *Rhône Valley, France* Vineyards spread out around the southern and western slopes of Mont Ventoux. When well made, the red wines have lovely juicy fruit or, in the case of Paul JABOULET and Pesquié, some real stuffing. Good, fresh rosés. Best producers: Anges★, Brusset, Cascavel★, Clos des Patris, Cave La Courtoise★, La Croix des Pins★, Fenouillet, Fondrèche★, Font-Sane, Gonnet★, Paul JABOULET★, Cave de Lumières★, la Martinelle★, le Murmurium, Pesquié★★, St Jean du Barroux, Cave Terraventoux, Unang, Valcombe★, VIDAL-FLEURY★, La Vieille Ferme★. Best years: (reds) **2012 11 10**.

VERDEJO From the brink of oblivion in the 1970s to some 17,000ha (42,000 acres) now, Verdejo has become the most commercially successful white grape in Spain, giving well-structured wines with grassy, apple-like flavours. Native to RUEDA and expanding into CASTILLA-LA MANCHA.

VERDELHO Best known as the grape that produces an off-dry style of MADEIRA fortified wine. Called Gouveio, it is used for white PORT. In Spain, as Godello, it makes fragrant, dry, often ageworthy whites in the Valdeorras (GALICIA) and BIERZO regions. WESTERN AUSTRALIA and NEW SOUTH WALES make big, sometimes oily, dry whites. Limited plantings in South Africa are used in white blends and a few varietal wines.

VERDICCHIO DEI CASTELLI DI JESI, VERDICCHIO DI MATELICA DOC *Marche, Italy* Verdicchio, grown in the hills near the Adriatic around Jesi and in the Apennine foothills enclave of Matelica, has blossomed into one of central Italy's most promising white varieties. Usually fresh and fruity, but some Verdicchio can age into a white of surprising depth of flavour. A few producers, notably Garofoli with Serra Fiorese★★, age it in oak, but even without wood it can develop an almost Burgundy-like complexity. A little is made sparkling. Best producers: (Jesi) Brunori★, Colonnara★, Coroncino★★, Fazi Battaglia★, Garofoli★★, Mancinelli★, Monte Schiavo★★, Santa Barbara★, Sartarelli★★, Tavignano★, Terre Cortesi Moncaro★, Umani Ronchi★, Villa Bucci★★, Fratelli Zaccagnini★; (Matelica) Belisario★, Bisci★, Mecella★, La Monacesca★★.

VIGNOBLE DES VERDOTS *Bergerac AOP and Monbazillac AOP, South-West France* David Fourtout makes all kinds of BERGERACs, from the everyday, good-value Clos des Verdots★ range to Château les Tours des Verdots★ (barrique-aged), to the top of the tree Verdots★★ and Le Vin★★. Outstanding MONBAZILLAC★★. Best years: (reds) (2012) **11 10 09 06 05 04**.

VERGELEGEN *Stellenbosch WO, South Africa* Historic farm with outstanding Sauvignon Blanc★★ – aggressive, racy, streaked with tropical fruit; the single-vineyard Schaapenberg Reserve★★ is flinty, dry and fascinating. White Vergelegen GVB★★★, a barrel-fermented Semillon- or Sauvignon-led blend, depending on vintage, ages superbly for at least 8 years. Also a ripe-textured, stylish Chardonnay Reserve★★. Of the reds, BORDEAUX blend Vergelegen GVB★★★ shows classic mineral intensity, and Merlot★★ and Cabernet Sauvignon★★ are often among South Africa's best. Single-vineyard Cabernet Sauvignon-based 'V★★★ is an attention-grabbing star. Also cracking MMV Brut★★ fizz. Best years: (premium reds) (2011) **10** 09 08 07 06 05 04 03.

VERMENTINO The best dry white wines of SARDINIA generally come from the Vermentino grape. The best examples – full-bodied and flavoursome – are from the Vermentino di Gallura DOCG zone in the north-east of the island. Vermentino di Sardegna DOC is lighter, less interesting. Also grown in coastal areas of LIGURIA (as aromatic Pigato) and TUSCANY, and in CORSICA. It is believed to be the same as Rolle, found in many blends in PROVENCE and the LANGUEDOC, and increasingly as varietal wines. Starting to appear in California, Australia and New Zealand. Best producers: (Sardinia) ARGIOLAS★, Capichera★★, Cherchi★, Contini★, Gallura co-op★★, Giogantinu★, Piero Mancini★, Pedra Majore★, Mura★, Santadi co-op★, Sella & Mosca, Vermentino co-op★★; (Tuscany) ANTINORI; (Provence) La Courtade★, Sarrins★; (Australia) YALUMBA.

VERNACCIA DI SAN GIMIGNANO DOCG *Tuscany, Italy* Famous Tuscan white wine: dry, variable and generally underwhelming, made from the Vernaccia grape grown in the sandstone hills around the town of San Gimignano. Up to 10% other grapes, e.g. Chardonnay, are allowed. There is a San Gimignano DOC for the zone's reds, though the best are sold as IGT Toscana. Best producers: Cà del Vispo★, Le Calcinaie★, Casale-Falchini★, V Cesani★, Guicciardini Strozzi★, La Lastra (Riserva★), Melini (Le Grillaie★), Montenidoli★, G Panizzi★, Il Paradiso★, Pietrafitta★, La Rampa di Fugnano★, Teruzzi & Puthod (Terre di Tufi★★), Casa alle Vacche★, Vagnoni★.

QUINTA DO VESÚVIO★★ *Port DOC, Douro, Portugal* Top vintage PORT (and DOURO wine★★) from the Symington stable that appears only when the high quality can be maintained. Best with at least 10 years' age. Best years: (Vintage) 2011 **10** 09 08 07 06 05 04 03 01 00 99 97 96 95 94 92 91 90.

VEUVE CLICQUOT *Champagne AC, Champagne, France* Owned by LVMH; high-quality reputation but erratic standards. The non-vintage is full, toasty and satisfyingly weighty, or lean and raw, depending on your luck; the vintage★ is back on form (★★ in 2004). Look out too for Cave Privée★★, recent releases of top older vintages. The de luxe Grande Dame★★★ is both powerful and elegant. Grande Dame Rosé★★★ is exquisite. Best years: 2004 02 00 99 98 96 95 90 89 88 85 82.

VIADER *Howell Mountain AVA, California, USA* Established in 1986 by Delia Viader. Excellent limited-production reds, including the signature Viader★★, an elegant, structured blend of Cabernets Sauvignon and Franc. Good Tempranillo★ and a dry rosé★ under the DARE label. Best years: (reds) 2010 **09** 08 07 06 05 03 01.

VICTORIA *Australia* Despite its relatively small area, Victoria has arguably a wider variety of land suited to quality grape-growing than any other state in Australia, with climates ranging from hot Murray Darling and Swan Hill on the Murray River to cool MORNINGTON PENINSULA and GIPPSLAND in the south. The range of flavours is similarly wide and exciting. With more than 750 wineries, Victoria leads the boutique winery boom, particularly in Mornington Peninsula. See also BEECHWORTH, BENDIGO, CENTRAL VICTORIA, GEELONG, GRAMPIANS AND PYRENEES, HEATHCOTE, RUTHERGLEN, YARRA VALLEY.

VIDAL-FLEURY *Rhône Valley, France* GUIGAL-owned, recently reinvigorated CÔTE-RÔTIE producer (classy La Chatillonne★★) and Rhône merchant; quality moving up steadily. Old favourites MUSCAT DE BEAUMES-DE-VENISE★ and red VENTOUX★ now joined by red and white★ CÔTES DU RHÔNE, CAIRANNE and GIGONDAS★. Best years: (reds) 2013 **12 11 10 09 07**.

VIEUX-CHÂTEAU-CERTAN★★ *Pomerol AC, Bordeaux, France* Slow-developing, tannic but delightful red with up to 30% Cabernet Franc and 10% Cabernet Sauvignon in the blend, which after 15–20 years finally resembles more a fragrant, refined MÉDOC than a hedonistic POMEROL. Best years: 2012 11 10 09 08 **07** 06 05 04 02 01 00 99 98 96 95 90 89 88.

DOM. DU VIEUX TÉLÉGRAPHE *Châteauneuf-du-Pape AC, Rhône Valley, France* The vines are some of the oldest in CHÂTEAUNEUF and the Grenache-based red★★ (sometimes ★★★) is among the best, most complex wines of the RHÔNE VALLEY, and lives for 20+ years. There is a small amount of white★★, which is rich and heavenly when very young but ages well, even in lighter years. New cuvée Piedlong★ replaces Roquète red since 2011. Good second wine, when not over-ripened, Télégramme. Also co-owns very fine les Pallières★★ in GIGONDAS. Best years: (reds) 2012 11 10 09 **08 07** 06 05 04 03 01 00 99 98 97 96 95 90 89 88 78.

VILLA MARIA *Auckland and Marlborough, New Zealand* Founder Sir George Fistonich also owns Esk Valley and Vidal (both in HAWKES BAY). Villa Maria Reserve Merlot-Cabernet★★★, Reserve Merlot★★, Esk Valley The Terraces★★★ and Vidal Merlot-Cabernet★★ are superb. Syrahs are among New Zealand's best: Esk Valley, Villa Maria Reserve and Vidal Legacy, all ★★. Reserve Chardonnay from Vidal★★ and Villa Maria★★ are suave and serious. The Villa Maria range includes various MARLBOROUGH Sauvignon Blancs, with Clifford Bay Reserve★★, Wairau Reserve★★, Graham Vineyard★★ and Taylors Pass★★ outstanding. Also from Marlborough, impressive Pinot Noir Reserve★★, Seddon Pinot Gris★, Reserve Riesling★★ and stunning botrytized Noble Riesling★★★. Best years: (Hawkes Bay reds) (2013) 10 **09 08 07 06 04**.

CH. DE VILLENEUVE *Saumur-Champigny AC, Loire Valley, France* Low yields and fully ripe fruit produce first-class SAUMUR-CHAMPIGNY★, with concentrated, mineral Vieilles Vignes★★ and le Grand Clos★★. Barrel-fermented white Saumur Les Cormiers★★ develops Burgundian complexity with age. Best years: 2013 11 **10 09 08 06 05 04 03 02 01**.

VILLIERA *Stellenbosch WO, South Africa* The speciality is Cap Classique sparklers: rich, biscuity Monro Brut★★ with 5 years on lees; additive-free Brut Natural Chardonnay★. Still whites include Sauvignon Blanc (Bush Vine★), consistent Riesling and delicious oaked Chenin Blanc★. Monro, a structured Merlot-led BORDEAUX blend, is best among the reds. Fired Earth★ is a tasty Late Bottled PORT style. Also 'mentor' to neighbouring M'hudi project (Platinum range Pinotage★, Cabernet Sauvignon★).

VIN SANTO *Tuscany, Italy* TUSCANY's 'holy wine' can be one of the world's great sweet wines – but the term has been wantonly abused (happily the *liquoroso* version, made by adding alcohol to partially fermented must, is no longer recognized as a legitimate style). Made from dried white or occasionally red grapes, fermented and aged in small barrels for between 3 and 10 years, the wines should be nutty, gently oxidized, full of the flavours of dried apricots and crystallized orange peel, concentrated and long. Vin Santo from red grapes (Sangiovese) is called Occhio di Pernice. Best producers: AVIGNONESI★★★, BADIA A COLTIBUONO★, Fattoria di Basciano★★, BIBBIANO★★, Bindella★★, Cacchiano★, Capezzana★★, Fattoria del Cerro★★, Corzano e Paterno★★, FONTODI★★, ISOLE E OLENA★★★, Romeo★★, San Felice★★, San Gervasio★, San Giusto a Rentennano★★★, SELVAPIANA★★, Villa Sant'Anna★★, Villa di Vetrice★, Volpaia★.

VINHO VERDE DOC *Minho and Douro Litoral, Portugal* 'Vinho Verde' can be red or white – 'green' only in the sense of being young. The whites are the most widely seen outside Portugal and range from medium-sweet but acidic to aromatic, flowery and fruity, often with a slight spritz. Some that fall outside the DOC regulations are sold as Vinho Regional Minho (Quinta do CÔTTO's Paço de Teixeiró). Best producers: Afros★, Quinta do Ameal★★, Quinta da Aveleda★, Quinta de Azevedo★/SOGRAPE, Quinta da Baguinha★, Quinta de Gomariz★, Quinta da Lixa, Quinta de Lourosa, Quintas de Melgaço, Anselmo Mendes (Muros Antigos★, Muros de Melgaço★), Palácio de Brejoeira, Provam (Portal do Fidalgo★, Vinha Antiga★), Casa de Sezim★, Quinta de Simães, Quinta do Soalheiro★, Quinta do Tamariz★, Casa do Valle★.

VINO NOBILE DI MONTEPULCIANO DOCG *Tuscany, Italy* The 'noble wine' from the gravelly clay hills around the town of Montepulciano is made from Sangiovese, known locally as Prugnolo Gentile, with the help of a little Canaiolo and Mammolo (and, sadly, Merlot). At its best, it combines the power and structure of BRUNELLO DI MONTALCINO with the finesse and complexity found in top CHIANTI. Improvement since the 1990s has been impressive. The introduction of Rosso di Montepulciano DOC (essentially a second wine) has certainly helped. Best producers: AVIGNONESI★★, Bindella★, BOSCARELLI★★, La Braccesca★★/ANTINORI, Le Casalte★, La Ciarliana★, Contucci, Dei★★, Del Cerro★★, Fassati★★, Gracciano★, Il Macchione★, Nottola★★, Palazzo Vecchio★★, POLIZIANO★★, Redi★, Romeo★, Salcheto★★, Sanguineto I e II★★, Trerose★ (Simposio★★), Valdipiatta★. Best years: (2012) 11 10 09 08 07 06 04 01 00 99 97.

VINSOBRES AC *Rhône Valley, France* Southern RHÔNE village whose hallmark is clear fruit. A good, fresh area for Syrah, which peps up the Grenache. Best producers: Chaume-Arnaud★, Constant-Duquesnoy, Coriançon★, Deurre★, Alain Jaume★, Moulin★, Péquélette, Famille Perrin★, Rouanne, la Vinsobraise co-op. Best years: (reds) 2012 11 10 09 07 06.

VIOGNIER Traditionally grown only in the northern RHÔNE VALLEY, most famously for the rare and expensive wines of CONDRIEU, Viognier is often a poor yielder, prone to disease and difficult to vinify. But the wine can be delicious: pear-fleshy, apricotty with a soft, almost waxy texture, usually a fragrance of spring flowers and sometimes a taste like crème fraîche. New, higher-yielding clones that limit its opulence are now being grown in Languedoc-Roussillon, Ardèche and the southern Rhône as well as in Spain, Portugal, Switzerland, Italy, Austria, the USA (WASHINGTON STATE and VIRGINIA, where Viognier can be world-class), Argentina, Chile, Australia, New Zealand and South Africa. Traditionally used in parts of CÔTE-RÔTIE to co-ferment with Syrah (Shiraz); this practice is now becoming popular in other parts of the world. Viognier is also increasingly being used as a blender with more neutral white varieties to inject perfume, texture and fruit.

VIRÉ-CLESSÉ AC *Mâconnais, Burgundy, France* Appellation created in 1998
out of 2 of the best MÂCON-VILLAGES. Originally, the rules outlawed wines
with residual sugar, thus excluding Jean Thévenet's extraordinary cuvées,
but common sense has prevailed. **Best producers:** A Bonhomme★★, Bret
Brothers★, Chaland★★, E Gillet★, Héritiers LAFON★, J-P Michel★, Roally★,
Thévenet★★, Cave de Viré★. **Best years:** (2013) 12 **11** 10 09.

VIRGINIA *USA* Virginia's surging wine industry has surpassed 250 wineries
in 7 AVAs, and is gaining international recognition as part of America's new
'wine country'. Aromatic Viognier produces some world-class examples and
earthy Cabernet Franc is promising, while varietal Petit Verdot yields some
enticingly aromatic reds. Many growers continue to tinker with other varieties
such as Petit Manseng, Nebbiolo and Tannat, which can be surprisingly
good. Increasing emphasis on vineyard-designated red blends. Virginia is also
producing some distinguished fizz. **Best producers:** BARBOURSVILLE★
(Octagon★★), Boxwood★, Breaux★, Chester Gap, Chrysalis, Glen Manor,
HORTON★, Keswick★, King Family★, LINDEN★, Pearmund★, Pollak, RdV★★, VIRGINIA
WINEWORKS/Michael Shaps★, Veritas★, Williamsburg★.

VIRGINIA WINEWORKS *Monticello AVA, Virginia, USA* Michael Shaps is one
of Virginia's star winemakers. In 2007 he created Virginia Wineworks,
the state's first custom-crush winery, where he provides facilities for
many in Virginia's new wave. He also makes beautiful Cabernet Franc★,
Petit Verdot and a Meritage red blend under his own name.

ROBERTO VOERZIO *Barolo DOCG, Piedmont, Italy* Famous and expensive
new-wave BAROLO producer. Single-vineyard Barolos include
Brunate★★, Cerequio★★, La Serra★★ and Riserva Capalot★★.
Successful Dolcetto d'Alba Priavino★, Vignaserra★★ (barrique-aged
Nebbiolo with a little Cabernet) and potent BARBERA D'ALBA Riserva Pozzo
dell'Annunziata★★. From vintage 2009 appears to be switching from
making heavyweight wines to something much lighter. **Best years:**
(Barolo) (2011) 10 09 08 07 06 04 01 00 99 98 97 96 95 93 91 90.

COMTE GEORGES DE VOGÜÉ *Chambolle-Musigny, Côte de Nuits, Burgundy,
France* De Vogüé owns substantial holdings in 2 Grands Crus, BONNES-
MARES★★★ and MUSIGNY★★★, as well as in Chambolle's top Premier Cru,
les Amoureuses★★★, epitomizing the silky style of great Burgundy. It is
the sole producer of minute quantities of Musigny Blanc★★, but since
replanting the wine is currently being sold as (very expensive) BOURGOGNE
Blanc until the vines are old enough. **Best years:** (Musigny) (2013) 12 11 10
09 08 07 06 05 **03 00 99 98 96 93 91 90**.

VOLNAY AC *Côte de Beaune, Burgundy, France* Elegant CÔTE DE BEAUNE reds:
attractive when young, good examples can age well. Top Premiers Crus:
Caillerets, Champans, Clos des Chênes, Santenots, Taillepieds. **Best
producers:** M Ampeau★★, d'ANGERVILLE★★★, BELLENE★, H Boillot★, J-M Boillot★★,
COCHE-DURY★★, V GIRARDIN★★, LAFARGE★★, LAFON★★★, Leroux★★,
Matrot★★, MONTILLE★★, Pousse d'Or★★, J Prieur★★, N Rossignol★★,
J Voillot★★. **Best years:** 2012 11 10 09 **08 07** 05 **02 99 96 95 91 90**.

VON SIEBENTHAL *Aconcagua, Chile* Tiny boutique winery founded by
Swiss lawyer Mauro von Siebenthal, who fell in love with the region.
Eclectic range, with consistently good Carabantes★ (Syrah blend),
Monteligˋ★ (Cabernet-Petit Verdot-Carmenère) and Parcela #7★★
(Cabernet-Petit Verdot-Merlot-Cabernet Franc). Toknar★★ is a rich
and vibrant 100% Petit Verdot.

VOSNE-ROMANÉE AC *Côte de Nuits, Burgundy, France* The greatest village in the COTE DE NUITS, with 6 Grands Crus and 13 Premiers Crus (notably les Malconsorts, aux Brûlées and les Suchots) that are often as good as other villages' Grands Crus. The quality of Vosne's village wine is also high. In good years the wines need at least 6 years' aging, but 10–15 would be better. Best producers: Arnoux-Lachaux★★★, Cacheux-Sirugue★★, S CATHIARD★★★, B Clavelier★★, Confuron-Cotetidot★★, Eugénie★★, GRIVOT★★★, Anne GROS★★★, A-F GROS★★, M GROS★★, F Lamarche★★, Dom. LEROY★★★, Comte LIGER-BELAIR★★, MÉO-CAMUZET★★★, MONTILLE★★★, MUGNERET-Gibourg★★★, Georges NOËLLAT★★, Dom. de la ROMANÉE-CONTI★★★, E Rouget★★★. Best years: (2013) 12 11 10 09 **08 07 06 05 03 02 01 00 99 98 96 95 93 90**.

VOUGEOT AC *Côte de Nuits, Burgundy, France* Outside the walls of CLOS DE VOUGEOT there are only 11ha (27 acres) of Premier Cru and 5ha (12 acres) of other vines. Clos Blanc de Vougeot was first planted with white grapes in 1110. Best producers: Bertagna★, Chopin★★, C Clerget★, Hudelot-NOËLLAT★★, VOUGERAIE★★. Best years: (reds) (2013) 11 10 09 **08 07 06 05 03 02 99**.

DOM. DE LA VOUGERAIE *Côte de Nuits, Burgundy, France* An estate created by Jean-Claude BOISSET in 1999 out of the numerous vineyards that came with Burgundy merchant houses acquired during his rise to prominence. Wines have been generally outstanding, notably Clos Blanc de VOUGEOT★★★ white, and le MUSIGNY★★★ and BONNES-MARES★★★ reds. Best years: (reds) (2013) 12 11 10 09 **08 07 06** 05 **03 02**.

VOUVRAY AC *Loire Valley, France* Dry, medium-dry, sweet and sparkling wines from Chenin grapes east of Tours. The dry wines acquire beautifully rounded flavours after 6–8 years. Medium-dry wines, when well made from a single domaine, are worth aging for 20 years or more, but avoid cheap examples. Spectacular noble-rotted sweet wines produced when conditions are right. The fizz, Mousseux and Pétillant (bottled at lower pressure), is some of the LOIRE's best. Best producers: Aubuisières★★, Bourillon-Dorléans★★, S Brunet★★, V Carême★, Champalou★★, F CHIDAINE★★, CLOS NAUDIN/Foreau★★, la Fontainerie★, Gaudrelle★, Gautier★★, P Gendron★, HUET★★, Pichot★, F Pinon★★, Taille aux Loups★★/BLOT, Vigneau Chevreau★. Best years: (dry) (2013) 12 **11 10 08 07 06**; (sweet) 2011 **09 04 03 02 01 97 96 95 90 89**.

VOYAGER ESTATE *Margaret River, Western Australia* Impressive cellar-door complex. Stellar, oatmealy Chardonnay★★★, vibrant, zingy Sauvignon Blanc-Semillon★★★ and Cabernet Sauvignon-Merlot★★★ are regularly some of WESTERN AUSTRALIA's best. Shiraz★ and Sauvignon★ are good.

WACHAU *Niederösterreich, Austria* This stunning 1350ha (3335-acre) stretch of the Danube is Austria's top region for dry whites, from Riesling and Grüner Veltliner. Best producers: ALZINGER★★, J Donabaum★, F HIRTZBERGER★★★, Högl★★, Jamek★, KNOLL★★★, NIKOLAIHOF★★, F X PICHLER★★★, Rudi PICHLER★★, PRAGER★★★, Schmelz★★, Domäne Wachau★. Best years: (2013) 12 11 10 **09 08 07 06 05 04 02 01**.

WACHENHEIM *Pfalz, Germany* Wine village made famous by the BÜRKLIN-WOLF estate. Its best vineyards can produce rich yet beautifully balanced Rieslings. Best producers: BÜRKLIN-WOLF★★, MOSBACHER★, Karl Schaefer★, J L Wolf★. Best years: (2013) 12 **11 10 09 08 07 05 04**.

WAGRAM *Niederösterreich, Austria* 2450ha (6050-acre) wine region on both banks of the Danube, stretching north-west of Vienna toward St Pölten. Known until 2007 as Donauland, Wagram is the source of fine Grüner

Veltliners and a steadily improving band of red wines from Zweigelt and even Pinot Noir. **Best producers:** A Bauer★, Ehmoser★, K Fritsch★, Kolkmann, Leth★, Bernhard Ott★★, Schuster.

WAIHEKE ISLAND *North Island, New Zealand*   Island in Auckland harbour, now home to over 30 wineries. Hot, dry ripening conditions make high-quality Cabernet-based reds that sell for high prices. Chardonnay, Sauvignon and Pinot Gris are now appearing, together with commercial plantings of stunning Syrah and Viognier. **Best producers:** Destiny Bay★★, MAN O'WAR★★, Mudbrick★, Obsidian★, Passage Rock★, STONYRIDGE★★★, Te Whau★. **Best years:** (reds) (2013) 10 **08 07 05**.

WAITAKI *South Island, New Zealand* A small emerging area in North Otago. Marginal in terms of climate, with high risk of frost, but with free-draining stony soils that often have a high limestone content. The star variety is Pinot Noir – tight, edgy, often with impressive floral/fruit aromas and chalky minerality – but tangy Riesling and Pinot Gris are also high performers. **Best producers:** Forrest★, Ostler★, Pasquale, Valli★★.

WALKER BAY WO *South Africa*   Maritime district on the south coast, home to a mix of grape varieties, but the holy grail of most producers is Pinot Noir, with the hub of activity in the Hemel en Aarde (heaven and earth) valley. Also steely Sauvignon Blanc, minerally Chardonnay, refined Pinotage and intense Syrah, among others. **Best producers:** Alheit★, Ashbourne★, Ataraxia★★, Beaumont★, BOUCHARD FINLAYSON★★, Brunia★, Creation★, Crystallum★★, Dom. des Dieux★, HAMILTON RUSSELL★★, Hermanuspietersfontein★, La Vierge★, NEWTON JOHNSON★★, Whalehaven★. **Best years:** (Pinot Noir) 2013 **12 11 10 09 08 07 06 05 04**.

WALLA WALLA VALLEY AVA *Washington State, USA*   Walla Walla has over 100 of WASHINGTON's wineries; vineyard acreage, although less than 5% of the state total, has trebled since 1999 – and is still growing, but most development is actually over the state line in Oregon. No one seems to take much notice. New, north-facing, high-altitude SeVein development above Seven Hills could be Washington's most exciting new vineyard. **Best producers:** ABEJA★, CAYUSE★★, DOUBLEBACK★, DUNHAM★, FIGGINS★, L'ECOLE NO. 41★★, LEONETTI CELLAR★★★, LONG SHADOWS★, Northstar★, PEPPER BRIDGE WINERY★, Reininger★, Charles SMITH★, Spring Valley★, Waitsburg Cellars★, Waters★, WOODWARD CANYON★★.

WARRE'S *Port DOC, Douro, Portugal*   Part of the Symington group, with top-quality Vintage PORT★★★ and a fine 'off-vintage' port from Quinta da Cavadinha★★. LBV★★ is in the traditional, unfiltered style. Warrior★ is a reliable ruby and Otima a solid 10-year-old tawny; Otima★ 20-year-old is much better. **Best years:** (Vintage) 2011 (09) **07** 03 00 **97 94** 91 85 83 **80 77** 70 66 63; (Cavadinha) (2010) (06) **01** 99 98 96 95 92 90 88 82 78.

WARWICK *Stellenbosch WO, South Africa*   Warwick produces the complex Trilogy★★ BORDEAUX-style blend and a refined, fragrant Cabernet Franc★. The Three Cape Ladies★ red blend comprises Pinotage, Cabernet Sauvignon and Syrah. Whites include an unwooded Professor Black Sauvignon Blanc★, full-bodied, lightly

oaked Chardonnay★ and unoaked First Lady Chardonnay★. Also involved in Vilafonté★ project with American Zelma Long. Best years: (Trilogy) 2011 **10 09 08 07 06 05 04**.

WASHINGTON STATE *USA* The second-largest premium wine-producing state in the US (after California), with more than 750 wineries. The chief growing areas are in irrigated high desert, east of the Cascade Mountains, where the COLUMBIA VALLEY AVA encompasses the smaller AVAs of YAKIMA VALLEY, WALLA WALLA VALLEY, Wahluke Slope, Horse Heaven Hills, Rattlesnake Hills, Red Mountain, Columbia Gorge, Snipes Mountain, Naches Heights, Ancient Lakes and Lake Chelan. Although the heat is not as intense as in California, long summer days with extra hours of sunshine due to the northern latitude seem to increase the intensity of fruit flavours, resulting in red and white wines of great depth. Cabernets Sauvignon and Franc, Merlot, Syrah, Chardonnay, Semillon and Riesling can produce very good wines here. A new move toward focusing on single-vineyard flavours is welcome. Puget Sound AVA is in much damper, cooler conditions west of the Cascades, and makes small amounts of pretty light stuff.

WEGELER *Bernkastel, Mosel; Oestrich-Winkel, Rheingau, Germany* The Wegeler family's 2 estates are dedicated primarily to Riesling, and dry wines make up the bulk of production. The Wegelers' share of the legendary BERNKASTELer Doctor has been in the family since 1903. Whatever their style, the best wines merit ★★ and will develop well with 5 or more years of aging. Best years: (Mosel) (2013) 12 11 **10 09 08 07 06 05 04**.

WEHLEN *Mosel, Germany* Village whose steep Sonnenuhr vineyard produces some of Germany's most intense Rieslings. Best producers: Kerpen, Dr LOOSEN★★★, MOLITOR★★, J J PRÜM★★★, S A Prüm★, Max Ferd RICHTER★★, Studert-Prüm, Thanisch Müller-Burggraef, WEGELER★, Dr Weins-Prüm★. Best years: (2013) 12 11 **10 09 08 07 06 05 04 01**.

ROBERT WEIL *Kiedrich, Rheingau, Germany* Huge investment from Japanese drinks giant Suntory, coupled with Wilhelm Weil's devotion to quality, clearly paid off, showing particular flair with majestic sweet Auslese, Beerenauslese and Trockenbeerenauslese Rieslings★★★. Other styles are ★, sometimes ★★. Best years: (2013) 12 11 **10 09 08 07 06 05 04**.

WEINBACH *Alsace AC, Alsace, France* This Kaysersberg estate is run by the Faller family. The extensive range (which includes cuvées Théo, Ste-Catherine and Laurence) is complicated, with Théo★★ being the lightest; Laurence★ wines are from the Altenbourg locale, but include a Grand Cru Furstentum Gewurztraminer; many of the Ste-Catherine★★ bottlings come from the Grand Cru Schlossberg. The top dry wine is the Ste-Catherine Riesling Grand Cru Schlossberg L'Inédit★★★. Quintessence★★★ is an SGN from Pinot Gris or Gewurztraminer. All the wines are exceptionally balanced and, while delightful on release, can age for many years. Best years: (Grand Cru Riesling) (2013) 12 11 **10 09 08 07 05 04 02 01 00 99 98 97 96 95 94 93 92 90**.

WEISSBURGUNDER See PINOT BLANC.

WELSCHRIESLING Unrelated to the great Riesling of the Rhine, this grape makes some of the best sweet wines in Austria and, as Graševina, some serious, weighty dry whites in Croatia. It is highly esteemed in Hungary as Olasz Rizling. As Riesling Italico it has virtually disappeared in northern Italy.

WENDOUREE *Clare Valley, South Australia* Small winery making impressive, ageworthy reds★★ from paltry yields off its own very old Shiraz, Cabernet, Malbec and Mataro (Mourvèdre) vines, plus tiny amounts of sweet Muscat★. Some of Australia's best reds, they can, and do, age beautifully for 30 years or more. Best years: (reds) (2013) 12 10 08 06 05 04 03 02 01 99 98 96 95 94 92 91 90 86 83 82 81 80 78 76 75.

WESTERN AUSTRALIA Warm-climate vineyards were established near Perth nearly 200 years ago; high-quality, cool-climate viticulture has been established in the state's south-west for just over 40 years, but Western Australia punches well above its weight. With just over 4% of Australia's grape crush it produces about 20% of Australia's premium wines. Thanks to the influence of the Roaring Forties, rainfall is more consistent and poor vintages rarer than in other parts of the country. With more than 400 producers, the focus of attention is on the GREAT SOUTHERN, MARGARET RIVER, Geographe and PEMBERTON.

HERMANN J WIEMER *Finger Lakes AVA, New York State, USA* Wiemer's family has 300 years' experience of winemaking in the MOSEL, so working with local Riesling pioneer Dr Konstantin FRANK was natural before he established his own winery in 1979. Fine sweeter styles (Auslese-style Late Harvest Riesling★★), though in recent years dry wines have shown more pizzazz. Good sparkling wines. Wiemer has handed the reins over to winemaker Fred Merwarth; the wines continue to excel.

WIEN *Austria* 560ha (1380-acre) wine region within the city limits of Wien (Vienna). The wines are mostly consumed young in the growers' Heurigen (wine inns). The 'Gemischter Satz' tradition of field-blend vineyards is being revived by many growers. Best producers: Christ, Cobenzl, Edlmoser, Mayer★, WIENINGER★★, Zahel. Best years: (2013) 12 11 10 09 07.

WIENINGER *Stammersdorf, Wien, Austria* Fritz Wieninger has risen above the parochial standards of many Viennese growers to offer a range of elegant, well-crafted wines from Chardonnay and Pinot Noir. The best range is often the Select★★, the pricier Grand Select★ being sometimes over-oaked. Also brilliant Riesling and 'Gemischter Satz' from the renowned Nussberg★★ vineyard. Best years: (2013) 12 11 10 09 07.

WILLAKENZIE ESTATE *Willamette Valley AVA, Oregon, USA* Bernard Lacroute purchased a cattle ranch in 1991 just outside Yamhill, and named the property after the ancient Willakenzie sedimentary soil. Eleven different clones of Pinot Noir are planted and estate-bottled Pinot Noirs from individual sites are the primary focus: Terres Basses★ and Triple Black Slopes★ are powerful long-aging styles. There is a small amount of rich Pinot Gris★ made from estate fruit and some delightful, rare, Pinot Meunier★ reds. Best years: (Pinot Noir) (2012) 11 10 09 08.

WILLAMETTE VALLEY AVA *Oregon, USA* Wet winters, generally dry summers, and a good chance of long, cool autumn days provide sound growing conditions for Pinot Noir, Pinot Gris and Chardonnay. The volcanic Dundee Hills is the most important sub-AVA; others are Yamhill-Carlton, McMinnville, and particularly the cooler Eola-Amity Hills, Ribbon Ridge and Chehalem Mountains. Best producers: ADELSHEIM★, ARGYLE★, BEAUX FRERES★★, BERGSTROM★★, Bethel Heights★★, BRITTAN★, Brooks★, Chehalem★, Cristom★★, DOMAINE DROUHIN★, DOMAINE SERENE★★, ELK COVE★, Evesham Wood★, Patricia GREEN★, PONZI★,

ST INNOCENT★, Shea Wine Cellars, Sineann★, Sokol Blosser, SOTER★★, WILLAKENZIE ESTATE★, Ken Wright★★. Best years: (reds) 2012 **09 08**.

WILLIAMS SELYEM *Russian River Valley AVA, California, USA* Exemplary Pinot Noirs (Rochioli Riverblock★★, Westside Road Neighbors★★ – can be ★★★) from various regions, including RUSSIAN RIVER VALLEY, SONOMA COAST and ANDERSON VALLEY. Zins are good too. Best years: (Pinot Noir) **2012 10 09 08 07 06 05 04 03 02 01 00 99 98**.

WIND GAP *Sonoma County, California, USA* Wind Gap sources grapes from vineyards across California that are influenced by wind gaps in the coastal hills. The wines are refreshingly low in alcohol and light on oak. Along with lovely Chardonnay★★ and vibrant single-vineyard Pinot Noir★★ from the SANTA CRUZ MOUNTAINS and Sonoma County, the winery also makes Grenache, Trousseau Gris and Syrah.

WINNINGEN *Mosel, Germany* Winningen's steep slopes, particularly the Ühlen and Röttgen sites, can produce excellent Rieslings, especially in a rich dry style. Best producers: Fries, Heddesdorff, HEYMANN-LÖWENSTEIN★★, Knebel★, Richter.

WIRRA WIRRA *McLaren Vale, South Australia* Outstanding producer with fine ADELAIDE HILLS whites – well-balanced and tangy Sauvignon Blanc★ and Riesling★ and tight, fine yet creamy Chardonnay★★ – and soft MCLAREN VALE reds led by delicious The Angelus (Dead Ringer outside Australia) Cabernet★★, chocolaty RSW Shiraz★★, rich, balanced Catapult Shiraz-Viognier★ and stylish, concentrated Woodhenge Shiraz★. Best years: (RSW Shiraz) 2013 12 10 **09 08** 06 05 04 03 02 01 98 96.

WISTON *West Sussex, England* Newcomer planted in 2005 and now producing excellent sparkling wines with ex-NYETIMBER winemaker Dermot Sugrue. Wines tend toward the dry side, but can be very good: South Downs Brut, Blanc de Blancs, Blanc de Noirs, Rosé★★.

WITHER HILLS *Marlborough, South Island, New Zealand* Large winery now owned by Lion Nathan breweries and struggling to hold on to its cult reputation created by founder Brent Marris (departed in 2007 to run his Marisco Vineyards/'The Ned'). Sauvignon Blanc now (since 2012) returning to drier style and single-vineyard Rarangi★ can be excellent. Chardonnay★ and Pinot Noir★ still do their best to maintain the original Wither Hills style. Best years: (Chardonnay) (2013) **12 10 09** 07 06.

WITTMANN *Westhofen, Rheinhessen, Germany* Inspiring, family-run bio-dynamic estate, succeeding equally with bold dry Rieslings★★, Chardonnay★★, Weissburgunder★★ (Pinot Blanc), and voluptuous Trockenbeerenauslese★★★. Best years: (2013) 12 11 10 **09 08 07 05**.

WÖLFFER ESTATE *Long Island, New York State, USA* One of the few wineries in LONG ISLAND's Hamptons, Wölffer created a sensation in the early 2000s when it released a 'Premier Cru' Merlot priced at a lofty $100. It is good – but overshadowed by the more modestly priced Estate Selection Merlot★, a rich Pinot Gris and a spritely rosé. Winemaker Roman Roth also has his own label, The Grapes of Roth, with an excellent MOSEL-style Riesling and snappy Cabernet Franc.

WOODWARD CANYON *Walla Walla Valley AVA, Washington State, USA* Big, barrel-fermented Chardonnays★ were the trademark wines for many years, but today the focus is on reds, led by Artist Series★★ Cabernet Sauvignon and Old Vines★★ Cabernet Sauvignon. Merlot★ is rich, velvety and perfumed. Good Cabernet Franc-based Estate Reserve★ and red BORDEAUX-style blend Charbonneau★. Best years: (top Cabernet Sauvignon) (2012) 11 10 **09 08**.

KEN WRIGHT CELLARS *Willamette Valley AVA, Oregon, USA* Ken Wright produces a dozen succulent single-vineyard Pinot Noirs. Now cutting back on the new oak and extraction, they range from good to ethereal, led by the Carter★★, Savoya★★, Guadalupe★★, McCrone★★ and Shea★★. Fine Chardonnay★★ and a crisp Freedom Hill Vineyard Pinot Blanc★, made in very small quantities. Best years: (Pinot Noir) 2012 11 10 **09 08**.

WÜRTTEMBERG *Germany* 11,360ha (28,070-acre) cooperative-dominated region centred on the river Neckar. 70% of the wine made is red, and the best comes from Lemberger (Blaufränkisch) or Spätburgunder (Pinot Noir) grapes. Massive yields often result in pallid wines, especially from the locally popular Trollinger grape. A few top steep sites are now producing perfumed reds and racy Riesling. Best years: (reds) (2013) (12) 11 **10 09 08 07**.

WÜRZBURG *Franken, Germany* The centre of FRANKEN wines. Some Rieslings can be excellent, but the real star is Silvaner. Best producers: Bürgerspital★, JULIUSSPITAL★★, Reiss, Staatlicher Hofkeller, Weingut am Stein★. Best years: (2013) 12 11 **10 09 08 07 06**.

WYNNS *Coonawarra, South Australia* Part of the giant Treasury Wine Estates, but Wynns' name is still synonymous with COONAWARRA. Investment in vineyard rejuvenation has paid off handsomely and the Wynns reds are now among Australia's finest reds. Top-end John Riddoch Cabernet Sauvignon★★★ and Michael Shiraz★★ show restraint and elegance: the Black Label Cabernet Sauvignon★★ struts a 50-year pedigree with dignity, while the Shiraz★ offers honest quality at a fair price. Each year Wynns selects a premium single-vineyard red (usually Cabernet, invariably ★★★) to show Coonawarra's potential. Also two V&A Lane reds★, attractive Chardonnay★ and delightful Riesling★. Best years: (John Riddoch) 2013 12 10 09 08 **06 05 04 99 98 96 94 91 90 88 86**.

XAREL-LO By far the most characterful, structured member of the classic Cava trio, this Catalan grape now dominates blends in top-end Cavas, some of them varietal, and is increasingly vinified as an unfortified white. Best producers: Gramona★★, Recaredo★★★.

YABBY LAKE *Mornington Peninsula, Victoria, Australia* Caused a sensation at the Melbourne Show in 2013 by winning Australia's most prestigious red wine trophy with a Pinot Noir (Yabby Lake Block 1) for the first time. Block 1, Block 2, Block 6 – these wines are chosen row by row and made into some of MORNINGTON PENINSULA's most expressive, scented and memorable Chardonnays★★★ and Pinot Noirs★★★. Single Vineyard★★ releases are also packed with flavour and personality. Also very tasty Pinot Gris★ and Syrah★. Red Claw is entry-level label. Also owns Heathcote Estate.

BODEGA YACOCHUYA *Salta, Argentina* A joint project formed in 1989 between the winemaker, philosopher and poet Arnaldo Etchart and enologist Michel Rolland. Yacochuya makes some of Argentina's most iconic, in-demand wines. The Yacochuya★★ (Malbec), when below 15% alcohol, is dark, ripe and complex, while the San Pedro de Yacochuya★ red blend never fails to impress. The Torrontés★ is also a delight.

YAKIMA VALLEY AVA *Washington State, USA* Important valley within the much larger COLUMBIA VALLEY AVA, encompassing top-notch Red Mountain AVA. Chardonnay, Merlot and Cabernet Sauvignon dominate plantings. More than 60 wineries. Top hop gardens too. **Best producers:** Airfield, Chinook★, DELILLE CELLARS★★, HEDGES★, OWEN ROE★, Powers.

YALUMBA *Barossa Valley, South Australia* Robert Hill Smith has taken his distinguished family firm to the pinnacle of Australian winemaking. There's an increasingly wide range under the Yalumba label, as well as a labyrinthine group under the banner of Hill Smith Family Vineyards. The latter includes Heggies (minerally Riesling★★, plump Merlot★★, opulent Viognier★★), Hill Smith Estate (Sauvignon Blanc★), Pewsey Vale (Riesling★★★) and TASMANIA's Jansz (vintage★★, non-vintage★). Flagship reds are The Signature Cabernet-Shiraz★★ (sometimes ★★★), Octavius Shiraz★★, Tri-Centenary Grenache★★ and The Menzies Cabernet★★, and all age well. Bush Vine Grenache★★ (sometimes ★★★), Virgilius Viognier★★ and Shiraz-Viognier★ are excellent too. High-quality Y Series varietals★ (sometimes ★★) are among Australia's finest quaffers. Also enjoyable Running with Bulls Tempranillo, Redbank, Mawson's, Oxford Landing (Sauvignon★) and Angas Brut. Museum Reserve fortifieds (Muscat★★) are excellent, but rare. **Best years:** (The Signature) (2012) (10) 09 08 **06 05 04 03 02 01 00 99 98 97 96 95 93**.

YARRA VALLEY *Victoria, Australia* Cool-climate Yarra is asking to be judged as Australia's best Pinot Noir region, but superb Chardonnay, fascinating Cabernet-Merlot and small amounts of world-class Shiraz are often more exciting. Fizz is also very good. A move toward single-vineyard wines is producing Yarra's most enthralling wines yet. Vineyards are now spreading to every corner of the valley, with much of the best fruit coming from less well-known zones: Upper Yarra, Kangaroo Ground, Denton and St Andrews. **Best producers:** Arthur's Creek★, Carlei★, COLDSTREAM HILLS★ (Reserve Chardonnay★★), DE BORTOLI★★, Diamond Valley★★, DOMAINE CHANDON/Green Point★★, Gembrook Hill★★, GIANT STEPS★★, Hoddles Creek★, JAMSHEED★★, Luke Lambert★★, Leayton Estate★, Mac Forbes★, Timo Mayer★★, Métier, MOUNT MARY★★, OAKRIDGE★★★, Payten & Jones★★, TARRAWARRA★★, Thick as Thieves★★, Toolangi★, The Wanderer★, Wantirna Estate★, Wedgetail★, Yarrabank★, Yarra Yering★★, Yeringberg★, Yering Station★★.

YATIR *Judean Hills, Israel* Situated in the Negev Desert, among Bedouin and camels, the vineyards in Israel's largest forest are up to 900m (3000ft) altitude. Flagship Yatir Forest★★, a BORDEAUX blend, is deep and supple, with ripe dark fruit backed by Mediterranean herbs. Full-flavoured Cabernet Sauvignon★, wild, spicy Syrah★, powerful Petit Verdot★ and delicate Viognier. **Best years:** (reds) 2010 09 08 **07 06 05 04**.

YEALANDS *Marlborough, South Island, New Zealand* Ambitious new winery with around 1000ha (2470 acres) of vineyards in the AWATERE VALLEY. Confidently zesty Sauvignon Blanc★, pretty Gewurztraminer, succulent Pinot Gris★, tangy dry Riesling and a light, aromatic Pinot Noir. Also some experimental varieties such as Grüner Veltliner and Tempranillo, both showing form. Also owns The Crossings and Crossroads brands. **Best years:** (Sauvignon Blanc) (2013) **12 11 10 09**.

YELLOWTAIL *Riverina, New South Wales, Australia* Yellowtail, Australia's fastest-growing export brand ever, has made the RIVERINA family winery, Casella, a major world player. Artfully crafted but overly sweet wines.

CH. D'YQUEM★★★ *Sauternes AC, 1er Cru Supérieur, Bordeaux, France* Often rated the most sublime sweet wine in the world. Despite a large vineyard (100ha/250 acres), production is tiny. Only fully noble-rotted grapes are picked, often berry by berry, and low yield means each vine produces only a glass of wine! This precious liquid is then fermented in new oak barrels and left to mature for 30 months before bottling. It is one of the world's most expensive wines, in constant demand because of its richness and exotic flavours. No Yquem was made in 2012. A dry white, Ygrec, is made most years. In 1999 LVMH, the luxury goods group, won a takeover battle with the Lur-Saluces family, owners for 406 years. **Best years:** 2011 10 09 **08 07 06 05 04 03 02 01 00 99 98 97 96 95 94 90 89 88 86 83 81 79 76 75 71 70 67**.

ZILLIKEN *Saarburg, Mosel, Germany* Estate specializing in steely Rieslings★★ (Auslese, Eiswein often ★★★) from the Saarburger Rausch. **Best years:** (2013) 12 11 10 **09 08 07 06 05 04**.

ZIND-HUMBRECHT *Alsace AC, Alsace, France* Olivier Humbrecht is a leading biodynamicist. Wines from 4 Grand Cru sites – Rangen, Goldert, Hengst and Brand – are superlative (Riesling★★★, Gewurztraminer★★★, Pinot Gris★★★, Muscat★★), as are wines from specific non-Grand Cru vineyards such as Clos Windsbuhl★★ and Clos Jebsal★★. Vendange Tardive and Sélection de Grains Nobles wines are almost invariably of ★★★ quality. Even basic Sylvaners★ and Pinot Blancs★★ are fine. Wines often have some residual sugar, but Olivier says that's just how they naturally turn out. **Best years:** (Grand Cru Riesling) (2013) (12) 11 10 09 08 07 05 04 03 02 01 00 99 98 97 96 95.

ZINFANDEL CALIFORNIA's versatile red grape can make big, juicy, briary fruit-packed reds – often farmed from very old vines – or insipid, sweetish 'blush' labelled as White Zinfandel, or even late-harvest dessert wine. Some notable Zinfandel is now made in Australia and South Africa. Best producers: (California) Bianchi, Brown★★, Cline★★, CHÂTEAU MONTELENA,

Dashe★★, DRY CREEK VINEYARD★★, DUTTON GOLDFIELD★★, Gary FARRELL★★, HARTFORD★★, Mariah★, Martinelli★★, Michael-David (Earthquake), NALLE★★, Oakville Winery, Peachy Canyon, Preston★, Rafanelli★★, RAVENSWOOD★, RIDGE★★★, Rosenblum★★, Saddleback★★, St Francis★★, SEGHESIO★★, Trinitas★★, TURLEY★★; (Australia) CAPE MENTELLE★★, Kangarilla Road, Nepenthe★★, Smidge, Tscharke. See also PRIMITIVO DI MANDURIA.

ZORZAL *Mendoza, Argentina* The irrepressible Michelini brothers continue to innovate in the region of Gualtallary, high in the UCO VALLEY. The thrilling new Eggo★★ (unoaked, fermented in concrete 'eggs') range offers stunning purity. Gran Terroir Malbec★★ and Pinot Noir★★ are very good. Entry-level Terroir Único range includes good Sauvignon Blanc★ and Malbec★.

ZUCCARDI *Mendoza, Argentina* The Zuccardi family have forged a global reputation for the unexpected and delicious. The recently revamped Zuccardi 'Q'★ varietals (Tempranillo★★) are fine and pure. Red blend Zeta★ (sometimes★★) improves with every vintage – and the new Emma Zuccardi★★ (Bonarda) and red blend Tito Zuccardi★★ promise to thrill. Some of Argentina's best sparklers, as well as tasty oddballs Caladoc and Ancellotta reds. New vineyards in the UCO VALLEY are increasingly providing the core of fruit for the high-end wines, such as Aluvional★★ (Malbec). Santa Julia brand delivers top-value varietals.

GLOSSARY OF WINE TERMS

AC/AOC/AOP (APPELLATION D'ORIGINE CONTRÔLÉE/PROTÉGÉE)
The top category of French wines, defined by regulations covering vineyard yields, grape varieties, geographical boundaries, alcohol content and production method. Guarantees origin and style of a wine, but not its quality. *See* page 24.

ACID/ACIDITY
Naturally present in grapes and essential to wine, providing balance and stability, a refreshing tang in white wines and appetizing grip in reds.

ADEGA
Portuguese for winery.

AGING
An alternative term for maturation.

ALCOHOLIC CONTENT
The alcoholic strength of wine, expressed as a percentage of the total volume of the wine. Typically in the range of 7–15%.

ALCOHOLIC FERMENTATION
The process whereby yeasts, natural or added, convert the grape sugars into alcohol (ethyl alcohol, or ethanol) and carbon dioxide.

AMONTILLADO
Traditionally dry style of sherry. *See* Jerez y Manzanilla in main A–Z.

ANBAUGEBIET
German for growing region; these names will appear on labels of all QbA and QmP wines. There are 13 Anbaugebiete: Ahr, Baden, Franken, Hessische Bergstrasse, Mittelrhein, Mosel, Nahe, Pfalz, Rheingau, Rheinhessen, Saale-Unstrut, Sachsen and Württemberg.

AUSBRUCH
Austrian Prädikat category used for sweet wines from the town of Rust.

AUSLESE
German and Austrian Prädikat category meaning that the grapes were 'selected' for their higher ripeness.

AVA (AMERICAN VITICULTURAL AREA)
System of appellations of origin for US wines.

AZIENDA AGRICOLA
Italian for estate or farm. It also indicates wine made from grapes grown by the proprietor.

BARREL AGING
Time spent maturing in wood, usually oak, during which wine takes on flavours from the wood.

BARREL FERMENTATION
Oak barrels may be used for fermentation instead of stainless steel to give a rich, oaky flavour to the wine.

BARRIQUE
The *barrique bordelaise* is the traditional Bordeaux oak barrel of 225 litres (50 gallons) capacity.

BAUMÉ
A scale measuring must weight (the amount of sugar in grape juice) to estimate potential alcohol content.

BEERENAUSLESE
German and Austrian Prädikat category applied to wines made from 'individually selected' berries (i.e. grapes) affected by noble rot (*Edelfäule* in German). The wines are rich and sweet. Beerenauslese wines are only produced in the best years in Germany, but in Austria they are a regular occurrence.

BEREICH
German for region or district within a wine region or *Anbaugebiet*. Bereichs tend to be large, and the use of a Bereich name, such as Bereich Bingen, without qualification is seldom an indication of quality – in most cases, quite the reverse.

BIODYNAMIC VITICULTURE
This approach works with the movement of the planets and cosmic forces to achieve health and balance in the soil and in the vine. Vines are treated with infusions of mineral, animal and plant materials, applied in homeopathic quantities. An increasing number of growers are turning to biodynamism, with some astonishing results, but it is labour-intensive and generally confined to smaller estates.

BOTTLE SIZES

CHAMPAGNE

Magnum	1.5 litres	2 bottles
Jeroboam	3 litres	4 bottles
Rehoboam	4.5 litres	6 bottles
Methuselah	6 litres	8 bottles
Salmanazar	9 litres	12 bottles
Balthazar	12 litres	16 bottles
Nebuchadnezzar	15 litres	20 bottles

BORDEAUX

Magnum	1.5 litres	2 bottles
Marie-Jeanne	2.25 litres	3 bottles
Double-magnum	3 litres	4 bottles
Jeroboam	4.5 litres	6 bottles
Imperial	6 litres	8 bottles

BLANC DE BLANCS
White wine made from one or more white grape varieties. Used especially for sparkling wines; in Champagne, denotes wine made entirely from the Chardonnay grape.

BLANC DE NOIRS
White wine made from black grapes only – the juice is separated from the skins to avoid extracting any colour. Most often seen in Champagne, where it describes wine made from Pinot Noir and/or Pinot Meunier grapes.

BLENDING
The art of mixing together wines of different origin, style or age, often to balance out acidity, weight etc. Winemakers often use the term *assemblage*.

BODEGA
Spanish for winery.

BOTRYTIS
See noble rot.

BRUT
French term for dry sparkling wines, especially Champagne.

CARBONIC MACERATION
Winemaking method used to produce fresh fruity reds for drinking young. Whole (uncrushed) bunches of grapes are fermented in closed containers – a process that extracts lots of fruit and colour, but little tannin.

CHAMPAGNE METHOD
Traditional method used for nearly all of the world's finest sparkling wines. A second fermentation takes place in the bottle, producing carbon dioxide which, kept in solution under pressure, gives the wine its fizz.

CHAPTALIZATION
Legal addition of sugar during fermentation to raise a wine's alcoholic strength. More necessary in cool climates where lack of sun produces insufficient natural sugar in the grape.

CHARMAT
See cuve close.

CHÂTEAU
French for castle: widely used in France to describe any wine estate, large or small.

CHIARETTO
Italian for a rosé wine of very light pink colour from around Lake Garda.

CLARET
English for red Bordeaux wines, from the French *clairet*, which was traditionally used to describe a lighter style of red Bordeaux.

CLARIFICATION
Term covering any wine-making process (such as filtering or fining) that involves the removal of solid matter either from the must or the wine.

CLONE
Strain of grape species. The term is usually taken to mean laboratory-produced, virus-free clones, selected to produce higher or lower quantity, or selected for resistance to frost or disease.

CLOS
French for a walled vineyard – as in Burgundy's Clos de Vougeot – also commonly incorporated into the names of estates (e.g. Clos des Papes), whether they are walled or not.

COLD FERMENTATION
Long, slow fermentation at low temperature to extract maximum freshness from the grapes. Crucial for whites in hot climates.

COLHEITA
Aged tawny port from a single vintage. *See* Port in main A–Z.

COMMUNE
A French village and its surrounding area or parish.

CO-OPERATIVE
In a co-operative cellar, growers who are members bring their grapes for vinification and bottling under a collective label. In terms of quantity, the French wine industry is dominated by co-ops. They often use less workaday titles, such as Caves des Vignerons, Producteurs Réunis, Union des Producteurs or Cellier des Vignerons.

CORKED/CORKY
Wine fault derived from a cork which has become contaminated, usually with Trichloroanisole or TCA. The mouldy, stale smell is unmistakable. Nothing to do with pieces of cork in the wine.

COSECHA
Spanish for vintage.

CÔTE
French word for a slope or hillside, which is where many, but not all, of the country's best vineyards are found.

CRÉMANT
French term for traditional-method sparkling wine from Alsace, Bordeaux, Burgundy, Die, Jura, Limoux, Loire and Luxembourg.

CRIANZA
Spanish term for the youngest official category of oak-matured wine. A red Crianza wine must have had at least 2 years' aging (1 in oak, 1 in bottle) before sale, a white or rosé, 1 year.

CRU
French for growth, meaning a specific plot of land or particular estate. In Burgundy, growths are divided into Grands (great) and Premiers (first) Crus, and apply solely to the actual land. In

Champagne the same terms are used for whole villages. In Bordeaux there are various hierarchical levels of Cru referring to estates rather than their vineyards. In Italy the term is used frequently, in an unofficial way, to indicate a single-vineyard or special-selection wine.

CRU BOURGEOIS
Term for a group of châteaux (over 200) in the 8 appellations of Bordeaux's Médoc, ranked below the Crus Classés (Classed Growths) and revised annually after official tastings.

CRU CLASSÉ
The Classed Growths are the aristocracy of Bordeaux, ennobled by the Classifications of 1855 (for the Médoc, Barsac and Sauternes), 1955, 1969, 1986, 1996, 2006 and 2012 (for St-Émilion) and 1953 and 1959 (for Graves). Curiously, Pomerol has never been classified. The modern classifications are more reliable than the 1855 version, which was based solely on the price of the wines at the time of the Great Exhibition in Paris, but in terms of prestige the 1855 Classification remains the most important. With the exception of a single alteration in 1973, when Ch. Mouton-Rothschild was elevated to First Growth status, the list has not changed since 1855. It certainly needs revising.

CUVE CLOSE
A bulk process used to produce inexpensive sparkling wines. The second fermentation, which produces the bubbles, takes place in tank rather than in the bottle (as in the superior Traditional Method). Also called Charmat.

CUVÉE
French for the contents of a single vat or tank, but

usually indicates a wine blended from either different grape varieties or the best barrels of wine.

DEGORGEMENT
Stage in the production of Champagne-method wines when the sediment, collected in the neck of the bottle during *remuage*, is removed.

DEMI-SEC
French for medium-dry.

DO/DOP
Spanish quality wine category, regulating origin and production methods. *See* page 38.

DOC
Italian quality wine category, regulating origin, grape varieties, yield and production methods. *See* page 31.

DOC/DOP
Portugal's top regional wine classification. *See* page 39.

DOCA
Spanish quality wine category, intended to be one step up from DO. *See* page 38.

DOCG
The top tier of the Italian classification system. *See* page 31.

DOMAINE
French term for wine estate.

DOSAGE
A sugar and wine mixture added to sparkling wine after *dégorgement* which affects how sweet or dry it will be.

EDELZWICKER
Blended wine from Alsace, usually bland.

EINZELLAGE
German for an individual vineyard site which is generally farmed by several growers. The name is preceded on the label by that of the village: for example, the Wehlener

Sonnenuhr is the Sonnenuhr vineyard in Wehlen. The mention of a particular site should signify a superior wine.

EISWEIN
Rare, chiefly German and Austrian, late-harvested wine made by picking the grapes and pressing them while frozen. This concentrates the sweetness of the grape as most of the liquid is removed as ice. *See also* Icewine.

ERSTE LAGE
In Germany's Mosel, this term is used to indicate outstanding sites.

ERSTES GEWÄCHS
An official classification used in the Rheingau in Germany. Top sites were chosen by a kind of popular vote. Growers tend to use the label only for their best wines. *See also* Grosses Gewächs.

ESCOLHA
Portuguese for selection.

EXTRACTION
Refers to the extraction of colour, tannins and flavour from the grapes during and after fermentation. There are various ways in which extraction can be manipulated by the winemaker, but over-extraction leads to imbalance.

FEINHERB
Disliking the term Halb-trocken, some producers prefer to use Feinherb. No legal definition but usually applies to wines with 9–25g per litre of residual sugar.

FILTERING
Removal of yeasts, solids and any impurities from a wine before bottling.

FINING
Method of clarifying wine by adding a coagulant (e.g. egg whites, isinglass) to remove soluble particles such as proteins and excessive tannins.

FINO
The lightest, freshest style of sherry. *See* Jerez y Manzanilla in main A–Z.

FLOR
A film of yeast which forms on the surface of fino wines (and some other wines) in the barrel, preventing oxidation and imparting a tangy, dry flavour.

FLYING WINEMAKER
Term coined in the late 1980s to describe enologists, many Australian-trained, brought in to improve the quality of wines in many underperforming wine regions.

FORTIFIED WINE
Wine which has high-alcohol grape spirit added, usually before the initial fermentation is completed, thereby preserving sweetness.

FRIZZANTE
Italian for semi-sparkling wine.

GARAGE WINE
See vin de garage.

GARRAFEIRA
Portuguese term for wine from an outstanding vintage, with 0.5% more alcohol than the minimum required, and 2 years' aging in vat or barrel followed by 1 year in bottle for reds, and 6 months of each for whites. Also used by merchants for their best blended and aged wines. Use of the term is in decline as producers opt for the more readily recognized Reserva as an alternative on the label.

GRAN RESERVA
Top category of Spanish wines from a top vintage, with at least 5 years' aging (2 of them in cask) for reds and 4 for whites.

GRAND CRU
French for great growth. Supposedly the best vineyard sites in Alsace, Burgundy, Champagne and parts of Bordeaux – and should produce the most exciting wines.

GROSSES GEWÄCHS/GG
A vineyard classification in Germany, devised by the VDP growers' association and now widely adopted. Wines must meet both quality and stylistic criteria: essentially for Riesling, dry and very sweet wines.

GROSSLAGE
German term for a grouping of vineyards. Some are not too big, and have the advantage of allowing small amounts of higher QmP wines to be made from the grapes from several vineyards. But sometimes the use of vast Grosslage names (e.g. Niersteiner Gutes Domtal) deceives consumers into believing they are buying something special. Top estates have agreed not to use Gross-lage names on their labels.

HALBTROCKEN
German for medium dry. In Germany and Austria medium-dry wine has 9–18g per litre of residual sugar, though sparkling wine is allowed up to 50g per litre. *See* Feinherb.

ICEWINE
A speciality of Canada, produced from juice squeezed from ripe grapes that have frozen on the vine. *See also* Eiswein.

IGT
Italian classification of regional wines. Both premium and everyday wines may share the same appellation. *See* page 31.

KABINETT
Term used for the lowest level of QmP wines in Germany.

LANDWEIN
German or Austrian 'country' wine. The wine must have a territorial definition and may be chaptalized to give it more alcohol.

LATE HARVEST
See Vendange Tardive.

LAYING DOWN
The storing of wine which will improve with age.

LEES
Sediment – dead yeast cells, grape pips (seeds), pulp and tartrates – thrown by wine during fermentation and left behind after racking. Some wines are left on the fine lees for as long as possible to take on extra flavour.

MACERATION
Important winemaking process for red wines whereby colour, flavour and/or tannin are extracted from grape skins before, during or after fermentation. The period lasts from a few days to several weeks.

MALOLACTIC FERMENTATION
Secondary fermentation whereby harsh malic acid is converted into mild lactic acid and carbon dioxide. Normal in red wines but often prevented in whites to preserve a fresh, fruity taste.

MANZANILLA
The tangiest style of sherry, similar to fino. *See* Jerez y Manzanilla in main A–Z.

MATURATION
Term for the beneficial aging of wine.

MERITAGE
American term for red or white wines made from a blend of Bordeaux grape varieties.

MESOCLIMATE
The climate of a specific geographical area, be it a vineyard or simply a hillside or valley.

MIDI
A loose geographical term,

virtually synonymous with Languedoc-Roussillon, covering the vast, sunbaked area of southern France between the Pyrenees and the Rhône Valley.

MOELLEUX

French for soft or mellow, used to describe sweet or medium-sweet wines, particularly in the Loire.

MOUSSEUX

French for sparkling wine.

MUST

The mixture of grape juice, skins, pips and pulp produced after crushing (but prior to completion of fermentation), which will eventually become wine.

MUST WEIGHT

An indicator of the sugar content of juice – and therefore the ripeness of grapes.

NATURAL WINES

Philosophical movement originating in France and subsequently catching on in Italy and elsewhere as a counterpoint to the mass of 'industrial' wine. (Artisan) members seek to bring out the true expression of the soil 'naturally', i.e. by minimal intervention both in the vineyard and in the winery, notably without the addition of sulphur dioxide. This process has yet to be made certifiable so is left to the producer to interpret, resulting in a broad range of quality, from the exceptional to vinegar.

NÉGOCIANT

French term for a merchant who buys and sells wine. A *négociant-éléveur* is a merchant who buys, makes, ages and sells wine.

NEW WORLD

When used as a geographical term, New World includes the Americas, South Africa, Australia and New Zealand. By extension, it is also a term used to describe the clean, fruity, upfront style now in evidence all over the world, but pioneered in the USA and Australia.

NOBLE ROT

(*Botrytis cinerea*) Fungus which, when it attacks ripe white grapes, shrivels the fruit and intensifies their sugar while adding a distinctive flavour. A vital factor in creating many of the world's finest sweet wines, such as Sauternes and Trockenbeerenauslese.

OAK

The wood used almost exclusively to make barrels for fermenting and aging fine wines. It adds flavours such as vanilla, and tannins; the newer the wood, the greater the impact.

OECHSLE

German scale measuring must weight (sugar content).

OLOROSO

The darkest, most heavily fortified style of sherry. *See* Jerez & Manzanilla in main A–Z.

OXIDATION

Over-exposure of wine to air, causing loss of fruit and flavour. Slight oxidation, such as occurs through the wood of a barrel or during racking, is part of the aging process and, in wines of sufficient structure, enhances flavour and complexity.

PASSITO

Italian term for wine made from dried grapes. The result is usually a sweet wine with a raisiny intensity of fruit. The drying process is called *appassimento. See also* Moscato Passito di Pantelleria, Recioto della Valpolicella, Recioto di Soave and Vin Santo in main A–Z.

PERLWEIN

German for a lightly sparkling wine.

PÉTILLANT

French for a lightly sparkling wine.

PHYLLOXERA

The vine aphid *Phylloxera vastatrix* attacks vine roots. It devastated vineyards around the world in the late 1800s soon after it arrived from America. Since then, the vulnerable *Vitis vinifera* has generally been grafted on to vinously inferior, but phylloxera-resistant, American rootstocks.

PRÄDIKAT

Grades defining quality wines in Germany and Austria. These are (in ascending order) Kabinett (not considered as Prädikat in Austria), Spätlese, Auslese, Beerenauslese, the Austrian-only category Ausbruch, and Trockenbeerenauslese. Strohwein and Eiswein are also Prädikat wines.

PRÄDIKATSWEIN

A higher quality category than QbA, with controlled yields and no sugar addition. QmP covers 6 levels based on the ripeness of the grapes: *see* Prädikat.

PREMIER CRU

First Growth: the top quality classification in parts of Bordeaux, but second to Grand Cru in Burgundy. Used in Champagne to designate vineyards just below Grand Cru.

PRIMEUR

French term for a young wine, often released for sale within a few weeks of the harvest. Beaujolais Nouveau is the best-known example.

QBA (QUALITÄTSWEIN BESTIMMTER ANBAUGEBIETE)

German for quality wine from designated regions. Sugar can be added to increase the alcohol content. Usually pretty ordinary, but from top estates this category offers excellent value. In Austria *Qualitätswein* is equivalent to German QbA.

QMP (QUALITÄTSWEIN MIT PRÄDIKAT)
The old (pre-2007) term for Prädikatswein.

QUINTA
Portuguese for farm or estate.

RACKING
Gradual clarification of wine: the wine is transferred from one barrel or container to another, leaving the lees behind.

RANCIO
Fortified wine deliberately exposed to the effects of oxidation, found mainly in Languedoc-Roussillon and parts of Spain.

REMUAGE
Process in Champagne-making whereby the bottles, stored on their sides and at a progressively steeper angle in *pupitres*, are twisted, or riddled, each day so that the sediment moves down the sides and collects in the neck of the bottle on the cap, ready for *dégorgement*.

RESERVA
Spanish wines that have fulfilled certain aging requirements: reds must have at least 3 years' aging before sale, of which one must be in oak barrels; whites and rosés must have at least 2 years' age, of which 6 months must be in oak.

RÉSERVE
French for what is, in theory, a winemaker's best wine. The word has no legal definition in France.

RIPASSO
A method used in Valpolicella to make wines with extra depth. Wine is passed over the lees of Recioto or Amarone della Valpolicella, adding extra alcohol and flavour, though also extra tannin and a risk of higher acidity and oxidation.

RISERVA
An Italian term, recognized in many DOCs and DOCGs, for a special selection of wine that has been aged longer before release. It is only a promise of a more pleasurable drink if the wine had enough fruit and structure in the first place.

SAIGNÉE
Rosé wine takes its colour from the skins of red grapes: the juice is bled off (*saignée*) after a short period of contact with the skins.

SEC
French for dry. When applied to Champagne, it means medium-dry.

'SECOND' WINES
A second selection from a designated vineyard, usually lighter and quicker-maturing than the main wine.

SEDIMENT
Usually refers to residue thrown by a wine, particularly red, as it ages in bottle.

SEKT
German sparkling wine. The best wines are made by the traditional method, from 100% Riesling or 100% Weissburgunder (Pinot Blanc).

SÉLECTION DE GRAINS NOBLES (SGN)
A superripe category for sweet Alsace wines, now also being used by some producers of Coteaux du Layon in the Loire Valley. *See also* Vendange Tardive.

SMARAGD
The top of the three categories of wine from the Wachau in Austria, the lower two being Federspiel and Steinfeder. Made from very ripe and usually late-harvested grapes, the wines have a minimum of 12.5% alcohol, often 13–14%.

SOLERA
Traditional Spanish system of blending fortified wines, especially sherry and Montilla-Moriles.

SPÄTLESE
German for late-picked (riper) grapes. Often moderately sweet, though there are dry versions.

SPUMANTE
Italian for sparkling. Bottle-fermented wines are often referred to as *metodo classico* or *metodo tradizionale*.

SUPER-TUSCAN
Term coined in the 1980s for top-quality wines that did not conform to local DOC regulations (usually Chianti) and were therefore classed as vini da tavola (table wine). Many are now sold under the regional IGT Toscana.

SUPÉRIEUR
French for a wine with a slightly higher alcohol content than the basic AC.

SUPERIORE
Italian DOC wines with higher alcohol or more aging potential.

SUR LIE
French for on the lees, meaning wine bottled direct from the cask/fermentation vat to gain extra flavour from the lees. Common with quality Muscadet, white Burgundy, similar barrel-aged whites and, increasingly, bulk whites.

TANNIN
Harsh, bitter, mouth-puckering element in red wine, derived from grape skins and stems, and from oak barrels. Tannins soften with age and are essential for long-term development in red wines.

TERROIR
A French term used to denote the combination of soil, climate and exposure to the sun – that is, the natural physical environment of the vine.

TRADITIONAL METHOD
See Champagne method.

TROCKEN
German for dry. In most parts of Germany and Austria, Trocken matches the EU definition of dryness – less than 9g per litre residual sugar.

TROCKENBEEREN-AUSLESE (TBA)
German for 'dry berry selected', denoting grapes affected by noble rot (*Edelfäule* in German) – the wines will be lusciously sweet although low in alcohol.

VARIETAL
Wine made from, and named after, a single or dominant grape variety.

VDP
German organization recognizable on the label by a Prussian eagle bearing grapes. The quality of estates included is usually – but not always – high.

VDQS (VIN DÉLIMITÉ DE QUALITÉ SUPÉRIEURE)
French quality wine category, phased out after the 2011 vintage.

VELHO
Portuguese for old. Legally applied only to wines with at least 3 years' aging for reds and 2 years for whites.

VENDANGE TARDIVE
French for late harvest. Grapes are left on the vines beyond the normal harvest time to concentrate flavours and sugars. The term is traditional in Alsace. The Italian term is *vendemmia tardiva*.

VIEILLES VIGNES
French term for a wine made from vines at least 20 years old. Should have greater concentration than wine from younger vines.

VIÑA
Spanish for vineyard.

VIN DE GARAGE
Wines made on so small a scale they could be made in a garage. Such wines may be made from vineyards of a couple of hectares or less, and are often of extreme concentration.

VIN DE PAILLE
Sweet wine found mainly in the Jura region of France. Traditionally, the grapes are left for 2–3 months on straw (*paille*) mats before fermentation to dehydrate, thus concentrating the sugars. The wines are sweet but slightly nutty.

VIN DE PAYS
The term gives a regional identity to wine from the less renowned districts of France. Many are labelled with the grape variety. Gradually being converted to new IGP classification. *See page 24.*

VIN DE TABLE
French for table wine; phased out after the 2008 vintage.

VIN DOUX NATUREL (VDN)
French for a fortified wine, where fermentation has been stopped by the addition of alcohol, leaving the wine 'naturally' sweet, although you could argue that stopping fermentation with a slug of powerful spirit is distinctly unnatural.

VIN JAUNE
A speciality of the Jura region in France, made from the Savagnin grape. In Château-Chalon it is the only permitted style. Made in a similar way to fino sherry but not fortified and aged for 6 years in oak. Unlike fino, *vin jaune* ages well.

VINIFICATION
The process of turning grapes into wine.

VINO DA TAVOLA
The Italian term for table wine, officially Italy's lowest level of production, is a catch-all that until relatively recently applied to more than 80% of the nation's wine, with virtually no regulations controlling quality. Yet this category also provided the arena in the 1970s and 80s for the biggest revolution in quality that Italy has ever seen, with the creation of innovative, DOC-busting 'super-Tuscans'.

VINTAGE
The year's grape harvest, also used to describe wines of a single year. 'Off-vintage' is a year not generally declared as vintage. *See* Port in main A–Z.

VITICULTURE
Vine-growing and vineyard management.

VITIS VINIFERA
Vine species, native to Europe and Central Asia, from which almost all the world's quality wine is made.

VQA (VINTNERS QUALITY ALLIANCE)
Canadian equivalent of France's AC system, defining quality standards and designated viticultural areas.

WEISSHERBST
German rosé wine, a speciality of Baden.

WO (WINE OF ORIGIN)
South African system of appellations which certifies area of origin, grape variety and vintage.

YIELD
The amount of fruit, and ultimately wine, produced from a vineyard. Measured in hectolitres per hectare (hl/ha) in most of Europe, and in the New World as tons per acre or tonnes per hectare. Yield may vary from year to year, and depends on grape variety, age and density of the vines, and viticultural practices.

WHO OWNS WHAT

With Constellation's decision to sell off a great chunk of its wine business, it becomes clear that some of the world's vast drinks conglomerates have become too big to be beneficial to wine. I'm not entirely sure they all know what they're doing and I'm certainly not sure they all have the interest of wine and wine quality – as against business and bottom line – at heart. It's not all bad news: in some cases wineries have benefited from the huge resources that come with corporate ownership, but I can't help feeling nervous knowing that the fate of a winery rests in the hands of distant institutional investors. Below, I list some of the names that crop up again and again in the world of wine.

Other wine companies – which bottle wines under their own names and feature in the main A–Z – are spreading their nets. GALLO has agreements with, among others, Da Vinci winery in Tuscany, MCWILLIAM'S of Australia and Whitehaven of New Zealand. California businessman Donald Hess owns Hess Collection in California, Peter LEHMANN in Australia, GLEN CARLOU in South Africa, and COLOMÉ and Amalaya in Argentina. Besides Ch. MOUTON-ROTHSCHILD, the Rothschild family have other interests in France, co-own OPUS ONE and, in partnership with CONCHA Y TORO, produce ALMAVIVA in Chile.

The never-ending whirl of joint ventures, mergers and takeovers has slowed down a bit, but the following can only be a snapshot at the time of going to press.

ACCOLADE WINES

Accolade was created when Constellation Brands (see below) sold 80% of its Australian, South African and European business to Champ, an Australian private equity group, in January 2011. Accolade's wine portfolio includes HARDYS, Banrock Station, House of Arras, BAY OF FIRES, Brookland Valley, HOUGHTON, Leasingham and Berri Estates in Australia, Mud House in New Zealand, Kumala and Flagstone in South Africa, Echo Falls and Stowells.

AXA MILLÉSIMES

The French insurance giant AXA's subsidiary owns Bordeaux châteaux PETIT-VILLAGE, PICHON-LONGUEVILLE, Pibran and SUDUIRAUT, plus Dom. de l'Arlot in Burgundy, Mas Belles Eaux in the Languedoc, TOKAJI producer Disznókö and PORT producer Quinta DO NOVAL.

CONSTELLATION BRANDS

US-based Constellation became the world's largest wine company in the first decade of the 21st century through a series of acquisitions in Australia, New Zealand, Canada, South America and South Africa. In 2004 Constellation acquired the prestigious Robert MONDAVI winery and all its entities, including OPUS ONE (a joint venture with the Rothschild family of Ch. MOUTON-ROTHSCHILD), as well as a 40% stake in Italy's RUFFINO (increased to 50% in 2010). Constellation's brands include Blackstone, CLOS DU BOIS, Estancia, FRANCISCAN, Mount Veeder Winery, RAVENSWOOD, Simi and Wild Horse in California, Hogue Cellars in Washington State, Le CLOS JORDANNE, INNISKILLIN, JACKSON-TRIGGS and SUMAC RIDGE in Canada, and Kim Crawford and NOBILO in New Zealand.

FREIXENET

This famous CAVA producer remains a family-owned business, with winery estates and interests around the world. In Spain, alongside FREIXENET Cavas, the portfolio includes Castellblanch, Segura Viudas, Conde de Caralt, René Barbier, Morlanda and Valdubón. Further afield it includes Bordeaux *négociant* and producer Yvon Mau, the Champagne house of Henri Abelé,

Gloria Ferrer in California, Viento Sur in Argentina and Australia's Wingara Wine Group (Deakin Estate, KATNOOK ESTATE).

JACKSON FAMILY WINES

The late Jess Jackson, founder of California's KENDALL-JACKSON, built up a large portfolio of independent wineries in California, including: Arrowood, Atalon, Byron, Cambria, Cardinale, Edmeades, Freemark Abbey, HARTFORD, La Crema, La Jota, Lokoya, MATANZAS CREEK, Murphy-Goode, Pepi, Stonestreet and Vérité. Further afield, Jackson also owns Calina (Chile), Yangarra (Australia), Ch. Lassègue (ST-ÉMILION) and Tenuta di Arceno (Tuscany).

LVMH

French luxury goods group Louis Vuitton-Moët Hennessy owns Champagne houses MOËT & CHANDON (including Dom Pérignon), KRUG, Mercier, RUINART and VEUVE CLICQUOT, and has established DOMAINE CHANDON sparkling wine companies in California, Australia and Argentina – and a new joint venture in China. It also owns Ch. d'YQUEM, CAPE MENTELLE in Australia, CLOUDY BAY in New Zealand, NEWTON in California, Numanthia in TORO, Spain, and TERRAZAS DE LOS ANDES in Argentina.

PERNOD RICARD

The French spirits giant owns Australia's all-conquering JACOB'S CREEK brand, along with Wyndham Estate and the Orlando, Gramp's, Poet's Corner and Richmond Grove labels. Pernod Ricard's portfolio also encompasses New Zealand's mighty BRANCOTT ESTATE, CHURCH ROAD and Stoneleigh brands, as well as Champagne producers G H MUMM and PERRIER-JOUËT, Californian fizz MUMM NAPA, Long Mountain in South Africa and a number of Argentinian producers, including Etchart and Graffigna. In Spain, Pernod Ricard controls CAMPO VIEJO, Alcorta, Azpilicueta, Siglo and Ysios, among others. In China it owns the impressive Helan Mountain winery in Ningxia province.

TREASURY WINE ESTATES

The wine division of Australian brewer Foster's, recently demerged and renamed Treasury Wine Estates, was founded on the twin pillars of Australia's Wolf BLASS and BERINGER in California. In 2005 Foster's won control of Australia's biggest wine conglomerate, Southcorp, and the group currently controls more than 50 wineries and brands. Australian brands include LINDEMAN'S, PENFOLDS, ROSEMOUNT, SEPPELT, WYNNS, COLDSTREAM HILLS, DEVIL'S LAIR, Annie's Lane, Baileys of Glenrowan, Leo Buring, Heemskerk, Jamiesons Run, Metala, Mildara, Greg Norman, Rothbury Estate, Rouge Homme, St Huberts, Saltram, Seaview, T'Gallant, Tollana, Yarra Ridge and Yellowglen. In California it owns, among others, Chateau St Jean, Etude, Meridian, Souverain, St Clement and Stags' Leap Winery. Treasury also owns MATUA VALLEY and Secret Stone in New Zealand, and Castello di Gabbiano in Tuscany.

INDEX OF PRODUCERS

343

OLDER VINTAGE CHARTS *(top wines only)*

FRANCE										
Alsace (vendanges tardives)	02	01	00	99	98	97	96	95	90	89
	8◆	8◆	8◆	6◇	8◆	8◆	7◇	8◆	10◆	9◆
Champagne (vintage)	02	00	99	98	97	96	95	90	89	88
	9◇	6◇	7◆	7◆	6◆	8◆	9◆	9◆	8◆	9◆
Bordeaux	03	02	01	00	99	98	97	96	95	94
Margaux	7◇	7◆	9◆	9◆	7◇	7◆	6◇	8◆	8◆	6◇
St-Jul., Pauillac, St-Est.	8◆	8◆	8◆	10◆	7◇	7◆	6◇	9◆	8◆	6◇
Graves/Pessac-L. (red)	6◇	6◆	7◆	9◆	7◇	8◆	6◇	8◆	8◆	6◇
St-Émilion, Pomerol	7◇	7◆	8◆	9◆	7◇	9◆	6◇	7◇	9◆	6◇
Bordeaux (cont.)	90	89	88	86	85	83	82	81	75	70
Margaux	9◆	8◆	7◇	8◆	8◇	9◆	8◇	7◇	6◇	8◇
St-Jul. etc.)	9◆	9◆	8◆	9◆	8◆	7◇	10◆	7◇	8◆	8◇
Graves/P-L (red)	8◇	8◆	8◇	6◇	8◇	8◇	9◆	7◇	6◇	8◇
St-Émilion etc.	9◇	9◆	8◇	7◇	9◇	7◇	9◇	7◇	8◇	8◇
Sauternes	03	02	01	00	99	98	97	96	95	90
	9◆	7◆	10◇	6◇	8◆	7◆	9◆	9◆	7◆	10◆
Sauternes (cont.)	89	88	86	83	80	76	75	71	67	62
	9◆	9◆	9◆	9◆	7◇	8◆	8◇	8◇	9◇	8◆
Burgundy										
Chablis	03	02	01	00	99	98	96	95	92	90
	7◆	8◆	4◇	9◆	7◇	7◇	8◆	8◇	8◇	9◇
Côte de Beaune (wh.)	03	02	01	00	99	97	96	95	93	92
	5◆	8◆	6◆	8◆	8◆	7◇	6◇	7◇	8◇	8◇
Côte de Nuits (red)	03	02	01	00	99	98	96	95	93	90
	8◆	9◇	7◆	7◇	9◆	7◆	9◆	7◆	8◆	9◆